World culture report 2000

World culture report 2000

Cultural diversity, conflict and pluralism

UNESCO Publishing

Director of Research:
Lourdes Arizpe
Executive Co-ordinator:
Ann-Belinda Preis
Graphs and cover:
Marina Taurus

Published in 2000
by the United Nations
Educational, Scientific
and Cultural Organization,
7 place de Fontenoy,
75352 Paris 07 SP, France
Text composed by Incidences
93170 Bagnolet, France
Printed by Corlet
14110 Condé sur Noireau

ISBN 92-3-103751-X

Preface

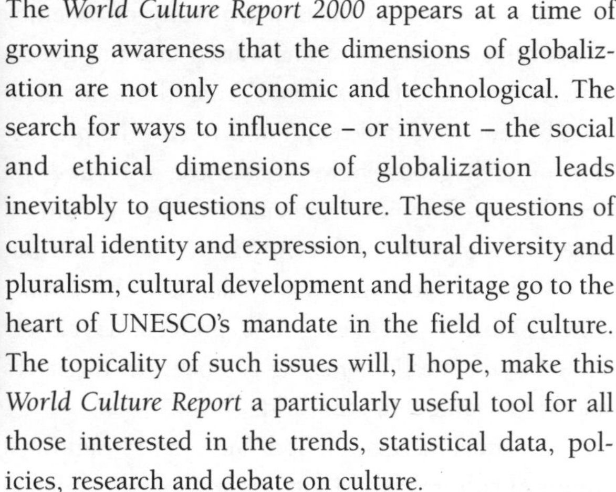

The *World Culture Report 2000* appears at a time of growing awareness that the dimensions of globalization are not only economic and technological. The search for ways to influence – or invent – the social and ethical dimensions of globalization leads inevitably to questions of culture. These questions of cultural identity and expression, cultural diversity and pluralism, cultural development and heritage go to the heart of UNESCO's mandate in the field of culture. The topicality of such issues will, I hope, make this *World Culture Report* a particularly useful tool for all those interested in the trends, statistical data, policies, research and debate on culture.

Cultural identity and expression are challenged in a number of ways by the processes of globalization. Those who are able to take an active part in global cultural exchange often experience culture as a process rather than as a product and their personal sense of cultural identity becomes a gateway of receptivity towards other cultures. But for those who lack the means of exchange or of self-expression, or who experience globalization as an inexorable and alien process, there can be a retreat into a narrow sense of cultural identity that rejects diversity. When this negative reaction is exploited politically or exacerbated by other factors, culture swiftly becomes intertwined with conflict.

Wherever there are risks of cultural tension and conflict, or indeed of creeping cultural uniformity, culture itself is central to the solutions. This is firstly a matter of finding ways to establish respect for all cultural identities and ways to reinvigorate cultural exchange. There is also the very useful function of culture as a lever for contesting the status quo. It can serve to challenge and to reappropriate the processes of change in creative and constructive ways.

Altering the course of global transformations is of course a far from easy task. The speed of social and economic change often goes counter to the rhythms of culture, which more often measure time in phases of experience, stages of life and even in generations than in the nanoseconds of the digital networks. UNESCO and its many partners have an urgent task in seeking ways of preserving the languages, customs, arts and crafts of the communities most vulnerable to sweeping change.

We may live in times when many of us enjoy extraordinarily extensive and varied cultural goods, but without constant renewal from the sources of tangible and intangible cultural diversity, the production of such goods, however massive, will mask an actual cultural impoverishment. The loss of cultural diversity is significant not only for culture itself but for human development as a whole. As with so many other global issues today, this problem is closely linked to the steadily growing gap between the haves and the have-nots in the world.

Unequal access to both new and traditional means of cultural expression implies not only a denial of cultural recognition, it can also seriously affect an individual's or a community's membership of, or exclusion from, the knowledge society. Culture has multiple and complex links with knowledge. The processing of information into knowledge is a creative and culturally informed act, as is the use to which that knowledge is put. A truly knowledge-rich world has to be a culturally diverse world.

It also has to be a world of cultural pluralism if we are to learn to live together. The *World Culture Report* looks at the ways in which a successful transition can be made within societies from the fact of cultural diversity to the fabric of cultural pluralism. By respecting the equal dignity of all cultures and by acknowledging their interdependence, paths to pluralism – which themselves are plural – preserve cultural identities within a framework of tolerance and diversity.

I believe that in this way, by preserving diversity and promoting pluralism, we can enable culture in the twenty-first century to fulfil one of its most important functions: bringing a measure of harmony into our lives.

KOÏCHIRO MATSUURA
Director-General of UNESCO

Acknowledgements

Special thanks to:

The Scientific Committee for collaborating in providing guidance for the report, and in particular:

Lourdes Arizpe (Mexico)
HRH Basma Bint Talal (Jordan)
Yoro Fall (Senegal)
Néstor García Canclini (Mexico)
Keith Griffin (United Kingdom)
Elizabeth Jelin (Argentina)
Junzo Kawada (Japan)
J. Mohan Rao (India)
Adriaan van der Staay (Netherlands)
David Throsby (Australia)

The Governments of Denmark and the Netherlands for providing financial support

The Governments of Canada, France, Italy and the Philippines for lending their expertise in the statistical methodological surveys

Youssef Chahine
Louis Emmerij
Anthony Giddens
Leo Goldstone
Norman Long
Paul Streeten

The UNESCO National Commissions

Institutions

Copenhagen Peace Research Institute (COPRI) (Denmark)
Human Development Report Office of the United Nations Development Programme
International Labour Organization (ILO) (Switzerland)
International Peace Research Institute (PRIO) (Norway)
Social and Cultural Planning Office (Netherlands)
Stockholm International Peace Research Institute (SIPRI) (Sweden)
The World Bank

Contents

11 List of tables and graphs
13 Acronyms used in the text
14 General Introduction
20 Internet haiku contest on cultural diversity

Part One. Cultural diversity, conflict and pluralism

24 Chapter 1. Cultural diversity, conflict and pluralism
Lourdes Arizpe, Elizabeth Jelin, J. Mohan Rao and Paul Streeten
- Columbian case study: after nature *Arturo Escobar* 28
- Nationalities and conflicting ethnicity in a time of transition *Valery A. Tishkov* 31
- Cultural fundamentalism *Verena Stolcke* 32
- The problem of defining the 'good' in pluralistic societies *Andreas Føllesdal* 36
- Women's place-based strategies against violence *Wendy Harcourt* 38

Part Two. Current debates

46 Introduction *Louis Emmerij*
48 Chapter 2. Redistribution, recognition, and participation: towards an integrated concept of justice
Nancy Fraser
58 Chapter 3. Globalization, inequality and the social investment state *Anthony Giddens*
66 Chapter 4. Globalization and cultural diversity *Elie Cohen*
- United States trade policy and culture: future strategies *William S. Merkin* 68
- Cultural diversity and international trade regulations *Ivan Bernier* 70
- The MAI: on the threshold of a cultural war? *Guiomar Alonso Cano* 77
- The dynamics of African film-making *Mbye Cham* 86
- Cultural diversity in national cinema *Lluís Artigas de Quadras* 89

92 Chapter 5. The culture of courage: *an interview with Youssef Chahine*
- The euphemism of globalization *Sabina Berman* 96
- Actors in the new millennium *Gong Li* 99

101 Chapter 6. Culture and poverty *Rodolfo Stavenhagen*
- Respecting the cultural diversity of local initiatives *HRH Princess Basma Bint Talal* 109

111 Chapter 7. Sustainable pluralism and the future of belonging *Arjun Appadurai and Katerina Stenou*
- The European exception *Antonin J. Liehm* 116
- To be Indian is already to be culturally diverse *Mallika Sarabhai* 121

Part Three. Cultural policies and cultural heritage

128 Introduction *David Throsby*

130 Chapter 8. Paying for the past: the economics of cultural heritage *Arjo Klamer and David Throsby*

- Heritage conservation and urban redevelopment: the case of Nagahama *Emiko Kakiuchi* 133
- Putting a value on the invaluable: the case of Fez Medina *Paola Agostini* 136
- Community mobilization for heritage conservation and development *Richard A. Engelhardt* 140

146 Chapter 9. An outline of UNESCO's actions in heritage conservation and rehabilitation *Mounir Bouchenaki*

- New advocacy and funding schemes for endangered cultural heritage *Kirstin Sechler* 148
- A risk map of the cultural heritage in Italy *Carla Bodo and Annalisa Cicerchia* 150

153 Chapter 10. Impact of recent developments in the notion of cultural heritage on the World Heritage Convention *Laurent Lévi-Strauss*

- Defining the concept of 'intangible heritage': challenges and prospects *Lyndel Prott* 156
- Renewal of the notion of authenticity *Laurent Lévi-Strauss* 160

164 Chapter 11. Heritage conservation and values in globalizing societies *Randall Mason and Marta de la Torre*

- Incentives in the protection of intangible cultural heritage *Junzo Kawada* 168
- Intangible cultural heritage: new safeguarding approaches *Noriko Aikawa* 174

Part Four. New media and cultural knowledge

184 Introduction *Isabelle Vinson*

186 Chapter 12. Using information technology to preserve and sustain cultural heritage: the digital collective *Maurita Peterson Holland and Kari R. Smith*

- Diasporic networks in cyberspace *Karim H. Karim* 188
- A need for self-representation in Arab African countries *Tahar Chikhaoui* 190
- Nisswa: an electronic cross-roads between local and global activism in the Arab world *Lamis Alshejni* 192
- Promoting civil society activism through the new media *George Yúdice* 193

197 Chapter 13. Museum strategy in the information society *Pierre Coural*

- Active learning *Ranjit Makkuni* 200
- True access? Gender participation and cultural comfort zones on the web *Katherine W. Getao* 203
- The Internet: not the swansong of the book *Alvaro Garzon* 204
- Cultural policies on the southern web *Heloisa Buarque de Hollanda* 206

Part Five. International public opinion and national identity

212 Introduction *Adriaan van der Staay*

215 Chapter 14. International public opinion and national identity: a descriptive study of existing survey data *Jos W. Becker*

- Happiness *Robert M. Worcester* 217
- Changing roles of women in Europe *Robert M. Worcester* 219
- Changes in Asia *Jos W. Becker* 243

Part Six. Measuring culture: national and international practice

254 Introduction *Leo Goldstone*

256 Chapter 15. Canada's national Culture Statistics Program: a quarter century of development *Paul McPhie with notes from Michel G. Durand, John J. Gordon and John Foote*

263 Chapter 16. The Philippine approach to cultural statistics *Jaime C. Laya*

- Culture statistics and poverty *Leo Goldstone* 264

267 Chapter 17. Towards an international system of culture statistics and indicators: the Italian experience *Paolo Garonna*

271 Chapter 18. Culture and its statistics: a glance at French experience *Paul Tolila*

- The *Index Translationum* on CD-ROM: an analytical tool *Sylvie Bosser* 274

278 Chapter 19. In search of indicators of culture and development: progress and proposals *Sakiko Fukuda Parr*

- Life expectancy as an integrating concept *Paul Streeten* 281

Part Seven. Statistical tables and culture indicators *Leo Goldstone*

288 Introduction

290 Culture indicator tables

291 Table symbols

292 Statistical tables

410 Index and sources of culture indicators

414 List of countries by region

List of tables and graphs

Tables

1 Geographic region with which one identifies (1995, in percentages) 221
2 Geographic region with which one identifies (1995, difference from mean percentage) 222
3 Correlations between various identifications (1995, all respondents) 222
4 Willingness to move in order to improve work or living conditions (1995, in percentages) 224
5 Willingness to move in order to improve work or living conditions (1995, difference from mean percentage) 225
6 Correlations between areas in view of willingness to move (1995, all respondents) 226
7 Correlations between identification and willingness to move (1995, all respondents) 226
8 Feelings about one's own country (1995, in percentages) 227
9 Feelings about one's own country (1995, difference from mean percentage) 228
10 Pride in national achievements (1995, in percentages) 229
11 Pride in national achievements (1995, difference from mean percentage) 230
12 Country rank by national feeling and pride in political, economic and cultural achievements (1995, rank orders) 231
13 Correlations between the rank numbers of countries on three indices (1995, Spearman rho) 231
14 Criteria for being a true national of a given country (1995, in percentages) 233
15 Criteria for being a true national of a given country (1995, difference from mean percentage) 234
16 Opinions on the influx of immigrants (1995, in percentages) 235
17 Opinions on the influx of immigrants (1995, difference from mean percentage) 235
18 Feelings about immigrants (1995, in percentages) 236
19 Feelings about immigrants (1995, difference from mean percentage) 237
20 Opinions on cultural diversity (1995, in percentages) 238
21 Opinions on cultural diversity (1995, difference from mean percentage) 239
22 Dimensions of attitudes on the basis of respondents' scores (1995, factor scores) 240
23 Correlations between dimensions of attitudes and personal characteristics of all respondents (1995, Pearson correlations) 240
24 Dimensions of attitudes on the basis of national scores (1995, factor loadings, 23 countries) 241
25 Correlations between dimensions of attitudes and characteristics of countries (1995, Pearson correlations, 23 countries) 241
26 Public expenditures on culture 1984–98, in millions of C$ 257
27 Direct economic impact of the culture sector on GDP by function, Canada 1994–95, in millions of C$ 259
28 Direct economic impact of the culture sector on employment by function, Canada 1994–1995 261

Graphs

1 Biodiversity and cultural diversity 26
2 Languages in former colonized countries 35
3 Major UN Human Rights Conventions 50
4 Golden Pen of Freedom Laureates 54
5 International poverty line 59
6 Global cinema market 88
7 International poverty line 105
8 International migration 114

9 UNESCO cultural conventions 135
10 UNESCO cultural conventions 137
11 UNESCO Cultural Conventions 2000 151
12 Cultural diversity and festivals 161
13 Living languages in the world 174
14 Living languages in the world (mother tongue) 199
15 Languages 199
16 Nobel Prize for Literature 204

Top tens

1 Plant species 1996 29
2 Forests (% of total area) 29
3 Employment-to-population ratio (female) 1997 52
4 Least income inequality 1988–98 55
5 Human Development Index 1999 60
6 Public expenditure on education (% of GNP) 1995–97 63
7 Cultural trade (% of GNP) 1997 75
8 Cultural trade (per capita) 1997 75
9 Feature films produced 1998 93
10 Feature films imported 1998 94
11 Cinema screens (per person) 1998 95
12 Cinema attendance (per person) 1998 98
13 Largest bilateral and multilateral donors 1999 103
14 Foreign born (% of population) 1995 112
15 Tourist arrivals 1998 118
16 Nationals visiting abroad (per inhabitant) 1998 120
17 Endangered heritage sites (World Monument Fund) 1999 147
18 Sites on the World Heritage List 158
19 Tertiary students in fine arts and humanities (% of all tertiary students) 1994–97 169
20 Natural heritage sites 170
21 Personal computers (per person) 1997 189
22 Televisions per person (annual rate of change) 1980–97 191
23 Mobile cellular phones (greatest rate of increase) 1995–98 194
24 Internet hosts (per person) 1997 198

Acronyms used in the text

AAMD Association of Art Museum Directors
ADB Asian Development Bank
AGFUND Arab Gulf Programme for United Nations Development Organizations
AIDS acquired immune deficiency syndrome
AMICO Art Museum Image Consortium
AMN Art Museum Network
APC Association for Progressive Communications
CBD Convention on Biological Diversity
CD compact disc
CHE complex humanitarian emergencies
CHIN Canadian Heritage Information Network
CIMI Consortium for Interexchange of Museum Information
CIOFF International Council of Organizations for Folklore Festivals and Folk Art
CVM contingent valuation method
DNA deoxyribonucleic acid
ECM European Charter of Museums
ECOSOC United Nations Economic and Social Council
EMII European Museum Information Institute
FAO Food and Agriculture Organization of the United Nations
G7 The G7 countries
GAD gender and development
GATT General Agreement on Tariffs and Trade
GCI Getty Conservation Institute
GUI graphical user interface
HDI Human Development Index
IAB Inter-American Bank
ICARE International Centre for Research in Art Economics
ICCD Instituto Centrale del Catalogo e della Documentazione
ICCROM International Centre for the Study of the Preservation and Restoration of Cultural Property
ICOM International Council of Museums
ICOMOS International Council on Monuments and Sites
ICTs Information and communication technologies
ICTM International Council for Traditional Music
IFPI International Federation of the Phonographic Industry
ILO International Labour Organization
IMF International Monetary Fund
ISPO Information Society Project Office
ISSP International Social Survey Programme
IST Information Society Technologies
ITU International Telecommunication Union
JPM J.P. Morgan
LEAP Local Effort and Preservation Project
LEG Leadership Group on Cultural Statistics of the European Union
LSB Litigation Settlement Body (WTO)
MAI Multilateral Agreement on Investment
MFN most favoured nation
MSU Member States of UNESCO
NACCS National Advisory Committee on Culture Statistics (Canada)
NCCA National Commission for Culture and the Arts (Philippines)
NGO non-governmental organization
NPO non-profit organization
OECD Organisation for Economic Co-operation and Development
PBP Proyecto Biopacífico
PCN Proceso de Comunidades Negras
RAMP religious and moral pluralism
RLG Research Libraries Group
SCRAN Scottish Cultural Resources Access Network
SDG Screen Digest
SID Society for International Development
UNCHR United Nations Centre for Human Rights
UNCTAD United Nations Commission on Trade and Development
UNDP United Nations Development Programme
UNESCO United Nations Educational, Scientific and Cultural Organization
UNFPA United Nations Fund for Population Activities
UNHCR United Nations High Commission for Refugees
UNICEF United Nations Children's Fund
UNPOP United Nations Population Division
UNRISD United Nations Research Institute for Social Development
UNSTAT United Nations Statistical Division
UPU Universal Postal Union
WAN World Association of Newspapers
WB World Bank
WBANK The World Bank
WCMC World Conservation Monitoring Centre
WCR World Culture Report
WHO World Health Organization
WID Woman in Development
WMF World Monuments Fund
WMW World Monuments Watch
WON Woman on the Net
WSL World Statistics Ltd
WTO World Tourism Organization
WTO World Trade Organization
WWW World Wide Web

General introduction

As the arrival of the third millennium turns a new page of history, people all over the world are setting their hand to writing it down. Communications, both instant and global, and travel and networking have created unheard-of spaces for experimenting with and inventing new ways of living together. The world is hearing a magnificent overture of cultural possibilities. People everywhere, however, are repositioning themselves in this vast global commons in order to preserve part of their traditions, while at the same time engaging in cultural exchanges and redefining their relationships with neighbours on this tiny planet. Cultural exchanges are in fact the axis of these new phenomena. The challenge for governments and civil societies is to find ways of channelling such exchanges through democratic practices that respect human rights, gender equity and sustainability.

Significantly, a majority of conflicts now arising within nation-states involve cultural matters: the ethnic war in Kosovo; the clash between Christians opposing the Sharia Muslim law as state law and Muslim local authorities in Kaduna, Nigeria; rioting against Chinese in Indonesia as a result of the economic crisis; and mobilization of three million Indians demanding political participation in Ecuador. And all these conflicts have erupted only in the very short time that has elapsed since the publication of the first *World Culture Report* two years ago.

Friction based on perceptions of cultural difference between nationals and migrants has also been in the news in developed as much as in developing countries in recent years. Many conflicts are also linked to urban movements which, in new democratic settings, are carving out a new political space for themselves, *inter alia* by reclaiming cultural forms of heritage and identity. We reiterate, then, the message of the first issue of the *World Culture Report*, that conflicts are not necessarily an obstacle to development. The question is one of knowing how governments are to channel them as a productive rather than a destructive force.

Responding to this challenge, the second issue of the *World Culture Report* focuses on 'Cultural Diversity, Conflicts and Pluralism'. It could be argued that this issue has been continuously dealt with over the past two decades. Programmes in international institutions have indeed conducted long-term research on the management of cultural pluralism. This problem, however, now has a much larger component of cultural concerns than ever before. What are the historical origins of cultural differences, increasingly evoked as reasons for conflict? How does cultural creativity generate a dynamics of cultural change that will invariably influence the way cultural groups define themselves? How has this dynamic evolved in the new political and social architecture of globalization?

The general principles for dealing with diversity were asserted with some authority by the World Commission on Culture and Development in 1995 and endorsed at the Intergovernmental Conference on Cultural Policies for Development in Stockholm in 1998. The report, entitled *Our Creative Diversity*, stated a commitment to respect cultures that in their turn have values of respect for other cultures. That commitment is increasingly valid. Yet the extremely rapid changes in today's governance and cultural environments are creating a relentless need for new concepts and new analytical methods.

At present, globalization, telecommunications and informatics are changing the way in which people identify and perceive cultural diversity. In particular, the outworn metaphor of the 'mosaic of cultures' or the 'global cultural mosaic' no longer describes different peoples' cultural preferences as they enter the world of the twenty-first century. Cultures are no longer the fixed, bounded, crystallized containers they were formerly reputed to be. Instead they are transboundary creations exchanged throughout the world via the media and the Internet. We must now regard culture as a process rather than as a finished product.

Accordingly, Part One of this report, which presents the result of our research and our reflection on the main theme, proposes a new metaphor of a 'Rainbow River' to describe the cultural state of the world, inspired in this by Nelson Mandela's superlative human wisdom. The Rainbow River represents us all, with our history, our families and our distant neighbours.

While there has been unanimity and praise for the general principle enunciated in *Our Creative Diversity* regarding cultural expression, by far the most controversial recommendation made in the report is the one relating to cultural rights. The Group of 77 opposed it, many governments were concerned that it would lead to an incompatibility with fundamental citizen rights, and lawyers and social scientists are now involved in a debate on cultural rights and wrongs.[1] The absence of consensus, even on the basic concepts that should underlie policy decisions, sent us back to the drawing board.

If cultural diversity is an irrepressible manifestation of the inventiveness of the human spirit, the creation of difference is equally inexorable. No attempt should be made to stifle or repress it. Yet the manner in which such difference is defined and acted upon by governments and social custom determines whether it is to lead to greater overall social creativity or else to violence and exclusion. Culture has always been regarded as an unquestionably consensual activity in cultural policies. Now a deeper look at what is happening today shows that even in art, culture is seen as a 'site of contestation'.[2] We have chosen this novel view of culture analysis as it is more in tune with the network of perspectives created by the contemporary flow of culture between countries and continents, and with the conflictual relationships in multicultural settings, especially in cities. However, we give it a more policy-oriented thrust by regarding culture as a 'site of negotiation', and one creating exciting new possibilities.

So it was back to the drawing board. Part One of the report explores new conceptual tools for policy such as cultural injustice and cultural recognition. This is not done in terms of management of cultural pluralism, but rather in those of the understanding of recent changes in perceptions of cultural differences, cultural origins and the reproduction of diversity. New discoveries on the origins of human diversification confirm that while we all belong to one species, yet an extraordinary variety of cultural paths has contributed to leaving an imprint of cultural diversity on the history of all peoples. A case-study from Colombia explores this new perspective and the promise of cultural diversity in strategies for long-term environmental sustainability. We should, accordingly, think of cultural diversity as having existed in the past, as assuming fuller form in the present, and as becoming a river in full spate in the future. Such diversity is, ultimately, a product of the human will. And having invented it, we should live with it.

Rethinking diversity also implies understanding today's irreversible changes in the roles of women and men in society and in long-term sustainability strategies. The types of activities in which women's movements around the world have been engaged in recent years are generating a new form of political experience that is not readily contained in traditional political categories. The networking, building of solidarity, advocacy, lobbying and reflection radiating from women's daily needs – their autonomy and individual rights, the home and the community – may be usefully labelled the 'politics of place'. Recent practices of women's strategies in relation to violence are analysed in this issue of the report.

We conclude by arguing that the acknowledgement, approval and even celebration of diversity, while it does not imply relativism, does imply pluralism. Cultural pluralism here refers to the way in which different nation-states, civil groups and national and international institutions understand and organize cultural diversity. No policy prescription can be ready-made in this respect; such an exploration has to be made in terms of the culturally-diverse histories of all countries. Although we consider policy recommendations important and necessary as a general goal, and therefore propose a set of guidelines called 'Equal Dignity for All', it is clear that such proposals are fully intelligible only in specific situations and that some degree of contextualization will always be necessary.

Part Two highlights six lively debates about crucial matters of international import already touched on in the previous part. The first of these is concerned with the crucial question of social justice and its two related components of redistribution and recognition. Justice today requires both redistribution and recognition and it is proposed that these should be integrated into a single framework so as to challenge injustice on both fronts.

The second debate makes the case for a new balance between state regulations and market dynamics in order to minimize both income gaps and the number of 'winners' in the rapidly globalizing economy. This balance will have to be found in what is termed a 'social investment state'. In such a state, emphasis would be placed on human and social capital so that people could create civil society networks to stimulate innovative approaches and provide an enabling approach to social policy.

The globalization issue is brought into the domain of cultural diversity by way of international trade and the notion of 'cultural exception' in the third debate. Recent years have witnessed an increase in the number of trade disputes, all the more acrimonious in that they challenge the right of nations to retain their consumption patterns, protect the private life of citizens, maintain the moral rights of authors, and stop the dissemination of new food technologies. The right approach is not to confront cultural fragmentation with globalizing economic forces but rather to synthesize identity claims and globalization.

'We are not all the same. Nevertheless we are not terrifying because of our differences. In fact, without difference, we should all be narcissistic.' The voice is that of Youssef Chahine, the well-known Egyptian film-maker. In his film on the life of Averroes, the philosopher who had to flee the Inquisition in medieval Spain, tolerance to new ideas becomes the overriding principle in respecting cultures in all political and religious contexts. His latest film, *L'Autre* (The Other), articulates the importance of recognizing the Other's difference, 'because it enlightens our recognition of his dreams and attachments'.

Further on, the report records the voices of many artists who are accustomed to working internationally. We asked them: what is happening to cultural diversity in terms of artists' work in the context of globalization? Their replies take the form of artistic analyses or personal statements.

Mallika Sarabhai, referring to a 'hybridizing' experience with the Nigerian performer, Peter Badejo, and the British director, John Martin, explains the special style of flows across and between their cultural backgrounds that developed through their collaboration:

It is not Indian, although there are very strong influences within it, nor is it Nigerian or British although those influences are also part of the 'recipe'. We developed it because we felt it spoke to us and through us without ever weakening our own cultural identities. We developed it because we believed this particular fusion would speak to audiences from a wide cultural catchment area.

Their performance was hugely successful in Britain, and in West Africa it was greeted rapturously.

Sabina Berman, a Mexican film-maker, is rather more sceptical about the image of globalization as the free flow of ideas back and forth between numerous cultural centres, given the extreme economic inequalities between Latin-American countries and the industrialized countries. Describing the cumbersome path out into the world for artists of this region, she captures the immediate challenge for Mexican films by stating that 'A country without films is like a house without mirrors to reflect the image of those who live there, so that they can see and reinvent themselves.'

Finally, the Chinese actress, Gong Li, sums up her vision for the twenty-first century by drawing attention to the wide variety of new roles that actors will have to play. Emphasizing the importance for actors of being observers of society and human nature, she concludes: 'They will no longer be mere stage performers. . . . A good actor is both an outstanding artist and an exceptional social activist.'

Poverty has been targeted by the United Nations and governments for immediate action, raising once again the issue of its relationship to culture. However, the contemporary debate – the fifth in our series – is as culture-bound as the versions of earlier times when it was argued that the poor were poor because of their cultural values. A way out of the poverty dilemma calls for a synthesis between the current orthodoxy and a return to the positive and production aspect of the welfare state, while strengthening human rights, democratic governments and popular participation.

The sixth and final debate highlights one of the cornerstones of this report, namely, the question of cultural pluralism. It is argued that globalization has, among other effects, increased the tension between migration and citizenship. The heterogeneity of political forms in the world today deserves wider and wider recognition. Cultural pluralism means granting cultural groups the right to diversity in the public sphere, and this may involve separating the question of the loyalty and attachment of people living in the same national territory from that of their rights as citizens.

Part Three focuses on cultural policies and cultural heritage. Responding to concerns expressed by governments and NGOs, a number of new analytical approaches are presented. The leading chapter proposes that treating heritage as capital assets will lead to better decisions regarding the allocation of resources for its preservation and protection. Strategies and new concepts evolving from the complexities of the role of heritage in a globalized world are discussed in the context of UNESCO's cultural heritage programmes, and in the light of new approaches to professional conservation. Several new models and methods now being applied in heritage management are also presented, including incentives for increased community participation and the use of the new information technologies to meet the urgent challenges of preserving important heritage sites and objects.

In view of the current worldwide interest in the preservation of intangible cultural heritage, Part Three also outlines the new perspectives of the continuous work UNESCO has conducted in this field, and describes new projects related to oral traditions and the safeguarding of other cultural expressions. The definitional and other challenges inherent in the development of a new international instrument for intangible cultural heritage are submitted to a critical analysis. As co-ordinator of this part of the report, David Throsby emphasizes the persistent, underlying theme of the chapters here – which indeed extends to the entire report – namely, the long-term concept of sustainability.

The new information and communication technologies (ICTs) that are bringing about decisive changes in the way cultures are created and communicated also have to meet new social demands. They may increasingly become vehicles for the empowerment of all who find that their rights are not being acknowledged. Thus Part Four presents a project to build 'Digital Collectives' of Native American cultures. A key question here is: 'When nature and culture are intertwined, where and how do we access, catalogue and preserve this knowledge so central to the web of life?' The different chapters explore the possibilities offered by the ICTs to do this through various museological, activist and research networks – the latter offering exciting explorations of new ways of reintroducing cultural components into the learning process.

In structuring the architecture of the new virtual communications and information circulation, the role of both public and private initiatives is equally important. A chapter on the experience of the Louvre Museum in setting up interactive educational services explains how strategic choices by corporate actors for data circulation heavily impacts on the relationship of the public to cultural knowledge. As can be seen already in several regions, new forms of cultural knowledge are also being created by on-line collaborative research experiences and a more sensitive approach to the cognitive aspects of the relationship of users to technology.

Many people believe that cultural diversity is on the retreat in the virtual world. On the contrary, as discussed in several contributions here, more and more pages and whole segments of the Internet are reactivating cultural exchanges and intensifying talks among members of ethnic groups scattered in farflung cities or countries. While greater imagination in the use of ICTs will very likely foster ever greater cultural diversity, the crucial policy-related question remains as to whether this will be enough to encourage a creative reshaping based on equality of access and new forms of democratic participation of citizens.

Discussions at international forums necessarily take a sweeping view of cultural phenomena. Part Five records many experiences that have not always been positive concerning the reality of globalization, based on existing survey data.

The present global development sees the continuing emergence of both old and new problems including inequality of opportunity and power, discrimination and conflict, and instability and extremism. However, the awareness of what is happening all over the world is rapidly becoming globalized too. A common theme underlying this study is the desire to see the widest possible diversity of people participating in the process of decision-making.

In this period of flux and cultural change, people's valuations can no longer be taken for granted. Asian values have long been widely debated in relation to the economic success of East Asia and the recent economic crisis there. Opinion surveys cited in this issue show that there is an underlying unity in Asian society's valuation of hard work and the importance of investing in the education of future generations. However, there is a striking diversity of valuations between, for instance, Chinese and Japanese respondents. A similar diversity of responses between older and younger generations points to rapid cultural change.

Opinion surveys in European countries, on the other hand, show that the influx of migrants and the rise of nationalism are the cause of considerable differences in the way nationals perceive themselves. Nationals and migrants have problems in relating to one another. Another opinion survey explores the degree of happiness felt by different nationalities. A significant, optimistic finding is that local and global loyalties are not necessarily mutually exclusive. In a number of countries people are able to link their identity vis-à-vis the national state to a simultaneous attachment to a wider international context. The comfortable distinction between the 'local' and the 'global' is swiftly fading; increasing numbers of people now insist upon being local and global at one and the same time.

While other UNESCO reports such as those on education and science can call on decades of statistics and debates to provide a clear state of the art, the field of culture and development is only now creating the art. The basic concepts, analytical methods and indicators are only now being constructed. In Parts 6 and 7 we address the issues of statistics and developing cultural indicators.

It is for this reason that the Scientific Committee for this report strongly urges Member States, universities and research centres as well as nongovernmental institutions to foster and carry out basic research in this field. It has been pointed out that UNESCO should not attempt to do what research institutions of Member States are already doing quite well. By multiplying the sources, methodologies and interpretations hailing from different countries, the *World Culture Report* will gain by offering precious and reliable data from culturally diverse contexts.

This issue of the report began with UNESCO's Member States being asked to provide basic information on topics that in some countries are quite sensitive. Impressively, more than one hundred countries answered the questionnaire. In some cases, special surveys were conducted to collect information. The report provides reliable, government-endorsed data on languages, religions, festivals and the most frequently visited cultural heritage sites. In this way, the *World Culture Report* promotes the generation of the culture and development indicators that are so crucial for policy decision-making. But even more importantly, it is helping to consolidate the basis for a conceptually agreed international framework on culture and development. Such a framework can only come from a consensus between scientists, policy-makers and stakeholders.

The work carried out so far in the context of the *World Culture Report* and at several associated research meetings has considerably sharpened our awareness of the complexities and pitfalls of such an enterprise. The recent seminar entitled 'Measuring Culture and Development: Prospects and Limits of Constructing Cultural Indicators', held as part of the joint UNESCO-World Bank-Government of Italy Conference entitled 'Culture Counts' in Florence in October 1999, consolidated a number of critical dimensions for the development of such a fully-fledged, international framework. The first of these, significantly, is cultural diversity, followed by cultural creativity, and now cultural income, expenditure and labour force as well which comprise the countries' 'cultural account'.

Cultural indicators cannot be constructed without solid theoretical and conceptual grounds to build on. Nor can they have any influence in the world if the concerns that are at the root of such explorations are not policy driven. Cultural concerns were absent from development planning for a very long time and it is only in recent years that these tasks have been taken up by governments and international agencies.

In this second *World Culture Report* these challenges are confronted and put to work at the same time. In order to debate these new ideas, the report should be exploratory; in order to measure cultural responses in the era of information and communication, it should be rigorous; and to propose policy-driven recommendations, it should be a 'site of cultural negotiation' for the new global cultural commons.

LOURDES ARIZPE
Chair of the Scientific Commitee of the
World Culture Report;
Professor, Researcher at the Centro Regional
de Investigaciones Multidisciplinarias (CRIM),
UNAM (Mexico)

ANN-BELINDA S. PREIS
Executive Coordinator,
World Culture Report Unit
Sector for Culture, UNESCO

Notes

1. See H. Nieć, *Cultural Rights and Wrongs*, Paris, UNESCO, 1998. Recent literature on this subject is vast.
2. This perspective arose out of cultural analysis, a new line of inquiry developed mainly at the University of Birmingham in Great Britain and in ethnic studies in the United States, as well as in other countries. See C. Willet, *Theorizing Multiculturalism: A Guide to the Current Debate*, London, Blackwell, 1998.

Internet haiku contest on cultural diversity

› UNESCO's *World Culture Report* surveys current trends in culture and development to foster intercultural co-operation. Authors and artists from the widest possible range of cultures are invited to contribute to it.

› The report has opted for cultural diversity as the main theme of its issue for the year 2000. An Internet haiku contest on cultural diversity was therefore launched to represent in poetic form what this diversity of cultural ways of living means for us all in the world.

› The haiku poetic form came into existence as a mode of collective writing in fifteenth-century Japan. In its original form it was frequently used to convey the beauty of nature in an extremely precise and simple form by addressing the things of everyday life. The art of haiku is that of a poet's feeling for words and for their exact positioning. The recent advent of global communications has transformed haiku into a universal form of poetic expression that is boundless in its inspiration as it circulates freely on the Internet.

› As the new millennium gets under way, the peoples of the world are looking about and finding more cultural diversity than ever before. Communications, travel and migration are bringing diverse cultures together. This edition of the report contains the thirty-one haikus that have been selected by an international jury as representing today's multicultural world.

› Following the launching of the contest, haikus were received by UNESCO from the following countries: Canada, Croatia, Cuba, Democratic Republic of the Congo, Ecuador, Finland, France, Greece, Hungary, India, Japan, Mexico, Morocco, New Zealand, Pakistan, Spain, Trinidad and Tobago, the United Kingdom and the United States.
iWe wish to thank all those who participated in the contest.

What is this bright smile
Over dark, feathery pines?
Why, a Kyoto moon.
Arthur Gillette

Together we grow
different cultures that we share
bring us completeness
Michelle Aumack

In this constant move
of sameness turning different
humanity lives
Anonymous

A different spring
than villagers see?
A temple pilgrim
Steve Mc Carty

Part One

Cultural diversity, conflict and pluralism

Chapter 1
Cultural diversity, conflict and pluralism

LOURDES ARIZPE
Chair of the Scientific Committee of the World Culture Report; Professor, Researcher at the Centro Regional de Investigaciones Multidisciplinarias (CRIM) UNAM (Mexico)

ELIZABETH JELIN
Sociologist and Researcher, Consejo Nacional de Investigaciones Cientificas y Tecnicas (CONICET) and Faculty of Social Sciences, University of Buenos Aires (Argentina)

J. MOHAN RAO
Professor, Specialist in Development Economics, University of Massachusetts (United States)

PAUL STREETEN
Professor Emeritus of Boston University, Boston (United States); Consultant to the United Nations Development Programme (UNDP)

'Our new task is to develop policies of recognition and of justice . . . that can be coherently combined with . . . equality.'

Introduction

Human beings have forever invented and exchanged cultural elements; hence cultural diversity has ever been a part of human experience. Such exchanges come in the wake of historical contacts with other local or regional groups, bringing some of them closer or causing conflicts of domination between them. Thus, the world does not consist of a mosaic of cultures but of a constantly changing river of cultures with its different currents forever mingling.

The 'Rainbow River', to borrow Nelson Mandela's metaphor of the 'Rainbow Nation' for South Africa, has not stopped flowing since it began in Central Africa 150,000 years ago. All human beings share the capacity to create cultures, which means they have a common creative potential. This is not to say that they all have or will have the same culture, and this for the very reason that they are creative.

The huge growth of new communications technologies over the past two decades has brought many parts of the world into close communication and may well fulfil the promise of a 'global village'. Many people feel that this will lead to forced cultural homogenization. However, no limits can be placed on people's creativity and capacity to alter their ways of being. Therefore, we can expect a continuing vitality of human cultural diversity. Fears of cultural uniformity are groundless because it is impossible to stem the flow of a river.

The persistence and renewal of diversity present new challenges in the contemporary international context, however. At the same time that globalization is creating new opportunities for cultural exchange, new forms of intolerance and aggression are appearing. Xenophobia and racism, ethnic wars, prejudice, stigmas and segregation and discrimination based mainly on ethnicity and gender, are generating violence and suffering almost everywhere.

All these phenomena amount to a refusal to recognize others as full human beings entitled to the same rights as oneself. Those responsible use 'difference' as an excuse for intolerance, hatred and the annihilation of others. Many also use 'difference' as an excuse for violent political struggles without realizing that a barrier that protects from the outside may well imprison from the inside.

The faster pace and huge volume of global interaction have prompted a greater awareness of cultural diversity. While it has given wider scope to the expression of such diversity, it has also permitted the representation of differences such as hierarchy, domination and conflict. In fact, one could look at the human trajectory as the history of different answers to the same questions. How do people behave towards those of a different community? How should they behave? These questions are every bit as relevant at the level of interpersonal relations as in interstate, international and intercultural contexts. Our choices in regard to our cultural heritages, in relating to others with different traditions and in drawing new three-dimensional cultural maps of the world, will shape the societies of the twenty-first century.

People, however, do not all have an equal capacity (or freedom) to choose. Inequality of access to resources, political power, information and the media strongly condition that capacity. These differences apply not just to individuals but also to groups. Women, in many societies, are being tied to 'keeping the traditions' when, in fact, it is these so-called 'traditions' that contradictorily keep them outside the spheres of power and participation. The representation of cultural differences as hierarchical conflict rather than as creative diversity reflects this inequality. This is at the base of what we understand to be cultural injustice.

Often, cultural injustice is blurred beneath definitions of diversity that turn norms into essentialist, never-changing values outside history and fixed by racial or even genetic characteristics. In fact, cultural diversity results from the inherent capacity of human beings to build creatively on the cultural legacies transmitted to them, thereby adding diversity to their ways of life. This continuous flow of variations can be halted only if invention, imitation or innovation are totally forbidden, as has happened in some world cultures. But then the human spirit, which is one of boundless creativity, has been killed.

Diversity usually clusters around a cultural core for geographical, historical or other reasons, so that a cultural boundary is deliberately marked that separates one cultural group from another. Now that cultural groups are repositioning themselves within this three-dimensional map, many people would like to know how such cultural diversity originated and what its dynamic is in our contemporary world.

How is cultural diversity generated?

Originally the word 'culture', as in agriculture or, in Spanish, 'puericultura' – the raising of children – implied the activity of cultivation. This is lost when cultures are taken to mean something fixed or inanimate, like rocks. On the other hand, cultivating the human spirit is endless, and when nurtured bountifully, can raise a person's feeling for love and life or a people's common endeavour to great heights. If we did not believe this we would not fight to preserve the great architecture of past and present civilizations or the cultural landscapes created by countless men and women joining hands to make the earth bountiful in food, beauty and remembrance. Indeed, there would be no World Heritage List from which new artists and architects could continue to draw inspiration for monuments in their own time.

The question of the origins of cultures has been frequently aired in the popular press in recent times. Scientific debates are revealing how humans evolved into different strands after their appearance in Africa, then dispersed to the Near and Far East and Europe. Racists may interpret these discussions as indicating that there are historic differences between 'races', a term now being substituted by them for 'culture' as an immovable object. In fact, very recent DNA findings and archaeological diggings have confirmed that we are all descended from one group of human ancestors who first appeared in Africa approximately 4.4 million years ago; about one million years ago they had spread to the whole of Eurasia; they were already in what is now Israel 1.4 million years ago and in Java 1.8 million years ago. Findings also show that other hominid species, such as the Neanderthals, existed as well.

Diversity, therefore, was already present as human life dawned. The difference between hominids and *Homo sapiens* was cultural. *Homo sapiens*, the group to which all human beings in the world today belong, showed a much greater capacity to make sophisticated weapons and household utensils and, notably, to evolve social organization and artistic creation.

One may well ask why this was so. Genetics explains that the human genome has gone through many mutations and probably gave our hominid ancestors advantages in acting together, hunting, taking care of children and elders and adapting or migrating to different environments. The rates of mutations, in fact, are one of the ways in which DNA analysis helps reconstruct the early history of human diversity. Genetic evidence indicates that diversity within sub-Saharan Africa was greater than outside Africa.[1] It also shows that DNA diversity outside Africa is a subset of that found within Africa, thus strengthening the argument that our earliest ancestors all came from this continent.

What happened next? There are two hypotheses, both based on genetic evidence. The first one suggests that the human species has existed as a single subdivided population for the past 100,000 years or so. Gene flow therefore played a major role in maintaining genetic similarity among regions. This means that there were considerable exchanges of men and women as marital partners. The second one – the 'weak Garden of Eden' hypothesis – holds that long ago humans separated into small regional groups with differing levels of gene exchange. In other words, some mixed more than others.

Archaeology has produced evidence that gender was the first form of human diversity. Men most probably developed hunting tools while women invented agriculture and ceramics. Thus, cultural practices led to a stronger marking of sexual differences – sexual dimorphism – between men and women than between the sexes in most of our primate cousins.

BIODIVERSITY AND CULTURAL DIVERSITY

countries with the greatest biodiversity	more than fifty languages currently spoken
Argentina	
Australia	x
Bolivia	
Brazil	x
China	x
Colombia	x
Costa Rica	
Democratic Republic of the Congo	x
Ecuador	
India	x
Indonesia	x
Kenya	x
Madagascar	
Malaysia	x
Mexico	x
Myanmar	x
Panama	
Papua New Guinea	x
Peru	x
Philippines	x
South Africa	
Thailand	x
United Republic of Tanzania	x
United States	x
Venezuela	x
Viet Nam	x
Zambia	

GRAPH 1
Countries with the highest number of plant and vertebrate species. The majority of them report having over fifty languages in daily use. The list of twenty-seven countries was compiled by combining two lists of Top Twenty Countries for vertebrate species and plant species, respectively. Thirteen countries were found on both lists (forty countries), which, when subtracted from the total, gave the final result of twenty-seven countries.

Source: See the Index of culture indicators and sources and Tables 6 and 30 in Part Seven of this report.

Biodiversity and cultural diversity

Although humans are an animal species, the genetic mutation which gave them the capacity to learn and transmit knowledge from one generation to the next explained their historical success in expanding human populations all over the globe. Unfortunately this capability is leading to the destruction of biological diversity on the planet, with unforeseeable consequences. The loss of cultural diversity should then be seen as proceeding in interaction with the loss of biodiversity.

However, while biodiversity has been estimated at more than 30 million species, human beings, now that the Neanderthals and the Pithecanthropecines have disappeared, are one single Homo species, having at present several thousand diverse patterns of living.

Many peoples, some of whom have been placed in the category of indigenous peoples in the contemporary world, have evolved cultures that were closely adapted to specific ecosystems; they include the !Kung peoples of the Kalahari desert and the Yanonama peoples of the Amazon. They are now threatened by the destruction of the ecosystems in which they live. Aboriginal peoples living in deserts, tropical rainforests, mangroves or coastal or arctic regions are directly affected by environmental depletion and/or intrusions by other populations whose main activities are extractive: miners, loggers, large-scale fishing enterprises and so on.

In brief, as Claude Lévi-Strauss has said, 'diversity is less a function of the isolation of groups than of the relationships which unite them'. Celebration of our cultural diversity is to be welcomed. But it has to be accompanied by emphasis on what we have in common as human beings.

Cultural variables

We have affirmed the existence of human diversity. Within the flow of human diversity, people construct identities; and all identities, by definition, indicate a relationship between two persons or groups. Being Ashanti or Ghanaian or African defines a certain kind of relationship to other local, regional or national groups. Every identity is relational. Identities accordingly imply an affirmation of difference and possibly an antagonism.

This basic distinction pervades normal life. Yet there is nothing in the basic nature of people that assigns them to such different categories. Peoples and cultures define and construct 'us' and 'them' as part of their historical and cultural interrelationships. Who is on which side of the divide – and what attitude one category exhibits towards the other – is variable and depends on historical and local circumstances.

The perception and categorization of differences have been the basis of domination. Within societies there are class, gender and age hierarchies. There are also ethnically defined hierarchies implying domination and discrimination. Ideologies of patriarchy and racial superiority have been used to justify these practices. Only gradually, and not universally, has the view of the essential equality of human beings come to be accepted as codified in the Universal Declaration of Human Rights.

Whatever criteria are used to define 'the other', the range of positions towards others is quite wide. At the interpersonal level, one extreme is caring 'too much'. Appropriation or identification is the mechanism at play. The other ceases to be different; there is no room for his or her subjectivity and distinct existence. At the societal and political level, claiming to protect the other as if he or she were in need of such protection transforms the other into an inferior being. Ultimately, positions of this sort end up abolishing difference and turn into a form of disguised ethnocentrism.

At the other extreme, 'the other' is seen as so different and so unworthy of life that his or her physical being, often not considered fully human, is destroyed. Genocide and killings are the result. Alternative ways out are sometimes offered to the potential victims: complete assimilation into another culture, resulting in destruction of their former identities. History is full of cases where languages have been forbidden, where attachment to certain political symbols meant jail or death, where religious practices and beliefs were hidden or abandoned, where dress-codes and even the length of hair were, and still are, fixed by rules set by those in power.

Imagining difference

Imagining difference is the first step in acceptance of others. They in turn have the same right to build their awareness in freedom as long as their actions do not prevent one from enjoying that same freedom. 'It is not that we must love one another or die. . . . It is that we must know one another and live with that knowledge. . . . We must learn to grasp what we cannot embrace. It is in this, strengthening the power of our imaginations to grasp what is in front of us, that the uses of diversity and of the study of diversity lie.

CLIFFORD GEERTZ[9]

Colombian case study: after nature

In Colombia, struggles for the defense of natural resources have taken on a decidedly cultural character, particularly in the context of biodiversity debates. Such is the case with the social movement of black river communities in the richly diverse rainforests of the Colombian Pacific. The growth of this movement since about 1990 has taken place against a complex backdrop. At the national level, significant events included the opening-up of the Colombian economy to world markets in 1990 and a substantial reform of the national Constitution in 1991, which granted black communities of the Pacific region collective rights to the territories they had traditionally occupied. Internationally, tropical rainforest areas were in the limelight because of their importance as the main source of biodiversity on the planet. The emergence of collective ethnic identities in the Colombian Pacific and similar regions thus reflects a double historical movement: the emergence of the biological as a global problem, and the bursting forth of cultural ethnic identities.

The social movement of black communities that has developed in the region comprises a network of more than 140 local organizations grouped under what is known as the Proceso de Comunidades Negras (PCN). Emphasis is given by the PCN to the social control of the territory as a precondition for the survival and strengthening of culture and biodiversity. In the river communities, activists and communities have worked together to understand the meaning of the new Constitution and to develop concepts of territory, development, traditional production practices and use of natural resources. This process led to the drawing-up of a proposal for a law of cultural and territorial rights called for by the 1991 Constitution (Ley 70, approved in 1993), and to consolidation of a series of politico-organizational principles that emphasize four fundamental rights, i.e. identity, territory, a measure of political autonomy, and a self determined vision of development.

Because of its rich natural resources, the Pacific Coast of Colombia is in the spotlight of national and international development establishments. Activists have sought to insert themselves in biodiversity-related discussions at all levels. One of the most important manifestations of this has been the active engagement of river communities and PCN activists with the government-run Proyecto Biopacífico (PBP), a project for the conservation of the region's biodiversity which accepted the black and indigenous movements as one of its most important partners for dialogue.

Of growing importance is the increasing transnationalization of the movement through participation in official forums such as the Convention of Biological Diversity (CBD) and in various international oppositional movement networks. At the same time PCN activists have run for local elections, continued to organize locally and nationally and sought funding for territorial demarcation. In the midst of this, there has been an escalation of violence in the region, some of it directed explicitly against activists and communities to discourage them from pressing for territorial demands. These tensions are related to the overall intensification of development, capitalism and modernity in the region.

PCN activists have progressively developed a political ecology framework through their interaction with community, state, NGO and academic sectors. Within this framework the territory is seen as a fundamental and multidimensional space for the creation and recreation of the ecological, economic and cultural practices of the communities. The territory is seen in terms of articulations between patterns of settlement, use of space and resources, and symbolic practices. It has been demonstrated that local communities have developed through the centuries a sophisticated local model of nature that integrates the biophysical, human and supernatural worlds and is significantly distinct from modern conceptions.

One of the major contributions of the PBP was researching the traditional production systems of the river communities; these are geared more towards local consumption than towards the market, and for this reason have generally been sustainable. Practices are characterized by low-intensity exploitation, shifting use of productive space over broad and different ecological areas, diverse agricultural and extractive activities, family and kindred-based labour practices, and horticulture. In many of the river basins these systems are not only under heavy stress, chiefly because of growing extractivist pressures, but are increasingly untenable, requiring novel economic and technological strategies that will also generate resources for conservation.

Activists have introduced a number of important conceptual innovations. The first of these is the definition of biodiversity as 'territory plus culture.' Closely related to it is a view of the entire Pacific rainforest region as a 'region-territory of ethnic groups', i.e. an ecological and cultural unit that has been painstakingly built up through the daily practices of the communities. The region-territory is also thought of in terms of 'life corridors' which bring together communities, their activities and the natural environment. Life corridors may, for instance, link mangrove ecosystems or extend from the middle of the rivers to inside the forest. Some are formed around particular activities, such as traditional gold mining or women's shell-collecting in the mangrove areas.

The region-territory is a management category that points toward the construction of alternative life and society models. It is an attempt to explain biological diversity from inside the ecocultural logic of the Pacific. The territory, conversely, is seen as the space actively used to satisfy community needs. For a given river community, the area of effective appropriation of resources has longitudinal and horizontal dimensions, sometimes encompassing several landscapes and river basins. The territory thus embodies a community's life project. It should be emphasized that the region-territory is not a separatist strategy. On the contrary, and much like the case of the Zapatista in Chiapas, the call for some measure of autonomy is a proposal for a genuine national pluralism that responds to the recognized multicultural character of the society. It is a contribution by the social movements to a wider democratizing project that incorporates grass-roots communities in ways that were unknown in the past.

Whereas the territory is the space of effective appropriation of the ecosystem, the region-territory is conceived as a political construction for the defence of the territories and their sustainability. To put it differently, and unlike conventional approaches, sustainability cannot be conceived in terms of patches or single activities or merely in economic terms. It must respond to the multidimensional character of the practices of effective appropriation of the ecosystem. The region-territory can thus be said to articulate the life project of the communities with the political project of the social movement. Similarly, the definition of biodiversity encompasses local principles of autonomy, knowledge, identity and economy. Nature is not an entity 'out there', but is deeply rooted in the collective practice of humans who see themselves as integrally connected to it.

With this concept in mind, the reductive view of biodiversity in terms of genetic resources to be protected through intellectual property rights becomes untenable. The struggle for territory is above all a cultural struggle for autonomy and self-determination. The strengthening and transformation of traditional production systems and local economies; the need to press on with the collective titling process; and working towards organizational strengthening and the development of forms of territorial governability are all important components of an overall strategy centred on the region.

ARTURO ESCOBAR
Professor, Department of Anthropology,
University of North Carolina (United States)

Plant species

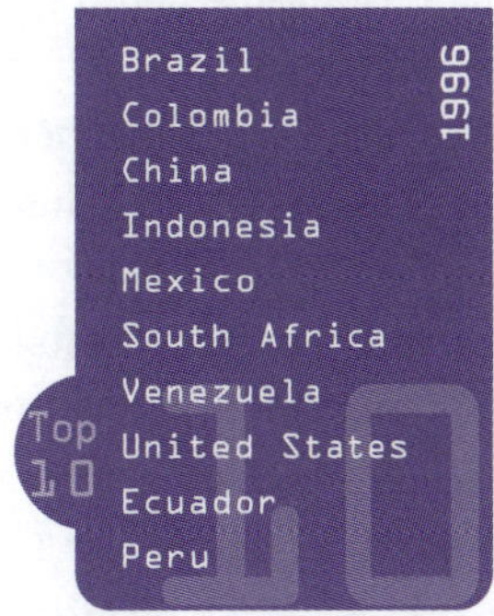

1996
Brazil
Colombia
China
Indonesia
Mexico
South Africa
Venezuela
United States
Ecuador
Peru
Top 10

Source: See the Index of culture indicators and sources and Table 30 in Part Seven of this report.

Forests

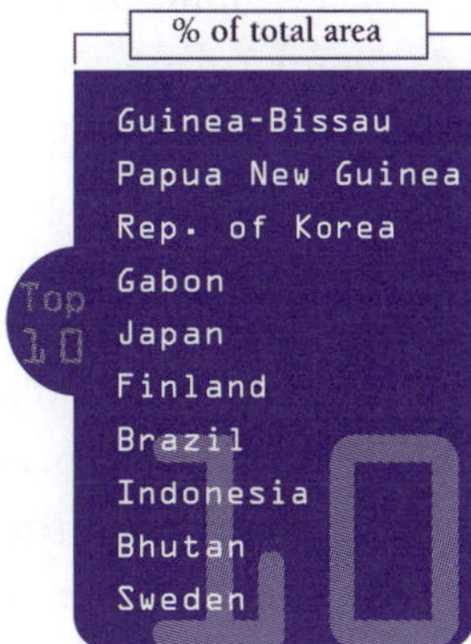

% of total area
Guinea-Bissau
Papua New Guinea
Rep. of Korea
Gabon
Japan
Finland
Brazil
Indonesia
Bhutan
Sweden
Top 10

Source: See the Index of culture indicators and sources and Table 30 in Part Seven of this report.

The pages of history contain many instances where groups have not just tolerated others but have based their mutual relationships on respect or even a shared closeness. The bases for such closeness are practices that accord dignity to the other while maintaining a creative openness as well. This attitude and this relation deserve a name: we shall call it conviviality. The challenge facing us today is to know how to deal with conflict, domination and cultural injustice in ways that will foster conviviality. It is an attainable ideal. We should do all in our power to ensure that our ability to create convivial relations – what we might call 'conviviability' – becomes a principle of development in global civil society.

Conflict and domination

A distinctive feature of developments over the last few decades has been a shift from class- and income-based conflicts to dissension over recognition and redress of cultural injustice. Conflict is normally viewed as destructive of the social order.[2] Yet it is not necessarily an obstacle to successful development.

One trend is clear: whereas violent conflicts formerly took the form of wars between nation-states, they are increasingly occurring as armed conflicts between parties that are not recognized states. Since 1945 civil or internal conflicts have been more common than international or interstate ones, a fact only recognized in the 1990s. The parties in these conflicts are generally referred to as 'ethnic communities', be they in Central Africa, the Balkans or parts of the former Soviet Union. Conflicts of this kind are the cause of increasing numbers of civilian casualties.

A paradox today is that ethnic and cultural demands have emerged out of a context of widespread acceptance of the principles that individuals and groups have equal rights, a right to dignity and to a social order that satisfies them; these are, in other words, the principles of the Enlightenment. Without this background, it is unlikely that ethnic groups would be able to articulate their demands as they do today. In fact, at the time of the Universal Declaration, progressive intellectual and political circles faced the challenge of creating the conditions for a new era of cultural pluralism. The recognition of pluralism was expected to become an antidote to the recurrence of massive crimes, genocide and cultural annihilation committed on the basis of ideologies and interests that implicitly or explicitly denied victims the status of human beings with rights. The ideology of universal human rights would thereby serve to protect potential and actual victims.

A specific trend, however, has developed in the contemporary world, leading to what has been termed 'cultural fundamentalism'. There is an assumption that relations between different cultures are by nature hostile and mutually destructive. This erroneous assumption leads, in political practice, to segregation and policies of exclusion, as the right-wing proposals for European immigration policies are showing. This assumption also leads to violent conflicts of the 'either-or' type where there is no room for bargains and negotiations. Within such a perspective, differences in ethnicity are seen as the underlying condition of violent conflict. People come to believe that the fundamental issue over which they are fighting is ethnic difference.[3]

This is unfortunate. It is also untrue. As most analysts and observers of contemporary violent conflicts are showing, domination and injustice, not ethnic differences, render people with different cultures antagonist towards one another. Conflict refers to opposition, disagreement and struggles. It exists in all realms of social life, in so far as diversity is constitutive of the human species. It is a significant force in social change and in cultural creativity, and often a force pushing for the redress of injustice. A society without conflicts would be odd indeed. But conflict becomes objectionable when it turns into violence, or when it is based on a denial of the dignity of others or even of their right to exist. It is not a matter of avoiding conflict, but of finding ways to pursue it without humiliation, violence or death.[4]

Generally speaking, conflict emerges as the contention for power between élites. Yet 'A conflict that begins as rivalry over the distribution of power within a political élite . . . is much more likely to gain popular commitment if it can be read in a different light, as a battle for national identity and pride, for

Nationalities and conflicting ethnicity in a time of transition

Recent violent conflicts and movements of people from other post-Soviet states have changed the ethnic composition of the population of Russia somewhat. Over 3.5 million ethnic Russians out of 25 million living in the new states moved there mainly from Central Asia, Kazakhstan, Latvia and South Caucasus. Several million other immigrants, mainly seasonal workers, entrepreneurs and cultural élite, have also come to live in Russia. They include about one million Azeris and half a million each in the case of Georgians, Ukrainians and Armenians.

Many are forced migrants from areas of conflict (Abkhazia, Karabakh, Tajikistan) or have been displaced internally following conflict in the North Caucasus (about 30,000 Ingush were expelled from North Ossetia while 500,000 Chechens and 200,000 Russians left war-torn Chechenia). There are new immigrants from countries in Asia and Africa (Afghan, Chinese, Kurds, Somalis and Vietnamese among others) who moved to this country seeking exile to the West and who are denied refugee status by the Russian authorities. Since 1991, a total of two million persons have emigrated from Russia including Jews, Ukrainians and Volga Germans.

In the early 1990s several major crises in centre-periphery relations due to a secessionist stance on the part of certain republics were settled in a number of ways. Following hard bargaining, the Republic of Tatarstan signed a special treaty (February 1994) which limits the power of the Kremlin and guarantees a high level of political sovereignty and economic and cultural control. In the ethnically diverse Northern Caucasus, the autumn of 1992 saw a violent conflict between neighbouring ethnic communities of Ossetians and Ingush in North Ossetia following a territorial dispute. The federal authorities failed to prevent the ethnic cleansing of the Ingush minority in the region.

In the Republic of Chechenia, secession followed the 'national revolution' of 1991, political anarchy and the expulsion of ethnic Russians. Then came a devastating war waged by the federal army in 1994–96. In late summer 1999 war broke out once again in Chechenia, resulting in over 40,000 deaths, 700,000 people driven from their homes and the total destruction of the capital city of Grozny and countless towns and villages. Strong pressure was placed on the Russian government by the international community to halt the violence against civilians and negotiate with the Chechen combatants.

The general trend in the late 1990s, however, saw a cooling of radical ethno-nationalism. This was aided by a modest economic upturn (despite the 1998 financial crisis) and by a growing public desire for order following drastic economic changes and violent political manifestations. This is noteworthy in the autonomous republics of the Volga region and in the Urals and Siberia where radical scenarios have given way to tough bargaining with the federal government in support of the social and economic interests of the local communities. Some territorial autonomies such as Buryatia, Chuvashia, Tatarstan and Yakutia are coming out in favour of a more pluralistic, inclusive cultural policy.

Russia is facing growing problems of chauvinism, xenophobia and religious extremism. The financial crisis, chaotic changes in federal cabinets and the struggle for power and privatizing resources have caused social tensions and stirred up the ultranationalist forces. An incoherent official policy towards questions of identity, coupled with the inadequacy of the law to carry out its function, have incited ultra-rightist activists, including the Cossack and other 'great Russian' chauvinist groups, to adopt anti-Semitic and anti-immigrant (mainly anti-Caucasian) positions. This has been the case above all in large cities such as Moscow and in the southern part of Russia where the population was suffering from Chechen raids in addition to floods of refugees. Chauvinism has proved to be a fertile ground where ultra-nationalist groups and part of the Communist opposition share a common cause.

Apart from the attempted breakaway by Chechenia, a real threat to civic peace in 1999 was posed by the Wahhabist strain of Islamic extremism. Nurtured and armed by certain forces abroad, mostly in Saudi Arabia, this trend has found a number of bases in Chechenia and Daghestan. Terrorist acts have been committed, including attacks on officials, abductions and taking of hostages and bombings.

An increasing role in conflict management and maintaining ethnic balance is being played by non-governmental organizations and other civic institutions. In fact, public organizations which in the past fanned ethnic tensions, such as the Confederation of the Peoples of the Caucasus, have faded from the political scene. National movements representing certain ethnic groups see their position and influence dwindling because such ethnic nationalist organizations have never stood for inter-ethnic accord or prevention of conflict. On the contrary, they have often adopted a destructive position; a case in point is the Ossetin organization 'Styrr Nykhas', which is hindering the efforts of the Ingush and Ossetin authorities to cope with the consequences of the conflict between the two groups and the return of Ingush refugees.

Such nationalist movements are now being replaced by NGOs and civic coalitions seeking peoples' diplomacy and ethnic accord. Unions and coalitions of a more constructive type are springing up at national and local levels. Local ethnic leaders too are beginning to show greater restraint in promoting 'national revival', preferring peace-making activities and cultural dialogue. Regular congresses are held in Pyatigorsk (Northern Caucasus) under the title 'Peace in the Caucasus through Education, Languages and Culture'. Public education projects are going ahead as part of UNESCO's Culture of Peace programme. Non-governmental organizations too are increasingly active in solving the problems of refugees. They have developed a network of legal consultation to provide new settlers with free legal advice and, if necessary, representation in court. Such activities are promoting a better culture of law in society.

VALERY A. TISHKOV
Professor, Director of the Institute of Ethnology and Anthropology, Russian Academy of Sciences (Russian Federation)

Cultural fundamentalism

A conceptual shift can be detected among the political right and centre in many countries toward an anti-immigrant rhetoric on cultural diversity which is based on certain assumptions underlying the modern concepts of citizenship, national identity and the nation-state. Immigrants from the poor South (and more recently from the East) in Western Europe are increasingly regarded as undesirable, threatening strangers. The immigrants already 'in our midst' are the targets of hostility and violence as politicians of the right and conservative governments fuel popular fears with a rhetoric of exclusion that extols national identity founded on cultural exclusiveness.

In some European countries, the media and politicians warn of the danger of cultural estrangement or alienation that immigrants provoke in the 'host' country. In other words, the 'problem' is not 'us', but 'them'. Although unemployment, the housing shortage and the deficient social services for which they are blamed are obviously not the immigrants' doing, 'they' are made the scapegoats for 'our' socio-economic difficulties.

The meaning of this culturalist rhetoric of exclusion has been controversial. I have argued that, rather than regard it as a new form of racism, this rationalization of anti-immigrant sentiment and policy can more readily be understood as a form of cultural fundamentalism. This is not merely a play on words. This culturalist rhetoric is distinct from racism in that it reifies culture conceived as a compact whole, bounded and territorialized. It is considered to be historically rooted in a set of traditions and values transmitted through the generations by drawing on the nineteenth-century ideology of the nation-state.

The conceptual structure of cultural fundamentalism is genuinely distinct from traditional racism as an apparently anachronistic resurgence, in the economically globalized world, of a heightened sense of primordial identity. Yet this contradiction between professions of equality of opportunity and individual freedom, on the one hand, and primordial or essentialized exclusions on the other is, in fact, intrinsic in modern liberalism.

There is an additional component of cultural fundamentalism. A key assumption concerning human nature can be found in political as well as popular discourse on extracommunitarian immigration by the early 1980s. Newspaper headlines, politicians and scholars, as well as the people in the street, invoke the term xenophobia alongside racism to describe mounting anti-immigrant animosity. Advocates of a halt to immigration, in effect, talk of a 'threshold of tolerance', alluding to what ethologists have called the territorial imperative – the alleged fact that populations (note, among animals) tend to defend their territory against 'intruders' when these exceed a certain proportion (estimated variously at between 12% and 25%) because otherwise severe social tensions are bound to arise.

'Xenophobia' literally means 'fear and hatred of strangers or foreigners or of anything that is strange or foreign' (*Webster's Third New International Dictionary*, 1986). Conservatives regard it as an attitude inherent in human nature, which accounts for an allegedly inbred tendency to value one's own culture to the exclusion of any other and therefore be incapable of living with others. This idea is, of course, a social myth rather than a natural fact, at least until a xenophobic gene has been discovered. Until then, xenophobia is to cultural fundamentalism what the bio-moral concept of 'race' is to racism, namely, the naturalist constant that legitimates and endows with truth value the respective ideologies.

Cultural fundamentalism, then, assumes a set of symmetrically opposed categories of people, namely, that of the foreigner, the stranger and the alien as opposed to the national and the citizen. The apparent contradiction in the modern liberal democratic ethos, between invoking a shared humanity based on the general idea that no human being is to be excluded, while at the same time speaking of cultural particularism in national terms, is resolved ideologically in the following way: a cultural 'other', the immigrant as an alien, and as such a potential 'enemy' who threatens 'our' national-cum-cultural uniqueness and integrity, is constructed out of a trait which is shared by the 'self'.

Understood in this way, national identity and belonging interpreted as cultural singularity become an insurmountable barrier to doing what comes naturally to humans (in principle) – namely, communicating.

Instead of arranging different cultures in clusters, cultural fundamentalism segregates them territorially. The fact that nation-states are by no means culturally uniform is ignored. Localized political communities are regarded by definition as culturally homogeneous. The presumed inherent xenophobic propensities – though they challenge the supposed territorial rooting of cultural communities, since they are directed against strangers 'in our midst' – reterritorialize cultures. Their targets are uprooted foreigners who fail to assimilate culturally.

Contemporary cultural fundamentalism posits nationality as a precondition for citizenship in a shared cultural heritage. Because racist doctrines have become politically discredited by the horrors of the Second World War, cultural fundamentalism as the contemporary rhetoric of exclusion thematizes, instead, familiar nationalist notions of cultural exclusiveness. Immigrants may continue to be identified by their phenotype, but what tends to be seen in their 'faces' nowadays is their status as aliens and their poverty, rather than their 'race.'

It will be interesting to follow the new controversies provoked by the United Nations population projections for Europe. Against the background of the ideology of cultural exclusivism just described, it should not come as a surprise that the growing need for immigrant labour in the wealthy countries, announced by the United Nations as well as by Eurostat, may bring about not only new state-designed natalist policies to induce greater procreative enthusiasm among national women: there are already signs that it may also make the ageing population more receptive to further cuts in retirement benefits so as not to be 'swamped' by undesirable aliens.

VERENA STOLCKE
Professor of Social Anthropology, Departamento de Historia de Sociedades Precapitalistas y Antropologia Social, Universidad Autonoma de Barcelona (Spain)

example' (Smith, 1997, p. 198). Thus, particular ethnic identities may emerge in the unfolding of conflict. Conflicts may sharpen the formation of identities with a return to their historical origins and a reinterpretation of an idealized past. Hence, what are called 'ethnic conflicts' are often conflicts over power or economic and environmental resources. Therefore, the underlying problem in relation to ethnicity and conflict is not ethnic difference per se, but political mobilization. War creates difference, and as the Yugoslav case shows, language difference is being manufactured as a result of war.

Ignatieff gives us a vibrant testimony of the dynamics behind such violent eruptions:

There is nothing in our nature that makes ethnic or racial conflict inevitable. The thesis that different races and ethnic groups can live in peace, even in harmony, is not a mirage. What is more, persistent hatreds, apparently unmovable, in ethnic war zones, following detailed analysis, are nothing more than an expression of terror generated by the collapse or absence of institutions that allow individuals to create civic identities sufficiently firm to balance out their ethnic affiliations. When individuals live in consolidated States – even if they are poor – they do not need to appeal to the protection of the group. The disintegration of states, and the resulting Hobbesian fear, is what produces ethnic fragmentation and war.[5]

Do all 'cultures' have the same value?

The basic dignity of all individuals and groups has been recognized, but this does not mean that all the cultures they identify with are of equal worth. 'Cultures' cannot be compared in this way for several reasons. Firstly, as explained in the text, they are not totalities that neatly delimit themselves from neighbouring 'cultures'; in fact, individuals in close contact with other cultures will tend to adopt traits belonging to those 'cultures'; hence most groups have variants of hybrid cultures within them. Secondly, basic cognitive and symbolic traits make any comparison of actual values or customs inappropriate. Thirdly, some values in some 'cultures' may not deserve respect. As Sowell puts it, 'if everything is respected equally, then the term respect has lost its meaning.'

THOMAS SOWELL[10]

Cultural and other injustices

Cultural conflicts today are invariably set in national or international contexts. They are part of the larger struggles over political power, economic resources and alternative visions of the social good. We live in a time of increasing disparities of income, wealth and access to information and the media. Economic inequalities among nations have increased in the past two decades. Moreover, this period has yielded new trends of increasing inequality within many rich and poor countries alike. Yet, as Fraser argues in Chapter 2 in this report, claims for justice must include not only issues of economic redistribution and political empowerment but also claims for cultural recognition.

Cultural opposition to what is perceived as a homogenizing global cultural trend has accelerated, just as the means of institutional redress of unequal access to economic resources has weakened or is attacked as ineffectual. The growing dislocations of power have accordingly coincided with growing cultural pressures. In this context, it has become imperative that we find the conceptual tools with which to understand cultural conflict, inequalities and injustices as part of a larger reality of growing inequalities and injustices in economic, social and political domains. In this larger arena the issues at stake are income inequality, lack of political power and lack of social recognition and respect.

We propose here to search for these tools, starting from a notion of 'cultural injustice' and proceeding from it to broaden the perspective. Cultural injustice refers to inequality in the resource base available to different groups that see themselves as sharing valued patterns of living. Such inequality may be historically inherited, but also includes cultural discrimination, namely, the closing of opportunities and of access to resources on the basis of cultural traits. The obverse face of cultural injustice is cultural privilege and domination.

Cultural injustice is rooted in patterns of representation, interpretation and communication. It includes cultural domination, non-recognition and disrespect. We must assume that justice today requires both recognition and redistribution. But there are interferences between them: recognition claims tend to promote group 'differences'. Redistribution claims, in contrast, often call for changing economic and social structures that exclude certain groups.

Examples of this are gender and cultural strategies for development. Gender has politico-economic dimensions since it structures the division of labour. On the other hand, gender discrimination is a cultural value as well. So remedies pull in opposite directions. There is a feminist redistribution-recognition dilemma: how can feminists fight simultaneously to abolish gender differentiation and valorize gender specificity?

The same kind of dilemma affects cultural diversity. How can indigenous peoples and cultural minorities fight simultaneously to have everything that the dominant cultures have, while at the same time valorizing their own cultural specificity?

This means that conflicts may arise between the preservation of cultural traditions and the attitudes and institutions that are needed for economic growth and development. As Amartya Sen[6] has argued, it is now for the people to decide whether to sacrifice material goods for the preservation of a culture or whether to sacrifice certain cultural features for greater prosperity. But we must first ask what margins people have for such decisions in today's structures of inequality.

Cultural diversity and inequality

There are two prevalent approaches to these basic issues of inequality. One seeks to redress inequalities through policies of redistribution and direct assistance to the needy. The other conceptualizes inequalities in terms of capabilities and access to opportunities. The means for building capabilities, as also for redistributive policies, necessarily include public action and institutions (primarily but not exclusively the state): access to education (in many countries, the opportunities for young girls have been practically nil, and thus policies to redress discrimination and exclusion have become urgent), access to health services, and opportunities to learn the skills needed to function in the modern world (including information technologies). It should to be noted that the effective implementation of a programme to reduce inequalities in capabilities and access requires macroeconomic policy and political regimes that facilitate rather than hinder them.

Processes of democratization are fundamental if the political regime is to play its part in redressing cultural and other injustices. However, political democratization is not just a means but also an end in itself. It allows individuals and groups the opportunity to help decide not just the policies that will be implemented but also the 'rules of the game'. As such, democratization can help establish a sense of 'ownership' of the policies and rules in place. This sense of ownership may also be instrumental in establishing a sense of belonging to the society.

The key concept here is that of citizenship. First and foremost, citizenship refers to the equality of basic rights to which individual members of a society are entitled. In a properly functioning democracy, the set of rights is not fixed but subject to widening and enlargement through participatory political practices. Yet there is another dimension of citizenship, one that is crucial to our concern with issues of cultural injustice. Citizenship has a collective aspect as well: it implies the recognition of the basic right to belong to political, social or cultural groups. The sense of belonging to such groups, the rights associated with it, and the legitimate recognition of this fact on the part of institutions of the state, constitute an integral part of the notion of justice that we are proposing. In the long run, this involves a process of empowerment of previously marginalized, excluded and disenfranchized groups.

Justice in the sense proposed here is an integral unity of cultural justice, citizenship rights and opportunities and capabilities to participate fully in the economic, political and cultural life of the community, whether as individuals or as members of groups. These elements define the basic building blocks of a society based on equality. To be effective, equality in this sense has to be built into the very institutional frame of a society and its governing processes and through which individuals and groups can pursue whatever it is they have reason to value.

This is not all, however. The central issue is one of knowing how to allow conflict that is rooted in diversity to retain its creative potential while preventing objectionable aspects – group violence, humiliation, even genocide – from surfacing. The core

LANGUAGES IN FORMER COLONIZED COUNTRIES

International language	Number of countries where the international language is: the leading language	an official language	the second leading language	among the five leading languages
Arabic	17	18	2	24
Spanish	17	18	3	19
English	7	23	3	25
French	1	20	2	9
Portuguese	1	5	0	3
Chinese	1	1	1	11
Russian	0	0	10	16
Turkish	0	0	2	4

GRAPH 2

This table shows the different historical patterns in which a colonial language has become a commonly used international language in countries colonized in the past 500 years and with a population of more than one million. One pattern is that of Arabic and Spanish. They are each the leading language in around twenty countries, reflecting a history where the colonial language was forcibly imposed and the indigenous languages were suppressed and sometimes wiped out.

A second pattern is that of English. It is the leading language in only seven countries but is an official language in twenty-three countries and among the five leading languages in twenty-five countries. This reflects a history where the colonial language was used for administrative and official purposes but people continued to speak their indigenous languages.

French is a more extreme version of the English pattern. It is a leading language in only one country and among the five leading languages in only nine countries. However, it is an official language in as many as twenty countries. Like English, it was used for administrative and official purposes, but it was very much the language of the élite and much less a lingua franca than English. To this day, the French spoken by an educated African is closer to Parisian French than the English spoken by an educated African is to BBC English.

Portuguese follows the French pattern, but covers only a few countries. If Portuguese America had broken up into as many parts as Spanish America, Portuguese would be an official language in many countries. However, the Portuguese colonial administration was much more centralized than the Spanish, and it transformed itself into only one country, Brazil, with a population equal to all the other countries of South America, which are Spanish-speaking.

Chinese has a different pattern altogether. It is one of the five leading languages in eleven countries, but almost none of this translates into an official language, a leading language or even a second leading language. In this case, Chinese was not the language of administration, but the language of commerce practised by a minority.

Russian takes on yet another pattern. It does not figure as an official language or a leading language, but, unlike Chinese, it is the second leading language in ten countries, nearly equal to the second-place slot of all the other colonial languages combined, and among the five leading languages in sixteen countries. Russian was not only the colonial language of administration and the official language, it was also the language of a state-imposed immigration. It remains the language of many who came to work in often sparsely populated provinces and who have now outstayed the colonial period.

Turkish is the eighth and last colonial language in the table. Turkish was the language of the Ottoman Empire and presents yet another picture in which the colonial language had very little impact at all. The Turkish rulers kept to themselves as long as the subject people paid their taxes and acknowledged sovereignty.

Source: See the Index of culture indicators and sources and Table 6 in Part Seven of this report.

of our answer is an integral notion of institutionalized justice and equality, political, economic and cultural. But implicit in our conception of how diversity may be guided to contain conflict while promoting creativity is also an affirmation of the idea of pluralism. Institutional mechanisms for equal treatment and against discrimination or segregation are only one side of this picture. Creation of avenues of dialogue and open communication – after all, culture is all about relating with one another – is the other, as we argue below.

Creative pluralism

Cultural diversity as a descriptive feature of our contemporary world is our point of departure. Diversity fosters creativity, manifested in the ability of human groups to adapt and transform their living conditions. As the world stands today, diversity and creativity are caught in the cage of inequality and injustice. To move forward, in fact, imagining difference is the first step, but it must be followed by acceptance of the Other. This requires recognition that others have the same right to build their conscious-

The problem of defining the good in pluralistic societies

The problem of deciding on the concept of the 'good' in pluralistic societies, for instance through the creation of overlapping consensus or intercultural communicative practices, is a difficult one to resolve through juridical or legislative measures. In any case, negotiating such differences cannot be done if a cultural canon is made into a metaphysical condition of being which is in principle opposed to cultural negotiation.

No position on these questions is possible without explicit or implicit valuations of 'the good life', not just for the individual but for society as a whole. It is possible, of course, to suppose that autonomous individuals should be free to pursue whatever they have reason to value.

At bottom, therefore, these questions can be answered only by considering the social necessity of sharing economic and ecological resources and the common institutional mechanisms which make that sharing possible. Without this sharing, the benefits of the social division of labour, even when this is immediately promoted by market competition, may eventually be jeopardized. But shared institutions do not automatically mean real democracy, in terms of individual rights, checks on majorities and curbs on money power. Shared institutions can be based upon domination and coercion or upon participation and co-operation. Their shape and scope depend on the particular configuration of power among individuals and groups and particular mechanisms for resolving conflicts of cultural norms and beliefs.

Disagreements about conceptions of what is good tend to increase the need for answers to questions exploring the legitimate use of state power. However, such disagreements also restrict what may be regarded as plausible answers among individuals of different views.

Given the variety of views about the good life and the number of divergent world-views, there will be disagreement about the absolute and relative importance of the interests we have. Reasonable disagreement is therefore to be expected about the value of a wide variety of goods under institutional control. Nevertheless, some goods, and access to such goods, may be recognized as forming bases for reasonable claims:

- ***Security goods.*** In order to ensure survival and basic security, spelled out in terms of basic capabilities, individuals should have control of foodstuffs, public health services and other goods.
- ***Human rights.*** These are regarded as universal in the world of states as we know it: all individuals have such rights. Minorities' interest in controlling cultural change may in principle ground rights of several kinds.
- ***Strategic goods.*** Income and wealth, social positions and educational opportunities can be recognized as valid across a broad range of cultures and conceptions of the good life.
- ***Political power.*** The reason for regarding political power as a good is not that individuals have a fundamental interest in self-legislation or autonomy. We have to accept, for purposes of justice, that individuals have an interest in influencing social institutions, particularly when alternative arrangements would place such authority with others. The present distribution of political power is steered away from citizens of poor states in favour of those in richer states and transnational businesses.

ANDREAS FØLLESDAL
Senior Researcher, ARENA
and Department of Philosophy,
University of Oslo (Norway)

ness freely as long as their actions do not prevent one from enjoying that same freedom.

'Conviviability' between people of diverse cultures is the utopia guaranteeing equality of life changes, but is incomplete if freedom is not incorporated in it. Heller states: 'It can only be incorporated provided entry into and exit from each and every culture – native or chosen – is a free act. If not . . . the freedom by individuals to assume multiple identities is regularly curtailed when absolute solidarity with one of those identities is demanded'.[7]

It is clear that we must insist on certain conditions for informed choice on cultural matters. The point is that the individual must perceive the alternatives as feasible and understand the consequences. Korsgaard expresses this succinctly:

> We may believe that a human being is free, if ever, when he or she not only has a range of options but an education that enables him or her to recognize those options as such and the self-respect that makes his or her choice among them a real one. Ignorance, lack of imagination and lack of self-respect are not just external constraints on the range of your options: they can cripple the power of choice itself. The possession of freedom of the will may itself be lucky.[8]

Cultural diversity has to be understood for what it is: conscious and deliberate choices that distinguish one culture from another. In places where cultures have historically intermingled for many generations, differences between them will be marked according to who, why and where they must be specified. Differences are then marked not only horizontally, between coexisting cultures but also in terms of scale, for clusters of cultures may also belong to broader cultural areas that are also regionalized according to areas of influence or power.

For example, a person may speak of the West when thinking in terms of macro-regional units, but may go on to distinguish between American and European culture; then subdivide the latter into Anglo-Saxon, Germanic, Latin or Nordic cultures; then subdivide Latin culture into, among others, French and Spanish; then the latter into Castilian and Catalan cultures, among others; then further subdivide these into the Catalan culture of Catalonia and that of Valencia and so on, seemingly endlessly, until he or she arrives at the Spanish saying, 'Cada cabeza es un mundo' (Every mind is a world).

Identity works in much the same way. A person may identify as a Mandingo in certain contexts, as a Senegalese in others and as an African in yet others. Having an identity requires defining that identity in relation to other local cultures and also to regional and international ones.

There are three general modes for dealing with diversity. The first one is relativism. Relativism takes the universality of culture – the fact that all human beings are 'cultured' beings, that is to say, that their actions have meanings within the groups to which they belong – to the extreme. If everything is culture, then there are no parameters to judge and compare traits and practices across cultures. Cultures are seen as closed systems of practices, beliefs and values. Boundaries among them are fixed. Relativism implies that the standards of one culture cannot be applied to others, thus any trait can be justified and interpreted only within a given culture. Cultures are their own justification.

At the other extreme, and far more pervasive in the world today, is a view of diversity that stems from an initial differentiation between 'majority' and 'minority' cultures, between 'mainstream' and 'marginal' cultures. The premise is that in any given society or country, there is a 'majority' or 'dominant' culture. Minorities, indigenous groups, migrants, in sum the 'others', are expected to adopt (or adapt themselves to) the dominant patterns.

There are two major problems with this absolutist approach to diversity. One is 'internal' and concerns the very idea of a homogeneous mainstream culture. In reality, the 'dominant culture' always involves social differentiation and hierarchical subordination within it. Not everybody is equal to participate on the same level in the benefits and the burdens of the group. Gender discrimination – that basic universal difference turned into a power relationship between men and women – is a deeply ingrained pattern in most if not all societies. It represents a universal pattern of injustice that has only recently started to become visible. Policies devised to redress it are very new and difficult to

Women's place-based strategies against violence

The concept of place is played out on three levels in women's lives and struggles. Women's bodies are the first environment or place. It is the female body that defines women as the other, as the reproductive being, the mother, as the sexually desired. It is the body through which women mediate all gendered interactions including those from which they defend and evolve their identity.

A second level is the domestic place of the home that for many women still defines their primary social and cultural identity and living domain. The home and immediate community are usually the safe places for women to express themselves. It is here that women foster their own sense of power and knowledge and sustain their own and their family's livelihoods as they balance their productive and their reproductive workspace. The 'usually' is an important proviso given that gender inequalities also lead to very unsafe home environments with domestic violence and oppression of women. Even if it is through resistance to these factors, women act and live largely in the home and so it is from this place that women draw their strength.

The third place is outside the home: the political and social public place, the male-dominated domain to which many women still have no access – and where most women find themselves silenced and where few women rule. The women's movement for many years now has been creating diverse avenues for entry into that place, even if too often marginal to the pulse of political power. They need to help redesign institutions where their voices will be heard in ways that can mediate and radically change the public political domain.

The politics of place is advanced in local struggles that are then connected up through networks, weaving together different groups in ways that cannot be easily placed in national, regional or international political categories. None the less they expand the struggle to levels beyond the local. The politics of place deliberately challenges the sense of polarity between local as 'here' and global as 'there'. Instead, the global is now being very closely mapped onto the local. People live with the global in their own lives and indeed shape the global at the local level. Using the opportunities offered by globalization – the shift in private and public discourses, new technologies, the ambivalence about the role of the state, the possibilities for linkages across geopolitical borders – women are responding to the changes, negative and positive, of globalization through the politics of place.

A place-based strategy for change in gendered difference towards greater equity is being mapped out by many women both as individuals and groups based on their everyday realities, their resistance to hierarchies and gender bias and their own activities. At the basis of this movement are the community women's groups networking within their community and among other women. Their activities defy definitions of women as simply the exploited victims of globalization. Instead they are creating and living the global in the local. By organizing into NGOs or community voluntary organizations they are resisting the worst forms of globalization in the work-, domestic- and market-place and are taking advantage of some of the opportunities of the new information technologies and access to different lifestyles, ideas and cultures.

One of the deepest and most difficult areas of conflict between the genders historically has been violence against women (VAW) – domestic violence, sexual harassment, civilian rape, and rape as an instrument of war. In the last decades it is in campaigns around VAW that women have fought many of the battles for their self-determination. Through diversified resistance, largely by women's groups in civil society, new political spaces have opened up that have forged legal, social and cultural change. These changes, however, must be constantly defended, since the globalization process is bringing about violence in women's lives in many new ways at all three levels of body, home and community, and public space. With globalization there has been a notable increase in domestic violence, rape, and drug and alcohol abuse, all of which have a detrimental effect on the well-being, health and self-determination of women at the receiving end of such aggression.

In contesting the growing violence which has come with globalization, and in reappropriating their bodies and safe spaces in home and community, women have brought the issue of violence out into the public space. Through the networking and linking of issues,

en have ensured that rape, domestic violence and harassment are
nger silenced or seen as isolated occurrences. Rape as a weapon
ar is now acknowledged in the mainstream press and by the
ic and, in the case of the former republics of Yugoslavia, swiftly
shed. Women's centres to help victims of rape in war have been
p in spite of ethnic divisions. NGOs around the world are both
ing immigrant women make other choices besides sexual
ices and recovering them from difficult situations.

The Fiji Women's Rights Movement (FWRM) provides a
lusive example of how the three environments of women are
ely interlinked in the politics of place. The FWRM grew out of two
ed needs: to protect women from domestic violence, and to save
n from being discriminated against as women workers in the tax-
zones. FWRM has included in its lobbying platform such matters
onstitutional reform, women's inequality in the workplace and
e, unpaid rural labour, and domestic and community violence.

Working with multiracial cross-section groups, FWRM has
istently lobbied for a minimum wage for garment industry
en, spearheaded enquiries into the conditions of women working
x-free zones and striven to obtain legal recognition for women's
id labour in the home, in subsistence farming and in agriculture.
have run a public media campaign on rape called 'Forceline' – a
term implying that rape is an acceptable cultural practice –
cted at schools, medical personnel, police officers and judicial
onnel, and rural women's groups. Drawing on international
ort, the group has become the voice of Fijian women in the
nal media and political arena. Thanks to its efforts to bring an end
ltural acceptance of wife-beating and rape, FWRM has opened up
paces in which women's three environments are politicized
ugh resistance to oppression.

NDY HARCOURT
der and development researcher and writer,
or, *Development*, and Director of Programmes,
ety for International Development (Italy)

implement because they represent a major challenge to an established power relation embedded in cultural practices.

The second problem is 'external', in other words it shows up vis-à-vis the 'others'. In one of its two forms, the absolutist approach stands for assimilationist policies that call for full incorporation of these others into the majority, seeking a path aimed at the destruction of diversity and otherness. Another form arises when the recognition of difference by mainstream society and power élites is based on a patronizing attitude while at the same time difference is also claimed by the subordinated other. The result of this patronizing attitude, when it is not accompanied by simultaneous movements towards full citizenship in the political arena and by economic policies of redistribution, is that cultural difference is turned into a barrier – both the majority and the minorities concur in establishing and maintaining the barrier, implying marginalization, discrimination and exclusion.

The perspective we are proposing here, that of creative pluralism, steers clear of both relativism and absolutism. Pluralism is not mere tolerance and indifference, which are the hallmarks of relativism. Nor is it a mere subterfuge for effectively assimilating or subordinating minority cultures into the 'mainstream' culture. Creative pluralism involves an active and dynamic coexistence of diverse groups. Creative pluralism incorporates conditions in the public domain that allow for creative contact and transformation. As noted by Appadurai and Stenou in Chapter 7 it enables culturally diverse groups to be organized in such a way as to be able to reproduce their identity while also evolving creatively over time.

Towards policies of equality and recognition

Our new task, then, is to develop policies of recognition and of justice that work together. Such policies must identify and defend those versions of the cultural politics of difference that can be coherently combined with the social politics of equality.

Cultural conviviality cannot be free of institutions. Nor can it be free of a historical inheritance that varies from one society to another. So there can be no general prescriptions about the form that these institutions should assume. Rules and institutions that constitute bargains of power and resources will always depend on a specific context. As such they will be conflict-ridden and there is no guarantee that they will either maintain or promote conviviality.

Socio-economic conflicts cannot be resolved once and for all nor resolved in ways that command unanimity. On the other hand, it is doubtful that a society's conflicts can be resolved for any duration if the effective capacities to participate in political and social life are distributed unfairly. Unequal capabilities, including those of cultural creation, are more likely to exacerbate conflict than to resolve it. As in economics, the political advantages enjoyed by some to the exclusion of others may cumulate over time to produce hegemony or irreconcilable conflict. Diversity reduces the probability of grave errors and of harmful cumulative processes. It provides a protective sheath of cultivated social prudence that is also likely to support economic and ecological prudence.

The presumption, then, is that both diversity and equality are conducive to harmony. Respect and reciprocity cannot, of course, be decided by law or institutionalized, although disrespect and hierarchy can be and often are. Nevertheless they may be promoted through a general principle of conviviability. Minimizing inequality in the social primary goods in Rawls's sense – not just rights and liberties but also powers and opportunities, income and wealth, and the bases of self-respect – is not only the most effective instrument in this regard but can also be institutionalized. Minimizing inequality is not merely justice as fairness in the Rawlsian sense but also the route to promoting conviviality and the legitimacy of a regime.

The failure to confront the unequalizing and disenfranchising effects of modern economic, political and informational processes is a root cause of the fact that conviviality and popular sovereignty have both remained unfulfilled promises. Minimizing inequality – not just absolute poverty – empowers the possibility of equal and effective participation and, thereby, of genuine cultural pluralism.

Policy recommendations: equal dignity for all

At the start of the twenty-first century, the world is returning to some of its fundamental, unresolved questions: the issues of liberty and equality, individual freedoms and collective responsibilities, sustainability and equity, and the role of government, democracy and justice. Cultural policies will play an increasingly important role in opening up the spaces for interactivity and negotiation in all these areas.

It is with this in mind that the following policy recommendations have been emphasized in the work done for this second World Culture Report.

1. Government policies should define cultural recognition as a basic right of human beings. This entails considering all members of a society and of a state as having equal rights as long as they respect fully the rights of others. In addition, every culture that respects others should have the right to equal acknowledgement of its identity. Every state should define the legislation, institutions and policy actions that best advance such principles.

2. Cultural justice is essentially indivisible. Hence it should be promoted as part of efforts to achieve economic, political and social justice.

3. Recognition is a basic need, but justice today requires both economic redistribution and recognition. Economic inequality and political marginalization are fundamentally inimical to both conviviability and human development. The emancipatory potential of both cultural recognition and politico-economical equality should be integrated into a single, comprehensive framework.

4. If people are made to feel inferior as individuals or as a group their capabilities will be impaired. The principle of permitting the full development of everyone's personality suggests an enabling approach to policy that builds on the needs, desires and aspirations of the people themselves. It regards people as autonomous agents with initiatives and responsibilities rather than as passive targets of policies.

5. Anti-discriminatory policies should be incorporated into education and all government programmes. This will affect all formalized relationships between citizens and the state. But the recognition of equal

dignity should be enforced not only in governance relationships, but should also become part of everyday life in society. Hence an informal, networked ethics of conviviability should be developed as a background to all social relationships.

6. Conviviability is based on the principle that all human beings have the same ability to create culture and hence to attain reason and to establish emotional ties with other human beings which, if lost, bring a sense of privation and pain. Pluralism in any given society becomes sustainable thanks to its capacity to absorb new and often unpredictable differences. 'To grasp what we cannot embrace' means imagining difference and living with that knowledge.

7. The capacity of human beings to feel empathy and compassion for others goes deeper than the mere coexistence of different ethnocultural groups and should be recognized as the basis for human conviviality in any society. Such feelings touch the most profound spiritual nature of men and women and should be given overt recognition in social and political discourse relating to a global society.

8. Cultural pluralism means granting cultural groups the right to diversity in the public sphere and this in turn involves recognizing some degree of political self-government for all such groups. This means sharing sovereignty by one method or another. However, the appropriate bundle of minority rights may vary among states.

9. The following policies may be established in order to protect minorities' interests concerning culture:

(a) the provision of a threshold of legal protections enabling minorities to explore, share and convey their culture to each other – their opportunities for communication among themselves are crucial;

(b) the protection of a culture from outside forces that would destroy its valued and valuable features – minority representation on political bodies is essential, particularly in view of the fact that conflicts can arise in unexpected ways;

(c) transparency regarding government action, including mechanisms to ensure minorities' access to channels of information, both to and from the government, about specific policies that concern them;

(d) mechanisms providing domestic minorities with leverage against government abuse – international audiences and advocacy networks can act to reduce the risks of a government misuse of domestic authority.

10. A balance between government, the private sector and civil society provides the social foundation for peace, prosperity, democracy and equality. In achieving this, it is necessary to create spaces for the continued activation of non-dominant cultural forms such as those that rely on relational notions of personhood and more collective or holistic conceptions of rights, responsibilities and organizations, as long as they respect the equal rights of others.

11. Educational strategies should take account of their impact on social attitudes and on the reframing of popular and mainstream identities in conjunction with the emergent culturally and place-based identities, such as those of ethnic movements. This does not apply only to minority groups; it also holds for the re-framing of popular identities in general.

12. Policies should support networks that are creating alternative visions of rights to subsistence, autonomy and the economy, and to nature in terms of ecological design principles that integrate human and ecological processes.

Notes

1. J. Mountain, 'Molecular Evolution and Modern Human Origins', *Evolutionary Anthropology*, Spring 1998, No. 2.

2. On the role of conflict as a valuable tie, see A. O. Hirschman, 'Social Conflicts as Pillars of Democratic Market Societies', in: *A Propensity to Self-Subversion*, Cambridge, Massachusetts and London, Harvard University Press, 1995; and P. Streeten, *Appendix to Gunnar Myrdal: The Political Element in the Development of Economic Theory*, London, Routledge and Kegan Paul, 1953. Hirschman's essay also contains a brief history of thought on the subject.
The discussion that follows is indebted to this essay.

3. Among the dangers of new forms of intolerance, the dogmatism of some self-defined communities is paramount. When ethnicity or any other cultural difference comes to be defined as 'essential', as part of 'human nature', it becomes the basis for claims in societal intergroup conflictive relations. Ethnic differences tend to turn into total identities, fundamental to the very definition of personhood within the group. Often such communities are defined or strengthened as part of the conflict itself and

may have weak historical roots. Leaders of such 'postulated' communities show a strong hand to their followers, denying the members their moral autonomy. Under such conditions, outside intervention and denunciation can easily be interpreted as disrespect for cultural diversity.

4. One significant analytical distinction is between 'divisible' and 'nondivisible' types of conflict. As Hirschman notes, conflicts about distribution can be negotiated, based on 'bargaining and arguing' (1995, p. 243). 'Highly varied though they are, they tend to be divisible; they are conflicts over getting more or less, in contrast to conflicts of the either/or, nondivisible category that are characteristic of societies split along rival ethnic, linguistic, or religious lines. Nondivisible conflicts have recently also become more prominent in the older democracies' (p. 244).

5. M. Ignatieef, *El Honor del Guerrer* [The Warrior's Honour: Ethnic War and Modern Conscience], Madrid, Taurus, 1999.

6. A. Sen, *Development as Freedom*, New York, Alfred Knopf, 1999, pp. 31–3.

7. A. Heller, 'The Many Faces of Multiculturalism', in R. Baubock, A. Heller and A. Zolberg (eds.), *The Challenge of Diversity*, Aldershot, Avebury, 1999.

8. C. M. Korsgaard, 'Commentary on G. A. Cohen and Amartya Sen', in M. Nussbaum and A. K. Sen (eds.), *The Quality of Life*, Oxford, Clarendon, 1983.

9. 'The Uses of Diversity', in *The Tanner Lectures on Human Values,* p. 264, Cambridge, Cambridge Univ. Pr., 1986.

10. *Migration and Cultures: A World View,* pp. ix–x, New York, Basic Books, 1966.

Bibliography

Allardt, E. 1993. Having, Loving, Being: An Alternative to the Swedish Model of Welfare Research. In: M. Nussbaum and A. K. Sen (eds.), *The Quality of Life*, pp. 84–8. Oxford, Clarendon Press.

Angier, N. 1999. Chimpanzees Doin' What Comes Culturally. *New York Times*, 17 June, p. A1.

Basque Government. Navarre Government and Basque Cultural Institute. 1999. *Sociolinguistic Study of the Basque Country*. Bilbao.

Boutros-Ghali, B. 1999. *Mes années à la Maison de Verre*. Paris, Fayard.

Castells, M. 1998. Informational Capitalism and Social Exclusion. *UNRISD News*, Autumn/Winter, No. 19.

Drobizheva, L. M.; Aklayev, A. R.; Koroteeva, V. V.; Soldatova, G. U. 1996. *Democratization and Profiles of Nationalism in the Russian Federation*. Moscow, Mysl. (In Russian.)

Escobar, A. 1999. After Nature: Steps to an Anti-essentialist Political Ecology. *Current Anthropology*, Vol. 40, No.1, February.

Goskomstat of Russia. 1998. *Population of Russia: 1897–1997. Statistical Handbook*. Moscow.

Hartman, G. 1970. *The Fateful Question of Culture*. New York, Columbia University Press.

Hills, J. 1998. Viewpoint on Social Exclusion: The Content Behind the Babble. *Social Sciences News from the ESRC*, January, No. 37.

Kaul, I.; Grunberg, I.; Stern, M. (eds.) 1999. *Global Public Goods: International Cooperation in the 21st Century*. Oxford, Oxford University Press.

Lieven, A. [n.d.] *Chechnya. Tombstone of Russian Power*. New Haven and London, Yale University Press.

Lukes, S. 1998. Berlin's Dilemma. The Distinction Between Relativism and Pluralism. *Times Literary Supplement*, March 27.

Mountain, J. 1998. Molecular Evolution and Modern Human Origins. *Evolutionary Anthropology*, Spring.

Putnam, R. D.; Leonardi, R.; Nanetti, R. Y. 1992. *Making Democracy Work: Civic Tradition in Modern Italy*. Princeton, Princeton University Press.

Rao, J. M. 1999. The Social Basis of International Cooperation. *International Social Science Journal*, December.

Sen, A. 1982. Equality of What? In: *Choice, Welfare and Measurement*. Cambridge, Mass., MIT Press.

——. 1999. *Development as Freedom*. New York, Alfred Knopf.

Smith, D. 1997. Language and Discourse in Conflict and Conflict Resolution. *Current Issues in Language and Society*, Vol. 4, No. 3.

Streeten, P. 1997. Some Reflections on Social Exclusion. In: C. Gore and J. B. Figueiredo (eds.), *Social Exclusion and Anti-Poverty Policy: A Debate*. Geneva, International Institute for Labour Studies, Research Series 110.

Tishkov, V. 1997. *Ethnicity, Nationalism and Conflict in and after the Soviet Union. The Mind Aflame*. London, Sage Publications.

——. (ed.) 2000. *Ways to Peace in the North Caucasus*. Moscow, Institute of Ethnology and Anthropology. (In Russian.)

Vyatkin, A.; Kosmarskaya, N.; Panarin, S. (eds.) 1999. *On the Move: Post-Soviet Migrations in Eurasia*. Moscow, Natalis Press. (In Russian.)

Zayonchkovskaya, Z. 1999. *Russia: Migration at Time Scale*. Moscow. (In Russian.)

Otherness of us,
people, planet, life to share
open like rose

Brad Burch

How big is the world!
s there room for me and you?
Yes, I think so too.

Anthony Vickers

Brotherhood and love
Linking arms around the world
Cherish all peoples

Shannon Kung

Full and peaceful Earth
Each intermingling along
Spins a peaceful song

Narin B. Stassis

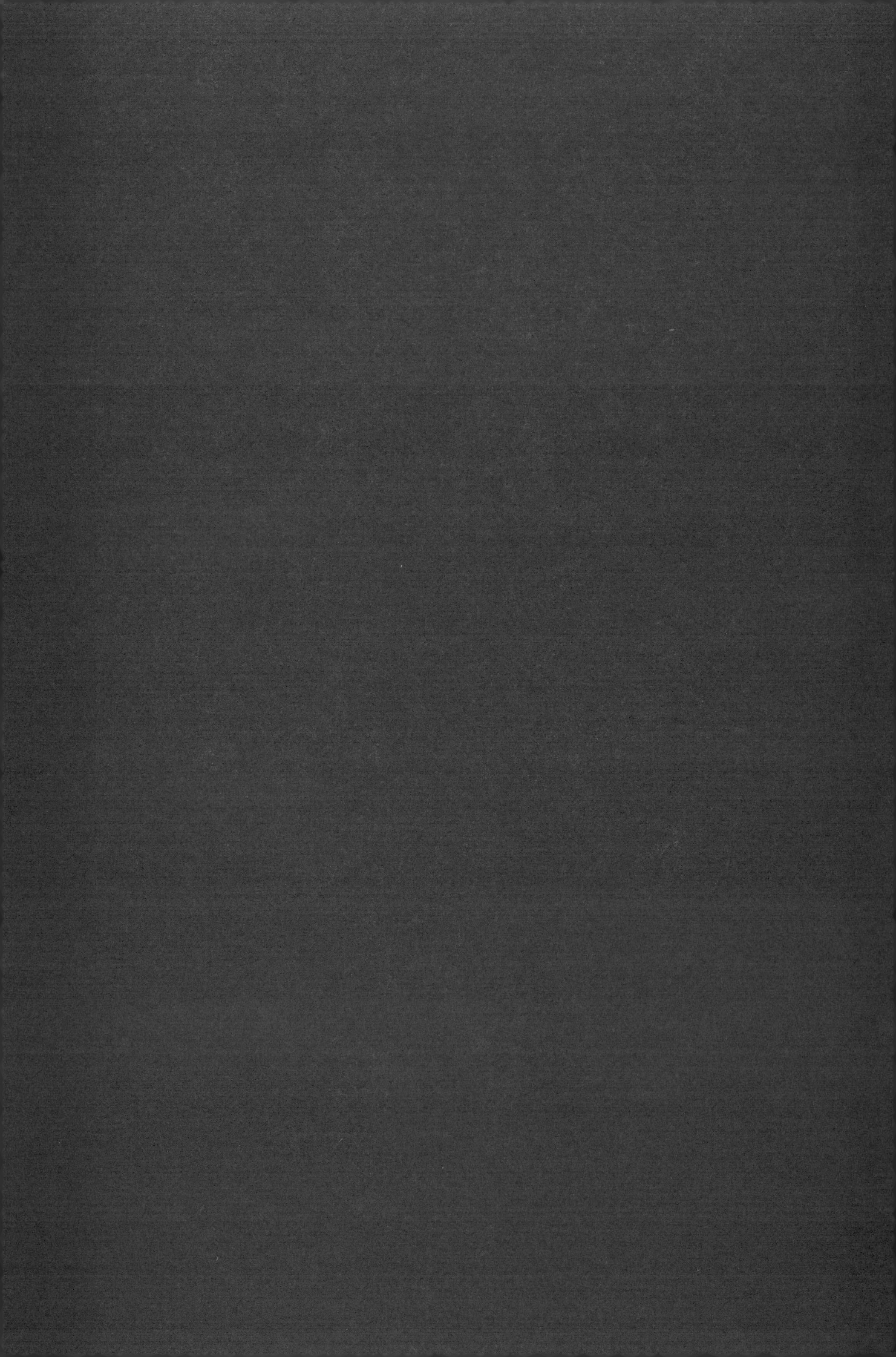

Part Two
Current debates

Introduction

Part One of the report gives an overview of the main theme of the second *World Culture Report*. It is clear that there are few certainties and quite a few questions, five of which are dealt with in this part, which for that reason is entitled 'Current Debates'.

There is first of all the crucial question of social justice and its two related components of 'redistribution and recognition'. Fraser, in a crucial contribution, argues forcefully and convincingly that justice today requires both redistribution and recognition and that these should be integrated in a single framework. Egalitarian redistributive justice is a well-known and recognized thing, even if it has come under attack by the current orthodoxy. The 'politics of recognition' is a new concept and refers to a 'difference-friendly' approach to such groupings as cultural, ethnic, racial and sexual minorities. Justice today needs both the politics of retribution and the politics of recognition. Fraser contributes to the current debate by arguing for a comprehensive framework that encompasses both redistribution and recognition so as to challenge injustice on both fronts.

The second consideration is the shifting balance between the state and the market in the provision of public goods. Giddens argues that a new balance between state regulations and market dynamics has to be found in what he calls a 'social investment state', which stimulates individual initiative and responsibility rather than passivity and resignation. The author observes that at the beginning of the twenty-first century we are confronted with wide-ranging social transformations: globalization, the rise of a new knowledge-based economy and the convergence of our active, reflexive citizenry. The advent of the knowledge economy is altering the rules of economic development. Societies can move from an agrarian to a knowledge economy without passing through a phase of old-style industrialization. Just as Fraser argues for a synthesis of redistribution and recognition, so Giddens, author of *The Third Way: The Renewal of Social Democracy,* attempts to identify a new synthesis between state and market in order to minimize both income gaps and the number of 'winners' in the rapidly globalizing economy that is accompanied by social, political and cultural globalization trends. Globalization is as much a differentiation process as a homogenizing force. The 'social investment state' places emphasis on human and social capital so as to enable people and to create civil society networks that will stimulate innovative approaches.

The third debate, initiated by Cohen, takes the globalization issue into the domain of cultural diversity by way of international trade and the 'cultural exception'. We have witnessed in recent years an increase in the number of trade disputes, all the more acrimonious in that they challenge the right of nations to retain their consumption patterns, protect the private life of citizens, maintain the moral rights of authors and stop the dissemination of new food technologies in the absence of irrefutable evidence that they are not noxious. We are also witnessing the rise of forces in civil society worldwide that successfully revolt against the homogenizing ambitions of the major players on the world scene. (An example of this is the failed attempt to introduce the Multilateral Agreement on Invesment (MAI), and the failure of the Millennium Round in Seattle.) Cohen argues that the right approach is not to oppose cultural fragmentation to the economic forces of globalization. It consists, once again, of a synthesis between identity claims and globalization. The principle of 'cultural exception' can function as a laboratory for a new concept of globalization that will reconcile open trade and cultural diversity.

We then come, fourthly, to an old debate in a new guise, that of poverty and culture. Stavenhagen, a well-known Mexican anthropologist, revisits this issue with the assertion that the contemporary narrative on poverty is as culture-bound as the versions of earlier times. He summarizes Oscar Lewis's thesis dating from the 1950s: the poor are poor because their cultural values prevent them escaping from poverty. The solution therefore lies in changing the culture of the poor. Stavenhagen argues that poverty among many world populations today – including migrant populations – is often related to structural racism, in other words, that most migrants to the industrial countries are poor and come from poor lands. If the poor of the rich countries are still poor and if poverty in the developing countries is not on the wane, it is because current policies have not been successful and alternative solutions must be found. Stavenhagen asserts that political cultures have ways of changing and that, in the face of persistent poverty, social philosophy is returning to some of its fundamental questions: the issues of liberty and equality, individual freedoms and collective responsibilities, the integration of humanity and nature, and the role of government, democracy and justice. In the author's view, a way out of the poverty dilemma calls for a synthesis between the current orthodoxy and a return to the positive and production aspect of the welfare state while strengthening human rights, democratic governments and popular participation.

The fifth debate is led by anthropologists Appadurai and Stenou. They examine the question of cultural pluralism and the fundamental rethinking this requires of our ideas of governance, belonging and political recognition. In this sense the nation-state plays a central role in the future of belonging. The authors claim that there has been a remarkable reticence to rethink the nature of sovereignty and more particularly to rethink the centrality of the nation-state as a co-ordinated locus of sovereignty, territorial integrity and the legitimate monopoly of force. Globalization has introduced two major complications in the field of cultural pluralism: it has intensified the tensions between migration and citizenship and it has intensified pre-existing tendencies towards nationalist xenophobia. Appadurai and Stenou introduce the term 'partial citizens' to pinpoint the fact that such migrants are not illegal, but face restricted rights in terms of employment, citizenship, duration of stay, legal rights and so on. The authors propose policy changes which require us to recognize three realities: (i) we must understand that we live in a world of heterogeneous political forms; (ii) cultural pluralism means granting cultural groups the right to diversity in the public sphere and this in turn means recognizing some degree of political self-government; and (iii) the question of loyalty and attachment to people living in the same national territory must be separated from the question of their rights as citizens.

Here, therefore, are lively papers about crucial matters already touched on in the previous part. To further illustrate many of the points made, this part includes an interview with Youssef Chahine, an Egyptian film-maker, and several boxes by other artists. Such discussions are of crucial importance in a world in which the majority of the population are minorities and where diversity can easily lead to conflict.

LOUIS EMMERIJ
Economist, former Special Adviser
to the President,
Inter-American
Development Bank (IDB) (United States)

Chapter 2
Redistribution, recognition and participation: towards an integrated concept of justice

NANCY FRASER
Henry A. and Louise Loeb Professor of Politics and Philosophy, Department of Political Science, New School for Social Research (United States)

'It is my general thesis that justice today requires both redistribution and recognition. Neither alone is sufficient.'

Introduction

In today's world, claims for social justice seem increasingly to divide into two types. First, and most familiar, are redistributive claims, which seek a more just distribution of resources and goods. Examples include claims for redistribution from the North to the South, from the rich to the poor, and (not so long ago) from the owners to the workers. To be sure, the recent resurgence of free-market thinking has put proponents of redistribution on the defensive. Nevertheless, egalitarian redistributive claims have supplied the paradigm case for most theorizing about social justice for the past 150 years.[1]

Today, however, we increasingly encounter a second type of social-justice claim in what has been called the 'politics of recognition'. Here the goal, in its most plausible form, is a difference-friendly world, where assimilation to majority or dominant cultural norms is no longer the price of equal respect. Examples include claims for the recognition of the distinctive perspectives of ethnic, 'racial' and sexual minorities as well as of gender difference. Moreover, this type of claim has recently attracted the interest of political philosophers, moreover, some of whom are seeking to develop a new paradigm of justice that puts recognition at its centre.

In general, then, we are confronted with a new constellation. The discourse of social justice, once centred on distribution, is now increasingly divided between claims for redistribution on the one hand, and claims for recognition on the other. Increasingly, too, recognition claims tend to predominate. The demise of communism, the surge of free-market ideology, the rise of 'identity politics' in both its fundamentalist and progressive forms – all these developments have conspired to decentre, if not to extinguish, the politics of redistribution.

In this new constellation, the two kinds of justice claims are often dissociated from one another – both practically and intellectually. Within social movements such as feminism, for example, activist tendencies that look to redistribution as the remedy for male domination are increasingly dissociated from tendencies that look instead to recognition of gender difference. And the same is true of their counterparts in the academy, where feminist social theorizing and feminist cultural theorizing maintain an uneasy arms-length coexistence. The feminist case exemplifies a more general tendency to decouple the cultural politics of difference from the social politics of equality.

In some cases, moreover, the dissociation has become a polarization. Some proponents of redistribution reject the politics of recognition outright, casting claims for the recognition of difference as 'false consciousness', a hindrance to the pursuit of social justice. Conversely, some proponents of recognition applaud the relative eclipse of the politics of redistribution, which for them smacks of an outmoded materialism that can neither articulate nor challenge key experiences of injustice. In such cases, we are effectively presented with what is constructed as an either/or choice: redistribution or recognition? class politics or identity politics? multiculturalism or social democracy?

These, I maintain, are false antitheses. It is my general thesis that justice today requires both redistribution and recognition. Neither alone is sufficient. As soon as one embraces this thesis, however, the question of how to combine them becomes paramount. I shall argue that the emancipatory aspects of the two paradigms should be integrated into a single, comprehensive framework. Theoretically, the task is to devise a two-dimensional conception of justice that can accommodate defensible claims both for social equality and for the recognition of difference. Practically, the task is to devise a programmatic political orientation that integrates the best of the politics of redistribution with the best of the politics of recognition.

My argument proceeds in three steps. In the first section, I shall outline the key points of contrast between the two political paradigms, as they are presently understood. Then, in the second, I shall problematize their current dissociation from one another by introducing a case of injustice that cannot be redressed by either one of them alone, but that requires their integration. Finally, I shall consider some normative philosophical questions (third section) that arise when we contemplate integrating redistribution and recognition in a single comprehensive framework.

Anatomy of a false antithesis

I begin with some denotative definitions. The politics of redistribution, as I shall understand it, encompasses not only class-centred orientations, such as New Deal liberalism, social democracy, and socialism, but also those forms of feminism and anti-racism that look to socio-economic transformation or reform as the remedy for gender and racial-ethnic injustice. Thus, it is broader than class politics in the conventional sense. The politics of recognition, in contrast, encompasses not only movements aiming to revalue unjustly devalued identities, for example, cultural feminism, black cultural nationalism and gay identity politics, but also deconstructive tendencies, such as queer politics, critical 'race' politics and deconstructive feminism, which reject the 'essentialism' of traditional identity politics. Thus, it is broader than identity politics in the conventional sense.

In general, then, I reject the familiar assumption that the politics of redistribution focuses exclusively on injustices of class, whereas 'identity politics' focuses instead on injustices of gender, sexuality and 'race'. Rather, I treat redistribution and recognition as dimensions of justice that can cut across all social movements. Understood in this way, the politics of redistribution and the politics of recognition can be contrasted in three key respects.

First, the two approaches assume different conceptions of injustice. The politics of redistribution focuses on injustices that it defines as socio-economic and presumes to be rooted in the politico-economical. Examples include exploitation, economic marginalization and deprivation. The politics of recognition, in contrast, targets injustices it understands as cultural, which it presumes to be rooted in social patterns of representation, interpretation and communication. Examples include cultural domination, non-recognition and disrespect.

Second, the two approaches propose different sorts of remedies for injustice. For the *politics of redistribution*, the remedy for injustice is politico-economical restructuring. This might involve redistributing income, reorganizing the division of labour, or transforming other basic economic structures. For the *politics of recognition*, in contrast, the remedy for injustice is cultural or symbolic change. This could involve upwardly revaluing disrespected identities, positively valorizing cultural diversity, or transforming entire societal patterns of representation, interpretation and communication in ways that would change everybody's identity.

MAJOR UN HUMAN RIGHTS CONVENTIONS

- Bhutan
- Botswana
- Eritrea
- Guinea-Bissau
- Indonesia
- Democratic People's Republic of Korea
- Lao People's Democratic Republic
- Malaysia
- Mauritania
- Myanmar
- Oman
- Pakistan
- Saudi Arabia
- Singapore
- Thailand
- United Arab Emirates
- United States

Graph 3
Countries that have ratified no more than half of the eight major UN Human Rights Conventions
Source: See the Index of culture indicators and sources and Table 14 in Part Seven of this report.

Third, the two political orientations assume different conceptions of the collectivities that suffer injustice. For the politics of redistribution, the collective subjects of injustice are classes or class-like collectivities which are defined economically by a distinctive relation to the market or the means of production. The classic case in the Marxian paradigm is the exploited working class. But the conception can cover other cases as well. Also included are racialized groups of immigrants or ethnic minorities that can be economically defined, whether as a pool of low-paid menial labourers or as an 'underclass' largely excluded from regular waged work, deemed 'superfluous' and unworthy of exploitation. When the notion of the economy is broadened to encompass unwaged labour, moreover, women too become visible as a collective subject of economic injustice as the gender burdened with the lion's share of unwaged carework and consequently disadvantaged in employment. Also included, finally, are the complexly defined groupings that result when we theorize about the political economy in terms of the intersection of class, 'race' and gender.

For the politics of recognition, in contrast, the victims of injustice are more like Weberian status groups than Marxian classes. Defined not by the relations of production, but rather by those of recognition, they are distinguished by the lesser esteem, honour and prestige they enjoy relative to other groups in society. The classic case in the Weberian paradigm is the low-status ethnic group whom dominant patterns of cultural value mark as different and less worthy. But the concept can cover other cases as well. In today's politics of recognition it has been extended to gays and lesbians, whose sexuality is interpreted as deviant and devalued in the dominant culture; to racialized groups, who are marked as different and lesser; and to women, who are trivialized, sexually objectified and disrespected in myriad ways. It is also being extended, finally, to encompass the complexly defined groupings that result when we theorize the relations of recognition in terms of 'race', gender and sexuality simultaneously as intersecting cultural codes.

Increasingly, as I noted at the outset, the politics of redistribution and the politics of recognition are posed as mutually exclusive alternatives. Some proponents of the former reject 'identity politics' as a counter-productive diversion from the real economic issues – claiming, in effect, 'It's the economy, stupid.' Conversely, some proponents of recognition reject difference-blind redistributive politics as assimilationist – claiming, in effect, 'It's the culture, stupid.'

This, however, is a false antithesis.

Exploited classes, despised sexualities, and bivalent collectivities: a critique of justice truncated

To see why the foregoing antithesis is false, let us imagine a conceptual spectrum of different kinds of social collectivities. At one extreme are modes of collectivity that fit the politics of redistribution: at the other are modes of collectivity that fit the politics of recognition. In between are cases that prove to be difficult because they fit both political orientations simultaneously.[2]

Consider, first, the redistribution end of the spectrum. At this end let us posit an ideal-typical mode of collectivity whose existence is rooted in the economic structure of society as opposed to the status order. By definition, then, any structural injustices its members suffer will be traceable to the political economy. The core of the injustice will be socio-economic maldistribution, while any attendant cultural injustices will derive ultimately from the economic structure. At bottom, therefore, the remedy required to redress the injustice will be redistribution, as opposed to recognition.

An example that appears to approximate the ideal type is the exploited working class, as understood in orthodox, Marxist economics. In this conception class differentiation is the artifact of an unjust political economy. The injustice is at bottom a matter of distribution, as the proletariat shoulders an undue share of the system's burdens while being denied its fair share of the system's rewards. To be sure, its members also suffer serious cultural injustices, the 'hidden injuries of class'.[3] But far from being rooted directly in an autonomously unjust status order, these derive from the economic structure, as ideologies of class inferiority proliferate to justify exploitation. The remedy for the injustice, consequently, is redistribution, not recognition. The last thing the proletariat needs is recognition of its difference. On the contrary, the only way to remedy the injustice is to restructure the political economy so as to put the proletariat out of business as a distinctive group.

Now consider the other end of the conceptual spectrum. At this end let us posit an ideal-typical mode of collectivity that fits the politics of recognition. A collectivity of this type is rooted wholly in the status order, as opposed to the economic structure, of society. Thus, any structural injustices its members suffer will be traceable ultimately to the society's institutionalized patterns of cultural value. The core of the injustice will be misrecognition, while any attendant economic injustices will derive ultimately from the status order. The remedy required to redress the injustice will be recognition, as opposed to redistribution.

An example that appears to approximate this ideal type is a *despised sexuality*, perceived through the prism of the Weberian conception of status. Here, the social differentiation between heterosexuals and homosexuals is grounded in a status order of society, in which institutionalized patterns of cultural value constitute heterosexuality as natural and normative, homosexuality as perverse and despised. The result constructs gays and lesbians as despised others who lack not only the standing to participate fully in social life but even the right to exist. Pervasively institutionalized, such heteronormative value patterns generate sexually specific forms of *status subordination*, including ritual shaming, imprisonment, psychiatric 'treatment', assault and murder; impaired rights of privacy, expression and association; diminished access to employment, health care, military service and education; impaired rights of immigration, naturalization and asylum; exclusion from or marginalization in civil society and political life; and invisibility and/or stigmatization in the media. These harms are injustices of misrecognition. To be sure, gays and lesbians also suffer serious economic injustices; they can be summarily dismissed from work and are denied family-based social-welfare benefits. But far from being rooted directly in the economic structure, these injustices derive instead from an unjust pattern of cultural value. The remedy for the injustice, consequently, is recognition, not redistribution. Overcoming homophobia and heterosexism requires changing the sexual status order, deinstitutionalizing the heteronormative value patterns and replacing them with patterns that express equal respect for gays and lesbians.

Matters are thus fairly straightforward at the two extremes of our conceptual spectrum. When we deal with collectivities that approach the ideal type of the exploited working class, we face distributive injustices requiring redistributive remedies. What is needed is the politics of redistribution. When we deal with collectivities that approach the ideal type of the despised sexuality, in contrast, we face injustices of misrecognition requiring remedies of recognition. What is needed here is the politics of recognition.

Matters become murkier, however, once we move away from these extremes. When we posit a type of collectivity located in the middle of the conceptual spectrum, we encounter a hybrid form that combines features of the exploited class with features of the despised sexuality. I will call such a collectivity 'bivalent'. Rooted at once in the economic structure and the status order of society, it suffers injustices that are traceable to political economy and culture simultaneously. Bivalently subordinated groups suffer both maldistribution and misrecognition in forms where neither of these injustices is an indirect effect of the other, but where both are primary and co-original. In their case, accordingly, neither a politics of redistribution nor a politics of recognition alone will suffice. Bivalently subordinated groups need both.

Gender, I contend, is a bivalent collectivity. Neither simply a class nor simply a status group, gender is a hybrid category rooted simultaneously in political economy and in culture. From the distributive perspective, gender structures the fundamental division between paid 'productive' labour and unpaid 'reproductive' and domestic labour, as well as the division within paid labour between higher-paid, male-dominated, manufacturing and professional occupations and lower-paid, female-dominated 'pink collar' and domestic service occupations. The result is an economic structure that generates gender-specific modes of exploitation, economic marginalization and deprivation. Here, gender appears as a class-like differentiation. And gender injustice appears as a species of economic injustice that cries out for redistributive redress.

From the perspective of the status order, however, gender encompasses elements that are more like sexuality than class and that bring it squarely within the problematic of recognition. Gender encodes pervasive patterns of cultural value which are central to the status order as a whole. As a result, not just women, but all low-status groups risk being 'feminized' and thereby demeaned. Thus, a major feature of gender injustice is androcentrism, an institutionalized pattern of cultural value that privileges traits associated with masculinity, while devaluing everything coded as 'feminine'. The result is to construct women and girls as subordinate and deficient others who cannot participate as peers in social life. Pervasively institutionalized, this androcentric value pattern generates gender-specific forms of 'status subordination' including sexual assault, domestic violence, lifelong tutelage, arranged marriages, dowry deaths, mass rape as a weapon of war, genital mutilation and sexual enslavement; hence, denial of bodily integrity, reproductive freedom and sexual self-determination; but also diminished access to housing, food, land, health care and education; impaired immigration, naturalization and asylum rights; exclusion from or marginalization in civil society and political life; media stereotyping and objectification; and harassment and disparagement in everyday life. These harms are injustices of recognition. They are relatively independent of political economy and are not merely 'superstructural'. Thus, they cannot be overcome by redistribution alone but require additional, independent remedies of recognition.

Employment-to-population ratio
female
1997
Top 10
China
Norway
Thailand
Sweden
United States
Azerbaijan
Denmark
Switzerland
Romania
Ukraine

Source: See the Index of culture indicators and sources and Table 28 in Part Seven of this report.

Gender, in sum, is a 'bivalent' mode of collectivity. It combines a class-like dimension, which brings it within the ambit of redistribution (with a status dimension), and simultaneously within the ambit of recognition. It is an open question whether the two dimensions are of equal weight. But redressing gender injustice, in any case, requires changing both the economic structure and the status order of society.

The bivalent character of gender wreaks havoc on the idea of an either/or choice between the politics of redistribution and the politics of recognition. That construction assumed that the collective subjects of injustice are either classes or status groups, but not both; that the injustice they suffer is either maldistribution or misrecognition, but not both; that the group differences at issue are either unjust differentials or unjustly devalued cultural variations, but not both; that the remedy for injustice is either redistribution or recognition, but not both.

Gender, we can now see, explodes this whole series of false antitheses. Here we have a collective subject that is a compound of both status and class, that suffers injustices of both maldistribution and misrecognition, whose distinctiveness is compounded of both economic differentials and culturally constructed distinctions. Gender injustice can only be remedied, therefore, by an approach that encompasses both a politics of redistribution and a politics of recognition.

Gender is not unusual in this regard. 'Race', too, is a bivalent mode of collectivity, a compound of status and class. Rooted simultaneously in the economic structure and the status order of society, racism's injustices include both maldistribution and misrecognition. In the economy, 'race' organizes structural divisions between menial and non-menial paid jobs, on the one hand, and between exploitable and 'superfluous' labour power, on the other. As a result, the economic structure generates racially specific forms of maldistribution. Racialized immigrants and/or ethnic minorities suffer disproportionately high rates of unemployment, poverty and over-representation in low-paying menial work. These distributive injustices can be remedied only by a politics of redistribution.

In the status order, meanwhile, Eurocentric patterns of culture value privilege traits associated with 'whiteness', while stigmatizing everything coded as 'black', 'brown', and 'yellow', paradigmatically – but not only – people of colour. The effect is to construct ethnic minorities, racialized immigrants, indigenous peoples, and/or metis as inferior and degraded others who cannot be full members of society. Pervasively institutionalized, Eurocentric norms generate racially specific forms of status subordination including stigmatization, assault, police brutality, enslavement, 'ethnic cleansing' and genocide; discrimination in housing, health care and welfare provision; diminished rights of immigration, naturalization and asylum; media stereotyping; devaluation of immigrant and/or minority culture; exclusion or marginalization in public spheres and political institutions; harassment and disparagement in everyday life; and denial of the full rights and equal protections of citizenship. Quintessential harms of misrecognition, these injustices can be remedied only by a politics of recognition.

Neither dimension of racism is wholly an indirect effect of the other, moreover. To be sure, the distributive and recognition dimensions interact with one another. But racist maldistribution is not simply a by-product of status hierarchy; nor is racist misrecognition wholly a by-product of economic structure. Rather, each dimension has some relative independence from the other. Neither can be redressed indirectly, therefore, through remedies addressed exclusively to the other. Overcoming the injustices of racism, in sum, requires both redistribution and recognition. Neither alone will suffice.

Class, too, is probably best understood as bivalent for practical purposes. To be sure, the ultimate cause of class injustice is the economic structure of capitalist society. But the resulting harms include misrecognition as well as maldistribution. And cultural harms that originated as by-products of economic structure may since have developed a life of their own. Left unattended, moreover, class misrecognition may impede the capacity to mobilize against maldistribution. Thus, a politics of class recognition may be needed to get a politics of redistribution off the ground.[4]

Sexuality, too, may be treated as bivalent for practical purposes. To be sure, the ultimate cause of 'heterosexist injustice' is what I call the heteronormative value pattern that is institutionalized in the status order of contemporary society. But the resulting harms include maldistribution as well as misrecognition. And economic harms that originate as by-products of the status order have an undeniable weight of their own. Left unattended, moreover, they may impede the capacity to mobilize against misrecognition. Thus, a politics of sexual redistribution may be needed to get a politics of recognition off the ground.

For practical purposes, then, virtually all real-world axes of subordination may be treated as bivalent. Virtually all implicate both maldistribution and misrecognition in forms where each of these injustices has some independent weight, whatever its ultimate roots. To be sure, not all axes of subordination are bivalent in the same way, nor to the same degree. Some, such as class, tilt more heavily toward the distribution end of the spectrum; others, such as sexuality, incline more to the recognition end; while still others, such as gender and 'race', cluster closer to the centre.

Nevertheless, in virtually every case, the harms at issue comprise both maldistribution and misrecognition in forms where neither of these injustices can be redressed entirely indirectly but where each requires some practical attention. As a practical matter, therefore, overcoming injustice in virtually every case requires both redistribution and recognition.

The need for this sort of two-pronged approach becomes more pressing, moreover, as soon as we cease considering such axes of injustice singly and begin instead to consider them together as mutually intersecting. After all, gender, 'race', sexuality and class are not neatly cordoned off from one another. Rather, all these axes of injustice intersect one another in ways that affect everyone's interests and identities. Thus, anyone who is both gay and working-class will need both redistribution and recognition. Seen this way, moreover, virtually every individual who suffers injustice needs to integrate both kinds of claims. And so, furthermore, will anyone who cares about social justice, regardless of individual, personal social location.

In general, then, one should roundly reject the construction of redistribution and recognition as mutually exclusive alternatives. The goal should rather be to develop an integrated approach that can encompass and harmonize both dimensions of social justice.

Normative-philosophical issues: justice as participatory parity

How can we develop such a two-pronged approach? How can we integrate redistribution and recognition in a single framework so as to overcome their current dissociation? In the remainder of this essay I want to consider two sets of issues: normative-philosophical issues, which concern the relation between recognition and distributive justice as categories in moral theory; and social-theoretical issues, which concern the relation between economy and culture.

The project of integrating redistribution and recognition in a single framework impinges on a continuing debate over three normative philosophical questions. First, is recognition really a matter of justice, or is it a matter of self-realization? Second, do distributive justice and recognition constitute two distinct, *sui generis*, normative paradigms, or can either of them be subsumed within the other? And third, does justice require the recognition of what is distinctive about individuals or groups, or is recognition of our common humanity sufficient?

With respect to the first question, I propose to understand recognition as an issue of justice, not of self-realization. Thus, one should not answer the question, 'What's wrong with misrecognition?', with the answer that it impedes self-realization by distorting the subject's 'practical relation-to-self'.[5]

GOLDEN PEN OF FREEDOM LAUREATES

1961	Ahmet Emin Yalman, *Hur Vatan*, Turkey
1963	U. Sein Win, *The Guardian*, Burma
1964	Gabriel Makoso, *Le Courrier d'Afrique*, Democratic Republic of the Congo
1965	Esmond Wickremesinghe, Assoc. Newspapers of Ceylon, Sri Lanka
1966	Jules Dubois, *The Chicago Tribune*, United States
1967	Mochtar Lubis, *Indonesia Raya*, Indonesia
1968	Christos Lambrakis, *To Vima*, Greece
1969	The Czechoslovak press fighting for freedom
1970	Alberto Gainza Paz, *La Prensa*, Argentina
1972	Hubert Beuve-Méry, *Le Monde*, France
1973	Anton Betz, *Rheninische Post*, Germany
1974	Julio de Mesquita Netu, *O Estado de Sao Paulo*, Brazil
1975	Sang-Man Kim, *Dong-A Ilbo*, Republic of Korea
1976	Raul Régo, *Republica - A Luta*, Portugal
1977	Robert High Lilley, *Belfast Telegraph*, United Kingdom
1978	Percy Qoboza, *The World*, South Africa and Donald Woods, *The Daily Dispatch*
1979	Claude Bellanger, *Le Parisien Libere*, France, posthumously
1980	Jacobo Timerman, *La Opinion*, Argentina
1981	José Javier Uranga, *Diario de Navarra*, Spain
1982	P. Joaquin Chamorro Barrios, *La Prensa*, Nicaragua
1985	Joaquin Roces, *The Manila Times*, Philippines
1986	Anthony Heard, *The Cape Times*, South Africa
1987	Juan Pablo Cardenas, *Analisis*, Chile
1988	Naji al-Ali, Palestinian Cartoonist, posthumously
1989	Sergei Grigoryants, *Glasnost*, USSR
1990	Luis Gabriel Cano, *El Espectador*, Colombia
1991	Gitobu Imanyara, *The Nairobi Law Monthly*, Kenya
1992	Dai Qing, *Guangming Daily*, China
1993	Pius Njawe, *Le Messager*, Cameroon
1994	Omar Belhouchet, *El Watan*, Algeria
1995	Gao Yu, Freelance Journalist, China
1996	Yndamiro Restano Diaz, *The Independent Press*, Cuba, Bureau of Cuba (BPIC)
1997	Mehmed Halilovic, *Oslobodenje*, Bosnia and Herzegovina; Heni Erceg, *Feral Tribune*, Croatia; and Dusan Mijic, *Nasa Borba*, Yugoslavia
1998	Doan Viet Hoat, *Dien Dan Tu Do*, Viet Nam
1999	Faraj Sarkohi, *Adineh*, Iran (Islamic Republic of)
2000	Nizar Nayouf, *Sawt Al-Democratiyya*, Syrian Arab Republic

GRAPH 4
Since 1961, the World Association of Newspapers, based in Paris, has awarded the Golden Pen of Freedom, its annual press freedom prize, to a journalist who has made an outstanding contribution to press freedom. The following table lists the thirty-nine recipients of the award who come from thirty-four different countries.

Source: World Association of Newspapers, 2000.

One should say, rather, that it is unjust that some individuals and groups are denied the status of full partners in social interaction simply as a consequence of institutionalized patterns of cultural value in whose construction they have not equally participated and which disparage their distinctive characteristics or the distinctive characteristics assigned to them.

Let me explain. To view recognition as a matter of justice is to treat it as an issue of status. This in turn means examining institutionalized patterns of cultural value for their effects on the relative standing of social actors. If and when such patterns constitute actors as peers, capable of participating on a par with one another in social life, then we can speak of reciprocal recognition and status equality. When, in contrast, institutionalized patterns of cultural value constitute some actors as inferior, excluded, wholly other, or simply invisible, hence as less than full partners in social interaction, then we can speak of misrecognition and status subordination.

Least income inequality
Top 10
1988 - 98
Slovakia
Austria
Norway
Finland
Czech Republic
Sweden
Belgium
Denmark
Poland
Hungary

Source: See the Index of culture indicators and sources and Table 28 in Part Seven of this report.

This account has a number of advantages. First, it permits us to sidestep unresolvable disagreements about self-realization and the good. Second, it explains why misrecognition is not simply a matter of prejudicial attitudes resulting in psychological harms but a matter of institutionalized patterns of cultural value that impede equal participation in social life. Finally, it avoids the patently dubious view that everyone has an equal right to social esteem. What it *does* entail is that everyone has an equal right to pursue social esteem under fair conditions of equal opportunity. And such conditions do not apply when, for example, the institutionalized patterns of cultural value pervasively downgrade femininity, 'non-whiteness', homosexuality, and everything culturally associated with them. When that is the case, women and/or people of colour and/or gays and lesbians face obstacles in the quest for esteem that are not encountered by others. And all individuals, including straight white men, face further obstacles if they opt to pursue projects and cultivate traits that are culturally coded as feminine, homosexual or 'non-white'.

Does it follow, turning now to the second question, that distributive justice and recognition constitute two distinct, *sui generis*, normative paradigms? Or can either of them be reduced to the other?

In my view, the answer is 'No'. As we saw, recognition cannot be reduced to distribution because one's status in society is not simply a function of one's class position. Witness the case of the African-American Wall-Street banker who cannot get a taxi to pick him up. In this case, the injustice of misrecognition has little to do with maldistribution. It is rather a consequence of institutionalized patterns of cultural value that constitute people of colour as comparatively unworthy of respect and esteem. To handle such cases, a theory of justice must reach beyond the distribution of resources and goods to examine patterns of cultural value. It must consider whether institutionalized patterns of cultural value constitute some social actors as less than full partners in social interaction.

Conversely, likewise, distribution cannot be reduced to recognition because one's access to resources is not simply a function of one's status. Witness the case of the skilled white male industrial worker who becomes unemployed due to a factory closing after a speculative corporate merger. In this case, the injustice of maldistribution has little to do with misrecognition. It is rather the consequence of imperatives intrinsic to an order of specialized economic relations whose *raison d'être* is the accumulation of profits. To handle such cases, a theory of justice must reach beyond cultural value patterns to examine the economic structure of society. It must consider whether economic mechanisms that are relatively decoupled from cultural value patterns and that operate in a relatively impersonal way deprive some social actors of the resources they need to participate fully in social life.

In general, then, neither distribution nor recognition can be reduced to the other. Rather than endorsing either one of these paradigms to the exclusion of the other, I propose to develop what I shall call a 'two-dimensional' conception of justice. A two-dimensional conception treats distribution and recognition as distinct perspectives on, and dimensions of, justice. Without reducing either dimension to the other, it encompasses both of them within a broader, overarching framework.

As already noted, the normative core of my conception is the notion of 'parity of participation'. According to this norm, justice requires social arrangements that permit all adult members of society to interact with each other as peers. For participatory parity to be possible, I claim, at least two social conditions must be satisfied. First, the distribution of material resources must be such as to ensure participants' independence and 'voice'. This I call the 'objective' condition of participatory parity. It precludes arrangements that institutionalize deprivation, exploitation and gross disparities in wealth, income, labour and leisure time.

In contrast, the second condition for participatory parity I call 'intersubjective'. It requires that institutionalized patterns of cultural value express equal respect for all participants and ensure equal opportunity for achieving social esteem. This condition precludes cultural patterns that systematically depreciate some categories of people and the qualities associated with them, whether by burdening them with excessive ascribed 'difference' from others or by failing to acknowledge their distinctiveness.

Both the objective condition and the intersubjective condition are necessary for participatory parity. Neither alone is sufficient. The objective condition brings into focus concerns traditionally associated with the theory of distributive justice, especially concerns pertaining to the economic structure of society and to economically defined class differentials. The intersubjective condition brings into focus concerns that have recently been highlighted in the philosophy of recognition, especially concerns pertaining to the status order of society and to culturally defined hierarchies of status. Thus, a two-dimensional conception of justice oriented to the norm of participatory parity encompasses both redistribution and recognition, without reducing either one to the other.

This now brings us to the third question. Does justice require the recognition of what is distinctive about individuals or groups, over and above the recognition of our common humanity? Here it is important to note that participatory parity is a universalist norm in two senses: first, it encompasses all adult partners to interaction; and second, it presupposes the equal moral worth of human beings. But moral universalism in these senses still leaves open the question whether recognition of individual or group distinctiveness could be required by justice as one element among others of the intersubjective condition for participatory parity.

This question cannot be answered, however, by abstract conceptual analysis alone. It needs rather to be approached in the spirit of pragmatism as informed by the insights of critical social theory. Everything depends on precisely what currently misrecognized people need in order to be able to participate as peers in social life. And there is no reason to assume that all of them need the same thing in every context. In some cases, they may need to be unburdened of excessive ascribed or constructed distinctiveness in order to be able to participate as full partners in interaction. In other cases, they may need to have hitherto underacknowledged distinctiveness taken into account. In still other cases, they may need to shift the focus onto dominant or advantaged groups, bringing out the latter's distinctiveness, which had been falsely parading as universality. Alternatively, they may need to deconstruct the very terms in which attributed differences are currently elaborated. Finally, they may need all of the above, or several of the above, in combination with one another and in combination with redistribution. Which people need which kind(s) of recognition in which contexts depends on the nature of the obstacles they face with regard to participatory parity.

Conclusion

Let me conclude by recapitulating my overall argument. I have argued that to pose an either/or choice between the politics of redistribution and the politics of recognition is to posit a false antithesis. On the contrary, justice today requires both. Thus, I have argued for a comprehensive framework that encompasses both redistribution and recognition so as to challenge injustice on both fronts.

I then examined two sets of issues that arise once we contemplate devising such a framework. On the plane of moral theory, I argued for a single, two-dimensional conception of justice that encompasses both redistribution and recognition without reducing either one of them to the other. And I proposed the notion of parity of participation as its normative core.

The key political question of our day is: How can we develop a coherent programmatic perspective that integrates redistribution and recognition? How can we develop a framework that integrates what remains cogent and unsurpassable in the socialist vision with what is defensible and compelling in the apparently 'postsocialist' vision of multiculturalism?

If we fail to ask this question, if we cling instead to false antitheses and misleading either/or dichotomies, we will miss the chance to envisage social arrangements that can redress both economic and cultural injustices. Only by looking to integrative approaches that unite redistribution and recognition can we meet the requirements of justice for all.

Notes

1. Research for this paper was supported by the Tanner Foundation for Human Values, Stanford University and UNESCO. I am grateful for helpful comments from Elizabeth Anderson, Richard J. Bernstein, Judith Butler, Rainer Forst, Axel Honneth, Theodore Koditschek, Steven Lukes, Jane Mansbridge, Linda Nicholson, Anne Phillips, Erik Olin Wright and Eli Zaretsky.
2. The discussion which follows substantially revises a section of my essay, 'From Redistribution to Recognition? Dilemmas of Justice in a "Postsocialist" Age', *New Left Review,* No. 212, July/August 1995, pp. 68–93; reprinted in N. Fraser, *Justice Interruptus: Critical Reflections on the 'Postsocialist' Condition,* London, Routledge, 1997.
3. R. Sennett and J. Cobb, *The Hidden Injuries of Class,* New York, Knopf, 1973.
4. I am grateful to Erik Olin Wright (personal communication, 1997) for help in formulating several of these points.
5. This formulation represents the alternative approach of A. Honneth as developed in *The Struggle for Recognition: The Moral Grammar of Social Conflicts,* trans. J. Anderson, Polity Press, 1995.

Chapter 3
Globalization, inequality and the social investment state[1]

ANTHONY GIDDENS
Professor, Director of London School of Economics and Political Science (United Kingdom)

'My suggestion is that a new balance between state regulation and market dynamics is to be found in a "social investment state".'

At the beginning of the twenty-first century we are confronted with wide-ranging social transformations: globalization, the rise of the new knowledge-based economy, and the emergence of an active, reflexive citizenry. Each of these refers to a complex of changes; moreover, each is connected with the others. The intensifying of globalization has been deeply influenced by the information technology revolution, while the knowledge economy itself is becoming globalized. At the same time the rapid diffusion of information dissolves tradition and custom, enforcing a more active, open approach to life. Fostering more rapid scientific innovation, globalization contributes directly to the creation of new risk situations; it places a premium upon the effective management of both the dynamic and the threatening sides of risk-taking. Countries and individuals differ widely in their capacity to cope with these challenges. Globalization thus produces 'winners' and 'losers', and becomes a source of new inequalities. If we are to confront these disparities we will have to adapt our policies and our institutions to the new situation.

Uneven globalization and development

The globalizing economy has a number of distinct features.[2] Science and technology, and human symbolic skills, play an increasingly essential role in productivity and therefore in economic growth. Productivity in the advanced economies, unlike in earlier stages of capitalist development, is no longer as dependent upon the addition of capital or labour to the production process. Information-processing activities are growing in importance as measured both in terms of contribution to the gross domestic product and the proportion of the workforce involved. A fundamental transition is taking place in the organization of production and of economic activity more generally, towards customized products, the flattening of economic hierarchies and the creation of networks linking firms or parts of firms. Along with these, a growing role is played by small and medium-sized businesses in generating economic development.

The dynamic sectors of the world today are in finance, computers and software, telecommunications, biotechnology and the communications industries. Industrial manufacture, of course, is still highly important, and to some extent has become redistributed to non-Western countries. However, most manufacturing processes have become closely integrated with information technology, as have retail and distribution. Moreover, ideas, image and brand name count for far more in generating profitability than efficiency of manufacture. Efficient manufacture is a bottom line, a necessary condition, but certainly not a sufficient one.

The advent of the knowledge economy is altering the rules of economic development. Societies or regions can move from an agrarian to a knowledge economy without passing through a phase of old-style industrialization. One example is the area around Chicago in the Great Lakes region, where agricultural markets led to financial markets. The much-elaborated 'Silicon Valley' of India, in the Bangalore area, is another illustration. Yet these new opportunities also make development more complex: in the context of a knowledge-intensive global economy, a burgeoning manufacturing sector and other achievements of old-style industrialization become almost meaningless as indicators of economic progress.[3]

Globalization is by no means wholly economic in its nature, causes or consequences. It is a basic mistake to limit the concept to the global marketplace. Globalization is also social, political and cultural. On all these levels, it is a highly uneven set of processes, proceeding in a fragmentary and oppositional fashion. Although mainly dominated by the industrialized nations, it is not simply the same as 'Westernization' – all the countries in the world today are affected by globalization processes. Developments in science and technology, for example, affect people's lives in richer and poorer countries alike and in a more immediate way than ever before. Yet how they affect people's lives differs, and this is because globalization is much less a homogenizing, than a differentiating, process.

Globalization is not developing in an even-handed way, and is by no means wholly benign in its consequences. To many people living outside Europe or North America, it looks uncomfortably like Westernization – or, perhaps, Americanization, since the United States is now the sole superpower, with a dominant economic, cultural and military position worldwide. Many of the most visible cultural ex-

INTERNATIONAL POVERTY LINE

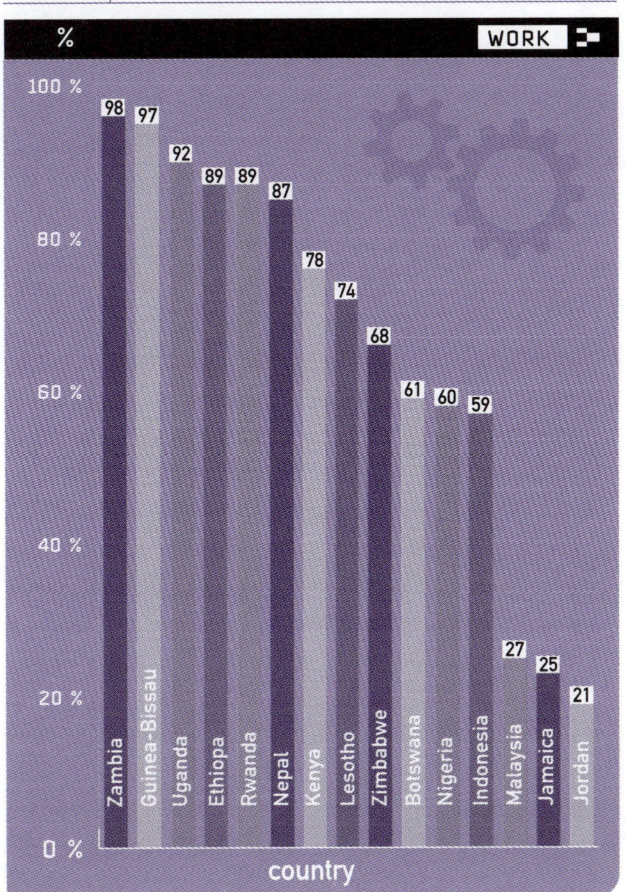

GRAPH 5
PERCENTAGE OF POPULATION LIVING BELOW AN INTERNATIONAL POVERTY LINE OF US$2 PER DAY IN FIFTEEN COUNTRIES

Countries for which poverty-level estimates are available and with fewer than three major social security benefits, e.g. old age and disability, death, family allowances, maternity, sickness, work injury or unemployment. In twelve of these fifteen countries, more than half of the population are living on less than US$2 per day, and in seven of these countries over three-quarters of the population are living below this very extreme poverty line, all without a working social security net.

Source: See the Index of culture indicators and sources and Tables 28 and 29 in Part Seven of this report.

pressions of globalization are indeed American: Coca-Cola, McDonald's or CNN. Most of the giant transnational corporations are based in the United States too. Those that are not all come from the rich countries, not the poorer areas of the world. A pessimistic view of globalization would consider it largely an affair of the industrial North, in which the developing societies of the South play little or no active part. This same view would see globalization as destroying local cultures, widening world inequalities and worsening the lot of the impoverished. The new imperatives of economic development, epitomized by the World Bank's structural adjustment programmes, seem to pay little attention to local demands and histories. Rather they impose a demanding economic regime – a 'golden straightjacket' in the words of *New York Times* journalist Thomas Friedman[4] – on countries which strive to participate in the global marketplace. Globalization creates a world of winners and losers, a few on the fast track to prosperity, the majority condemned to a life of misery and despair.

And indeed the statistics are daunting. The share in global income of the poorest fifth of the world's population has dropped from 2.3 to 1.4% over the past ten years. The proportion taken by the richest fifth, on the other hand, has risen. According to the 1998 United Nations *Human Development Report*, in 1960 the 20% of the world's population who lived in the richest countries had thirty times the income of the poorest 20%. By 1995 they had eighty-two times the income. There are striking and increasing disparities within countries as well. In Brazil, for instance, the poorest 50% of the population received 18% of the national income in 1960. By 1995, they received only 11.6%, while the richest 10% of Brazil's population were taking home 63% of the national income. In Russia, the richest 20% of the population now receive eleven times more of the national income than the poorest 20%.[5]

The gap between the richest and poorest countries in the world is huge and it has continued to grow. Over the past thirty years, income per capita in the developing countries has grown faster, on the average, than in the industrial ones. But the countries at the bottom of the economic scale have had growth rates that are either non existent or negative. In 1965, the average income per capita in the G7 countries was twenty times that of the seven poorest countries. By 1997, it had become nearly forty times as much. (To find a true comparison, these figures would have to be adjusted for the differences in the cost of living, which would reduce the difference considerably. But it is still very high.)

Disparities are also obvious regarding consumption levels and basic infrastructure. Today the wealthiest one-fifth of the world's population consumes 58% of total energy while the poorest fifth consumes less than 4%. The wealthiest one-fifth have 74% of all telephone lines, the poorest fifth 1.5%.[6] In many less-developed countries, safety and environmental regulations are low or virtually non-existent. Some transnational companies sell goods there that are controlled or banned in the industrial countries – poor-quality medical drugs, destructive pesticides or high tar- and nicotine-content cigarettes. As two writers recently put it, rather than a global village, this is more like global pillage.[7]

Along with ecological risk, to which it is related, expanding inequality is the most serious problem facing world society. It will not do, however, merely to blame it on the wealthy. Of course the Western nations, and more generally the industrial countries, still have far more influence over world affairs than do the poorer states. But globalization is becoming increasingly decentred – not under the control of any group of nations, and still less of the large corporations.

Human Development Index

Top 10 — 1999

Canada
Norway
United States
Japan
Belgium
Sweden
Australia
Netherlands
United Kingdom
France

Source: UNDP, *Human Development Report*, 1999.

States and markets: finding the right balance

The need for redistribution on a global scale calls for new approaches to development policy. Globalization seems to diminish the ability of state governments to implement such policies, by affecting patterns of national sovereignty, including not only government and the state, but the very substance of international relations as well. Nation states are, and will remain, powerful, and their leaders have a major role to play in responding to the changes transforming world society. However, governments are losing some of the economic power they once had to control their own affairs. Thus globalization 'pulls away' from the nation state. But it also 'pushes down', generating new pressures towards, and possibilities for, local autonomy and identity, including local forms of nationalism. At the same time, globalization 'squeezes sideways', giving rise to new economic or cultural regions that sometimes cut across existing national borders. Sovereignty is no longer an all-or-nothing matter – if it ever was: boundaries are becoming fuzzier than they used to be. Yet the nation state is not disappearing, and the scope of government, taken as a whole, expands rather than diminishes as globalization proceeds. Nations retain, and will do for the foreseeable future, considerable governmental, economic and cultural power over their citizens and in the external forum. They will be able to continue to wield such powers, however, only in active collaboration with one another, with their own localities and regions, and with transnational groups and associations.

To accept such a conclusion does not imply that national governments have to adopt a diminished role in the world. Reform of the state can give government more influence than before, rather than less. There is a difference between a *big* state, as measured by the number of its functionaries or the size of its budget, and a *strong* state. A state may be at the same time oversized and ineffective. In many areas the 'big institutions' can no longer provide as they did before. The advent of new global markets and the knowledge economy, coupled with the ending of the Cold War, have affected the capability of national governments to manage economic life and provide an ever-expanding range of social benefits. A different framework is needed, one that avoids both the bureaucratic, top-down government favoured by the old left, and the aspirations of the right to dismantle government altogether.

A new and different balance between states and markets for provision of public goods has to be found. Markets have, or can have, beneficial outcomes that go beyond productive efficiency. A successful market economy has an important 'hidden curriculum'. If adequately regulated, market exchange is essentially peaceful. Market relations have often been imposed by the use of force. Yet once a working market economy has been established, people who stand in exchange relationships have little cause to resort to force. 'Gangster capitalism', where rent-seeking is backed by the use of violence, is a specifically abnormal and unstable form of market structure.

In addition, market relations allow free choices to be made by consumers, at least where there is competition between multiple producers. In spite of the influence of advertising and other attempts by producers to shape tastes and needs, such choice is real. Markets can also favour attitudes of responsibility, since participants need to calculate the likely outcomes of what they do, whether they are producers or consumers. This factor helps explain other aspects of the liberating potential of markets, since the decisions of individuals are not made by authoritarian command or by bureaucracy.

A successful market economy generates far higher economic prosperity than any other system. In effect, there is no longer a rival system in place, save in the residues of post-communist economies. A primary reason for the economic success of market exchange is that market mechanisms provide continuous signals for producers, traders and consumers, and do so in combination with market-clearing tendencies. Command economies were not able to provide for continuous adjustments. Combined with entrepreneurial energy, a market economy is vastly more dynamic than any other type of economic system. Yet that very dynamism, intrinsic to the creation of wealth, generates major social costs that markets themselves do not meet, such as the social disruption caused by job loss through economic slump or technological change. Market economies generate externalities whose social implications have to be dealt with by other means. Also, markets cannot nurture the human capital they require: government, families and communities must do this.

Yet the idea that the state should be reduced to a 'caretaker' capacity is plainly inadequate. The 'minimal state' ideology ignores the limitations of markets just as thoroughly as the traditional left does the pathologies of the state. To be able to carry out the tasks upon which free market philosophy concentrates – creating an effective system of law and policing, guaranteeing freedom of contract – the state needs to do a great deal more besides. Government must play a basic role in sustaining the social and civic frameworks upon which markets actually depend.

The social investment state

Finding the right balance between markets and states is a huge topic, and it would be out of the question to discuss it in any detail here. A need for reform of the state apparatus has become clear in recent years. My suggestion is that a new balance between state regulation and market dynamics is to be found in a 'social investment state' which would promote individual initiative and responsibility, rather than passivity and resignation.[8] As a generic project, state reform should not be concerned with making it cheaper, but with reconstructing social policies to reproduce more effective social outcomes. A society that employs a high level of the population, for example, should be able to release greater expenditures for education, health care and other social programmes. But state expenditures must be carefully directed and must be seen as a form of investment. The guiding principle for investment policy, private as well as public, should be: wherever possible invest in human (and social) capital. This principle would apply to welfare systems, as well as to other aspects of society. Old-style welfare, based on transfer payments, bureaucratic services and social engineering, should cede to the generation of active well-being, lifelong learning and devolved welfare provision by a social investment state.

Education obviously has to be the key force in *human* capital development. It is the main public investment that can foster both economic efficiency and civic cohesion. Education is not a static input into the knowledge economy, but is itself becoming transformed by it. Education has traditionally been seen as a preparation for life – an attitude that persisted as it became more and more widely available. Now it needs to be redefined to focus on capabilities that individuals will be able to develop through life. Orthodox schools and other educational institutions are likely to be surrounded with, and to some extent subverted by, a diversity of other learning frameworks. Lifelong learning is far more than just a slogan. In the old economic order, the basic competencies needed for jobs remained relatively constant. Now, learning (and forgetting) have become integral to work in the knowledge economy. A worker creating a novel multimedia application cannot succeed by using long-standing skills: the tasks in question did not even exist yesterday.

Yet the knowledge economy requires more than individual skills. The cultivation of social capital is just as important. The 'new individualism' that goes along with globalization is not refractory to co-operation and collaboration co-operation (rather than hierarchy) is positively stimulated by it. 'Social capital' refers to trust networks that individuals can draw upon for social support, just as financial capital can be drawn upon to be used for investment. Like financial capital, social capital can be expanded: invested and reinvested. Since the moment when it was first introduced by the sociologist James Coleman,[9] the idea of social capital has been so widely deployed that some think it has been drained of much of its value. Yet its usefulness resides in the wide application it can have. Social capital refers to relationships of trust that facilitate co-ordination or co-operation. As such, it is of prime importance in civil society, the very basis of the everyday civility crucial to effective public life.

In the context of the new economy, social capital has a more specific significance. It is the basis of the networks that play a major role in innovation. In the old economy, innovation was often the result of separate processes of research, development and production. In the knowledge-based economy, innovation stems more from networks and collaborative ventures. Co-ordination costs are lowered through shared norms rather than through bureaucratic hierarchy. Research has indicated that the development of active partnerships is one of the main factors explaining differences in rates of innovation.[10] Firms are increasingly turning to networks of suppliers and customers to develop novel ideas and technologies. There were only 750 inter-firm alliances in the United States during the 1970s. Between 1987 and 1992, there were 20,000. The range of industry ties with universities has also grown rapidly. Recognition of the importance of ongoing networks of learning and innovation has proceeded further in the private sector than in government in most countries. But governments should be looking for policies that enhance such alliances as well.

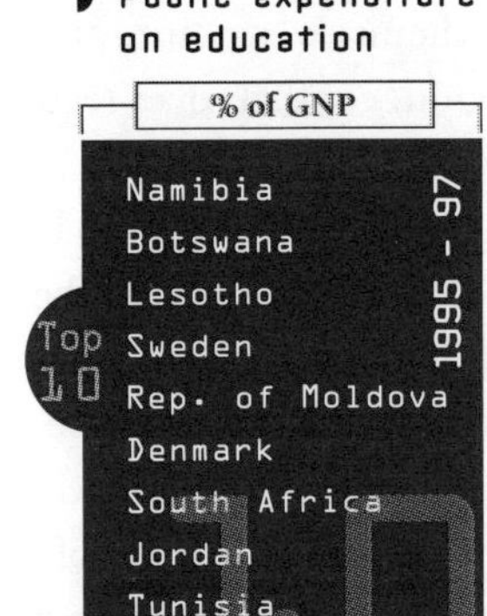

Public expenditure on education
% of GNP
Top 10
1995 - 97
Namibia
Botswana
Lesotho
Sweden
Rep. of Moldova
Denmark
South Africa
Jordan
Tunisia
Uzbekistan

Source: See the Index of culture indicators and sources and Table 24 in Part Seven of this report.

Equality and pluralism

The principle of 'Wherever possible, invest in human capital' strongly suggests an *enabling approach* to social policy, that is, building upon the action strategies of the poor. The finding that most welfare claimants are much more active than was previously believed might imply that support should be reduced. The real conclusion to be drawn is just the opposite: the fact that most claimants actively look for ways to become independent shows that investing in them pays. The same point applies to those who have no chance of going from welfare to work: children, the disabled or sick, the elderly and others. There should be no suggestion that they should be penalized as part of the transition from passive to active welfare policies. But it still makes sense to help mobilize their action potential and reduce dependency.

How should we think of equality as the aim of social policy itself? The economist Amartya Sen developed the concept of 'social capability', which makes an appropriate starting point. Equality and inequality do not refer merely to the availability of social and material goods – individuals must have the capability to make effective use of them. Policies designed to promote equality should be focused upon what Sen calls the 'capability set', the overall freedom a person has to pursue his or her well-being. Advantage and disadvantage should similarly be defined as 'capability failure' – not only loss of resources, but loss of freedom to achieve as well.[11]

Treating increasing equality as securing a fairer distribution of social capability means accepting that the same set of resources can produce varying outcomes for people, depending upon how far they can convert them into effective freedoms. The favourite pastime of the Australian tycoon Kerry Packer is said to be watching sports on TV while eating take-home pizzas. A welfare recipient might do the same thing – but within quite a different framework of available choices.[12]

Freedom defined as social capability is not plucked out of thin air, nor is it close to the self-seeking agent presumed in neo-liberal economic theory. Individuals, as the communitarians say, exercise freedom precisely through their membership of groups, communities and cultures. Freedom to do whatever one wants, in relation to oneself, one's own body, or to others – in other words libertarianism – is alien to the left, and should remain so. It is not individual choice that is at the core of pluralism, but the diversity of cultures and groups to which individuals belong.

As the political philosopher Michael Walzer has pointed out, too many old leftists made equality the enemy of liberty. 'Political conflict and the competition for leadership always make for power inequalities and entrepreneurial activity always makes for economic inequalities. . . . None of this can be prevented without endless tyrannical interventions in ordinary life. It was an historical mistake of large proportions, for which we [on the left] have paid heavily'.[13] Freedom and equality, especially in contemporary social contexts, have a complex and social character, but Walzer's claim that they 'can emerge coherently out of a full-scale pluralism'[14] seems entirely justified. For too long, pluralism was either downplayed in favour of equality, or politicians sought to achieve equality through the state – rather than by grounding their projects in the associations of civil society.

Conclusion

A redefined balance between government or political power, the economy and civil society can provide the societal foundation to achieve prosperity, democracy and equality. Plainly we do not have an effective balance at the moment. Some states are in a better position to address this problem than others. There is a North/South division along these lines. Some have spoken of the new fault-line in global social relations as running between a 'zone of peace' in the industrialized North, contrasted to a 'zone of conflict' in the South. In the former, democracy, civil order and a market economy all appear firmly established. In the latter, democracy is advancing only with difficulty, and religious, ethnic and economic conflicts are common. As Claude Ake, expressing a 'view from Africa' puts it, many countries of the South are 'in the grip of strong centrifugal forces, including secessionism. The South is deeply divided by religious differences that are often politicized. It is prone to violent, atavistic nationalism, territorial disputes, and struggle over natural resources.'[15]

Globalization puts further pressures on developing countries, which tend to have even less control over their domestic economic affairs.[16] The global marketplace and its accompanying processes of technological change are swamping nascent forms of governance which need to be strengthened. Where there is as yet no developed civil society, and hence little democracy, there is also little chance of effective economic development either. International collaboration is needed if we are to foster democracy and fight poverty globally. Alleviating poverty would demand large-scale investment in human capital and infrastructure, linked to social and political criteria as well as economic considerations. Most of the problems that inhibit the economic development of the poorer countries, however, do not arise in the global economy itself or from self-seeking behaviour on the part of the richer nations. They lie mainly in the countries concerned themselves, in authoritarian government, corruption, conflict, over-regulation and a low level of emancipation for women.

It is extremely difficult indeed to break away from circumstances that essentially take the form of a vicious circle of deprivation. Resources coming from the outside can at most help trigger the necessary indigenous changes. Just as welfare dependency can discourage effect and reinforce a sense of incapacity within nations, the same can happen on an international basis. Directing investment to human resources, promoting active supply interventions, and coupling these with structural changes in state and civil society, are even more crucial in the less developed countries than in the more economically advanced ones.

Notes

1. This essay is based on ideas that I discuss in more detail in *The Third Way and Its Critics*, Cambridge, Polity Press (forthcoming).
2. See M. Castells, 'The Informational Economy and the New International Division of Labor', in M. Carnoy, M. Castells, S. S. Cohen and F. H. Cardoso (eds.), *The New Global Economy in the Information Age*, Philadelphia, Pennsylvania State University Press, 1993, pp. 15–43.
3. G. Gereffi, 'Rethinking Development Theory: Insights from East Asia and Latin America', *Sociological Forum*, Vol. 4, No. 4, 1989, pp. 505–533.
4. T. Friedman, *The Lexus and the Olive Tree*, London, Harper Collins, 1999.
5. United Nations Development Programme (UNDP), *Human Development Report 1998*, New York, Oxford University Press, 1998, p. 29.
6. T. Friedman, op. cit., p. 259.

7. J. Brecher and T. Costello, *Global Village or Global Pillage: Economic Reconstruction from the Bottom Up,* Boston, South End Press, 1994.
8. I have given a more detailed outline of the concept of social investment in *The Third Way: The Renewal of Social Democracy,* Cambridge, Polity, 1998.
9. See J. Coleman, *Foundations of Social Theory,* Cambridge (Mass.), Harvard University Press, 1990.
10. See J. E. Fountain, 'Social Capital: A Key Enabler of Innovation', in L. M. Branscomb and J. H. Keller (eds.), *Investing in Innovation,* Cambridge (Mass.), MIT Press, 1998, pp. 85–101; and M. E. Porter, 'Clusters and Competition', in *On Competition*, Boston (Mass.), Harvard Business Review Books, pp. 197–287.
11. A. Sen, *Inequality Reexamined,* Oxford, Clarendon Press, 1992.
12. M. Latham, *Civilising Global Capital,* Sydney, Allen and Unwin, 1998, p. 38.
13. M. Walzer, Pluralism and Social Democracy, *Dissent,* Winter 1998, pp. 47–53.
14. Ibid., p. 50.
15. C. Ake, 'A View from Africa', in H. H. Holm and G. Sorensen (eds.), *Whose World Order?* Boulder, Westview Press, 1995, p. 25.
16. K. Griffin and A. Rhaman Khan, *Globalization and the Developing World: An Essay on the International Dimensions of Development in the Post-Cold War Era,* p. 43, New York, UN Human Development Report Office, 1992. (Human Development Report Office Occasional Papers 2.)

Chapter 4
Globalization and cultural diversity

ELIE COHEN
Director of research at the Centre National de Recherche Scientifique,
Member of the economic advisory council attached to the Office of the Prime Minister (France)

'... the principle of cultural exemption could work as a test-bed for a new concept of globalization which would reconcile the norm of open trading with that of cultural diversity ...'

Has globalization gone too far?[1] That such a question should be raised by an American neo-classical economist is one of the many signs that the triumphant march towards globalization no longer even sparks off academic debate. It is not that the opening-up of economies and the unrestricted flow of goods, technologies or capital are being challenged; it is not that recurring financial crises undermine its legitimacy; it is not even that there might be alternative economic organization patterns creating the same kind of wealth. It is simply a sign that globalization has turned into common economic law, and this is all the more questionable since globalization claims to control human activities by imposing the same hierarchy of collective preferences or by replacing political options with the impersonal rule of the market. In other words, people may want to liberalize trade, lower tariff barriers and set up a regulatory authority without necessarily accepting that trade criterion alone should prevail, at all times and in all places.

Recently there has been a marked increase in the number of trade disputes, all the more bitter in that they challenge the right of nations to retain their modes of consumption, protect private life, maintain authors' 'moral rights' and halt the dissemination of new food technologies in the absence of irrefutable evidence that these are not noxious. We are also witnessing the emergence of international public opinion capable of rallying to put a stop, for example, to the homogenizing ambitions of the Organisation for Economic Co-operation and Development (OECD) to regulate direct investment through the Multilateral Agreement on Investment (MAI), or the further extension of the realm of trade, as in Seattle. Lastly, we are witnessing an unabashed proliferation of demands for 'cultural exemption'. So, gradually, and following pressure from national and international public opinion and in the wake of early rulings made by the WTO Litigation Settlement Body (LSB), a debate on the coexistence of cultural diversities (expressing national or sub-national identities) and the homogenizing dynamics of globalization is now being held in public.

This debate took shape during the OECD negotiation on the MAI.[2] A second crucial episode occurred in Seattle with the victory of the assorted NGO coalition comprised of American blue-collar unionists and militant defenders of Third World social and environmental causes. In our report we shall try to show evidence that the MAI functions as an analytical element in current tension between the way globalization works and the demand for cultural diversity. We shall then move on to show how WTO's dynamics, notably on the occasion of the 'Millennium Round', generate potentially tense situations of conflict. Finally, we shall see how a new, combined approach to the requirements of both globalization and demands for respect of diversity could be used for purely cultural activities.

But firstly, what are the issues? The public arena is littered with ill-defined concepts such as globalization, cultural diversity and claims to identity; the concepts involved need to be clarified from the outset.

Globalization and cultural diversity: definitions

Globalization is presented as an established fact, a constraint one should adapt to, a symbol of modernity to be attained or a 'recipe' for improved performance depending on the context. The only thing capable of resisting globalization, it is generally felt, is the assertion of an identity – in other words, of a difference. The requirement that all things must converge is then vehemently questioned in the name of differences between economic regimes and pluralism in development processes.

Cultural identity, which is merely another way of expressing the unavoidable specificity of lifestyles, patterns of work and consumption as well as political and administrative institutions, is often used as an obstacle to globalization. Under the guise of cultural exception, it adopts the more restrictive meaning of a protection system for various artistic creation activities. The debate clearly compounds common sense concepts and categories, the positive and the normative, and theoretically and statistically established trends together with mere fantasies. The first task is self-evident: to sort out what is deliberately confusing.

GLOBALIZATION, CONVERGENCE, 'ONE BEST WAY'

Until recently, globalization was either credited with every possible virtue in the name of market efficiency, or denounced as a vector of cultural homogenization, institutional equalization and loss of sovereignty. Yet it is not a product of the last ten or twenty years. In many respects, developed countries have merely caught up with the level reached before the First World War.[3]

Where then is the novelty? At a guess, it is threefold. (1) Many more countries, even whole continents, have become involved in a process of economic interdependence through trade, capital flows and migrations. The *terra incognita* on the world trade map is shrinking fast: self-sufficiency and self-centred development strategies appear less viable or, at any rate, less manageable. (2) History has taught us that there have been many paths towards economic growth; the Japanese used neither the German nor the American model. And yet, some would like to turn a specific model – the American economy in its maturity – into the perfect economic model for the age of globalization. From this point of view history itself and the whole sequence of institutional mediations are actually discarded. This means that any approach using technological, economic and financial developments to reproduce policies or levels of achievement in a mechanical fashion fails to perceive the significance of institutional mediation. Similar constraints do not produce either the same policies, or the same attitudes, or the same results in different national economic systems. (3) The revolution brought about by information, transport and finance technologies has produced a symbolic representation of globalization that partakes of imaginary construction as much as of

United States trade policy and culture: future strategies

In the view of the United States, the so-called cultural industries (film, radio, television, book publishing, magazines and sound recordings) are part of the entertainment/media industry. From a trade policy perspective, these sectors are treated in the same way as any other commercial activity, no differently than, say, steel or autos. From an economic perspective, it is not hard to understand why the United States and others feel this way. These sectors generate significant numbers of jobs and revenue and are extremely successful in global markets. Measures or policies which are implemented around the world in the name of promoting or protecting culture, but which end up restricting the movement of cultural products from one country to another, are viewed very critically by the United States. Harsh American reactions to these types of measures or policies are based not just on the commercial harm being inflicted on United States economic interests, but also because actions by one country set precedents for others around the world to impose similar restrictions on United States access to those markets.

Given these vastly different attitudes to culture in the United States and around the world, it is not surprising that efforts in the past to negotiate resolutions to disputes that arise over culture usually fail. In my experience as a trade negotiator, it has proven fruitless to attempt to address these issues solely on merit, since the countries involved in the dispute will never view culture from a common vantage point. Whatever sympathy may exist in the United States for a country's concern to maintain a separate cultural identity in the face of the daily onslaught from the entertainment and media industries of the United States and elsewhere is usually overwhelmed by commercial and trade policy considerations.

Complicating the situation for negotiators is the fact that the affected industries are seldom prepared to compromise on these matters. Those companies that benefit from policies designed to promote or protect cultural industries tend to view them as essential for their livelihood and certainly as a major factor in their profitability. They have little, if any, interest in supporting any changes to these policies that would allow more competition from the United States and elsewhere, thus reducing their profits.

On the other hand, United States companies chafe at any restrictions on their access to world markets, believing that they are being forced to bear the costs associated with attaining a country's cultural policy objectives. Making compromise even more difficult is the concern held by many American companies and policy-makers that whatever arrangement is worked out with one country will end up setting a precedent which will encourage similar policies to be implemented or maintained around the world, resulting in further damage to United States commercial interests.

Many United States industries believe they are being forced to bear the brunt of the financial costs associated with achieving these cultural policy objectives, either through outright trade restrictions or by limitations on their ability to compete in the global market place. Countries must be willing to consider shifting some of the financial burden of paying for the costs associated with these cultural policies from the United States and other foreign commercial interests. It is unreasonable for any country to expect the United States to underwrite the majority of the costs maintaining these policies.

Clearly a middle ground must be found whereby the legitimate cultural needs of a country can be attained with a minimum of impact on international trade and investment flows. I believe it is unreasonable for countries to demand *carte blanche* to promote and protect their cultural industries. But it is also unreasonable to demand that cultural products be given exactly the same treatment as the products of any other commercial activity.

WILLIAM S. MERKIN
President and Chief Executive Officer,
Strategic Policy Inc. (United States)

economic reality. At the same time, uniformity and homogeneity loom large as the concept of globalization is maintained by the United States, whose development model is conveyed by its culture, its grip on international organizations, the strength of its financial sector and its near monopoly of the management consulting industry. Herein lies the first contradiction: a variety of socio-economic systems and political and institutional arrangements seems to produce an identical level of growth performance. Globalization does not contain uniformity – in other words the American model – in a genetic code, and yet, carried by many vectors, this one model tends to prevail. A given (American) economic system has found itself erected as a model – and then formulated in a series of recipes which prescribe 'one best way'.

In our approach to globalization, we shall therefore make a preliminary distinction between words and facts. Secondly, we shall have to pinpoint the forces that make systems converge. Finally, we shall consider the normative dimension.

IDENTITY, CULTURE, DIVERGENCE AND EXCEPTION

In attempting to account for the diversity of institutional arrangements, we have referred to the concept of culture. But more generally speaking, what do we actually mean by identity, culture, divergence and cultural exception? I have chosen a broad definition of culture in this paper to include lifestyles, patterns of interaction and co-operation within a community and the way such interactions are justified by a system of values and norms; I use a positive approach.[4]

By identity, we mean transmitted, inherited – and not chosen – features such as ethnic and sexual characteristics, but also identity in the sense of identification. What is of interest to us is the development of the identity claim, long considered as the antithesis of democratic and secular universal values and which has now become an integral part of the fight for democracy. As Bernard Manin has pointed out, 'secularization of politics and referral of religion or ethnic difference to the private sphere are artefacts contrived to secure ultimate equality between individuals'. How can this revival of the identity claim be accounted for?

Huntington and Touraine provide an initial response: as the core conflict between employers and proletariat disappears from industrial societies and as the East–West conflict also fades away at the international level, the integrating effect of this double polarization has collapsed and new types of conflicts are now emerging and spreading: war between civilizations[5] on the one hand, and regionalist, environmentalist, feminist and homosexual movements on the other. Hobsbawn[6] and Gellner[7] offer a second answer: national or even sub-national identities are constructed identities, fabricated by political élites. These élites reinvent a past, a national epic; they revive traditions and adopt symbols to promote identification.

Cultural exception can now be understood both as a means to protect a new or long-standing identity, and as a way of trying to invent one. It can therefore be a downright protectionist contrivance. Japan and Korea, in their catching-up phase, have often put forward the specificity of the Nippon spirit or the quality of Japanese rice in order to protect nascent industries or powerful lobbies. Conversely, it may reinforce an identity claim as in Catalonia, Quebec or Scotland and, to some extent, in Malaysia, with the promotion of Malaysian capitalism. What is called cultural exception may in fact conceal intentions that are purely and simply anti-democratic. Challenging universal values or human and social rights in the name of Asianism, 'communitarianism' or Confucianism – such stances may actually be an attempt to dodge shared responsibilities. Finally, cultural exception is called upon to promote timeless intellectual works or to highlight a cultural and linguistic heritage. The principle involved is both identity-promoting and economic: when one language dominates in such a way that it verges on a monopolistic hegemony, then competition and difference can thrive only through positive discrimination.

These points having been clarified, we may now proceed to ask the following three sets of questions. (1) Have we ever experienced, in the past twenty years, an upheaval in trade and capital flows such that we had to give up the analysis tools of 'inter-nationalization of economies' and devise new

Cultural diversity and international trade regulations

'Managing a world of converging economies, peoples and civilizations, each one preserving its own identity and culture, represents the great challenge and the great promise of our age.'
Renato Ruggiero, Director-General of WTO, 1997

In recent years the question of preserving cultural identity in a context of economic globalization has reached a scale that would have been difficult to imagine in the early 1980s. It now ranks among those issues (together with the environment and work) which the Director-General of the World Trade Organization (WTO) described in May 1998 'as exerting growing pressure on the international trading system, which are a genuine source of concern for the public at large but for which a solution cannot be found merely within the trading system itself' *(WTO Focus,* No. 31, *June 1998, p. 2).* The basic problem is that of the approach to be adopted to cultural products in international trade agreements. For the time being a feature of the importance given to the latter in such agreements has been one of fairly considerable ambivalence. Although cultural products are in principle catered for as any other products, they are quite often the subject, according to specific contexts and fields, of clauses denoting exceptions or reservations.

Two radically opposed views regarding cultural products underpin this debate. On the one hand, cultural products are seen to be entertainment products which are similar, in commercial terms, to any other products and therefore entirely subject to the rules of international trade. On the other hand, cultural products are seen as assets which convey values, ideas and meaning, or in other words, instruments of social communication which contribute to fashioning the cultural identity of a given community. As such, they must accordingly be excluded from the field of international trade agreements.

A closer examination of the status granted to cultural products in international trade agreements reveals, first and foremost, an absence of any genuine consensus as to the way they should be dealt with. As the WTO negotiations have shown, this is all the more preoccupying as the main arguments regarding the way cultural products should be treated are not truly satisfactory. Neither the argument for their total exclusion from international trade agreements nor that of their assimilation to any other product within the context of those same agreements would appear realistic in this regard.

When considered as commercial goods, cultural products may be difficult to exclude totally from the scope of international trade agreements, although this is less so in the case of bilateral agreements. If they are used to obtain a commercial gain and are the subject of trade at international level, they bring into question various and sometimes conflicting interests which can be reconciled only within an appropriate legal framework.

The principal countries exporting cultural products would be opposed to any exclusion of the latter from the legal framework governing international trade. Leading these countries is the United States, for which all cultural goods and services are a major export sector, as well as other countries such as Brazil, Japan and Mexico. The latter would certainly take a dim view of their exports being brought into question for cultural reasons that lie outside any regulation. Several countries that have developed a significant presence on the international market for cultural products could also be very concerned at such a trend. David Throsby, in a contribution to the first *World Culture Report* (1998), pointed out that even the developing countries, whose cultural production is becoming increasingly well-known throughout the world, could recognize what the advantage would be if a broadly open market were preserved in the cultural field.

Furthermore, those countries whose domestic market cannot sustain varied cultural production and which need foreign cultural products to respond to domestic demand would also find it to their advantage to be assured of unrestricted access to foreign cultural production. However, they could not be assured of such access if cultural products had to be totally excluded from the legal framework governing international trade. Even a principle of non-discrimination as fundamental as that of the status of most favoured nation could not be invoked in such a case.

Beyond strictly economic considerations, it should be underlined, lastly, that the complete exemption of cultural products from international trade agreements can have the dangerous consequence of opening the door, in legal terms, to restrictions that are more justified for commercial or even ideological reasons than for cultural ones. Even an exception such as Article XX (b) of GATT 1994, relating to 'restrictions imposed for the protection of national treasures of artistic, historical or archaeological value', is the subject of limitations regarding their use as a means of arbitrary or justified discrimination or as a disguised restriction on international trade. From that angle, it would be surprising, to say the least, that the whole range of cultural products could benefit from exemption, the scale of which would be left to the judgement of whomsoever invoked it.

If, however, total exemption of cultural products from international trade regulations does not appear to be a realistic solution, it does not mean that a strictly commercial view of cultural products should be adopted. Such an approach would, on the contrary, be dangerous. Over several years, evidence suggests that cultural production has increasingly become the concern of the cultural industries. The fact is that while this phenomenon of industrialization and commercialization of cultural production has considerably broadened access to production, it has also, paradoxically enough, restricted the scope of cultural production to what industry regards as commercially profitable. In this regard, it would seem reasonable to say that there is a serious risk for the preservation of cultural diversity.

An attractive, easy approach would be to make a distinction between so-called products of higher culture, such as opera, theatre, dance, painting and sculpture, whose cultural nature is clear-cut, and popular consumer products such as books, periodicals, cinema, television, records and the multimedia which belong more to the realm of so-called entertainment. However, to adopt that solution would mean forgetting that a major part of the culture which individuals acquire today stems precisely from mass cultural products. Therefore, distinguishing between cultural products is not a solution.

In actual fact, it is not so much cultural products as such that create a problem, in terms of international trade regulation. The problem lies more in national measures aimed at those products. Various means have been envisaged whereby these products could benefit from a particular status. It might be possible, for example, to make greater use of the reservation mechanism, whether such reservations be closed, that is to say, valid only for the past and for specific measures, or open, that is to say, valid for both the past and the future and for a given sector. (The refusal to make any specific commitments in relation to a given sector could be assimilated here as a form of reservation.)
The disadvantage of such an approach is that it opens the door to renewed pressure as negotiations go on with a view to eliminating such reservations.

Another solution would be a cultural exception clause the form and scope of which would be nearer to those of the general exceptions of GATT 1994. Such a clause would have to be monitored none the less. It could not be used for setting up measures which would be a means of arbitrary or unjustified discrimination or a disguised restriction on trade, and could be maintained only if there were other means less harmful to trade for achieving the specified legitimate objective. The ideal solution, however – the only one likely in the long term to provide a response to the current conflict on the attention given to cultural products in international trade agreements – would be a particular convention bearing on international trade in the cultural sector, namely, a convention which would set out clearly the justification for and limitations of a particular status for cultural products by emphasizing the need to preserve cultural diversity. Such a convention could be negotiated in a quite separate framework from that of WTO – here UNESCO comes to mind in particular – but it would have to be a last resort to respond to the problems raised within the framework of WTO and find its place within the latter.

IVAN BERNIER
Professor, Faculty of Law, Laval University (Canada)

ones capable of describing 'globalization'? (2) Does globalization threaten patterns of national growth and social regulation? Is it therefore imposing an ever-expanding form of institutional order? (3) Can the identity claim coexist with the universal values of market and democracy, and if so, under what conditions?

REPRESENTATIONS AND REALITY OF GLOBALIZATION

The image of an economy-in-flux, freed from both national ties and political authority, is now commonplace.[8] In many countries, the idea is accompanied by a good deal of fearful apprehension about globalization, the loss of sovereignty, the anarchy of markets and the global village. A world without boundaries, companies unincorporated in any country or the idea of government by law and by market reflect the same image. To avoid the imprecision fostered by the prevailing discourse on globalization, we must first distinguish between what is the continuation of an internationalization that has been going on since 1945 and a possible breakdown in the world economic order that occurred during the 1980s to the disadvantage of governmental authority and the advantage of impersonal forces in a global market.

For the sake of clarity, we will argue on the basis of theoretical models and see whether available empirical data may help us move forward.[9] In the first model, the *international economy*, the main components are national economies. Growth in trade and investment, admittedly, is perceived as contributing to international integration, specialization and the division of labour, but basically, the relation between and within nations still remains the determining factor, whether in international arrangements or at a national level. This model suggests that transnational corporations develop, trade and invest throughout the world, but nevertheless retain a clearly identifiable national basis and are bound by national regulations. Lastly, since the end of the nineteenth century, the international economy may be called integrated in so far as the communications revolution (telegraphy) made real-time transactions possible and was also open to trade and capital flows.

The *globalized economy* is a theoretical model quite different from the international economy and is constructed in contrast to it. In the globalized economy, national economies merge and rearrange at world level through a series of processes and exchanges. Such economic organization raises, first, the issue of government: who is capable of governing an array of transactions and processes which have a powerful impact on nations while escaping their authority? Moreover, in this model, transnational corporations become global because they sever their links with a domestic base, deny any territorial allegiance and are motivated only by principles based on optimization of their assets worldwide. Thereafter, any concerted national policy efforts become either impossible[10] or counterproductive.[11] Lastly, such a model implies that the distribution of power between authorities on the national level and between nations on the international level is radically altered. Nation-states can no longer claim sole power on the international level; they are forced to come to terms with regional and international organizations, including global corporations.[12]

Our past research has established that the current wave of globalization has not had any drastic effect either on trade or on direct investment (1% of world GDP), or on international controls (the last General Agreement on Tariffs and Trade (GATT) agreements were adopted unanimously by the contracting parties). So, why does something appear to be different? First of all, the developments described do add up. While no single trend in trade movements alone explains a globalization phenomenon, their combination has created a new environment. There is evidence of a widening of trade, simultaneously geographical (China, Latin America) and sector-based (services, agriculture, intellectual property), together with a deepening of integration (new WTO rules) and a recent speeding-up of developments (telecommunications and finance as vectors). In a nutshell, economies have grown more interdependent and regional integration has become a reality.[13]

One of the apparently soundest arguments of those who defend the theory of a globalized economy is the development of global corporations. Yet extensive study of their activities, assets and location would appear to point to the conclusion that genuinely global firms are few and far between and that, furthermore, wherever they operate they comply with national regulations. In actual fact, current developments correspond more to the open international economy model of the post-war years than to a globalized economy model.

And yet, simple observation of the powerlessness of political authorities with regard to economic disruptions, the reality of financial integration, the devastating effect of frenzied speculation and the advances of deregulation policies combine to weaken this theory. However, deliberate actions in the industrialized countries initiated deregulation first in the United States and in Europe, permitted the flow of capital to become freer and stepped up privatization of public assets. The fight against stagflation, government bankruptcy and bureaucracy justified a reversal of objectives invented and implemented by political élites in the developed countries, and not by impersonal market forces or the diktats of international organizations. Naturally, the situation is not the same in the case of developing countries.

Such objections disarm neither the critics nor the advocates of globalization. The most radical objection to statistical counter-evidence lies in the fact that the dynamics of globalization is presented as an emerging process, not yet fully-fledged in its consequences, which is all the more innovative in that it so closely relates to modernity. In this model, globalization is mainly a cultural phenomenon that economists assess very inadequately. Zaki Laïdi has described five hypothetical situations related to globalization: 'common forms', by which he means the proliferation of global places such as airports and hotels; 'global daily life', expressed, for instance, by major sporting events; 'global influences', as on the occasion of high-society tragedies such as Princess Diana's death; the more conventional 'market hypothesis'; and lastly, what he calls the 'discursive' hypothetical situation, which he believes appears in the use of homogenized forms of expression and parallel development and planning projects.

Laïdi's idea is certainly attractive; it undoubtedly helps to explain the concept of globalization in terms other than purely economic ones and emphasizes factors which affect our imaginations on a planetary level. These factors, in turn, strengthen spontaneous market trends and governmental policy strategies in terms of deregulation. But finding an opposing factor for every one of these factors would be all too easy. Hypothetical forms of representation might be contrasted with the revival of folk traditions and the construction of sub-national identities. Daily life on a global level might be confronted with shrinking horizons as evidence of 'localism' and an expanding definition of what is 'foreign'. 'Global influences' are short-lived, and we should be cautious, in the long run, about epiphenomena. The market hypothesis used as a basis for the development of global products runs counter to the notion of local identification producing a constant flow of piecemeal consumer habits. Evidently, the right approach would be, not to contrast cultural fragmentation with the economic and conceptual dynamics of globalization, but rather to mix them. As we shall see, a strong sense of cultural identity does not hinder the free play of economic globalization. Similarly, living in a closed economy and being affected by global cultural events are perfectly compatible.

Let us return, however, to the issues raised by the facts and trends. Economists would at first seem to be well-equipped for tackling these issues. If the economy really worked as taught in the schools, and if consumers were the hedonistic and calculating atoms they are purported to be, there would be no rational explanation for border-effects[14] or margin-effects, perceived by many as non-tangible barriers to trade. All things being equal, how can one explain that those who live in a given country prefer to buy goods from and to trade with neighbouring regions rather than foreign neighbours, even when this means paying prices that are nearly 38% higher? At the very least, such behaviour is a strong argument against the idea that globalization is marching on irresistibly. An explanation should be sought first in the existence of de facto protective measures: non-tariff barriers and exchange-rate fluctuations. But even when these factors have been eliminated, there remain a number of factors related perhaps to distance, but more particularly to a marked preference, in domestic consumption, for intra-national trade, local brands and national networks. So-called 'border effects' are therefore not merely an invisible protection or the inertia of behaviour patterns, but the result of differences in tastes, traditions and cultures. Furthermore, what holds true for goods is all the more so for services.

Globalization no doubt indicates a rise of interdependence, new consumer and labour trends and the emergence of more widely-held theories, even though these should be regarded with caution and debated, and then put into perspective in view of a countertrend towards cultural differentiation. But still globalization challenges the social, institutional and redistributive choices of nations, according to some critics whose analysis is radical: if taken literally, there is a contradiction between the universal dimension of the market and the universal dimension of democracy. We shall discuss this issue in the following section.

GLOBALIZATION AND QUESTIONING OF MODELS FOR NATIONAL GROWTH AND SOCIAL REGULATION

Has globalization gone too far? Rodrick[15] thinks so. His argument is straightforward: with respect to salaries, employment and social benefits, globalization produces winners and losers. Even if international trade does not play a determining role in absolute quantitative terms, as we have already clearly established, Rodrick believes it produces a three-fold effect.

First, international trade operates by altering 'the elasticity of demand for labour by replacing national labour by foreign labour'. No economist would challenge this replacement process, which has had different effects in the United States and in Europe. Whereas the Europeans maintain high labour costs for their unskilled jobs, bearing the cost of competition from low labour-cost countries through additional unemployment, the Americans let the wages of unskilled workers fall, nor are they capable of preventing the relocation of those activities most liable to be affected by such a labour-cost differential.

Second, when nations are engaged in trading, Rodrick adds, 'a gradual erosion of national standards and institutions' can be observed. Whether it be collective bargaining rules or environmental protection regulations, globalization allegedly brings down the level of everything. This is a provocative assumption which deserves further discussion. At this stage, it is worth noting that an economist is taking for granted a state of affairs that is far from being the case in Europe, where environmental protection rules and standards are constantly being enlarged.

Social welfare is the third area where the negative effects of globalization are experienced. For a long time social benefits were extended to cover more and more people, in accordance with a spirit of access for all, while today access has been restricted and individuals must pay for private insurance benefits. Thus the very legitimacy of international trade has been undermined. There are two sides to this argument: the first, which is analytically questionable, involves the substance itself, that is to say, a decline in social welfare, while the second hinges on cause and effect. It is well known that not one developed country has fully achieved satisfactory control of health expenditure, and that the payment of retirement pensions, whether under equalization or capitalization schemes, ultimately implies a sharing of income between generations. However, and this is the second aspect, the mere fact that the belief echoed by Rodrick is widely held makes it something tangible, and thus globalization serves as a scapegoat when national social welfare systems come under attack.

However, Rodrick is guilty of 'economism' along with the German theorist of social democracy, Fritz Scharpf, who considers globalization and European integration as the vector of social deregulation and as a challenge to national social compromises. According to Scharpf, the construction of Europe, which in itself is the vehicle of globalization in Europe, jeopardizes the neo-corporatist model, endorses the weakening of the traditional labour community and trade unions, and will ultimately herald the disappearance of the European social model. However, both authors have detected the real issue in national economic regimes. While submitted to the same market pressures, exposed to the same scientific and technical drive and sharing the same managerial cult of efficiency, the nations, their élites and their institutions nevertheless provide answers to their specific problems.

TRENDS TOWARDS GLOBALIZATION, DIVERSITY OF REGIMES AND DIFFERENTIALIST CLAIMS

Many capitalist regimes still offer, in specific forms, a combination of property rights, labour relations, monetary relations and a hierarchy in the actions of the regal-redistributive-regulating state. Many authors have identified 'national technological strategies',[16] described the diversity of financial systems on the basis of their being market-led, state-led or bank-led[17] and compared major brands of national capitalism.[18] But this acknowledgement of differences, differentiation or even divergence usually leads to two opposite conclusions: differences are seen either as mopped up by globalization and cast away into a prehistory of capitalist national brands, or else they persist – and the dynamics of globalization continue to be adopted and reinterpreted by national economic regimes[19].

At this point in the argument, the relation between globalization-enhancing trends and cultural-differentiation processes would appear as increasingly complex. They could be placed on a matrix combining economics and culture in the axes of universalism versus particularism. However, when political institutions are involved, a difficulty arises. One cannot

Source: See the Index of culture indicators and sources and Table 15 in Part Seven of this report.

Source: See the Index of culture indicators and sources and Table 15 in Part Seven of this report.

assume a priori that the universal values of the market and those of democracy are in any way compatible. Strictly speaking, authoritarian and democratic regimes should also be plotted on opposing axes, which would then transform the matrix into a tridimensional system. But in actual fact, there is little likelihood of finding authoritarian market-oriented regimes implementing cultural universalism and so our economics/culture matrix will require only minor corrections.

Economic globalization is opposed either by closed economies or by systems with government control of the opening-up of the economy. What runs counter to fragmentation of identities is the universal value of democracy together with cultural convergence. Economic globalization may very well coexist with the need for an identity: this is the case of authoritarian Islamist regimes involved in the international economy. There may be economic as well as cultural globalization. In other words, an open society may evolve which produces and consumes global products or global culture (world music, TV soap operas, etc.). A closing of the national economy may occur along with a fragmentation of identity (e.g. the Democratic People's Republic of Korea). There may be economic control and 'world culture'. This is a situation frequently found in countries that are 'catching up' in their economies, and they indulge in mercantilist or aggressively protectionist policies (post-war France, subsequently Japan and then the Republic of Korea).

Putting globalization problems as well as cultural identity and differentiation issues into perspective, while not offering definitive answers has, in our opinion, at least one merit: they can be used as a guide through the debates on the new world economic order emerging before our very eyes and combining globalization and diversity, and there will be less confusion between factual data, positive analysis and normative analysis. Mistaking hearsay for reality is less likely to occur, even though strongly-held concepts may, in the end, seem to become materially real. Finally, opinion, even when conveyed by national institutions, may be held separate from theoretical knowledge – even if it is hard to go against the opinion of the Washington consensus.

The MAI and the Millennium Round, each, in its own way, has had a practical, multilateral answer to the issue of the relationship between globalization and cultural diversity. The failure of the MAI and the rise in trade conflicts show, to say the least, that globalization cannot proceed unless new rules are set for the game.

The MAI analyser, or the assertion of cultural diversities

From the outset, the goals of the OECD appeared as legitimate: namely, the establishment of a 'constitution for a unified world economy'.[20] The reasons for this seemed to follow from recent economic developments. The volume of direct investment abroad had increased fourfold between 1982 and 1994 and annual flows had reached record levels in 1996 at $350 billion. Nearly 1,600 bilateral agreements governing foreign investment in the host countries had accumulated over successive phases. In May 1995 negotiations began at the OECD on a technical basis and with very little involvement by government authorities. After the Uruguay Round and the birth of the World Trade Organization (WTO), the development of a framework guaranteeing the security of direct investment seemed a logical step forward. In a context of globalization, trade in goods was seen as only one facet of the integration of economies; direct investment, it was believed, must undergo major expansion.

Agreement on the principles for controlling capital flows for financing direct investment did not a priori raise a problem in so far as these principles were to be aligned on the founding texts of the GATT or the WTO or with regional agreements like those of the European Union. The principles can be listed as eight clauses: (1) national treatment; (2) most favoured nation clause; (3) protection of investments; (4) a clause governing the limitations restricting performance conditions; (5) a ban on uncompensated expropriation of assets; (6) a ban on restrictions on repatriation of profits or capital transfers; (7) settlements of disputes between investors and states referred to the courts; and (8) a more immediately controversial clause directed at protecting investors against untimely changes in the rules of the game, the famous Clause 8 on 'set-back' and 'immobilization' provisions which, in fact, stipulates that states should abrogate discriminating legislation or should refrain from passing laws with a similar effect.

It seemed no more than good economic sense to organize investment flows in the context of globalization on legally well-established principles, no more than a logical determination to avoid proliferation of unbalanced bilateral agreements and possible agreements on exemptions for cultural industries as concluded in the Marrakech agreements. Who would have thought that negotiations that began so auspiciously could turn into something else, become so passionate, mobilize governments and, in the end, completely fail? What could account for such an explosion, such a failure, such a movement of international opinion,[21] or such incensed papers as 'L'AMI, c'est l'ennemi'?[22] Why such a triumph of international civil society over government technocracy supposedly subservient to international 'business'?[23] And furthermore, how can it be explained that France's withdrawal from the process was enough to paralyse the MAI and that negotiations were not resumed? Was consensus on the liberalization of direct investments so weak that refusal of it by France and by citizens' organizations sufficed to make it collapse?

For the moment we shall put aside the minor issues that were important, but could not of themselves justify going to such extremes. The forum – OECD – may well not have been the most appropriate: one does not negotiate an investment code among the

The MAI: on the threshold of a cultural war?

The seeds of the Multilateral Agreement on Investments (MAI) were planted in the OECD in the 1960s when member countries adopted two binding codes on investment liberalization (the Code of Liberalization of Capital Movements and the Code of Liberalization of Current Invisible Operations). However, the absence of enforcing mechanisms made compliance very difficult – hence, the interest raised during the Uruguay Round in starting new negotiations on a free-standing, enforceable multilateral investment agreement. That interest also mirrored the rapid ascendance of direct foreign investment to a central place in the world economy, growing three times as fast as total investment. At the end of 1996, the total stock of direct foreign investment by companies outside their home countries was over US$3 trillion, with OECD members owning 85% of all such investment. It was in this context that the MAI was to set the stage for eliminating the remaining barriers against foreign investors, and the OECD was seen as the appropriate forum in which to carry out the negotiations. In the original mandate, this free-standing international treaty was to be open to all OECD members and the European Communities and to accession by non-OECD member countries which were to be consulted as the negotiations progressed.

The year 1995 also saw the creation of the World Trade Organization as part of the Uruguay Round. Its functions were to oversee the rules of international trade by helping trade to flow smoothly, settling trade disputes between governments and organizing trade negotiations. One of the first items on the agenda immediately after its creation was clearly the pursuit of an investment agreement but WTO members were unable to agree on terms of reference to initiate negotiations. Opposition by developing countries was a major obstacle to such negotiations.

According to the OECD, multilateral investment rules were aimed at enhancing investors' confidence by providing a stable framework of clear and transparent rules applicable to all. Such a framework would have high standards for the liberalization of investment regimes and protection and would include an effective dispute settlement procedure. The MAI proposal would apply the principle of 'National Treatment', requiring governments to grant foreign investors the same benefits as domestic ones. It would also apply the most favoured nation principle to investment rules, imposing equal treatment among all foreign investor and target countries. It would also include a ban on 'Performance Requirements' to prevent governments from imposing performance measures on investors. Several other principles pointed at the overall goal of applying the deregulatory agenda of WTO in the area of investments by creating a set of global rules to replace a patchwork of some 1,600 bilateral investment treaties.

However, MAI proved to be Pandora's box. Dismantling barriers to foreign corporations and investors from member countries was the tip of the iceberg of a far more complex issue relating to technological change, liberalization of international trade and investment, the role of the state, public service, and the balance between public interest and market forces. Governments were taken by surprise. Some negotiating countries in the MAI believed that the reference to national public interest was necessary, and fought for the possibility of providing 'exceptions' or 'reservations' to protect culture, public health, the environment and social rights.

Pages and pages of proposed exceptions from the general rules were put forward. One of the most controversial was the French text entitled 'Special clause for cultural industries'.

As internal controversy on the MAI could not be solved by the negotiating delegations, the whole issue was referred early in 1998 to world public opinion which took it up with great interest ('L'AMI, c'est l'ennemi' [The MAI/'friend' is the enemy], *Le Monde*, 10 February 1998; ' . . . a sort of coup d'état of multinationals,' J. Estefania, *El País*; ' . . . like turning copyright works into commodities and investments,' J. Ralite, President of the États Généraux de la Culture).

The French campaign against the MAI brought many movements within the United States together, including Public Citizens Global Trade Watch, which saw the MAI as 'a treaty of corporate rights and government obligations which ignores the concerns of citizens', or 'a step backwards in international human rights' (Harvard Law School, Human Rights Clinical Project Program). Other interest groups also rallied against the MAI in Australia, Canada, India and New Zealand, using the Internet as a powerful vehicle for getting their messages across to their political representatives and the printed media.

Solid opposition to the treaty led negotiators in April 1998 to decide on a six-month delay to allow countries to seek domestic support and carry out consultations with other countries. This moratorium led to the decision by France to pull out of the negotiations as announced by Prime Minister Lionel Jospin just days before the MAI talks were to resume on 20 October 1998. Canada's Minister of Culture, Sheila Copps, supported France's decision, saying, 'It gives strength to the argument that there are some legitimate national concerns around cultural sovereignty.'

Internal discussions about culture and free investment rules behind OECD closed doors in the context of the MAI have had far less impact than their resultant effects and the process they set in motion. In other words the MAI negotiations released to the outside world what they could not resolve internally. Indeed culture proved to be but one of many conflicting areas, which included labour rights, national sovereignty, environment and so forth. However, culture was the kingpin of the confrontation. Indeed, it was in the name of culture that France blocked the negotiations.

Unlike the aftermath of the General Agreement on Tariffs and Trade (GATT), a new dynamics around culture took root in the MAI. What we are currently seeing is a repositioning of actors on a new stage. Different actors from the private, public and third sectors and intergovernmental organizations (IGOs) are building alliances and devising and applying new strategies. The treatment of culture in the upcoming round of multilateral negotiations on trade and investment will have decisive consequences on the economic hegemony of the markets and culture at global level. Some leading world newspapers would have it that we are on the threshold of a 'cultural war'. The MAI has set the stage. At stake is not only the huge economic potential of content or cultural industries, but also and no less important the power to define and impose meanings about how we see the world and what really matters in life. In short, culture has become a 'War Room' over the power to define and control both the 'content' and the 'message'.

GUIOMAR ALONSO CANO
Programme Specialist, Sector for Culture, UNESCO

members of a club of rich countries (twenty-one contracting parties) at a point in time when direct investment has begun to move in the direction of the countries with emerging economies (i. e. China). Similarly, when public negotiations are involved, it is, to say the very least, unwise not to organize press conferences. Had they wished to give the impression that an opaque process governed by an illegitimate board was challenging fundamental acquired rights, they could not have better succeeded.[24] And the method itself that consisted in drawing up a restrictive list of the exceptions while giving a completely open mandate in all other fields, would at that point appear to be a blind delegation of sovereignty.[25]

This, then, is how the very economics promulgated by the text, along with its general principles, its limited exclusions, its uncontrolled delegation of authority, all negotiated in an un-transparent technocratic environment, managed to unite a holy alliance of political sovereignists, environmentalists, cultural exception activists and even social progress advocates.

The flap among the sovereignists is easily understandable if Clause 7 is taken literally. It formalizes a de facto dissymmetry between business corporations and states. Under the proposal, states could be sued whenever any legislative or regulatory measure they might adopt could be interpreted as restricting free enterprise. In the eyes of the sovereignists and the environmentalists, the well-known case of Ethyl Corporation was evidence that the threat is real. This is because, under the clauses of the North American Free Trade Agreement (NAFTA), Canada was taken to court by an American firm: a Canadian law banned the use of a certain additive in the fuel manufactured by Ethyl Corp., and so the corporation felt injured. It could be pointed out that the procedural 'legalization' of disputes between companies and states in court is not unprecedented; the European Union, for one, already operates along such lines. It could also be pointed out that, over time, a number of laws or regulations supposedly of general intent were actually conceived so as to discriminate against foreign companies. But when a poorly informed public suddenly discovered that firms could take states to court and even prevent them from legislating, the measures were considered scandalous.

Clause 8 specified the danger that the sovereignists had identified, which then aroused the anger of the environmentalists and the champions of social progress. What does a so-called 'immobilization' clause really mean? Literally, that a state cannot modify a piece of legislation if it alters the conditions under which a foreign firm operates. Here again, it is possible to see what the authors of the clause meant to say. It would be far too easy for countries to attract investors through special fiscal, social and environmental conditions and then change the rules once the investment had been made. But as it was worded, the clause was literally outrageous, since it could potentially enable any foreign investor to challenge a country's environmental legislation, development of social benefits or even new forms of freedom. The OECD rightly retorted that the intention of the MAI was to secure equal terms for local and foreign firms alike without claiming extra-territorial status for foreign firms. But once again, the prospect of exceedingly vague legal principles coupled with powerful dispute settlement mechanisms accounts for the fears raised.

Finally, Clause 5, which prohibits nationalization without compensation, caused the defenders of Third World sovereignty to rise up in arms. They rightly sensed a restriction on the power of the élites of developing countries to plan and build the society they want; but opposition to this clause verges on the extremes of the sovereignty discourse. Indeed, if arbitrary action and predation are allowed in the name of legitimate political objectives, then foreign investors cannot at the same time be expected to be the victims.

Above and beyond Clauses 5, 7 and 8 which triggered the strongest protest, every other clause gave rise to heated debate. This was the case with Clause 1, called the national treatment clause, which mobilized the 'cultural exception' activists. How indeed can the active creation of works of art in national languages be supported (i.e. paid for) if culture is reduced to cultural industries and if the latter fall under common trade regulations? But conversely, how can the difference between the work itself and the product be established? Should the original work necessarily be expressed in the national language? Is a cultural product of entertainment like any other product? All these questions were answered in Marrakech, as we shall see, but the answer remained tentative and thus sowed the seeds for potential conflicts. Furthermore, any cultural exception with a limited time-scale and an ambiguous definition condemns those working inside such a system to permanent insecurity. This is what the protest against the MAI really expressed.

Similar debates surrounded Clause 2 – called the most favoured nation clause. How will sovereign states be able to boycott a nation that practises apartheid, engages in terrorist activities, violates human rights or even massacres part of its population if commercial considerations come first? This radical example shows how commercial standards, being prerequisites for any civilized trading system, become major obstacles to the promotion of a more equitable and more peaceful world.

This first planet-wide social movement against public technocracies arraigned as corporations' accomplices was a reaction expressing anxiety about globalization. Have we not gone too far, have we not given too much power to corporations, and have we not, in so doing, set relations between states and corporations off balance? Does not the relinquishing of whole sectors of national sovereignty, while no supranational political body accountable to an electorate has been created, mean that democracy has been bartered for litigation and jurisprudence?

Before answering such questions, we need to assess their impact more carefully. After all, the MAI might be an isolated event which should not be over-interpreted. As for the cultural exception so often defended by the French (even if it has rallied fresh supporters), it has long been a standard issue in international trade negotiations. But in the space of a few years or even a few months, trade-related tension has developed and an injured sense of national identity has been exacerbated in the context of a looming financial crisis.

There are, in fact, more and more jarring notes in the concert of praise for globalization. Different eating habits, divergent views on the protection of private life, clashing intellectual property regimes, conflicting constructions on science appropriation and, lastly – without claiming to be comprehensive – national claims to specifically designed development routes: these and other issues have bogged down the globalization agenda and are putting considerable pressure on the future negotiators of what is called the 'Millennium Round'.

The Millennium Round: scheduled convergence

The Marrakech agreement includes a 'built-in agenda' that makes it binding on the contracting parties to continue negotiations for reducing obstacles to trade in the agricultural and service sectors. Moreover, as the negotiations on dismantling tariff barriers to trade have reached their limit with the lowering of tariff peaks and tariff consolidation, the debate will now focus on deepening and extending trade regulation. Competition and investment protection policies will ultimately replace tariff agreements. In fact the 'Millennium Round' involves a more drastic change. What is at stake is no less than the drafting of a constitution for an open planet-wide economy, since all the items mentioned so far are on the WTO's de facto agenda.

In a report drafted for the Conseil d'analyse économique (CAE), Pierre Jacquet has pointed to the differences between the GATT system and the WTO system. Although they originated from the same point, there is more disparity than continuity between these two regulatory bodies for international trade. According to Jacquet, there are five characteristics that describe the shift in logic that has occurred in thinking from the GATT to the WTO:

- With the introduction of services and the multiplication of non-tariff barriers to trade, tariff negotiations are being replaced by negotiations on norms, standards and barrier-dismantling processes. In other words, access to markets is becoming a higher priority than tariffs.
- It is not so much a question of deregulating, but rather of replacing regulations adopted in a strictly national context by others agreed at the proper level, that is to say world level; this notion applies particularly to intellectual property.
- A sector-based approach in negotiations is justified by the complexity of trade, competition, and regulatory

and standardization issues, and this excludes 'trade-offs', which were still possible during an era of GATT-style enlightened mercantilism. With the WTO there is no possibility for bartering; audiovisual and cinematographic cultural exceptions can no longer be exchanged for a freeze on maritime transport, such as occurred during the Uruguay Round, since, by definition, sector-based negotiations are now considered to be independent of each other.

- An important point is that the WTO operates through the multilateral consolidation of regional agreements, rather than through brand-new negotiations between all the contracting parties. This means that the WTO can turn the advances of the Europeans against them by invoking the principle of the universality of trade concessions. Any community advance thus accelerates the opening-up of the world economy. Instead of blocking multilateralism, regional unions are in fact becoming its stepping stones.
- The last and by far the most important aspect, the Marrakech agreement, led to the creation of the LSB which sets the law in the field of litigation; day by day, jurisprudence is being produced which is gradually evolving into a doctrine. The LSB formally took over from the GATT's panels, but the impact of its immediately enforceable rulings has significantly contributed to bringing trade disputes into a legal environment and out of the arena of political compromise.

In short, the GATT was based on three basic principles, accepted by all, and with predictable processes involved: (1) enlightened mercantilism, (2) rules of the game for confident and reliable access to markets, and (3) arbitration function for the settlement of disputes. The entire concept behind the WTO is different. Grounded in the liberal concept of unilateral disarmament, it has developed through the autonomous action of laws. What is left in terms of political initiative is merely to decide on the timetable for sector-based negotiations. Let us now examine three aspects more closely.

Firstly, while the GATT was able to prosper without making free trade a precondition, the WTO upholds unilateral disarmament as an economic principle,[26] in the name of economic rationality, historical experience and statistical evidence. As we have already seen, the sector-based organization of negotiations precludes the reciprocal bartering of advantages and therefore the practices of enlightened mercantilism. If we pause to consider the domestic impact of multilateral trade policies, the loss of this leverage point hampers political action. Moreover, the regionalization-multilateralization relationship already mentioned has weakened the incentive for European citizens to open up trade within the framework of a single market, because such initiatives would *ipso facto* benefit other countries without any advantages in return.

Secondly, moreover, the fact that regular meetings to organize customs deregulation have been eschewed may be construed as simply a means of defusing the situation, but in fact, periods of peaceful trading between two cycles provide the time that is needed for significant political action to win social acceptance of the new economic order. Today, processes of constant monitoring make it possible to do away with the necessity of cyclical meetings and actually force lobbies to defend their positions constantly, in particular, through the rulings of the LSB.

Lastly, the process for the settlement of disputes is surely the most far-reaching innovation of the WTO. This is not only because a dispute may at any time be brought before the LSB, thereby destabilizing the rules for players. It is even more so because in the absence of specific political terms of reference regarding the scope and depth of more open trading and institutional convergence, the LSB is, and will increasingly be, a creator of legislation through its jurisprudence. And the major institutional innovation embodied by the LSB brings us to the heart of the problem, namely coping judiciously with the tension between the pressures of globalization and the demands for preserving cultural differences. The strategy actually chosen by the governments that finalized the Marrakech agreement was to keep trade policy and its impact out of the political sphere. Government leaders, confronted with hormone additives in beef, cultural exception, or ecological and social questions, and for lack of any explicit political agreement on substance, have adopted the agreement on the settlement of trade disputes.

It is as if there really had been a recognition of the diversity of the objectives to be pursued for liberalizing trade and even their potentially conflicting natures: yes to trade liberalization but no to child labour, yes to freedom of location but no to ecological dumping, yes to celebration of cultural diversity by unmasking protectionist strategies, yes to the precautionary principle but also to the unlimited commercial power of transnational corporations. Yet since contradiction cannot be resolved through mere statement of principles, codes of conduct or self-regulation, trade wars are the logical outcome. On the other hand, the WTO has given birth to the LSB. Consequently, disputes arising from diverging hierarchies of values and radically opposed collective preference patterns can now be referred to the commercial law process. The WTO's major political innovation has therefore been to offer prospects of limitless expansion to the 'litigation business'.

But is this situation really so deplorable?

As demonstrated by the example of European construction, the multilateral framework and the legal settlement bodies may in fact advantageously replace bilateral negotiations and state regulation. Without the European Commission and the European Court of Justice, it would never have been possible to dismantle so many protective measures, harmonize so much legislation and, finally, manage to organize the regulation of trade, support and competition. The single European market as well as the Euro have proved to be major political advances precisely because trade and monetary issues were technically addressed and delegated to agencies whose legitimacy and credibility are unchallenged. Community machinery made it possible to keep lobbies away from national authorities and incorporate them into a European regulation process. At the same time, the European Court of Justice has considerably raised the price to be paid by states for non-compliance with common standards.

At this stage in our investigation, three questions arise: (1) What are the appropriate world governance forums? (2) What are the prerequisites for establishing a negotiated world order? (3) How can tension between the drive towards globalization and the need to claim identity be reconciled?

Who should handle the tension between globalization and diversity?

A few years ago international political discourse gave a new lease on life to the word 'governance'. The World Bank in particular took up the term. Political theorists and specialists in local politics (as opposed to centralized government) were the first to use the term to describe any public action not strictly identified with the public authorities. The conjunction of the actions of central and local public authorities, the independent initiatives of divisions of local authorities responsible for services and public or privately-run utilities, the impact on the local public sphere of decisions taken by hybrid organizations generated by private and state partnerships, and the role of associations – successively protesters, partners and managers – all such actors and actions contribute in a real sense to local public activity that some authors put under the heading of 'governance'.

The concept then transferred to the realm of international relations. Here, anything that falls outside a strict definition of sovereign authority to include the complexity of interdependence between different levels of government and the diversification of agents acting inside a specific economic space seems to create a need for new concepts. In this respect the way in which Susan Strange has examined the question and suggested replacing the study of international relations by that of the international system is an interesting illustration. The departure from a Westphalian order governing relations between nation-states and the entry into a world in which international public action is produced by interaction between states, firms and international organizations would seem to justify this approach.

Now no one would deny that in recent decades, significant transfers of power have increasingly been made to international organizations and regional groups. Every state today is limited by a tightly knit network of international agreements that restrict its scope of action, facilitate intercommunication, protect the common heritage and shelter it from the undesirable initiatives of neighbouring states. The corollary of this trend towards internationalization of public affairs is that there has been a noticeable boom in non-elected authorities, not accountable to any voter constituency and whose actions affect the lives of citizens who then spontaneously appeal to national political authorities who can do precious little about it.

We can now see how the concept of 'governance' has shifted from the use being made of it by the World Bank. The term gradually became displaced from an observation of different forms of government to a setting-up of 'best practices', and this in turn has led to 'one best way' – a far cry from the governance advocated by the World Bank. But as everyone knows, a recommendation from a powerful moneylender is virtually an obligation. The notion of governance has accordingly paved the way for the wide acceptance of a ready-to-use tool kit. The increase in domestic concerns of a cultural, social and environmental nature, together with the responsibility and transparency issues raised by globalization and the increasing power of international organizations, have created a climate of tension which national governments must resolve partly at the multilateral and partly at the national level.

DEALING WITH TENSION: FIVE TYPICAL CASES

The examples presented in this paper, together with the proposed elements of analysis, would seem to suggest five ways of reducing tension between globalization and identity claims. Once the globalization process is acknowledged as a fact of life, the following options are open to us: we can influence public opinion; we can overhaul the concept of globalization, giving it a new political framework; we can allow the law and the market to work freely; we can rely on the evolution of international public opinion; or we can encourage international organizations to set limits to their actions without any multilateral political intervention.

Relieving tension between domestic public opinion and government leaders who endorse globalization is the first case in point. The idea is simple enough. It has many historical precedents and is somewhat akin to enlightened despotism. It consists in extolling the virtues of globalization through numerous economic studies which demonstrate its benefits, while saying nothing of the sector-based, geographical and social costs. History teaches us that people are sensitive to this kind of discourse in times of economic growth, whereas they may reject it violently in times of recession. One has only to remember the widespread enthusiasm that greeted speeches about 'economic horror' in France in 1996, the Korean demonstrations against the IMF and Mahathir's diatribes in Malaysia. In any case, political consent should always be preferred to despotism, however enlightened it may be.

Along the same lines and whatever the degree of public acceptance, it may be possible to continue with the current way of thinking which, for states, means setting in motion the process of trade liberalization and delegating implementation along with broad powers of interpretation to the international organizations. This approach would amount to accepting the automatic effects of programmed liberalism: the dynamics of regulation through laws and markets, market-led economic integration, law and litigation. In this case, however, increasingly frequent clashes, manifestations of tension and possible regression are to be expected. One of the ways of limiting domination by a strictly market-based mentality would be to incorporate certain environmental, social and cultural obligations in the WTO constitution. But the risk would be twofold: either a duplication of the hierarchy of criteria (the ILO and UNESCO have barely developed their admittedly timid arguments), or an overburdening of the institution with a subsequent loss of efficiency.

On the other hand, we could rely on a growing trend in international public opinion in favour of imposing restrictions on the influence of laws and markets, on the one hand, and a voluntary relinquishing of competence by national governments, on the other. It is an attractive prospect: if states are unable to restrain the influence of laws and markets because they are driven by world-wide trends, why not rely on the emergence and gradual development of a planet-wide civil society? All things considered, is the MAI not pointing in that direction?

The problem could also be actively dealt with by seeking political agreement on the degree of opening hoped for, and the required level of standardization of the rules of the game; this would mean bringing the issues into the political sphere once again. Agreement on the objectives of globalization or at any rate agreements on interim objectives, such as preservation of cultural diversity, sustainable development and protection of emerging industries in the take-off phase, might be envisaged.

Finally, political initiative could be focused on procedures rather than on substantive issues, by promoting international organizations dedicated to specific issues and by setting a recognized hierarchy of norms. It would indeed be wise not to put undue demands on an operational institution such as the WTO, but instead to set up as many institutions as there are problems to be solved, while providing for a cooperation procedure beforehand. In this respect, the social standards laid down by the ILO should be made more binding, and exemptions for cultural goods, which UNESCO could sponsor, should be introduced. Similarly, it will no doubt be necessary one day to create an organization to take charge of the natural heritage and the protection of the planet Earth. Then, the trade disputes which will undoubtedly arise in an increasingly integrated world economy will not be the responsibility of the market alone. A balance will then be achieved through confrontation between organizations that think differently and propose differing projects and co-ordination and appeal bodies in charge of reconciling the diversity of values.

CONDITIONS FOR ESTABLISHING A NEGOTIATED WORLD ORDER

Our attempted analysis of trade disputes and their settlement procedures should not lead to mistaken assumptions. The financial scale of litigation cases is small, but this should not conceal the fundamental nature of conflicts which all relate to 'being' rather than to 'having'. And politics is not governed by an economic rationale. In the conflict on hormone additives in beef, everything seems to be done on either side to fuel the fire, turning a minor trade dispute into a holy war between the hegemonic MacWorld and Granny's home cooking.[27]

The euphoria generated by globalization, to which hasty commentators are all too often prone, should not conceal the fact that throughout economic history, all present-day major powers underwent a protectionist and mercantilist phase as they began to expand, while tariff liberalization often covered non-tariff barriers. Consequently, globalization can never be achieved once and for all. Unless adequate care is taken, periods of expansion may be followed by periods of recession.

There have already been major achievements in opening up trade, and the European experience is exemplary: now that it has dismantled excessive protectionism, the nature of liberalization is going to change. It will both widen and deepen. None the less, the most serious danger would be to prejudge the extent of change and take for granted a triumphant march of unilateral liberalization and multilateral consolidation of progress achieved in the regional context with the blessing of the law and jurisprudence. Governments cannot proceed in the face of domestic public opinion with mere speeches on future benefits: these will only fall on the current victims' deaf ears. Finally, the passion aroused over protection of identity weighs more heavily than well-construed interest: witness the force of re-emerging nationalistic stereotypes.

Cultural exemption

If we were to focus the entire range of observations, contradictions and tentative solutions presented in this paper on one single case, the 'cultural exemption' issue would doubtless come romping home.

Initially, a relatively unimportant economic issue[28] provoked recurrent commercial strife, nurtured, on the one hand, by passionate protest from actors and creators in the name of cultural and linguistic identity, and, on the other, by a questionable policy asserting the universal principle that everything has market value. This ended in an unsatisfactory compromise which inevitably paved the way for the next round of battle. We might recall here that it was only on the occasion of the Uruguay Round that the issue of national restrictions on the broadcasting of foreign works was raised, on the initiative of the United States and in response to the 'TV without

Frontiers' directive, and that the GATT adopted a temporary compromise which, on the one hand, recognized a 'general exception' for national regulatory systems for 'the protection of national treasures of artistic, archaeological or historic value', and on the other, a specific provision for the cinema, while all other sectors of cultural activity continued to be ruled by the general provisions of the agreement. The GATT provisions, in particular, made it binding on member countries, if the most favoured nation clause were not applied, to abide by the national status clause. The trade dispute, revived during the MAI negotiations, was then consequently scheduled for Seattle. On what basis could a new agreement be concluded and in which forum?

Economic analysis does provide several theoretical bases for thinking out the concept of 'cultural exception', especially for audiovisual products. A sector such as the cinema can be characterized as an increasing-yield industry, because the cost of shooting a film remains the same whether 10,000 or one million people pay to see it. It is therefore in the producer's interest to aim at a wide market from the start. The increasing yield creates an entry barrier which may justify government intervention either to make a national industry competitive on the world market or to protect it. Furthermore, it can be assumed that there is a demand for diversity in cultural goods and that uncontrolled market pressures can stifle local productions. Competition between amortized products and original products may make it difficult to see whether film-goers are 'prepared to pay the price'. Lastly, national culture is also public property that produces external effects, and letting market forces dominate would therefore be less effective than granting subsidies. Yet, tariff protectionism cannot adequately solve the problems, although it may be legitimate to subsidize the creation and dissemination of cultural works with an increasing yield. The problem is then to see who should determine the criteria for awarding subsidies and who should assess their use and effectiveness. In the absence of this assessment, the promotion of cultural exception amounts to the same thing as protectionist measures.[30]

Moreover, when actual practices are reviewed, a less Manichean image than that which is commonly conveyed comes to light: the conflict does not simply oppose disinterested advocates of the promotion of intellectual works and the aggressive militants of totally free enterprise, which, as we have just seen, is not even justifiable in theory. Cultural sovereignists may be closet protectionists and militant free traders may want to defend the interests of a monopolistic industry. In actual fact, a protectionist policy applied to films and audiovisual material by means of production subsidies and broadcasting quotas, in a country such as France, neither stops the decline in number of original works created in the national language nor produces exportable works. Rather, production costs have become inflated due to guaranteed broadcasting and production subsidies. On the other hand, the sheer scale of the English-speaking world, the power of the multinationals of make-believe[31] and their contribution to the American trade balance weigh heavily in favour of unequal development and the extension of standard trade rules to the cultural industries. Whether it be the handing out of subsidies on the one hand, or monopoly profits on the other, the issue cannot be settled in purely economic terms. This means that demands for the dismantling of state funding for creation or even for equal dissemination rights for the monopolists and the dominated alike are difficult to justify.

What's in a word?

Language, in this area as everywhere else, both reflects and influences prevailing opinion. The use of the word 'exception' to describe the treatment of cultural goods in international trade conveys a somewhat negative sense, that culture is the misfit, a hindrance to the achievement of an otherwise perfect uniformity in the world trading system. If the protection of cultural values and the pursuit of other cultural objectives were accepted as a legitimate element alongside the pursuit of economic value in influencing trade policy at an international level, perhaps the term 'cultural recognition' would provide a more positive orientation in describing efforts to deal with this matter in negotiations between countries.

DAVID THROSBY[29]

Let us now consider what the objectives and impact of a cultural exception policy might be in terms of national public policies. No one denies that the national language, works of the mind and consequently the cultural industries are the backbone of a national identity. Defending creation, supporting diversity and plurality in audiovisual production and protecting the national broadcasting industry are legitimate policies. But once agreement on the general considerations has been achieved, the real difficulties begin. Were the issue simply to protect creators' original works, the difficulty would be manageable. No one objects to the sponsorship and private grants and gifts for opera or the graphic arts. No one questions the right of states or foundations to encourage literary, musical or architectural creation. Finally, no one challenges the protection of the national heritage through regulatory measures, limitations on property rights and restrictions on the movement of goods.

In fact, the problem arises mainly for the cinema and for audiovisual material, which are not only the Seventh and Eighth Arts, so to speak, but also powerful industries as well. The various attempts to classify works on the basis of genre, quality or originality have proved inconclusive. Consequently, the countries which defend cultural exception constantly waver between promoting the national language, national producers and films shot on national territory. Those countries too are uncertain as to which incentives to select: general measures, targeted support or tax incentives. Lastly, those countries intervene in all or part of the production process, as the particular link considered to be crucial in production may vary from one period to another.

Hence the real question is whether the cultural benefits of protection are greater than the cost of doling out subsidies. But that kind of question calls for a political answer. It is simply not true that the only way to promote cultural diversity is by establishing a legal framework for encouraging intellectual works whose innate qualities would indeed already guarantee them an audience, a market and economic viability. Nor is it fair to say that the Colbertist tradition in France, defended as reflecting French national genius in the past but challenged today in all economic sectors, should be unhesitatingly maintained for the cultural industries. In the final analysis and in such sensitive sectors, pending adoption of a new common rule, the WTO cannot be left to settle such issues as these on its own.

In pluralist democratic societies, a widely held belief may induce a practical result, even if it is based on erroneous economic calculations and an incomplete image of public policy effects. Consequently, cultural exception policies may enjoy such support and popularity that political authorities will ultimately accept to bear their prohibitive financial cost. What can the WTO possibly do in such a context? It is currently bound by the Marrakech agreements, which include a temporary cultural exception clause. In view of the failure of the MAI, the issue was again raised in Seattle. But the subject was no longer an uncharted ocean; forces had made their appearance; commitments had been made and even the experts had learned to mistrust optimistic assessments of the benefits of maximum trade disarmament. For cultural issues, at least, a new agreement will require that the primacy of a democratic state over a corporation be recognized: no legal order can possibly make them equal. It will also mean accepting the preservation of the national institutions which endeavour to promote national works' and agreeing that national firms which benefit from this specific status be protected accordingly. At the same time, countries such as the United States, which have made their cultural industry into one of the strong points of their specialization, can hardly accept exclusion from conventional trade procedures. A solution might be to work out, in an appropriate context such as UNESCO, a positive definition of what comes under preservation of cultural diversity justifying cultural exception. Otherwise, one day, the matter will be referred to the LSB which will issue a ruling based essentially on legal and commercial considerations. However, to safeguard their legitimacy, universal commercial values should come to terms with cultural diversity and universal democratic values.

So, the principle of cultural exemption could work as a test-bed for a new concept of globalization, which would reconcile the norm of open trading with that of cultural diversity, the standard of specialized

The dynamics of African film-making

In the eyes of the many Africans who feel disempowered, political independence has meant a further decline in the quality of their life. It brought with it World-Bank-mandated structural adjustment and privatization programmes which benefit only a minority, increased economic polarization and hardships, sociocultural dislocations, further alienation from state political power seen as repressive and unresponsive to the needs of the majority, and a general sense of betrayal and disillusionment. This has translated into a strong, albeit repressed, undercurrent of discontent and imperative for fundamental change, and an increasing awareness of the potential and possible power of individuals when they are organized.

In considering film-making in particular, and the other creative arts in general, one is looking at particular insights into ways of thinking and acting on individual as well as collective realities, experiences, challenges and desires over time. African participation in the global civilization of cinema as producers and transmitters of their own images is, however, a relatively recent phenomenon. Egyptians started making films in 1928. However, it was only at the end of the 1950s and the start of the 1960s, following political independence in many African countries, that we began to witness the emergence of a significant corpus of films produced and directed by Africans.

African film-making, then, is in a way a child of African political independence. It was born in the era of heady nationalism and the nationalist anti-colonial and anti-neocolonial struggle, and it has been undergoing a process of painful growth and development in a post-colonial context of general socio-economic decay and decline, devaluation and political repression and instability on the continent. One is therefore talking here about a very young, if not the youngest, creative practice in Africa.

However, in spite of its youth and the variety of overwhelming odds with which it has to struggle, cinema by Africans has grown steadily over this short period of time to become a significant part of the global cinema civilization to which it brings many significant contributions. More specifically, it is part of a worldwide film movement aimed at constructing and promoting an alternative popular cinema, one that corrects the distortions and stereotypes propagated by dominant Western cinemas, and one that is more synchronized with the realities, experiences, priorities and desires of their respective societies.

We have then, in the landscape of African cinema at the end of the 20th century, the coexistence of three principal competing modes of film-thinking and -practice that are by no means uniform, fixed and stable. They have historically interacted and continue to do so in various ways to shape and transform the contours and contents of the landscape of cinema in Africa. This is a much contested and dynamic terrain, one that is in constant flux, with many internal pressures, demands and challenges to be negotiated continually, in addition to the effects of a constantly changing global political and media economy.

Southern Africa already enjoys a fairly well-developed production infrastructure, with skills and resources that film-makers from other parts of the continent and Southern Africa have in fact already begun using, thus enhancing the possibilities and prospects of South-South co-operation.

One of the major challenges for African cinema in the new millennium is to devise more effective and sustainable ways and mechanisms with which to break out of its traditional confines of festivals, schools, universities, museums and community centres into cinema theatres both in Africa and elsewhere. This question of the marginal status of African films within the global industry is the subject of much debate and strategy-making in African cinema circles. Efforts to remedy the situation place a major premium on the importance of distribution and the need to shift ever so slightly away from the current emphasis on production.

The issue of marginalization relates equally to the participation of women in African film practices. To date, African film-making has been predominantly a male activity with very few women figuring in prominent positions as directors, producers, writers, editors, camera persons and the like. Things are changing, albeit not fast enough. The past ten years have witnessed the emergence of a steadily growing body of work in various domains of cinema by women from different parts of the continent. This corpus of work has begun to effect some significant shifts and revisions in African cinematic conventions and practices, not unlike what transpired in African literature in the European languages when women came into the field in full force in the late 1970s.

The handful of women pioneer film-makers such as Thérèse Sita Bella from Cameroon, Safi Faye from Senegal and Sarah Maldoror from Guadeloupe/Angola, have now been joined by more than thirty film directors and many more women working in other aspects of film-making, video and television. Kenya stands as an instance of female dominance in terms of numbers and prominence.

In African cinema, the future may well be feminine.

Like some of their male counterparts, African women film-makers engage the broad range of issues and topics thrown up by the experiences and challenges of life in Africa across broad time spans. However, unlike many of their male counterparts, some of these women film-makers bring to these issues and topics a particular female and gender sensibility whose absence in male-directed films has severely handicapped film discourse on such issues and topics.

Many African film-makers consider cinema not only as entertainment, but more significantly as a vehicle of social, cultural, political and personal discourse and praxis. They use film to critically engage, celebrate and interrogate certain aspects of African cultural beliefs and traditions, while they exploit the resources of these traditions to make films that comment on the contemporary social, cultural, political, historical and personal realities, experiences and challenges of Africans. Thus, African cinema is part and parcel of the wider social and collective effort on the part of Africans to bring about a better life for the majority of Africans. African cinema is, as the Fulani say of art in general, 'futile, utile, instructive'. It is entertainment, it is educational and it is functional.

The themes that dominate African film narratives mirror the problems, challenges, experiences and desires of African individuals and societies over time, with particular emphasis on the operations and consequences of colonialism and its legacies.

The city as a site where traditional moral values and practices are tested, degraded, compromised or transformed is a theme that a number of African creative practitioners – oral narrative performers, writers, dramatists and film-makers – have privileged in many narratives.

Women film-makers bring a particular spin to this schema. *Saikati* by Kenyan film-maker Anne Mungai casts a specific glance at this phenomenon in contemporary tourist Kenya, with a specific focus on women. *Saikati's* world is the world of the Maasai *maara* surrounded by vast plains and animals of all sorts, a family enclosure within a small village, daily treks to and from school, and traditional Maasai dress, cosmetics and jewelry. Mungai here attempts a balanced look at female prostitution in urban Kenya and at the 'push-and-pull' factors that account for rural-urban drift.

In 1996, Safi Faye brought out her first feature fiction film, *Mossane*. Adapted from Faye's own Serère legends, the film imaginatively conflates myth, legend and reality to weave a narrative about personal desire, female choice, agency and identity, patriarchy, tradition and modernity. The narrative codes and structures as well as the visual style of *Mossane* favour female voices and desires, while effectively interrogating and subverting the limiting effects of tradition and its patriarchal supports. *Mossane* undertakes a forceful, articulate and highly compelling critique of the sociocultural status quo and its denial and containment of individual desires and aspirations. Like Saikati and many other young African female protagonists in film, *Mossane* is a symbol of new womanhood inscribed in the discourse of female-directed films.

More recently African cinema has been inundated with films on experiences of immigration as more and more film-makers and others relocate to Europe with hopes of relatively easier access to production resources. New diasporas are springing up everywhere, swelling the ranks of those already established there and giving rise to new and changing identities. The diversity, dynamics and complexities of these processes constitute the narrative focus of a large number of African films in the past ten years. *Toubabi* (1993) by Senegalese Moussa Touré emphasizes the traps of the French urban subculture of drugs, pimping and prostitution with a focus on its African victims who become ethically and morally debased even while professing superficially to hold on to their African-ness.

MBYE CHAM
Associate Professor,
Department of African Studies,
Howard University (United States)

GLOBAL CINEMA MARKET

COUNTRY	share earned by US films (%)	share earned by domestic films (%)
Philippines	35	50
Malaysia	45	4
China Hong Kong SAR	49	42
Norway	58	9
Japan	59	30
Italy	60	26
France	64	27
Indonesia	65	7
Republic of Korea	66	26
Australia	68	4
Argentina	70	13
Switzerland	70	2
Denmark	74	14
Germany	75	10
Sweden	76	15
South Africa	77	4
Spain	79	12
Finland	80	10
Poland	83	11
Canada	85	8
Thailand	85	10
United Kingdom	85	9
Hungary	90	6
Netherlands	90	9
Colombia	92	1
Mexico	92	4
Venezuela	94	1
Brazil	95	3
Portugal	95	2
United States	96	—

Graph 6

US films dominated the global cinema market in 1998. In only three of the thirty countries in this table, China Hong Kong SAR, Malaysia and the Philippines – all in Asia – do US films account for less than half the cinema box office receipts. In twenty-one of the countries, US films account for more than two-thirds of receipts. In only five countries, China Hong Kong SAR, France, Italy, Japan and Republic of Korea do receipts from domestic films account for more than a quarter of box office receipts. (Comparable data were not available for India, which has a vast domestic film industry).

Source: *Screen Digest*, 1999.

international organizations with that of the WTO, and the national democratic norm with the universal concept of cultural rights. As Bairoch points out, economic experience teaches us that the world has lived more often under protectionist rule than in free trading systems, and that free trade should never be taken as established once and for all.[32] The ongoing process of national fragmentation underlines how strong a claim the right to be different actually is. If agreement is not reached through enlightened negotiation, one may expect a violent backlash. Merely celebrating cultural diversity will not do. What is needed today is no doubt an 'economic constitution for an open world', but it must be a world which can combine the values of trade, democracy and identity.

After Seattle

Seattle will no doubt be remembered as an 'unconscious' deliberate mistake. Heralded as the place where an economic constitution for our planet was to be written, it allowed the establishment, instead, of an international NGO, whose objectives were utterly contradictory; it rekindled the North/South conflict and revealed the American tendency to return to aggressive bilateralism. It became the scene of European divisions as well: it depicted an imaginary, omnipotent WTO incapable of mastering the forces it had helped to liberate when finally put to the test.

The Seattle episode would seem to indicate that while an agreement on opening up trade requires further debate, the major regional groups none the less now feel that they can move alternatively from bilateral regionalism to multilateralism, from a deliberate political decision or an automatic policy through settlement of disputes, and from enlightened despotism to an electioneering policy.

One thing is certain: if the field is abandoned now to the defenders of idiosyncrasies, exceptions and exemptions of all kinds, if the search for mutual agreement on a common law and arbitration procedures becomes inaccessible, then we will probably bring about a return to what we were trying to avoid: a power struggle, purely and simply. In that case, Seattle will be remembered not as a moment of renewed public awareness worldwide, but as the triumph of

Cultural diversity in national cinema

Understanding cultural trade mechanisms is essential to preserving a pluralistic and diversified supply of creative works. However, the main difficulty would appear to be the absence of indicators to identify a specific consumer demand for cultural goods and services.

Since audiovisual goods represent half of the world's 'copyright core business', it is legitimate to approach this particular trade from the perspective of the cinema industry, especially if one takes into account the fact that a film is not just a work of art (*une œuvre de l'esprit*) in itself, but also an efficient vehicle for other forms of artistic creation.

One of the ways of keeping a community's identity alive is to translate its cultural expressions into images, which implies the capacity to produce them locally. In other words, a structured national cinematography sector is necessary on a local basis. However, this capability exists only in about one hundred countries around the world. Over a third of all countries, representing almost 465 million persons (8% of the world's population), have no cinematographic image to reflect their own culture, although several have implemented national policies giving priority to video and numeric image technologies, thus dividing production costs and multiplying local audiences considerably.

A characteristic feature of the situation in the 40 countries that do have a stable annual film production of between 10 and 200 films is dependence on direct government financing coupled with a high degree of legal protection which is even more important than public funding.

The volume of national film production appears to be related more to the number of inhabitants and their urban concentration than to national wealth measured in terms of gross national product or even the indicator for human development of the UNDP. Correlation with the number of books published is also far higher than with the percentage of youth attending primary school.

For medium-producing countries, the existence of sub-regional co-operation plans for financing technical structures and laboratories as well as training centres – the most expensive and fragile components of any cinematography sector – is essential.

A second condition for preserving cultural pluralism through cinematography is the capacity to exchange films between different national markets. In spite of the fact that the eight largest Hollywood film studios dominate the world market for cinema (85%), there is still a comfortable margin for non-commercial and national productions intended for large audiences. Medium-producing countries thus have their own 'peripheral market', be it geographic, linguistic or based on cultural affinity, which is an additional financial asset.

The regional flow of films and cinematography rights should therefore be given the closest attention at the forthcoming negotiations on international commerce conducted by the World Trade Organization, particularly in the discussions on the exchange of cultural goods and services.

LLUÍS ARTIGAS DE QUADRAS
Programme Specialist,
Cinema and Audiovisual, UNESCO

A worldwide survey on national cinema was recently conducted by the Culture Sector of UNESCO, the results of which were published in May 2000. A free copy is obtainable by e-mail from <ll.artigas@unesco.org>

modern neo-protectionism dressed up in the virtues of cultural identity, sustained development and prudence.

Those who, instead, intend to work on a new international commercial and legal order, will simply have to put Seattle behind them and return to the drawing board – and consciously and thoughtfully come up with regulated globalization, respectful of cultural diversity.

Notes

1. D. Rodrick, *Has Globalization Gone Too Far?*, Washington, D.C., Institute for International Economics, 1997.
2. In 1995, the twenty-nine OECD countries started a round of negotiations on the terms of liberalization of direct investment flows. An initial Multilateral Agreement on Investment (MAI) was drafted in March 1997. The planet-wide protest movement secured a first victory with the postponement obtained at the ministerial session of 27–28 April 1998. The French Government, following the *La Lumière Report* of September 1998, decided to terminate its participation in the process launched by the OECD.
3. UNCTAD data, *World Investment Report,* United Nations, 1994.
4. UNESCO, *World Culture Report,* 1998, UNESCO Publications, Paris, 1998.
5. S.P. Huntington, *The Clash of Civilizations and the Remaking of the World Order,* Simon and Schuster, New York, 1996.
6. E. Hobsbawn, *Nations and Nationalism since 1780,* Cambridge, Cambridge University Press, 1990.
7. E. Gellner, *Nations and Nationalism,* Oxford, 1983.
8. There is no mistaking the theories of Kenichi Ohmae and Robert Reich.
9. P. Hirst and G. Thompson, *Globalization in Question,* Cambridge, MA Polity Press, 1996.
10. P. Kennedy, *Préparer le XXIe siècle,* Paris, Odile Jacob, 1994. (French translation.)
11. O. Kenichi, *The Borderless World,* New York, Harper Business, 1990.
12. J. Stopford and S. Strange, *Rival States, Rival Firms,* Cambridge, Cambridge University Press, 1991.
13. See E. Cohen, *La tentation hexagonale: la souveraineté à l'épreuve de la mondialisation,* Paris, Fayard, 1996.
14. J. Ceglowski, 'Has Globalization Created a Borderless World?', *Federal Reserve Bank of Philadelphia Business Review,* March/April 1998, pp. 17–27.
15. Op. cit.
16. G. Dosi, 'Technological Paradigms and Technological Trajectories: A Suggested Interpretation of the Determinants and Directions of Technical Change', *Research Policy,* No. 11, 1982.
17. J. Zysman, *Governments, Markets and Growth: Financial Systems and the Politics of Industrial Change,* Ithaca, Cornell University Press, 1983.
18. C. Johnson, *MITI and the Japanese Miracle,* Stanford, Stanford University Press, 1982.
19. S. Berger and R. Dore, *National Diversity and Global Capitalism,* Ithaca, Cornell University Press, 1996.
20. Phrase coined in 1996 by Renato Ruggiero, WTO Director-General.
21. See 'The MAI and the Clash of Globalizations' by S. J. Kobrin in *Foreign Policy,* Autumn 1998, pp. 97–109: '600 organizations in nearly 70 countries expressing vehement opposition to the treaty, often in apocalyptic terms'. Guy de Jonquières from FT talked of 'network guerrillas', saying 'a coalition of strange bedfellows arose in opposition to the treaty, including the AFL-CIO, Amnesty International, Australian Conservative Foundation, Friends of the Earth, Oxfam, Public Citizen, Sierra Club, Third World Network, United Steelworkers of America, Western Governors Association and World Development Movement.'
22. Jack Lang launched his withering attack in *Le Monde* of 10 February 1998, thereby contributing to the crystallization of a movement which, in France, mainly involves cinema and television professionals. The French title translates into a play on words: *The MAI (='friend', from the French acronym, AMI) is the enemy.*
23. Lori Wallach made these points under the heading 'Le nouveau manifeste du capitalisme mondial' in *Le Monde Diplomatique* in February 1998. It was taken up in a full-page advertisement in the *International Herald Tribune* on 17 February 1998 under the title 'Should Corporations Govern the World?'
24. The fact that the President of the Foreign Affairs Committee of the French National Assembly declared, without being contradicted, that 'he had heard of this negotiation from artists who had come to tip him off', had a disastrous effect.
25. In the MAI draft agreement a distinction was made between 'general exceptions' for the sake of national security, 'temporary safeguards' for temporary recovery of the balance of payments, and 'specific exceptions' when there was a wish to preserve national specificities.
26. Pierre Jacquet et al. argue that 'Economic analysis indicates that being the first to liberalize in activities with economies of scale offers strategic advantages, and

experience has shown that countries which have managed to develop a degree of expertise in liberalization derive substantial benefits from it.'

27. *International Herald Tribune,* 23 August 1999.

28. Trade in cultural goods (equipment and services in the book and periodical sectors, music, cinema, photography, radio and television) increased threefold between 1980 and 1991 to the amount of $196.5 billion. The figures may seem high, but for a country such as France, the trade deficit was only $2.8 billion, and for the United States the deficit, not the surplus, was $7.9 billion (UNESCO data). If we take a more closely focused view of the audiovisual sector, then the European (the 'Twelve') deficit was only $5.6 billion in 1996. There is nevertheless a trend that worries European creators: Hollywood derives half its income from exports, and the European audiovisual deficit is increasing: (in billions of $) 3.6 in 1992, 4.8 in 1995, 5.6 in 1996.

29. *Economics and Culture,* [n. d.], Cambridge, Cambridge University Press.

30. The economic argument is based on an article entitled 'La guerre des cultures aura-t-elle lieu?' *in Ramses,* 1999, pp. 275–91.

31. R. Barnett and J. Cavanagh, *Global Dreams, Imperial Corporations and the New World Order,* New York, Simon and Schuster, 1994.

32. P. Bairoch, *Victoires et déboires, histoire économique et sociale du XVI*[e] *siècle à nos jours* (3 vols.), Paris, Gallimard, 1997.

Chapter 5
The culture of courage: an interview with Youssef Chahine*

'I believe tha[t] we maintai[n] our specificit[y] withi[n] our universa[l] nature.

Globalization

When we speak of globalization with reference to global communication – which would facilitate understanding between different people – we should indicate what vector and what language are being used, as the word can have many meanings depending on who is speaking.

To my mind, globalization has never stood for anything. I am an Alexandrian. When I am asked where I learnt to speak Italian, I reply that I learned it in the streets in fights with little Italians who were every bit as urchin-like as myself. We also spoke a little Greek and a little French and Arabic, and English of course. There was even some Maltese in the mix. We had a kind of mutual understanding. When asked what we were, we answered 'I'm Alexandrian'; we didn't say 'I'm Egyptian', but rather, 'I'm Alexandrian'. As if the city were a republic on its own. This was the case almost everywhere in Egypt, this tolerance for all cultures: there were always add-ons or complements, if you like.

So when one speaks of globalization, and of the possibility of improved communication, what is the message? This is the real question. Is it the communication of evil, violence and selfishness?

I believe it is very, very difficult to speak of globalization. The term is almost measureless. What rules are involved and what is the true connotation of the word? It is too glib to say that the world has become a small village or a global village. But could it be a small village which is fond of its image and where people recognize themselves in others? Remember that my latest film is entitled *L'Autre* ('The Other'). Does it describe a world of ceaseless minor conflicts and wars that go on and on interminably? How can one claim to be global and at the same time say 'I want to kill you'? To me it just doesn't make sense. What are the rules? Is one global simply from an economic standpoint? For example, globalization interpreted by some regimes encourages the enrichment of those who are

* From an interview conducted on 28 April 1999.
Y. Chahine is a film director in Egypt.

already 'globalized', while accentuating isolation of those who have never benefited from its effects.

It would be oversimplifying to talk of globalization and not explain the rules. So I would like someone to tell me – UNESCO, for example – what the rules are and what they signify. Suppose there's an announcement about the frontiers being opened, what effect will it have on the average poor Egyptian? Is it going to help him or not? Is it going to affect his life of drudgery and undernourishment?

Likewise, cultural globalization is a wonderful notion, but is there really a desire for it to be understood in the way that we would like people to understand it? I probably eat differently from you and of course I was educated differently. So what are the routes which have been opened by globalization?

When we fail to understand what is going on around us, we inevitably feel wary and threatened. The word 'globalization' should be clearly defined. If I fail to understand, then suddenly I hear that there is a cultural exception which I inevitably adapt to my own circumstances. As long as things are not made clear, I shall be on the defensive since I do not know what is expected of me. You know, there are cows born in Egypt that remain Egyptian because they don't have any choice. But I myself can choose between three different things: my mother is Greek, my wife French and I myself am of Levantine origin.

Being referred to as a cultural exception does not make one automatically ultra-nationalist or ultra-terrorist. Journalists, for instance, should be careful of the language they use. If they mention 'Islamic terrorists', they should provide some indication for all other types of 'terrorist' such as 'Jewish terrorists', 'Catholic terrorists' or 'Baptist terrorists'. The fact is that there are terrorists everywhere, in all religions. Why should this specificity be applied in certain cases only? A terrorist is a terrorist, it's as simple as that.

I myself am not Muslim, but I have lived at the heart of Islam, a religion that is highly respectable like all the others. Besides, culturally speaking, the world's three great religions have all borrowed from Akhenaton. In Akhenaton you will find the same kind of love, directed towards one God. At the basis of all globalization, if you like, we should all be armed in the same way. And for this, education is vital. But is education open to everyone in this world? If not, whom can we hope to convince? Nobody makes the rules, so we continue to speak and to write without them.

How can we render globalization accessible and comprehensible to everyone? Could it be via films or televised series? Mind you, television is a weapon which can be mortally dangerous but also immensely educative. At present, 99% of all programmes misinform us, so who gives UNESCO the right to tell us what to do? Yet unless we decide to respect a minimum moral code, we are all going to lose out.

Feature films produced

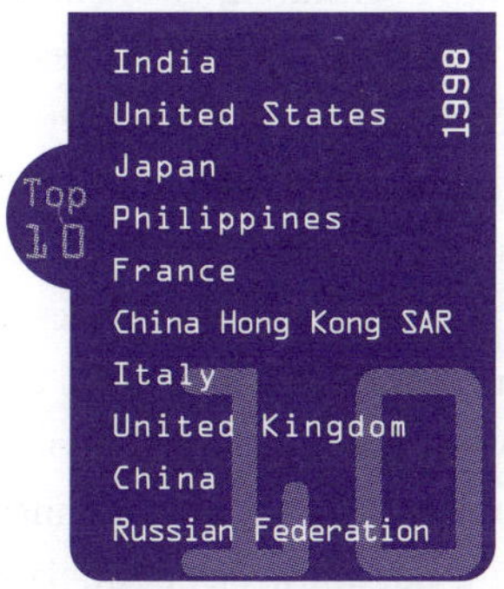

Top 10 — 1998
India
United States
Japan
Philippines
France
China Hong Kong SAR
Italy
United Kingdom
China
Russian Federation

Source: See the Index of culture indicators and sources and Table 4 in Part Seven of this report.

In my films I am unable to describe a future that is black, because I don't believe it will be so. We are still in the electronic Middle Ages, but we can easily overcome this. The battle is not lost: UNESCO has a vital role to play in ensuring that the sources of information are honestly and evenly distributed. Rules will also have to be introduced to limit the amount of disinformation, and such rules should respect the specific nature of creativity.

In the field of cinema, for instance, we need to work in an atmosphere of mutual respect even if we do not know the Other. It is important to recognize the Other's difference because it enlightens our recognition of his dreams and attachments. Our differences belong to ourselves, and as long as they do not endanger the Other, they are of no concern to anyone else.

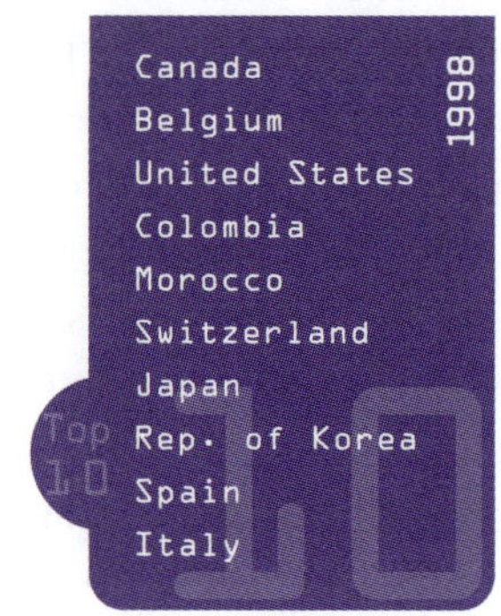

Feature films imported
Canada
Belgium
United States
Colombia
Morocco
Switzerland
Japan
Rep. of Korea
Spain
Italy
1998
Top 10

Source: See the Index of culture indicators and sources and Table 4 in Part Seven of this report.

When we have children, we should try to discover their particular desires and modes of thought as early as possible. Today the Internet is a grave danger whereby children can accidentally come across the 'benefits' of violence through games. Some of these are dreadfully violent; consequently, rules should be set with the aid of UNESCO to combat the dangers related to the new communication technologies.

The same applies to all the cultural means at our disposal. We should not allow our politicians to use a medium such as television or the media in general simply for their own personal needs. The same talking space should be made available throughout the world to allow all people to express themselves, thus avoiding favouritism.

I personally began to learn what globalization was all about when I noticed that preference in the world of the cinema is given to those who have no links with it and are able to impose their own point of view and persuade others that their system is the best. Maybe you do not drink water from the Nile, but perhaps from the Mississippi or the Danube. We are not all the same. Nevertheless we are not terrifying because of our differences. In fact, without difference, we should all be narcissistic.

To my mind the most profound interaction between people of different cultures that can be attributed to globalization is not the fruit of it. In the domain of the cinema, it should be sufficient to call this interaction the Cannes Film Festival or, in the case of music, the Bayreuth Festival. Globalization does not mean that people meet more often. In the past such interactions were called encounters, and I feel that this word is more meaningful. The word 'globalization' is misleading and can lead to confusion.

I believe that I could have made *L'Autre* a very long time ago, because in it I speak of ourselves vis-à-vis the Other. As an Egyptian-Alexandrian, I have never been frightened by the Other; I would never ask the Other what his religion is or why his skin is white or black. The only question is whether I liked that person or not. The notion of globalization would not encourage me to ask more.

Can we show that globalization is truly beneficial? It is fine to be a humanist and I would be the first to admit this – Moses said so, and Jesus and Mohammed too. Is this globalization? Likewise, in our own arrogant way, we believe that we represent the three greatest religions in the world, while eliminating three-quarters of the globe, be they Buddhists, Taoists or others.

A glance at the statistics for the screening of foreign films in the United States shows a total of less than 1%. The country protects its cinema industry very well while at the same time demonstrating verbal open-mindedness on the international scene. The agro-food industry too proves the point in its trade relations with the European continent.

The American monopoly of the film industry also influences distribution. I deplore the fact that I am unable to see African or Tunisian films at least once a year to discover how others think. In every country in the world, there is somebody making extraordinary films. But since the economic stakes in the United States are considerable, the audience targeted is likely to be the 11–18 year olds. Older people, it is felt, go to the cinema less often since they are too busy worrying about life.

It is not easy to speak of culture nowadays as it is excessively bound up with the economy. I believe we should be more aware of what we are doing since everything we do has an impact on others. The question is to know whether the other counts in our eyes or not and whether or not, in that case, he is an 'enemy'. Rules are needed to define the notion of 'enemy'. The issue needs to be talked through. The question is to know at what moment one wants to be part of the world, rather than speak of globalization or other such terms.

One may be tempted to abandon one's principles. In my profession as film-maker, if I feel that I can't make a particular film, I'm still not sure I am going to be able to resist whatever negative pressure is being applied. But, thanks be to God, I have been able to resist up to now by saying 'No' while limiting my own demands and needs. I have no need for big hotels or cars. A car is simply a means of transport from one place to another, and whether it is shiny or not is of no importance. What counts is to be able to get to the laboratory or wherever and to be satisfied with the result of one's work. However, I understand that there are people who consider that they don't need to think at all, but prefer to be told what to do in order to be fortunate enough to work.

In my own case, I once left the country and went into voluntary exile because somebody dared tell me that I only did things my own way. So I answered that I wouldn't make a film that had come out of somebody else's head, since I can't interpret for another person whose thoughts I don't know. It is unfair to prevent a large number of people from seeing somebody's work just because it doesn't please the minority.

Once, one of my films was crudely refused a particular category in an international film festival: so I decided to present it in another category where it was an outright success. My film had been refused on the grounds that it was extremely poor. 'You had better hide it,' I was told. Later they made excuses and said they had been mistaken about my film. Concrete examples should be given when one speaks of globalization. Does globalization affect me directly? And in what way? My answer would be that it all depends on the moral force in each particular individual. What is the source of this moral force? There must be rules somewhere for us to consult. Somebody has to be able to say 'No' just as parents do to their children. Now that parents have negligible influence over their children, it falls to organizations to say what is good and what is bad. To my mind, a great deal remains to be done as far as setting standards is concerned.

Creativity and globalization

Economically speaking, globalization is obviously a threat. A concrete example of this is the process by which films are made. Thirty years ago, I set up a company; at that time you could found a company with a capital of 14,000 French francs, which is what I did. For thirty years, I was able to make films, even if it was in co-production with other countries. It enabled me to offer an opportunity to at least two young people each year to be trained. They made their first film with me, not because I had the money, but because I knew where to beg, including from UNESCO, but at least in true logic they could create their film and put it together economically. Creating films was, I believe, very important for all of us. If the person who produced it was talented, then so much the better! And if that person had been trained for seven or eight years in specialized cinema institutes, but had not managed to make a film, then it was tragic. I have been able to make films for the past thirty years now because I was given such an opportunity, the same as I have in turn given to more than twelve young people in fact.

Now, the world of cinema proclaims that, as a result of globalization, the only way forward is to create large companies, since only businessmen can help us out of this crisis. However, as we very well know, economists promise us the moon and, as ever, it is only months or years later that we're able to check that their predictions have failed. Meanwhile, many people have suffered and their films have not been made.

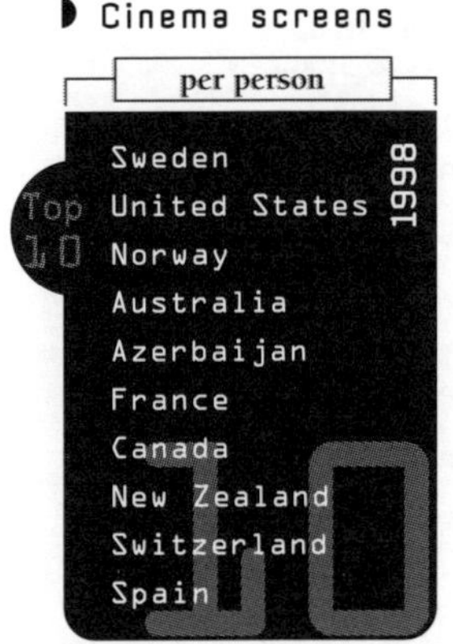

Cinema screens
per person
Top 10
1998
Sweden
United States
Norway
Australia
Azerbaijan
France
Canada
New Zealand
Switzerland
Spain

Source: See the Index of culture indicators and sources and Table 4 in Part Seven of this report.

The euphemism of globalization

Globalization appears to have brought about four major changes. Over the past ten years the cultures in which my friends live and work have been invaded, more than ever, by artistic productions from the industrialized countries, that transform their audiences and oblige them to change their way of working. Their own works receive more invitations from abroad, yet always in the narrow, élite context of the festival and conference circuit. A few new sources of funding have opened up, generally through government funds in developed countries such as France and Japan, but hardly what one would call a gold mine. And, finally, it has perhaps become easier to export oneself as a creator to the industriazed countries, but this generally means leaving one's idiosyncratic baggage, one's cultural identity, behind.

My friend Francisco Franco, a Mexican stage director whose plays are exceptionally successful, told me: 'I communicate easily with my audience because I feed my soul on the same things that they feed on. A lot of rock music in English, a lot of American TV shows and movies and a pinch of Mexican "ranchera" music and "telenovelas".' A year ago I watched a rehearsal of what was to be his next production and was surprised to learn that he was using the music of Canadian singer and songwriter Leonard Cohen. I asked Francisco why he was using English-language songs to accompany a Mexican play and he replied: 'It's only natural. The play is about urbanites in their thirties. If they listen to rock music it will most likely be English or American.'

Mirna, a late twentieth-century Venezuelan film director, won a European film award and the doors of the industrialized countries opened to her. Mirna wants to make films with larger budgets than she can ever hope to raise in the very modest Venezuelan film 'industry' and wants her films to be seen by as many people as possible, preferably all over the world.

She has an opportunity to make films in France, but they have to be in French and her Venezuelan origins will be reflected only in one of the characters. Another offer has come from Hollywood. This would be a feminist comedy in which she will be able to use her experience as a woman, but where Venezuela is not even mentioned. The Hollywood producer was quite clear: 'We want stories in English featuring North American characters.' Or as another Hollywood producer put it: 'The US audience has to be able to identify at least with the lead actor. Only then do we give a thought to the international audience.'

I thought to myself: we identify with Schwartzenegger without any trouble, so why shouldn't they identify with a Colombian hero? So I asked: 'How can the American public identify with Mozart but not, for example, with Sor Juana? Why with John but never with Juan?' There is a Eurocentric definition of the 'universal' in 'First World' minds that would be worth analysing on another occasion. In any event, the filter to the world, in films and theatre, is the United States of America. You have to become North American (or be adopted as an honorary North American, like Mozart or Frida Kahlo) to gain planetary stature.

Renowned Mexican poet and scriptwriter Beatriz Novarro (*Lola, Danzón, El Jardín de Edén*) put it this way: 'What the First World does, when you have proved that you are talented, is give you a chance to make films, and all they want in exchange is your identity. They say: here, this fine mirror is for you, but we don't want to see your reflection in it.'

So the path out into the World for the Latin American artist passes through two types of customs control. One requires the artist to leave behind what makes him or her different before going abroad to ply his or her trade. This is the customs control of the mass culture business. The other type of control imports finished works and requires them to be 'typical' and easily identifiable, 'very Mexican', 'unquestionably Guatemalan' or 'as Argentinian as the tango'. This is the customs control of the élitist international festival circuit.

As I said earlier, in the mass culture business you have to be North American before you go global. The music field is a source of hope for films and theatre. In music the Anglo-American filter has opened up its pores to let in a wide variety of cultures. Perhaps one day the filter will also let in films and plays by Latin Americans, with recognizable national flavour.

This has been known to happen. I can think of two cases: *Como Agua para Chocolate*, written by Laura Esquivel and directed by Alfonso Arau, with a Mexican theme and flavour, and *La Muerte y la Doncella*, a play by Ariel Dorfman that captures Chile's dilemma in the face of its recent past. But was it to let bygones be bygones or to demand retribution?

Another possibility exists, however, and there have already been a few examples. As the diversification that promises what we call 'global culture' gains ground, the possibility of the major film centres making films about Latin American subjects looms into view. They will be in English more likely than not, perhaps in French, but probably not in Hindi.

In the distant future one can possibly imagine North American audiences reading subtitles, but in the not-so-distant future one can see them identifying with Frida Kahlo in a film which Roberto Schneider from Mexico is preparing in Los Angeles in English. It recently happened with a number of films, screen versions of novels: two novels by renowned Chilean novelist Isabel Allende, filmed in Hollywood: *La Casa de los Espíritus* and *De Luz y Sombra*; and *Gringo Viejo*, a novel by Mexican author Carlos Fuentes, adapted for Hollywood by Argentine director Aída Bornik.

Says Joanne Zipel, New York-based manager in the film and theatre business: 'In the long run we – audiences and artists – get used to seeing Latin American stories told in English.' That means that, as part of what it considers universal, Hollywood accepts Latin American stories as well as European ones. We shall see General Buendía de Macondo speaking English, with as little surprise as we saw 18th-century French people speaking English in *Les Liaisons Dangereuses*, or modern-day Greeks speaking English in *Z*. It is a foregone conclusion in Hollywood: English is the modern-day Esperanto, the language of the global village.

It sounds just wonderful when they say that globalization means a worldwide market governed only by the laws of free competition. In practice, from the viewpoint of the Latin American film-maker or playwright and given the extreme economic inequalities between our countries and the 'First World', globalization is a euphemism for ruthless imperialism. For the time being there is no sign that the near future will bring the much-heralded flow of ideas back and forth between numerous cultural centres. The general impression is more that of intense radiation emanating from a single centre.

Inevitably there is a tendency to turn to various forms of protectionism to help the small domestic film and theatre 'industries'. In Argentina the Government of Carlos Saúl Menem imposed a tax on cinemas to contribute to revitalizing the country's film industry. There are more and better films, but there are still too few Argentinian channels exporting them. Following Argentina's example, in 1999 film-makers in Mexico clamoured for a similar tax, in addition to the requirement that cinemas show at least 10% of Mexican productions. Voting on both questions caused considerable controversy. Film theatre owners organized an opinion poll among film-goers that included the question: Should the government intervene in the selection of films to be shown? The question was carefully worded in such a way as to bring back dark memories of past times when governments interfered massively in people's lives. They might have asked: Should the government take steps to promote the making and screening of Mexican films?

Films are the modern mode of telling stories in the most popular way and with the greatest impact. A country without films is like a house without mirrors to reflect the image of those who live there, so that they can see and reinvent themselves. Or worse still, a house in which the mirrors are full of the reflections of others, reflections that make those who live in the house feel inadequate and alienated.

SABINA BERMAN
Playwright,
Film director (Mexico)

In my own particular case, as the owner of a 14,000 Franc company, I suddenly learned that a new law pushed through by the United States, no doubt, stipulated that no company valued at less than 400 million francs would enjoy any privileges. Now not all film industries are designed in the same way, nor are all of them self-financed, as in France, for instance. This raises a number of questions: Where are the 400 million francs to come from? And why do businessmen suddenly want to invest in the cinema? The answer to both questions is: 'He who pays the piper plays the tune.' I have attended key meetings with prime ministers, finance ministers and other high-ranking officials and have told them frankly that they cannot speak of the cinema without taking account of such mechanisms.

To use a metaphor, if a particular person is asked to describe his work and says 'I am a poet', I am a little surprised because it is not for him to say he is a poet. That's for me to judge. 'I write poetry' is not the same thing as saying 'I am a poet'. It is up to others to say you are a poet or film-maker. As far as the cinema is concerned, you are able to make films or you are not.

Personally I go through all sorts of trials when I decide to produce a film. After all, people don't know what to do with me, nor do they know what to do without me. I have been around for fifty years and they can hardly say that I'm talking nonsense!

The source of my creativity is the weapon I use to fight barbarity. I have none other. That is why my fight has been such a personal one. No one has the right to tell me what to do. When they tried to influence the very source of my creativity, I felt like leaving the country. I have no desire to use my weapon beyond the bounds of my reality; in other words, I do not want to work outside Egypt. I don't want to be American, nor do I want to be French, and yet I don't want anyone to tell me that I am forbidden to work in my own country.

I am Egyptian and I will definitely not allow anyone to influence me. I will do anything to maintain my 'identity' although the word has become commonplace. In my films I have no wish to speak about people I don't know very well, and I want to be able to speak about the place where I was born and the feelings this inspires in me, because I can't speak in any other way.

This is vital to me. I have no wish to be dishonest, no wish whatever! I believe I have acquired a certain amount of knowledge. I am ageing 'to the best of my abilities', as they say in English, but I can't allow myself to be dishonest. After all, a film is seen by an audience of at least twenty million people. There is a moral code to be respected, even if I don't like using such expressions. Morality, to my mind, is not related to who made love to whom and under what tree, but to something altogether lovely. There are ways of communicating through love, but one should not lie when speaking of things that one doesn't understand oneself.

In any case what matters is that my own difference belongs to me. For writers like Freud or Jung we are all different and I thank God for those differences because if I were only capable of loving myself alone, the situation would be catastrophic; I would be totally selfish and never understand anything about the Other. Freud also said that the Other was oneself. There is no getting round it, universality is just that. If I became interested enough in the Other I would discover that he or she is at least as interesting as three-quarters of the people in the world. In this sense, we can say that we are not all that different from one another. We resemble each other in that we are different, yet universal. Personally I do not consider that people are different. The Other does not frighten me. I believe that we maintain our specificity within our universal nature.

Speaking for myself, I have more dictionaries in my library than novels. When I write, there are differ-

Cinema attendance
(per person)
1998
Top 10
United States
Singapore
Australia
New Zealand
Canada
Panama
China Hong Kong SAR
Ireland
India
France

Source: See the Index of culture indicators and sources and Table 4 in Part Seven of this report.

Actors in the new millennium

My hope is that the twenty-first century will be a peaceful one with advanced science and technology being used to benefit and serve humankind. Computers will enter into every aspect of human life. Is humanity to lose part of its creativity and imagination as a result of the emergence of the computer? Is humanity's traditional way of thinking to be replaced by it? These are some of the questions that face us.

Computers were created by human beings in order to strengthen and enrich imagination and creativity. The tremendous progress made in science and technology should not discourage people from thinking. On the contrary it should speed up their studies, their work and their lives by making everything far more convenient.

Yet human beings are animals who live in communities. Each person belongs to a particular group. One of the negative effects that the twenty-first century could have on humankind, as a result of the rapid development of science and technology, might be that computer screens replace other people and become the centre of their lives, with face-to-face contact in decline and greater isolation. In large, technologically advanced cities, this phenomenon is already proving harmful to the growth and development of children, particularly those attending school, in that they are missing the important lesson of direct communication between human beings.

Actors need a varied experience of life, a vivid imagination and a keen sense of observation. The ability to communicate with other people and understand them is particularly important to the actor. In my opinion, no matter how times change, and no matter what progress is made in science and technology, the one thing an actor should never allow to happen is to lose genuine contact with the world.

Advanced science and technology are beneficial for the creation of films. They can help to turn our dreams into reality, to shoot scenes that cannot be shot in the real world and to make our productions more artistic and elegant. The world is a stage upon which we encounter the changing times, follow passing trends and take in the latest developments. Actors have to experience everything that life has to offer. But while following the latest trends, we must yet be aware of the past and of our history, which are the greatest asset and source of inspiration for an actor.

Actors in the twenty-first century should be observers of society and human nature. They should observe the social scene, show concern for their friends and take an interest in everything that is going on in the world. With the spread of science and technology, there may be less to observe than before, as communication between human beings grows less intense. Thus observation will increasingly become important for an actor.

My first lesson as an actress was to learn to observe life. I observed everyone, both those I knew and those I did not know, striving to share their happiness, anger, grief and joy – the whole range of human feelings – to guess their profession, character and love-life and to visualize how they lived so that I could bring those persons I had seen and imagined into my performance in films. An intelligent and talented actor should play many different roles requiring a full knowledge of human nature and thought. Only thus can the actor create living and artistically convincing characters.

Actors in the twenty-first century will have to play a wide variety of roles, relying on their powers of observation. They will no longer be mere stage performers, but will have to utilize their prestige and intelligence to make a greater contribution to society. A good actor is both an outstanding artist and an exceptional social activist.

GONG LI
Actress (Hong Kong SAR)

ences in the language I use: Arabic, English or French. On consulting a dictionary, we discover that a word may be far more precise in one language than in another. That is why I respect all languages. I write in three languages. It drives my production assistants crazy. When I want to write a pleasing dialogue, there is no better language than Arabic, Egyptian Arabic. For romanticism, I write in French, because I generalize somewhat. The choice of French is linked to my wife. For true precision, I write in English because it is the first language that I studied in English schools. Since I know that texts are translated into five or six languages at UNESCO, it is essential for me to indicate what word is employed and in which language. There are some words that carry greater weight in a particular language than others. I prefer to read philosophy in French. As for Italian, I know a few words thanks to Pavarotti. What a superb language!

I learned English thanks to an English lady on a train which wasn't going very far but which stopped in every little village. After the first village, she and I were still face to face. She looked at me and said, 'Don't you find it absurd that we have been together for a good quarter of an hour on this train and still don't know anything about each other?' We have been friends ever since. Imagine, on a train like that, me knowing nothing about her and she knowing nothing about me.

I have taught a lot, for at least thirty years, and I am still very optimistic about future generations and their refusal to let anyone manage their lives. I doubt whether the administrator will win the upper hand over the creator.

My job teaches me that if I am going to tackle such and such a subject, I have to evolve. In terms of globalization, I need to know what this means and what keys of comprehension are at my disposal in order to transmit a particular message. What is the exact meaning of the much-used expression 'cultural globalization'? I don't claim to know. But I do know one thing, and that is that the association of 'cultural' and 'globalization' needs to be profoundly examined and analysed before we can start using it. Let us not forget that others used the expression before us just as others lived before us. We are the product of history of all kinds, including artistic and cultural. My film begins with the same message: 'You may have a computer, but I invented the alphabet.'

We cannot claim privileges in the name of our own contribution to history. Others have had the opportunity to invent many other things, such as the great Egyptian culture which so influenced the Greeks and the Romans and finally reached us by way of the Arabs. The twelfth century, which was the great Arab period, was the setting for a film of mine, *Le Destin*.

We owe a great deal to Averroës who had already conceived of the separation of church and state, yet who was a profoundly religious man. Likewise the texts of the Bible, the Koran and the Torah basically resemble each other. The Old Testament contains magnificent stories of courage. All you need to do is understand them without transforming them. When a word is used, I like someone to explain to me what is meant by that word. When we say, for example, 'She's a beautiful girl', it's a bit vague. Are we referring to her face or her eyes? I pay great attention to eyes because our eyes are for seeing with. And they are much more beautiful when we have love in them.

That's a word we haven't used yet: the only real globalization which should affect us is that of learning to love.

Chapter 6
Culture and poverty

RODOLFO STAVENHAGEN
Social Scientist, Professor,
El Colegio de Mexico (Mexico)

'There is more to a relationship between culture and poverty than the idea that the poor necessarily share a common culture . . .'.

The academic discourse on poverty has always been one-sided: it expresses the perceptions and concerns of the 'haves' regarding the 'have-nots'. What shall we do with the poor? How *dangereuses* are the *classes laborieuses*? Are they lazy, brutish, incapable and criminal; or hard-working, decent and salvageable? Will the poor, alas, always be with us? Are they a transitory phenomenon on the gold-paved globalized super-highway? Or are they the logical by-product of capitalist accumulation? Are they a necessary reserve army of labour, or a useless and redundant burden on society? Are the poor preordained to suffer in this world in order to achieve paradise at some later stage? Will they rise in revolutionary anger, shake off their secular chains and break the power of the rich once and for all? Will the poor be able to redeem themselves or will somebody (the Salvation Army or the World Bank) come along to do it for them?

Surely, contemporary discourse on poverty is as culture-bound today as previous versions were in earlier times. Before any significant progress can be made towards the eradication of poverty – which has become a top item on the international agenda since the Copenhagen Summit on Social Development in 1995 – account must be taken of the implicit and explicit cultural values associated with the concept itself, its definition and measurement.

The current debate on the poverty issue reflects the concerns and priorities of the people who decide on poverty reduction strategies and social development policies. The poor have been identified as that part of the population which lives below an arbitrarily defined poverty line (PL) as measured in monetary income. The difficulties involved in this approach are obvious: what are the criteria by which a poverty line is established? Usually it expresses the cost of a basic food basket and some additional amenities. If this line is raised or lowered by any value, the number of 'poor' will vary accordingly. Within the population defined as poor, differences may be as large or larger than between the upper levels of the poor and the lower levels of the non-poor. The monetary income used to establish the line and measure poverty levels may not only leave out important non-monetary aspects of levels of living, but may also ignore social and cultural features of group life that are an integral part of any balanced conception of poverty. Finally, if the unit of measurement is the household or the family, individual differences within these units may be blurred, whereas if it is the individual, the family unit (an indispensable tool for understanding poverty at all) will be ignored. The poverty line approach is not very useful for guiding social policies because it takes no account of specific group differences in social, cultural or ethnic terms and usually ends up by providing a rationale for consumer subsidies.

Another widely-used approach considers the poor as the population unable to fully satisfy basic human needs. This view, while more adequate but less amenable to statistical calculations than the PL approach, is not without problems of its own, to the extent that there is hardly agreement on what constitutes basic human needs, let alone how to satisfy them. In general, there seems to be a consensus that basic needs (BN) are more than simply material requirements for survival (daily calorie intake, minimum health standards, protection against extreme environmental hazards, etc.) which human beings are said to share with animals and which by that definition make them universal in nature.

Some authors refer to 'absolute' basic needs, which all individuals share, and below which the material survival of a human being is impossible. Others insist that needs are relative to the social and cultural context in which they are defined, and this refers particularly to the social and cultural needs of the person, including identity, dignity, recognition, belonging, knowledge and so forth, which go beyond material requirements but are equally important for survival in any given collectivity. Everybody seems to agree, however, that while needs may be widely shared across cultures (food, shelter, security), the satisfaction of human needs varies greatly in accordance with cultural differences and the nature of diverse human societies. For example, how the need to satisfy hunger is met may differ significantly in terms of what are considered edible and/or tasty foods. How such foods are acquired, prepared, distributed, consumed and disposed of varies greatly from one culture to another. Satisfying hunger also varies according to whether food is acquired directly from nature (as among subsistence farmers, who still represent the majority of the rural population worldwide) or bought for a price in a market (which means being able to buy food). Thus, while needs may be universal and absolute – to a certain extent – need satisfaction is essentially a cultural matter and a function of different kinds of social arrangements.

The poverty debate relates mainly to societies with significant internal inequalities, where access to resources, income and entitlements is unequally distributed among the population and in which governments are held to be at least partly responsible for redressing economic and social imbalances. At the world level, of course, some countries are classified as poor or poorer and others as rich or richer in average per capita income or national product terms. Accordingly, some become the target of specific actions in the field of international co-operation, and others, whose population might be ranked a notch higher, will not be so rewarded.

Leaving aside the unresolved discussion on what constitutes absolute levels of poverty, the problem is usually dealt with in relative terms, and this leads to a parallel and not unrelated issue, that of inequality among the members of any given nation or society. People's perception about what it means to be poor is of course conditioned by its opposite: what does it mean to be rich or affluent? In general, it appears that poverty is perceived more acutely in societies in which income, wealth and standard of living differences are high, than in those in which the distance between the upper and the lower strata is less obvious. Again, such a generalization may be tempered by other conditions: whether the rich are ostentatious or discreet in their behaviour, whether the physical and social distance between rich and poor is greater or lesser, whether the avenues for upward mobility are open or the society is rigidly stratified, and whether the shared values in a given society accept poverty as a fatality or reject it as unacceptable and on what grounds. Different combinations of these elements lead to different understandings of poverty, and therefore also, probably, to different sets of policies to combat it.

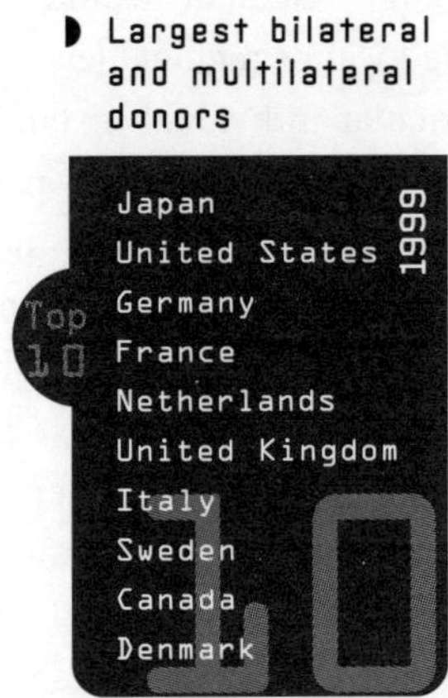

Source: OECD, *DAC Report*, 1999.

Whereas poverty indexes frequently provide us with distribution curves of the number of individuals to be found at any one level, social research shows that poverty is not distributed haphazardly among any population. Poverty, however defined, is a social phenomenon and tends to cluster in clearly identified groups of people. No serious policy to combat or eradicate poverty will be successful if it ignores this simple fact, but a look at some of the contemporary literature on poverty shows that this is not so obvious after all. Most of the aggregate data on poverty is provided by household surveys in which a number of variables are introduced and through which statistical correlations may be constructed, such as age, gender, employment, income, education, age and, in some cases, race or ethnicity. Comparing different households will provide a fairly good idea of levels of living, but when intra-household differences are introduced, the picture may vary. Thus, when gender is introduced as an analysis control, women tend to rank higher on the poverty scale than males in most instances. Recent research has focused increasingly on these issues, thus raising the question of why these differences occur, which in turn leads to the study of the sociological and cultural determinants of gender discrimination in different societies. But in a number of studies there is disagreement about how gender is conceptualized. A comparative survey in six African countries on how gender issues are dealt with in the World Bank's poverty assessments gave inconclusive results (Whitehead and Lockwood, 1999). Another analysis of the Bank's poverty assessments in Africa argues that 'the setting of an arbitrary poverty line affects who is identified as poor: in the assessments it is most usually a substantial share of the population rather than a clearly defined sub-group' (Hanmer, Pyatt and White, 1999, p. 804).

A number of studies show that during the 1980s and 1990s income inequality worsened in most countries as well as between countries. In fact, poverty is often the expression of other forms of group inequality and social exclusion; it is associated with various forms of discrimination, unequal access to essential social services and to participation in government and basic political and decision-making processes. The poor and disadvantaged groups are frequently identified in class terms (landless peasants, urban squatters in the informal economy) or in ethnic terms (racial and cultural minorities, indigenous and tribal peoples).

This 'horizontal inequality' has been identified as one of the key elements in the root causes of the multiple and complex humanitarian emergencies (CHE) that are besetting the world at the turn of the century. A case in point is the group of indigenous peoples of Latin America. A comparative study carried out by the World Bank in Bolivia, Guatemala, Mexico and Peru has concluded that poverty among Latin America's indigenous population is pervasive and severe, and that the living conditions of the indigenous population are generally abysmal, especially when compared to those of the non-indigenous population. Furthermore, the study found that there is a strong correlation between level of schooling attained, indigenous origin and poverty (Psacharopoulos and Patrinos, 1994). These findings and others raise anew the question of the relationship between poverty and ethnicity or culture. In the case of Latin America, the disadvantaged position of indigenous populations in the national societies is rooted in a long history of oppression, exploitation and discrimination which would be sufficient to account for the origins of marginalization and destitution, but might not explain the persistent contemporary poverty that so much of the existing literature on the subject has documented. The *indigenista* policies of Latin

American governments were designed to assimilate indigenous populations into the national mainstream, but would cultural assimilation by itself be able to reduce poverty? The indigenous live, for the most part, in rural areas where poverty is greatest, but even in Bolivia's urban areas 'a disproportionate share of indigenous people are poor relative to the overall population. Even after controlling for schooling attainment, indigenous individuals have a 16 percentage point greater probability of being poor than non-indigenous individuals' (ibid., p. 94).

If poverty affects disproportionately a segment of the population defined – as in Latin America – in cultural terms, we must consider the dynamics of group discrimination and 'horizontal inequality'. Unless we take the theoretically flawed and empirically disproved view that the indigenous have fewer 'natural' capabilities or are less productive, ceteris paribus, than the non-indigenous and that their 'reward' is therefore greater poverty, we must consider the social and economic mechanisms of inclusion and exclusion in a country such as Bolivia, where indigenous poverty is pervasive despite the fact that the indigenous are the majority population, and that they probably participate to a greater degree in national affairs than in any other Latin American country.

Poverty, as all specialists agree, is a complex and multi-dimensional phenomenon. If it is to be seen in its structural and collective context, and not just as one of the (perhaps transitory or permanent) attributes of de-contextualized individuals, then we must consider the structural relations of specific groups with other groups (for example, landowners and farming communities), or the culturally determined relations of individuals within certain groups (for example, do village communities or extended families habitually take care of the sick, the elderly, the unemployed?). Much of the current data on poverty differentials come from household surveys, and the literature on the subject clearly indicates that the composition of households varies considerably across cultures. How comparable in sociological terms are a household in the inner city of a large North American metropolis and a rural extended family in central Africa or the Indian subcontinent?

Probably no single element would suffice to reduce poverty at the local or regional level, although it might help a particular individual or family. But a package of measures intended to help a particularly vulnerable group of rural poor must necessarily involve the active participation of the people themselves in the design, implementation and evaluation of the project in order for it to be 'context sensitive'. Unfortunately, international and government bureaucracies usually have little time or inclination to take such matters into account, and thus the Third World has been littered over the past few decades with small, large and monumental 'development failures' that have left most poor people no better off than before. The success stories have been when people were able to take their fate into their own hands within the framework of their own culture. International agencies have been slow to learn this lesson, but things are beginning to change. Indeed, the concept of 'empowering the poor' is being widely promoted through nongovernmental organizations (NGOs) and other agencies and is now considered an indispensable element in poverty reduction or alleviation programmes. Empowering the poor means social organization and mobilization, community participation, leadership training, facing the power structure, institution-building and, in general, *conscientização*, to use Paolo Freire's well-known concept.

Over the past few decades, social scientists have studied conditions of poverty in different regional contexts. Regardless of differences, however, certain common patterns recurring among poor families and in poor communities have caught the attention of researchers. Does poverty lead to certain predictable forms of behaviour or recurrent types of social relationships, similar value systems and attitudes? Some authors, following the pioneering work of Oscar Lewis in the 1950s, identify such common traits as the expression of an underlying 'culture of poverty' which poor people around the world are said to share despite other social and cultural variations that may distinguish them. Indeed, comparative micro-level research on poor families and communities shows striking similarities in some aspects and underlines differences in others. For example, family-based social safety nets, communal solidarity, 'jobbing' (doing any kind of work available at almost any wage), widespread attitudes of fatalism and hopelessness, and a youth culture in which violence, drugs and delinquency often appear prominently (particularly in urban areas) are, among others, features that are seen repeatedly in poor households around the world.

However, the concept of the culture of poverty – aside from certain elements – has been more often wielded by the general public than by knowledgeable researchers as a suggested explanation of poverty itself. The poor are presumed to be poor because of certain values in their culture which prevent them from rising out of poverty. The solution to the problem, then, is in the hands of the poor themselves and the way to achieve this is by changing their culture. The poor are expected to do this on their own, or else it is left to various kinds of social agents (government employees, NGOs, religious missionaries, educators, etc.). Indeed, in the debates concerning development and underdevelopment which occupied academic attention from the 1960s onward, there was much talk about cultural obstacles to development. Mainstream sociological thinking considered that 'development' was a good thing and that 'the West' knew how to do it. The problem was how to transfer this knowledge to the culturally limited peoples of the underdeveloped countries. When we look at some of the ideas espoused nowadays by international financial agencies, we find that thinking on these issues has not changed much since colonial and immediate post-colonial times, though some 'politically correct' lip-service is now paid to the recognition of and respect for indigenous traditional values. It is assumed that once the culture of poverty changes, poverty as such will progressively disappear. This approach reduces the lessening or elimination of poverty to a question of cultural policies, or more simply, to an issue of changing attitudes. While poverty and its reduction is certainly also a cultural issue, the 'blame the victim' approach that the culture of poverty argument implies is unacceptable on both moral and practical grounds. There is more to a relationship between culture and poverty than the idea that the poor necessarily share a common culture which prevents them from climbing higher on the social ladder.

How is the 'culture of poverty' to be changed without attacking the root causes of poverty? Poverty is not only a lack of material goods or incomes, it is linked to various forms of marginality, discrimination and social exclusion of specific populations or groups. In the United States, for example, income levels and standards of living vary considerably among the population in terms of racial and ethnic characteristics. Hispanics and Blacks tend to occupy the lower strata. The UNDP's *Human Development Report* indicates that the Human Development Index (HDI) for whites in the United States is among the highest in the world (similar to that of the population of Canada, which occupies first place on the HDI), whereas that of Hispanics and Blacks is closer to the population of Trinidad and Tobago, which rank approximately thirtieth on the scale (UNDP, 1993). Other studies show that educational achievement is also lower among these minority groups.

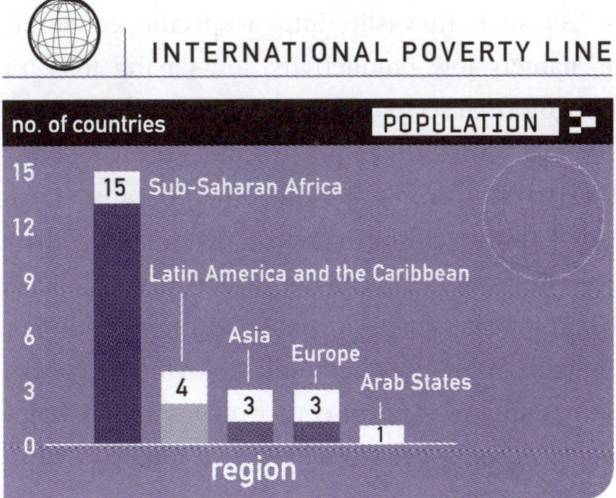

GRAPH 7
Countries where more than half of the population lives below an international poverty line of US$2 per day. among the 72 countries for which data are available.

Source: See the Index of culture indicators and sources and Table 28 in Part Seven of this report.

Academics have long argued whether these differences in economic and educational group outcomes are to be attributed to genetic, psychological, cultural, structural or other factors. The genetic argument can safely be eliminated as unscientific and unsustainable despite a spate of recent literature attempting to 'prove' the innate inferiority of this or that minority group (e.g. Herrnstein and Murray, 1994). The knotty relationship between psychological, cultural and economic factors is more difficult to disentangle. When a specific ethnic group finds itself traditionally marginalized, victimized and disadvantaged, it is clear that the cultural values and the collective psychology of the group are affected, and this in turn reinforces social exclusion mechanisms. In a number of North American and European countries that have become hosts to massive migrations from the Third World, these mechanisms operate to the disadvantage of numerous minority groups who are often further burdened by the workings of different expressions of racism in the host society.

In fact, poverty in many parts of the world, particularly among migrant populations, is often related to structural racism. It is not racial, cultural or ethnic differences by themselves which become the major causes of racism, discrimination and xenophobia. A more crucial factor is that most migrants to the industrial countries are poor and come from poor lands. As such they slip into a specific economic niche, namely low productivity, low-paying jobs, or into the informal sector of the economy, and they tend to gather in virtual urban ghettos, not because of any kind of natural ethnic bonding, but because most other avenues are closed to them. How well known are the descriptions of ethnically or racially distinct urban housing projects, shanty towns or deteriorated inner-city neighbourhoods where unemployment is high and hopes are low. And, of course, drugs and violence proliferate, if only because alternative life opportunities are not available.

If racism is understood as a set of beliefs and practices whereby certain ethnic groups are discriminated against in a given society because of their real or imagined racial and/or ethnic characteristics, then the new name of racism at the end of the twentieth century is no longer colonialism or Nazi ideology, but rather xenophobia and social exclusion related to international migrations, the emerging of new kinds of ethnic or racial minorities, and the persistent and growing inequalities between the haves and the have nots in a globalized economy.

In this context, particular attention has been given in some countries to the tendency to blame immigrants, foreigners and racial and ethnic minorities, particularly when they are poor, for all kinds of social problems and public ills. Scapegoating minorities is not a new phenomenon, of course, but when it occurs in times of economic depression or crisis it leads easily to restrictive immigration and social policies that express and also strengthen rejectionist perceptions and discriminatory attitudes among the host populations. Moreover, in such an environment it becomes easy for the judicial authorities to 'criminalize' certain ethnic and racial minorities. When 'undocumented' foreign workers are said to be taking 'our' jobs or 'illegally' using 'our' social services paid for by 'our' taxes, then the stigmatized ethnic or racial group as a whole is tainted by alleged criminal behaviour and becomes an easy target for unscrupulous public officials or political zealots. This occurs frequently, for example, with Mexican migrants in the United States (but the victims are also often bona fide Hispanic United States citizens). The youth of ethnic and racial minorities frequently engage in non-standard activities (the Rastas in the United Kingdom, the Mexican Cholos in the United States), which then becomes labelled as 'deviant' that becomes easy, in the end, to classify as *delinquent* behaviour. Members of such identified youth groups, particularly when they live in poor areas, become suspects and are often treated as potential criminals by police and local authorities, irrespective of whether they have in fact engaged in any criminal activity (Stavenhagen, 1999).

The world is a mosaic of cultures and societies, and even within the framework of economic globalization, cultural diversity remains vivid and remarkable. Variations in situations of poverty reflect this diversity. In many cases, in the poor countries, poverty may be due to natural factors such as droughts, floods, desertification or endemic illness. More often than not, however, poverty is caused by human factors: skewed distribution of resources, income and wealth, insufficient capital assets, the workings of exploitative economic relations, inadequate social arrangements, inefficient economic and political institutions, lack of political will, vested interests, or simply by some basic human failings such as greed, intolerance, indifference, egotism and corruption in some, or idleness, passivity, hopelessness and despair in others.

If the poor in the rich countries cannot be wished or washed away, and if in the poor countries poverty is increasing both in quantity and intensity as a by-product of globalization, then surely current strategies to combat this world scourge have not been successful and alternative solutions must be found. Some scholars propound a market-plus strategy, which means preserving and building upon market-oriented development processes but adding a 'social' component by increasing social expenditures, recalling the state into service to carry out certain necessary public investments, and building social service institutions in partnership between governments, business, civil society and the international community, all this with due respect for local and national cultural traditions (Dyke, 1998).

Many proposals have been presented over the years to deal with this problem, and there is agreement that these are not merely technical issues to be handled in a technocratic way. There are no ready-made recipes to deal with poverty in general. On the contrary, these are political issues that must be solved by political will, which in turn depends on the values and world-view of whoever is in a position to decide matters of national and world concern. As so many have pointed out, in the West, 'communitarianism' has been replaced by 'libertarianism', social responsibility by individualism, collective good by private profit, the work ethic by consumerism, and as Bauman states, the once widely held consensus in favour of collective responsibility for individual misfortune by the present consensus against that principle. When the socially excluded are blamed for their exclusion by the power structure which refuses to recognize its own responsibility in creating the conditions for exclusion, then the time has surely come to take a good, hard look at the hegemonic cultural values which make this possible. Therefore UNESCO's report on culture and development calls for a new global ethic without which a solution to these problems can hardly be feasible (World Commission on Culture and Development, 1995).

As the new millennium dawns, with a widely felt need to revise the parameters of neoliberal economic policies at the international level, people around the world are struggling to find answers to failed development strategies, persistent poverty and lacerating inequalities. The search for alternative development has taken many forms. One approach stresses sustainable growth that will be responsive to ecological considerations, meaning that the environment will be preserved for present and future generations. This concern was stressed in the Rio Environmental Summit of 1992 and in subsequent conferences. The poor are the immediate victims of environmental deterioration (air and water pollution, deforestation, desertification, toxic wastes), and where poverty is widespread, environmental damage increases. This vicious circle must be broken by adequate environmental policies and the creation of a worldwide environmental culture. It has taken nearly three decades since the Stockholm Conference in the early 1970s for the relationship between the environment and poverty to become an important issue on the international agenda, but the battle has not yet been won, basically for two reasons: first, rich countries have demonstrated their indifference with respect to the environmental deterioration of the developing countries, and second, many governments in the developing countries think that imposing environmental safeguards and conditions on development strategies will frighten away highly solicited foreign investments. In the absence of adequate development alternatives, poor people themselves are forced to seek livelihoods which are incompatible with environmental preservation (for example, logging in tropical forests).

Another approach relates to agricultural development. Global markets and transnational agribusiness promote monoculture for export which, while it may generate much-needed foreign exchange, has helped destroy both the local farmers' subsistence agriculture and an ecologically integrated agricultural environment, pushing millions of people off the land and into urban shanty towns. For thousands of years, subsistence agriculture's main purpose was to feed rural families. But peasant societies also had to provide a surplus to other sectors of the economy, which has frequently led to the pauperization of peasant communities and to increased hunger and food insecurity among farmers. As Barraclough points out, there are social origins to hunger and poverty among rural folk: 'Food insecurity is more associated with individual and national poverty than with an overall shortage of food globally or even nationally' (Barraclough, 1991, p. 5). An end to hunger would imply farming strategies for equitable and ecologically balanced agricultural development rather than the current fashionable growth with rural poverty that prevails in the strategies of so many developing countries. This requires a thorough rethinking of peasant society in the modern world and a complete overhauling of images of modernization and development. Farming is still, after all, the major single occupation in the world, and rural poverty is concentrated in the countries of the Third World (World Bank, 1996).

While the incidence of poverty is related to many factors, and now increasingly to global macroeconomic forces, the struggle against poverty must also take place at the local level in communities and villages and neighbourhoods where the everyday issues must be tackled. One widely held view is that people-oriented, environment-centred and poverty-concerned development with popular and democratic participation should focus on local issues: access to land, water, forests; preventing and combating pollution, fostering health services for everybody; making education available to all children and adults, particularly girls; training youth for leadership roles; promoting equal rights for women and girls respecting the specific rights of indigenous peoples; creating opportunities for the development of productive activities; strengthening solidarity networks; improving community social services; enabling the redistribution of resources; furthering autonomous governance and democratic decision-making processes; exercising respect for local traditions; using, whenever possible, traditional knowledge and skills; establishing and strengthening local institutions. Some years ago, all this was put forward under the catchy title, 'Small is beautiful', and while social and economic analysis has moved on towards other formulations, hegemonic thinking in the development field in recent decades has grandly ignored the local level, meaning also the poor and the marginalized. Research has shown that local cultures can be the focus of endogenous, people-centred development efforts, and in recent years some international agencies have become increasingly responsive to this challenge, much in advance, it must be acknowledged, of many governments.

To the extent that the elimination of poverty is closely related to power structures and political will, many authors insist on the need to overhaul the state and governmental structures. After a few decades of development thinking in which the role of the state was pushed aside, there seems to be increasing awareness that states do after all have a responsibility and a role to play in promoting socially equitable development policies. This issue is related to the political culture of the times. With the demise of the centrally planned economies, much social thinking associated with social welfare, socialism and the responsibility of states for the collective well-being of their populations was downgraded, when not degraded, as unrealistic, nostalgic and useless. State intervention was actually considered inimical to the flowering of individual effort and personal liberties. True democrats, it was held, would not want to reconsider the state as a necessary institution in the struggle against poverty; the invisible hand of the market would take care of these problems which, at any rate, concerned only the poor themselves. But political cultures have a way of changing, and in the face of the dramatic and persistent presence of poverty in the world, social philosophy is returning to some of its fundamental questions: the issues of liberty and equality, individual freedom and collective responsibility, the integration of humankind and nature, the role of government, democracy and justice. Before effective means to eliminate poverty in the world can be implemented, some of these issues need to be resolved at the intellectual level (Sen, 1992).

Many of these problems have been taken up at the more immediate level by numerous social and political movements worldwide. Indigenous and tribal peoples are struggling for the defence of their environments and natural resources. Urban shanty-town

Respecting the cultural diversity of local initiatives

It is widely acknowledged in development circles that structural adjustment programmes and opening up the world to global markets and free trade may well have contributed to rising unemployment and increased poverty levels among the world's population. And while it is important to remove barriers to trade and promote the role of the private sector as a means of stimulating economic growth, it is equally important to focus on meeting basic human needs. If we do not change our current course of action by mustering the necessary political will, I believe that there is real danger of further marginalization of the world's most vulnerable groups. This is because the poor and the poorest of the poor simply do not have the same access to funding and resources as the rest of society, nor do they possess many of the necessary skills to survive in a global economy and environment.

In Jordan, like anywhere else, we face severe challenges to our development efforts. We are a small country with few natural resources, located in a part of the world that has experienced much conflict and uncertainty. Our own attempts to undergo structural adjustment and economic reform are helping us to turn our economy around after many long years of recession; however, levels of unemployment and poverty remain high and there is much national debate about the appropriate mechanisms to address such issues.

In Jordan, there has always been a well-respected and dedicated nongovernmental organization (NGO) movement. With the rise of civil society over the last decade, we have witnessed the increasing importance of women's roles in social, economic and political affairs. This participation has contributed greatly to the diversification of developmental efforts, especially in rural areas.

Over the years, it has become apparent that a number of factors are required to stimulate local development. For instance, we have seen that the role of local women's committees and the pioneering work of strong, capable rural women leaders has enabled a culture of trust, respect and credibility to be established among different partners in development. This in turn has ensured not only a wide outreach of programmes and activities but also an environment that respects creativity and initiative.

As women realize their potential and become more aware of their rights and inherent abilities to foster change, new development models are emerging from specific cultural settings that cater to the diversity of needs at local levels. It is no longer culturally acceptable to impose development ideas on local communities. Instead, development organizations must work 'with' their partners and not 'for' them. It is also important to increase human capabilities and foster local leadership so that communities can determine their own speed of growth and find their place within the global community.

One of the many difficulties facing NGOs in the developing world lies in their capacity to access funding. This is largely dependent on meeting Western international donors' requirements. Meeting those requirements can sometimes undermine local efforts and erode the trust and credibility that has been established within communities over many years. In development work, many painful choices have to be made. It is sometimes necessary to decide to forfeit access to funding in order to maintain cultural integrity. And yet, the cost of not keeping up with development trends is harmful to development organizations as well as to their partners and clients.

Helping to ease traditional societies into the modern era requires careful consideration and a deep respect for local culture and customs. While the trend towards sustainability and best practice is developmentally sound, the transference of such practices and concepts to the local level takes time. Development is about widening human capabilities and choices. To ensure participation and empowerment of local communities, it is important to develop local leadership as a means of drawing on local resources and initiative. Much of my current work involves capacity-building to enable communities to recognize and cultivate their own resources and funding for projects. Each community, each project should be not only sustainable, but also culturally relevant.

It is our responsibility to identify development models that work locally and to promote them while being aware that each community has the choice to implement only those aspects that it deems to be relevant, and not necessarily the whole package. Concepts conceived by development thinkers at the international level do not always resonate with local priorities. We should be aware of this. As we move into the future, we must continue to find a balance in order to bridge global and local realities and devise innovative ways to insure a mutually beneficial dynamic between the two.

HRH PRINCESS BASMA BINT TALAL
Chairperson, Board of Trustees,
Jordanian Hashemite Fund for Human Development
(Jordan)

dwellers organize for land titles and housing and social services. Women's organizations have succeeded in putting the issue of women's rights and gender relations on the international agenda. Peasant associations claim access to land and credit. Street children call for attention to their plight. Laid-off workers and unions demand changes in the economic strategies of the new global business élite. Ethnic minorities stress the recognition of multicultural citizenship rights. Religious organizations preach non-violent resistance to oppression and a profound commitment to the poor (as does the Catholic theology of liberation in Latin America). And the weak, the excluded and the oppressed everywhere place the issue of human rights (including economic, social and cultural rights) at the forefront of their social and political agendas. Some are impatient with the slow progress made to reduce poverty. They demand more rapid and dramatic changes and they are sometimes willing to go far in order to make their statements. Revolutionary, utopian and millenarian ideologies have been able to inspire numerous followers around the world, and political violence is frequently the language in which they frame their aims and aspirations, as the experience of the Indians in Chiapas has shown after their armed uprising against the Mexican State at the beginning of 1994.

Truly, at the beginning of the twenty-first century, a new political culture appears to be emerging, without which any serious hope that poverty will disappear from the world in the short run is bound to fail.

Bibliography

Banton, M. 1983. *Racial and Ethnic Competition*. Cambridge, Cambridge University Press.

Barraclough, S. 1991. *An End to Hunger? Social Origins of Food Strategies*. London, Zed Books.

Bauman, Z. 1998. *Work, Consumerism and the New Poor*. Buckingham, Open University Press.

Dyke, N. B. (ed.). 1998. *Persistent Poverty in Developing Countries: Determining the Causes and Closing the Gaps*. Queenstown, Aspen Institute.

Herrnstein, R. J.; Murray, C. 1994. *The Bell Curve*. New York, Free Press.

Hanmer, L. C.; Pyatt, G.; White, H. 1999. What do the World Bank's Poverty Assessments Teach Us about Poverty in Sub-Saharan Africa? *Development and Change*, Vol. 30, No. 4, October.

Psacharopoulos, G.; Patrinos, H. A. (eds.). 1994. *Indigenous People and Poverty in Latin America: An Empirical Analysis*. Washington, D.C., The World Bank.

Sen, A. 1992. *Inequality Reexamined*. Cambridge, Harvard University Press.

Stavenhagen, R. 1999. Structural Racism and Trends in the Global Economy. Unpublished paper, International Council on Human Rights Policy.

UNDP. 1993. *Human Development Report 1993*. New York, Oxford University Press.

UNDP. 1999. *Human Development Report 1999*. New York, Oxford University Press.

Whitehead, A.; Lockwood, M. 1999. *Gender in the World Bank's Poverty Assessment*. Geneva, UNRISD.

The World Bank. 1996. *Poverty Reduction and the World Bank. Progress and Challenges in the 1990s*. Washington, D.C., The World Bank.

World Commission on Culture and Development. 1995. *Our Creative Diversity: Report of the World Commission on Culture and Development*. Paris, UNESCO.

Chapter 7 Sustainable pluralism and the future of belonging

ARJUN APPADURAI
Samuel N. Harper Professor, Department of Anthropology, University of Chicago; Director, Globalization Project, Centre for International Studies (United States)

KATERINA STENOU
Director, Division of Cultural Pluralism, Sector for Culture, UNESCO (France)

'The question of loyalty and attachment for the people living within any particular national territory must be separated from the question of their rights as citizens.'

The terrain of terms

Pluralism today – in the sense of cultural pluralism – is intimately bound up with the theory and practice of the modern nation-state – and its sustainability requires some fundamental rethinking of our ideas of governance, belonging and political recognition. In this sense the nation-state and its forms are a central part of the argument of this essay about the future of belonging.

Cultural diversity, for anthropologists, refers to some socially stable arrangement for the coexistence of groups with different cultural identities. This co-existence has to have sufficient longevity, security and sustainability to allow the identities in question to be reproduced. For a cultural identity to be more than just a slogan, it must evolve creatively over time, and since relations between groups are always evolving, the challenge is how to guide this evolution in a creative and sustainable manner. This is the key to the idea of sustainable diversity or pluralism. Thus, while diversity may refer to a social fact or state, pluralism is a norm and a dynamic process that requires openness to changing cultural values both within and across societies. In our usage, pluralism, both within and across states, is a way of talking about diversity in a dynamic and open-ended manner and implies the challenge of sustainability.

The problem of sustainable pluralism is further complicated because we now know that cultural systems change over time while retaining certain distinctive characteristics. Thus for cultural diversity to be reproduced, not only must we have conditions for culturally defined groups to survive and reproduce themselves, but the relations through which they relate to one another must also be reproducible over time. These patterns of reproduction are neither mechanical nor predictable since they involve complex patterns of cultural evolution that emerge from the relations between local and global factors, between culture and history and between state policies and public opinion. Thus, to make the ecological metaphor specific for a moment, not only must the diversity of species be maximized, the ecosystems in which they cohabit – such as rainforests or deserts or lakes – must also be reproducible over time.

Today this sort of sustainable pluralism requires nurturing partly within the framework of one nation-state or other. The word pluralism is thus appropriate to describe this model of sustainable diversity since it occurs in relation to the jurisdiction of societies organized as nation-states. Sustainable pluralism thus defines a situation in which a finite number of culturally diverse groups are organized to relate so that each has maximum opportunity to reproduce its identity and to evolve creatively over time. The other dimension of the challenge of sustainable pluralism refers to relations between states and across the planet. But the prior issue is how to do it within particular national societies, organized politically as states. Pluralism across and among states, as it affects their relationship with one another, is not addressed in detail in this essay, although it poses important questions in itself.

While there is a growing consensus among various global political and economic élites about the virtues of economic globalization – free trade, open markets, cross-border investments and highly interconnected financial markets – there has been a remarkable reticence to rethink the nature of sovereignty and, in particular, to rethink the centrality of the nation-state as a co-ordinated locus of sovereignty, territorial integrity and the legitimate monopoly of force. There is no easy way to think about sustainable pluralism without conducting a parallel debate about new forms and structures of sovereignty which are 'open' and 'reformed' in some of the same ways as the global economy is now imaged and imagined. Sustainable pluralism, both within and across current national boundaries, requires a new ecology of sovereignty.

Globalization and cultural pluralism

As far as cultural pluralism is concerned, globalization has introduced at least three major complications. It has deeply intensified the tensions between migration and citizenship. It has exacerbated the national politics of identity. And it has intensified pre-existing tendencies towards nationalist xenophobia. These three effects are themselves interconnected and each requires some discussion.

Source: See the Index of culture indicators and sources and Table 6 in Part Seven of this report.

First, migration is an ancient feature of human history. But the politics of migration began to change in the era of modern imperialism in which several European nation-states sought to practice democracy at home and imperialism abroad. In the era of globalization, this contradiction takes on fresh force as population movements interact with new ideologies of open frontiers and free trade as well as with new forms of ethno-nationalism. On the one hand, the increasing integration of global markets and the increased pressures on all national economies to be globally competitive has meant new incentives to import 'guest' populations, both in menial occupations abandoned by national citizens and in high-skill occupations which do not have enough trained nationals to fill them. These labour flows (both high- and low-end) have produced a whole new world of migrants and citizens who are partial citizens. The term 'partial citizens' can be used to pinpoint the fact that these migrants are not illegal from the point of view of the host country, but that they face various kinds of restrictions on the conditions of their employment, citizenship, duration of their stay, legal rights, tax liabilities and so on. Needless to say, Indian engineers in Silicon Valley, Filipino maidservants in Milan, Sri Lankan chauffeurs in Kuwait, Senegalese janitors and Nigerian artists in Paris do not have exactly the same problems. But in so far as they are legal workers in their new economies, they present various challenges to societies committed to democracy and the rule of law for all citizens. Partial citizens open up questions of rights and duties in the gray zones of national legal and political norms about citizenship. Globalization has made it increasingly difficult to treat migrants as absolute non-citizens. In turn, this means that the idea of 'the people', with some sense of historical, cultural and physical intimacy, is called into question, and the boundaries of national citizenship become, to some extent, blurred.

Second, cultural minorities – especially refugees, guestworkers and other underprivileged groups – are increasingly enabled to articulate their cultural rights as human rights in national or international courts. Thus the question of the right to cultural difference – whether in clothing, prayer, diet, housing, marriage or language – has become a matter of distributive justice. In so far as it has become adjudicable in courts of law, largely as a matter of human rights, it has been brought squarely into the legal/political sphere. As a result, such arguments acquire a doubly worrisome aspect for national citizens. They threaten the unspoken ethnic assumptions about membership in the nation and they open the door to claims on other entitlements (such as welfare, credit or housing) that are otherwise not open to partial citizens. Globalization affects these debates over citizenship in two ways: first as an economic force that provides incentives for economic migration, and second as a circuit through which such discourses as those of 'human rights' spread rapidly to new national and cultural contexts.

This leads to the third complication that globalization introduces into the problem of cultural pluralism, namely, the problem of xenophobia. As migrant groups, driven or seduced into new national societies by the forces of globalization, press ever stronger cultural demands in the name of cultural rights as human rights, they force the implicit ethnic bases of all nationalisms into view. The debate over the use of the headscarf in French schools brings out the delicate links between public life, 'Frenchness' and the racial/religious standing of minorities in France.

Throughout the world, we now see societies in which several generations of migrants are dealing with the tensions between a new host country and a land of origin and memory. The tensions in Hong Kong between old and new migrants from mainland China, and the question of whether Cantonese or Mandarin speakers will dominate the new Hong Kong is one example. The ambiguous role of Indians in the new South Africa is another example, where history, memory and the complex relations between different populations of the British Empire still affect the question of who the privileged citizens of the new South Africa shall be. In the United States, and especially in the border states of Texas and California, the cultural privileges of Spanish speakers are a matter of internal debate among different generations of Mexican-Americans, as well as between them and the white American majority. In every one of these cases and others besides, the cultural privileges of immigrant populations are tied up with labour flows, economic changes and market shifts that create new aspirations and uncertainties. Europe, in general, faces such problems in many of its wealthier countries as the new and expanding idea of the European Union opens borders that were previously relatively hard to cross. In all these new situations, economic incentives and global pressures are at odds with national politics and local cultural fears, including fears about globalization.

An approach which is built on understanding this convergence of internal and external threats to national identity may have more explanatory potential than the two dominant approaches to contemporary cultural conflicts, the 'clash of civilizations' approach of Huntington (1998) and the more interesting *Jihad vs. McWorld* hypothesis of Barber (1996). True, there are culture debates and conflicts (which can invade the sphere of domestic politics and international relations). Indeed, the spread of global capitalism, especially in its consumerist forms, provokes culturalist defences. But the underlying structural problem is the conjuncture of the external behemoth of the global economy (and its attendant 'American' values) and the internal 'Trojan Horse' of migrant claims to fuller citizenship in a new home.

The link between these internal and external forces of globalization is provided by the large variety of 'diasporic nationalisms' that now criss-cross the world's public spheres. Consider the number of groups who live in a global diaspora while harbouring hopes of a nation-state of their own: Armenians, Kashmiris, Kurds, Sikhs and Sri Lankan Tamils are among the most prominent of these. But there are many others who live in exile, nurturing counter-nationalisms that are equally threatening to their home societies and their host societies. Such counter-nationalisms, unlike earlier forms of exile politics, are now globally networked, widely diasporic and transnationally interactive. They inhabit what we have called 'diasporic public spheres', public spheres constituted across national lines and often for explicitly transnational purposes.

INTERNATIONAL MIGRATION

			IMMIGRANTS	
COUNTRY	no. immigrants (thousands)	Main country of origin	as % of total population	as % of labour force
United States	798	Mexico	9.3	10.8
Germany	615	Poland	9.0	9.1
Russian Federation	583	Kazakhstan	...	...
Mexico	480	United States	...	...
Japan	275	China	1.2	1.0
United Kingdom	237	United States	3.6	3.6
Canada	216	China Hong Kong SAR	17.4	18.5
Ukraine	130	Russian Federation	...	...
France	102	Algeria	6.3	6.1
Australia	86	New Zealand	21.1	24.6
Netherlands	77	Turkey	4.4	2.9
Switzerland	73	Yugoslavia	19.0	17.5
Austria	53	Turkey	9.9	9.1
Croatia	52	Bosnia and Herzegovina	...	...
Belgium	49	France	8.9	7.9
Denmark	49	Somalia	4.7	3.1
Kazakhstan	38	Russian Federation	...	...
Sweden	33	Yugoslavia	6.0	5.2
Belarus	31	Russian Federation	...	...
Norway	22	Sweden	3.6	2.8

Graph 8

International migration has increased considerably in recent years, sometimes with signifiant cultural, social and political consequences. The following table shows the inflow of foreign population and the main country of origin for twenty countries in 1999 in descending order. It also shows the percentage of the population and the labour force made up of foreign nationals. Migration is occurring on a global scale, in Central and Eastern Europe, in North America, in East Asia and in Australia. The immigrants come from a wide range of countries, some for work, some for asylum and some for leisure. But only in Australia, Canada and Switzerland do immigrants account for more than 10% of the population.

Source: OECD and UN Population Division, 1999.

These diasporic public spheres cannot be understood without recognizing the role of electronic media in creating new forms of imagined communities which cross national boundaries, maintain cyber-contact and visualize new social identities and projects through mass media, such as television, e-mail, fax and telephone. These communities, in which travel and face-to-face links are complemented by electronic mediation, allow physically dispersed and politically fragmented communities to strengthen older ties or to create new ones. The forms of cultural citizenship that characterize this world in motion are critically dependent on electronic forms of mediation, communication and identification.

Public diversity and cultural citizenship

In multi-ethnic democracies such as the United States, minor identities are created by making them matters of culture (in the sense of lifestyle) rather than of politics. But this usually means that such minor groups are pushed out of the national public sphere (Parekh, 1997). This is the vital point about the co-production of majorities and minorities in the emergence of modern nation-states. The public sphere that emerges in modern nation-states is rarely a multicultural space. Minorities are usually free to express their cultural identities in the private sphere, in institutions close to the family, kinship groups and neighbourhood. Whenever the public sphere, meaning behaviour in public, is involved, national culture is dominant and minority practices are discouraged. From the perspective of the minority, this national culture looks very much like majority culture, but from the point of view of the majority, it is naturalized as 'national' culture.

What is the nub of the problem of diversity and the state? Public diversity poses two sources of anxiety to modern nation-states. The first is that organized cultural minorities whose practices and preferences are granted legitimacy in the public sphere become potential claimants on a variety of institutional spaces and practices regulated by the state, including jobs, housing, credit, tax benefits, educational subsidies, political representation, linguistic preferences and the like. Since these resources are rightly seen to be finite, this arena is perceived by those who control the state as a zero-sum game, where new claimants need to be minimized. This anxiety is fundamentally economic; we shall return to it shortly.

The second anxiety is more fundamental. It pertains to the problem of 'peoplehood' and of the ethnic character of the state. To grant public and political recognition to cultural diversity is to raise a potential threat to national integrity, since all nations rely on some form of cultural identity as the dominant component of national identity. Public cultural diversity threatens to expose the ambiguities that inform the idea of the 'people' in all modern nation-states. The main ambiguity is this: for the idea of the 'people' to have real power as the foundation of territory and sovereignty, it must be based on some naturalized principle (of blood, kinship, race, language and so on) which is, in essence, ethnic. At the same time, in the social theory of democracy, the people are abstract, their characteristics are universal, and, in principle, any person could be part of the 'people'. In other words any person could be a citizen. And here is the nub of the contradiction in the modern, democratic theory of citizenship. From the point of view of the liberal conception of citizenship, the qualities of citizens are entirely formal and thus open to anyone. But from the point of view of nationalism, there is something special about the people within this or that national territory. What can this special characteristic be, if it is not ultimately ethno-national or cultural? Thus, the central dilemma of modern democratic citizenship, namely, that it is simultaneously open and closed, is brought to the fore when cultural minorities seek a share in the public sphere, and that is why their claims are so unsettling.

We can now return briefly to the ways in which globalization exacerbates the problem of cultural minorities and the public sphere. Because globalization increases the number and variety of 'partial citizens', and because these globally circulating citizens also constitute diasporic public spheres with multiple national attachments and loyalties, they constitute a circulatory, external threat to the idea of national 'peoplehood', unlike internally generated

The European exception

'If everything had to be started all over again, then one would have to start with culture,' was a statement attributed to Jean Monnet towards the end of his life. I find this difficult to believe. Firstly, the father of what was to become the European Union had other things on his mind. The two world wars, for instance, were still very present in the minds of the ex-belligerents. The main concern at the time was to prevent European coal and steel from ever being used again to build machines of destruction when the idea of a united Europe was in gestation. In short, any claim that culture was the first priority would have been considered out of place and in bad taste when millions of people did not even have a roof over their heads. In any event, and no matter how advanced its construction was, the European Union would hardly have agreed to lend an ear to such a suggestion. Even today, it is hardly ready to do so.

What the founding fathers had in mind was to create an economic Europe, a true common market leading to a single currency and perhaps later to a type of federation. Despite all the obstacles, often considered insuperable, these initial objectives have been very largely attained.

On the other hand, culture in the strict sense has never been considered as more than merchandise by Brussels, a commodity to which the same rules should apply as to any other product, in other words the highest possible common denominator that can be produced, distributed and consumed as if it were a car, a textile or a food product. The reference model at the outset was the United States, particularly since the latter had managed to produce a homogeneous culture from a wide range of heterogeneous ingredients and a common language accessible to the majority of people, by complying with and marrying cultural needs.

There was another obvious model: the Soviet Union. It too had dreamed of a vast centralized market, standardized production regulating demand, a single currency and a federation. In the field of culture, it had wagered on a single common language, a 'Soviet' culture and even a *homo sovieticus* engendered by an awesome assembly of cultures. The dream fell through. However, when considering Europe, one cannot help but wonder if the idea was really such an aberration or if it could have worked had it been tackled differently, for instance if private property, market competition and the job market had not been suppressed.

Europe did not commit such mistakes and has no reason to do so. Consequently, does it have a better chance of giving birth to a real European culture and a true European person? I firmly believe in a European Common Market and an economic Europe, just as I believe in a political Europe for the future as an inevitable evolution in some shape or form. However, my Europe is not a Soviet Europe, democratic in nature, economically viable and prosperous. My Europe is comprised of thirty-five to forty different cultures and identities, expressing themselves in as many languages and with just as many pasts, memories and traditions, the whole thing achieving unity through a common geographical and historical paradigm, and indeed a common memory.

I would like to give two examples to clarify my remarks. A few years ago, in Stockholm, I was asked whether I feared that, if Sweden joined the Common Market, it would lose its identity. I answered by quoting the example of the Austrian Empire: a vast common market which was functioning well, an economic and political lingua franca and a monarchy, bicephalous towards the end, and controlled from a single capital. Different cultural identities developed side by side to the benefit of all. It could have continued in this way, if Vienna had had the intelligence to understand that cultural autonomy had to be transformed into political autonomy in order to bar the way to destructive nationalist movements.

My second example is very different. An emigrant of European origin, with an experience similar to mine, quickly realizes on arrival in the United States that there is a difference between the inhabitants of the South (former Confederates) and the 'pure Yankees' or the Californians, or even the inhabitants of the Middle West. The reason is, I believe, that an American from the southern United States keeps in mind, as if it were coded, the tragic experience of a country torn apart and occupied, at the cost of tens of thousands of dead on his own territory – of women raped, of armed robberies and of scenes of plunder perpetrated by foreign soldiers. The Southern States are an exception – I am obviously speaking of the white population here – in the success story of the young history of America. Europeans are also heirs to a distant but vivid memory. Their tragic past is an integral component of what I call the European paradigm, shared by all the peoples and cultures of Europe, different as they are.

At its very beginning, the European Union probably underestimated the issue of the multiple identities that comprised its very essence. Having understood that this multiplicity could engender nationalism and bloodshed, it then believed that common economic interests could serve to counterbalance this danger and that a European identity would relegate those diverse identities little by little to the background. This is a legacy, inspired by a nineteenth-century Marxist concept whereby the defense of common economic interests and the elimination of rivalries in this domain were meant to erase national and cultural differences, at the same time preventing conflicts.

But Europe is not a melting pot and will never become one, since its identity is defined expressly through the multiplicity of its cultures. It is not by eliminating identities which have been formed over centuries, indeed millennia, that we can achieve cultural integration, and by so doing, limit the dangers of nationalism but rather by doing just the opposite, that is, reinforcing the cultural dimension of these components. Thanks to a weakening in deadly economic rivalries, this has become possible for the first time in the history of Europe.

Such a result can be achieved only through positive, dynamic cultural interventions and a policy aimed at reinforcing cultural identities within the framework of mutual knowledge and understanding. The various European populations should have access both to their own culture and to the culture of others. Exchange programmes for young people, and in particular those relating to education and tourism, are undeniably promising steps. However, we can perceive and regret the current tendency towards cultural standardization that future European executives are exposed to during their training. We cannot insist too much on the enriching nature of cultural exchange and accordingly on the major importance of improved understanding of the notion of European identity.

ANTONIN J. LIEHM
Political Scientist; former Professor,
École des Hautes Études en Sciences Sociales,
former Editor of *Lettre Internationale* (France)

minorities who constitute a more domestic and more domesticable threat. Of course, such tensions are worsened when claims to public (cultural) diversity are produced in the interaction of external and internal minorities who may share cultural affinities even when their history and form of citizenship is different. This, for example, is the challenge that Turks pose to the German state, since more- and less-recent Turkish migrants constitute a complex alliance of minorities with a common cultural characteristic, which is their Turkish identification and (for some) their Islamic commitment.

In general, problems of diversity in the public sphere of democratic societies are greatly complicated when generational differences among cultural minorities create differences in their relationships to national citizenship. In these cases, the cultural minorities themselves become sites of intense 'internal' cultural debates, as well as of struggles against one or more states. Diasporic public spheres are frequently characterized by debates between 'youth' and 'elders' within diasporic communities about such essential matters as marriage, consumption and the politics of the homeland.

The very idea of cultural rights (by definition, group rights) represents a radicalization of liberal social theory and moves significantly beyond the ideas of tolerance and recognition. It recognizes that the right to culture in everyday life is fundamentally political and requires a significant degree of autonomy: legal, juridical and spatial. It puts the state under a strong obligation to provide the spaces for cultural expression. In its radical form this conception of cultural citizenship (Rosaldo, 1997; Stavenhagen, 1998) actually demands the voluntary sharing of state power in areas of law, language and territory. Though there may be various means for putting this idea of sharing state power into practice, it puts cultural minorities and the state into a common political space, recognizing the cultural biases of most states and the political requirements of cultural diversity. As we have already observed, access to electronic media can directly affect the capability of individuals and groups to articulate, promote and institutionalize new forms of cultural citizenship.

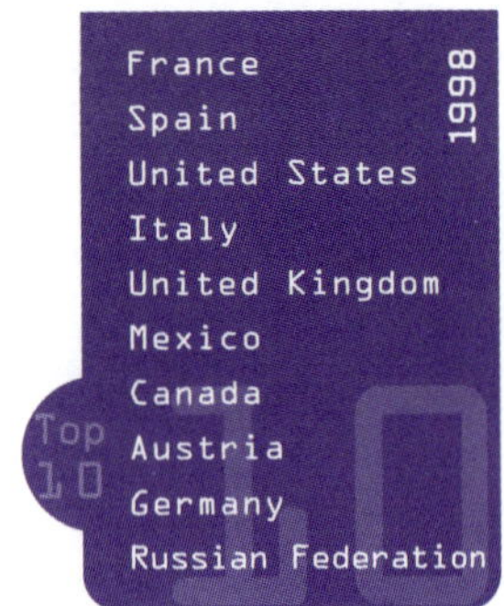

Tourist arrivals
1998
France
Spain
United States
Italy
United Kingdom
Mexico
Canada
Austria
Germany
Russian Federation
Top 10

Source: See the Index of culture indicators and sources and Table 18 in Part Seven of this report.

Even a more moderate interpretation of the idea of cultural citizenship – which stops short of restructuring the reach of the state – suggests a principle that is the sine qua non of cultural diversity as a rights-based aspiration, namely, the principle that genuine cultural diversity must be recognized in the public sphere. In turn, given its own cultural-ethnic underpinnings, the state cannot be a mere referee of recognition and cultural toleration. It needs to rethink the nature of its own cultural jurisdiction. We shall return to this point in the conclusion.

The political economy of dignity

Too many discussions of cultural pluralism fail to recognize what may be called 'the political economy of dignity'. That is, they do not recognize that collective cultural rights, as they have been discussed here, cannot rely entirely on normative calls to tolerance, to recognition or to states to allow minorities to 'enjoy their own cultures'. Although the symbolic core of cultural dignity is an end unto itself and thus cannot be reduced to matters of wealth and stratification, dignity as a part of the public sphere must be placed within the wider context of inequality, both political and economic.

It is a truism that something like half of the world population (a total which has just crossed the six billion mark) lives in poverty, by measures agreed upon by the World Bank, UNDP's *Human Development Report* and other reputable measurements. This shocking fact should caution us against hoping that subscription to certain norms of cultural diversity (difficult enough in itself) will easily translate into public policy. Whether we consider the inequality within nations or between nations, we can easily see why resources for the active support of minority cultural spaces are hard to come by.

These facts about radical inequality (and poverty) have been seriously exacerbated by the globalization of the world's economy in the last few decades. Even the sources such as the World Bank, whose success is measured by higher hopes for economic globalization, have conceded that inequality within and between countries has grown as a result of the tighter integration of the global economy and the more promiscuous flow of global capital, even if poverty has not increased in absolute terms. So, global poverty was already unacceptably deep and inequality is growing. What does this mean for the future of cultural pluralism? We wish to address three implications of this harsh state of affairs for the rights of cultural minorities in the public sphere:

- First, although states are being invited by various international resolutions as well as by internal pressures from their own minorities, to show active respect for the cultural rights of minorities, their worries about global competitiveness and about investing in globally valuable skills, occupations and institutions will necessarily reduce their incentives to invest in the future of cultural pluralism.
- Second, on a worldwide basis, it has been widely recognized by development economists such as Amartya Sen and many others that the levels of poverty in many societies make it impossible for ordinary people to voice and articulate their cultural aspirations in any meaningful way.
- Third, and perhaps worst, the overwhelming economic disenfranchisement of a large part of the world's population makes it difficult for cultural minorities to assure 'internal' democracy. Here we face the single hardest dilemma about cultural pluralism. Even when states and international bodies are able to make sincere commitments to diversity, how can they ensure that democratic debate occurs both within and across communities? This is a thorny problem for democratic theory and practice and is most often recognized in examples like bride-burning, female circumcision and other abhorrent practices which are sometimes argued to be part of some cultural repertoire that demands non-interference. The standard solution to this dilemma is simply to reject those 'cultural' arguments that violate widely accepted 'universal' standards. But since universal standards are undeniably historical and contextual in their origins, this is never a reliable argument. What is clearly preferable is to foster a level of democratic debate within specific cultural communities so that their own inner life is likely to be as democratic as possible. But this is hardly likely in a situation where the bulk of people in many culturally defined communities depend for their very lives (and livelihoods) on the goodwill of their leaders, their patrons and their representatives.

The democratization of cultural debate about what constitutes acceptable practice and what ought to change depends on the economic dignity and financial enfranchisement of ordinary people in as many cultural communities as possible. Thus, apart from the direct ethics of suffering, justice and equality, there is another reason to support all reasonable means of poverty reduction: this is the only way to secure the ability of ordinary people to participate in debates about culture within their own communities and thus to assure them that arguments for cultural rights are not just the slogans of self-elected élites which actually harm the interest of whole groups within the community, such as women, the poor, children, the aged or any other victims of internal discrimination.

For all these reasons, it is not meaningful to speak of cultural rights or, more broadly, of sustainable pluralism outside of a linked commitment to the political economy of dignity. This means that cultural rights, and even human rights more generally, should be integrally connected to the welfare and well-being of all citizens and to the reduction of poverty as a global priority. Within this broader commitment to economic transformation, there is a special need to invest in the resources through which the ethos of cultural pluralism can be globally disseminated, and this involves investing in the imagination as a social faculty.

The infrastructure of the imagination

We build here on earlier work (Appadurai, 1996) which argues that the imagination is increasingly a social faculty, a property of groups and is no longer simply a feature of the mental life of gifted individuals (although it certainly is that as well). In the era of globalization, the imagination is the site of social negotiations between local and global forces and is the battleground on which progressive social movements fight the forces of propaganda, bigotry and fear. The imagination – as a popular and collective faculty – is affected by mass media as well as by local knowledge, by formal education as well as by everyday experience, by traumatic experiences as well as by more secure and stable memories. Particularly because of the complexities of mass media – their variety, their power and their reach – the collective imagination of ordinary people in many societies is full of paradoxes: it is simultaneously more cynical and more gullible; more open and more suspicious; more forgetful (of various histories) and yet more obsessed with memory than ever before (Huyssen, 1999).

Many forces, both official and popular, compete to shape the imagination as a social practice. Among these are the global entertainment industries, the world of news, the institutions of education and science as well as the informational contexts of everyday life, such as the street, the café and the marketplace. One among these forces, which we may collectively describe as the infrastructure of the imagination, is what we call art. The work of artists has a special relationship to the problem of cultural pluralism for reasons that have to do with the ways in which art capitalizes the imagination of its viewers.

Art – whether high or popular art, adult or children's art, museum or street art, plastic or performance art, ephemeral or monumental art – has a special potential in relation to making pluralism sustainable. To see why this is so, we need to attend to one specific and defining feature of all ethnophobic movements, which is that they tend to see themselves in terms of histories rather than in terms of horizons or possibilities. Put more simply, cultural consciousness can turn predatory when it sees itself primarily as

Nationals visiting abroad
per inhabitant
1998
Singapore
Switzerland
Austria
Belgium
Germany
Ireland
United Kingdom
Denmark
Sweden
Rep. of Moldova
Top 10

Source: See the Index of culture indicators and sources and Table 18 in Part Seven of this report.

a living form of a specific (often ethnic) heritage. When ethnic or cultural identity is organized as a project or projection, as a future, as the expression of a horizon rather than a heritage, its relations to other ethnic projects can be potentially more plastic. Horizons leave room for dialogue and negotiation and for the creation of spaces for overlapping consensus (in Rawls's sense), spaces that are not seen in a zero-sum metric. Heritage as the sole fuel of cultural diversity tends to be closed, finite, fixed and beyond negotiation. It is more open to hostile ethnic mobilization. This is a delicate point since it is unlikely that human beings will ever become free of what Maurice Halbwachs called 'the prestige of the past' and of history, memory and heritage, nor should they be. But in so far as cultural memory has tended to become exclusive and hostile, it needs to be counterbalanced by the future as a horizon of group identity. It is worth noting here that the Greek etymologies that underpin the word 'horizon' simultaneously connote boundaries and openness.

Such a future-oriented infrastructure for the workings of the imagination of cultural difference will need to develop deep flexibility as regards the possibilities of difference, of otherness and of alterity. And such flexibility is not just a matter of seeing good images of the Other, or subsidizing the artwork of minorities, or circulating the work of one cultural

To be Indian is already to be culturally diverse

Indian! To the majority of people across the world it conjures up an image of one culture, one people: 'Indian' dance, 'Indian' music, 'Indian' food. Before considering cultural interaction with other countries, it is vital, and surprising to many, to understand that India is itself a vast pluriculture. Having 20% of the world's population does not translate into one homogeneous culture. Aryan, Dravidian and Sino-Tibetan peoples, speaking twenty-two languages and some nine hundred dialects, have a diversity of behaviour-patterns, dress, cooking, story-telling, singing and dancing that is unimaginably extensive. To be Indian is already to be culturally diverse.

My performing arts company is in Gujarat in Western India, but half my genes are from my mother's very different South India. In the company there are six languages from all over the nation, and each brings from his or her village, city or state other influences and experiences. There is no tension in this: it is part of the enrichment of creating contemporary Indian culture, and our work benefits enormously from this diversity of input, even if we have to translate ideas into six languages before work can begin!

In this India my own principle performance vocabulary is *Bharata Natyam*, from Tamil Nadu in the south. At the same time some of my closest colleagues are experts in the folk performance tradition, *bhavai*, from the north-west states of Gujarat and Rajasthan. Does this detract from my own performance? Not at all. By seeing, performing and discussing this (equally Indian) style, my own work expands, because, finally, culture reacts to whatever is around it. Indeed, culture for us is precisely that reaction filtered through the vocabularies of those who experience it. There is a fear that the flood of new 'global' culture may endanger Indian identity.

Back in my company we are regulary enriched by a constant influx of foreign artists. They too are enriched by the exchange. They are learning possibilities of behaviour and expression, and they transmit their own expertise. Are their productions a dilution of our culture? Not at all – they are very distinctly Indian.

There are those who argue that only local work can really fulfil the potential of the performing arts, and that this should be the sole aim of performance work. They stand firmly, and understandably, against the diluting effects of globalization. Yet in taking this stand they unfortunately also oppose the fascinating and valuable work of directors, choreographers and other artists who search for universality in their work as something that can be understood across cultures.

Wearing T-shirts and singing *bhajans* is possible. Wearing *kurta-pyjama* and accessing the Internet is equally possible.

Like so many artists through the ages we have recognized elements in each other's work which we find exciting, enriching and generously open to us and to our audiences. It would have been relatively easy to simply juxtapose our work on stage, but that would have missed the point of creating together, and become only anthropological study. What has been developed through our collaboration is a style, which flows across and between our cultural backgrounds. It is not Indian, although there are very strong influences within it, nor is it Nigerian or British, although those influences are also part of the 'recipe'. We developed it because we felt it spoke to us and through us without ever weakening our own cultural identities. We developed it because we believed this particular fusion would speak to audiences from a wide cultural catchment area.

The artist seeks to internalize all of these in order to speak, communicate and celebrate. That is the strength of artists, and as long as they do this they will enjoy the winds of many cultures, converting them to new energy but not being blown away by any of them. We are, in most cases, no longer forced to abide by one set of cultural references, for we are surrounded by many.

For the artist to ignore this is to push art to the periphery of society as some sort of nostalgic reminder of what we once were. But art must speak now in a language for now, so artists must also rediscover and reform their language constantly. This in no way means discarding traditional forms; the artist must become alert to the many languages within our contemporary society in order to speak of them, and must be steeped in the culture and rhythms of wherever he or she is based. The artist today must be globally aware but locally rooted.

MALLIKA SARABHAI
Dancer, Academy of Performing Arts,
Usmuanpura (India)

tradition or region to another – although these are all good things. It requires something more deep and more abstract, which is the habit of imagining things other than as they are or as they appear. All art, whether abstract or realistic, modern or folk, representational or abstract, feeds the sinews of such flexibility. Art does not just stock the imagination with images of forms and possibilities. It opens the senses to the habit of the new, the different, the unimagined and even the unimaginable. In this way, art is anticipatory of new possibilities not by providing a preview of the future, but by improving our collective capabilities for imagining other worlds, other forms, other shapes and other designs.

Here lies the key to the relationship between art and sustainable pluralism. Pluralism in any given society becomes sustainable because of its capability to absorb new differences and often unpredictable ones. In an age in which cultural groups may shift styles, when new groups arrive suddenly and depart unpredictably, when youth revise their identities at blinding speed, when cultural identities can shift or realign themselves both internally and externally, the Other is a moving target, so no design for cultural pluralism which is strictly geared to the present can ever be adequate, for the relations among culturally diverse groups will always evolve to create new forms and possibilities for cultural identity. The sustainability of any particular pluralist equilibrium will require the imaginations of ordinary people to be supple and thus open to new regimes of diversity. To prepare people to recognize, appreciate, criticize and celebrate such emergent cultural forms, no practice can be better preparation than the making and viewing of art, of all types, in all contexts, by all people. For art, along with the forms that it offers to the imagination, is nothing less than an archive of possible forms, and sustainable pluralism requires us to be open to new cultural projects without knowing in advance how they will look and feel. Needless to say, art is only one part of the infrastructure of the imagination. The flame of inventiveness that needs to be stimulated applies to new projects and possibilities in science, religion, politics and education as well. In this sense, art is a point of entry into a wider dynamics of inventiveness in the social structure which involves the infrastructure of the imagination as a whole.

Towards a new architecture of belonging

There is much debate about the crisis of the nation-state in the era of globalization. From one point of view, it is clear that the nation-state faces unprecedented new challenges. On the other hand, in many regards, it is alive and well. What is clear is that it is changing its form, structure and function in important ways. The changes that are most relevant to the future of sustainable pluralism require us to recognize three realities:

1. We are living in a world of heterogeneous political forms, including nongovernmental organizations (NGOs), diasporic nationalist movements, transnational political alliances and interest groups, and cross-border authorities and regulations. Thus, we are entering a world of multiple forms of sovereignty of which the classical nation-state is clearly only one, even if it is the most powerful of these.
2. Cultural pluralism means granting cultural groups the right to diversity in the public sphere and that this in turn means recognizing some degree of political self-government for all such groups. This means sharing sovereignty by one or other method.
3. The question of loyalty and attachment for the people living within any particular national territory must be separated from the question of their rights as citizens. That is, the problem of government must be delinked in some way from the problem of national identity. States, in this process, must be weaned away from being the trustees of the nation (seen as an indivisible cultural entity) and begin to think of themselves as trustees of cultural pluralism and as the guarantors of its sustainability.

Bibliography

Appadurai, A. 1996. *Modernity at Large.* Minneapolis, University of Minnesota Press.

Barber, B. 1996. *Jihad vs. McWorld.* New York, Ballantine Books.

Huntington, S. 1998. *The Clash of Civilizations and the Remaking of World Order.* New York, Touchstone.

Huyssen, A. 1999. Present Pasts: Media, Politics, Amnesia. *Public Culture*, Vol. 12, No. 2. (Special issue on globalization.)

Parekh, B. 1997. *A Commitment to Cultural Pluralism.* (Paper prepared for the UNESCO Intergovernmental Conference on Cultural Policies for Development, Stockholm, Sweden.)

Rosaldo, R. 1997. Cultural Citizenship, Inequality and Multiculturalism. In: W. V. Flores and R. Benmayor (eds.), *Latino Cultural Citizenship: Claiming Identity, Space, and Rights.* Boston, Beacon Press.

Stavenhagen, R. 1998. Cultural Rights: A Social Science Perspective. In: H. Nieć (ed.), *Cultural Rights and Wrongs: A Collection of Essays in Commemoration of the 50th Anniversary of the Universal Declaration of Human Rights.* Paris and Leicester, UNESCO Publishing and Institute of Art and Law.

His tea glowed in me
and the **drum beat** ever known
a stranger's house, home

Sharath Srinivarsan

Sense of belonging
Various colours and shapes
Where do you fit it?

Pate Gaye Y. Ritchie

World without cultures
Branches without autumn leaves
Sand without seashells

Karolyn Schenk

Dew drops on the leaves
Sun rays falling on the drops
Diamonds on the tree

Asim Majeed

Part Three
Cultural policies and cultural heritage

Introduction

In a rapidly changing world, cultural heritage is playing an increasingly important role in providing people with a sense of who they are, where they have come from and what their lives mean. Heritage buildings, locations and sites, artworks and artifacts as well as languages, customs, communal practices, traditional skills and so on are all becoming more widely recognized as essential means of articulating identity and meaning for local communities, regions, nations and humankind as a whole. At the same time the world's cultural heritage is exposed to ever-growing threats from a variety of sources, including the ravages of air pollution and other environmental hazards, the pressures of the explosion in international tourism, destruction by war and human conflict, lack of resources for conservation and, in many cases, sheer neglect.

To be able to comprehend these changes and manage them in ways that will enhance the cultural and economic value of heritage, new analytical approaches are required, incorporating expanded notions of cultural heritage which go beyond the static monument-oriented views of the past and take account of the interests of a wider variety of stakeholders. Such approaches will help in developing better cultural policies for implementation at local, national and international levels. It is important that policy programmes and strategies recognize the role of both tangible and intangible heritage in representing cultural diversity within society and enhance the possibilities of access to heritage resources for every member of the community.

This part of the report contains contributions describing some of these newer ways of thinking about heritage. Several themes emerge. The first concerns the economic dimension of heritage protection. Conservation is costly and resources are always limited. Klamer and Throsby argue that treating heritage as capital assets will enable better decisions to be made about the allocation of resources to its preservation and protection. But in this process, the economic rate of return cannot be allowed to dominate all other considerations; rather, the concept of heritage as cultural capital invites a balanced assessment of both the cultural and the economic value to which heritage gives rise.

The second theme deals with the definition of heritage, which has evolved over time to admit a much wider range of cultural phenomena representing continuing processes connecting past, present and future. This expansion of the heritage domain has profound implications both for policy development and for conservation practice; in both cases, new strategies are evolving which have to be more sensitive than in the past to the subtleties and complexities of the role of heritage in a globalized world. The chapters by Bouchenaki and Lévi-Strauss describe how these developments have affected the actions of UNESCO, the leading international organization in the heritage field, while the chapter by Mason and de la Torre discusses needed reforms in the approach of professional conservation practice.

A third and more persistent theme underlying all these chapters is that of concern for the long term, encapsulated in the notion of sustainability. Just as the principles of sustainable development have been applied in the case of environmental resources, so also can we articulate similar principles outlining society's responsibilities to care for its cultural heritage.

Finally, this part draws attention to a number of specific new approaches to heritage management. These include: new methods for generating local interest in and support for heritage projects, as in the World Monuments Watch List of 100 Most Endangered Sites, and UNESCO's Local Efforts and Preservation (LEAP) project for community mobilization which has been piloted in the Asia/Pacific Region; the application of economic evaluation methods to heritage projects where non-use benefits are involved, illustrated by the World Bank project for the preservation of the Fez Medina in Morocco; new models for using cultural heritage as part of an urban development strategy, illustrated by a case-study of the Japanese town of Nagahama; new methods developed in Italy for synthesizing cultural mapping with geographic information systems to provide a map identifying degrees of risk to heritage assets across the country; and a new focus on providing incentives for practitioners whose work involves traditional skills which form part of the intangible cultural heritage, as well as an outline of new safeguarding approaches and new perspectives launched by UNESCO.

DAVID THROSBY
Professor of Economics
Macquarie University, Sydney (Australia)

Chapter 8
Paying for the past: the economics of cultural heritage

ARJO KLAMER
Professor of the Economics of Art and Culture
Erasmus University, Rotterdam (The Netherlands)

DAVID THROSBY
Professor of Economics
Macquarie University, Sydney (Australia)

'Considering heritage items as cultural capital also introduces the long-term nature of the benefits that heritage provides

Introduction

The house is burning down. What should you save? That old chest of drawers that has been in the family for generations? The silverware? The family albums? The fire is raging. You cannot take everything. You have to choose. What is worth so much that it simply must be rescued? Then again, you could choose to step away from the heat, let everything burn, and look forward to a future that is not burdened by mementos of the past.

People all over the world face a similar decision when 'an act of progress' is about to destroy historic artefacts or locations. In some cases the choice is obvious: certain objects, structures and sites, even though they may have outlived their original purpose or usefulness, are recognized to be of such significance that preserving them is regarded as essential. Such heritage items, from the Book of Kells to the Great Wall of China, are so strongly identified with specific cultures or with the broader values of human civilization that to allow them to deteriorate or disappear would be unthinkable. But the case for preservation is not always so obvious, especially with items of more recent origin. For example, what should become of the empty factories and smokestacks left in the wake of technological progress? Should they be preserved as monuments to the industrial age? Or should they be torn down and replaced with new structures that would be more appropriate in a post-industrial society?

An obvious difficulty with such decisions is the fact that we cannot predict how peoples' evaluations of heritage might change over time. A case in point is the Dutch windmills. In the mid-nineteenth century, the advent of steam pumps made windmills obsolete. Dutch farmers wanted to pull them down because these structures had become useless to them and were a nuisance on their land. But groups of conservation-minded citizens campaigned to save the mills, buying up a number of them to prevent their destruction. A few decades later the Dutch Government stepped in and took over responsibility for their preservation. Now most Dutch people, perhaps even the farmers, appreciate the sight of windmills in their landscape, and, even more significantly, these objects have become an internationally recognized symbol of the Netherlands.

The windmills happened to be saved, but other old buildings and sites are torn down or allowed to deteriorate. The loss of the old would seem to be the price of progress; this is only to be expected in a future-oriented century. Paradoxically, the twentieth century also made major efforts towards the preservation and conservation of the past. International organizations – ICCROM, ICOM, ICOMOS, UNESCO and others – national governments, semi-governmental and non-governmental organizations and agencies, corporations and private citizens are active in supporting museums (the primary institutions for the collection and conservation of relics of the past), maintaining archaeological sites and historic buildings, organizing conferences and workshops, and lobbying politicians and bureaucrats. Change apparently also inspires people to re-evaluate their past and appreciate their cultural heritage.

What should be saved and what should be let go in the name of progress? The decision may be a matter of emotion or artistic judgement. Inevitably, it will also be a matter of cost. The present paper examines the economic dimensions of cultural heritage decisions and discusses the uses and limitations of economic analysis in considering heritage issues. Our discussion is primarily directed towards tangible cultural heritage, broadly defined as those items, structures, sites and so on that are considered culturally significant to a defined group of people. Our interpretation of heritage includes both movable items, such as free-standing artworks and artefacts, and immovable heritage items such as buildings, sites and urban locations. Our definition does not include natural heritage such as landscapes or environmental features, although there may well be important connections between environmental and cultural phenomena in particular cases. Neither does our consideration extend to intangible cultural heritage such as customs, mores, oral traditions, language, literature or music, although it should be recognized that the discussion of heritage in general applies equally to tangible and intangible forms.[1]

Why economic questions are important for cultural heritage

Arguments for heritage preservation are usually based on artistic, historical, archaeological and cultural assessment. Hence conservation decisions have largely been the province of art historians, archaeologists, architects, urban planners and cultural theorists, either in their own right as cultural workers on heritage projects or in museums and galleries, or as expert advisers to governments or other agencies. However, it is undeniable that there are significant economic dimensions to heritage decisions, even if one uses the word 'economic' simply to denote 'financial'. Consider the case of Venice. Its value as heritage is beyond question, whether in terms of individual buildings or, more importantly, as an aggregate whose cultural value as a whole would generally be regarded as even greater than the sum of its parts. Yet in the management of the city, officials face choices that are clearly economic in nature. The resources available to maintain the city are by no means unlimited. Moreover, whatever financial revenues are brought in by tourism must be weighed against the cost of maintenance resulting from the large crowds and the inevitable wearing away of culturally significant property. And there are questions as to how far 'user-pays' solutions can be employed in Venice in charging tourists for their cultural experiences as a means of contributing to the city's upkeep. It is not surprising, then, that cultural managers, not just in Venice but around the world, are becoming increasingly aware of economic considerations in their daily work.[2] Nor is it surprising that economists themselves have recently begun to take a greater interest in studying heritage matters, given the fascinating economic problems that arise in this field.[3]

We shall here identify several issues and concepts fundamental to economic analysis that are helpful in looking at cultural heritage decisions. First, the science of economics highlights the phenomenon of scarcity and the choices it necessitates. Accordingly, economists are inclined to insist upon the sobering fact of the scarcity of material and human resources available for allocation to heritage conservation. We cannot conserve everything, hence a choice must be made. Second, resources are costly; if they are used for the maintenance and preservation of heritage, they are not available for other uses, so they incur opportunity costs. The range of tangible and intangible costs involved in heritage decisions is extensive and multifaceted. Third, this analysis will demonstrate that cultural heritage as an asset is comparable to Nature; if no resources are invested for upkeep, such heritage will lose its value, deteriorate and perhaps disappear altogether. Fourth, the analysis calls attention to the preferences of potential 'consumers' of cultural heritage. Experts and enthusiasts may value a monument highly, but economic analysis will pose the question whether those who pay (e.g. taxpayers) are willing to keep paying. A problem arises when taxpayers' preferences are out of line with those of the heritage experts who are making decisions and spending money on their behalf. In that case those who care are not the same as those who pay. And this is a problem from the economic point of view.

In a world in which we may assume that individual utility-maximizing behaviour motivates action, economics is biased towards market solutions for the allocation of scarce resources. Economic orthodoxy states that freely functioning markets are the best means for the desires of consumers for goods and services to be matched by the willingness of producers to supply those goods and services. According to this orthodox view, markets are not only efficient in their allocation of scarce resources, but they also ensure that those who pay the price are the very same people who benefit from the transaction. After all, participation is voluntary: nobody is forced to pay, so when people pay, they do so because they believe they will gain something.

However, economists have also acknowledged that market economics do not always work. For example, corporations may wield excessive power and charge exorbitant prices, and neither producers nor consumers may be well enough informed to make good decisions. Peoples' preferences may be distorted by misleading advertising; market arrangements may clash with spiritual and human values (this is why trading in human beings and, in most countries, human organs is outlawed); and some economic activities may produce unintended spillover effects on others. Finally, some goods that everyone wants, like clean air or a safe country to live in, may not be tradable on a market at all. The last example concerns what are termed collective or public goods: once such goods are produced, everyone may benefit from them without being made to pay, and no one can be excluded from enjoying their benefits.

Cultural heritage may be said to fall into this last category of non-tradable goods, and a certain economic problem, even a failure, characterizes the market for cultural heritage. The benefits of cultural heritage items are generally so diffuse that we could not expect them to be negotiated in market transactions. Consider an old monument in the middle of a town square. The people of the town, at least the majority of them, may care for the monument, and may be willing to pay for its maintenance – but will they continue to do so if they realize that others may enjoy the monument without paying anything at all? But how could future generations of townspeople be charged for the benefits *they* will enjoy? There is no market arrangement that assures that all those who benefit pay the price. A similar question arises about the pyramids of Egypt. Are the Egyptians to pay for the costs of their upkeep, when people all over the world value their preservation? If we were to leave the preservation of the town's monument or the Egyptian pyramids to market forces alone, it is likely that neither would be sufficiently cared for and both could eventually disappear.

Nevertheless, when a heritage item does have a direct value in use for individuals, markets can come into play. People will buy paintings, go to exhibitions in museums or visit historic buildings and sites because 'cultural consumption' seems important to them. Their willingness to pay real money for these experiences may be sufficient to define property rights, set up a market and determine a price. In fact, by establishing these 'use values', the market is enlisted to help finance the maintenance of many

Heritage conservation and urban redevelopment: the case of Nagahama

Nagahama is a small town of 50,000 inhabitants located in Shiga Prefecture in Japan. Since Hideyoshi Toyotomi built a castle there at the end of the sixteenth century, it has been a thriving commercial centre. During the 1980s, however, like other towns in Japan, Nagahama stagnated and went into economic decline. In 1988 a project was initiated there to reverse this decline through the rehabilitation of the cultural heritage and the encouragement of a particular cultural industry.

At the junction of two main streets in the town centre stands a building dating from the Meiji era originally constructed as the Kurokabe Bank. In 1987 it was scheduled for demolition, but the Nagahama town council stepped in and called for proposals to restore it. Accordingly, the council, together with eight private companies, set up a new 'third-sector' enterprise called Kurokabe Inc. to undertake the restoration project. The companies and the town invested 90 million yen and 40 million yen respectively to establish Kurokabe Inc., which purchased the building the following year. It was decided to use both the traditional and the modern crafts of glassware as the basis for the town's development strategy. The former Kurokabe Bank was converted into the Kurokabe Glassware House selling high-grade imported glassware; a new glassware workshop was built; and a restaurant converted from a warehouse was opened, serving food with glass tableware made by local artists. With these three buildings, Kurokabe Inc. started Kurokabe Square in 1989, and in the short period of only nine months had attracted one hundred thousand visitors. Since then Kurokabe Inc. has gone on to renovate some thirty old houses nearby and has opened shops, restaurants and galleries. At the present time Kurokabe Square itself comprises thirty buildings, mostly converted from old structures such as warehouses, merchant houses and so on. By 1998 annual sales had reached almost 900 million yen and visitors were numbered at 1.8 million per year.

The success of the Kurokabe Square project can be attributed to several factors. The judicious mix of old and new – historic sites put to new uses – was a good one. In addition the management strategy using a third-sector enterprise provided an ideal vehicle for co-operation between private and public sectors. Furthermore, in promoting glass, the project was able to develop simultaneously the creation, display and sale of glassware, thus providing for a balanced expansion of an important cultural industry.

Kurokabe Square has proved to be a catalyst for further cultural development in the town. The project has attracted more people to pre-existing performing arts events such as the *Bonbai* (potted plum trees) exhibition in spring, a boys' *kabuki* performance on the decorated float of the *Hikiyama-maturi* Festival and a fireworks festival in summer. Visitors to the Square are also attracted to other nearby cultural sites such as temples, shrines, museums, historic sites and parks. Prompted by the success of Kurokabe Square, the town council and private sector are considering further capital-investment projects, including new museums and venues, to follow up the cultural and economic development of the town.

All things considered, the Kurokabe Square project in Nagahama is a telling example of the way in which cultural heritage restoration and reuse can be combined with a specific cultural industry to promote urban regeneration and revitalization. Kurokabe Inc. also provides a model for public/private co-operation in managing this type of urban development project: it is a model that could well be applied in other parts of the world.

EMIKO KAKIUCHI
Institutional Relations Officer,
Institute of Advanced Studies,
United Nations University, Tokyo (Japan)

heritage items throughout the world, for example, through visitation charges levied on tourists at museums, galleries and sites.

Thus, when considering the economic dimensions of a heritage item, whether a painting by Van Gogh or a building such as the Taj Mahal, we must recognize the difference between the item's direct use values which can indeed be expressed through market transactions, and those non-market benefits or 'non-use values' which cannot be traded. Now let us consider more closely how non-use values function. People all over the world may derive pleasure and satisfaction from simply knowing that Van Gogh's paintings and the Taj Mahal exist. Economists refer to this phenomenon as *existence value*. Additionally, people may hope that one day they might be able to purchase a Van Gogh (or see one in a museum) or visit the Taj Mahal, or they may like to know that these opportunities are available to others. Such benefits are known as *option values*, since they reflect the value to individuals of preserving an option for future consumption either by themselves or by other people. Similarly, many people are concerned that heritage items should be passed on intact to future generations, just as we today have inherited items from the past. In other words, people attribute a value to the Van Gogh and the Taj Mahal because they can be bequeathed as a historical legacy to the future; these benefits are called the bequest value of heritage items. The question for economists is how to determine these values, both use and non-use, when the preservation of some heritage asset is at stake.

Assessing economic and cultural value

It is apparent that one of the most fundamental questions in any discussion of heritage conservation relates to assessing the value of the particular item. Indeed, as we noted earlier, an assessment of value is essential to the very definition of cultural heritage itself. How can an item be given a value reflecting the many different types of benefits that it might bestow? Even a superficial consideration of this question brings to light the tension that exists between the economic value of cultural heritage and what might be thought of as its cultural value. This issue is not new: the great nineteenth-century economist and art critic John Ruskin railed against the classical political economists for trying to place a commercial value on everything. He asserted that art transcended such worldly measurements.[4] Here we shall consider how modern economics tries to grapple with the question of valuation.

Let us begin with a very simple case. As regards direct-use values for which markets exist, economists know that the price mechanism, operating via voluntary exchange, establishes an objective measure of value. When several parties bid for a good that is unique or costly due to high production costs, the price will be accordingly high. If a Monet is offered for sale, its value is obvious from the price that someone is willing to pay for it. That price will be affected by a number of factors, some 'economic', some 'cultural'. For instance, one of the economic influences on price will be a market assessment of the value of the Monet as a financial asset: is its value likely to rise further in future, providing a handsome capital appreciation to the purchaser even if he or she locks the painting away in a bank vault, and even cares nothing for its qualities as art?[5] At the same time, the price the Monet fetches at auction will reflect something of the position this artist has been accorded in the pantheon of painters, and how this particular work is ranked within his œuvre; thus price is also influenced by what could be regarded as purely cultural or aesthetic considerations. Furthermore, price is affected by authenticity; an exact copy of the Monet will sell for a mere fraction of the price of the real thing, even though it may be indistinguishable from the original.

Similarly, the direct-use value of immovable heritage is measurable by market price. These include the entrance fees people pay to visit historic sites, museums, exhibitions and so forth, or the rental paid by tenants in a building classified as a historical monument and which has been refitted as commercial space; such prices indicate the direct and tangible economic value of the services produced by these heritage items.

But we have already pointed out that direct-use value, which we expect to be reflected in market prices, is only one component of the value of an item of cultural heritage. To derive the total economic value we must add the non-use values as well, and these may in many cases be far greater than the market price. Economists have developed techniques for measuring non-use value, principal among which is the contingent valuation method (CVM). Essentially CVM entails asking consumers, under hypothetical conditions, how much they would be willing to pay in order to maintain the intangible benefits they enjoy from a particular heritage item, or how much compensation they would be willing to accept for the loss of those benefits. Thus, for example, the inhabitants of the town with the ancient monument in the square might be asked how much they would be willing to contribute to a fund to provide for the upkeep of the monument, and their responses could be expected to reflect the value they place on the monument as a symbol of a shared cultural heritage. But some of the difficulties associated with CVM immediately suggest themselves. For example, people might conceal their true willingness to pay, believing that even if they paid nothing, the monument would still be preserved via the contributions of others (the 'free-rider' problem). Furthermore, the hypothetical nature of the question might cause respondents not to take it seriously, and hence not to express their real valuations. Additionally, how could a researcher be sure that all potential beneficiaries, or all possible sources of non-use value, have been accounted for in any experiment or survey, so that the aggregate willingness to pay really does measure the total non-use value of the item?

Despite these difficulties, CVM techniques, which have been extensively used in valuing environmental amenities, have recently begun to be applied to the valuation of cultural heritage.[6] Economics also offers other techniques for evaluation, such as impact studies (measuring the broad economic impact of investment in cultural heritage), hedonic market methods (the valuation of non-market goods is inferred from demands for other related goods) and referendums (people are asked to vote on public expenditures on cultural heritage). None of these techniques is perfect, but used together they can provide important indications of the non-use values attached to cultural heritage and as such can inform and enlighten decisions that might otherwise be based on purely financial outcomes.

Yet a nagging question remains. Suppose that all possible use and non-use values have been measured in an exercise aimed at assessing the value of an item of cultural heritage, such that the total valuation represents the true economic 'price' that people are prepared to pay for the item's tangible and intangible benefits, measured in terms of the other material goods and services they are collectively prepared to give up in order to obtain those benefits. Is this the full story? Or is there simultaneously some other value scale that also reflects the worth of the item, measured according to a quite different set of criteria? For want of a better term, we might call that other measure the item's 'cultural value'. Suppose, for the moment, that we limit this to purely aesthetic value, however it might be determined. We must ask whether there is any reason why a ranking, say, of

UNESCO CULTURAL
CONVENTIONS
COUNTRIES
Bhutan
Chad
Eritrea
Guinea-Bissau
Lesotho
Liberia
Republic of Moldova
Namibia
Rwanda
Sierra Leone
Singapore
Somalia
Trinidad and Tobago
United Arab Emirates

GRAPH 9
COUNTRIES THAT HAVE RATIFIED NONE OF THE UNESCO CULTURAL CONVENTIONS:
Protection of the world cultural and natural heritage (1972), Protection of cultural property in the event of armed conflict (1954), and Means of prohibiting and preventing the illicit import, export and transfert of cultural property (1970).

Source: See the Index of culture indicators and sources and Table 13 in Part Seven of this report.

Putting a value on the invaluable: the case of Fez Medina

In the ancient Moroccan city of Fez Medina – a city said to be outside time – mules still lug goods through crowded narrow streets and metalworkers bang on copper in tiny storefronts. In 1976, Fez Medina's historical and cultural importance led UNESCO to declare it a World Heritage Sites. But today Fez Medina – a religious centre for more than a thousand years, a showcase of architectural beauty and a cultural relic of Morocco – is also a city in serious disrepair, threatened by a crumbling infrastructure, devastating pollution and poverty.

With the approval of two loans for a total of $14 million in 1998, the World Bank contributed to the international effort to restore and rehabilitate the walled city while preserving its artistic, spiritual and cultural prominence. The Rehabilitation of Fez Medina project will assist in preserving and improving the Medina of Fez, with particular attention to the historic housing stocks and the quality of urban environment by means of direct intervention and efforts to increase private conservation efforts.

An empirical study was undertaken by the World Bank using the contingent valuation method (CVM) and a Delphi exercise (solicitation of opinion of experts) to measure some of the economic benefits accruing to the project's successful completion. These methods have been used to value public goods by establishing what people would be willing to pay for specified improvements on them (in this case the reconstruction of the Fez Medina). The methods are thus aimed at eliciting willingness to pay in dollar amounts.

Economic benefits from the project involving the Fez Medina can be divided into five categories depending upon the beneficiary. In category 1 are those benefits accruing directly to residents of Fez; in category 2 are those accruing to Moroccans who are not residents of Fez; in category 3 are those accruing to foreign visitors to Fez; in category 4 are those accruing to foreign visitors to Morocco who do not visit Fez during their current trip; and in category 5 are those accruing to non-Moroccans who do not visit Morocco. The present study did not consider any of the potential benefits to Moroccans (categories 1 and 2), but concentrated rather on attempting to quantify as far as possible the potential benefits likely to accrue to non-Moroccans if the project were undertaken.

For the CVM component of the study, a sample of 600 adults was surveyed representing both tourists and those visiting Morocco for business or other purposes in June–July 1997. Respondents were provided with information about the Fez Medina and the proposal for its rehabilitation. They were asked how much they would be prepared to contribute, by way of a special fee, to help finance the project. In the Delphi study a sample of thirty CVM experts was surveyed in order to obtain their estimates of what they thought mean and median willingness to pay for the Fez rehabilitation project might be among European residents.

The results of this study suggested that the economic benefits deriving from the project are extremely high once the use and non-use values of this cultural heritage are considered. Extremely conservative estimates (based on the CVM and Delphi analysis) showed that:

- for foreign visitors to Fez, the total annual value of the Fez Medina project is equal to about $11 million;
- for non-Fez foreign visitors to Morocco, the total annual value of the Fez Medina project is equal to almost $47 million; and
- for European (including Norway and Switzerland) households, the total annual value of the Fez Medina project amounts to several hundred million dollars.

Even if only a fraction of the amount of benefits received by visitors (an annual total of about $58 million) could be captured in Morocco – for example by increasing the tourist tax – it would generate a substantial annual income flow which could be used to finance the required conservation investment for Fez and other sites and far outweigh the project cost of $14 million.

It is important, though, to remember that economic analysis should not be the only method used in deciding if it is worthwhile pursuing a project. Other criteria, including social, cultural and political aspects, should be considered. Economic analysis is only one of the many useful tools available to help decision-makers make more informed decisions. (For further details of this study, see Ismail Serageldin, *Very Special Places: The Architecture and Economics of Intervening in Historic Cities*, Washington D.C., World Bank, 1999.)

PAOLA AGOSTINI
Environmental and Natural Resources Economist,
World Bank, Washington D.C. (United States)

paintings according to purely aesthetic criteria would, other things being equal, be the same as a ranking in terms of economic value. There may be a correlation, perhaps a high correlation, but there is no reason why the two lists should coincide perfectly. In other words, a measurement of an item's aesthetic value, which clearly has some importance in its own right and may exercise some influence over people's decision-making, including their economic decision-making, may nevertheless not be fully captured by an economic valuation, no matter how thoroughly that valuation might have been calculated.

The final conclusion of these considerations is to argue for a dual approach to the valuation of cultural heritage. There is no doubt that experts and decision-makers in art history, conservation, archaeology, urban planning and so on can scarcely afford to ignore the economic dimensions of the decisions they make in valuing cultural heritage, especially if those decisions have policy implications for the organizations or government authorities which they serve. By the same token, economists assessing the value of items of cultural heritage cannot assume that all cultural dimensions are expressed, even in principle, by their evaluation techniques. A comprehensive assessment needs to account for both the economic and the cultural values of the item under consideration.

Nevertheless, it must be recognized that measurement problems are likely to present substantial difficulties in any real-world application. Finding

UNESCO CULTURAL CONVENTIONS

COUNTRIES

Argentina	France	Nigeria
Armenia	Georgia	Oman
Australia	Greece	Pakistan
Belarus	Guatemala	Panama
Bosnia and Herzegovina	Guinea	Peru
Brazil	Hungary	Poland
Bulgaria	India	Qatar
Burkina Faso	Iran (Islamic Republic of)	Romania
Cambodia	Iraq	Russian Federation
Cameroon	Italy	Saudi Arabia
Canada	Jordan	Senegal
Colombia	Kyrgyzstan	Slovakia
Costa Rica	Latvia	Slovenia
Côte d'Ivoire	Lebanon	Spain
Croatia	Libyan Arab Jamahiriya	Syrian Arab Republic
Cuba	Luxembourg	Tajikistan
Cyprus	Madagascar	Tunisia
Czech Republic	Mali	Turkey
Democratic Republic of the Congo	Mexico	Ukraine
Dominican Republic	Mongolia	United Republic of Tanzania
Ecuador	Nicaragua	Uzbekistan
Egypt	Niger	Yugoslavia
Estonia		

GRAPH 10
COUNTRIES THAT HAVE RATIFIED THE THREE UNESCO CULTURAL CONVENTIONS
Protection of the world cultural and natural heritage (1972), Protection of cultural property in the event of armed conflict (1954), and Means of prohibiting and preventing the illicit import, export and transfert of cultural property (1970).

Source: See the Index of culture indicators and sources and Table 13 in Part Seven of this report.

an economic value is more straightforward, because at least there exists a quantitative rule by means of which different aspects of value can be reduced to a common denominator. Thus, whether one is dealing with the direct costs of conservation or the opportunity costs of resources involved in heritage activities, or whether one takes into account market price as a measure of tangible benefit or willingness to pay as an indicator of intangible worth, the economic value of a heritage item can, at least in principle, be aggregated by reference to a standard yardstick, namely money, a commodity which is readily exchangeable for all other material goods and services in the economy. On the other hand, however, the cultural value of heritage is by its very nature non-material and multi-faceted, and includes, among other things, aesthetic, historical, spiritual, social and symbolic elements. Furthermore, not only are there multiple dimensions to the notion of cultural worth, but there are no consistent or agreed value scales against which these characteristics can be measured. And even if systematic measurement within individual characteristics were possible, attempts to combine them into a single measure of cultural value would be a daunting task indeed.

Heritage as asset

Money spent on cultural heritage is sometimes compared to money spent on ice cream: once it is eaten, it is gone and all that remains is a sweet memory. But, cultural heritage is not like ice cream. Money spent on it is not money wasted because the value it produces remains or perhaps increases. Cultural heritage, so economists propose, is therefore better thought of as an asset like a machine or Nature. A cathedral or a palace is real estate whose investment value is likely to increase over time; the same applies to the art collections of museums such as the Louvre or the Prado. In economic terms, these buildings and collections are capital stock that provide a flow of services over an extended period of time. Money spent on such capital is thus money invested. Money spent on the improvement of an archeological site adds to the value of that site, that is, increases the flow of services.

However, we economists will hasten to add that cultural heritage usually differs from other capital stock like houses and factories because it generates cultural value and, in some cases, economic value like income. Therefore it is better to call it 'cultural capital', defined as an asset which embodies or contributes to cultural value, as discussed in the previous section. Because items of cultural capital specifically invoke cultural value in this way, they are distinguished as assets from other forms of physical economic capital. A building of no cultural significance exists just as a building, valued as an asset simply for its economic worth, and it provides a flow of services whose value could be measured entirely in economic terms. But a building that is classified historically next door has an asset value measurable in both economic and cultural terms and provides services with both economic and cultural dimensions. Thus in assessing the latter building's asset characteristics, such as its rate of depreciation, optimal level of maintenance and the rate of return it earns, we should be mindful that cultural as well as economic value must be taken into account.[7]

Considering heritage items as cultural capital also introduces the long-term nature of the benefits that heritage provides. In particular it stresses the fact that those of us alive today have inherited these cultural assets as a result of the investment and conservation decisions of the past, and that our actions in either caring for or neglecting the assets during our custodianship of them will affect the extent to which future generations can benefit from them. The management of resources over time in the light of future benefits which the uses of those resources may yield is an important question of economic efficiency. It is also an issue that raises ethical questions: to what extent does the present generation have a moral or ethical responsibility to provide for future generations? This is by no means a new idea. In the middle of the industrial revolution, John Ruskin warned his contemporaries against the destruction of beautiful old things for the sake of progress when he wrote:

> [Be] it heard or not, I must not leave the truth unstated, that it is again no question of expediency or feeling whether we shall preserve the buildings of past times or not. *We have no right whatever to touch them.* They are not

ours. They belong partly to those who built them, and partly to all the generations of mankind who are to follow us (Ruskin, 1880, p. 197; emphasis in original).

The phenomenon of inter-generational equity – fairness in the treatment of future inhabitants of this planet – is a crucial aspect of sustainability, a concept that has been widely discussed in relation to management of natural resources and ecosystems. Indeed, some parallels might be drawn between decisions relating to natural capital – defined as the stock of natural resources such as minerals, forests, fish stocks, soil fertility, environmental features and the ecological systems of air, land and water that support them – and those relating to cultural capital as defined above. Here again the question of equity comes to the fore. It can be suggested that, just as we have a responsibility to care for the natural environment if humankind is to survive and prosper, so also do we bear a similar responsibility towards the cultural environment, in particular towards heritage. Thus, for example, just as it is generally accepted that precautions are warranted if our actions threaten a biological species with extinction, so also might it be proposed that caution be exercised in the management of heritage assets which, if destroyed, could never be replaced.

Policy issues

In this paper we have interpreted cultural heritage in economic terms as a case characterized by significant market failure. When markets fail, some alternative arrangement is required in order to bring about a socially desirable outcome. Since there is generally very little one single individual acting alone can do to rectify a problem on the scale of an entire market, some form of collective intervention is needed. It may be effected through governments acting at local, regional, national or international levels on behalf of their constituencies to purchase, maintain, restore, subsidize and provide or regulate access to heritage items of all sorts. Alternatively, or in addition, collective action to remedy market failure in the heritage area may occur voluntarily through the activities of NGOs, corporations, community groups, philanthropists or foundations, many of which already provide financial support, expertise and voluntary labour to museums, galleries, sites, buildings, archaeological projects and so forth.

From an economic point of view, it can be argued that the active involvement of individuals and non-profit organizations presents advantages over government involvement. When governments provide the funds for the upkeep of a monument or the purchase of a painting for a museum collection, every taxpayer must pay, although perhaps only a few of them will benefit. And how many really care? Even when research points to a willingness to pay for cultural heritage or to significant economic advantages of a given public investment in cultural heritage (e.g. from tourist revenues), economists will worry about such things as distorted incentives and rent-seeking behaviour (the efforts of people pressuring politicians for a so-called public good while benefiting themselves from the government action). When individuals or foundations invest funds in cultural heritage, such worries tend to disappear, because in that case we can be assured that those who pay are also those who care. Certainly other people may benefit from such an investment, but that is apparently the purpose of the benefactors. For example, when English citizens donate money to the National Trust they clearly want others besides the members of the Trust to be able to appreciate British heritage.

Sociologists recognize in such private initiatives the operation of the so-called 'third sphere' or, to use a more popular term, 'civil society'. Distinct from the market and government spheres, this sphere consists of voluntary associations such as families, societies and non-profit organizations. Interactions are based on reciprocity in the form of gifts, as when citizens donate money to foundations or other NGOs which, in turn, donate funds for cultural heritage projects. Private initiatives are not limited by national boundaries. The American Getty Foundation, for example, supports cultural heritage projects all over the world. Sociologists will always point out that third-sphere activities usually express a sense of responsibility and of involvement that easily gets lost when markets or governments dominate. Conversely, foundations may lose the motivation and the persuasion to solicit funds for cultural heritage projects when govern-

Community mobilization for heritage conservation and development

Cultural heritage conservation depends upon the commitment and involvement of local communities. Policy-makers as well as conservators have come to recognize that for protection regulations to be effectively implemented and socially acceptable, populations living in or near heritage sites must be given a leading role in the development of conservation policies as well as in the management of the sites.

It is within this context that UNESCO has formulated the Local Effort And Preservation (LEAP) Project to model and test a process whereby local communities are encouraged to assume an active stewardship over the heritage and are empowered to develop that heritage in a responsible, profitable and sustainable manner. LEAP is a development project that demonstrates that the preservation of heritage is not a luxury for developed economies. The project's full title is 'Integrated Community Development and Cultural Heritage Preservation through Local Effort'. It models preservation as an activity that can bring economic opportunities and serve as a tool for job creation, income generation and thus poverty alleviation, based on traditional technologies, locally available materials and the human resources of a local community.

In order to accomplish this, the LEAP programme aims to empower inhabitants in local communities to:

- understand and advocate the sustained conservation of locally-significant monuments, sites and the material and intangible traditions uniquely associated with local culture;
- play a leading role in actual hands-on conservation and preservation work, as well as in the interpretation of the heritage values which are to be safeguarded; and
- develop the means through which they can benefit financially from the enhanced conservation of the heritage.

The programme was first developed and tested in the Asia-Pacific region. Analysing the situation of the current populations of most heritage sites in Asia and the Pacific, we find that they are direct descendants of the original builders of that heritage. Accordingly, future economic and social development in heritage sites in the region based on traditional, indigenous cultural values and practices are likely to be the most acceptable and sustainable solutions in the long run. This is an underlying assumption of the project.

However, within the region, the permutations and combinations of local settlement and the heritage are complex. The people living on historic cultural sites in Asia/Pacific typically find themselves in at least one of the following four situations with respect to the site. They may be:

- urban inhabitants of the historic towns or the centres of ancient cities such as Kathmandu (Nepal), Lijiang (China), Hoi An (Viet Nam) or Vigan (Philippines). In such cases, the local populations often live in – and may in fact be the proprietors of – the protected buildings.
- communal inhabitants of religious or otherwise public historic monuments who continue to use historic monuments for the purposes for which they were built. Luang Prabang (Lao PDR) and Kandy (Sri Lanka) are examples of sites where such occupation and stewardship of heritage sites is a continuing tradition.
- rural inhabitants of cultural landscapes such as the rice terraces of the Philippines Cordilleras, the Tonle Sap floodplains of the Angkor region in Cambodia, Inle Lake in Myanmar, Lake Toba on the Island of Sumatra in Indonesia, Mustang in Nepal, or the Hunza and Swat Valleys of Pakistan. The fact that the inhabitants use traditional farming techniques and traditional equipment is often in large part responsible for maintaining the authenticity of the landscape.
- people who live on or near archaeological sites, who are often unaware that there is history contained in the ground below them (at least until antique hunters apprise them of the fact). Fortunately, because traditional domestic architecture construction techniques throughout the region are typically non-invasive, the underground archaeological remains at such places as Ban Chiang (Thailand), Khar Bulgas (Mongolia), or the Plain of Jars (Lao PDR) are still intact.

There are a number of threats to the continued survival of historic properties and the stock of regional cultural capital. These threats include population growth, environmental degradation, the transformation of subsistence farming and the loss of traditional land-use methods and, finally, the pressures of unsustainable tourism development.

The basic approach used for implementation of the LEAP project involves initiating a variety of community participatory activities which act as the catalyst for local community interest groups to assess the unique characteristics, strengths and economic potential of the elements making up their physical as well as intangible cultural heritage, and then to design a community action plan to self-develop these elements in a way that is both profitable and sustainable. Through the project, assistance is provided in the form of practical, technical peer advice and, if needed, small start-up grants or loans.

The project's implementation strategy has an overtly political objective: it demonstrates how heritage conservation can be an effective tool for job-creation and income generation, and thus for poverty alleviation, by promoting custodianship over the heritage and by empowering local communities to develop their heritage in a responsible, sustainable and profitable manner. Through this strategy, heritage preservation becomes a development activity that stimulates economic opportunities by using traditional skills and indigenous resources available in the community.

Activities vary from site to site, depending upon circumstance and need, and are continually evolving, yet are built around three thematic 'entry points':

1. Practical training in heritage preservation and management is provided through reinforcement of local-level endogenous capacity. This means working with, among others, local town and site managers, neighbourhood wardens, local businessmen and women, women's and youth groups and temple priests in order to develop popularly-accepted zoning and environmental management plans for both preservation and development of historic areas. The resulting preserved areas can be as small as a neighbourhood street or park, or large enough to encompass the entire community and its surrounding landscape. This strategy includes training in the use of basic management tools such as mapping and computer-aided geographic information systems in order to demystify these technologies and make their advantages available to local citizens so that they may become competent managers of their own habitats.
2. Fostering community participation in heritage preservation, particularly in urban areas, through public-private partnerships to develop this heritage in an economically sustainable way (which may or may not involve adaptive reuse of the facilities), and through these efforts engender a stewardship ethic. Public archaeology programmes based in local schools, open to the community-at-large, have proven useful in generating an ethic of local stewardship over a common, shared heritage.
3. Recruiting the potential of cultural tourism as a tool for the preservation and enhancement of both the physical and intangible heritage. This involves developing training for and promotion of community-based tourism-related occupations grounded in the interpretation of local culture and history. Such promotion efforts also restore pride in local heritage, inspire the desire to manage the heritage well and thus attract business to restored historic areas. The project is stimulating a paradigm shift in heritage conservation from an élite technical specialization practised only by a handful of experts to a popular grass-roots movement where individuals assume responsibility for, and local communities take on the stewardship of, the heritage.

If the LEAP project proves to be successful in linking economic development with the preservation of culture and heritage, then something very important and far-reaching will have been accomplished. Heritage preservation will be brought into universal play throughout the Asia/Pacific region as a tool for an endogenous and sustainable economic and human development that is appropriate to a particular locale.

RICHARD A. ENGELHARDT
UNESCO Regional Advisor for Culture in Asia and the Pacific, UNESCO Principal Regional Office for Asia and the Pacific (Thailand)

ments already tax citizens for precisely the same purpose.

At the beginning of the twentieth century, third-sphere initiatives were significant for establishing cultural heritage on an agenda. Dutch citizens founded private societies to preserve the windmills and the British set up their heritage trust funds. These initiatives were taken by citizens for the sake of the common good. Shortly thereafter governments began to assert an expanded role for the state in the realm of heritage. Policy-makers began to show an interest in heritage, and civil servants devised a variety of policies to manage that interest, including direct ownership of cultural heritage sites or buildings, the subsidization of private owners (including societies and foundations), tax breaks, regulations (including listing) and the organization and financing of information and education programmes.[8] In the economic appraisal of these policies, two questions arise: first, the value of the project under consideration must be compared with alternative projects or programmes, and second, the effects of policies on the incentives of those who care for and benefit from heritage assets must be explored. Let us pose these questions for the principal policy options listed above.

When a cultural heritage site or other item is under public ownership, the market is by-passed and the government is left to determine how much expenditure is justified.[9] Do taxpayers agree, especially if the main beneficiaries of the expenditure are foreign tourists? Might there be some better way of spending the money? It is easier to ask these questions than to answer them, although economists can help to assign a value to the heritage which may assist decision-making. The incentive question arises in this case because of the absence of competition; the willingness of people to volunteer time and money to support the heritage item may be reduced when an all-powerful government is in charge. The general conclusion is that alternative forms of intervention to direct ownership may be preferable in many cases, although it has to be recognized that public ownership is generally indicated when the collective nature of the asset is beyond question (as in the case of national monuments or significant national institutions) or when handling the asset is too complex to be left to private parties (as in the case of city squares and ancient temples).

Governments can also subsidize organizations or individuals who take care of cultural heritage items. In such cases the government relinquishes some control, leaving decision-making in the hands of the subsidized organizations or individuals themselves. In these circumstances there may be a danger of rent-seeking behaviour by those caretakers anxious to increase the amounts of subsidy they receive. As Sir Alan Peacock has observed: '[Art administrators] delude themselves into believing that they are perpetually underfunded [and] conduct continuous action designed to remove the constraint' (1997, p. 227). One mechanism for providing an incentive to the private parties to continue to seek support elsewhere is for the government to award subsidies in the form of matching grants, that is, grants that will match funds that are raised in the private sector.

Subsidies show up in the government's budget. Their allocation usually requires decisions from policy-makers and the responsible government officials. But governments can also use a less obvious instrument in the form of tax measures. These include granting non-profit status to heritage organizations, allowing reductions in value-added and property tax, and providing for tax-deductible donations and the like. Lower tax revenues will result, but the amount of the decrease will not appear in the government's budget. So, for example, a tax-deductible gift of a million dollars to a museum will cost the treasury half a million in tax revenues if the marginal tax rate is fifty per cent, but the collective taxpayers who have contributed that half a million to the museum do not get the credit for their generosity, because it does not show anywhere explicitly. Nevertheless, economists tend to favour tax measures in bringing about economic change because such measures are most effective in stimulating the incentives of individuals and organizations. Thus in the case of cultural heritage, an individual who considers donating a valuable painting to a local museum may be encouraged to do so if he can deduct the value from his income before taxes. Policy-makers, on the other hand, tend to prefer subsidies because they suggest more direct influence and also because they show explicitly how much the government cares for its cultural heritage.

Regulation entails the formulation and enforcement of rules, codes and standards governing any action that might affect some item of cultural heritage. A distinction can be made between hard and soft regulation (Throsby, 1997). The government may legislate that a heritage item must not be destroyed and that it will be properly conserved, with the threat of punishment for those who break this law; this is hard regulation. Soft regulation consists of voluntary covenants and treaties and lacks any punitive element. An important regulatory tool is listing, i.e. placing heritage assets on an official list. When an item is included in an official list of cultural heritage, its owners are obliged to conserve it. Various requirements may be specified with a listing, such as the stipulation that no alterations be made that affect the original state of the item. Listing is a case of hard regulation because legal enforcement is possible; however, inclusion in an international list such as the UNESCO World Heritage list is a soft regulation in so far as the only possible serious sanction is the threat of being dropped from the list. Although listing may be considered an honour, it carries a responsibility too. It may also affect the price of a heritage asset, raising it in some cases (when the kudos attached to listing enhances the property's attractiveness to buyers) and diminishing it in others (when listing makes a property more difficult to sell).

Governments can also support the cause of conservation of cultural heritage by drawing attention to and giving information about threatened assets. Listing itself is one tool for this purpose; once an item is listed, more people will give it their attention by visiting it or wanting to read about it. Education is yet another tool. Recently, concerted efforts have been made to set up websites that give information about heritage assets as a means of educating the public about their importance. Although in general more information and more attention is better, some sites could probably do with less: the masses of people that visit Venice and Florence actually pose a threat to the preservation of these historic cities.

The above catalogue of instruments provides an overview of the tools which may be used by governments in giving effect to cultural heritage policy as viewed from the standpoint of economics. Consideration of these tools raises several further issues. First, there is the question of whose preferences should determine government policy towards heritage. In liberal democratic societies, governments are expected to reflect the broad will of the community in making decisions on economic, social and cultural issues. Nevertheless, there may be cases where it is felt that the public is ill-informed, uncaring or entirely ignorant about certain matters, making it necessary for governments to assert what might be regarded as a more enlightened view. Heritage is a case in point. Perhaps only a few people such as art historians, archaeologists, museum directors, curators and so on are competent to recognize the true value of heritage and give advice to governments. If so, heritage would be an example of what economists refer to as merit goods, i.e. goods whose benefits are so generally regarded as meritorious that it is appropriate for governments to provide support for them, even if people do not demand those benefits directly themselves. The economic difficulty with merit goods is that it is impossible to judge what constitutes an optimal level of provision.

The issue of whose preferences should count raises the question of the international spread of responsibility for heritage, to which we have already referred. If the Italian Government, for example, had no money for its heritage programmes, other countries might wish to assume this responsibility, since in so many respects Italian cultural heritage is the cultural heritage of the Western hemisphere. Likewise, the selling of Tibetan heritage items to non-Tibetans is a cause for international concern. These cases require international policies co-ordinated by bodies such as UNESCO, but their implementation remains problematical in the absence of effective international financing and enforcement mechanisms.

Conclusion

Economists have an important role to play in discussions and decisions about cultural heritage. We have argued in this paper that economists cannot claim to have the final word on these matters. Economic studies in the field of cultural heritage are far from conclusive and leave room for speculation and opinion. They usually fail to account, for example, for the special cultural values of cultural heritage items. Nevertheless, economic questions on value and incentives cannot be avoided when people decide to commit scarce resources to the cause of cultural heritage. Yet too often advocates of heritage projects from a conservationist perspective will emphasize cultural values without any regard to the economic values involved, including the economic value of alternative projects. And too many government programmes are designed without consideration of the incentives affecting other interested parties.

It is true that economists are preoccupied with market solutions and profit. They prefer to emphasize the bias of economists in favour of individual responsibility and democratic decision-making, because economic reasoning is all about incentives and the choices that individuals make. That is why non-market actions in the third sphere accord with the economists' bias. Where possible, economists prefer individuals and private organizations to take initiatives and assume responsibility. And if they do so by means of donations, voluntary work and non-profit status, then so much the better. Even so, economists generally acknowledge that governments have an indispensable task in taking possession of some projects, stimulating private parties, controlling the field of cultural heritage by means of regulations and information and providing resources where required to protect and advance the collective interest in looking after the cultural heritage of the world.

Bibliography

Bianca, S. 1997. Direct Government Involvement in Architectural Heritage Management: Legitimation, Limits and Opportunities of Ownership and Operation. In: J. M. Schuster et al. (eds.), pp. 13–31.

Bille Hansen, T. 1997. The Willingness-to-pay for the Royal Theatre in Copenhagen as a Public Good. *Journal of Cultural Economics*, Vol. 21, pp. 1–28.

Frey, B. S.; Pommerehne, W. W. 1989. *Muses and Markets: Explorations in the Economics of the Arts*. Oxford, Basil Blackwell.

Ginsburgh, V. A.; Menger, P.-M. (eds.). 1996. *Economics of the Arts: Selected Essays*. Amsterdam, North Holland.

Grampp, W. D. 1973. Classical Economics and its Moral Critics. *History of Political Economy*, Vol. 5, pp. 359–74.

Hausman, J. A. (ed.) 1993. *Contingent Valuation: A Critical Assessment*. Amsterdam, North Holland.

Hutter, M.; Rizzo, I. (eds.). 1997. *Economic Perspectives and Cultural Heritage*. London, Macmillan.

Klamer, A.; Zuidhof, P.-W. 1999. The Values of Cultural Heritage: Merging Economic and Cultural Appraisals. In: Getty Conservation Institute, *Economics and Heritage Conservation*, pp. 23–61. Los Angeles, GCI.

Martin, F. 1994. Determining the Size of Museum Subsidies. *Journal of Cultural Economics*, Vol. 18, pp. 255–70.

Mossetto, G. 1992. A Cultural Good Called Venice. In: R. Toure and A. Khakee (eds.). *Cultural Economics*, pp. 247–56. Berlin, Springer Verlag.

Peacock, A. 1997. Towards a Workable Heritage Policy. In: M. Hutter and I. RIZZO (eds.), pp. 225–35.

Peacock, A. (ed.). 1998. *Does the Past Have a Future? The Political Economy of Heritage*. London, Institute of Economic Affairs.

Prott, L. V. 1998. International Standards for Cultural Heritage. *World Culture Report*, pp. 222–36, Paris, UNESCO.

Ruskin, J. 1880. *The Seven Lamps of Architecture* (new edition). Orpington, George Allen.

Santagata, W.; Signorello, G. 1998. Contingent Valuation and Cultural Policy Design: The Case of 'Napoli Musei Aperti'. Paper presented at Tenth International Conference on Cultural Economics, Barcelona, Spain, 14–17 June.

Schuster, J. M. et al. (eds.). 1997. *Preserving the Built Heritage: Tools for Implementation.* Hanover, University Press of New England.

Throsby, D. 1997. Making Preservation Happen: The Pros and Cons of Regulation. In: Schuster et al. (eds.), pp. 32-48.

—— 1999. Cultural Capital. *Journal of Cultural Economics,* Vol. 23, pp. 3–12.

Notes

1. For further discussion of the definition of heritage, see contributions to Hutter and Rizzo (1997); see also Prott (1998) and Klamer and Zuidhof (1999).
2. For further discussion of Venice, see Mossetto (1992) and papers given at a conference on 'Venice as a City of Art', ICARE (International Centre for Research in Art Economics, University of Venice), 13–15 May 1991.
3. See, for example, contributions to Schuster et al. (1997), Hutter and Rizzo (1997) and Peacock (1998).
4. See Grampp (1973).
5. For an analysis of the determinants of the prices of artworks of various sorts, see, for example Frey and Pommerehne (1989, Ch. 6) and contributions to Ginsburgh and Menger (1996).
6. For a fuller account and assessment of CVM methodologies, see Hausman (1993); for some recent applications to the evaluation of cultural projects, see Martin (1994), Bille Hansen (1997), and Santagata and Signorello (1998).
7. For a fuller account of the concept of cultural capital in economics and other disciplines, see Throsby (1999).
8. In its main points, this list follows the classification of instruments articulated by Schuster et al. (1997).
9. For a discussion of public ownership and operation of cultural heritage assets, see Bianca (1997).

Chapter 9
An outline of UNESCO's actions in heritage conservation and rehabilitation

MOUNIR BOUCHENAKI
Director, Cultural Heritage Division,
Assistant Director-General for Culture a.i.
UNESCO (France)

'Methods o[f] approach an[d] means o[f] access t[o] fundin[g] sources ar[e] now fa[r] mor[e] complex.

In 1959 Egypt and the Sudan submitted to UNESCO an urgent request for help in safeguarding the sites and monuments of Nubia that were threatened with submersion by an artificial lake resulting from the construction of the Aswan Dam. It was the first time since it was founded in 1945 that UNESCO had received such a request; how was the Organization to respond?

On 8 March 1960, the Director-General of UNESCO, Vittorino Veronese, appealed to 'governments, institutions, public and private foundations and all persons of goodwill' to provide their technical or financial contribution to efforts aimed at preserving the Nubian sites and monuments from disappearance. The ceremony to launch this appeal was attended by André Malraux, who exalted 'action by which man wrenches something from death'. The campaign to safeguard the monuments of Nubia had thus begun, and represented an entirely novel concept in UNESCO's approach to cultural heritage.

Until the 1960s it had been widely accepted that all monuments located within the borders of a particular state were the sole concern of that state which was therefore responsible for their upkeep. However, the Nubian campaign introduced a new concept according to which these monuments could be seen as belonging to the cultural heritage of humanity and were therefore of concern to the entire international community and, consequently, to UNESCO. Nevertheless, it was clear that a state, Egypt in this case, should bear a reasonable share of the burden and should undertake to fulfil all the commitments it had accepted during the campaign.

This campaign was pursued for some twenty years and its completion was heralded as a complete success by the international community. We may now attempt an analysis of the reasons for the campaign's success, but we must also bear in mind the difficulties and delays which marked its inception. It would, in fact, be illusory to believe that, in the wake of the launching of the appeal by UNESCO, funds were immediately made available: almost two years went by before financial contributions began to come in. However, the determination displayed by the Egyptian and Sudanese authorities in creating the necessary infrastructure played a vital role in the strategy for fostering public awareness in favour of that first campaign. Over and above the technical achievement the campaign brought about, it offered a striking example of international information and promotion successfully conducted for the benefit of a conservation project. Pursued in two phases, Abu Simbel and Philae, it achieved its objectives by collecting more than $40 million from public and private international sources, out of a total cost of some $70 million.

On the strength of the success achieved by that campaign, many states turned to UNESCO to seek support from the international community for their most prestigious sites. In particular, we should recall that in the wake of the disastrous floods which ravaged Florence and Venice in 1966, an appeal was launched for international solidarity. As regards Venice there is ample evidence, some thirty years later, of how several dozen monuments were restored, including the Doges' Palace which regained much of its splendour thanks to an international effort on the part of the Italian Government and UNESCO. Several support committees were set up in most of the European countries as well as in the United States in order to provide a vital contribution to the safeguarding of many of Venice's monuments and works of art. Nevertheless, the problem still remains of protecting the city as a whole against high tides; these call for work on a gigantic scale and plans are still under review. Such action affecting the lagoon was not, in point of fact, among the objectives of the campaign, which was confined to safeguarding the monuments. The same was true of the temple of Borobudur in Indonesia and the archaeological site of Carthage in Tunisia. These two campaigns were completed successfully, once again due to the efforts of the international community and to an accurate definition of the tasks involved and the objectives to be achieved.

Endangered heritage sites (World Monument Fund)

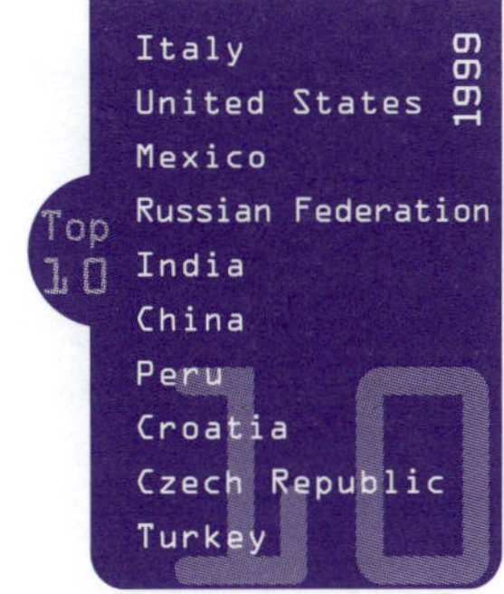

1999
Top 10
Italy
United States
Mexico
Russian Federation
India
China
Peru
Croatia
Czech Republic
Turkey

Source: See the Index of culture indicators and sources and Table 12 in Part Seven of this report.

Could the same be said, however, of the other international campaigns decided on by the General Conference? More than twenty campaigns are currently under way and are faced with varying degrees of difficulty in their implementation. These difficulties first became apparent in the early 1980s and were analysed by a special committee appointed by the Executive Board. An in-depth study submitted to the Board at its 125th session, together with an information document prepared by Belgium, Canada, Tunisia and Turkey, entitled *Strategy for International Safeguarding Campaign*, reflected a common opinion advocating a reduction in the number of future campaigns. Furthermore, some management experts had suggested a review of ongoing campaigns in order to reappraise their aims and means. By that time it had become clear that safeguarding urban sites such as those of the Medina in Fez, the Old City of Havana and the Kathmandu Valley, called for countless tens, not to say hundreds of millions of dollars. In order to safeguard the Medina in Fez, for example, the master plan of 1975–79 provided for an estimated budget of $650 million, but which today has been revised upwards to $1 billion. What countries or

New advocacy and funding schemes for endangered cultural heritage

In 1995 the World Monuments Fund launched the World Monuments Watch (WMW) programme to provide a forum for a growing constituency of stakeholders in the protection and preservation of significant cultural heritage and to cultivate and disseminate information on new and exemplary approaches to the challenges facing the field today. The WMW list of 100 Most Endangered Sites is published biennially from applications received from around the world. To date, government agencies have submitted almost 65% of the applications to this programme – evidence that the need is great and the resources few.

The WMW programme and its List of 100 is first and foremost a public–awareness-raising tool and a call to action to local communities, decision-makers and commercial interests. Sites are selected by an independent panel of nine experts representing major international preservation agencies and related professions. The List of 100 is not a permanent designation (like UNESCO's World Heritage list) but is intended as a mechanism to empower concerned organizations, government agencies and individuals to address serious problems at important sites at a very critical moment.

The first two Lists issued in 1996 and 1998 contained a total of 175 sites. These represented 75 countries, with site types ranging from sacred to archaeological to industrial. In the majority of sites there were urgent problems caused by exposure to the elements: air pollution, vandalism and population pressures. Site nominators sought recognition and assistance in carrying out emergency conservation treatment, preservation and master planning, condition surveys and implementation of improved site protection and infrastructure.

The announcement of the third biennial List of 100 for the years 2000–2001 is an opportunity to assess the accomplishments at sites over the programme's first four years. Of the 175 sites, 75% have reported some form of progress, with 40 sites completely removed from the dangers they faced at the time of listing. Although the main accomplishment of the List of 100 is the ability of the nominator to utilize the site's listing to raise awareness, in some cases sufficient activity cannot be achieved without financial assistance. While not specifically a grant programme, WMW recognizes the need for immediate financial assistance to galvanize efforts and address emergency conditions at certain sites. The World Monuments Fund has raised private funds from foundations, corporations and individuals to support work at approximately half of the sites on each endangered list.

Private sector response to the challenge issued with the announcement of each new List of 100 has been impressive. From single grants from individuals to a multi-million dollar commitment by a major corporation, financial resources are being identified and dedicated to improving the condition and ensuring the future of sites through the WMW programme. To date, 139 grants totalling $7 million have been awarded to 84 sites in 49 countries.

Governments have been the largest single partner group to receive these funds and the one most likely to respond with additional financial and in-kind assistance for the project. This demonstrates one of the most striking results of the programme – the effectiveness of placing small but strategic amounts of grant money at sites. Seed funding has been surprisingly successful in increasing the opportunity for local partners to leverage funds – increasing the means of a local organization or a government agency to accomplish a larger goal. Reports show that over $17 million were received by WMF-funded projects from other local sources as a direct result of WMF's initial investment.

The vast majority of grant funds have been directed to emergency conservation work and evaluation and planning programmes. But funds have also been used by site representatives for creative projects that develop site programmes in challenging new directions, such as public awareness raising, training, maintenance planning, tourism impact studies and fund-raising campaigns.

Raising the issues facing a site to an international and diverse audience through the WMW programme has become an important tool in the efforts to address the myriad of new challenges confronting cultural heritage sites around the world. Threats of population pressures, urbanization and the negative effects of tourism are presenting increasingly pressing problems for cultural heritage resources. Successful examples of creative financing, interdisciplinary approaches and diversification of traditional roles or responsibilities must be part of the expanding dialogue to find viable solutions.

KIRSTIN SECHLER
Director
World Monuments Watch Programme
World Monuments Fund, New York (United States)

institutions are actually able to secure funding of this magnitude? Can it reasonably be expected to come from donations?

Two factors need to be taken into account. The first is that donations for the benefit of the cultural heritage, whether from public institutions or private bodies, have become scarcer. In the 1960s, at a time of economic prosperity, a single campaign was launched appealing for the attention and generosity of the public at large and governments in particular. A trend rapidly emerged and some thirty campaigns were proposed in the 1980s. Despite efforts to make such campaigns attractive, they are unfortunately just too numerous for the general public, already mobilized to contribute to a growing number of worthwhile causes.

The second factor to be borne in mind is that fund-raising has now become a sophisticated process with precise rules and pre-investment fund requirements. However, given the financial difficulties facing international and governmental organizations, particularly UNESCO and ICCROM, as well as non–governmental organizations (ICOMOS, ICOM and IFLA), it has become increasingly difficult to devise authentic fund-raising programmes such as those commonly found in Japan, the United Kingdom and the United States. The task of UNESCO's Secretariat, which is responsible for implementing the action plans of safeguarding campaigns, has therefore become particularly onerous, and in circumstances in which the Secretariat, moreover, is technically under-equipped. The difficulties encountered are all the more serious in that public opinion in the various Member States involved in an international safeguarding campaign continues to believe that UNESCO, like a bank, should provide the necessary resources, particularly financial, recalling here the case of the first campaign which is still regarded as a quasi-mythical precedent.

The real situation, as clearly revealed by the in–depth study of 1987, is that fund-raising for the whole range of campaigns usually meets only approximately 2% of the declared needs. This alarming state of affairs led the General Conference to decide to suspend any new campaign launch during the six-year period covered by the Third Medium-Term Plan (1990–1995). The decision was renewed for the subsequent Medium-Term Strategy (1996–2001). A single exception was allowed by the General Conference, namely the launching of the International Campaign for the Safeguarding of the Archaeological Site of Tyre and its Environs (Lebanon), which had been approved in 1982 but was not implemented until March 1998 on account of the war that had brought disorder to the country for more than fifteen years.

The major phase involving implementation of infrastructure and rehabilitation continues to be a stumbling-block for international campaigns. The very scale of the urban restructuring needed to protect the sites and their environment means that safeguarding operations extend well beyond mere aesthetic intervention. It is precisely because all these campaigns, through their specific sites, comprise a socio-economic problem of development, including modification of the architectural and urban functions of the buildings concerned, that they result in real restructuring operations on human settlements and therefore call for major investment. In this regard financial development institutions such as UNDP, the World Bank, the Asian Development Bank (ADB), the Inter-American Bank (IAB) and AGFUND among others are being approached increasingly to provide funds for projects for safeguarding heritage. Examples include the cases of Quito (Ecuador) with funding of $40 million from the IAB, Fez with the World Bank ($15 million), in the near future the vicinity of the Taj Mahal through ADB, and possibly the monuments of Ethiopia through the European Union and the World Bank.

UNESCO has played a pioneering role in the protection of historical urban centres by securing the adoption of action plans stipulating an integrated conservation approach on the basis of the Warsaw-Nairobi Recommendations of 1976 and the Toledo-Washington ICOMOS Charter of 1987. The experts called in by UNESCO have studied the complex nature of historical urban sites. They have taken into account the subtle, fragile balance that contributes to authentic social conviviality. Strategies of rehabilitation and renovation have been devised, particularly for historical cities such as Sana'a in

A risk map of the cultural heritage in Italy

Italy has a huge endowment of architectural and archaeological heritage, just as it has a wide range of natural hazards (earthquakes, volcanoes and so on) and man-made risk. Protecting the country's priceless heritage assets against natural disaster, vandalism and theft is a high priority. But public decision-makers lack vital information about the exact location of Italy's cultural heritage and the degree of risk to which it may be exposed. The Istituto Centrale del Catalogo e della Documentazione (ICCD) of the Ministry of Heritage and Cultural Activities has a large database, dealing mainly with movable heritage and archaeological goods, but this has been compiled primarily for scientific purposes, and a complete inventory of built heritage in Italy is still lacking.

In 1997, therefore, the Istituto Centrale del Restauro of the Ministry for Cultural Goods and the Environment finalized the first stage of a project designed to create an information system where comprehensive data on the cultural heritage could interact with information on the different typologies of risk in the country. The result is a Risk Map which superimposes the distribution of cultural heritage onto a geographical information system providing an assessment of various types of danger to heritage assets in the different regions of the country. The aim of the Map is mainly to create a sort of 'civil protection system' for the Italian heritage but it can also be put to use for cultural tourism and local development purposes as well.

Data used to compile the heritage component of the Risk Map are drawn from the harmonization of information contained in Italy's two most authoritative nation-wide tourist and archaeological guides. This rather pragmatic choice of sources, which incurred some criticism because of its supposed lack of scientific exhaustiveness, was motivated by the need for a quick and reliable information basis upon which public decisions could be made. The basic data cards are drawn up using the national cataloguing system, and further research is in progress to deal with the socioeconomic aspects of the listed artistic and historic buildings. More than 51,000 monuments are contained in the database, including 17,000 churches, 8,200 villas and palaces, 5,200 buildings with wall paintings, and almost 2,000 museums and libraries.

Territorial danger data and indicators are classified as follows:

- *static-structural data* based on an in-depth study of the major phenomena that influence the stability of buildings, namely earthquake activity, volcanic activity, landslides and slips, flooding and coastal dynamics;
- *environmental factors* including an erosion index, a blackening index based on atmospheric particulate emissions and a physical stress index; and
- *anthropic danger* indicating the risks from human-related factors, including depopulation or overpopulation, tourism pressure and liability to theft.

The Risk Map proved its usefulness during the recent earthquakes in the Umbria and Marche regions by providing both central and local authorities with a means of rapid and effective recognition of the heritage items potentially hit by the seismic events.

There are many other parts of the world where cultural heritage is exposed to danger from natural disaster and human activity. The Risk Map method developed in Italy could well find application in other places and assist in the management of heritage in other parts of the world.

CARLA BODO and ANNALISA CICERCHIA
Researchers, Italian Institute of
Prospective Studies and Economic Analysis,
Department of the Treasury (Italy)

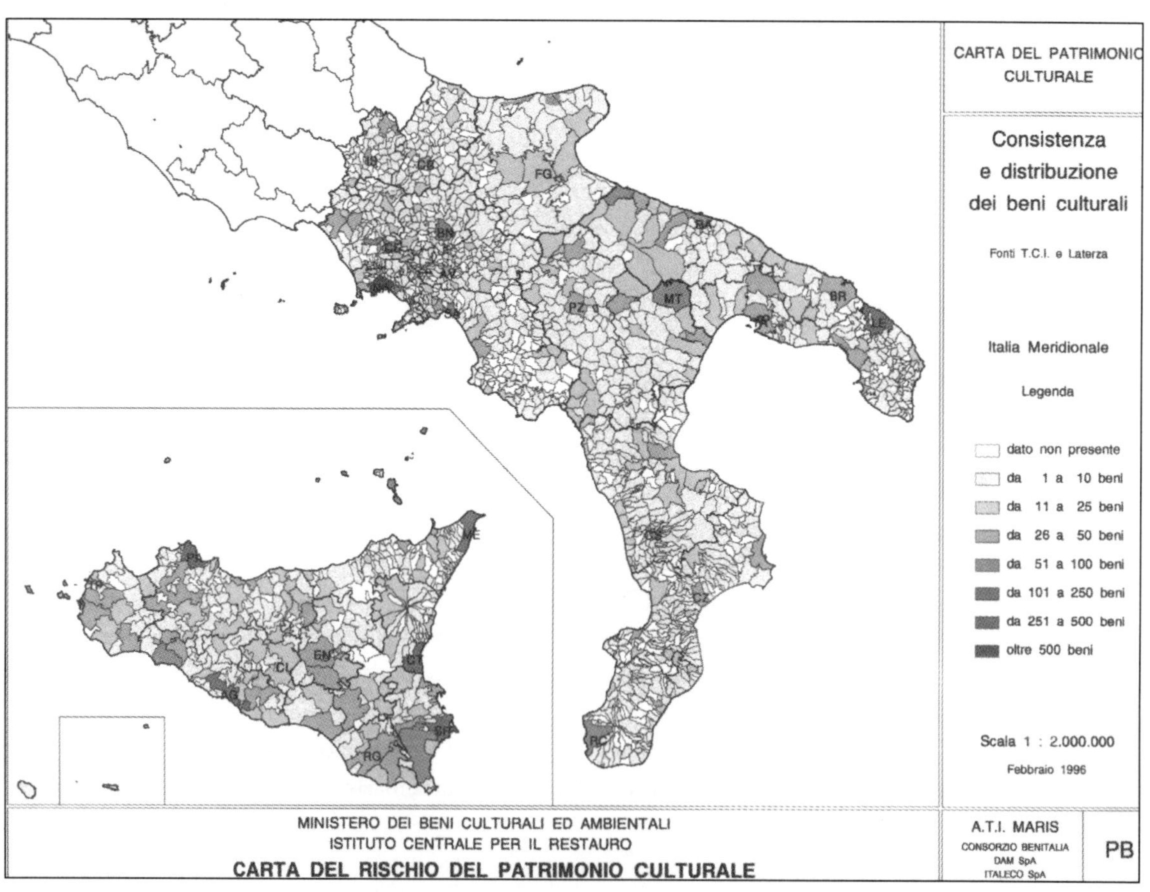

UNESCO CULTURAL CONVENTIONS 2000

REGION	Protection of the world heritage (1972)	Protection of cultural property in armed conflict (1954)	Prevention of illicit trade / transfer of cultural property (1970)	Total number of ratifications	Maximum possible number of ratifications	Ratification rate (%)
	NAME OF THE CONVENTION					
Africa	39	19	19	78	144	54.2
Asia	42	26	26	93	141	66.0
America	31	13	22	66	99	66.7
Europe	42	35	27	104	132	78.8
World	154	93	94	341	516	66.1

GRAPH 11
RATIFICATION OF UNESCO CULTURAL CONVENTIONS: 2000
Ratification of the UNESCO cultural conventions has now reached two-thirds of the maximum possible, and ratification of the central convention on the protection of the world heritage has reached 90%. The rate of ratification has been highest in Europe.

Source: See the Index of culture indicators and sources and Table 13 in Part Seven of this report.

Yemen and Fez in Morocco, according to a more global and overall vision of the development of the city in its broadest surroundings. So, for example, the plan of action for the architectural heritage of the old city of Sana'a advocated operations which were the result of a subtle combination of various sectors of intervention within a broad geographical context. Over the period 1985–1995, investments granted to the historical centre of Sana'a amounted to some $20 million, mainly through public funding. Some of the most significant consequences have been a marked re-evaluation of land prices today and the change of attitude on the part of the population, which is now more sensitive to the enhancement of the city and its durability.

It should be noted that international solidarity for the benefit of saving heritage has not been manifested merely in the context of the campaigns referred to above. The Convention concerning the Protection of the World Cultural and Natural Heritage, adopted by the General Conference of UNESCO in 1972, provided for the first time a permanent legal, administrative and financial framework for international co-operation. It also represents a more substantial innovation in that it linked two sectors that had hitherto been regarded as quite separate, namely, protection of cultural heritage and that of natural heritage. It also introduced the concept of world heritage whose scope overreaches any political or geographical frontier. A fundamental objective of the Convention is also to foster greater awareness among all peoples of the irreplaceable value of that heritage and the grave dangers that menace it. It is aimed at completing, strengthening and stimulating national initiatives, rather than competing with or replacing them. Ultimately, however, responsibility for preserving a specific heritage lies with each individual country.

In adopting the Convention on the Protection of the World Cultural and Natural Heritage, the Member States recognized and codified the general principles which underpin the operations described above, namely that each State would be responsible to the rest of humanity for the various components of the heritage that lie within its borders. They also recognized that the international community was under obligation to help a state assume such responsibility if its own resources were inadequate. Consequently, new possibilities have opened up for the funding of operations concerning the safeguarding of sites figuring in the World Heritage list. Once again, however, the resources available to the World Heritage Committee to cope with all requests for technical co-operation are inadequate. They have nevertheless enabled substantial support to be provided particularly in the case of situations where the heritage is exposed to what are regarded as serious threats, as was the case recently in Dubrovnik and Angkor. Furthermore, substantial support in the context of operational safeguarding actions has at last come from the voluntary contributions of Member States which have agreed to create funds-in-trust with UNESCO. This is the case, to cite but one example, of the substantial funds-in-trust established by Japan for funding operations on several major sites in Asia, and more recently on a site in Europe.

In summary, we may conclude that the development of strategies for heritage conservation and rehabilitation is a field which continues to be marked by a degree of uncertainty, particularly in difficult world economic circumstances. Methods of approach and means of access to funding sources are now far more complex and require fund-raisers to display not only real professionalism in their field, but also a very sound knowledge of the cultural assets to be protected. The fact remains, none the less, as recently pointed out by Gérard Bolla in an article entitled 'Cultural Heritage: Successes and Failures of International Solidarity', that:

> it is operational action in the field, of which the most striking example is still the rescuing of Abu Simbel, which gave UNESCO the image of a cultural organization that is capable of launching restoration activities on a vast scale and of bringing them to a successful conclusion. It has often been asked how UNESCO had succeeded in conducting many varied safeguarding campaigns, in spite of the inherent difficulties involved. In actual fact, the answer to this question lies in the two qualities which are indispensable for the implementation of multilateral projects for preservation of the heritage: cultural sensitivity and rigorous execution.

Chapter 10
Impact of recent developments in the notion of cultural heritage on the World Heritage Convention

LAURENT LÉVI-STRAUSS
Deputy Director,
Division of Cultural Heritage, UNESCO (France)

'The World Heritage List should therefore . . . remain completely open, as its development will depend both on future archaeological and scientific discoveries.'

The period from the 1950s to the late 1970s saw the adoption by the international community of the major conventions, recommendations and charters for the protection of the cultural heritage, including the Hague Convention for the Protection of Cultural Property in the Event of Armed Conflict (1954), the International Charter for the Conservation and Restoration of Monuments and Sites (1964), the Convention on the Means of Prohibiting and Preventing the Illicit Import, Export and Transfer of Ownership of Cultural Property (1970), and, lastly, and doubtless the most famous of all, the Convention concerning the Protection of the World Cultural and Natural Heritage (1972), better known as the World Heritage Convention.

It should be noted, however, that these international legal instruments, in spite of their wide range, defined their purpose and field of application according to a relatively restricted notion of cultural heritage limited to physical dimension alone. This vision of the heritage was no doubt inspired by Article I of UNESCO's Constitution. In the field of culture, this founding text gave the Organization the task of 'the conservation and protection of the world's heritage of books, works of art and monuments of history and science'. It was not until 1989 that the General Conference of UNESCO adopted the Recommendation on the Safeguarding of Traditional Culture and Folklore, and not until 1997 that it promulgated the implementation of a system of institutional recognition of the 'oral and immaterial heritage of humanity'. Of all these international conventions, the

World Heritage Convention has undoubtedly enjoyed the greatest success, not only through the public interest it has aroused, but also within the international community itself, since it has already been ratified by more than 85% of the Member States of the United Nations and UNESCO.

This success can be attributed to several factors. Firstly, the field of application of the 1972 Convention is not limited to specific circumstances such as armed conflict or illicit trafficking, where the heritage must benefit from special protection; rather its purpose is general and timeless. Secondly, this Convention provides both for a decision-making body which ensures its permanent relevance, namely the World Heritage Committee, and more importantly, for its own financial means, the World Heritage Fund, based on specific contributions from its states parties. The Fund is in a position to provide the assets recorded on the World Heritage list with financial assistance on a relatively modest scale (of the order of several tens of thousands of dollars for any given case), but operates rapidly and according to relatively simple procedures, thereby providing often invaluable assistance to cultural administrations with very limited means or in emergency situations. A third reason is its originality: the cultural heritage and the natural heritage are assured the same protection. The works of man and those of nature are perceived as two indissociable facets of one and the same resource which must be protected simultaneously. In 1972, this was an innovative measure of great originality.

Finally, the fourth reason for its continued success since the recording of the first sites on the World Heritage list by the Committee in 1978 can be attributed to a gradual deviation in purpose and to a partial change in ultimate aims, detectable when its implementation over more than twenty-five years is studied. The provisions of the 1972 Convention centred around two principal objectives: identification of certain cultural and natural assets of exceptional interest, for which preservation was required so that they would remain an integral part of the heritage of all humanity, and the concomitant implementation of the legal and financial means required for safeguarding them at both national and international levels. However, without underestimating the effectiveness of protection that the Convention could afford for the conservation of many assets – if only by reminding the states parties of the obligations they had contracted for the protection of their heritage – the initial aim of guaranteeing their physical conservation by granting collective financial assistance involving the international community as a whole was gradually weakened as the number of such assets on the World Heritage list increased. In fact, the 1972 Convention had been devised and elaborated in the 1960s, at a time when the threatened disappearance of the monuments of Nubia under the waters of the Aswan Dam and the major international campaign organized by UNESCO to save them had for the first time demonstrated how irreparable a loss the destruction of such monuments would have been for humanity. After this, the authors of the Convention believed it was necessary to organize and facilitate the repetition of the previous prodigious effort of international mobilization and solidarity on behalf of other assets of comparable importance. The success of the international campaigns for Borobodur and Carthage, coming shortly in the wake of the Nubian project, showed that this type of large-scale intervention could be systematically repeated with comparable success. However, it soon became clear that operations on a similar scale for the benefit of sites and monuments recorded on a World Heritage list would not be possible; the list was lengthening apace, and indeed by 1999 had reached a total of 582 cultural and natural assets. Thereafter, recourse would have to be limited to the relatively modest resources of the World Heritage Fund.

Accordingly, the World Heritage list gradually lost part of its initial aim of providing operational protection and shifted towards new ground, that of international public recognition of the monuments and sites on the list of humanity's most exceptional assets. The steady strengthening of this aspect of the World Heritage List, often referred to in such terms as a collection of the 'wonders of the world' or 'jewels in the crown', not only increased public interest year after year but also nurtured among the states parties, and today even among cities or regions, a vibrant spirit of emulation, if not actual competition, for inclusion on the List. Instead of a gradual slowing down over time of inscriptions on the List as might have been expected, the evidence suggests that, on the contrary, more and more proposals for inscription are being submitted every year to the Committee and that, furthermore, the proportion of proposed and listed sites is in no way decreasing. These facts, and particularly the success the Convention has had among states and the public at large, coupled with the fact that thirty or more cultural sites are proposed for inscription each year, have made the World Heritage List an excellent pointer to the evolution of attitudes to the cultural heritage among the international community since the late 1970s.

In its earliest years the Committee set about considering what would be the best methods for drawing up a balanced list to provide an accurate picture of the heritage of humanity. In subsequent years, several attempts were made to define more clearly the most appropriate methodological approach for comprehending the cultural heritage of humanity in all its diversity, drawing up a kind of inventory and thereby identifying what was missing from the List so that it should be properly balanced and truly representative of the world's various cultures. Several delegates from the states parties stressed that care should be taken to ensure that such a task did not result in a stereotyped list of the treasures of the world heritage, particularly at a time when the very notion of cultural heritage was changing. In point of fact, a number of specialists feared that the systematic inventorying of sites and monuments might ultimately attach too much importance to the traditional categories of 'classical' art history, centred around the study of major monuments and 'leading' civilizations. This came at a time when the organs of the Convention, and particularly the Committee, wanted to pause and study the possibility of extending the List to other types of assets and other cultures which were beginning to be perceived as poorly represented or even completely unrepresented.

The new approach suggested that attention be given, first of all, to the very concept of world heritage and the ultimate aims of the Convention, and particularly to whether appropriate links existed between the definition of cultural assets specified by the Convention, the criteria for the inscription of those assets, and their effective inscription on the List. What was the ultimate purpose of the World Heritage List? How could a truly comprehensive, coherent vision be given of the world's cultures? How could serious omissions be avoided? It was in the light of these questions that a meeting of experts representing the various regions of the world was organized in June 1994. At the end of their discussions, the experts stressed that the development of knowledge and reflection within the international scientific community had led over the previous twenty years to changes in the notion of cultural heritage. This meant abandoning the almost exclusively 'monumentalist' vision on which the List had hitherto been drawn up, and adopting a more anthropological, global approach to the material manifestations of the world's various cultures.

In fact, the history of art and architecture, archaeology, anthropology and ethnology are no longer concerned with studying isolated monuments, but rather with assessing complex, multidimensional cultural ensembles which are a spatial expression of social organization, lifestyles, beliefs, skills and representations of the various cultures, past and present, throughout the world. A material vestige should not be observed in isolation, but in its context and through an understanding of the multiple relations it maintains reciprocally with its physical and non-physical environment.

The experts also highlighted the fact that the List presented serious examples of imbalance. Europe, Christendom, the ancient cities and religious buildings of extinct civilizations, monumental architecture and historical periods were very largely over-represented to the detriment, in particular, of the archaeological and technical heritage, the heritage of non-European cultures and spirituality and, more generally, the heritage of all living cultures, especially those of so-called 'traditional' societies. They also pointed out that the cultural heritage of Africa and Oceania were particularly poorly represented in spite of their archaeological, technical, architectural and spiritual wealth, their original modes of territorial and

Defining the concept of 'intangible heritage': challenges and prospects

UNESCO's first *World Culture Report* in 1998 emphasized the preservation of cultural diversity, not just because of the human rights of minority groups, but because of the importance to human intellectual and cultural resources of preserving customs, languages and lifestyles which, after enduring for thousands of years, are now dying out at an alarming rate. These other ways of living in the world may one day prove to be crucial to human survival. A technological calamity, massive climate change or even genetic mutation may so irrevocably alter the world we live in that we may need all the different approaches possible to enable humankind to adapt to it.

Globalization of communications and trade has also created a fear that the wonderful diversity of human culture will be irreversibly affected, and this has led to increasing insistence being placed on their uniqueness and value. Environmental concerns have also played a role here: various organizations such as UNESCO's Science Sector, FAO, the Bio-Diversity Convention and the UNESCO World Conference on Science (Budapest, 1999) are stressing the importance of diverse forestry and agricultural practices for the general ecological welfare of the human race and of all species.

The phrase 'intangible cultural heritage' comes from the Japanese translation into English of their own pioneering legislation on this topic in 1950. The definition of the 'Principles and Guidelines for the Protection of the Heritage of Indigenous Peoples' (United Nations) includes in this heritage, *inter alia*, 'knowledge, the nature or use of which has been transmitted from generation to generation', 'literary and artistic works which may be created in the future', and 'music, dance, song, ceremonies, symbols and designs, narratives and poetry; all kinds of scientific, agricultural, technical and ecological knowledge, including cultigens, medicines and the rational use of flora and fauna'. The title of UNESCO's *Recommendation on the Safeguarding of Traditional Culture and Folklore 1989* reflected sixteen years of difficult debate. For anthropologists, 'folklore' was a technical term of art, but even they were not agreed on its exact meaning. Many groups feel that the common understanding of the word is degrading and should be avoided. For this reason the term 'folklife' is used in the United States. There has also been a debate between the partisans of 'people's culture' and those of 'high culture' associated with the élite of a society such as performing arts developed for royal courts alone.

Some overlap can be seen with what European States have treated for generations as 'intellectual property rights'. However, such rights are generally organized as rights of individuals, while the concept of heritage is related to the community. There is much discussion in international law today concerning 'individual' and 'collective' rights – it is an important aspect of the discussions going on in relation to the proposals for protecting the rights of indigenous peoples. Even the use of the term 'rights', it should be noted, employs a concept not inherent in social systems where social relations are seen as obligations rather than as rights.

Tribal peoples are deeply aware of the 'interconnectedness' of all things, a view described as the 'one web of life'. This is worlds apart from the compartmentalization of Western thinking: a concentration on particular aspects which divorces them from their contexts. Similarly there is a distinction between views of 'ownership' and 'custodianship', as well as protection of the intangible heritage conceived in terms of processes rather than of things. Contemporary anthropology shows that it is the social process, rather than the item produced, which needs to be preserved to ensure the continued creativity of the community. This is also the approach of many indigenous peoples. Whereas the Western paradigm turns all things into objects such as 'knowledge', 'life forms' or 'commerce', the traditional communities tend to regard all things as processes such as 'knowing' or 'coming to know', 'living', and 'safeguarding'.

Preserving the products of folklife by recording them or storing them in a museum is much less difficult than preserving the social processes which create them. Very often skills are transmitted by the elderly in the community who, after a lifetime of experience in the culture, have developed a particular expertise and the responsibility for its transmission. Invasive social processes such as globalization, tourism and commodification may well interrupt that transmission by weakening respect for the elders and their traditions in favour of the radical, the new and the exotic. In many traditional communities there is a sharp division between the roles attributed to men and to women.

New ideas of gender equality, promoted by human rights organizations, for example, may interfere with the traditional roles and tasks. The intrusion of individualism into community-based systems may make decisions on the preservation and development of traditional cultures particularly complex.

Such changes render it necessary to study society-wide processes and make value judgements about the empowerment of local communities, of women, and of the young and about how none the less to ensure respect for traditional culture and transmission of its unique elements.

How can we define the 'intangible cultural heritage'? First, there must be a careful survey of the cultural elements to be protected. While states speak for their peoples on the international level, it is essential that individuals and communities articulate their needs. Different communities may be at one on the need for protection, but not in respect of the same heritage elements.

The full concept of intangible cultural heritage covers an enormous area. A few examples: traditional language and oral heritage; traditional religion and ritual; designs and themes (some of which may be sacred or secret), music, poetry, drama, dance, styles of dress, crafts and skills (in building, weaving, carving, etc.), cuisine, tracking and hunting, husbandry, textiles, medical practice, methods of conflict resolution and so on.

Objectives in preserving these elements vary. For the bearers of these lifestyles it may be to preserve traditional wisdom and a treasured way of life for future generations. It may be physical survival, since traditional adaptation to the environment may avoid a lifestyle which is ultimately unsustainable. A state's objective may be to continue cheap local medical care for subsistence populations. For others the objective may be to gain time to fully inventory and exploit resources such as traditional knowledge of plant properties (medical, biological, agricultural) so as to appropriate them for economic gain. For scientists it may be to enable research into sustainable lifestyles or the diversity of human development as evidenced, for example, in the thousands of languages now under threat of extinction, or to rescue oral history and customary law before it disappears. It may include the survival of species unknown outside their community as part of the Earth's biological resources. Yet other groups may want to use traditional elements in their culture as a source of income to be authorized for use by others or reserved for themselves to provide economic resources. It may be to preserve a unique mode of life as a source of dignity, cultural pride and identity or, conversely, to use it as a tourist attraction to generate income.

At the same time it will be important to consider what threats the different aspects of heritage are confronted by, how serious and urgent these threats are and, most importantly, what other interests would be affected by their protection.

Where there are so many different actors and interests, unlikely to be compatible with one another, it is questionable whether all the objectives can be achieved; the means to be used may vary substantially. In one context the survival of an ecologically viable unit will be essential to ensure the provision of certain plants which are required for crafts such as paper- or textile-making, or for traditional healing or for traditional foods. In another we will be seeking the survival of a minimum number of speakers using their mother tongue. In yet another context we will be searching how to give community support to bearers of traditional know-how, which might well involve the award of prizes, craft fairs, artist-in-residence programmes, encouragement of folk festivals or even the return from outside the community of objects without which traditional ceremonies cannot be held. Other interested parties may want to extend the use of existing legal structures such as patent and copyright law to traditional knowledge.

The means of protection should not damage the community's social processes by preserving, as quaint survivals of a former lifestyle, only cultural elements which have long since ceased to play a part in the cultural life of their creators. Above all, the desire to preserve should aim to empower those persons who are bearers of traditional culture to continue to provide alternative models of behaviour and different criteria of 'success' to those portrayed by competing lifestyles.

LYNDEL PROTT
Director of the Section of
International Standards, UNESCO Culture Sector

spatial occupation and their systems of exchange networks for goods and ideas.

It was therefore unanimously agreed that the World Heritage List should not be a mere catalogue, or worse still a list of 'best monuments' or architecture. Changing attitudes meant that the notion of 'masterpiece' which underpinned some of the selection criteria was in fact not a determining factor for the assessment of heritage, and that folk arts, 'traditional' architecture, and examples of civil engineering were becoming more and more widely recognized. It was agreed that the choice of assets to be inscribed on the List should not be merely aesthetic, but also distinctly historical and anthropological, in so far as it would be related more to the inherent meaning of the works and their economic, social, cultural and symbolic significance than to their form.

With this in mind, it was felt that the World Heritage List must reflect in an all-encompassing, multidimensional and non-simplifying way the cultural diversity of humanity and therefore its intellectual, religious, aesthetic and sociological dimensions. Far from being a mere account of artistic events, it should, on the contrary, record the major manifestations of the diversity of cultures which make up humanity as a whole, including the living cultures. The World Heritage List should therefore also remain completely open, since its development will depend both on future archaeological and scientific discoveries and on developments in human thought and sensitivity more generally.

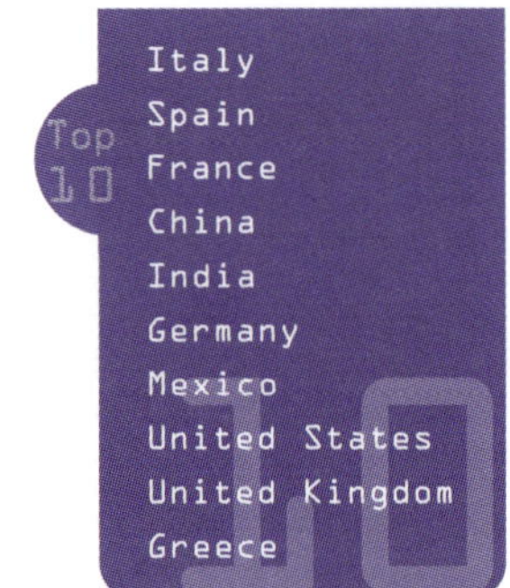

Top 10
Italy
Spain
France
China
India
Germany
Mexico
United States
United Kingdom
Greece

Source: See the Index of culture indicators and sources and Table 12 in Part Seven of this report.

To implement the new approach used in defining the cultural heritage, several measures were adopted in 1994 by the World Heritage Committee to identify the types of heritage that were poorly represented on the List, to review inscription criteria to take account of them more effectively, and to attenuate the conflict between nature and culture as established by the Convention. The first of these measures was implemented through a series of meetings in various regions of the world, particularly in Africa and Oceania, to identify the categories of cultural heritage that are abundant there but scarcely, if at all, represented on the List; these meetings were concerned particularly to identify archaeological heritage, traditional skills and technical heritage, spiritual and religious heritage, human establishments and cultural landscapes, cultural itineraries and trading routes.

The second measure adopted by the Committee involved a review of the cultural criteria for inscription in order to extend them in four directions (see Annex, p. 163). Firstly, a new drafting of criterion (i) replaced the notion of artistic masterpieces with that of a masterpiece of the human creative genius. It also led to a redrafting of criterion (ii). In its earlier version, where unidirectional influences operate, this criterion favoured the 'leading specimens of series', namely masterpieces whose model went far back in time and space. This centrifugal conception of cultural relations was clearly unacceptable. By giving unilateral preference to prototypes and models, UNESCO ran the risk of implicitly recognizing the frequently denounced concept of 'dominant cultures'.

Secondly, a concept of culture emerged that was nearer to the globalizing definition provided by anthropologists, illustrated first of all by the review of criterion (iii), in which the notions of traditional culture and living civilization are expressed. This trend also underlines the successive amendments made to criterion (iv), which now includes the technical heritage and landscapes, and to criterion (v), which, while initially referring to human establishments, was extended to occupation of territory.

Thirdly, this new, more anthropological, more global approach also naturally led the Committee to re-examine in depth the content and limitations of the field of application of criterion (vi). Unlike the first five criteria, this one does not refer to the physical components of the asset but to its immaterial values: 'associated with events or living traditions, ideas, beliefs and artistic or literary works of exceptional universal significance'. The use of this criterion means that the immaterial values of certain assets are not completely overlooked in the implementation of the Convention. In fact, it had soon come to light that sites such as Independence Hall or the Island of Gorée, *inter alia*, had to feature on the List more for their intellectual, moral or symbolic value than for the value of their physical components alone. The fact remained, nevertheless, that the restrictive definition of cultural heritage given in Article I of the Convention, confined to the physical heritage alone (monuments, sites and ensembles), required that the use of criterion (vi) be clearly specified.

Consequently, the inscription of the Genbaku Dome at Hiroshima in 1996, following that of the Auschwitz Concentration Camp in 1979, raised the question once again as to whether a site devoid of physical elements corresponding to one of the first five criteria could be inscribed to take account only of the human destruction which had taken place there and of which it remained the symbol, even if its place and significance in the history of humanity were unquestionable. On that occasion, the Committee expressed the fear that what some observers had already referred to as the 'battlefield syndrome' might develop in the future. They were referring to an ever-increasing number of proposals for the inscription of sites testifying to conflicts and massacres whose geopolitical connotations, the scar on the memory of the descendants of the victims or merely the founding role in the formation of a national identity, actually went far beyond the strictly historical and cultural value of the material vestiges that remain today. The Committee believed that if the World Heritage List were to be reoriented towards a list of 'places of memory', it would stray too far from the ultimate aims of the Convention. It decided, therefore, that criterion (vi) could justify an inscription only under exceptional circumstances and when it would be applied concurrently with other cultural or natural criteria.

Finally, this new more anthropological approach to the heritage was to acquire even greater meaning after ratification in 1992 of the Convention by Japan which had required a thorough reappraisal of the criterion of authenticity of cultural assets as applied up to that time. This criterion had originally been defined in reference to a European concept of formalized authenticity by the Venice Charter and had already raised a series of difficulties, particularly when monuments built of perishable materials such as wood or adobe had been proposed for inscription. In the case of sites built of wood, the replacement, even on a large scale, of structural elements had not been considered as causing any loss of authenticity; however, the Committee had expressed more serious reservations with regard to buildings where mud was the main component. In Japan some of the most ancient and most venerated temples have been rebuilt in an identical manner, either periodically for ritual reasons or quite simply on account of the natural deterioration of their perishable materials or because of fire, earthquakes or typhoons; thus Japan's adhesion to the Convention made it inevitable that the notion of authenticity in the Convention should be reassessed. The Nara Conference organized in 1994 therefore led to a review of the application of this notion in a more open and less European-centred manner (see the box entitled 'Renewal of the notion of authenticity'). Nevertheless, there is reason to regret that a more comprehensive reappraisal has not yet been undertaken of the very concept of authenticity and of the values and representations that could replace it in cultures where it does not exist. This has now become a prerequisite through recognition of attitudes and practices in Japan that are completely different from those of Europe, but in no way less respectful of ancient monuments.

The last of the measures adopted by the Committee in 1994 concerned the conflict between nature and culture. In recent years, implementation of the Convention has revealed the gradual reconciliation between cultural and natural heritage which has already led to the adoption of a new category of cultural landscapes and will probably lead, sooner or later, to integration within a single and continuous

Renewal of the notion of authenticity

Ratification of the World Heritage Convention by Japan in 1992 raised a fundamental conceptual issue, namely, that of the definition of authenticity which cultural property should possess in order to be included in the World Heritage List, as defined up to then in part (b) of paragraph 24 of the 'Guidelines for Implementation of the Convention'. The notion of authenticity applied by the Convention was inspired by the Venice Charter and attached importance to the conservation of original building materials. Articles 9 and 12 placed emphasis on the 'exceptional nature of restoration', 'respect for early materials' and the rule whereby elements used for replacing missing components should be distinguishable from the original parts.

How could such principles be maintained exclusively in view of the beauty and historic value of the monuments of Japan, which have come down to us today in an intellectual and material context that is quite alien to Western principles? On the one hand, as pointed out by Mr Nobuo Ito of the University of Kobe at the Nara Conference in 1994, the Japanese language and many other Asian languages do not have a word for 'authenticity'. Furthermore, it is quite clear that the perishable vegetable material with which almost all historic buildings in Japan are built requires regular restoration work and the replacement of certain parts. In some instances, periodical dismantling and reconstruction are part of the very nature of the monument. It remains perfectly clear, however, that buildings such as the Horyu-ji, the oldest wooden buildings in the world, which date back to the eighth century, and the Ise sanctuary, which was rebuilt following a ritual procedure in identical form in 1993 for the sixty-first time, are masterpieces whose authenticity cannot be questioned.

That is why the Declaration adopted at the end of the Nara Conference advocated a broader concept of authenticity to show due consideration, not only for materials, but also for the design, form, use and function, interpretations and techniques of, and finally the 'spirit' and 'impression' emanating from, the monument. In Article 11, the Declaration also recognizes that value judgements and notions of authenticity differ from one culture to another and may not therefore be based on a single set of criteria; this article is essential for a less European-based implementation of the Convention.

It is clear that recognition by the Convention of the ancient monuments of Japan has enabled substantial progress to be made towards achieving a more subtle and diversified understanding of cultural heritage. Furthermore, these developments extend well beyond the matter of authenticity. They call for close consideration to be given to other issues in these two intellectual universes, issues as fundamental as relationships between form and substance, identity and change, and philosophical conceptions of being and time.

Laurent Lévi-Strauss

ensemble of the two previously distinct series of criteria used for the inscription of cultural assets and natural assets. This may help to narrow the gap established by the Convention between nature and culture and to take greater account of their interpenetration and indissociable character in many types of assets and in the conceptions of many human societies, particularly those referred to as 'traditional'.

It has now been six years since these decisions were taken by the World Heritage Committee. It is not yet clear what results they have yielded. While new types of assets such as cultural landscapes, civil engineering and the industrial heritage feature more prominently on the List, the monumental heritage of Europe continues to predominate in comparison with other assets, in terms of both the number of sites already inscribed and the new proposals submitted each year. While some indicative lists have so far adopted a thematic and anthropological approach to the heritage, many others tend rather to reflect a juxtaposition of monuments established within a purely historical and national frame of reference. This would seem to be due to a twofold problem. The first aspect, of a conceptual nature, concerns the very identification of the types of assets corresponding to this new approach to the heritage. The other, as we shall see, hinges on the increasingly strong identity value which the cultural heritage has acquired in recent years.

In spite of the developments described above and which have now drawn the notion of cultural heritage recognized by the Convention closer to that adopted by the scientific community, their practical application, particularly the establishment of the World Heritage List, is still the subject of the debates and controversy which are going on today in that same scientific community. For example, there is evidence, according to regions, of two types of difficulties which are in fact symmetrical and inverse. The first relates to what might be seen as an inevitably restrictive definition of the heritage in many developing countries which paradoxically have not yet divested themselves of the classical monumental vision, in spite of the wealth of their non-monumental heritage. As a result, regions which have no monu-

Graph 12
Cultural Diversity and Festivals UNESCO
Member states wer sent a questionnaire on festivals and heritage sites. An overwhelming level of reponse (78%) came from Member staes where over fifty languages are spoken.

mental heritage continue to be underrepresented, even though they have traditional human establishments and ecosystems, methods of land and space occupation, and non-built sites of great cultural and spiritual significance which could legitimately claim to feature on the List.

The second difficulty, conversely, concerns what has become a perhaps too-extensive definition of heritage in other countries. The debates and controversy aroused in some Western countries by certain inscriptions, particularly of industrial sites, have revealed the limitations of a trend which had developed rapidly in recent years and sometimes resulted in a single globalizing concept of heritage that included virtually the whole range of testimony of human activity. The heritage talks organized by the French Ministry of Culture and Communication in November 1998 therefore raised the issue of a potential 'monumental abuse' at a time when, as Régis Debray pointed out, cranes, fishing vessels and hangars are now frequently classified as historical monuments. Furthermore, the increasingly affirmed identity aspect of the cultural heritage in a world seeking its points of reference means that proposals for inscription are also becoming a component of the image which countries wish to give of themselves and which they want to see recognized by the international community. This phenomenon may partly account for the growing success of the Convention, the ever-increasing number of assets proposed for inscription, and its 'world prize list' connotation which is gradually acquiring greater importance in public opinion than actual protection activities.

We are therefore witnessing a kind of 'snowball effect' as regards inscription proposals, encouraged by a considerable number of new cultural sites recorded each year: over the last six or seven years, 85 to 90% of the proposals submitted have been assessed favourably and have resulted in an inscription. The identity dimension of the cultural heritage and the limited number of sites actually refused have therefore nurtured a kind of 'inscription fever' which has now affected even municipal councils, particularly in Europe where the cultural administrations are among the best equipped for preparing inscription files and where monuments, in the most traditional sense of the term, are most numerous. That, broadly speaking, explains why the share of the European monumental heritage inscribed on the List has increased steadily. Nevertheless, we can hope that the World Heritage Committee will succeed in solving these difficulties in the forthcoming years and that the World Heritage List will be better balanced and more representative.

This task would seem all the more necessary as, in sizeable areas of the world, archaeological riches, lifestyles and methods of subsistence, and examples of original relationships with the environment which testify to the prodigious wealth of human diversity and creativity, are neither recognized nor protected. We must therefore take account forthwith of the renewal in scientific thought, without overlooking the risk of the rapid disappearance of these inestimable testimonies of the heritage of humanity. Efforts must therefore be made to speed up implementation of a strategy for drawing up the List to make it fully representative of the diversity of human societies and the multiplicity of original responses they have contributed throughout their history to questions which perhaps, more than ever, are those that face us today: how are we to live with nature and how should we live with other human beings?

Annex: Extract from the cultural criteria of the World Heritage Convention

24. A monument, group of buildings or site [as defined above] which is nominated for inclusion in the World Heritage List will be considered to be of outstanding universal value for the purpose of the Convention when the Committee finds that it meets one or more of the following criteria and the test of authenticity. Each property nominated should therefore:

(a) (i) represent a masterpiece of human creative genius; or

(ii) exhibit an important interchange of human values, over a span of time or within a cultural area of the world, on developments in architecture or technology, monumental arts, town-planning or landscape design; or

(iii) bear a unique or at least exceptional testimony to a cultural tradition or to a civilization which is living or which has disappeared; or

(iv) be an outstanding example of a type of building or architectural or technological ensemble or landscape which illustrates (a) significant stage(s) in human history; or

(v) be an outstanding example of a traditional human settlement or land-use which is representative of a culture (or cultures), especially when it has become vulnerable under the impact of irreversible change; or

(vi) be directly or tangibly associated with events or living traditions, with ideas, or with beliefs, with artistic and literary works of outstanding universal significance (the Committee considers that this criterion should justify inclusion in the List only in exceptional circumstances and in conjunction with other criteria, cultural or natural);

and

(b) (i) meet the test of authenticity in design, material, workmanship or setting and in the case of cultural landscapes their distinctive character and components (the Committee stressed that reconstruction is only acceptable if it is carried out on the basis of complete and detailed docu-

Chapter 11 Heritage conservation and values in globalizing societies

RANDALL MASON
Senior Project Specialist, Getty Conservation Institute[1] (United States)

MARTA DE LA TORRE
Group Director, Information and Communications, Getty Conservation Institute (United States)

'We argue that values and valuing processes are the foundation of the whole notion of heritage and thus of the practice of conservation'

Taking heed of globalization

Heritage conservation concerns the management, treatment, interpretation and fate of material heritage – old, beautiful or otherwise meaningful things such as buildings, objects and landscapes – and thus constitutes an important part of the sphere of material culture. Because all cultures practise some form of conservation, issues concerning cultural change are pressing matters for the conservation field worldwide. How, then, is the signal cultural process of contemporary society – globalization – refracted through the lens of heritage conservation? How has globalization affected the practice of heritage conservation? And what are the prospects for material heritage and conservation in a globalizing world? This paper will explore some of the dimensions of globalization most relevant to the practice of heritage conservation and suggest future directions and issues for the conservation field as it takes heed of globalization.

The philosophy, planning, policy and practices of the conservation field are rooted in, and in many ways still dominated by, canons and assumptions formulated a century ago in Western Europe and North America. Conservation professionals have made notable strides in ways of conserving material heritage – the technical aspects, that is – but less often in the conservation field have we asked, 'Why conserve?' Nor have we seriously considered such vastly complex questions as 'What should be conserved?' and 'Who decides?' As a group, we are inherently 'conservative' and reluctant to change.

It has to be acknowledged, though, that heritage conservation is strongly influenced by social, economic and broad cultural contexts, precisely the contexts and processes falling under the rubric of globalization.[2] These present the conservation field with a number of novel challenges vis-à-vis the role that conservation plays in society. Is the meaning and efficacy of material conservation being eroded by globalization? Such is the argument from some quarters: globalization 'de-territorializes' culture, and by extension makes material culture on all levels less central to social life. We would argue the contrary, however: the cultural imperatives to select, protect and interpret certain aspects of the material world – or, in other words, conserve heritage – are even more important now for cultures in a globalizing world.

Challenges to conservation in a globalizing world

The notion of globalization has been a lightning rod for debate and discussion about culture, economics, politics and society for the past generation.[3] Even defining the term is an adventure. Sociologist Roland Robertson described globalization as 'the twofold process of the particularization of the universal and the universalization of the particular.'[4] This neat formulation places heritage conservation – long focused on particularity, uniqueness and 'cultural significance' – at the very centre in debates about the effects of globalization. What roles does heritage play in globalizing society? Are they fundamentally different or are they new? Such questions must be paired with the central political issue of globalization, as framed for instance by the critic Fredric Jameson: 'Is [globalization] a matter of transnational domination and uniformity or, on the other hand, the source of liberation of local culture from hidebound state and national forms?'[5] Heritage conservation, deeply invested in collective remembering at all scales, is one arena in which these questions must be asked. For the purposes of this essay, it suffices to say that the tangle of processes associated with globalization presents the field with challenges so deep and transformative that they suggest the need for a new paradigm.

What does globalization mean specifically for material heritage, its conservation and its role in society? One can identify a few specific aspects of the complex of processes grouped under 'globalization' directly relevant to the efficacy of cultural heritage conservation.

- Increased mobility of many kinds (people, goods, capital, ideas and information) is made possible by the proliferation of information technology as well as by deregulation and marketization.
- The interpenetration and mixing of cultures, whether under the guise of hybridization or homogenization, is bound to be a contentious and uneven process.
- The increased pace of cultural change [6] exacerbates problems with conservation's traditional role of fixing the cultural meaning of heritage sites and objects.
- The rising influence of market economics and business thinking enables market logic and economic values to dominate other kinds of social relationships and value systems. The influence of the market on the cultural sphere has been widely criticized by academic observers, but very often embraced by cultural organizations.[7]
- Globalization and its results are uneven, which is to say that power imbalances are marked and seemingly widening; we in the conservation field should therefore be aware of them and try to correct them.

Taken together, these processes demand a rethinking of traditional relationships between, on the one hand, objects, buildings, territory, the environment and culture groups, and, on the other, the role of material heritage conservation (particularly immovable heritage) in the process of continually reconstituting culture groups (maintaining them in some ways, changing in others) through processes of remembering, commemoration, ritual, artistic production, architecture and so on.

Later in this essay we argue that material heritage conservation is a more pressing need in light of economic and cultural globalization. Further, it is suggested that ensuring cultural diversity, pluralism and access be counted among the essential goals for the heritage conservation field, and that meeting these goals will in effect make heritage conservation sustainable as a functional part of civil societies. How will the conservation field advance toward these goals? It will be by focusing attention on the values underpinning the heritage as much as by materially protecting heritage objects and sites themselves. The plan of this essay is as follows: first, several propositions and assumptions linking heritage conservation to broader social concerns will be clarified. These are needed to understand how traditional notions of conservation (scientific and craft-based) can be extended to embrace social issues. Second, some of the connections between cultural diversity and heritage conservation are discussed. Finally, an argument is presented for a culture- and values-centred approach to the practice of heritage conservation, enabling it to be more responsive to the problematics of global culture, more effective in producing cultural expressions relevant to contemporary life, and ultimately more sustainable.

Propositions

As starting points, the following two propositions describe some of the assumptions behind research being undertaken at the Getty Conservation Institute (GCI) and elsewhere to link material heritage conservation to broader social and cultural contexts. These assumptions lay the groundwork for dealing with the articulations between globalization and conservation processes.

First, the having, creating and caring for heritage is, in a sense, a basic social need. The need to remember, to reinterpret the past individually and collectively, and to do so using material culture (among other means) is a social phenomenon woven into the very fabric of modernity. The existence and conservation of material heritage is thus observable in most modern cultures.[8] This thesis has been advanced from a number of different disciplinary perspectives, including anthropology (the definition of culture as things, ideas, habits and practices passed from one generation to the next), sociology (the essential social phenomenon of collective memory), environmental psychology (human beings' transcultural attachment to, and use of, crafted objects and architectural space), social history (interpreting and generating knowledge about the past) and art history (the social functions of representation, the production of commemorative and mnemonic art works).[9]

This basic need to relate to the past is not a 'basic human need' in the same vital sense as housing, ample food, sanitation or public health. But it is life sustaining and akin to the recognition of basic human rights. Indeed, the Universal Declaration of Human Rights includes cultural access as an essential human right.[10] In other words, the creation and conservation of heritage is essential to the long-term health of a society, though it might seem dispensable in a short-term, crisis-driven view. (This suggests the importance of thinking in terms of sustainability vis-à-vis heritage conservation, a theme covered later in this essay.) Conditions for human thriving and civil society are multifaceted, and in the course of advocating strongly for the satisfaction of biological needs, one should not abdicate other essential arguments about social needs as if they constituted an either/or choice.

The second assumption is that heritage and heritage conservation are best understood as social processes and not in physical terms as a set of static artifacts with fixed meaning. This suggests that the goal of conservation is to preserve what is relevant – in other words, what is valuable – to the particular culture in a particular time and place, not simply preserving a certain collection of things. To emphasize the importance of seeing conservation through a sociological lens, it is useful to speak of a 'heritage-creation process' of which material conservation is one element.[11] In the same vein, other scholars have written of the sociocultural 'construction' or even the 'invention' of heritage.[12]

In recent generations, culture has come to be understood and modelled as a continuous, contingent, politicized process. Phenomena related to heritage should be seen in this light, too. Emphasizing the fluid qualities of culture and heritage helps to explain, for instance, divergent meanings attributed to particular heritage objects and sites, or the different ideas of what constitutes heritage in different societies (or in the same society over time), or the different role of conservation (how marginal? how central?) in the time and place of a particular society. A corollary to the understanding of heritage as a process is the idea that heritage conservation is only partly understood and incompletely conceived if it is seen as dealing only with the material aspects of the object. On the contrary, the challenge is to understand that heritage objects, buildings and sites – embedded in social, economic, political and geographic contexts – are part of the larger flow of culture.

Values and valuing as central to conservation

Building on these propositions, we argue that values and valuing processes are the foundation of the whole notion of heritage and thus of the practice of conservation. Further, discussion and research concerning the role of values in heritage conservation are essential for the future efficacy of the field.

What exactly do we mean by 'values'? A value is a good, in the sense of a positive characteristic rather than in the specific sense of a tangible, tradable, economic good. Obviously, judgement of what is good is very open to interpretation and stems from beliefs and needs held internally by an individual, yet shaped strongly by external society. Values are at the heart of the heritage-creation process noted above: a certain few things are defined by a society as heritage – and thus worthy of conservation – only if they are perceived as possessing value. Discussion of values as a motivating factor for all kinds of social action has been widespread in recent years.[13] And in the conservation field, values-centred approaches to project planning are gaining support.

Heritage, by definition, is something of historic value. But analysis cannot stop there: values are plural and heritage is multivalent. A particular heritage object, building or site can be seen as having simultaneously historical value (commemorating a person or event or idea), aesthetic value (pleasing the senses), spiritual value (serving as an object of veneration or place of worship), community or political value (aiding the coherence of a social group or some other political goal), educational value (interpreting the object yields knowledge), and of course economic value (of which there are many kinds, roughly categorized as use values and potential values).[14] Within each of these categories of value, one often finds a plurality of interpretations and evaluations as well. The different coexistent values are not always commensurable; in fact, they often diverge and conflict. Realizing the economic values of a particular historic building, for instance, might destroy its historical, spiritual or aesthetic values (reusing a church as a discotheque, for instance).

In reality, different stakeholders attach many different, even divergent, values to the same object/place at the same time. One of the most striking examples of this phenomenon is the value attached to Jerusalem and to the Temple Mount in particular. The various structures, archaeological layers and events associated with this place are imbued with strongly felt and often divergent values: spiritual, cultural, social, political and even economic. The site is cherished simultaneously by Christians, Jews and Muslims for quite different but equally heartfelt reasons, and any attempt to conserve, develop or interpret any element of the site provokes heated debate and even conflict.

Clashes between differing heritage values constitute a major issue practically, politically and conceptually. Speaking of 'values' suggests a certain allegiance to subjectivity but this does not necessarily point the way toward radical subjectivity. Indeed, the aim of recognizing the subjectivity of values is far more prosaic: the idea is not to raise deep, insoluble epistemological questions regarding the existence of heritage, the legitimacy of its conservation and the inescapable power relations in which conservation is embedded, but rather to understand better how decisions are and should be made about heritage matters 'on the ground'. Investment decisions, policy priorities, architectural design and consensus reached on community priorities are all underpinned by values and valuing processes, yet conservation professionals lack the tools and concepts for gauging and understanding the interplay of values.

Clearly, the plurality of values found in the Temple Mount or any other heritage site or object paves the way for conflict over competing and sometimes incommensurable values and over the fate of heritage objects and places, and the meanings attached to them. These conflicts are heightened in a globalizing society, in which (as noted above) mobility, markets and cultural mixing increase the pace and intensity of changes in all sectors of life (economic, cultural and political). Here is the challenge: without a

Incentives in the protection of intangible cultural heritage

Cultural heritage is usually classified as either tangible or intangible. In fact, however, this distinction is not absolute: the two spheres are continuous and sometimes overlapping. In the case of historic buildings, there is a continuum between those which represent a purely materialized heritage, such as the Pyramids of Egypt, and those which are preserved through the intervention of a certain intangible cultural heritage, like the wooden Shintoist shrine of Ise in Japan, which has been renewed since the end of the seventh century by rebuilding exactly the same model every twenty years. The Mosque of Djenne in Mali, made of unbaked clay, is maintained carefully through regular repair by the faithful. Other domains of intangible cultural heritage include spoken language, narrative arts and the performing arts. Most of the latter are supported by a set of objects from tangible culture such as musical instruments, masks, costumes and other properties. These objects are often made by a limited number of trained workers whose techniques have been transmitted from generation to generation as an intangible cultural heritage. Thus although the products are tangible, the techniques employed to produce them are intangible, so that both the products and the techniques must be preserved.

Some kinds of intangible cultural heritage are in danger of disappearing. Japanese examples include 'Bunraku' or traditional puppet theatre, street performers' arts, strolling players and blessing arts for ceremonial occasions. Bunraku, created in the seventeenth century, was prosperous until the 1960s, but its survival is now in danger. Another example is folk tales. This too was very common all over Japan, with local varieties, until the 1960s, but has suffered as a result of the radical changes which have occurred since then in everyday life.

Two kinds of solutions may be suggested for conserving intangible cultural heritage. First, for the performing arts with a steadfast traditional style and a fixed content based on a written text such as Bunraku, it is important to conserve and transmit the complete performing style as a living specimen of a cultural heritage. This calls for long-term training of novice players, for which a large and financially sound training institution is preferable. The same can be said for the ancient Hue court music of Viet Nam; thanks to the efforts of UNESCO, and with the financial support of the Japan Foundation, the National University of Hue has begun the training of court music successors.

Second, the telling of folk-tales has to be performed as oral communication in an intimate relationship between tellers and listeners. Here the form and spirit of the traditional culture is to be handed down. According to the tradition, the content should be current and even the 'classic' numbers are to be told without a fixed text by means of a vivid 'oral composition' or the improvised use by each teller of a formula taken from the conventional stock. Thus, in Japan, many regional or trans-regional and library-based associations of storytellers are actively at work, training novices in folk tales and in storytelling or organizing occasional sessions of storytelling for audiences of adults or children. Although such activities are just developing in Japan, they are already very successful in many other countries for the preservation of the oral heritage, especially in Germany and the United States.

The essence of intangible cultural heritage lies in the fact that it is carried out by living practitioners and that there is a living audience to enjoy it. Thus to mummify intangible cultural heritage in order to preserve it is to run the risk of dishonouring it; it should always be alive in the contemporary context, and should remain creative as it has always been.

Another example from a different country illustrates the creative succession of an intangible cultural heritage. Under the leadership of Dr Mahaman Garba, a renowned musician and ethnomusicologist at the Centre de Formation et de Promotion Musicales of Niamey in Niger, young musicians of Niger, who have inherited their ancestral musical traditions in the form of instruments, tunes and rhythms, are adding new instruments such as the keyboard and electric guitar and new musical elements such as rap to create music with new words appropriate to the current life of the people of Niger. These young musicians have now successfully released the first commercial recordings of their music in a country where such an undertaking had never before been attempted, owing to technical and financial difficulties.

The skills involved in traditional handicrafts are threatened by changing economic conditions. Hand weavers in India are unable to compete with the large-scale manufacturers of cloth, and despite the existence of training centres, the survival of their craft is precarious. Another example is the construction of Japanese wooden boats equipped with the 'ro' stern oar; it is becoming increasingly difficult to obtain the 'funa kugi' or iron nail of the particular bent form needed for these boats, and as a result the boats are on the point of disappearing. However, if there is sufficient demand and an assured income, even a highly specialized handicraft can hope to survive. One example is the making of the 'akeni' trunk for Sumo wrestlers in Japan. This is the traditional suitcase made from beautifully lacquered bamboo; for many years now only one craftsman has made this trunk, but because continuing income is assured, his son is taking over from him.

The preservation of intangible cultural heritage will succeed only if the right incentives are provided. Enlightened educational activities by UNESCO and other organizations are one strategy. Another is the provision of economic incentives through tourism, a positive force for the revivification or renewal of cultural heritage and for the cross-cultural mutual understanding of cultural diversity. By promoting incentives for cultural heritage practitioners, we can expect to contribute to cultural and economic advancement as follows:

First, by encouraging pride in cultural identity and respect for other cultures, we contribute to preventing conflict. The case of is a good example; it can animate communal or inter-generational circles in the context of intimate vocal communication, respecting traditional style and motifs, while using contemporary topics and making people aware of their own cultural heritage.

Second, developing traditional handicrafts in a new context is an effective countermeasure to the destruction of the natural environment. Handicrafts that make use of vegetal and other recyclable materials produce many useful items which cannot be replaced by plastic or metal goods. An illustration of this is the subtle and astonishingly wide use of calabash and wild grass straw among people of the African savannah.

Third, encouraging traditional handicrafts is a way of reviving the dignity of human labour, which in the modern economy tends to be downgraded and undervalued. Respect for human labour, especially of women, is a prerequisite for human development. And the revitalization of cultural heritage has an important role to play here in helping human development to acquire real sustainability.

JUNZO KAWADA
Professor of Cultural Anthropology,
Faculty of International Studies,
Hiroshima City University (Japan)

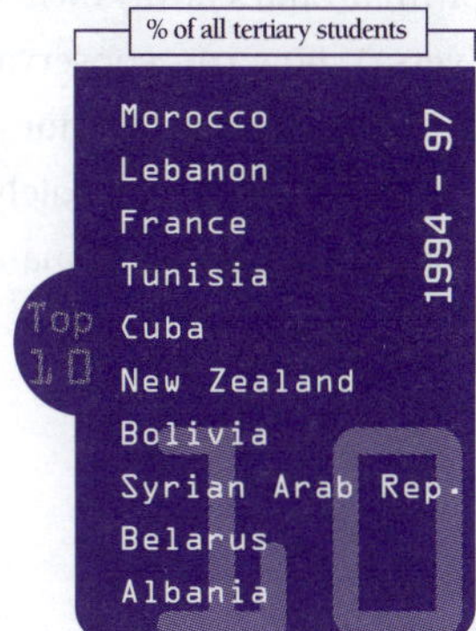

Tertiary students in fine arts and humanities
% of all tertiary students
Top 10
1994 - 97
Morocco
Lebanon
France
Tunisia
Cuba
New Zealand
Bolivia
Syrian Arab Rep.
Belarus
Albania

Source: See the Index of culture indicators and sources and Table 24 in Part Seven of this report.

priori denying the legitimacy of one or another type of value, or ranking them in some kind of pre-existing hierarchy of values (i.e. spiritual values always win over economic values, or vice versa), how can conservation decisions be managed so that many (all?) values are accounted for and given voice? This is not solely an intellectual question; it is manifestly a matter of management and conservation of real places and things.

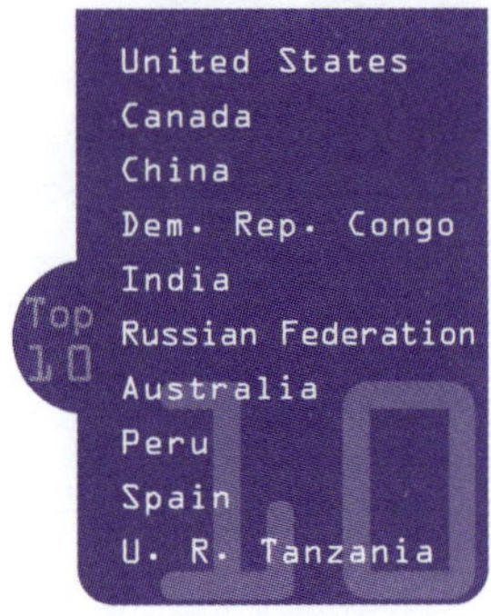

Natural
heritage sites
Top 10
United States
Canada
China
Dem. Rep. Congo
India
Russian Federation
Australia
Peru
Spain
U. R. Tanzania

Source: See the Index of culture indicators and sources and Table 12 in Part Seven of this report.

In asking these questions about values, the relationships between economic values and other values loom large. Economic values are clearly ascendant in globalizing society. The tendency in many policy and decision-making circles is to let economic considerations and market mechanisms reign.[15] Among conservation professionals, by contrast, the tendency has been to dismiss economic values as 'derived' from cultural values, and therefore to consider that they merit little or no consideration in weighing conservation decisions. This may be defensible rhetorically as a matter of conservation philosophy or theory, but any engagement with the actual world of competing values and stakeholders must engage the massive and popular influence of economic values – which often threaten the very cultural values that are the *raison d'être* of heritage conservation and the currency of diversity and pluralism. The end goal, within conservation, should be the preserving of a diversity of values within the practice and discourse of conservation – and it would be perilous to exclude the very real influence of economic values in this calculation.[16]

Cultural diversity and conservation

Cultural diversity is 'an all-pervasive, enduring characteristic of societies' and it has emerged as a social norm (in response to the massive economic, social, cultural and technical transformations of recent decades).[17] Recent public discussions about cultural diversity have driven home the principle that diversity is a good thing. In questioning exactly how conservation can advance the cause of diversity, one needs a deeper sense of why cultural diversity is desirable and what its different faces are.

At first glance, diversity and culture could be seen as having a tense relationship. Any culture is presumed to have some internal coherence and unity – as opposed to diversity – owing to the notion that a culture is discernible only if it can be distinguished from other cultures. On the other hand, many scholars have argued that diversity is critical to the survival and thriving of human societies. This is a commonly held belief, and indeed is fundamental to this report. The need for diversity is argued from ecological perspectives (cultures diversify as they adapt to different environmental circumstances); and from political perspectives (post-colonial arguments insist that diverse cultures should be cultivated against the homogenizing, repressive forces of dominant Western cultures). Economist Stephen Marglin even goes so far as to assert that, 'Cultural diversity may be the key to the survival of the human species.'[18] Empirically, the need for cultural diversity would seem to be expressed in the reality that multicultural societies and states have long existed in all parts of the world.

Anthropologist Ulf Hannerz has detailed a number of reasons why cultural diversity is needed in contemporary society.[19] Globalization, at first glance, is assumed to lead to a homogeneous, one-world culture that quashes diversity. In assessing the threats globalization poses to diversity, Hannerz sees reasons why diversity will not wither away: creativity and intercultural contact create culture at a rapid rate, which increases as part of the sweep of globalization. In other words, cultural innovation is more rapid than homogenization, and so diversity wins out; or, to use an ecological metaphor, new cultures evolve faster than they become extinct, which is the opposite of ecosystems. Also, the existence of a 'cultural record' (in other words, heritage) acts as a brake, so that cultures do not erode or disappear as fast or as completely as if globalizing forces had free reign. Calls to valorize and defend cultural diversity at all scales seem to emanate from the very processes of globalization.

Another line of thinking about globalization stresses the complexity of the social processes involved and finds that these processes are, to some extent, always accompanied by their opposites. For instance, the creation of homogeneous global cultures spread through market forces ('McDonaldization') is accompanied by opposing forces of differentiation, hybridization or outright resistance (witness the recent attack against a McDonald's restaurant in France, and protests at the December 1999 World Trade Organization meetings in Seattle). And while cultural fusion, pluralism and other democracy- or market-driven creation of new cultural forms are evident all over the globe, so are forces of chauvinism, 'cleansing' and commercial homogenization. Such opposing tendencies can be observed in many spheres of society.[20]

This pairing of opposite processes is also true regarding heritage conservation. The supposed tendency of globalization and its technologies to 'de-territorialize' culture and reduce attachments to local space, objects and territory is opposed by efforts to seek greater attachment to place. Witness the growing interest in preservation of landscapes and localities (as opposed to individual buildings and monuments), or the wide popular use of terms like 'sense of place' and other ways of expressing the attachments felt to places. Another tension arises from the way in which heritage objects are often defined as 'irreplaceable' while scholars increasingly speak of heritage as 'produced' in a continual process embedded in time and place. This suggests two categories of cultural heritage: one considered irreplaceable because of symbolic or artistic value (monuments, masterworks, landmarks and sacred sites); and another, ambient kind of heritage that is continually reproduced, which stresses utility values (the constant stream of new museums in which the experiences if not the artifacts themselves are seen to be replaceable; innumerable 'Main Street' shopping districts) and can be seen as 'replaceable,' or at least 'substitutable'.

Diversity means many things and its meaning is contingent upon different geographical and social milieux. Different norms of conformity and innovation must be allowed for cultures at all scales; this refers back to the argument that access to one's culture and freedom in cultural production are among the basic human rights and needs. In the contemporary United States, for instance, it is safe to say that innovation and creativity are highly prized (especially in the creation of new products and markets); whereas in Tibet, for example, allegiance to stable and well-defined spiritual traditions may be more prized than innovation and experimentation.

Looming behind the realization of many different notions of diversity, though, is the question of the scale at which diversity is desired and pursued. All conservation projects are rooted in their local context. It is common to find the different stakeholders in a heritage site having quite different interpretations of the site's cultural values, some favouring the meanings that fill out our global sense of diversity, others toeing the line of old orthodoxies of patriotism or ethnic chauvinism. In many instances, heritage sites skirt locality altogether and intentionally cultivate national identity. And there is also the notion of the 'global ecumene'[21] in which a truly global idea of cultural diversity is situated. Some heritage – by UNESCO's definition, those sites inscribed on the World Heritage List – are seen to be universally and uniformly meaningful at all scales.[22]

On the face of it, heritage conservation would seem to work against diversity. By maintaining older, existing cultural expressions and forms, conservation would appear to divert resources from the creation of new expressions and cultural forms. However, the two impulses work together in fundamental ways. First, conservation, far from setting existing cultural works in stone, is emphatically a means of reinterpreting and reproducing cultural meanings in the here and now. Acts of conservation do not simply 'maintain' a cultural artifact and its meanings and values; conservation is itself an act of interpretation, selection and valorizing and can respond quite directly to calls for greater diversity. Second, maintaining the 'stock' of a culture through conservation is a fundamental condition for cultural continuity, but also for creativity, which continually draws on this stock (consciously or not). In this sense, speaking of material heritage as a form of 'cultural capital' is useful for conceptualizing the ways in which heritage is valued, managed, accumulated and invested in by various stakeholders (that is, it can be viewed as a kind of capital asset having both economic and cultural values simultaneously[23]).

New ideas for conservation

Clearly, calls for diversity and the realities of globalization present great challenges to the heritage conservation field. In order for the field to evolve and adapt to the new, complex, in some ways contradictory conditions of globalizing culture, it is argued here that the conservation of values should take centre stage. The practice of conservation should not be limited to means of preventing and arresting material decay and ensuring the existence of and access to heritage in museums, protected historic districts and landscapes and so forth, though these will still be needed and must be cultivated; they are the historical strengths of the conservation field. But to supplement these mainly technical achievements, a more values-based model of conservation must be devised, the tools for which are interpretation, education and community engagement, as much as scientific research, documentation methods, connoisseurship and material treatments. In the future, conservation skills will need to encompass all of the following: a truly multidisciplinary understanding of the role material heritage plays in contemporary society, planning methods for garnering community input and negotiating among many stakeholders, methods of scholarly and popular interpretation and presentation of historic, cultural and other values, and pedagogical programmes and methods for transmitting the messages of heritage conservation beyond the field narrowly defined. A conservation paradigm based on preserving and transmitting knowledge and values – ensuring access to them – suggests that the distinction generally made between material heritage and immaterial expressions of heritage needs to be less rigid and more open.

How is values-driven conservation different from traditional models and why is it better suited to addressing the demands of cultural diversity in the context of globalization? A discussion of values connects the material and interpretive acts of conservation more closely to the social, cultural, economic and moral goals that drive these acts. Also, focusing conservation discussions on values – which, as argued above, are varied and plural – reinforces the interdisciplinary nature of conservation practice, constituting a kind of lingua franca for the various competing stakeholders with an interest in heritage (community members, tourists, business people, officials and politicians, economists, anthropologists, archaeologists, conservators, curators, artists and the like). Values present a useful discursive and heuristic tool for identifying and binding together a broad community around issues related to heritage.

The processes of constructing, ascribing and assessing value are the keys to defining, creating and conserving heritage and they should be a guide to making decisions, devising plans and clarifying priorities. Conservation driven by, and attuned to, values – of the present and for the future – will lead to somewhat different conservation outcomes and will require different ideas, tools and skills on the part of the conservation community and decision-makers.

The fact that values are always in flux requires that choices constantly be made among them. Values must inform policy, which in the broadest sense is about choosing among alternatives. Choices vis-à-vis heritage conservation need to be made for three different reasons: scarcity of resources (there are not enough funds to invest in all worthy conservation projects); abundance of potential heritage objects and places (the current theory of history holds that everything is historic, so the potential universe of heritage is enormous) and the need to identify some objects/places as more significant than others, in order to constitute them as 'heritage'; and the fact that any potential heritage object/place is valued in multiple ways, simultaneously, and that not all of these values can be realized at once.

The issue of how choices are made, on what basis and by what means and politics of negotiation are therefore very important to situating conservation in the broader social context. We in conservation would be glad for the certainty to be gained by being able to measure values objectively and plug them into an equation, and from this calculus be led along a clear path of action that conforms with the field's broadest goals (diversity, pluralism and access). But many kinds of value, by their very nature, are susceptible only to subjective means of expression. Further, values are so varied that many argue that they are incommensurable and cannot be traded with one another. Choices among heritage values have traditionally been made by connoisseurs, scholars or politicians and for their own, fairly narrow reasons. As a matter of socio-political process, these decisions have been made in a 'black box'. For the sake of cultural diversity, decisions need to be more transparent and more inclusive (without excluding experts).

Sustainability as a guide

As a matter of conservation practice and decision-making, values provide a language but not a guide to action. The notion of sustainability can be introduced to make this connection. Sustainability has become a leading cause in environmental conservation, and has effectively bridged the ecological concerns of environmental conservationists with broad, powerful forces of economic development and public policy. Increasingly, the notion of sustainability is being applied to the understanding of the role of culture in development.[24] Invoking the mantra of 'sustainability' requires some careful definitions. What is being sustained? In this case, it is culture that is being sustained first and foremost (as contrasted with sustaining ecological health, or capital accumulation and economic growth – but culture is not totally separate from these). A more emphatic shift needs to be made in reformulating the notion of sustainability to pursue the goal of how culture, and its evolution, can be sustained. Ensuring diversity, pluralism and access would be three useful tests for gauging the sustainability of cultural policies, decisions and trends. Values-centred conservation is envisioned as a paradigm that is more sustainable vis-à-vis culture because, as argued above, it better serves the goal of ensuring equity of access to culture.

Whatever the context of its use, the idea of sustainability is fundamentally about complexity and dealing with complex systems.[25] This is particularly well-suited to heritage conservation, which, as argued here, is driven by exceedingly complex interplays of different, shifting values. In this sense, sustainability represents a distinct advance on more linear ways of thinking about conservation (e.g. ensuring an adequate supply of resources for future consumption; increasing the number of listed properties or the amount of money invested as measures of success). The conservation field's response to globalization, in other words, should not necessarily find us arguing for the resources to protect more heritage, or that the existing heritage needs to be more completely protected. We need to know more about how conservation decisions are made and how they affect various stakeholders, in order to know what values and things need protecting. This definition also makes clearer why sustainability is an idea well-suited to the understanding of cultural conservation. What is culture if not a vastly complex system?[26]

A second idea fundamental to any use of 'sustainability' is long-term thinking. The norm of inter-generational (long-term) equity is a central part of the notion of sustainability, whether applied to ecology, investment or culture.[27] For the purposes of this essay, equity refers to cultural diversity and access, and simply preserving material artifacts so they persist through time cannot provide such access. Far more important is preserving the profusion of values, meanings, ideas and interpretations attached to the artifacts – in other words, the culture borne through the artifacts. 'Preserving' in this sense is not confined to putting values under glass, but rather means sustaining their expressiveness – whether it is language, music, artifacts, buildings or working landscapes – and access to it.

Intangible cultural heritage: new safeguarding approaches

Intangible cultural heritage encompasses the most fundamental aspects of living culture and tradition. Its manifestations are broad and diverse, whether related to languages, oral traditions, traditional knowledge, creation of material culture, value systems or the performing arts. Intangible heritage, along with tangible heritage, serves to reinforce cultural identity, diversity and creativity. The Kyrghyz epic story *Manas* is as much a monument as the Egyptian pyramids.

Interest in the concept of intangible heritage has been growing worldwide and has been most notably apparent in UNESCO's governing forums since the mid-1990s. There is a growing interest too in relation to cultural dynamics in contemporary society and particularly an increasing awareness of ethnic identity. To some extent, this awareness has emerged as a result of weakened frameworks of nation-states following the end of the Cold War era. A reaction to this situation has been the increasing assertion of ethnicity through intangible cultural expressions which embody, in addition to historical roots, genuine spiritual and ethical values.

There is greater awareness in many nations today of the urgent need to act to safeguard and promote their unique forms of cultural expression. Significantly, such action enriches cultural diversity throughout the world. Intangible heritage, as a mainspring of creativity, in turn contributes to the diversification of contemporary creativity. Indeed, the value of intangible heritage particular to a given locality is becoming increasingly recognized in reaction to the phenomenon of 'globalization'.

Two approaches

Two major approaches to the safeguarding of intangible cultural heritage are: (a) transforming it into a tangible form and (b) keeping it alive in its original context. The first of these implies documenting, recording and archiving and aims to guarantee the perpetual existence of intangible heritage. If Homer had not written down the *Iliad* some four centuries after the historical events, then the legendary battle scenes with the heroic characters of the Trojan War and the Mycenaean treasures would have been lost to us for ever.

The second approach seeks to keep intangible cultural expressions alive by encouraging revitalization and inter-generational transmission. In this way, custodians of the heritage – bearers, actors and creators of various cultural expressions – are given recognition and incentives not only to preserve but also to improve their skills and artistry.

Both approaches are complementary and indispensable for the safeguarding of intangible cultural heritage. UNESCO decided more recently to privilege the second option, giving due consideration to the Organization's previous focus on documentation and research as reflected in the 1989 *Recommendation on the Safeguarding of Traditional Culture and Folklore*. The Organization's decision to give precedence to this option came also in response to opinions expressed by the 1993 International Expert Meeting which drew up a new guideline for the programme.

Experts recommended that UNESCO undertake activities to encourage guardians and creators of intangible cultural heritage. The crucial role of populations and communities who produce and reproduce different cultural forms was also underlined. Experts finally recommended that priority be granted to the revitalization of these cultural expressions in their original contexts (thus avoiding so-called 'folklorization').

Partnerships

In order to revitalize traditional popular cultures, UNESCO encourages governments to give incentives to cultural groups, local communities and practitioners of the intangible culture in the form of official recognition, legal protection, special health care provisions, tax deductions or subventions. It also urges governments to introduce the intangible culture into education curricula and to promote festivals, competitions and television programmes.

Many governments are already committed to safeguarding intangible culture as their national heritage. The main results of a recent worldwide survey sent by UNESCO to its Member States, to which 103 members responded, speak for themselves:

LIVING LANGUAGES IN THE WORLD

Geographical region	Living languages
Asia	2,165
Africa	2,010
Pacific	1,300
America	1,000
Europe	225
World	6,700

Graph 13
Living Languages in the World

Source: *Cambridge Encyclopaedia of Language*, 1997.

- In 57 states, intangible cultural heritage is part of national cultural policy;
- 31 states have an infrastructure tailored to preserving intangible heritage;
- 49 states have the means to train collectors, archivists and documentalists;
- 54 countries run courses in or out of school on intangible culture;
- 47 countries have national folklore councils or similar co-ordinating bodies;
- 80 states provide moral or economic support to individuals and institutions promoting intangible heritage;
- of 63 countries providing support for artists and practitioners, 28 give state support, 14 give honour or status, and 5 give state positions;
- in 52 states, national legislation contains provisions on the 'intellectual property aspects' of intangible heritage;
- 80% of events to disseminate intangible heritage are identified as festivals or fairs;
- 66% of institutions disseminating intangible heritage are cultural and educational organizations.

Despite its intergovernmental nature, UNESCO's partnership with civil societies has recently expanded. Today the Organization co-operates with many NGOs such as the Summer Institute of Linguistics, the International Council for Traditional Music (ICTM), and the International Council of Organizations for Folklore Festivals and Folk Art (CIOFF) which are renowned for their activities in safeguarding and promoting intangible cultural heritage.

An international conference organized jointly by UNESCO and the Smithsonian Institution in Washington, D.C. in 1999 confirmed the urgent necessity to work closely with communities, cultural groups and practitioners. In considering intangible culture as manifest in community activities which express, reinforce and reflect widely shared values, beliefs, ideals and practices, the conference recommended UNESCO to create and increase its co-operation with grass-root NGOs and NPOs.

A new project entitled 'Proclamation of Masterpieces of the Oral and Intangible Heritage of Humanity' aims to encourage governments, NGOs, local communities, groups and individuals to preserve and promote their unique individual heritage.

The Spanish author, Juan Goytiso and other residents of Marrakesh (Morocco), including Mustapha Zine (notary) and Jaafar Kanssoussi (historian), created an NPO called the Association to Protect Popular Cultural Expression Performed in Jema'el Fna Square. It also enjoys the enthusiastic support of Carlos Fuentes, the Mexican writer.
The Association documents popular cultural performances, mobilizes schoolchildren to visit the Square, organizes exhibitions, is campaigning for a National Day for Jema'el Fna Square, and produces television programmes and films.

New perspectives

Conservative or nostalgic views of intangible heritage too often regard it as static and merely historical. They are primarily concerned with 'authenticity'. In contrast to monumental culture, intangible heritage is often dynamic and constantly evolving in view of its close connection to living practices of community life.

If this heritage is to remain a living part of community life, t should play a significant social, political, economic and cultural role there. Traditional knowledge, for example, can contribute to resolving problems of inter-ethnic conflict and environmental protection. Traditional cultural expression, on the other hand, must readapt and be relevant to contemporary life if its survival is to be ensured. The challenge is one of pursuing dynamic, community-based and collaborative approaches to intangible cultural heritage so as to ensure its continuity and vitality for future generations.

NORIKO AIKAWA
Director,
Intangible Heritage Section, UNESCO

Is cultural diversity one of the norms implied in sustaining culture? Yes, but there are enormous problems in how to gauge cultural diversity. First, as noted above, there are many different sorts of diversity: how can different cultures and cultural expressions be distinguished from one another, let alone compared? Different cultures are comfortable with different levels and kinds of diversity. How much diversity is enough? At some point is too much diversity a bad thing?[28] Little is understood of the 'ecology' of cultural heritage, and heritage conservation is thus pursued without much certainty about the effect of its actions on the whole 'system' of culture. To improve the field's knowledge in this regard, one of the acute research needs is to map the system in which cultural heritage conservation interacts with economic, political, social, geographical and other systems in contemporary society.[29]

Prospects for heritage conservation

Heritage, and our collective need for it, will not fade away, nor will the complexity of decisions about what to conserve and how to conserve be magically clarified. Ultimately, the answers to heritage conservation decisions and policies, and their sustainability, will be found in and by communities themselves.[30] The judgements of conservation professionals, universal declarations, the work of transnational organizations such as GCI and UNESCO and public policies should not provide more than guidelines, advice and shared ideas. We can provide maps, but each community must choose its own course.

Conservation will continue to serve as a hedge against cultural loss, because material culture, environmental ties and aesthetic satisfaction remain important to individual and collective quality of life. As the traditional attachments between territory and culture are eroded by globalization's celebration of flows, intentional attachments to material heritage will seem more important. Despite the predictions of some,[31] the fact remains that space, artifact and territory still matter in global society – and by many accounts they matter more than ever. Heritage will also be seen, ideally, as a source of creativity, a way of replenishing and investing in our stock of cultural capital, which, as the cultural economist Arjo Klamer puts it, is 'the ability to be inspired'.[32] In both senses – as a hedge against loss and a source of new cultural forms – conservation is cast as a desirable kind of cultural production.

The goal of diversity in the context of the global ecumene can be achieved and sustained only with heritage conservation as one of its means. Diversity can be cultivated through conservation as long as decisions about which values, which meanings and which parts of material culture should be conserved are made explicit and abide by wide commitments to diversity, pluralism and creativity.[33] By contrast, the 'marketization' of cultural spheres often works against the collective, democratic ideals behind diversity, pluralism and access by creating markets in which culture becomes a product whose price increases in direct proportion to its standardization. What can the conservation field do to ensure that cultural diversity is enriched by our work? First, cultivate an awareness of values (both within our field and in public understanding of our work), and thereby provide a means for different disciplines, fields and stakeholders to speak a common language.[34] Second, broaden the focus of the field from safeguarding things in and of themselves. Conservation of material heritage is a means to an end: cultural confidence, or cultural sustainability, or even more broadly, diversity, pluralism and access. To do this, the conservation field needs to collaborate with and learn from other fields and disciplines. Third, work more assiduously with allied disciplines and with communities, in a collaborative, context-sensitive mode of conserving the heritage that replaces the traditional delivery of expert opinions with support for community values.[35] The immediately attainable goal is to ensure the plurality of voices and values embodied in the process of creating and conserving heritage.

Notes

1. This paper presents the views of the authors, not necessarily the position of the Getty Conservation Institute (GCI). The mission of the GCI is to advance the practice of material heritage conservation worldwide. The Institute's activities are designed to serve the conservation field in meeting current challenges and thinking creatively about the future. The Institute has been pursuing the links between contemporary social dynamics and the practice of conservation through research efforts on the economics of heritage conservation, the role of values in the construction of heritage and in conservation decisions and in various of the Institute's educational efforts.

2. Indeed, we propose a more encompassing definition of heritage conservation: it has traditionally been confined to technical and scientific efforts to arrest or prevent material decay of objects and buildings, but this traditional focus is under pressure to expand and look outward. In this expanded sense, conservation would also be taken to include, for instance, the interpretation of heritage, lists and other policies and laws regarding the definition and care of heritage, discourse regarding philosophies and attitudes toward heritage and its care, the political and institutional arrangements and dynamics supporting heritage and the financing and investment of all these activities. (The GCI is undertaking research to identify and characterize these other parts of the heritage conservation process that link traditional, hands-on conservation practice to the social contexts that shape the need and the opportunities for it.)

3. There is an immense variety of commentary on globalization. See, for instance, Appadurai (1996), Castells (1999), Hannerz (1996), Jameson and Miyoshi (1998), Sassen (1993 and 1999) and Tomlinson (1999).

4. Jameson in Jameson and Miyoshi, 1998, p. xi.

5. Ibid., p. xiii.

6. Anthropologist David Maybury-Lewis uses the notion of 'cultural confidence' for the idea that it is the pace of cultural change that can produce feelings of dislocation and cultural loss, as much as the actual content of the change (see Avrami, Mason and de la Torre, 1999).

7. Among the critics, consider Jameson's account of the collapse of critical distance between the capitalist economy and culture (Jameson, 1984) or Zukin's account of cultural institutions' role in urban development (Zukin, 1995); advocates include many museum directors (Vidarte, 1999).

8. Most, if not all, cultures in the world are modern to some extent. It has been argued that 'traditional' or 'native' cultures fully remote from the influences of modernity do not exist (Tomlinson, 1999).

9. For example, see Boyer (1994), Csikszentmihalyi (1993), Halbwachs (1980), Susman (1984) and Yates (1966).

10. Consult [http://www.un.org/rights/50/decla.htm]. See Article 27 specifically, and other, indirect references to the rights of cultural access and participation throughout the Declaration.

11. The idea of a heritage-creation process is discussed in Avrami, Mason and de la Torre (1999).

12. Hobsbawm and Ranger (1983); Lowenthal (1985).

13. The GCI has been pursuing research on the importance of values in heritage conservation; see Avrami, Mason and de la Torre (1999). Examples of the prominence of 'values' as a discourse in other, varied fields and sectors include the following quote prominently displayed on the website of the Ford Foundation: 'Values – judgments about what is right and important in life – help steer our lives and institutions.' (Susan V. Berresford, President, Ford Foundation, http://www.fordfound.org on 15 September 1999). Harvard Divinity School publishes a periodical titled *Religion and Values in Public Life*. Books centred on the notion of values appear not only in the economics and philosophy fields, as expected, but in disciplines ranging from literary criticism to architecture to conservation biology.

14. For typologies of value see Frey (1997), Kellert (1996), Klamer and Zuidhof (1999), Lipe (1984), Marquis-Kyle and Walker (1992), Riegl (1982) and de la Torre (1997).

15. This tendency is well documented in the American context in books such as Kuttner (1999).

16. For information on the GCI's research project on these issues, see Mason (1999).

17. Pérez de Cuellar (1995), p. 17.

18. Marglin (1990), p.16.

19. Hannerz (1996), Chapter 5.

20. See, for instance, the work of sociologist John Tomlinson (1999) summarizing debates about the globalization of culture, or the work of Saskia Sassen on centralization and marginality in recent reorganization of the global economy (Benedikt, 1997).

21. The term is used by Hannerz but is also employed more widely, as in the journal *Ecumene*.

22. See Arizpe (1999).

23. See Throsby (1999b) for a detailed discussion of the application of the 'cultural capital' notion to cultural heritage.

24. In addition to the first *World Culture Report* (UNESCO, 1998) and the report of the World Commission on Culture and Development (Pérez de Cuéllar, 1995), the World Bank has staged several conferences and publications concerning the role of culture in development (see for instance Serageldin and Martin-Brown, 1999). For an alternative, critical view see Apfel Marglin and Marglin (1990).

25. Bradbury (1998).

26. The GCI is currently pursuing research on the meaning and use of 'sustainability' as a norm in the heritage conservation field.
27. Throsby (1997 and 1999a).
28. Even environmental conservationists working to ensure biodiversity do not seem sure of these issues of measuring diversity and creating clear norms, although they have the benefit of detailed, scientific understanding of the ecological systems in which their conservation efforts are embedded.
29. The GCI plans a research effort to begin such a mapping exercise (see forthcoming white paper entitled 'A Conceptual Model of Conservation in Society').
30. 'Communities' as used here refer to local, regional and national scales.
31. For instance, Morley and Robins (1995, cited in Tomlinson, 1999).
32. Mason (1999).
33. See Arizpe's article on conviviability (UNESCO, 1998).
34. There is little empirical data on the role that different values play in heritage conservation (for one of the few published examples, see de la Torre, 1997). Values are only beginning to be a subject of conceptual, theoretical and epistemological interest within the conservation field (see Benedikt, 1997; English Heritage, 1997; Kellert, 1996; Rosvall, 1999). Hearing about empirical studies done by others around the world would be welcome. The authors would appreciate knowing about other empirical studies about heritage values that have been completed (contact us at GCIEconomics@getty.edu).
35. Place Matters, a programme of identifying cultural landmarks in New York City, is an excellent example of focusing on community values instead of relying on experts in deciding what the city's landmarks should be, thus decentring the responsibility to decide which values will be preserved. See Kaufman, 1998.

Bibliography

Apfel Marglin, F.; Marglin, S. (eds.). 1990. *Dominating Knowledge: Development, Culture, and Resistance.* Oxford, Clarendon Press.

Appadurai, A. 1996. *Modernity at Large: Cultural Dimensions of Globalization.* Minneapolis, University of Minnesota Press.

Arizpe, L. 1999. Cultural Heritage and Globalization. In: E. Avrami, R. Mason and M. de la Torre (eds.), *The Values and Benefits of Cultural Heritage Conservation: Research Report.* Los Angeles, Getty Conservation Institute.

——. 1998. 'Convivencia': The Goal of Conviviability. In: UNESCO, *World Culture Report: Culture, Creativity and Markets.* Paris, UNESCO Publishing.

Avrami, E.; Mason, R.; de la Torre, M. (eds.). 1999. *The Values and Benefits of Cultural Heritage Conservation: Research Report.* Los Angeles, Getty Conservation Institute.

Benedikt, M. (ed.). 1997. *Center 10: Value, a Journal for Architecture in America.* Austin, University of Texas Press.

Benhamou, F. 1997. Conserving Historic Monuments in France: A Critique of Official Policies. In: M. Hutter and I. E. Rizzo (eds.), *Economic Perspectives on Cultural Heritage*, pp. 196–210. London, Macmillan.

Boyer, M. C. 1994. *The City of Collective Memory: Its Historical Imagery and Architectural Entertainments.* Cambridge, MIT Press.

Bradbury, R. 1998. Sustainable Development as a Subversive Issue. *Nature & Resources*, Vol. 34, No. 4, October–December, pp. 7–11.

Castells, M. 1999. *The Information Age: Economy, Society and Culture.* Cambridge, Blackwell. 3 vols.

Csikszentmihalyi, M. 1993. Why We Need Things. In: S. Lubar and W. D. Kingery (eds.), *History From Things: Essays on Material Culture.* Washington, D.C., Smithsonian Institution Press.

English Heritage. 1997. *Sustaining the Historic Environment: New Perspectives on the Future (An English Heritage Discussion Document).* London, English Heritage.

Frey, B. S. 1997. The Evaluation of Cultural Heritage: Some Critical Issues. In: M. Hutter and I. E. Rizzo (eds.), *Economic Perspectives on Cultural Heritage*, pp. 31–49. New York, St. Martin's Press.

Halbwachs, M. 1980. *The Collective Memory* (translated by F. J. Ditter, Jr. and V. Y. Ditter), New York, Harper and Row. (First published 1950.)

Hannerz, U. 1996. *Transnational Connections: Culture, People, Places.* London/New York, Routledge.

Hobsbawm, E.; Ranger, T. (eds.). 1983. *The Invention of Tradition.* Cambridge, Cambridge University Press.

Jameson, F. 1984. Postmodernism, or the Cultural Logic of Late Capitalism. *New Left Review*, Vol. 146, pp. 53–92.

Jameson, F.; Miyoshi, M. (eds.). 1998. *The Cultures of Globalization.* Durham/London, Duke University Press.

Kaufman, N. 1998. Heritage and the Cultural Politics of Preservation. *Places*, Vol. 11, No. 3, pp. 58–65.

Kellert, S. R. 1996. *The Value of Life: Biological Diversity and Human Society.* Washington, D.C., Island Press.

Klamer, A.; Zuidhof, P. W. 1999. The Values of Cultural Heritage: Merging Economic and Cultural Appraisals. In: R. Mason (ed.), *Economics and Heritage Conservation: A Meeting Organized by the Getty Conservation Institute*, pp. 23–61. Los Angeles, Getty Conservation Institute.

Kuttner, R. 1999. *Everything for Sale: The Virtues and Limits of Markets*. Chicago: University of Chicago Press.

Lipe, W. D. 1984. Value and Meaning in Cultural Resources. In: H. Cleere (ed.), *Approaches to the Archaeological Heritage: A Comparative Study of World Cultural Resources Management Systems*. New York/Cambridge, United Kingdom/Cambridge University Press.

Lowenthal, D. 1999. Stewarding the Past in a Perplexing Present. In: E. Avrami, R. Mason and M. de la Torre (eds.), *The Values and Benefits of Cultural Heritage Conservation: Research Report*. Los Angeles, Getty Conservation Institute.

—— 1985. *The Past is a Foreign Country*. Cambridge, Cambridge University Press.

Marglin, S. 1990. Towards the Decolonization of the Mind. In: F. Apfel Marglin and S. Marglin (eds.), *Dominating Knowledge: Development, Culture and Resistance*. Oxford, Clarendon Press.

Marquis-Kyle, P.; Walker, M. 1992. *The Illustrated Burra Charter*. Sydney, Australia ICOMOS/Australian Heritage Commission.

Mason, R. (ed.). 1999. *Economics and Heritage Conservation: A Meeting Organized by the Getty Conservation Institute*. Los Angeles, Getty Conservation Institute.

Morley, D.; Robins, K. 1995. *Spaces of Identity: Global Media, Electronic Landscapes and Cultural Boundaries*. London/New York, Routledge.

Mumford, L. 1938. *The Culture of Cities*. New York, Harcourt Brace and Company.

Pérez de Cuéllar, J. 1995. *Our Creative Diversity: Report of the World Commission on Culture and Development*. Paris, UNESCO Publishing.

Riegl, A. 1982. The Modern Cult of Monuments: Its Character and Its Origin. (Translated by K. W. Forster and D. Ghirardo), *Oppositions*, Vol. 25., pp. 21–51. (First published in 1903.)

Rosvall, J. 1999. *The Heritage Restoration Facing a New Challenge: Sustained Development*. (Paper presented at the European Historical Heritage as Employment Generating Source Conference, Caceres, Spain, 28–30 April 1999.)

Sassen, S. 1999. *Globalization and Its Discontents: Essays on the New Mobility of People and Money*. New York, New Press.

——. 1993. *The Global City: New York, London, Tokyo*. Princeton University Press.

Serageldin, I.; Martin-Brown, J. (eds.). 1999. *Culture in Sustainable Development: Investing in Cultural and Natural Endowments*. (Proceedings of the Conference Sponsored by the World Bank and UNESCO held at the World Bank, Washington, D.C., 28–29 September 1998.) Washington, D.C., World Bank.

Sheets, P. D. 1992. *The Ceren Site: A Prehistoric Village Buried by Volcanic Ash in Central America*. Fort Worth, Harcourt Brace Jovanovich College Publishers.

Susman, W. 1984. *Culture as History: The Transformation of American Society in the Twentieth Century*. New York, Pantheon.

Throsby, D. 1999a. Cultural Capital. *Journal of Cultural Economics*, Vol. 23, pp. 3–12.

——. 1999b. *Cultural Capital and Sustainability Concepts in the Economics of Cultural Heritage*. Los Angeles, Getty Conservation Institute. (Unpublished research report.)

——. 1997. Sustainability and Culture: Some Theoretical Issues. *International Journal of Cultural Policy*, Vol. 4, pp. 7–20.

Tomlinson, J. 1999. *Globalization and Culture*. Chicago, University of Chicago Press.

De La Torre, M. (ed.). 1997. *The Conservation of Archaeological Sites in the Mediterranean Region*. Los Angeles, Getty Conservation Institute.

UNESCO. 1998. *World Culture Report: Culture, Creativity and Markets*. Paris, UNESCO Publishing.

Vidarte, J. I. 1999. Culture, Renewal and Development. (Speech presented at the Culture Counts: Financing, Resources, and the Economics of Culture in Sustainable Development Conference sponsored by the World Bank and the Government of Italy in co-operation with UNESCO, Florence, 4–7 October 1999.)

Yates, F. A. 1966. *The Art of Memory*. Chicago, University of Chicago Press.

Zukin, S. 1995. *The Cultures of Cities*. Cambridge, Blackwell.

Our differences
are always **making anew;**
the one to **behold**

Gale Oxley

My lunch – soup, his – rice
Smells mingle in the lunch room
Canadian **food**

Grace Darney

Amidst city glow
They exude humanity
[illegible] kind

Red White Black and Brown
All the colours of the world
Come together now!

Melissa Guinand

Part Four
New media and cultural knowledge

Introduction

The superhighways of communication formed by the extraordinary expansion of the information and communication technologies (ICTs) offer us new opportunities and spaces to exchange, create, debate, act and expand our knowledge of the surrounding world, pushing out the horizon of our lives. Today, the main focus of attention is on electronic trade and economic issues. However, the cultural aspects of the development of ICTs are no less important in view of the consequences for human society and the role of ICTs in the globalization process.

ICTs' relations with culture raise major questions as mentioned in Part One of this report. The first and most urgent of these is whether the intensive use of ICTs will accelerate cultural homogenization headed by those who dominate the infrastructure and hence access, thereby causing the loss of cultural identities. Although there are reassuring signs that ICTs will foster respect for different types of cultural expression and representation, will that be enough to encourage a creative cultural reshaping based on equality of access and new forms of democratic participation by citizens?

A second major concern is that in purely market-oriented societies, culture circulation may become exclusively aligned to the exchange of goods with consequent restriction on access to culture. This question is reflected in the discussion in Part Two on cultural exception primarily as it affects cultural industries. However, marketed cultural products are only a part of what is on the web. Public resources, individual creativity and non-profit community initiatives make up a large part of what may be termed cultural contents. Such initiatives are contributing to building up a huge new corpus of cultural knowledge that directly reflect the priorities and desires of different societies.

Although new forms of solidarity encourage the creation and circulation of cultural knowledge, will this equal sharing of a new corpus of cultural knowledge help to avert either inequalities and tensions between cultural identities or the conflicts that may result from them?

Three major themes run through the contributions in this Section, which sets out to answer some of the main questions facing policy-makers in the information society. The first theme concerns the efforts made to sustain the cultural diversity and creative empowerment of cultural and linguistic communities in the new media. Today, cultural projects and initiatives have to cope with new social demands as shown in the paper by Holland and Smith, which proposes a digital collective model for preserving the cultural heritage of native Americans and renewing collection-based knowledge. Cultural grounds (linguistic, religious and ethnic) thus provide the basis for collective initiatives to restructure social, economic and political action. Yudice's survey of Afro-American presence on the web shows how these communities have cleverly occupied web space, proving that web cultural exposure does not necessarily conflict with market interests. This is also exemplified by Karim's survey of the action of diasporic communities on networks. ICTs are a form of empowerment for those who feel that their rights are not being acknowledged or for whom cultural differences lead to social and economic inequality. Access to the Internet may be seen in some cases, such as the 'Movimento dos Sem Terra' in Brazil, as a non-violent way of bringing pressure to bear on the authorithies. In certain cultural environments, the new media are also helping to replace distorted images of reality such as the role of women in the development of the Arab world described by Alshejni. These new ways of sustaining cultural diversity may well generate greater awareness of one's otherness and overcome cultural misunderstandings as Chikhaoui argues.

The second theme is the respective role of public and private initiatives in regard to ICTs. A public-service-oriented policy has guided the Louvre's presence on the web since 1995. The paper by Coural shows how, in a globalized world, corporate strategic choice for a unique format of data circulation strongly influences public attitudes concerning cultural knowledge and conditions of access. ITC's are obviously improving the individual's ability to freely access knowledge generated outside traditional institutions and national systems. However, while conditions of knowledge production are changing, access to knowledge – book and computer literacy, as stated by Garzon – remains the key to inclusion and participation in the life of the nation.

The third theme concerns the new forms of cultural knowledge that are being created by on-line collaborative research experiences and a more sensible approach to the cognitive aspects of the technology-culture relationship. Getao's paper points out how culturally-sensitive technological environments described as 'cultural comfort zones' may not only encourage gender participation but condition true access to resources available on ICTs. Technological research is aiming at the creation of 'intelligent environments' that are responsive to human needs, requests and cultural situations. Makkuni's research on new learning environments indicates attempts by a few researchers to explore new ways of reintroducing cultural components in the learning process. Coural too argues that new working environments, such as virtual spaces, are responsible for a critical assessment of traditional epistemological tools.

The major objective of all ICT-related policies is still to preserve the cultural diversity inherent in every society in the world by responding to social demands.

ISABELLE VINSON
Programme Specialist, Research
and Development Unit,
Sector for Culture, UNESCO

Chapter 12
Using information technology to preserve and sustain cultural heritage: the digital collective

MAURITA PETERSON HOLLAND
Associate Professor and Assistant to the Dean for Academic Outreach,
School of Information, University of Michigan (United States)

KARI R. SMITH
School of Information Research Intern,
University of Michigan (United States)

'How will ou institutions an technologie preserve celebrate, reflec and perhap even stimulat culture's variet and dynami change?

If we believe that culture is 'a mass of interplaying stimuli' (UNESCO, *World Culture Report* 1998), then how will our institutions and technologies preserve, celebrate, reflect and perhaps even stimulate culture's variety and dynamic change? Society has usually left this challenge to its libraries, archives and museums; these institutions accumulate artefacts of culture, based on this or that criterion. Libraries collect books and records of language and customs; archives collect documents, image and sound recordings, transcripts and manuscripts; art museums collect paintings, sculpture and so forth; natural history museums collect practical implements, costumes and other samples of everyday life. The materials in these institutions are treated as 'special': they are untouchable for the viewer, stored in special conditions rather than displayed, and described by means of a special vocabulary. The arrangement and labelling system reflects rational Western philosophy, but it is generally arcane to the visitor.

There are also many materials not kept in these kinds of institutions that may provide important cultural information and hold intrinsic value for a community of people. And there are also intangible cultural treasures that cannot be put into a physical space for storage and conservation. Often people think that these things are too valuable to lose and wonder what they can do. With the advent of digital technology, we can now bring together the representations of this diverse array. We can make connections among the virtual objects and link their use, geographic origin and role in a specific culture. We can document origins and include common descriptive material, and we can directly engage the viewer. Using digital capture of voice or text, visitors can even add their own observations about the virtual materials. People can share their personal connections to artefacts and places. At the same time, they document their use of language in relating experiences and in describing objects. This paper will examine one specific case: a project to inscribe, using computer technology, the culture of the indigenous people of America, the Native Americans. It proposes the adoption of a digital collective model that may be used by other groups, applied as a holistic design.

Dynamic culture

Can we capture culture? There are a multitude of cultures, all rooted in history and tradition. Yet each living culture is dynamic, requiring practice and renewal if it is to survive. It is this balance between maintaining a distinct identity and incorporating change that assures the robust vitality of cultures. As Stavenhagen (1998) observed:

> There is . . . a danger . . . which is to treat culture as an object, a 'thing' which exists separately from the social space in which various social actors interrelate. Anthropology reminds us that the ethnic (i.e. cultural) identity of any group depends not so much on the content of its culture as on the social boundaries that define the spaces of social relationship by which membership is attributed to one or the other ethnic group.

The cultures of indigenous peoples are rooted in both the natural and spiritual worlds. In fact, nature and culture are inextricably joined in cultural expression. Posey calls this linking of the two a 'web of relations.

Institutions of memory and knowledge

When nature and culture are intertwined, where and how do we access, catalogue and preserve this knowledge so central to the web of life? For centuries, archives, libraries and museums have been the keepers of certain selected cultural artefacts and materials. However, objects from indigenous peoples challenge these institutions of memory and force us to think about the ways they preserve, conserve, exhibit, describe and make memory itself accessible. Influenced by technology and by competition for viewing audiences, museums are now experimenting with immersive exhibit design and instructive, rather than descriptive, labels. They encourage visitors to interact with the exhibit and with each other.

New technologies can also have a destabilizing effect by causing a paradigm shift or offering unexpected opportunities. In a web environment, institutions now have a global audience. Exhibits need not have a fixed viewing time because web-based exhibits are accessible at all hours and for many years; collections too numerous or large to be incorporated in a museum's physical space may be brought together on the web. Even buildings, equipment and historic monuments that stand outside the museum walls, or that no longer exist, can be selected and organized into collections and exhibits.

There is growing popular interest in saving the material that acts as a document of individual and societal activity. New fields such as organizational archaeology, information architecture and digital librarianship strive to provide ways of keeping documentary track of people and organizations and the activity and artefacts they create. New institutions are formed to address the deeply-felt need to document the perspective of a particular tradition or heritage. Materials deposited at physical sites are both more and less accessible to visitors, because contextual fragmentation occurs as each community struggles to maintain physically some small amount of material evidence.

Native American culture in museums

Where should Native American cultural materials be housed? There are several problems that confront those who seek to confine Native American culture within institutional boundaries. Native American materials are widely distributed in private collections and public museums, in Native-controlled or reservation museums and cultural centres and in non-Native facilities. The level of collection, preservation, description, access and interpretation varies as much as the venues themselves. For example,

Diasporic networks in cyberspace

A diaspora is usually defined as an ethnic group that lives in a number of countries where its present members or their ancestors may have arrived as immigrants. The varied cultural expressions of these intercontinental communities are inflected by the strength of their links with the homeland and other parts of the diaspora, the period of migration and the intensity of interactions with other groups. Most of these communities have been unable to sustain transnational cultural production and distribution in the past due to the lack of centralized organizations and adequate funding, and sometimes because of government restrictions.
They have therefore attempted to locate the technologies that facilitate efficient and inexpensive exchanges among their small, far-flung groupings. Consequently, South Asians and Arabs living in Europe were among the first to adopt home video systems and digital satellite broadcasting.

The new media seem especially suited to the needs of diasporic communities. The structures of electronic systems have the capacity to support ongoing communication between widely-separated transnational groups. The decentralized nature of on-line networks stands in contrast to the highly controlled model of broadcasting. Technologies such as the Internet are also interactive besides being relatively inexpensive and easy to operate.

Diasporic cybercommunities centred around very specific topics are attempting to bring communal knowledge to bear on contemporary issues. News groups such as soc.culture.sierraleone, soc.culture.jewish, and alt.religion.zoroastrianism allow people interested in these topics to communicate from wherever they have access to Usenet. 'Shams' is a newsgroup providing for discussion of issues relating to the rights of women in Muslim law; 'Bol' is a Listserv for issues of gender, reproductive health and human rights in South Asia; and 'KoreanQ', also a Listserv, caters for lesbian and bisexual women of Korean origin. Co-operative arrangements between students and professionals of recent Chinese origin working in high technology sectors in Canada, the United Kingdom and the United States have led to on-line magazines that express their particular concerns. These new arrivals feel that their needs are not being met by the content of the thriving print and broadcast Chinese ethnic media, which is produced largely by older groups of immigrants from China. Despite being separated by large distances, the virtual editorial teams are electronically publishing regular issues that cover events in the homeland and in the Chinese diaspora.

Individual members of various diasporas are also participating in cross-cultural teams of virtual librarians to develop banks of on-line research resources. For example the Australia-based Asian Studies WWW Virtual Library project includes expert contributors with origins in Azerbaijan, Bangladesh, East Timor, Eastern Turkestan, Hong Kong SAR, Japan, Nepal, North Korea, South Korea, Sri Lanka and the South Pacific region who are living in Western countries. Several other virtual librarians are linked from various developed and developing countries. The project, which seeks to provide hypertext guide and access tools to scholarly information on Asia, is aimed at academics, librarians, journalists and graduate students. The respective virtual librarians manage specialist information modules and offer access to thousands of on-line materials. 'Native Web' is another cross-cultural venture. Operated from the United States, it provides links to electronic resources on indigenous cultures in the Americas. People of native and non-native backgrounds from South, Central and North America collaborate in providing content. Interactive on-line systems are also enhancing intercultural communication. The use of the Internet Relay Chat and the Relay program on Bitnet, two systems consistently used by university students in various parts of the world, allow for communication within and outside diasporas.
A cross-cultural management course being taught at the Wilfrid Laurier University in Canada uses the Internet to provide students with inexpensive contact with other cultures.

A number of diasporic websites are designed to correct what are considered misperceptions by outsiders and to mobilize external political support. Several web pages of the transnational Roma ('gypsies'), who have been vilified for centuries in a number of countries, function in this manner. The Council on American-Islamic Relations runs an electronic mailing list that provides updates on issues affecting Muslims and encourages subscribers to lobby relevant media, community and government organizations to redress what it views as unjust treatment. Several groups, such as the Tamil or Kurdish diasporas, also use on-line media to challenge propaganda and to carry out polemics against other websites.

The Canadian Government's General Social Survey for 2000 is asking questions for the first time on access to new media according to respondents' racial and national origins. A fuller picture of transnational communication would also require information about the quantity of electronic memory devoted to the diasporic materials produced on various types of new media. This would help to make comparisons with the size of the overall digital content being produced globally. International collaboration would be required to define content categories such as history, heritage, culture, institutional organization, directories and current information.

At the conceptual level, the transnational virtual communities appear to have much more stable and authentic sets of symbols, histories and cultural relationships compared to the on-line groups that are centred only on the single issues related to their members' professional or recreational interests. The production and dissemination of diasporic cultural materials in a transnational context presents a unique alternative to the cultural industries of global corporations. However, the very strength of the communications conglomerates and their increasing commercialization of on-line media are factors that may have an immense impact on the evolution of diasporic content. Whereas improvements in infrastructure and software may benefit transnational groups, commercial contingencies may overwhelm community considerations in the organization of networks and in the production and distribution of content. Another development to watch is the growing control that governments are exercising over on-line networks: this may eventually affect the cross-border ability of transnational cultural communities to maintain and extend effective electronic links.

KARIM H. KARIM
Professor in the Mass Communication
Programme, Carlton University, Canada

museums such as the National Museum of the American Indian (Washington, D.C. and New York), the Heard Museum (Phoenix, Arizona), Mashantucket Pequot Museum and Research Center (Mashantucket, Connecticut), Woodland Cultural Centre (Brantford, Ontario) and the Museum of Indian Arts and Culture (Santa Fe, New Mexico) provide careful descriptive control, appropriate presentation and physical security for the materials in their collections. Yet many Native American materials are not publicly accessible for lack of intellectual access, exhibit space, proper conservation or the like. Because many Native Americans rarely leave their tribal homes, few have the opportunity to view their own tribal heritage when it is located in a number of different museums far away.

Small repositories located closer to Native Americans are widely distributed around the United States; local collections are housed on reservations, sometimes in stores, often in churches, but rarely in dedicated facilities with trained curators. In addition, many of the thirty Native American tribal colleges lack the financial means to acquire and maintain collections. Although the collections they do possess may be rich in historical cultural content, they lack archival and curatorial expertise.

Native American collections have provoked a certain number of differences of opinion – and even conflict – with what is generally accepted museum practice. For example, the Native American Graves Protection and Repatriation Act of 1990 (NAGPRA) mandated that museums make available to tribes certain holdings within their collections. A difficulty for institutions with Native American collections is that many of the objects require regular use and care. For example, medicine bundles must be refreshed and restored through appropriate ceremony. Care and sensitivity to tribal culture and use of artefacts may require sharing between a museum and a tribe.

Some native people have won the right to remove accessioned objects from museums in order to carry out certain ceremonies or traditions. Gurian cites the Dog Soldiers of Northern Cheyenne using a pipe from the Smithsonian's National Museum of Natural History as an example: 'many native people have successfully argued that accessioned material should be used in the continuance of ceremony and tradition, that rather than relinquishing the artefacts to be preserved (and lose their usefulness), the reverse is true – the material is stored in trust waiting for the time when it must again be used.'

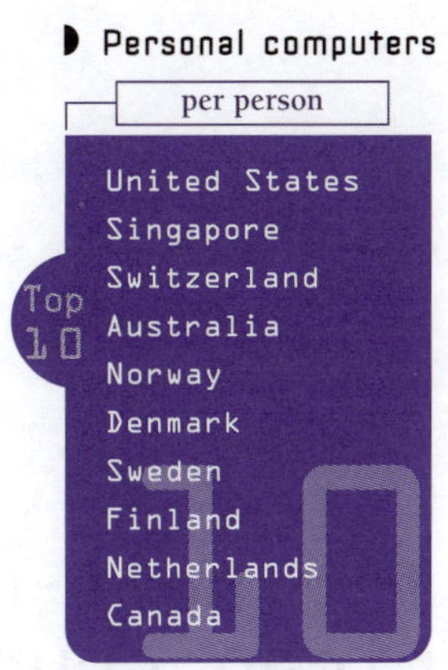

Personal computers
per person
Top 10
United States
Singapore
Switzerland
Australia
Norway
Denmark
Sweden
Finland
Netherlands
Canada

Source: See the Index of culture indicators and sources and Table 20 in Part Seven of this report.

Native American educational systems and tribal governments are interested in forging collaborative efforts to develop computing networks and information systems. Our work with Native Americans on information-technology-based initiatives involving cultural heritage (University of Michigan) confirms a pattern of widely-dispersed oral and artefact materials in personal collections and in public and private institutions. It reveals a grass-roots interest among teachers, schoolchildren and community members for accumulating and sharing digital surrogates of their heritage materials. It also confirms that artisans and elders frequently have knowledge that is undocumented and integral to understanding the materials.

Restoring the 'why' and the 'how' to objects, rather than just identifying the 'what', is the task of documenting culture. The case is eloquently stated by Doxtator (1997):

> Other ways in which the Iroquoian women's mind interacts with land are in the forms of language, place names that reference and act as triggers for personal and collective stories; the creative power of the spoken word; and on the making of concrete objects which in and of themselves become cultural metaphors that can evoke a great deal of cultural knowledge.

A need for self-representation in Arab African countries

Images today are an essential vehicle of cultural expression. An image deficit results in an identity problem, understood not in the political or cultural sense on the international stage, but as an anthropological problem of presence to oneself. Our societies are finding it difficult to project back on to themselves their own image; they are still impenetrable and consequently have insufficient self-knowledge. It is not that we have a false image of ourselves that can be treated or rearranged. The problem goes deeper than that: we lack images.

The two situations are intrinsically different. The absence of the self to the self is a fundamental matter, a vital issue in the sense that no life is possible without a presence to the self in some form or other. Our societies move, work, produce and speak but do not see themselves moving, working, producing and speaking. Yet to act and not see oneself acting is tantamount to inaction or doing nothing that can have an impact on one's personal destiny. A large production of images of the self by the self necessarily generates an awareness of one's otherness. The construction of the personality depends on the development of this otherness. The image is essential if one is to see oneself as another person. If, at the level of the individual, the image is permanent and cumulative, at the level of the community it must be multiple and repeated. Hence the importance of constituting a stock of images. It is, of course, a political problem. If the only images available are those of the state and the state happens to be cut off from society, the problem remains unsolved. The images of the state are of value only if they reflect the state of society.

On the other hand, this deficit is aggravated by a perversion: the image of the self created by another. Such images may not be common, but they exist. They are not perverse in themselves since each individual or culture necessarily possesses a particular image of the other that says more about their own culture than about the culture it is supposed to represent. It is perverse only because it fills the void: the image has literally been displaced. Hence this complexity. Instead of existing alongside the image of the self seen by the self, the image of the self as seen by another takes its place and blurs both the vision that is lacking and the lack of a vision. It is only false in that, owing to the deficit of images of the self by the self, it is not in the right place. This explains the totally anachronistic, naive and rather grotesque character of accusations of exoticism or neocolonial folklore. The overlapping of an almost non-existent image, all the more desirable because never attained, with an image that is more present and more effective but comes from elsewhere, is at the root of all cultural misunderstanding.

TAHAR CHIKHAOUI
President of the Association
Tunisienne pour la Promotion
de la Critique Cinématographique, Tunisia

She goes on to describe the richness of the relationship between the individual mind, the land and collective wisdom. '[The fact of] women sharing a mind with the earth is also part of the structuring process of using, imparting and retaining knowledge. Knowledge is made up of networks of shared cultural metaphors stored in the memories and thoughts of interconnected individuals.'

Maintaining contemporary Native American culture

Can we document and perpetuate the culture of Native Americans, whose language, land and livelihood are threatened by absorption into more dominant and economically viable groups? There are approximately two million Native Americans in the United States; about one million live on reservations. They are members of more than 500 tribes, each with its own unique traditions, celebrations, ceremonies and language. Some tribes consist of less than a few hundred people, while the largest, the Navajo, numbers approximately 250,000 on a reservation that extends across four States. The pressures to conform to the mainstream culture are enormous, and the odds of success in maintaining tribal identity may make the task appear futile.

The complex task and, some would argue, responsibility of maintaining, affirming and evolving cultural identity and traditions in the face of severe economic and social pressures is a frequent topic of conferences and publications and the specific mission of some organizations. In recent years with the advent of powerful technological tools for communication, there would seem to be hope for maintaining richly diverse communities. As Native Americans know, culture cannot be contained in institutions, nor can intangible cultural heritage be put into a physical space for storage and conservation. Rather, traditions, ceremonies, languages, tribal living experiences and links with the Earth are holistic and dynamic. But perhaps, with information technology as the catalyst, children, tribal elders and teachers can now create a powerful cultural resource that will sustain, empower and make it possible to evolve far into the future.

Culture in a digital collective

How can a piece of culture be preserved and even nurtured and changed in a digital environment? This question cannot be answered by describing computing processing capacity or by defining software and communication bandwidth, although these are necessary elements. Rather, the question might best be approached by considering the vision of what we want to achieve. Digital technology, especially on the World Wide Web, gives every person with a networked computer the opportunity to consume what is on the Web and to produce and add to it. The Web also connects content with personal response and shared experience. The Web promotes the participation model set forth by Matusov and Rogoff (1995) that demonstrates that a visitor-learner can become the educator or the storyteller, the missing link in identifying use or provenance, and a valued member of a (museum or cultural) community. Most importantly, the visitor-learner can become a collaborator. We may want to create an immersive experience where we can meet, speak, document, view, work together and maintain a memory of those activities.

Televisions per person
annual rate of change
1980 - 97
Top 10
China
Sri Lanka
Senegal
Oman
Ghana
Mongolia
India
Thailand
Guinea
Benin

Source: See the Index of culture indicators and sources and Table 3 in Part Seven of this Report.

Nisswa: an electronic crossroads between local and global activism in the Arab world

Throughout the history of colonization, resistance and nationalism, Arab women have been the object of cultural heritage, a flag of Arab identity. Used by both the 'outside' (global) world and the 'inside' (Arab) world (two spheres relative to our argument here), women have suffered from political distortion at international and local levels and have rarely managed to express themselves. They have often been used to represent the 'degradation' of Arab society by outsiders. On the other hand, and more recently, they have been used to express cultural diversity and resistance to external influences, not to mention political openness and desire for progress. Manipulated to play the role of Arab individual and communal identity in international relations, Arab women are put in a position of power for change, which is why their emancipation is critical to the development of the Arab world as a whole. Long ago, Arab women became aware of their role and began the struggle for their rights and the progress of their countries. Today, with globalization and information technology, their role can be far more influential.

During the 1950s and 1960s, Nasserism spread throughout the Arab world calling for unity, progress and the education of both sexes. Women were regarded as equal citizens and as essential for national development. Recently women have become better organized, conducting scientific research and constituting NGOs. Gender inequality remains rooted (there is a high degree of illiteracy with women at 64% and men at 32%, although every year more women are graduating from the universities), yet there is real awareness of a gender problem.

Today the Third World has greater access to knowledge than ever before. There are many issues that women cannot address in their everyday reality that, paradoxically, they can discuss internationally. There is still widespread ignorance on the outside as to the Arab reality in terms of gender. Accordingly, the international, global, multicultural world lacks an Arab culture as lived and viewed by women. Arab women must contribute to the construction of the 'global world' so that it will reflect an Arab culture aware of its own bias. Such a mechanism would be doubly beneficial: Arab women's contribution to world global construction would enhance their empowerment locally, while their grass-roots activity would be represented in the 'global world'.

In 1997 a partnership between UNESCO and the Society for International Development (SID) launched the Women on the Net (WoN) project. The main focus of this initiative was to create a democratic gender-balanced culture on the Internet, empowering women through the use of new technologies with greater concern for women in the South and marginal groups in the North. The project provided diverse perspectives of women from culturally diverse settings worldwide.

The Internet gives all users an equal voice. However, how can its use be democratic and gender-equal when what is missing is the reality of facts?

Many Arab women activists, understandably, regard the Internet as an élite domain. Yet many NGOs in the Arab world use it to research material, receive news and, more importantly, disseminate local information which otherwise would be next to impossible.

Nisswa ('women' in ancient Arabic) is meant to be a virtual association that aims to address gender and development (GAD) in the Arab region by advocating gender equity, which will lead us to ask for change in all sectors of organization of Arab society: initiating a critical discourse on the development process in Arab countries and discussing development from a gender perspective; creating information on activities aiming for more visibility of women's work and way of life (http://www.nisswa.org).

The gender bias in Arab countries is a vital factor for social change. Even if Internet remains a virtual world, its political qualities make it the perfect medium for Arab women's advocacy of their rights.

LAMIS ALSHEJNI
Volunteer, Women and Development Network
at the Society for International Development, Italy

Promoting civil society activism through the new media

The Internet is daily news. New millionaires are made as new media companies release their IPOs and as Internet portals are created by venture capital, telecommunications and entertainment conglomerates. The protests in Seattle re-enact the Zapatistas' 'digital revolution' now turbo-powered to mobilize global solidarity against the absorption of life, work and leisure by the market and the profit motive. Those networks of solidarity actors known as civil society – women, environmentalists, indigenous organizations and a myriad of affinity associations – seem to realize their organizational ideals in the open-ended connections provided by the web. A do-good culturalist bias leads some to think that markets and mores go their separate ways, but quite often they hitch their prospects to each other. Civic action in the media can legitimize the market, which in turn foots the bill for broadcast expenses. MTV websites, for example, preach the virtues of diversity and tolerance to a global audience. African-American feminist writer Bell Hooks, has even proposed a cultural criticism show for the Network (http://www.thepages.mtvn.com).

Does this necessarily lead to co-optation? While it is wise to proceed with caution when dealing with the entertainment industry, it is worth noting that the energy and anger of rap, reggae, rock and their sundry fusions with local musics pack a visceral cultural-activist punch unavailable to Culture and Heritage listserves and sites. Community and commitment are not always divorced from e-commerce: Tarika's CDs, which offer a critique of colonialism and racism in Madagascar as well as the 'historical connections' of the Malayo/Polynesian diaspora which are recaptured in their Malagasy roots music, can be purchased on their websites:

- http://www.froots.demon.co.uk/tarika.html and
- http://www.tarika.demon.co.uk.

This cultural activism has been taken to new levels by two Brazilian 'cultural groups'. The Grupo Cultural Olodum and the Grupo Cultural AfroReggae, both tapped the Afro-diasporic references of their music for civic and political ends and were recently featured in a concert in Rio de Janeiro to showcase the *Som das ONGs* [Sound of the NGOs] (AfroReggae bulletin <afroreggae@ax.apc.org> 16 July 1999). Their entry into the Internet is a logical progression. Scheduling performances, organizing civic and political events, communicating with funders, and now making their music available by download require the ubiquity of the web.

In 1979 Olodum was organized as a *bloco afro* or Carnival group, but soon thereafter became 'an organization that is dedicated to improving the lives of Afro-Brazilians, through embracing their culture, championing personal rights, and educating the people (*History of lodum*, http://www.e-net.com.br/olodum/report.html). The music itself is an expert demonstration in the sampling of culture, particularly from the African diaspora.

People around the world are likely to know of Olodum for their participation in Paul Simon's 'The Obvious Child' in his 1991 *Rhythm of the Saints* album and their appearance in Michael Jackson's music video *They Don't Really Care About Us* directed by Spike Lee. As an NGO, partly financed by a percentage of their record sales, they have also conducted campaigns to combat racism, AIDS, cholera, urban blight and youth homelessness. Olodum hopes to expand the reach of this activism through its Creative School, which aside from offering training in social education, English, Portuguese, History, Afro-dance, percussion and craftsmanship, also furthers the project of cultural awareness by introducing the community to the new media: computers, the Internet, video and CD-ROM. Its Afro-Brazilian Database includes information on Afro-Brazilian culture, science, religion, economy, politics and international relations (*What We Do*, http://www.e-net.com.br/olodum/do.html).

Grupo Cultural AfroReggae (GCAR) was born in 1993 as the police, in pursuit of the local narco-trafficking gang, entered their neighbourhood Vigário Geral. Angered by the continual harassment of the largely black population of the *favela*, AfroReggae sought to use culture as a way to instill self-esteem and woo youth away from narco-traffic and violence. This was made possible by a dense network of connections with local and international NGOs, human rights organizations, politicians, newspaper reporters, writers, academics and entertainment celebrities. The basic principle of their work is embodied in their practice of *batidania*, a portmanteau neologism that suggests that *cidadania* or citizenship dwells in the *batida* (beat) and *batucada* (music and rhythm of Afro-Brazilian dance) of *favela* youth that had been blamed for initiating a wave of *arrastões* or looting rampages on the beaches of middle-class Rio. Like Olodum, AfroReggae has extended this consciousness-raising activity to concrete civic action in health, AIDS, human rights and education and, in particular, training for a range of jobs in the service and entertainment sectors (percussion, dance, capoeira) ('Programas', http://www.afroreggae.org.br/index1.htm).

AfroReggae's expansion to other poor communities has led it to prioritize its Communications Program, which links it to 'an almost infinite network of people'.

These groups are capable of sophisticated self-analysis. They are aware of the danger of putting all the eggs of their activism in the basket of civil society and of the depoliticizing risks of absorption by the entertainment industry. To take control over its new contract with Universal Records (and to maintain the legality of GCAR's income-producing activities) AfroReggae has had to create a parallel for-profit corporation. They recognize that the industry 'capitalizes on some aspects of black culture, while relegating others.' The trick is to take intelligent advantage of exposure, for example, on MTV, while making sure to promote those artists who can get their message across.

GEORGE YÚDICE
Director, Privatization of Culture Project for Research on Cultural Policy, New York University (United States)

Do people want to participate and share in the emerging networks? One of the most far-reaching examples at the national level is the Museum of the Person established in Brazil (Museum, 1999). Using simple oral history documentation techniques, this project collects stories and photos from citizens across the country. The conjunction of the various narratives enables the reader to absorb a multiplicity of views. The collective effect is a documentation of life and language across all economic, geographic and social layers. In a cultural context, these multiple points of view reinforce appreciation of the differences among people and strengthen individual values and beliefs.

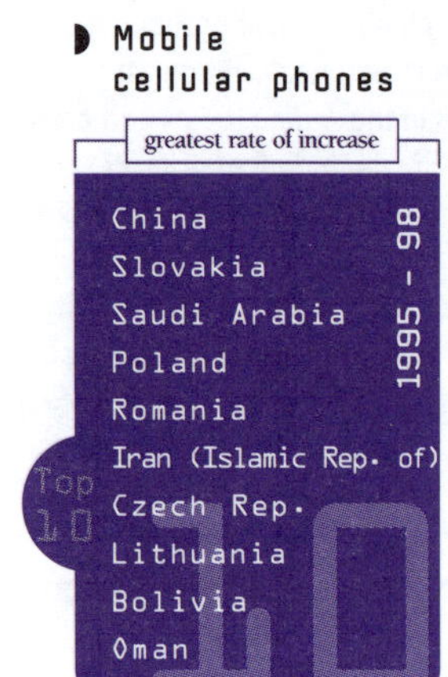

Mobile
cellular phones
greatest rate of increase
China
Slovakia
Saudi Arabia
Poland
Romania
Iran (Islamic Rep. of)
Czech Rep.
Lithuania
Bolivia
Oman
1995 - 98
Top 10

Source: See the Index of culture indicators and sources and Table 20 in Part Seven of this report.

These few observations about the capacity of information technology, the broad scope of cultural heritage and the behaviour and activity of people on the World Wide Web would indicate that culture can indeed be facilitated in a digital environment. We have developed a model for collecting, storing, accessing, interpreting and sharing cultural heritage called the digital collective and presented below.

The digital collective

What is a digital collective? In selecting the term 'digital collective', we weighed the words carefully. 'Digital' was chosen because it is the form of all objects and materials whether digitized in a conversion process or digitally-born. A collective is defined as a 'collection of individual persons or things; constituting a collection; gathered into one; taken as a whole, aggregate, collected' (Oxford English Dictionary, 1989). We are thus proposing, with a digital collective, an organizational structure, a database, that will draw in contributions from individuals and collectors and encourage comment and connections among viewers and materials in the collective. The collective will consist of digital 'surrogates' of objects donated by individuals and institutions. Physical items will be digitally recorded or 'captured' and returned to the owner; digital objects may be donated directly. Donors will also be asked to assign their copyright permissions to the collective. When necessary and appropriate, access restrictions may be placed on materials in the collective. The collective will provide information about physical storage locations for the material if this was given at the time of donation. As a general policy, the collective will not store physical materials; however, in practice, some visual and sound materials for which no digital standard exists may be stored temporarily until long-term digital preservation is possible.

The collective will be directed by a team of content specialists, community members and technology and organization professionals. Applying the best practice from oral history and anthropology as well as from archival and library-collection development, they will be responsible for determining the scope and organization of the database, soliciting materials and applying appropriate collection guidelines for accepting content. They will also be responsible for registration of artefacts, creating exhibits and displays, designing educational programming and products, maintaining the electronic records and digital 'surrogates' and the organization and management of the archival materials. A registrar will maintain the collective's database files, applying appropriate 'metadata'; the 'metadata' will include the terminology of the community or persons who donated the material. All descriptive information and associated materials may be in languages of the donor's choice and ability. We foresee that the collective will be multilingual in both the materials and their descriptions.

The Internet will be integral to the collective. Since the Internet is based upon distributed input in digital form, it permits both production and consumption of information; it makes possible a model for organizing and sharing images, sound files and other materials from a number of different sources. However, the Internet and the World Wide Web need not be the only distribution point for the digital collective. Its multiple input sources and collections are not bound by specific locations or particular time. Rather, materials may be viewed and manipulated in a number of formats and technologies including CD-ROM, CAVE Automatic Virtual Environment or holography, and may be stored or transmitted without regard to file size. In order to provide broad access, products will be created from the materials in the collective. These products may include, for example, a website, a CD-ROM or a digital exhibit within a traditional gallery space.

Through wide access via the Internet, it is also possible to solicit content and contextual information for the digital collective. Users will at times become the experts by adding to the records concerning particular items in the collective. For example, an elder may share a recollection of a particular day when an object in the collective was created, a child may add the sketch of a plant from which a native dye is made and a shepherd may describe a technique of shearing sheep for wool that will be dyed and woven. People will provide valuable information that goes far beyond curators' knowledge. This additional material, reviewed by a curator, may then become part of the collective. In this way people will be drawn to the collective as well as committed in their ownership of it.

Privately- and publicly-held materials submitted by individuals and institutions will become content for the digital collective. We are accustomed to donors providing objects and provenance information to museums and archives; however, curators usually then decide how to handle the contributions. In the digital collective, we envision donors and users directly contributing digital objects, descriptions and comments, and also building exhibits and designing and offering educational programmes.

It will be possible to link materials traditionally separated by institutional or cultural boundaries in the collective's database. In addition, contextual information can be added in the collective. For example, there are many objects in museums that are documentary in nature; this information is not usually described or displayed with the object. Similarly, there are many objects in archives that have artifactual as well as informational value, but the object may not be fully described according to museum standards. The digital collective will link objects with informational materials in various formats. This will enhance the contextual description of the objects and encourage ongoing contributions.

The project recognizes that accessibility and longevity depend on compliance with emerging standards for networked information. Many projects are currently under way that are formulating and promoting descriptive, digitization and format standards. They include UNESCO's Memory of the World programme, the Canadian Heritage Information Network (CHIN:http://www.chin.gc.ca), the Scottish Cultural Resources Access Network (SCRAN) (http://www.scran.ac.uk) and ICOM's Handbook of Standards for documenting collections, especially the pan-African AFRICOM (http://nic.icom.org/afridoc) and Central Asia's HeritageNet. The National Library of the Czech Republic has also contributed standards and guidelines for digitizing rare library materials (Knoll, 1998).

The collective's diverse digital objects must be linked to appropriate structural 'metadata' or associated in a logical way. Because the content and the descriptive material in the digital collective will be gathered by the team and by users, natural and controlled vocabularies will coexist. In fact, no one language for the collective will be imposed, although there will be standard vocabulary for description and access. Multilingual descriptive and content materials will better represent the original materials; ultimately, multilingual contributions may record changes in language and in cultural uses of objects.

Non-web products derived from the collective, such as CD-ROMs and videos, will also be available for locations where non-networked systems are more appropriate. Larson (1998) describes several such applications among Alaskan native communities. The School of Information at the University of Michigan has recently produced a CD-ROM (*The Living Tradition*, 1999) celebrating the cultural heritage of the Yup'ik Eskimos who live along the west coast of Alaska. The CD includes images from a travelling exhibit of Yup'ik masks created by the National Museum of the American Indian in New York and a series of stories from elders, songs and dances, and school lessons. The CD-ROM links to the web for access to additional information and materials.

The collective might also have exhibits or viewing rooms where materials from the collective would be displayed in apparently physical ('virtual') form. Models might also be fabricated using tools that generate physical parts from digitized objects. It may host special exhibits, discussion groups, open or closed conferences and events and activities suggested by the communities who access the collective. Repositories of lesson plans may be stocked for access. The collective, because it is digital, will also take advantage of rapidly evolving technology for sharing and using information, frozen neither in time nor in place. Immersive environments, collaborative tools and integrated media will encourage a broad range of input from oral storytelling to multi-sensory productions.

Bibliography

Abdelaziz, A. 1997. *Memory of the World: Preserving our Documentary Heritage*. Paris, UNESCO.

Brand, S. 1999. *The Clock of the Long Now.* New York, Basic Books.

Carlston, D. 1998. Storing Knowledge. In: M. MacLean and B. H. Davis. (eds.), *Time & Bits: Managing Digital Continuity*. Los Angeles, Getty Conservation Institute.

Chideya, F. 1999. *The Color of Our Future*. New York, William Morrow.

Doxtator, D. 1997. *Godi'nigoha': The Women's Mind.* Brandford, California, Woodland Cultural Centre. (Exhibition catalogue).

Gurian, E. H. 1999. What is the Object of this Exercise? A Meandering Exploration of the Many Meanings of Objects in Museums. *Daedalus*, Summer.

Haber, A. 1997. *Information: Welcome from the Director.* El Pais Virtual Museum of Art. Accessed on 19 May 1999. http://www.diarioelpais.com/muva2/#

Kenniston, K. 1999. *Can the Cultures of India Survive the Information Age?* Accessed on 31 May 1999. http://web.mit.edu/kken/Public/papers6.htm

Knoll, A. 1998. *Digitization of Rare Library Materials. Storage and Access to Data.* Prague, National Library of the Czech Republic; Albertina icome Praha Ltd (CD-ROM), accessed on 22 May 1999. http://www.unesco.org/webworld/mdm/czech_digitization/index.html

Larson, M. A. 1998. *Keeping our Words as Keepers of Words.* Paper presented to Society of American Archivists Annual Conference.

Living Tradition of the Yup'ik Mask. 1999. CD-ROM. Ann Arbor, Michigan, University of Michigan School of Information.

Long Now Foundation (www.longnow.org). San Francisco, California. (Accessed on 21 May 1999).

Matusov, E.; Rogoff, B. 1995. Evidence of Development from People's Participation in Communities of Learners. In: J. L. Falk and L. D. Dierking, *P ublic Institution for Personal Learning: Establishing a Research Agenda.* Washington, D.C., American Association of Museums.

Murray, J. H. 1997. *Hamlet on the Holodeck: The Future of Narrative in Cyberspace.* Cambridge, Mass., MIT Press.

Museum of the Person (www.museudapessoa.com.br). (Accessed on 24 May 1999).

Native American Graves Protection and Repatriation Act of 1990 [H.R. 5237], 104 Stat. 3048, Public Law 101-601, 16 Nov. 1990.

Pérez de Cuéllar, Javier. 1995. *Our Creative Diversity: Report of the World Commission on Culture and Development.* Paris, UNESCO.

Posey, D. A. 1998. Can Cultural Rights Protect Traditional Cultural Knowledge and Biodiversity? In: H. Nieć (ed.), *Cultural Rights and Wrongs: a Collection of Essays in Commemoration of the 50th Anniversary of the Universal Declaration of Human Rights.* Paris, UNESCO Publishing. Leicester, Institute of Art and Law.

Stavenhagen, R. 1998. Cultural Rights: a Social Science Perspective. In: H. Nieć (ed.), Stet. Paris, UNESCO Publishing. Leicester Institute of Art and Law.

World Culture Report: Culture, Creativity and Markets. UNESCO 1998. Paris, UNESCO Publishing.

Chapter 13
Museum strategy in the information society

PIERRE COURAL
Director, Audiovisual and
Cinematographic Production Unit,
Louvre Museum (France)

'. . . the new communication and information technologies raise questions as to the contents being circulated by museums to reach a wider and more diversified public.'

If museums are so incredibly fashionable today it is because they have directly benefited from the astonishing circulation of images that began over a century ago with the advent of photography, spread mainly by means of published books and followed by the audiovisual media and, more recently, by multimedia. What makes a museum attractive often hinges on subtle dialectics between the desire to know and the assurance of recognizing. It is also due to the fact that museums have adapted well to the expectations of the educational and associative sectors, the tourist industry and the leisure society. The development of cultural and educational services in the world's principal museums is a sign of the growing awareness in museum institutions of the need for cultural dissemination.

But the new communication and information technologies raise questions as to the contents being circulated by museums to reach a wider and more diversified public; subject, moreover, to this subtle interrogation are the museum strategy and policies being employed to take advantage of the information society.

The Louvre, a case in point

At the Louvre, service is intended first and foremost for various public audiences; it aims to respond to the diversity of their expectations, the complexity of their circumstances and the multiplicity of their commitments. The role of museums in the information society is complex and seemingly remote from what it was up to recent times. Is the Internet likely to undermine the traditional concept of art and culture and reduce it to an industrial asset? What status and social use will museums be able to boast of in the information society of the future?

New technologies were first introduced into the Louvre during the 1970s with the development of documentary informatics. Documentary tools were developed, using several major national documentary bases such as Joconde, Carrare and Pharaon (http://www.minist.cult.fr). These professional databases were intended primarily for internal consultation of collections. This was followed by the development of computerized inventories for the graphic arts which posited from the very outset the principle of databases open to public consultation (135,000 drawings). Today, the policy regarding production of computerized documentary resources continues to be the museum's main concern with, more particularly, the issue of the transfer of annotated inventories on to a computerized medium.

The worldwide advent of the Internet network determined that access to knowledge has become more important than production of knowledge. The Internet provided the Louvre with a new means of viewing its relationship with the public. For users of the global village, the Louvre's first step was to create the Louvre.fr website in 1995 for the information of visitors. It is available in four languages (English, French, Japanese and Spanish) and is one of the most frequently visited sites in France with over three million users a year.

It was also decided to create a site specifically dedicated to the educational world, Louvre.edu. The site was devised as a 'publication base' providing teachers and students with iconographical and textual resources and video material. Over 300 educational institutions took part in a pilot project in 1999. The development model for Louvre.edu is that of a galaxy of sister-sites, either upstream (the Europa.edu project) or downstream, particularly for the regions.

Another important target consists of scientific teams working on art. Providing them with access to certain computer resources or scientific documents and enabling people to work together on exhibitions, publications and symposiums are current objectives. This has led to the creation of Louvre.org, a site giving the scientific community ready access to documentary resources and an opportunity to undertake new ventures.

None of these projects are problem-free. First of all, a taxonomic assessment of the criteria and notions required in terms of scientific publishing and dissemination through these new networks should be conducted without delay. Questions should be asked as to the importance to be attached to annotated catalogues, Internet databases and internal collection management bases. The Internet is making us readjust our values as regards encyclopaedic knowledge. Most analysts are agreed that the giants of the encyclopaedic tradition of the future will no longer be the *Larousse* or the *Encyclopedia Universalis*, but rather the 'search engines' called Yahoo or Lokace. Knowledge will rest not so much on the accumulation of information as on our capacity to access it.

The globalization of culture

To return to the central issue of my paper, namely 'must we follow or lead?', the Louvre has given priority to an active but tempered policy. The Louvre still devotes some 60% of its cultural-product investment funds to the audiovisual media. This amounts to approximately 1 million francs a year.

In a world in which political influence frequently seeks to permeate cultural considerations and to transform aesthetics into what poet Paul Valéry termed an 'industry of beauty', the question arises, not only of an economic or at least an operational model, but also of strategies of alliances and the search for common objectives. The situation is fairly clear. The main issue today is a debate between those who are rich in heritage but poor in technology, and those who are rich in technology and poor in heritage.

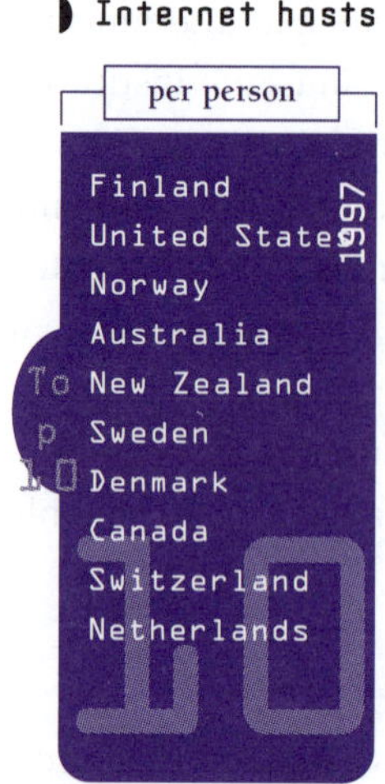

Internet hosts
per person
1997
Top 10
Finland
United States
Norway
Australia
New Zealand
Sweden
Denmark
Canada
Switzerland
Netherlands
10

Source: See the Index of culture indicators and sources and Table 20 in Part Seven of this report.

There is also a dividing line between those countries for which culture and education are, at least theoretically, the political responsibility of the State – namely countries that are governed by Roman law – and those for which culture lies chiefly in the hands of local authorities or quite simply with the private sector and associations, i.e. countries governed by common law and subscribing to the liberal tradition. A few examples selected from North America and Europe may serve to illustrate whatever concern the international situation may be causing and will highlight the independent options taken in policies adopted at the Louvre.

The situation in North America

Museum strategy in the information society in North America depends, firstly, on the special position the information society enjoys there. The Internet is led technologically, economically and socially by the North American continent. This could well lead to an imbalance at the heart of this new society, with consequent risks in terms of cultural diversity, perhaps calling for some strengthening of multipolar policies.

A second point is that museums, especially in the United States, do not enjoy the same privileged status as those in Europe. They are mainly governed by associations and foundations which take charge of heritage policy.

For example, the Getty Foundation has been actively involved in the work of the Consortium for Interexchange of Museum Information (CIMI) on developing the CIMI Z 39.50 standard, a specific standard regarding the interoperational use of museum databases and the adaptation of document formats such as XML or meta-data such as the Dublin Core. These specific standards, based more often than not on an assortment of public standards, have made it possible to conduct a form of privatization of databases. It will be noted that the operational activity of the CIMI is managed by the Research Libraries Group, Inc. which specializes in the exploitation of scientific, university and artistic databases. This is the background to the presentation of North American museums on the Internet. Three main sites now make up its backbone, one of which is the Art Museum Network (AMN), which we in Europe continue to call the American Museum Network since it essentially comprises the site of the Association of Art Museum

LANGUAGES

Common language	no. of countries*
English	35
Arabic	27
Spanish	22
Russian	18
French	13
German	13
Fulfulde	10
Armenian	7
Kurdish	7
Tatar	7
Turkish	7
Serbo-Croatian	7

Graph 15
Countries where a common language is among the five leading spoken languages

* Out of 150 countries with a population of over 1 million.
Source: See the Index of culture indicators and sources and Table 6 in Part Seven of this report.

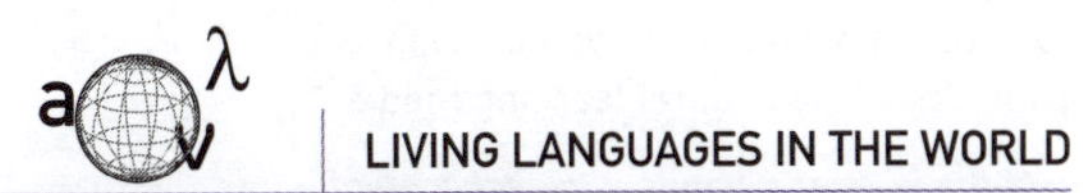

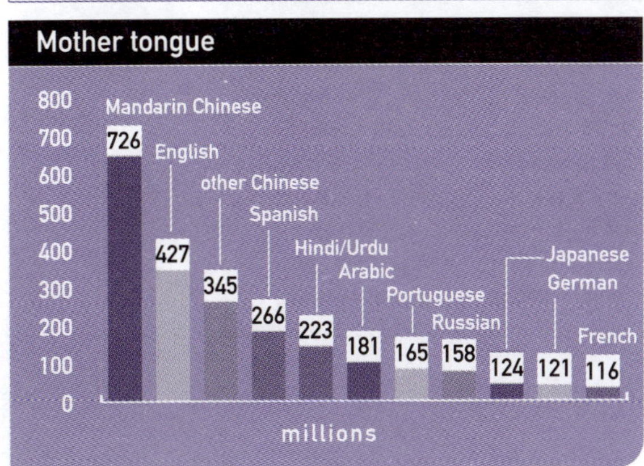

Graph 14
Languages spoken as a mother tongue by more than 100 million people

Source: *Cambridge Encyclopaedia of Language*, 1997.

Active learning

Against the static backdrop of present-day computer-based learning systems, we are proposing a new paradigm for presentation of and interaction with cultural content called 'Active Learning'. The next wave of cultural learning media will flow from a re-examination of the relationship of the human body to technology and the creation of tools that will bridge physical and virtual worlds.

Active learning

The invention of the 'graphical user interface' (GUI) some twenty years ago revolutionized how people interacted with computing media. The GUI created the desktop computing paradigm which in turn led to the design of the present form of learning system: the learner interacts with a digital document presented on a workstation using hardware (television monitor, keyboard and mouse), and software (button pushing, windows and point and click). These forms duly stabilized while speed increases improved the expressive capabilities of digital documents. These began as text-centric documents, were later transformed from text into picture documents, and ultimately became multimedia. The improvement in document forms was mirrored in richer presentation of content and the ability of documents to capture and disseminate knowledge. Similarly the nature of the cultural content being disseminated changed from descriptions of artifacts to presentations showing how artifacts are situated in the world of artistic process and cultural practice. With the advent of the Net, digital documents make it possible to access not only the descriptions of cultural practice but also to connect to images of living practitioners, cultural places and events.

However impressive the present form of display technology and speed of information transfer may be, important aspects relating to the physical dimensions of humanity have been overlooked by the modern document. The workstation disembodies the learner. Presentations become 'screen-centric'. The workstation becomes the focus of people's offices and homes. While presentations on-screen are animated and rich, the learner's body is usually static. Interaction is reduced to button-pushing while the expressive potential of the human hand is completely ignored. The sense of touch is reduced to mere mouse-clicks. In short, the learning experience with computing tools is static.

The worlds of art and architecture, performing arts and craft have given us countless examples of learning spaces and craft objects that are in tune with human physicality. We believe that new, beyond-the-desktop paradigms will follow a re-examination of the relationship of the human body to physical space and physical interfaces with digital representations. New bridges must be designed to span physical and virtual spaces. New graspable, touchable, adornable interfaces need to be explored to give users kinaesthetic contact with the learning content. In this way, the learning experience can exchange its present static form for something richer and more dynamic. We call this expressive cultural learning experience Active Learning.

Research questions

Research questions in the active learning space include correlating physical space with learning space, developing the relationship of the learner's hand with digital content, expanding multimedia interactions and bridging computer and traditional media.

- *Correlating physical space with learning space:* Immersion in the current form of computing presentations occurs within the boundaries of a rectangular screen. Can we not extend the notion of immersion to expand beyond the boundaries of a screen to include the overall environment including architectonic space, sense of enclosure, backdrops in physical space, environmental lighting and audio systems and aroma effects? Building such a rich presentation would advance the expressive capabilities of the cultural learning media.

- *Relationship of the learner's hands to digital content:* The world's music and art traditions have shown us the value of hand skills and hand literacy as forms of expression. Yet our present digital tools are designed to eliminate hand skills and all contact with content. Despite the hundreds of hand positions that are possible, interactions with current learning systems are reduced to point and click and button-pushing.

Could we not employ gestures to provide kinaesthetic forms of interaction with digital content? Could we not also explore the relation between the forms of hand-held interfaces corresponding to the dimensions and spaces created by the hand and body? Could we not study and incorporate the attributes of texture and touch in the design of hand-held interfaces?

- *Multimedia interactions:*

Contemporary multimedia technology has undoubtedly increased screen-based display space and provided users with speedy access to images and sounds. While there is a rich output flowing from system to user, input from user to system is keyboard-, mouse- and text-based.

What if, instead of relying on text-based retrieval and button-pushing, the learner could interact through expressive gestures? Might not gestural interaction allow the learner to access pictures through pictures, and sounds through sounds? Could we not explore 'multimedia' search engines?

- *Bridges between computer media and traditional media:*

Early attempts at computing focused on emulating the properties of paper media, namely, creating digital screen design based on paper-based presentation models. While designers captured the main features of the paper medium in digital media, the subtler aspects of paper interaction were overlooked, such as the fact that a paper document is tactile and sensuous and participates in fluid, social learning interactions.

Can we not therefore seek to bridge the gap between traditional media and computing display media?

Exploring such questions led us to a vision of the active learning experience that would incorporate spatial dimensions and the body in the act of communication and, eventually, to the Crossing exhibit project.

The Crossing exhibit project

The term 'Crossing' is related to the Sanskrit term for a pilgrimage site as a crossing-point to a space for learning, reflection and transformation. The Crossing project aims to create a physical/virtual multimedia exhibit to be situated in Bombay, New York and Paris so that learners may connect with the living knowledge traditions of Banaras (India), a pilgrimage site and 2000-year-old centre of learning located close to the River Ganges.

The Crossing exhibit re-'presents' the complex learning spaces of Banaras by means of living multimedia documents and interfaces. Through the design of physical and virtual learning spaces and live, real-time multimedia net-based connection to the spaces of Banaras, as well as interpretation by knowledge practitioners, the exhibit aims to immerse people in the transformative dimensions of the place.

In terms of layout the Crossing exhibit consists of a collection of physical virtual spaces, each one interpreting learning themes related to the pilgrimage site. Some of these spaces and interfaces are dynamically-created physical space.

In each learning space, large screens of multimedia imagery engulf the user. The screens create a sense of enclosure that defines physical space, while providing surfaces for the projection of content. In many instances, the enclosures are dynamically created through the robotic control of unfurling screens based on the user's proximity to certain spaces in the exhibit.

In contrast to the desktop model of interaction, in which the user is situated outside the display screen, the spatial enclosures and projections situate the user 'inside' the knowledge space. Such spaces when carefully designed can immerse the user in the content. Even in a simple case of a workstation surrounded by enclosing projections, the latter, by defining the limits of a physical space, can provide a valuable peripheral context for the workstation's screen-based presentation.

We also propose, for interface research, to shift from button-pushing to kinaesthetic, high-touch interfaces.

The active learning experience shifts the information-access paradigm from button-pushing on glass screens to interacting with smart, high-touch, physical objects that relate to the body and the content. We believe that kinaesthetic interaction will intensify the user's engagement with the content. The new physical, graspable, adornable, 'gesturable' interfaces in turn provide the tools for the user to interact with the physically immersive knowledge spaces of the future.

RANJIT MAKKUNI
Researcher in Multimedia,
Xerox Palo Alto Research Center,
Palo Alto (United States)

Directors (AAMD). This project is largely funded today by Intel Corporation which, through this medium, is developing its plan for a commercial museum with ArtMuseum.net.

The second is exCalendar.net, the official site for exhibitions of the major museums in the world. In its public version, the site is an information tool providing up-to-date news of exhibitions around the world. In its professional version, exCalendar aims to become a forum for discussion and the programming of exhibitions. European museums have remained largely aloof from this project in the belief that a plan might arise for setting up a government of museums via the Internet, which would lie outside their power in technical, organizational and linguistic terms.

The third is the Art Museum Image Consortium (AMICO), which offers access by contractual licence to approximately 50,000 images in the educational sector. The RLG Inc. is the principal agent for these transfers of rights. AMICO operates as a consortium whose members – the museums – contribute a minimal number of images and texts in addition to an annual financial contribution. The exploitation rights are given to AMICO which transfers them to RLG Inc. which then markets them to sub-licensees. AMICO requires contributors to supply their data according to a particular format specific to the AMICO library. The publishers' software for management of museum collections is gradually beginning to integrate this standard in the formatting of records of databases.

In contrast to the case of the Canadian Heritage Information Network (CHIN) which has managed, with considerable talent, to develop a coherent project for the benefit of Canada's museum community, the American model, however efficient it may be seen to be, has not yet succeeded in extending its influence very far internationally. The main European actors have continued to maintain an 'empty chair' policy; at the same time no substantial European initiative has yet taken shape. Recent awareness of the urgent need for a joint proposal on the part of the European museums with regard to the Internet would seem to be a prerequisite for redressing international equilibrium and developing a multipolar policy.

The situation in the European Community

In Europe, museums long ignored one another and it is thanks to the European Commission that attempts have since been made to establish closer links. For many years museums were faced with two options: either collaborate with the highly resourceful Information Society Directorate-General, i.e. industrialists in the information society, or with the impoverished Education and Culture Directorate-General in charge of culture, the audiovisual media and sport, and whose successive commissioners have never given much attention to the new technologies. The main programmes comprise *Kaleidoscope* for the living arts, *Ariane* for literature and *Raphael* for the cultural heritage. In 2000 new impetus will transform *Raphael* into a programme that is particularly adapted to the development of networks of professionals in the age of new networks. It is thanks to support for this programme that an association of British museum documentalists has just launched the European Museum Information Institute (EMII). The year 2000 will also herald the launching of a preliminary Commission outline plan for culture: Culture 2000. Unfortunately, apart from cultural co-operation agreements, no part of the proposal focuses specifically on the link between cultural heritage and the new dissemination technologies.

Devised as a preliminary sister site to Louvre.edu, an online educational service on the artistic heritage of Europe (Europa.edu) proposes to present the main centres of creation that have left their mark on the artistic history of Europe by means of a vast chronological and geographical overview. Each site is represented by a selection of major works and monuments, while a library groups the textual resources available in five languages. Users can create files to prepare a presentation or devise an Internet site. The site is expected to open in June 2000. In view of the preliminary results of the Connect initiative, the European Parliament may pass a real framework programme which would intervene in parallel with Culture 2000 and help cultural institutions to carry out their educational tasks.

True access? Gender participation and cultural comfort zones on the web

In order to introduce information technology into a culture, one can choose either to leave the technology as it is and transform the people so that they can use it, or to transform the technology so that people can comfortably use it as part of their own culture. If we are to achieve long-term success, we must nurture a culturally diverse World Wide Web (WWW) and provide metaphors to enable web users to interpret it. Lack of cultural spaces in which to nurture the use of the web by culturally diverse people will limit its effectiveness. I shall describe this problem in greater detail in order to propose an agenda for the extension of cultural comfort zones to web users from different nations.

Despite the formidable technical barriers (lack of technical and educational infrastructure for information and communication technologies), it is clear that many people in poorer countries are accessing and benefiting from the web. However, I believe that if the use of the web is to become truly worldwide, then we must address both the cultural and the technical issues.

Some important cultural shifts have taken place since the popularization of the World Wide Web. Some of these are trivial, such as the invention of a whole new 'cyber-vocabulary', while others are very profound.

The nature of the Internet and the web have opened them up to a completely new type of participant. The June 1996 edition of *Working Woman* focused on the use of the web by women. In her editorial, Lynn Povich made an important point regarding this new breed:

> Men had a jump on us with hardware. Historically, so few women studied engineering and computer science that men took the lead in creating and developing the computer industry. You can see it in the hardware firms and even in the large software and chip companies – there are hardly any women running them. Only now are women graduating from college in the sciences in substantial numbers. Only now are girls encouraged to be technoliterate. . . . But the new world of multimedia and the Internet is another thing entirely. It demands content and therefore levels the playing field a bit. Because women hold senior positions in publishing, the arts, advertising, the media and marketing, we are as able as men to design a product, whether it's a home page, an on-line service or a CD-ROM.

The entry of women as real players in the web has been perhaps the most profound change in the use of ICTs by any group. The Society for International Development (SID) with its Women in Development (WID) network has been working since 1984 to culminate in the recent co-ordination of the Women on the Net (WoN) project. The project brought women from every continent and the most culturally diverse backgrounds together to dialogue in cyberspace. Many interesting issues arising from this dialogue have been published. The Internet struck a cultural chord in women and welcomed them to the use of ICTs in order to enhance their lives. This cultural transformation illustrates the truth that people are drawn to applications and possibilities rather than to technology. Powerful, culture-friendly applications of ICTs are needed that will naturally draw in the people whom we target to benefit most of all from the technologies.

Language and culture are allied and we must allow for language diversity on the web if we are to make it readily accessible to people all over the world. We also need to recognize that cultures already have rich multimedia forms that can be incorporated into the web culture. For example, the Kiswahili culture of East Africa is essentially non-confrontational. Therefore, one way of passing a message is to wear the traditional East African cloth, the Khanga, which carries a printed proverb to communicate a positive or negative message to the family and community .

It is also necessary to take account of the different world-views from which people approach the content of the web. For example, how should one reconcile differing responses to technology, such as whether Africans should join the debate concerning the Artificial Intelligence Machine, or reject it on the grounds of a specific African sensibility?

We can better appreciate and benefit from a world-view when it is contained in a cultural context. We hear one another better if we acknowledge one another's culture. By creating cultural, linguistic, national or special-interest communities around websites and/or clearing-houses, we can provide an easier and safer web entry point for culturally sensitive populations. We can create visual and cultural clues to allow people to move from their point of greatest cultural control, i.e. their home, out to their community and ultimately to the world itself.

Cultural comfort zones are needed in the form of interface languages and metaphors that can successfully mediate the potential clash between cultures. It is no accident that the smallest unit of the World Wide Web is called a 'home page'. I believe that the geographical metaphor can be useful with respect to culture. Geographically, the home is the place of greatest cultural control, because this is where the individual has greatest choice in the selection of language, cultural behaviour and cultural artefacts. The community also tends to have greater cultural harmony because many people are able to choose to live in a place where they are culturally comfortable. From these zones one is able to move out into the world, recognizing that every time one crosses a boundary one has to exercise greater cultural tolerance because one is entering a new culture.

To overcome the cultural divide, Web researchers and developers must provide metaphors to help Web users to comfortably navigate through culturally diverse materials. Most of all, we need to keep the dialogue going between cultures. WWW will then truly reflect the world.

KATHERINE W. GETAO
Senior Lecturer,
Institute of Computer Science,
University of Nairobi (Kenya)

The Internet: not the swansong of the book

Traditionally, the use of books became possible when the reader mastered the discipline of reading. Imperceptibly, the apprenticeship of reading has passed from the linear discourse on the written page to the simultaneous perception of several windows on a screen: this new way of grasping messages is more than a method. It is a new attitude and a new way of thinking. The result is that literacy training is becoming more difficult in the developing countries and less durable in the industrialized ones, which themselves are now facing an illiteracy problem. So what does the future hold for traditional books?

While the Internet is proving to be a technique that can advance the culture of the written word, for the time being the ultimate outcome is hard to perceive. The first signs are on the whole encouraging. We have already called attention to them, but there are others that threaten the quality of the written message at least according to today's criteria and equal access in the light of language pre-eminence: the abundant harvest of information, data and exchanges on the Net takes place in a small number of languages, the frequency of use of a language on the Internet being proportional to the technological capability and equipment of its users. Moreover, the use of these languages is far from being particularly correct: abbreviations, borrowings from other languages, and neologisms are linguistic mutations specific to the Net and amount in essence to deformation of the language. The correction of the asymmetrical origin of contents, the languages in which they are expressed and access to the network represent a formidable challenge to the international community.

Penetrating the meaning of a text is also an opportunity to reflect in order to grasp all the shades of meaning and develop critical analysis. The comparison of the written word with the individual's own experienced reality is an exciting challenge. For its part the most recent invention of contemporary communication, the Internet, has not excluded the written universe – far from it. On the contrary, the written message lies at the very heart of its existence. Nevertheless there is no reason to suppose that the Internet can replace the book as an instrument of reflection, deepening of content or critical analysis. Privileging from the outset the informative function of the written text as the heir to the old telegram, cable or fax, the 'Net' has projected the written message into this ephemeral, rapid and volatile dimension of cyberspace and the screen.

It goes without saying that the post-television generation is creating a closer association between the screen and the written text, but it does not seem to possess the traditional instruments needed to make correct use of its own language. Cut off in a sense from the laborious discipline of a linear apprenticeship of reading, it has difficulty in grasping the meaning of the written message, which is replaced by a global perception specific to the numerous windows of computer technology. The Internet has opened up a vast range of technical possibilities which will no doubt help to change the content and form of the message, but we cannot yet speak of an 'Internet culture' as we do of a 'book culture'. Until this technology (which for the time being is no more than that) emerges as a different form of universal expression (and perhaps a different way of learning to read), the focus must still be placed on effective training in reading and writing. But whatever medium is chosen, the unique instrument for the precise expression of thought and the beauty of the message continues to be language, just as learning to read and write continue to be the only solid foundation for the qualitative use of all the new communication technologies.

ALVARO GARZON
Director, Section for Books and
Cultural Industries,
Sector for Culture, UNESCO (Columbia)

NOBEL PRIZE FOR LITERATURE

COUNTRY

Australia	France	Italy	South Africa
Belgium	Germany	Japan	Spain
Chile	Greece	Mexico	Sweden
Colombia	Guatemala	Nigeria	Switzerland
Czechoslovakia	Iceland	Norway	United Kingdom
Denmark	India	Poland	USA
Egypt	Ireland	Portugal	Union of Soviet Socialist Rep.
Finland	Israel	St. Lucia	Yugoslavia
			Stateless*

GRAPH 17

NOBEL PRIZEWINNERS FOR LITERATURE IN THE TWENTIETH CENTURY COME FROM THIRTY-TWO COUNTRIES

* Ivan Bunin was officially declared stateless by the Nobel Institute at his own request.

Source: Nobel Foundation, 1999.

The current grouping within the new Prodi Commission of DG 10 (Culture) and DG 22 (Education) under the authority of one commissioner shows that adequate funding for culture accrues when it is combined with education.

On the issue of the information society, it was Commission policy to distinguish between political objectives and industrial issues. The first consideration was economic, and aimed at developing an industry of content in Europe in the cultural and public sector. This initiative can be traced back to the DG 13, in charge of telecommunications, information and research through the IMPACT programme, launched in 1988, which intended to establish a European industry and market for information services. From 1989 onwards, the programme led to the adoption by the Commission of an important text, *Guidelines for Greater Synergy Between Public and Private Sectors on the Information Market*. The ratification of the Maastricht Treaty led to the Birmingham Declaration of the European Council in October 1992 on the issue of citizenship in the Union. What measures should be taken to be 'closer to citizens' in the age of new networks? By instituting European citizenship in October 1997, the Amsterdam Treaty recognized the right for every citizen to education, culture and information. Access to public data, particularly of a cultural nature, then appeared as a tangible proof of, and the price to be paid for, the new right to European citizenship.

Commissioner Martin Bangemann, in charge of industrial affairs and information technologies, visualized a way of combining political and industrial issues in the information society. He set up the Information Society Project Office (ISPO), an authoritative structure that guided the launching by DG 13 of the Information Society Technologies (IST) programme with a budget of 3.6 billion euros. This may be viewed in the light of the 46 million euros of the IMPACT programme in 1988 or with the case of Culture 2000 which was refused 95 million euros. In the part of the programme dealing with consumption in the 'Information Society', special attention is given to the cultural heritage. The third key-action, to which 564 million euros have been allocated, focuses on 'Multimedia content and tools'. The purpose of this is to improve the functional aspect, facility of use and acceptability of future projects and services related to information in order to permit linguistic and cultural diversity, to contribute to the valorization and exploitation of the European cultural heritage, to stimulate creativity and to improve education and training systems for lifelong learning. A number of aspects have a direct bearing on heritage and culture: access to the scientific and cultural heritage; digital preservation of the cultural heritage; cultural information systems; and transparent incorporation of heritage systems in new digital applications in libraries. The fifth key-action focuses on 'The city of tomorrow and the cultural heritage'.

Over the past fifteen years, the European Commission has sought to develop a relationship between the community of European museums and the new technology industries. However, its efforts have been in vain, and the failure of the Florence Memorandum of Understanding in 1998 is a good illustration of this. DG 10 (Culture) and DG 22 (Education) were caught unawares by DG 13 which, between 1996 and 1998, invited museums and industrialists to establish closer links in order to define a set of common rules regarding access to data produced by cultural institutions. These rules were brought together in the Memorandum of Understanding which was signed by over 450 institutions in March 1998.

Following publication of the Memorandum, it seemed that the European Commission could count on a basic consensus whereby it could then lay down new rules of access to the European cultural heritage and develop a culture and knowledge industry. However, the museums gradually tired of being treated as mere 'reservoirs of information'. Furthermore the launching of a European Charter of Museums (ECM) led to questions regarding European initiatives.

The MEDICI programme, successor to the Florence Memorandum of Understanding, was launched in October 1998 to establish closer links around the notion of 'fair revenue' between museums and industry. As a result of this, an active policy on the part of institutions means that a response can now be

Cultural policies on the southern web

There can be no doubt that easy access to information nowadays offers positive prospects for the democratization of information and communication. At the same time it raises the urgent issue of the globalizing nature of a web-type environment for Third World users. One question that unavoidably arises in this connection has to do with whether, and if so how, identities are being reforged in this deterritorialized, fragmented, global universe which is constantly permeated with massive flows of information. How do Web users see themselves; how do they 'construct' their place in this unpredictable context?

Traditionally, identification processes and representations of identity drew on a number of parameters, rather than just one: belonging to a region, nation, age group or genealogical family. In the Internet environment, precisely the opposite is the case: concepts of time and place no longer provide bearings.

The structure of homepages (it is no coincidence that the English word 'home' is used) in this regard provides an excellent area to analyse the way in which subjectivities and assertions of identity are portrayed in the decentralized web space. Another striking point here is the way in which the 'home' unit, a small territory that is clearly personal and more precisely defined than 'local' (in current use in negotiations with the symbolic global universe), has become firmly established.

As a backdrop to this, our chief concern is the emergence of new forms of inequality on the web and, counterbalancing these, creative opportunities and new ways of defending equal rights for everyone to access the new technologies. Highly relevant to the above is the fact that English is the default language. As we know, the United States is the only country not required to use a suffix with electronic addresses circulating on the network.

This example is particularly pertinent because it refers not only to difficulties in accessing information located on the web but also points up possible reactions which are among the most interesting now emerging. I am referring to a fascinating negotiation on national languages in some Spanglish or Portinglish dictionaries on the web. Spanglish is the Spanish used by a browser who is not fluent in English. If one accepts the premise that cyberspace is (at least so far) an American dominion and hence uses the English language, Spanglish would seem to offer no resistance to English vocabulary while at robustly the same time rejecting English grammar and syntax.

Hence, such web users acquire the English vocabulary they find and then subject it to the logic and grammar rules of their vernacular languages, thereby shaping new inflections and geopolitical and linguistic territorialities. It is true that new easy-to-read translated programmes and software have been launched. But there is a significant loss in translation in terms of style, irony and, at the end of the day, power of communication.

Further, it is increasingly important to look into the hegemony of English on the Web as more and more users who are not proficient in English join in. A case in point would be Brazil: the figures bear out this relative decrease in proficiency. In 1996, 62% of Brazilian web users spoke English. In 1997, the figure fell to 58% and in 1998 to 55% (http://www.ibope.com.br/digital/cade98/adpkd4.htm). These facts point to a trend towards the popularization and educational diversification of users as well as to a broadening of scope beyond finance and business where the basic language is English.

If, for instance, we consider the potential of the Net as a political forum which looks like an increasingly attractive proposition, we find a worrying indicator: according to Sonia Aguiar from the Brazilian Institute for Social and Economic Analyses (IBASE, http://www.ibase.org.br/), only 30% of the topics discussed in conferences listed on the AlterNex network, the Brazilian member of the Association for Progressive Communications (APC), in February 1995, were in Portuguese.

Now to come to a specific case, a virtual library (http://www.ufrj.br/pacc) has been set up for information and communication on cultural studies in the framework of the Brazilian National Research Council's (CNPq) Prossiga project, the country's most ambitious programme in support of scientific work and communication (http://www.prossiga.cnpq.br).

The choice of cultural studies for an information and research project on the Internet was a deliberate strategy. It was an attempt to respond to the dynamics of social expansion in relation to the new technologies, new information flows and global cultural processes which require a rigorous reshaping of the very concept of identity.

In this connection, a consideration of the definitions (or their absence) that scientific communities give of the nature of cultural studies in different local and national contexts shows interesting variations. In Latin America, these studies became broader in scope and gained more acceptance in the second half of the 1980s just when the process of political liberalization in southern Latin America was in full swing. It was at that point that the Latin American academic debate began to take on board new issues flowing from the reorganization of national boundaries and the new ways that civil society had found to dialogue with the state. These new forms of dialogue became more intense as the state showed little capacity to meet the demands of civil society, thus making the latter turn increasingly to the international sphere and impressing upon political and academic circles the need to consolidate a global civil society.

One instance of this effectiveness lies in the boost that Internet access gives to NGOs, trade unions and grass-roots movements or fringe cultural productions at relatively low cost. Since 1985 IBASE has been a pioneer in the use of electronic communication for social action, the idea being to intervene and stimulate public debate on issues and projects able to radicalize democracy in its various forms.

A classic case in point in Brazil was the international mobilization and impact achieved through the Internet by the landless peasants' movement, the 'Movimento dos Sem Terra' (MST), which from 1979 (a period when these kind of claims were beginning to gain more attention in national political spheres) struggled for hundreds of peasant families to take part in the organized occupation of uncultivated land. From 1996 onwards, there began an intensive daily publication on the Net of newspaper articles, reports, declarations and articles in English, Portuguese and Spanish, as well as faxes and e-mails. Amnesty International joined in and circulated a document decrying the killing of rural workers and also lent its e-mail and automatic reply service to the movement. In 1997 MST achieved international visibility and local negotiating power.

This example demonstrates the strategic prospects offered by the network concept. Such a netwar could decisively influence what a population knows of itself or of the outside world. It could become involved in foreign policy, propaganda and political decision-making. In short, the Internet's potential for mobilization and intervention appears boundless.

A brief overview of the main Brazilian sites that fit the conceptual ethnic and gender frameworks – both in terms of civil society organization sites and artistic and cultural production sites – shows the variety of possible uses that can be made of the network. Here we see a fairly active use of virtual public space to design new identities and cultural policies and strategies. One of the most outstanding is the fairly academic NGO 'Documentação Indigenista e Ambiental' (www.cr-df.rnp.br/~dia), which since 1991 has developed an extensive multimedia indigenous databank on the Internet. The site comprises a vast collection of data, statistics, and maps of indigenous lands. It also provides opportunities for producing films and photographs and doing research to safeguard indigenous memory and disseminate it to the general public. The special feature of these kinds of databanks on the network, away from university circles and not using the traditional logic of archives and libraries, is that they gather selective information or do research to make diagnoses to meet immediate demands.

The emergence of these new opportunities makes it increasingly important to survey and analyse the material accommodated on the Internet and to design citizen-friendly scientific policies for the Web.

HELOISA BUARQUE DE HOLLANDA
Co-ordinator, Programa Avancado
de Cultura Contemporanea,
Universidade Federal do Rio de Janeiro (Brazil)

given to the new requirements of public communication in the age of new technologies.

In the United Kingdom, thanks to funding from the Millennium Committee, which since 1994 has received 28% of National Lottery takings (or almost £1.5 billion), projects relating to the information society have been funded autonomously and on a large scale. The most striking example is undoubtedly the Scottish Cultural Resource Access Network (SCRAN) (http://www.scran.ac.uk) launched in 1996.

SCRAN is a project very comparable to Louvre.edu by its concepts and purpose; it is an on-line educational server for educational material on the history and heritage of Scotland. From a publishing standpoint, the Louvre, unlike SCRAN, regards the role of text as being of considerable importance; furthermore, SCRAN sees a danger of proliferation where the Louvre sees a right of appropriation, i.e. the possibility of reutilizing downloaded media. Our views also differ on a similarly important issue. While the Louvre Museum, in spite of its apparently powerful position, has been able to raise new funds amounting only to slightly more than 20% of the cost of Louvre.edu, that is to say, one million francs, SCRAN has an overall budget of £15 million (150 times more). Their budget is covered to the amount of 50% by the Millennium Committee. Hence, SCRAN has been able to develop over 200 projects in collaboration with museums, libraries, archives and universities.

It is quite clear today that the era of splendid isolation is now over and that mergers or closer links must be established to ensure the rapid creation of the foundations of a European museum structure on the Internet. Three specific channels are emerging: (a) public information, with programmes, products and provision of a public dimension for professional debates on conservation, restoration and education; (b) the education sector, in a preliminary phase, taking account at national or regional level of the objectives resulting from educational diversity; and (c) technical and scientific standardization of art history.

The start of such an initiative would seem to be taking shape due to the impetus of the Berlin museums: e-museums, a multi-public site for information on the current activities of museums and major exhibitions, projects and achievements in regard to on-line services. This site should come into operation in spring 2000.

It is likely that a European awakening will help to establish a pole capable of coexisting on an equal footing with North American initiatives. The situation in the rest of the world does not strike us as favourable, and the generous, democratic image with which the Internet all too often covers itself is unfortunately still not in conformity with the facts.

Black, White, Yellow, Brown:
when seen from Culture's apex
the view is perfect.

Pervaiz Salik

You understood me
Just drinking tea together
it was five dirhams

Meghann Ormond

In same dwelling-house
a community in the flat
of two countries.

Dusko Matas

The ways of our time
When a happy world babbles
For whole days in rhyme

Jean-Pierre Tsambe Imanja

Part Five
International public opinion and national identity

Introduction

In this report many experiences with the reality of globalization, and that have not always been positive, are recorded. The results of massive and rapid change seem to impose a more prudent approach to development. A discerning view would imply a middle position between the excessive utopianism of the first half of last century and the sense of drift of the second. It would also try to strike a balance between short-time solutions and long-term policy. In present global development, old and new problems are re-emerging: inequality of opportunity and power, discrimination and conflict, and instability and extremism. The two magic formulas of market and democracy do not automatically produce miracles. A new world of risks and gains also brings with it new demands for continuity, stability and security.

The awareness of what is happening all over the world is rapidly becoming globalized itself. A technical revolution in communications is drawing millions, and very soon billions, of people into its network. The flow of news and transmitted experiences is unprecedented. Unheard-of places are suddenly becoming household words. This unprecedented opening up of the local or the national horizon to events that are out of reach may prove unsettling both to ordinary people and to those in power.

The present report attempts to come to grips with changes in comprehension and control that are vital to us all. Through the report also runs a common theme, i.e. the wish to let the widest possible diversity of people participate in the process of prudent decision-making.

The reactions of populations to major changes in their circumstances will express themselves in valuations. These valuations are no longer to be taken for granted. The constant flux of events, but also the constant creativity of mankind in coping with these and producing new solutions, place a burden on countless individuals to make choices and select their preferred approach to this new world. This massive process of creation and selection is regulated by traditional institutions less than before. It manifests itself in a free-floating mass of immediate reaction which one could describe as the public mood. This mood is less predictable than before. Recent demonstrations against globalization and the World Trade Organization in Seattle or public protest against xenophobia in Vienna have shown how surprising public opinion may be.

In this period of flux and cultural change it has become relevant to policy-makers to acquire adequate indications about the way public opinion is evolving. Monitoring changes in public opinion, not only by scrutiny of the content of the media but also by approaching people directly, has become an indispensable tool in the process of evaluation in most open societies. Though haphazard in many instances, public opinion research is frequently used in exploring issues. Very often the results show discordance between the views of policy-makers and opinion leaders, on the one hand, and what people really have to say, on the other. The results are sometimes far more moderate and sensible than expected. The findings may even point to tensions and judgements that were previously ignored: as such, public opinion is, and rightly so, one of the elements to be assessed realistically when policy proposals and decisions are being made. A systematic use of opinion research in the policy-making process may help democracy adapt to less structured conditions.

The question of Asian values, which are exercising policy-makers and as discussed in the *World Culture Report 1998*, is a case in point. An earlier general assessment of the unity and diversity of values in Asia is now specifically corroborated by Japanese research summarized in this report. Yes indeed, there may be some underlying unity in the valuation of (hard) work in Asian society and the importance of investing in the education of future generations. But even more striking is a diversity of valuations between, for instance, Chinese and Japanese respondents. In the same way, the diversity of responses between the older and younger generations indicates rapid cultural change. It is not yet possible to ascertain whether this change consistently moves in one specific direction. But diversity and change there are. These findings place the discussions about Asian values in an interesting dynamic context.

Turning now to some specific issues discussed in the other chapters of the *World Culture Report 2000*, it should be pointed out that they can be only partially be considered in relation to data on public opinion. The reason is quite simple: it has not been possible to design new research for this report. One has to make do with secondary analysis of data collected as part of existing studies.

However, a few findings may shed additional light on current debates. Although for the present, armed conflicts between nation states appear to be superseded by certain forms of civil war, and as such are leading to new problems, the rise of nationalism in the face of citizens coming from other states is a growing problem. Migrants have to reckon with the new state they are living in. The importance of values underpinning the national culture should not be underestimated. The general attitude towards migrants depends very much on the way in which nationality is perceived by national citizens. In this situation two values would appear to be strategic: the attitude of nationals to their own identity, and their attitude to outsiders. Is one's self closely identified with one's national culture? What is the level of nationalism? Is self-perception or group identity based on more or less immutable (ascribed) identity values or on values that can also be acquired by foreigners? And when considering ways of recognizing differences and giving access to citizenship, will public opinion accept others as fellow citizens on a general or a partial basis, or on individual or collective terms? There is no all-inclusive answer to these questions. There are considerable differences between the ways nationals perceive themselves and the way they approach others. This diversity is confirmed by the public opinion research presented here.

A further issue highlighted by opinion findings is the supposedly mutual exclusion of global and local identifications. It is becoming clear that the usual opposition of cosmopolitan attitudes and localism needs rethinking. In a number of countries the populations appear to be able to link their identification vis-à-vis the national state with considerable readiness to accept their simultaneous attachment to a wider international context. This popular and patriotic cosmopolitanism stands in contrast to popular and fanatic nationalism, which could also be called 'cultural fundamentalism'.

In considering these moods and values, we should note the fundamental change in the world situation. Migration is no longer a theoretical or distant phenomenon, but a reality that involves even secluded local communities. While migration may not be the preferred solution of the migrants themselves, neither is it the preferred solution of many ordinary people in the receiving countries. Policy-makers should accordingly take problematical attitudes on both sides into account, paying particular attention to the predominant attitudes of the receiving side.

Leaving aside further specific problems drafted in this report, and taking together the findings of the previous and the present *World Culture Reports*, we may expect public opinion to be basically supportive of the further democratization of society. On the basis of public opinion research we should also be aware of the potential for conflict if democracy does not find any practical solutions for the negative aspects of globalization.

Finally, as pointed out in *World Culture Report 1998*, the absence of data from large areas of the world means there are still zones of silence in terms of public opinion research. Indeed current debates would be strengthened if world public opinion were underpinned by systematic, broadbased research.

ADRIAAN VAN DER STAAY
Social Scientist; Former Director of the Social and Cultural Planning Office, and Professor Extraordinary in Cultural Policies and Cultural Criticism, Rotterdam University (Netherlands)

Chapter 14
International public opinion and national identity: a descriptive study of existing survey data

JOS W. BECKER
Social and Cultural Planning Office (Netherlands)

'We propose to go on covering "cultural issues" from the angle of people's values as indicated by their ideas, wishes, judgements, perceptions and beliefs.'

INTRODUCTION

RESEARCH ON DIVERSITY, CULTURAL PLURALISM AND DISCRIMINATION

Part Four of the first *World Culture Report (1998)* was devoted to the study of public opinion and global ethics. Chapter 16 offered an overview of values and beliefs, of the populations of various countries and regions of the world (van der Staay, 1998) and was based on international surveys of public opinion. These data were meant to supplement the research-measuring aspects of culture in a more objective way, as reported in Part Seven of the 1998 Report. The study of values was also meant to concentrate people's thoughts as a counterbalance to the voice of 'authority', meaning the points of view upheld by academics and politicians, universities and international institutions, and influential conferences and books (*World Culture Report*, 1998, pp. 250–1; McKinley, 1998, pp. 322–40; Goldstone, 1998, pp. 349–88). We propose to go on covering 'cultural issues' from the angle of people's values as indicated by their ideas, wishes, judgements, perceptions and beliefs.

In guiding the preparation of this report, UNESCO proposed a series of possible subjects: diversity, cultural pluralism, discrimination, equality of access, the local and global in technology, access to knowledge, matters concerning cultural heritage and so on. Not all of these subjects can be covered by general survey research. For instance, when issues of policy or technology are concerned, specialized research among policy-makers or technicians offers more accurate insight.

No new research was undertaken in drafting the 1998 chapter. Existing data were analysed instead, notably the *World Values Survey* dated 1990–93. Since then only a limited number of new data have become available.[1] Promising research on national identity was carried out by members of the *International Social*

Survey Programme (ISSP) in 1995. Among other subjects, this survey covers citizen's orientation towards their city and homeland and the world outside, feelings of nationalism and evaluation of cultural differences between nations, and tolerance or intolerance towards immigrants and minorities. Twenty-four countries participated; this is a fairly large number, although appreciably smaller than the forty-eight countries that took part in the *World Values Survey*. Feelings of nationalism and attitudes towards minorities, like localistic or cosmopolitan attitudes, are of special interest to the present *World Culture Report*. The fact that only a limited number of countries participated seems less of a drawback than it might otherwise have been. We therefore think that extensive use of the relevant ISSP data is a reliable approach.

EARLIER EFFORTS: PRINCIPLES, THE CONCEPT OF VALUES, SOME IMPORTANT RESULTS

We propose to begin this chapter by mentioning some of the principles that guided our earlier efforts and by enumerating a few of the conclusions that were reached. Having presented the reader with a short summary, we then extend and deepen the knowledge of international public opinion on an international scale.

In 1998 the cultural areas in which beliefs could be held were delineated in conformity with the main concerns for cultural policy, as expressed in the report *Our Creative Diversity.* The authors of that report stressed the need for the containment and limitation of social conflict and the furtherance of co-operation between different people with different interests and from different cultures. In order to achieve this objective, attention should be paid to human rights and responsibilities, democracy and the rights of civil society, the protection of minorities, commitment to the peaceful resolution of conflict and to fair negotiation and equity within and between generations.

Among all these topics, equity (or social harmony) and social justice can be realized only on the basis of shared commitments or, stated in somewhat different terms, on the basis of a core of shared ethical values and principles (Pérez de Cuéllar, 1995, pp. 34, 40–6). The World Commission's list of basic concerns represents the values which should guide research and analysis.

In the social sciences, the concept of *value* may be interpreted in many ways. Some of these were reviewed in van der Staay (1998, pp. 252–3). Eventually the author decided to use a short yet comprehensive definition that could be universally accepted. Values were regarded as ideas of what is desirable in society. Desirability might refer to a favourable state of affairs, for instance adequate housing for the population, or a certain level of public health. It could also refer to desirable ways of thinking and behaving, in fact to various kinds of morality. We propose to adhere to this definition.

If it is to become a value, an idea should be widely shared by individuals. In addition, values are general in nature and thus sufficiently abstract to be applied to a wide range of practical situations. Values are commonly divided into universals and particulars. Whereas universals are valid for the whole of society, particulars apply only to certain areas, as do medical ethics. We will concern ourselves here exclusively with universal values. Values serve as guidelines for policy, thought and behaviour. They can also be used as standards to judge particular instances of these phenomena.

It was supposed that the dissemination of values was affected positively by globalization, the process in which ideas as well as behaviour are disseminated on a grand scale. Globalization is the outcome of intensified communication. Communication in turn is stimulated by an increasingly efficient technological infrastructure, facilitating the exchange of information and geographical mobility.

The results of globalization in terms of value are twofold. In general, globalization leads to the adoption of ideas and beliefs from other countries or cultures and thus to cultural homogeneity. It is also possible, however, that confrontation with other cultures causes people to resist the acceptance of 'foreign' ideas and practices. In this instance national pride or pride in a country's cultural heritage comes to the fore, and cultural diversity rather than homogeneity results. Therefore, the possibility of growing

Happiness

What is happiness, and what are the factors that govern its attainment?

Happiness is a state of mind, a subjective rather than objective measure of contentment, of the quality of life, of satisfaction with one's health, wealth, status and achievement.

According to a MORI poll carried out in Britain in 1993, when asked 'Overall in the last week, how have you been feeling? Have you been very happy, fairly happy, neither happy nor unhappy, fairly unhappy or very unhappy?', eight out of ten people (79%) reported they had been happy, 13% unhappy and the rest were neutral. Interestingly, there were no 'don't knows'. Women (82%) were a shade more likely to report being happy than men (76%). The least happy were those in the 35–44 year age group (20%). Surprisingly, marriage did not make very much difference, as 79% of those who were married said they were happy, while nearly as many single (78%) and separated/divorced (76%) were happy too.

These findings apply only to Great Britain. When international comparisons are made, the following picture emerges. The measure of happiness and reported state of health correlate highly over countries (about 0.84). However, there seems to be little relationship between trust in institutions and a nation's reported state of happiness.

What does seem to matter is people's perception of their own social status, which is naturally tied to income in most cases. Nearly eight in ten of those who describe themselves as upper class report that they are happy, while only one in five of those who claim to be lower class report being happy.

Religion seemed to make relatively little difference, although those who describe themselves as 'very' religious are significantly more likely to describe themselves as happy than those who are 'not at all' religious.

ROBERT M. WORCESTER

diversity exists, despite the presence of culturally unifying forces.

The generally experienced need for a common cultural background as a basis for social harmony and co-operation, added to the undecided balance of cultural homogeneity and diversity, enabled the authors of the previous *World Culture Report* to gain insight into the phenomena of cultural unity and diversity. Almost all of van der Staay's chapter on public opinion and global ethics was devoted to analysing data on beliefs from this point of view.

In accordance with the main concerns of *Our Creative Diversity*, data were analysed on the subject of people's essential needs, on some of their ideas concerning politics, on tolerance, especially towards foreigners or immigrants, on the family and some gender issues and on the environment. Some conclusions were reached.

First of all, the division between unity and diversity is not clear-cut. No statements on values could be found to indicate that they were completely accepted by the inhabitants of one geographical region or separate country and categorically rejected by the citizens of another. The researchers succeeded only in pinpointing some values that were fairly generally held (unity) and other values that populations quite clearly disagreed upon (diversity). In all other instances, it could be maintained only that where unity could not be claimed to exist, an impressive diversity was absent in any case. The general picture was of a fairly broad dispersion of values that might be interpreted as a stage in an evolution towards further cultural unification. How far such unification was to proceed could not be determined at the time.

Some ideals seemed to be widespread as regarded special fields of interest:

- the ideal of democracy, though *not* accompanied by a truly universal endorsement of human rights;
- the ideal of tolerance was upheld, though only partly applied to foreigners (not in the labour market) and not to all minorities, such as homosexuals;
- the ideal of women's emancipation;
- the acceptance of paid work by married women, although traditionally perceived drawbacks were still emphasized;
- a fairly liberal view on marriage with some emphasis on marital fidelity;
- the desire to protect children from harm.

It could be added that the environment was indeed considered a problem, but to a far lesser degree than specialists in the field and environmentalists appeared to think.

OLD AND NEW CONCERNS

The concerns guiding the compilation of the chapter in the 1998 Report also underlie the present effort to provide a new overview of public opinion. Given the still pressing need for social harmony and international co-operation, a continuing interest in cultural unity and diversity will come as no surprise to the reader. Here is the question that was central to the analysis given in the previous culture report:

To what extent does similar thinking prevail in various countries or larger regions of the world with regard to topics addressed by the *World Culture Report*, and to what extent do countries diverge in this respect?

This question refers to agreement and disagreement on values. If countries differ strongly on the question of whether, for instance, divorce should be permitted, cultural diversity is assumed to exist. If differences are small, cultural unity appears to be the rule. This view of the data is rather 'formal'. The researcher simply 'counts' the differences of various magnitudes or, using an even simpler procedure, takes a statistical measure of dispersion into account. This last procedure was, with some embellishment, used in 1998. Instead of concentrating on the agreement on values, attention could also be shifted towards the value of agreement. In this case one is interested in the opinions people harbour on the importance of their own nation, on citizens of other nations and on members of minority groups within their own country. Are people always concerned for social harmony, or do situations occur in which they reject other groups or even favour conflict? Does the country one belongs to represent an important value?

Such considerations lend importance to the following question: to what extent are citizens

Changing roles of women in Europe

Recent research into the role of women in society uncovered evidence of considerable cultural diversity even between the industrialized countries of Western Europe. These data are taken from MORI's multi-national study for the Whirlpool Foundation carried out in 1995 focusing on the role of women in society. Sample groups of women and men were interviewed in France, Germany, Italy, Spain and the United Kingdom and some of the questions were the same as those in a Louis Harris survey conducted the previous year in the United States.

When women aged 18–65 were asked in a cross-national European study (five countries, 1995), 'Which if any of these groups of people lend the greatest support in various ways to women generally in their lives?', it appeared that 'their family' was seen as most supportive, named by between 71% and 80% of those responding; in Britain, 64% also saw 'their friends' as lending support, whereas the figures were only 23% for Italy and 17% for Spain.

Attitudes to work and career too were different according to sex. In the United States, working women were almost evenly divided as to whether they regarded their work as 'just a job' or as 'a career'; in Germany, by contrast, it was 'just a job' by a margin of more than four-to-one, and in Italy by almost three-to-one.

This seemed to reflect a generally stronger feeling in the United States than in Europe that a job, especially a full-time one, is a good thing in itself rather than simply an economic necessity. When asked what they would ideally do with their time if money were not a consideration, 33% of men and 15% of women aged 18–55 in the United States said they would prefer to work full-time; these figures were far higher than in Europe; in Italy, for example, less than half as many men or women would choose to do so.

One striking conclusion to be drawn from this comparison is that in both Britain and Italy there was equal preference for part-time work among both men and women, while in the other countries, notably Germany, the figures were close, not to say identical. Even within Europe, the survey brought out considerable differences in what women hoped to get from their work. In Britain, flexible working hours were clearly most highly valued, with job security ranking second, while fewer than one in three attached importance to having stimulating or challenging work. In Italy, however, interesting work was a matter of concern to 51%, and in France to 44%. In Spain, job security was thought to be the most important aspect of work. British women put high priority on employer provision of childcare.

ROBERT M. WORCESTER

oriented towards their own country or towards other areas both closer and further removed from the sphere of their personal life? How strong are their feelings of nationalism? How can their attitudes towards ethnic minorities; be described?

The remainder of the chapter will be divided into four broad paragraphs: identification with geographical areas, especially the country one lives in; ideas on the importance of one's own country and feelings of nationalism; ideas on citizenship and opinions on minorities; and the relationship between attitudes and the characteristics of individuals and countries. Overviews and conclusions are added.

NATIONAL AND INTERNATIONAL IDENTIFICATION

VARIOUS IDENTIFICATIONS

How strong is the bond between the individual and the place where he or she lives: neighbourhood, city, province, country or even the surrounding continent? How willing is he or she to exchange one of these for another if such a move provides him or her with a better job or better living conditions? Does loyalty to a place constitute a barrier to mobility? The answers to these and related questions provide insight into the relationship between the individual and a number of geographical entities, including his country. On this subject some survey questions were asked. For instance, how close did the individual feel to various areas ranging from neighbourhood to continent?[2]

It may be useful to point out that these and other questions were subject to so-called *local adaptation* in different countries. In general this principle means that the formulation of questions is adapted to the country in which the survey is being held. Of course the adaptation should leave international comparability unharmed. With regard to geographical orientations, the concept of 'province' was sometimes used, while the word 'state' was inserted for the United States. If necessary, the actual name of the country was mentioned. The tables in this chapter refer to the concept of 'continent', whereas the word itself was not used in formulating the questions. The researchers spoke of East Asia, Europe or North America. Even this detailed designation is, of course, not meaningful for all the countries. The inhabitants of Australia or the United States could well argue that their country corresponded more or less to a continent. In this respect some care will have to be taken in interpreting the data.

DIFFERENCES BETWEEN COUNTRIES

The averages calculated for the twenty-four countries showed that identification with country was the strongest (Tables 1 and 2).[3] An average of 41% felt very close to their country. Approximately 30% held this feeling towards neighbourhood, hometown or province. Attachment to the continent was the weakest of the series (21%).[4]

The data clearly show that a general sense of belonging is country specific to some extent. The inhabitants of some countries seem to feel a consistently high attachment to all the areas offered for their consideration, while other nations are considerably less attracted to all of the areas. It might be assumed that a generalized need to belong makes itself felt more in some national cultures than in others. If this need appears to exist it could be assumed that national identity shows the characteristic of conformism. Cultures showing the need to belong to a relatively weak degree might be labelled individualistic where identity is concerned. For instance, the scores of Austria, Bulgaria, Hungary and Japan are consistently above the general mean. These nations seem to be inclined towards conformism. The inhabitants of Canada, the United States and most western European countries show a measure of attachment consistently below the general mean. In these cases, individualism could be considered as much more dominant.

The mean percentage for identification with the neighbourhood is 29%. In Austria the score is 50% and in Norway 12%. In general it would seem that identification with the neighbourhood is rather weak in sparsely populated countries or in countries where large areas are sparsely populated such as Australia, New Zealand, Norway and Sweden. A large spatial distance between isolated dwellings

TABLE 1
GEOGRAPHIC REGION WITH WHICH ONE IDENTIFIES (1995, IN PERCENTAGES)

	Respondent feels very close to					
	neighbourhood	hometown	province	own country	continent	country and continent
Japan	42	37	41	60	27	0.36
Philippines	28	15	16	22	6	0.41
Australia	13	19	23	61	7	0.29
New Zealand	16	20	20	56	15	0.36
United States	15	13	14	35	18	0.55
Canada	22	19	25	35	16	0.50
Norway	12	18	25	52	21	0.27
Sweden	18	15	17	33	9	0.39
Ireland	41	34	37	54	8	0.29
Great Britain	18	13	12	24	4	0.33
Netherlands	20	15	10	28	10	0.44
Germany						
East (former)	25	23	21	28	12	0.51
West (former)	26	20	16	24	12	0.38
Austria	50	44	48	56	27	0.47
Italy	30	40	35	43	23	0.43
Spain	44	48	46	43	21	0.35
Hungary	53	59	59	80	76	0.60
Poland	26	25	21	55	29	0.43
Czech Republic	36	39	22	48	30	0.57
Slovenia	33	33	29	49	25	0.45
Bulgaria	55	62	58	72	58	0.53
Russian Federation	30	32	25	42	8	0.22
Latvia	28	40	26	41	13	0.37
Slovakia	24	37	22	42	23	0.34
mean percentage	**29**	**30**	**28**	**45**	**21**	

Source: SCP (ISSP 1995).

probably makes the social unit of the neighbourhood less important.

Identification with the country is markedly present in Hungary (80%), Japan (60%) and Poland (55%). In the Philippines, the attachment is the lowest (22%). An explanation for these differences is difficult to devise. Japan and the Philippines, for instance, are both East Asian countries, but they seem to be opposites where the relationship between the individual and the country is concerned. Great Britain, the Netherlands and former West Germany have a fairly long history as independent nations, yet their populations do not seem to identify strongly with the country as a whole. From whatever angle one views the data, a consistent explanation is hard to find. We are probably confronted with peculiarities of national cultures.

RELATIONSHIP BETWEEN IDENTIFICATIONS

The relationship between the different identifications is perhaps of more interest than the somewhat elusive national differences. Let us suppose that an individual is strongly oriented towards his immediate neighbourhood: is it still possible for him to identify intensely with his country? Or, and this is perhaps a more important question, can an individual identify with his country and still feel an attachment towards a larger part of the world? In other words, can a 'good'

Table 2
Geographic region with which one identifies (1995, difference from mean percentage)

	Respondent feels very close to				
	neighbourhood	hometown	province	own country	continent
Japan	12	7	13	15	6
Philippines	–2	–15	–12	–23	–15
Australia	–16	–11	–5	16	–13
New Zealand	–13	–10	–8	11	–5
United States	–15	–17	–14	–10	–3
Canada	–7	–11	–3	–10	–5
Norway	–17	–12	–3	7	0
Sweden	–11	–15	–11	–12	–11
Ireland	12	4	9	9	–13
Great Britain	–11	–17	–16	–21	–17
Netherlands	–9	–15	–18	–17	–11
Germany					
East (former)	–4	–7	–7	–17	–9
West (former)	–3	–10	–12	–21	–9
Austria	20	14	20	11	7
Italy	1	10	7	–2	2
Spain	14	18	18	–2	0
Hungary	24	29	31	35	55
Poland	–3	–5	–6	10	8
Czech Republic	7	9	–6	3	9
Slovenia	3	3	1	4	4
Bulgaria	26	32	30	27	38
Russian Federation	0	2	–3	–3	–13
Latvia	–1	10	–2	–4	–7
Slovakia	–6	7	–6	–3	2
mean percentage	**29**	**30**	**28**	**45**	**21**

Source: SCP (ISSP 1995).

Table 3
Correlations between various identifications (1995, all respondents)

	Neigbourhood	City	Province	Country	Continent
Neigbourhood	1				
City	0.59	1			
Province	0.44	0.60	1		
Country	0.28	0.40	0.48	1	
Continent	0.24	0.30	0.36	0.43	1

Source: SCP (ISSP 1995).

Dutchman also be a 'good' European, or does national identification preclude a positive attitude towards supranational entities? In an age of globalization it is not without interest to note that the identifications with various geographical areas tend to go together. This can be inferred from the correlations mentioned in Table 3. The correlations are calculated from all respondents in the survey, pooled irrespective of their country.[5] The correlations for the separate countries are given in the last column of Table 1. The coefficients are positive without exception. Attachment to the hometown, for instance, does not prevent the respondent from feeling very close to his country or even to the surrounding continent. It is true that this attachment generally declines with geographical distance. The correlation between 'neighbourhood' and 'hometown' is fairly high (0.59), while that between 'hometown' and 'province' is somewhat lower (0.44), and so on. The general conclusion from Table 3 cannot, however, be other than that the identifications do not replace or substitute each other, but rather coexist.

COUNTRY AND INTERNATIONALISM

In view of co-operation and integration at the international level, the positive relationship between identification with the nation and the surrounding continent is of special interest. Table 3 shows a correlation of 0.43, which may be called high considering the fact that surveys usually yield lower coefficients. It is therefore quite possible that an individual feels very close to his country while regarding himself as, for instance, a European. Naturally this finding does not represent an 'iron law'. The correlation is far from perfect. For instance, not every Dutchman will show great attachment to Europe. This type of research highlights only fairly clear regularities. Nevertheless it may be concluded that international integration is not without a foundation in the sphere of public opinion.

Migration

WILLINGNESS TO MOVE

If people could improve their working or living conditions, how willing or unwilling would they be to migrate inside or outside their country? The researchers confronted the respondents with the same range of areas as for the questions about identification.[6]

Generally speaking, willingness to move is not very widespread, even if a better life were the reward. Depending on the area, about 10% to 20% of those questioned are very eager to change abode. The distance to be covered is important. The exchange of one neighbourhood for another meets with the least resistance: 18% would be very willing to do this, while 6% to 7% might be prepared to move to another country or even continent (see the general means of Tables 4 and 5). Not surprisingly, high preparedness for mobility and strong identification are inversely related.

The differences between the countries are far smaller than in the case of identification. Most of the scores are less than 10% above or below the general mean for the twenty-four countries. The inhabitants of the United States appear to be quite mobile where the move to another neighbourhood, city or state is concerned. Russians seem to be rather averse to mobility (Table 4).

POTENTIAL MIGRANTS

Acceptance of geographical mobility is a generalized phenomenon as in the case of identification. The more one would like to go to another neighbourhood, the more one accepts the move to another city, province, country or continent (Table 6). General attitudes – favourable or unfavourable – towards mobility seem to exist. Most of the people willing to move to another country would also be prepared to go and live in another part of the world. (The correlations between 'country' and 'continent' mentioned in Table 4 are quite high.) They are the potential 'true emigrants' among the respondents. In the twenty-four countries taken together, 5% of the indivuduals questioned are very willing to move to another country and equally willing to go and live on another continent.[7] Extremely poor countries whose standard of living is a strong motive for migration did not take part in the survey. Even in these countries, the percentages of 'potential movers' may well be fairly low, but if all of such people acted out their inten-

TABLE 4
WILLINGNESS TO MOVE IN ORDER TO IMPROVE WORK OR LIVING CONDITIONS (1995, IN PERCENTAGES)

	Respondent is very willing to move to another					
	neighbourhood	town	province	country	continent	country and continent
Japan	11	8	7	2	3	0.81
Philippines	13	10	8	9	7	0.81
Australia	19	12	8	5	5	0.91
New Zealand	21	13	12	7	6	0.87
United States	35	24	21	6	6	0.91
Canada	31	19	16	11	10	0.86
Norway	25	13	8	5	4	0.89
Sweden	22	12	10	12	9	0.87
Ireland	16	11	9	8	7	0.87
Great Britain	24	16	13	9	8	0.90
Netherlands	25	19	16	9	8	0.88
Germany						
East (former)	18	8	6	4	3	0.85
West (former)	23	13	10	7	5	0.83
Austria	15	9	7	5	3	0.75
Italy	24	16	13	10	7	0.83
Spain	18	16	13	9	8	0.90
Hungary	11	7	6	3	2	0.71
Poland	16	11	9	8	6	0.86
Czech Republic	16	8	6	4	3	0.79
Slovenia	11	8	6	4	3	0.78
Bulgaria	15	12	9	10	8	0.89
Russian Federation	5	4	3	4		
Latvia	8	5	2	3	3	0.73
Slovakia	18	12	12	9	6	0.79
mean percentage	**18**	**12**	**10**	7	6	

Source: SCP (ISSP 1995).

tions, the flow of economic migrants would become impressive. This appears to be happening in some parts of the world. The closer the respondent feels to a given area, the less willing he is to move to another one (Table 7).[8]

National feelings: the native country evaluated

SOME CONSIDERATIONS AND INDICATORS

When asked to make an evaluation of their country, people may feel they are lucky to be living there and not elsewhere. The recognition of a country's virtues – or the condemnation of its vices – may be directed at particular aspects of the national institutions, culture, manners or way of life. This section offers a description of the way in which people evaluate their native country in terms of general concepts and specific achievements.

People were asked to react to evaluative statements about their native country. These were subject to local adaptation, [my country] being systematically replaced by the name of the country in which the survey was held:

- I would rather be a citizen of [my country] than of any other country in the world.

Table 5
Willingness to move in order to improve work or living conditions (1995, difference from mean percentage)

	Respondent is very willing to move to another				
	neighbourhood	town	Province	country	continent
Japan	–8	–4	–3	–5	–3
Philippines	–6	–2	–2	3	1
Australia	0	1	–2	–2	–1
New Zealand	3	1	3	0	1
United States	16	12	11	0	1
Canada	12	7	6	4	4
Norway	6	1	–2	–1	–1
Sweden	4	0	0	5	3
Ireland	–2	–1	0	1	1
Great Britain	6	4	4	3	3
Netherlands	7	7	7	2	2
Germany					
East (former)	0	–4	–4	–3	–2
West (former)	4	1	0	0	0
Austria	–3	–3	–3	–2	–3
Italy	6	4	3	3	1
Spain	0	4	4	2	2
Hungary	–7	–5	–4	–4	–3
Poland	–3	–1	–1	1	1
Czech Republic	–2	–4	–3	–3	–2
Slovenia	–7	–4	–3	–3	–3
Bulgaria	–3	0	0	3	2
Russian Federation	–14	–8	–7	–3	–6
Latvia	–11	–7	–7	–4	–3
Slovakia	0	0	2	2	0
mean percentage	**18**	**12**	**10**	**7**	**6**

Source: SCP (ISSP 1995).

- Generally speaking [my country] is a better country than most other countries.
- The world would be a better place if all the other countries were more like us [name of nationality].
- People should support their country even it is in the wrong.

Only one of the statements was negatively formulated:

- There are some things about [my country] today that make me feel ashamed of [my country].

Judgements vary in intensity. They may be moderate and firmly rooted in observable fact. People may, however, also harbour extreme and unrealistic ideas about their native country's excellence, in which case concepts such as nationalism or chauvinism apply. The strong wording of most statements – especially those of support for a country even if it is in the wrong, on the country as an example for the whole world and on the country generally being better than others – makes them suitable indicators for nationalism. A question on the desirability of national unity will be added to the tables.[9]

Other questions, i.e. those concerning reasons for national pride, were formulated in a simpler manner. They aimed at making specific evaluations of a country's achievements, institutions and culture. What made people proud of their country?[10] Was it the way democracy was upheld, the country's polit-

Table 6
Correlations between areas in view of willingness to move (1995, all respondents)

	Neigbourhood	City	Province	Country	Continent
Neigbourhood	1				
City	0.76	1			
Province	0.65	0.77	1		
Country	0.42	0.49	0.56	1	
Continent	0.38	0.44	0.51	0.85	1

Source: SCP (ISSP 1995).

Table 7
Correlations between identification and willingness to move (1995, all respondents)

	Respondent identifies with:				
	neigbourhood	city	province	country	continent
Would move to another:					
neighbourhood	–0.32	–0.26	–0.25	–0.20	–0.18
city	–0.25	–0.27	–0.28	–0.19	–0.17
province	–0.20	–0.20	–0.27	–0.21	–0.19
country	–0.13	–0.13	–0.13	–0.25	–0.22
continent	–0.06	–0.06	–0.04	–0.04	–0.09

Source: SCP (ISSP 1995).

ical influence, its economic effort, the level of social security or the fair and equal treatment of various groups? Were science, art and literature, and achievements in sport, history or the armed forces an important reason for pride? The answers to the questions, cross-tabulated by country, are to be found in Tables 8 to 11.

SEPARATISM

In some countries the question about separatism was not asked. The rejection of separatism is quite high. In Canada, Great Britain and Russia, however, the independence of some of the nation's territories does not appear to be absolutely unthinkable. One could argue that separatist movements are active in these countries, thereby making separatism familiar to the public at large.[11]

NATIONALISM

The incidence of truly nationalistic feelings seems to be limited. To some extent people express preference for citizenship of their own country, about 47% agreeing strongly with the relevant statement. It might indeed be difficult for citizens to imagine themselves as having a different nationality. Other statements of a clearly nationalistic content meet with far less favour. That their native country is better than most others in the world is a view strongly held by an average of 18% of those questioned. An average of 12% would be inclined to defend their country against their better judgement. Only 9% seemed to believe that the world would be a better place if the citizens of other countries were more like themselves.

Nationalism may not be very widespread, but the tendency to feel ashamed about one's country is also weak. The average score seems fairly high (21% for 'agree strongly') but this mean is influenced by the high scores of a small number of Eastern European countries. Embarrassment at certain national characteristics is – as is to be expected – inversely related to the other items in Tables 8 and 9. The higher the regard an individual has for his country, the less reason he sees to be ashamed of it.

Some countries are characterized by a fairly high incidence of nationalist sentiment. Some 72% of the Japanese would not like to be a citizen of any other country in the world and 52% think of Japan as a better nation than many others. These percentages are quite high (Table 8). A fairly high regard for one's own country is also found in Australia and the United States. Some Western European countries show a remarkably low regard in this respect: Italy, the Netherlands and Spain. The Spaniards and the Dutch do not seem to find much fault with their countries, whereas the Italians are fairly critical of their nation. Some 32% of Italians sometimes feel ashamed at some aspects of their society. In general a critical attitude towards one's country is prevalent in Eastern Europe: former East Germany (35%), Latvia (39%), Russia (42%) and the Slovak Republic (40%). The levels in this respect are fairly low in Hungary (9%) and Slovenia (8%) (Table 8).

NATIONAL PRIDE

What national achievements are deemed most important by the public? Generally speaking, national achievements in the political or socio-economic fields cannot be considered as an important reason for pride (Table 10 and Table 11). An average of only about 10% consider democracy, political influence, economic effort, social security or the fair and equal treatment of groups as reasons for being very proud of their country. Cultural effort seems to carry far greater weight. Averages of between 24% and 34% are proud of their country's science, art and literature, and achievements in sport or history (Table 10). On the

TABLE 8
FEELINGS ABOUT ONE'S OWN COUNTRY (1995, IN PERCENTAGES)

	Respondent agrees strongly:					
	one nation is essential	wants to be a citizen of [my country]	own country better	own country is example	supports even when wrong	feels ashamed about some things
Japan	91	72	52	15	12	28
Philippines	93	30	13	7	7	7
Australia	95	66	38	13	7	12
New Zealand	97	52	28	10	6	15
United States	94	71	40	15	11	17
Canada	76	53	36	16	5	14
Norway	95	45	18	5	6	11
Sweden	90	38	12	6	5	26
Ireland		46	17	9	5	15
Great Britain	70	43	15	10	7	20
Netherlands	94	17	8	3	2	5
Germany						
East (former)	92	41	11	7	9	35
West (former)	84	34	10	6	5	27
Austria	92	58	29	24	13	14
Italy	84	28	7	4	8	32
Spain	84	25	6	5	7	5
Hungary		62	7	6	28	9
Poland	85	52	11	8	19	25
Czech Republic	87	47	7	4	10	35
Slovenia	96	48	6	7	15	8
Bulgaria		66	22	13	40	30
Russian Federation	76	44	20	9	30	42
Latvia	82	49	11	6	13	39
Slovakia	92	43	8	5	11	40
mean percentage	**88**	**47**	**18**	**9**	**12**	**21**

Source: SCP (ISSP 1995).

whole the army does not appear to be an important reason for national pride (mean percentage 17%).

DIFFERENCES BETWEEN COUNTRIES

Pride in democracy and the country's political influence are found only to a certain degree in Canada (34% and 24%, respectively) and the United States (29% and 22%). Taking strong pride in the fair and equal treatment of social groups is a fairly rare phenomenon. The scores of Ireland and Bulgaria might be called somewhat high. The results for the other countries are unremarkable (Table 10).

The country's scientific effort is thought to be important in the United States (51%), Australia and New Zealand (both 40%) and Canada (38%). For some of the Eastern European countries, science is not a reason for pride.

The people of Bulgaria, Ireland and New Zealand show pride in their country's achievement in sports (scores above 60%), while the inhabitants of Poland and former West Germany do not rate the country's success very highly.

The nation's art and literature are thought to be especially important by the Irish (59%).

The British (48%), the Americans (49%) and, rather unexpectedly, the Irish (40%) take pride in their army.

History is important to the Bulgarians (65%), the

TABLE 9
FEELINGS ABOUT ONE'S OWN COUNTRY (1995, DIFFERENCE FROM MEAN PERCENTAGE)

	Respondent agrees strongly:					
	one nation is essential	wants to be a citizen of [my country]	own country is better	own country is example	supports even when wrong	feels ashamed about some things
Japan	3	25	34	6	1	7
Philippines	5	–17	–5	–2	–5	–14
Australia	7	19	20	4	–5	–9
New Zealand	9	5	10	1	–6	–7
United States	6	24	22	6	–1	–4
Canada	–12	6	18	7	–6	–7
Norway	7	–2	0	–3	–6	–10
Sweden	2	–9	–6	–3	–6	5
Ireland		–1	–1	0	–7	–6
Great Britain	–18	–4	–3	1	–4	–1
Netherlands	6	–30	–10	–6	–10	–17
Germany						
East (former)	4	–6	–7	–2	–3	14
West (former)	–4	–13	–8	–3	–7	5
Austria	3	11	11	15	2	–8
Italy	–4	–19	–11	–5	–3	11
Spain	–4	–22	–12	–4	–5	–16
Hungary		15	–11	–3	16	–12
Poland	–3	5	–7	–1	7	4
Czech Republic	–1	0	–11	–5	–2	14
Slovenia	8	1	–11	–2	3	–13
Bulgaria		19	4	4	28	8
Russian Federation	–12	–3	2	0	18	21
Latvia	–6	2	–7	–2	1	18
Slovakia	4	–5	–10	–4	–1	19
mean percentage	**88**	**47**	**18**	**9**	**12**	**21**

Source: SCP (ISSP 1995).

British, the Czech people, the Irish and the North Americans (scores 50% or more).

Only a few of the national differences mentioned in the tables could be highlighted. Separate findings are legion. Their interpretation is not always easy. Looking at the tables the reader might feel at home with some of the results, he might feel equally baffled by others. The following paragraph gives the reader a comprehensive overview. The construction of certain indices from survey-questions and the ranking of countries will contribute to this end.

RANKINGS FOR NATIONALISM AND PRIDE

Three indices were constructed by adding up the reactions to separate items, i.e. nationalism, pride in political and economical achievements, and pride in cultural achievements. Each of these 'instruments', or batteries, is based on three survey questions.

- The index for *nationalism* consisted of the reactions to the statements about the native country being the best in the world, the idea of the native country as a salutary example to others and the conviction that one should support the country under any circumstance.
- The index for *political and economic achievements* consisted of pride in democracy, in economic achievements and in the social security system.
- The index for *cultural achievements* consisted of

TABLE 10
PRIDE IN NATIONAL ACHIEVEMENTS (1995, IN PERCENTAGES)

	Respondent is very proud of:									
	democracy	political influence	economic effort	social security	fair treatment	scientific effort	sports	art and literature	army	history
Japan	17	8	28	9	11	33	29	36	10	33
Philippines	13	6	10	10	11	11	26	19	13	33
Australia	16	6	6	11	12	40	46	28	28	28
New Zealand	13	15	17	6	14	40	66	42	32	29
United States	29	22	29	14	18	51	38	31	49	50
Canada	34	24	13	32	0	38	32	32	20	40
Norway	19	20	21	12	9	19	48	19	8	23
Sweden	12	5	2	15	8	26	31	16	6	17
Ireland	18	20	27	16	21	27	69	59	40	53
Great Britain	15	9	7	9	15	31	24	24	48	50
Netherlands	19	4	13	22	13	22	24	12	5	20
Germany										
East (former)	6	11	23	7	5	25	32	25	5	10
West (former)	17	11	29	24	7	24	7	16	6	8
Austria	22	14	26	39	19	39	46	38	14	40
Italy	4	2	5	3	3	18	29	47	9	40
Spain	10	6	7	8	10	12	26	25	13	26
Hungary	3	2	1	1	11	26	40	34	6	30
Poland	4	6	4	2	7	9	8	14	14	27
Czech Republic	4	7	7	3	2	11	19	33	3	50
Slovenia	4	4	5	4	11	12	46	25	19	30
Bulgaria	10	8	8	4	22	19	66	47	28	65
Russian Federation	4	6	4	1	3	25	33	37	14	45
Latvia	15	12	8	5	12	13	21	37	7	31
Slovakia	4	3	5	4	7	7	19	26	12	37
mean percentage	**13**	**9**	**13**	**11**	**10**	**24**	**34**	**30**	**17**	**34**

Source: SCP (ISSP 1995).

pride in science and technology, in the arts and literature and in the country's history.

In each of these three cases the strongly affirmative answers – strongly agree, very proud – were counted per respondent. All three indices ranged from 0 (no affirmation) to 3 (three affirmations). The construction of the indices was not based on the usual approach of attitudinal research, but on the correspondence between indicators and concepts at face value.[12] For each country and index, the mean scores were calculated. After that the means were rank ordered. Table 12 shows these rankings. The number 1 refers to the highest score and number 24 to the lowest. The countries are placed in order of ranking on nationalism.

Had nationalism been a consistent phenomenon, the rankings would have corresponded. If the public in a given country had had truly nationalistic feelings, the rankings on each of the three indices would be consistently high. People would not only regard their country as the best in the world, they would also be proud of everything their country and its culture had to offer. In fact, this is the case in only a limited number of cases. According to the findings presented in Table 12, the overall correspondence between the rank orders is actually quite weak. It is possible, however, to distinguish a few groups of countries.[13]

- Austria, Bulgaria, Ireland and the United States rate fairly high on all three of the indices. These

TABLE 11
PRIDE IN NATIONAL ACHIEVEMENTS (1995, DIFFERENCE FROM MEAN PERCENTAGE)

	Respondent is very proud of:									
	democracy	political influence	economic effort	social security	fair treatment	scientific effort	sports	art and literature	army	history
Japan	4	–1	16	–2	0	9	–5	6	–7	–1
Philippines	0	–4	–3	–1	0	–13	–8	–11	–4	–1
Australia	3	–4	–7	0	2	16	12	–2	11	–6
New Zealand	0	5	5	–5	4	16	32	12	15	–5
United States	16	13	17	3	8	27	3	1	32	16
Canada	21	14	1	22	–10	14	–2	2	3	7
Norway	6	10	8	1	–2	–5	14	–11	–9	–11
Sweden	–1	–5	–11	4	–3	2	–4	–14	–11	–17
Ireland	5	11	15	5	11	3	35	29	23	19
Great Britain	2	–1	–6	–2	5	7	–10	–6	31	16
Netherlands	6	–5	0	11	3	–2	–11	–18	–12	–14
Germany										
East (former)	–7	1	10	–4	–5	1	–3	–5	–12	–24
West (former)	3	1	16	13	–3	0	–28	–14	–11	–26
Austria	8	5	13	28	9	15	12	8	–3	6
Italy	–9	–7	–8	–8	–7	–6	–5	17	–8	6
Spain	–3	–4	–6	–3	–1	–12	–9	–5	–4	–8
Hungary	–10	–8	–12	–10	0	1	5	4	–11	–4
Poland	–9	–3	–9	–9	–4	–15	–26	–16	–3	–7
Czech Republic	–9	–3	–5	–8	–8	–13	–15	2	–14	16
Slovenia	–9	–5	–8	–7	0	–12	12	–5	2	–4
Bulgaria	–3	–2	–5	–7	11	–5	32	17	11	31
Russian Federation	–9	–3	–9	–10	–7	1	–1	7	–3	11
Latvia	2	2	–4	–6	1	–11	–14	7	–10	–3
Slovakia	–9	–6	–7	–7	–4	–17	–15	–5	–5	3
mean percentage	**13**	**9**	**13**	**11**	**10**	**24**	**34**	**30**	**17**	**34**

Source: SCP (ISSP 1995).

TABLE 12
COUNTRY RANK BY NATIONAL FEELING AND PRIDE IN POLITICAL, ECONOMIC AND CULTURAL ACHIEVEMENTS (1995, RANK ORDERS)

	Nationalistic feelings	Political and economic achievements	Cultural achievements
Japan	1	12	11
Bulgaria	2	14	3
United States	3	3	2
Austria	4	1	4
Australia	5	7	10
Canada	6	2	5
Russian Federation	7	24	8
New Zealand	8	13	6
Hungary	9	20	13
Poland	10	21	23
Great Britain	11	9	9
Ireland	12	4	1
Norway	13	8	19
Philippines	14	11	15
Slovenia	15	18	18
Latvia	16	15	14
Germany			
East (former)	17	17	20
West (former)	21	6	24
Slovakia	18	19	16
Sweden	19	10	21
Czech Republic	20	23	12
Italy	22	22	7
Spain	23	16	17
Netherlands	24	5	22

Source: SCP (ISSP 1995).

countries could be called consistently nationalistic.

- Former West Germany and the Netherlands are fairly averse to nationalism, but accentuate economic effort and social security as a reason for pride. In this respect these countries resemble each other fairly closely.
- In New Zealand and Russia low regard for the economy combines with fairly high scores for nationalism and cultural achievements. In view of Russia's economic situation this result can be readily understood. As for New Zealand it should be pointed out that the survey was carried out in the mid-1990s, when the country's economy was performing badly.

The scores of the remaining countries are fairly unsystematic, which makes allocation to a distinct category difficult. Some of the results call for separate discussion. Japan, for instance, takes first place for nationalism, but shows medium scores for political, economic and cultural achievements. In this case nationalism appears to be a relatively autonomous cultural trait. Not a few of the Eastern European countries – former East Germany, Latvia, Slovenia, and the Slovak and Czech Republics – show middling scores for nationalism and to some extent refrain from regarding their economies, political systems and cultures as reasons for pride. The cultural climate could be described as 'lukewarm' in these respects. As noted above, Bulgaria is an exception in Eastern Europe. The same, although to a lesser degree, might be said of Hungary. Nationalist feelings are fairly strong. Economic pride is low, but the score for cultural pride is located in the middle of the range.

NATIONALISM AS A TRADITION

Are the data really as fragmented as they appear? Social scientists are justly renowned for providing their readers with exasperating answers to their questions. The answer to this particular question is 'Yes and No'! Yes, the data are as diverse as the above-mentioned grouping of countries indicates and No, a certain rudimentary structure underlies this diversity. The rank numbers on nationalism do not correlate with those on economics. The value 0.34; this coefficient, Spearman rho, is not significant (Table 13). The same goes for the correlation between economics and culture (0.33). The correlation of 0.65 between nationalism and culture, however, is significant. Countries showing high nationalism need not

TABLE 13
CORRELATION BETWEEN THE RANK NUMBERS OF COUNTRIES ON THREE INDICES (1995, SPEARMAN RHO)

	nationalism	politics/ economics	culture
nationalism	1		
politics/economics	(0.34)	1	
culture	0.65	(0.33)	1

Source: SCP (ISSP 1995).

boast of their economy and related matters. These countries tend, however, to be proud of their past culture, art, literature, history and science, whether this sentiment is founded on fact or not. Nationalism should therefore be regarded as part of a rather traditional complex of thinking. This complex is not particularly influenced by perceived successes regarding more modern phenomena of democracy, social security and, to some extent, economic growth or national wealth.

Citizenship and minorities

WHO BELONGS TO THE NATION? INCLUSION AND EXCLUSION

The public gave its opinion on the requirements for citizenship. When does a person truly belong to a certain country? Of course formal citizenship is an obvious condition to be fulfilled. The category of true citizens could be limited to the passport carriers. Other conditions should also be met, however, such as having an adequate knowledge of the language or personally identifying with the nation. Points of view on these subjects indicate who belongs to the nation and who does not. The views on citizenship are also of some interest for the study of people's attitudes towards immigrants and ethnic or cultural minorities. Is it easy or difficult to become a citizen?

This section also reports on people's wishes concerning the influx of migrants. Should their numbers be limited or not? In addition, some conclusions are drawn with relevance to favourable or unfavourable attitudes towards foreigners. Finally the desirability of minorities maintaining their own traditions is discussed.

The researchers used two groups of individual characteristics in formulating statements.[14] The survey questions were subject to local adaptation. The name of each specific country was mentioned in 'the local questionnaire'.

One of the sets of statements referred to a dimension called formal or objective citizenship. The statements read as follows: 'It is important to have been born in a country. It is important to have the citizenship of a country. It is important to have lived in a country for most of one's life.'

One could also be of the opinion that these characteristics may not be acquired by newcomers, or not be acquired at all. People underlining their importance harbour exclusive ideas on citizenship. They make it hard for immigrants to become full members of the receiving society. This consequence can be intentional or unintentional.

Three other statements referred to personal achievement or to what could be called subjective citizenship, in other words, qualities that can be acquired more easily. In principle the transition from one society or culture to another runs a smoother course. The statements read as follows: 'It is important to be able to speak the language of a country. It is important to respect the political institutions and laws of a country. It is important to feel like a citizen of a country.'

A seventh item referred to religion. How important was it to belong to the country's most important religion? This item seemed to be a part of the group indicating objective citizenship. More detailed analysis, however, showed unsystematic differences between countries.[15] For this reason the item is omitted from some parts of the following analysis.

FEELINGS AND LANGUAGE

From Table 14 the reader can decide which of the requirements are thought to be more important than others. In general the public gives more weight to subjective or inclusive qualities than to the exclusive ones. Surprisingly enough, official citizenship does not rate very highly. Religion is least important (Tables 5, 14 and 15). Feeling like a citizen and having a good knowledge of the language are the most important factors (mean percentages in more than 24 countries of 62% and 59% respectively). Respect for the law – also 'inclusive' – and having official citizenship show a 'mean importance' of slightly over 50%, while around 40% of the respondents attach great weight to being born in a certain country or to having lived there for a long time. Only 20% think that being an adherent of the dominant religion should be a qualification for citizenship.

TABLE 14
CRITERIA FOR BEING A TRUE NATIONAL OF A GIVEN COUNTRY (1995, IN PERCENTAGES)

	Respondent considers as very important:						
	to feel like a citizen	to speak the language	to respect the law	official citizenship	being born in a country	long-time resident	religion
Japan	56	39	27	49	37	33	11
Philippines	64	62	54	65	71	58	57
Australia	72	61	69	66	29	27	15
New Zealand	67	61	59	55	41	35	16
United States	62	71	65	75	41	44	39
Canada	63	49	65	59	25	23	15
Norway	62	74	80	60	35	33	10
Sweden	56	71	84	53	27	29	8
Ireland	67	15	43	65	58	49	32
Great Britain	53	65	57	54	50	42	22
Netherlands	47	67	40	39	23	21	3
Germany							
East (former)	47	53	48	49	43	35	14
West (former)	45	55	55	45	27	28	17
Austria	68	67	56	67	46	50	32
Italy	57	48	50	45	44	43	26
Spain	45	32	33	34	37	34	18
Hungary	85	79	29	45	41	47	20
Poland	72	54	34	44	43	38	27
Czech Republic	71	75	44	51	38	47	11
Slovenia	63	71	49	50	43	41	17
Bulgaria	78	60	54	53	59	51	45
Russian Federation	65	57	54	47	40	45	17
Latvia	62	61	58	41	36	41	14
Slovakia	73	71	49	54	37	39	12
mean percentage	**62**	**59**	**52**	**53**	**40**	**39**	**21**

Source: SCP (ISSP 1995).

DIFFERENCES BETWEEN COUNTRIES

Differences between countries are generally fairly minor. Some of the major ones may be of interest to the reader.

Language is thought to be fairly *un*important in Ireland and Spain. The Hungarians, on the other hand, regard language as important, and consider that 'feeling like a Hungarian' should be a precondition for citizenship.

Official citizenship is important to the inhabitants of the United States. The citizens of Bulgaria, Ireland and the Philippines feel by and large that citizens should be born in the country where they claim citizenship. Religion is thought to be important in Bulgaria, the Philippines and the United States.

RESTRICTION OF IMMIGRANTS

In most countries, people are opposed to the arrival of more immigrants. An overall 62% want less immigration (Tables 16 and 17). In Bulgaria (78% for restriction), the Czech Republic (74%), East Germany (79%), Hungary (84%), Italy (76%) and former West Germany (76%) people seem to be especially reluctant to admit more immigrants. Other societies are relatively open-minded in the matter: Canada (41% for restriction), Ireland (22%), Japan (42%) and Spain (40%).

Table 15
Criteria for being a true national of a given country (1995, difference from mean percentage)

	Respondent considers as very important:						
	to feel like a citizen	to speak the language	to respect the law	official citizenship	being born in a country	long–time resident	religion
Japan	–6	–20	–25	–3	–3	–6	–10
Philippines	1	3	2	12	30	19	36
Australia	9	2	17	14	–11	–12	–6
New Zealand	4	2	6	2	1	–4	–5
United States	–1	12	12	23	1	5	18
Canada	1	–10	12	6	–16	–16	–6
Norway	0	15	28	8	–6	–6	–11
Sweden	–7	12	31	0	–13	–10	–13
Ireland	4	–45	–10	13	18	10	12
Great Britain	–10	6	4	1	9	3	1
Netherlands	–16	8	–12	–14	–17	–18	–17
Germany							
East (former)	–15	–6	–4	–3	3	–4	–7
West (former)	–18	–4	3	–8	–14	–11	–4
Austria	6	8	3	14	5	11	11
Italy	–5	–12	–2	–8	4	5	5
Spain	–17	–27	–19	–19	–4	–5	–3
Hungary	23	20	–23	–8	0	8	–1
Poland	9	–5	–19	–9	2	–1	6
Czech Republic	8	16	–9	–2	–2	8	–10
Slovenia	0	12	–3	–3	2	2	–3
Bulgaria	16	1	2	1	18	12	25
Russian Federation	3	–2	2	–5	–1	6	–3
Latvia	–1	2	5	–12	–5	2	–7
Slovakia	10	12	–3	1	–3	0	–9
mean percentage	**62**	**59**	**52**	**53**	**40**	**39**	**21**

Source: SCP (ISSP 1995).

The wish to decrease the number of immigrants and the idea that political refugees should be prevented from staying do not always correspond. The people of a given country can be reluctant to accept more immigration and yet make an exception for immigrants that come for political reasons.[16] Political refugees seem to be most welcome in the Scandinavian and Western European countries. Latvia (66% for expelling refugees), the Philippines (64%) and Slovenia (55%) seem to be relatively closed to this idea.

ATTITUDES TOWARDS IMMIGRANTS

Respondents were shown the following statements: 'Immigrants increase crime rates'; 'Immigrants take jobs away from people who were born in this country'; Immigrants are generally good for the economy of this country'; 'Immigrants help to open this country to new ideas and cultures'.[17]

The belief that immigrants play a role in increasing the crime rate is fairly generally held. Some 51% of all respondents think this is true, 42% say that immigrants take jobs away from other citizens, and about 40% deny that immigrants have any beneficial influence on the national economy. The positive influence on culture is much more widely acknowledged. Only 26% deny that immigrants stimulate the emergence of new ideas in society (Tables 18 and 19).

The incidence of feelings seems to follow a fairly

Table 16
Opinions on the influx of immigrants (1995, in percentages)

	restrict immigration	restrict no. of political refugees
Japan	42	33
Philippines	62	64
Australia	61	34
New Zealand	62	25
United States	64	25
Canada	41	18
Norway	63	12
Sweden	69	12
Ireland	22	10
Great Britain	61	26
Netherlands	61	16
Germany		
East (former)	79	8
West (former)	76	12
Austria	56	14
Italy	76	32
Spain	40	19
Hungary	84	24
Poland	63	23
Czech Republic	74	19
Slovenia	64	55
Bulgaria	78	29
Russian Federation	58	28
Latvia	70	66
Slovakia	67	37
mean percentage	**62**	**27**

Source: SCP (ISSP 1995).

Table 17
Opinions on the influx of immigrants (1995, difference from mean percentage)

	restrict immigration	restrict no. of political refugees
Japan	–20	6
Philippines	–1	37
Australia	–1	7
New Zealand	–1	–1
United States	2	–2
Canada	–21	–9
Norway	0	–14
Sweden	6	–14
Ireland	–41	–17
Great Britain	–1	–1
Netherlands	–1	–11
Germany		
East (former)	17	–19
West (former)	14	–15
Austria	–6	–12
Italy	13	5
Spain	–22	–8
Hungary	22	–2
Poland	0	–4
Czech Republic	12	–8
Slovenia	2	29
Bulgaria	16	2
Russian Federation	–4	1
Latvia	8	39
Slovakia	5	10
mean percentage	**62**	**27**

Source: SCP (ISSP 1995).

clear pattern in the countries surveyed. Generally negative attitudes towards immigrants tend to be present to a fairly high degree in Eastern European countries.

The relationship between immigrants and the crime rate is perceived as relatively weak in Canada (20% think this relationship important) and Ireland (13%).

The competition for scarce jobs is seen as a relatively unimportant phenomenon in Japan (15%), Norway (20%) and Sweden (16%). These are not the same countries as those denying a positive influence on the economy as a whole. This idea is least subscribed to in Australia (15%), Ireland (21%) and New Zealand (17%).

The contribution of immigrants to the culture of the host country is denied in Eastern European countries. In the remainder of the countries surveyed, especially in Australia, Canada, Ireland, New Zealand and Sweden, the idea of cultural enrichment is much more widely accepted.

Cultural diversity: desired assimilation

Some of the data are of prime importance for the theme of cultural diversity. If a country's inhabitants insist on immigrants adapting themselves fully to the 'national way of life' and on their adoption of all of the country's current beliefs, tolerance of cultural diversity can rightfully be called low. Acceptance of

Table 18
Feelings about immigrants (1995, in percentages)

	They increase crime rate	They occupy scarce jobs	They have no positive economic influence	They have no positive cultural influence
Japan	65	15	23	20
Philippines	28	36	39	28
Australia	31	36	15	5
New Zealand	24	40	17	8
United States	33	48	33	16
Canada	20	25	13	8
Norway	69	20	51	21
Sweden	59	16	38	12
Ireland	13	38	21	10
Great Britain	26	50	39	18
Netherlands	37	28	38	17
Germany				
East (former)	68	53	38	20
West (former)	55	26	28	15
Austria	63	38	26	25
Italy	64	37	59	38
Spain	28	45	38	18
Hungary	74	63	64	54
Poland	75	59	34	18
Czech Republic	68	42	68	51
Slovenia	59	60	52	45
Bulgaria	83	71	63	41
Russian Federation	63	54	53	41
Latvia	60	57	58	47
Slovakia	68	55	64	51
mean percentage	**51**	**42**	**40**	**26**

Source: SCP (ISSP 1995).

diversity is indicated by the acceptance of minority culture. The survey contained statements on the issue of cultural assimilation, formulated as follows:

1. It is impossible for a person who does not share this country's customs and traditions to become fully a national.[18]
2. Ethnic minorities should be given government assistance to preserve their customs and traditions.[19]

The respondents also chose one of two contrasting statements:

1. It is better for society if groups maintain their distinct customs and traditions.
2. It is better if groups adapt and blend into the larger society.

The answers in favour of cultural diversity are shown in Tables 20 and 21. About 30% think it possible for people who do not share fully in a country's customs and traditions to become national citizens in the true sense of the word; 46% favour policies aiding minorities to retain many of their own customs; 48% think it better for society if groups maintain their own traditions. In general, support for diversity is not entirely absent.

The results per country present the reader with an interesting pattern. In most of the tables already mentioned, Western European countries and English-speaking countries outside Europe, including Canada, have proved quite tolerant of immigrants or foreigners. According to Tables 18 and 19, these coun-

TABLE 19
FEELINGS ABOUT IMMIGRANTS (1995, DIFFERENCE FROM MEAN PERCENTAGE)

	They increase crime rate	They occupy scarce jobs	They have no positive economic influence	They have no positive cultural influence
Japan	14	–27	–17	–6
Philippines	–23	–6	–1	2
Australia	–20	–6	–25	–21
New Zealand	–27	–2	–23	–18
United States	–18	6	–7	–10
Canada	–31	–18	–28	–19
Norway	18	–22	10	–5
Sweden	7	–26	–2	–15
Ireland	–39	–4	–20	–16
Great Britain	–25	8	–1	–8
Netherlands	–14	–14	–3	–9
Germany				
East (former)	16	11	–3	–6
West (former)	3	–16	–13	–11
Austria	12	–5	–15	–1
Italy	13	–5	19	12
Spain	–23	3	–2	–8
Hungary	23	21	23	28
Poland	24	17	–7	–8
Czech Republic	16	0	27	25
Slovenia	8	18	12	19
Bulgaria	32	29	23	15
Russian Federation	12	11	12	15
Latvia	9	14	18	21
Slovakia	17	13	24	25
mean percentage	**51**	**42**	**40**	**26**

Source: SCP (ISSP 1995).

tries rate low on the expression of unfavourable ideas on immigrants. When it comes to the question whether one can be a citizen even without possessing a full knowledge of national traditions, respondents consider this to be a realistic possibility. Either the scores are above the general mean or only slightly below it. Norway and Sweden are exceptions in this respect (Tables 20 and 21).

Western European and English-speaking countries in particular, however, while favourably inclined towards foreigners, give but scant support to a policy to help minorities to retain their own culture. Moreover, their attitude towards the idea that cultural diversity could be beneficial to society should also be regarded as rather cautious (Tables 20 and 21). In other words, these countries are less tolerant of cultural diversity than might be inferred from earlier findings.

Eastern European countries offer a quite different picture. They tend to emphasize the value of national culture (see the section on national pride). Moreover, the prevailing mood towards immigrants could not be called positive in all respects. Yet attitudes towards a 'cultural policy' are favourable in these countries and the idea of cultural diversity appears to be accepted to some degree.

The difference in actual immigration may account for this pattern. Australia, Canada, New Zealand and the United States are 'classic' immigration countries. Parts of Western Europe have been

TABLE 20
OPINIONS ON CULTURAL DIVERSITY (1995, IN PERCENTAGES)

	Citizen need not share national traditions	Policy for minority traditions should exist	Maintain minority traditions
Japan	29	60	85
Philippines	24	67	54
Australia	42	16	17
New Zealand	46	18	44
United States	42	17	42
Canada	51	19	36
Norway	16	20	25
Sweden	18	20	19
Ireland	44	52	40
Great Britain	25	16	20
Netherlands	21	21	29
Germany			
East (former)	36	70	62
West (former)	41	41	53
Austria	25	40	43
Italy	36	61	37
Spain	35	59	52
Hungary	26	77	61
Poland	24	71	53
Czech Republic	24	44	50
Slovenia	21	72	55
Bulgaria	5	53	55
Russian Federation	29	75	82
Latvia	14	68	71
Slovakia	44	56	62
mean percentage	30	46	48

Source: SCP (ISSP 1995).

confronted with immigration in recent decades. In consequence the countries experienced the practical difficulties of absorbing large groups of new citizens from foreign parts. This experience is reflected in public opinion. It cannot be said that Eastern Europe is a major focus for mass immigration. Accordingly, cultural assimilation is not at issue and a rather lenient attitude is easily adopted.

One might look at the findings in yet another way. The concept of minority may have different meanings in different countries. In most Western countries, 'minority' refers to immigrants of the first and second generations. The minorities in Eastern Europe, however, have been residing for a long time in a given country. Support for their specific culture, even in the form of a policy, could well be part of a tried and tested way of thinking and influencing opinion. In view of many of today's conflicts, it regrettably must be said that, especially in this case, opinion does not always go hand in hand with actual behaviour.

Accounting for attitudes

INDICATORS

The attitudes of persons are closely linked to their characteristics, e.g. sex, age or education. Do different categories of individuals hold different views about national identity? The climate of opinion in countries can be explained by country-specific characteristics, e.g. national income, the education system or population density.

In this regard, the following opinion criteria were chosen for consideration:

- orientation towards the country
- index for nationalism
- index for pride in political and economic achievement
- index for cultural achievement
- the view that the number of immigrants should be lower
- an unfavourable attitude towards minorities
- the idea that assimilation or integration is desirable
- index for exclusive requirements for citizenship
- index for inclusive requirements for citizenship.[20]

Sex, age and education (number of years in full-time education following sixth birthday) were used as the personal characteristics of respondents.

The scores of the national samples on the opinions were taken to represent national characteristics. These are found in nearly all of the foregoing tables. The percentage of Dutch respondents who feel very close to their country is an example. The statistical tables of the *World Culture Report 1998* provided further national data (Goldstone, 1998). The gross national product (GNP) served as an indicator of

Table 21
Opinions on cultural diversity
(1995, difference from mean percentage)

	Citizen need not share national traditions	Policy for minority traditions should exist	Maintain minority traditions
Japan	–1	14	37
Philippines	–6	21	6
Australia	12	–30	–30
New Zealand	16	–29	–4
United States	12	–29	–6
Canada	21	–27	–12
Norway	–14	–26	–23
Sweden	–12	–26	–28
Ireland	14	6	–8
Great Britain	–5	–31	–28
Netherlands	–9	–26	–18
Germany			
East (former)	6	23	14
West (former)	11	–5	5
Austria	–5	–6	–5
Italy	6	14	–10
Spain	5	12	4
Hungary	–4	30	14
Poland	–6	25	5
Czech Republic	–6	–2	2
Slovenia	–9	26	7
Bulgaria	–25	7	7
Russian Federation	0	29	34
Latvia	–16	22	23
Slovakia	14	10	14
mean percentage	**30**	**46**	**48**

Source: SCP (ISSP 1995).

wealth. The percentage of GNP spent on education indicated a country's educational level. The capacity to absorb immigrants was measured by the percentage of the foreign-born population and by population density. It was supposed that a large number of foreigners and a high population density limited the capacity to admit immigrants and contributed towards negative feelings. In view of the attitude towards a country's cultural achievement, the number of UNESCO cultural heritage sites was selected as an indication of historical and cultural richness.

Two types of analysis were carried out: one on the basis of individuals, irrespective of their countries, and another on the level of the countries with the country specific variables.

THE INDIVIDUAL LEVEL

All respondents were pooled, irrespective of their country.[21] Next the opinions were reduced to three complexes, or general attitudes, by means of factor analysis, namely a) nationalism, b) attitudes towards minorities and c) attitudes regarding the assimilation of foreigners as desirable.[22]

The statistical technique used, factor analysis, calls for a brief explanation. It is assumed that respondents represent a larger cultural pattern. The analysis aims at describing the pattern in terms of a limited number of dimensions on the basis of chosen indicators. The importance of each indicator for a particular dimension is expressed by a coefficient or factor loading. The dimensions or general attitudes are themselves scales, which for instance means that individuals can exhibit high or low nationalism, think positively or negatively about minorities, and view assimilation as desirable or undesirable. Furthermore, the dimensions are independent of each other. A person experiencing strong nationalism can still be well disposed towards foreigners, or can bear them ill-will. Pronounced nationalism can be found together with emphasis on assimilation or with tolerance of diversity. Establishing which of the possible combinations is important, however, calls for further analysis.

Dimensions can be correlated with characteristics of respondents, for example with their age. The same reasoning applies to the level of countries. In this case, however, the number of observations is far smaller. On the individual level, calculations are based on 23,000 respondents, whereas on the level of countries the number of observations is only 23.[23]

In Table 22 the coefficients indicate how important various opinions are for these general complexes or dimensions.[24] The higher the coefficient, the more the corresponding opinion contributes to the general complex. Coefficients of 0.4 or higher are important. Coefficients of between 0.3 and 0.4 should be considered weak. Coefficients at a still lower value are unimportant and are therefore omitted from the tables.

Table 22
Dimensions of attitudes on the basis of respondents' scores (1995, factor scores)

	high nationalism	minority negative	assimilation desired
country oriented	0.46		
nationalism	0.61		
pride pol eco	0.67		
pride cult	0.72		
less immigrants		0.75	
neg feelings		0.77	
assimil desired			0.90
excl citizenship	0.50	0.40	(0.32)
incl citizenship	0.51	(0.37)	(0.37)

Source: SCP (ISSP 1995).

Table 23
Correlations between dimensions of attitudes and personal characteristics of all respondents (1995, Pearson correlations)

	High nationalism	minority negative	assimilation desired
sex [a)]	(–0.00)	0.02	(0.00)
age [b)]	0.16	0.11	0.09
education [c)]	–0.03	–0.09	–0.04

a) direction: male
b) direction: old
c) direction: many years in education

Source: SCP (ISSP 1995).

The first complex is dominated by nationalism, taking great pride in the country's efforts and imposing stringent requirements for citizenship. Shades of meaning in this case are unimportant. It does not matter whether the achievements are economic, political or cultural. The difference between inclusive and exclusive criteria is disregarded. People are proud of everything the country has to offer, and newcomers wishing to become nationals should make a considerable effort. Hence the choice of the general label of 'nationalism'.

The second complex concerns ideas about foreigners, notably immigrants. It is characterized by the wish to limit the number of immigrants and by prejudice towards minorities. The requirements for citizenship are quite important. The tendency to confront newcomers with exclusive demands – and hence to make their integration difficult – has slightly more meaning than the inclusive requirements.

The demand on minorities to shed their own culture and absorb the host country's ways and mores is extremely important in the third and last complex. High requirements for citizenship seem to play some role, although their coefficients cannot be called impressive. The message is that foreign residents should adapt.

Table 23 shows the relationship between the complexes and respondents' sex, age and educational level.[25] This relationship is extremely weak. Because of the large number of respondents (24,000 on pooled and weighted data), most of the correlations reach a certain level of significance.[26] Nevertheless their values are low. They range between 0.00 and 0.16. Age seems to be the most important personal characteristic. The older the individual, the more nationalism he experiences, the less favourable he is towards minorities and the more he wishes them to adapt. People with higher education are less nationalistic than those at a lower educational level. They feel more positive towards minorities and are less desirous of adaptation. There is virtually no link between a person's sex and his or her ideas. The only – very marginal – tendency is for men to be somewhat more prejudiced towards minorities than women.

Owing to the diminutive size of the correlations, these conclusions can be regarded only as weak tendencies. Rather than emphasize these regularities, it is safer to conclude that the idea of nationalism and the attitude towards minorities are independent of important personal characteristics. This type of thinking could be a trait of the individual's personality and/or may have been formed in the early stages of socialization.

THE LEVEL OF COUNTRIES

The reduction of data on attitudes to single complexes gives results of rather similar dimensions, as we have already seen in the case of individuals.[27] The contribution of the separate indicators, however, yields interesting differences (Table 24).

On the level of countries, nationalism is char-

Table 24
Dimensions of attitudes on the basis of national scores (1995, factor loadings, 23 countries)

	high nationalism	minority negative	assimilation desired
country oriented	0.59	0.52	
nationalism	0.84		
pride pol eco	(0.31)	–0.79	
pride cult	0.85		
less immigrants		0.45	0.76
neg feelings		0.84	(0.36)
assimil desired		–0.75	0.48
excl citizenship	0.60		
incl citizenship			0.93

Source: SCP (ISSP 1995).

Table 25
Correlations between dimensions of attitudes and characteristics of countries (1995, Pearson correlations, 23 countries)

	High nationalism	minority negative	assimilation desired
gnp [a)]	0.06	–0.53	–0.12
density [b)]	–0.33	0.05	–0.29
foreigners [c)]	0.17	–0.71	0.13
% edu [d)]	–0.02	–0.23	0.36
heritage [e)]	–0.35	0.02	–0.22

a) gross national product per capita in US $
b) population per sq km
c) % of population foreign born
d) % of gross national product for education
e) number of cultural heritage sites

Source: SCP (ISSP 1995); *World Culture Report 1998.*

acterized by an orientation towards the homeland, by nationalism as a separate attitude, by a high regard for national culture and by emphasis on exclusive criteria for citizenship. The coefficient for pride in the economy that was meaningful in the case of the individuals is much less important here (Table 24).[28] Whereas individuals do not draw a sharp distinction between the two sources of national pride, countries do. A country is of course different from an individual. An interpretation must therefore be found on another level than that of the mental process. In a large number of countries, ideas about the importance of the nation's culture and history are in all probability linked to nationalism by tradition and propaganda.

The attitude towards minorities is more sharply defined than in the case of the analysis for individual respondents. A negative attitude goes together with strong attachment to the homeland, the idea that immigration should be limited, and low economic pride. The results are suggestive of disappointment with material progress and with social conditions being compensated for by cautious or negative feelings towards foreign elements in society. As shown above, this combination is frequent in Eastern European countries. In line with this finding, the desire for assimilation is – as in Eastern Europe – at a low level (the number is negative.) The complex of assimilation is defined by a cautious attitude towards the admission of immigrants and emphasis on inclusive citizenship. The reading of this pattern is clear. If foreigners are to be admitted at all, they should integrate by learning the language and acquiring the culture.

As in the case of the analysis on individuals, the correlation with background variables is disappointing. In Table 25 only two coefficients are significant, i.e. those for the national product and the percentage of foreigners, both combined with ideas about minorities.[29] (The coefficients are printed in bold type, and non-significant coefficients are given without the customary brackets.) The poorer the country, the more negative its opinion on minorities. And yet – at first sight surprisingly – the more foreigners there are, the more positive its opinion is. This may be easily explained. Rich countries attract more immigrants than poor ones. It has already been shown that in these countries – for instance those of Western Europe – some tolerance towards minorities prevails. Another underlying mechanism might also be at work. If a country is accustomed to a fairly large proportion of foreigners, feelings of fear may abate and opinions become more tolerant.

All in all, Table 25 is perhaps more interesting for what it does not say than for what it does say. Nationalism and the demand for integration cannot be explained by important national characteristics.

Nationalism in particular seems to be a free-floating part of a culture. It may or may not prevail in a country irrespective of, for instance, wealth or educational level. This finding emphasizes the traditional character of the phenomenon.

Contrary to common opinion, high population density is not automatically reflected in negative attitudes towards foreigners. Nor does high density of foreign residents necessarily lead to nationalism. This proportion is even positively related to favourable ideas about minorities. Again, the weight of country-specific traditional thinking might overshadow possible effects. In any event, the widely-held view that high population figures and a large foreign population inevitably lead to social tension does not appear to be based on fact.

Perhaps less important is the finding that cultural capital as represented by the number of heritage sites bears no relation to nationalism. It may even be true that the fewer such 'monuments' there are, the higher the ratio of nationalism is. Either this indicator is not appropriate or the nationalistic appeal of culture and history is a fiction.

Finally a word on education is called for. It might be supposed that traditional thinking retreats as education advances. Observation of the development of countries appears to bear this out. The insight is not necessarily groundless. However, in the case of nationalism and tolerance it may be prudent not to rely too much on the blessings of such a positive effect. Highly educated persons may well be less xenophobic and more tolerant than others, but the relationship is a rather tenuous one. Moreover, such a result is valid for a particular moment in time. A rise in educational level means that a growing number of individuals join the ranks of the better educated. However, the 'newcomers' may in fact bring with them attitudes, feelings and habits that they already possessed. This seems to be the case with participation in culture. In many cases people who are not used to visiting the theatre do not acquire the habit following higher studies. On the level of countries the situation is more visible. No relationship could be shown to exist between the educational level of a country and its attitudes, especially nationalism. It follows that a country's education systems may be highly developed, yet entertain a climate of opinion that has nationalistic and intolerant traits.

A general overview

IDENTIFICATION TOWARDS THE COUNTRY

Of five possible orientations to geographical entities – starting with an individual's neighbourhood – the one involving the country proved to be the strongest. The bond between an individual and the nation seemed to be especially intensive in Bulgaria and in Hungary: in the latter, 80% of the population felt very close to their own country, in Bulgaria 72%. The orientation proved weak in Great Britain – 24% of the British felt very close to the national level – and in former West Germany, also 24%. Feelings of closeness were at their lowest in the Philippines with 22%. The figure for Japan is fairly high – 60% – but the figure cannot be called extreme.

IDENTIFICATIONS COMBINED

Considering the enlargement of scale and the supposed trend towards globalization, it is little short of remarkable that the various orientations actually supplement each other. A feeling of being close to one's neighbourhood does not preclude a strong attachment to city or country. The combination of a strong orientation towards the country with a strong attachment to the surrounding continent – however the concept of continent is defined – is even quite frequent. It can be concluded that international integration has its basis in the sphere of public opinion.

IMMIGRATION

Willingness to move is weak, in general, even if a better life is the reward. The exchange of one neighbourhood for another meets with the least resistance: 18% would be very willing, while 6% to 7% might be prepared to move to another country or even continent.

As a rule, feelings of belonging to a given area were negatively related to preparedness to move to another. People feeling very close to their country were unwilling to emigrate to another one or to

Changes in Asia

In 1996 the Japanese Dentsu Institute for Human Studies conducted a comparative analysis of global values. This research effort was to be the first of a series. Representative samples of citizens from Tokyo, Bangkok, Beijing, Bombay, Jakarta and Singapore were interviewed. The Institute reported its first findings in *Tokyo and Five other Asian Cities: Diversity and Common Ground*. The last words of the title in particular – common ground – seemed to indicate common changes.

Much of the common ground could be found in the ideas about good health and having good human relationships on the whole and positive ones within the family. These were thought in all the countries to be the most important values. Financial wealth and ambition were only slightly less favoured. The same went for values such as convenience, comfort and success at work.

It is perhaps not surprising that people thought of all these things as almost equally desirable. Some interesting diversity came to light, however, when the questioning went into greater detail. Respondents were asked to enumerate their three favourite ways of spending time during the coming five years. Some 26% of the Japanese wanted to spend their time on their jobs. Surprisingly, this percentage was the lowest in the series, with 60% for China (Beijing) the highest. When it came to spending time on hobbies and leisure, 70% of the Japanese felt inclined to give these priority, against 14% of the Indonesians and 5 % of the Indians. Dentsu concluded that the Japanese had become more oriented towards leisure and play and that their traditionally high professional orientation had weakened, especially among the younger generation. One might say that in these respects China differs fairly sharply from Japan. It is remarkable that the Chinese seemed to take intellectual effort very seriously: 38% considered taking classes and learning as something to do in the next five years, while 42% thought studying in general was important.

Could ideas about the family and on the roles of men and women still be called traditional? Not necessarily. In all five cities a majority of respondents favoured the idea that the roles of men and women should be left to individuals to decide, as opposed to the view that men should do professional work and women should take care of the home. Freedom of choice was also favoured in the case of having children. In four out of five countries it was thought that married couples should be able to decide whether or not they would have children.

Nevertheless, traditional opinions on the family were also found. About two-thirds thought that children should look after their parents in old age. This feeling was somewhat weaker in Indonesia (57%), while Japan proved to be a notable exception with only 15%.

It is not so easy to place sacrifices for childrens' education between the contrasting concepts of tradition and modernity. People took this consideration to heart. Only small categories – generally less than 10% – felt they should not invest heavily in studies. Between 60% and 80% favoured the proposal that money should be available for education even if this meant financial difficulties for parents.

In the realm of government some type of welfare state was preferred to individualism and 'market ideology'. A society with full social benefits was preferred to a system featuring low taxes and individual autonomy. Improving the standard of living by market regulation was preferred to an approach based on free competition. Personal freedom should be restricted if it is in the public interest. Half to two-thirds of the respondents supported 'collective policy arrangements'. The Japanese differed from the Asians in one respect. They found it difficult to choose between the regulation of individual rights and 'fewer rules and more personal freedom'.

Democracy was supported. Only small minorities wanted a strong leader to carry out rapid social reform. This wish was strongest in Bombay (35%) and weakest in Japan (5%). The percentages of the other cities ranged from 11% to 18%. The majority of the respondents were of the opinion that the wishes of citizens should be reflected in government policy. The Japanese in particular doubted whether their government would heed their wishes. In a follow-up survey conducted in 1997 it appeared that only 14% of the Japanese believed that the political system truly reflected the will of the people. Compared to European cities, this percentage was significantly low.

The Dentsu findings suggest that new, more individualistic family values seem to be taking hold in Asia. As to a more relaxed attitude to work, the Japanese example appears to be of some relevance. Democracy is an important value. The same applies to the welfare state, which is not in contradiction with Asian values. A certain measure of cultural change can be discerned. So far, the full adoption of societal solutions common to Europe and the United States is supported by minorities only. It would appear that Asian countries are taking over elements of Western culture which they like or can easily incorporate into their own society. The principle of selection leading to diversity would appear to be as important as the tendency towards cultural unity.

Jos W. BECKER

another continent. It can therefore be concluded that being 'internationally minded' implies feelings of sympathy but does not mean that people will be moving all the time. Aspiring to be an emigrant is still exceptional, although this phenomenon should not be disregarded. Most of those who are willing to move to another country would also be prepared to go to live in another part of the world. They are the potential 'true emigrants' among the respondents. Taking all twenty-four countries together, 5% of the respondents are willing to move to another country and very willing to go to live on another continent. Present figures may appear to be low, but if all potential migrants were to behave as they thought fit, the stream of economic migrants would swell markedly, which in fact appears to be the case here and there in the world.

NATIONAL FEELINGS

Large numbers of people prefer to be citizens of their own country. The idea that one's own country is better than any other country is fairly widespread. Japanese and Americans in particular like to live in their native countries (Japan: 72%; US: 71%) and think their country is the best (Japan: 52%; US: 40%). The Dutch and Spaniards could consider living elsewhere; 28% of the Spaniards and 17% of the Dutch would not have any other nationality; 8% of the Dutch and 7% of the Spaniards think their country is the best in the world.

On the whole, criticizing one's own country is not a common practice. Quite a few Eastern Europeans, however, see reasons to be ashamed of their country (Czech Republic, 35%, former East Germany, 35%, Latvia, 39%, Russia, 42% and Slovenia, 40%). Admiration need not be given unreservedly. The Japanese see some reason for embarrassment. The people of the United States, however, do not. Conversely, discreet emphasis on a country's good points need not imply a critical attitude. For instance, only 5% of the Dutch experience some feeling of shame towards their own society.

National pride derives more from a country's culture and history than from its economy and politics. Past culture and history can be regarded as ascribed characteristics, whereas economics and politics are signs of achievement or effort. On the average, culture is a reason for pride for 24% to 30%, while the economy scores about 10%. Tradition is therefore considered of more importance than actual effort.

Some 29% of the inhabitants of the United States are proud of their country's democracy, while 34% of Canadians adhere to this view. Pride in this regard is especially low in Hungary (3%) and Italy (4%); pride in the country's political influence gives more or less the same picture: Canada, 24%, Italy, 2%, Hungary, 2% and the United States, 22%.

Economic effort is thought to be important in Austria (27%), Ireland (27%), Japan (28%), the United States (29%) and former West Germany (29%). The percentages are universally low in Eastern European countries.

Art and literature are important to the Bulgarians (65%) and the Irish (59%); the Dutch (12%) and former West Germans (16%) do not regard those as reasons to stress their country's excellence.

People do not seem to judge their country in terms of the way various groups are treated. The national scores for 'the fair and equal treatment of groups in society' are low and do not differ much. The percentages for Bulgaria and Ireland are fairly high at about 20%. The idea of social justice is perhaps better indicated by pride in social security. Pride is on a high level in Austria (39%) and Canada (32%). The percentages for the Netherlands and former West Germany are quite high (22% to 24%).

On an index of nationalism, the composition of which was explained above, Bulgaria, Japan and the United States rank highest, with Italy, the Netherlands and Spain ranking lowest. For economics and culture, other indices were constructed. Some combinations of the scores for all three indices show that Austria, Bulgaria, Ireland and the United States rate fairly high on all three; these countries could be called consistently nationalistic. The Netherlands and former West Germany – accentuating economic effort – resemble each other fairly closely.

Rankings for nationalism do not correspond to those for economics. A country in which nationalistic thinking is prevalent does not have to be extremely proud of its economic efforts. Rankings for nationalism do, however, correspond to those of an index for culture and history. It might therefore very well be imagined that a high regard for traditional values encourages nationalism. In general a country may do very well in the economic field, without that success stimulating nationalistic feelings. On the whole, the phenomenon of nationalism is, in all probability, part of a wider complex of traditional thinking, somewhat removed from fact and reality.

CITIZENSHIP

Ideas on citizenship and attitudes towards minorities reveal something about exclusive and inclusive thinking in countries. It is possible to require that a person be born in a country or be a long-time resident or a passport carrier before being recognized as a full citizen. Such demands are quite exclusive. It is also possible to require mastery of the language, respect for the laws or even a purely subjective sense of citizenship, i.e. that a person should feel like the citizen of a given country. These are examples of inclusive thinking, in so far as they can largely be met by a person's own efforts.

Ideas on citizenship seem to be more inclusive than exclusive; in other words, it might be easier to link nations than might be supposed. Feeling like a citizen and having a sound grasp of the language are most important (mean percentages for more than 24 countries of 62% and 59% respectively). Respect for the law – also 'inclusive' – and having official citizenship show a 'mean importance' of slightly more than 50%. Around 40% of the respondents attach great significance to being born in a certain country or to having lived there for a long time. Only 20% think that adherence to the dominant religion should qualify a person for citizenship. Surprisingly, official citizenship or possession of the passport of a given country is not the most important characteristic.

The Japanese accord a relatively low priority to knowledge of the Japanese language and even to respect for Japanese law. This may indicate a conviction that being Japanese is an extremely privileged situation beyond the reach of a foreigner, despite all his or her efforts. These thoughts are of course located in the ideological sphere only. It is to be doubted whether a foreigner could break Japanese law without being sanctioned.

Language is thought to be fairly unimportant in Ireland and Spain. Hungarians, on the other hand, think the contrary. They also hold that 'feeling like a Hungarian' should be a precondition for citizenship.

Official citizenship is emphasized by the inhabitants of the United States. The citizens of Bulgaria, Ireland and the Philippines feel fairly strongly that citizens should be born in their own country.

Religion is regarded as important in such different countries as Bulgaria, the Philippines and the United States.

ATTITUDES TOWARDS IMMIGRANTS AND MINORITIES

This lenient view of citizenship does not mean that immigrants are welcome everywhere and that the presence of foreigners is favourably regarded. Here the practical problems of assimilating large numbers of newcomers come into play.

In most countries people are opposed to the influx of more migrants. An overall percentage of 62% want less immigration. This reluctance is probably felt most acutely with regard to so-called economic immigrants. Opposition to political refugees is much less marked. About 27% want them to leave.

Aversion to extended immigration is probably connected with perceptions of practical problems. The belief that immigrants play a role in increasing the crime rate is fairly generally held. Some 51% of all respondents think that this idea holds true. A full 42% say that immigrants take jobs away from other citizens and about the same percentage (40%) deny any beneficial influence from immigrants on the national economy. A positive influence on culture, however, is much more widely accepted. Only 26% explicitly deny that immigrants stimulate the emergence of new ideas in society, with 74% admitting this influence or taking a neutral view.

Negative feelings towards immigrants tend to be present to a fairly high degree in Eastern European countries.

The relationship between immigrants and the crime rate is perceived as relatively weak in Canada (20% think this relationship important) and Ireland (13%).

The competition for scarce jobs is seen as a relatively unimportant phenomenon in Japan (15%), Norway (20%) and Sweden (16%). These are not exactly the same countries as those denying a positive influence on the economy as a whole. This idea is least subscribed to in Australia (15%), Ireland (21%) and New Zealand (17%).

In Eastern European countries again the contribution of immigrants to the culture of the host country is denied. In the remainder of the countries surveyed, especially in Australia, Canada, Ireland, New Zealand and Sweden, the idea of cultural enrichment is much more widely accepted.

The balance between required assimilation and cultural diversity favours the latter. About 30% think it possible for people who do not share a country's customs and traditions to become a national citizen in the true sense of the word. This is an instance of exclusive thinking. This 30% is somewhat lower than the 46% favouring a policy to aid minorities in retaining much of their own customs and tradition; 48% think it better for society if groups maintain their own traditions. In general, support for diversity is not entirely absent.

CULTURAL POLICY

Should governments assist minority groups in retaining their own culture? Western European countries and the English-speaking countries outside Europe give but scant support to policies aimed at helping minorities to retain their own culture. Eastern European countries have a more positive attitude towards such cultural policies. This difference in attitudes may be due to the fact that migration towards Eastern European countries is actually quite low. The problem of integrating new citizens does not arise, thereby favouring liberal attitudes to diversity.

EXPLANATION

Cultural patterns in this context may be said to comprise the dimensions of nationalism, attitudes towards minorities and attitudes towards their integration. The separate indicators are subsumed under these headings. The three general cultural complexes have little relation to social categories. Age groups appear to be of some importance. The older an individual is, the greater is his sense of nationalism, the less favourably disposed he is to minorities and the more he wants them to adapt. Highly educated people feel less nationalistic than those with lower levels of schooling. Their attitude towards minorities is more positive and they are less desirous of adaptation. Men and women hold similar opinions on this subject.

At the country level attitudes are also weakly related to a country's characteristics. The poorer a country is, the less favourable is its climate of opinion regarding minorities. The more foreigners live in a country, the more favourable is the climate of opinion. This particular relationship may be due to the influence of Western European countries that are prosperous, attract immigrants and are reasonably well disposed towards them. One may also surmise that in countries with many foreign residents the population is accustomed to their presence.

Contrary to what is commonly supposed, a high population density does not foster negative attitudes towards foreigners. Neither does a high proportion of foreign residents fuel nationalism. The weight of traditional thinking might overshadow possible relationships in these cases. The often-heard contention, that the country is so densely populated and has so many foreign residents that social tension is inevitable, does not seem to be founded on fact.

Cultural capital as represented by the number of heritage sites bears no relation to nationalism. It may even be true that the strength of nationalism is inversely proportional to the number of 'monuments' there are. The nationalist appeal to culture and history may well rest on fictitious grounds.

One might suppose that traditional thinking diminishes as educational level rises. This appears to be the lesson to be drawn from the development of countries. In the case of nationalism and tolerance, however, it would be prudent not to rely too much on the blessings of such a mechanism. Highly educated individuals feel less nationalistic and show more tolerance than persons at a lower educational level, but the relationship is weak. At the level of countries, the relationship between the educational level and attitudes, especially nationalism, appears to be absent. However highly-developed a country's educational system is, the reigning climate of opinion can still show nationalistic and intolerant traits.

Conclusions

The country seems to be the focal point of the individual's loyalty. This does not mean that negative feelings towards enlargement of scale and so on are the rule. Attachment to one's own country frequently accompanies a positive attitude towards larger, surrounding areas and – it may be inferred – international co-operation.

People generally show regard for their country. Considerable numbers like to live there and cannot imagine what it would be like to live elsewhere. Extreme nationalistic or chauvinistic feelings, however, occur infrequently.

Ideas about the excellence of a country's past culture and history are the foundation of chauvinistic feeling. Together these beliefs form a traditional complex of thought, focused on national glory. The complex is traditional in the sense that a country's excellence is seen to emanate from characteristics that are already present and can therefore be regarded as being ascribed.

Economic achievement is only a marginal cause of national pride. Economic effort, social security, democratic politics and fair and equal treatment of groups do not appear to be part of the tradition of nationalism.

Almost all the countries surveyed are reluctant to admit more foreign immigrants. Economic immigrants are particularly unwelcome. Many countries, on the other hand, tend to be lenient towards political refugees. Attitudes to foreigners already in residence can be called relaxed to a degree. Official citizenship is less important although, it should be added, it has some significance. Foreign immigrants especially are blamed for supposedly contributing to crime. Taking scarce jobs from indigenous workers is a less frequent reproach. Immigrants' contribution to the openness and the multi-cultural character of society is frequently mentioned as a quality.

Acceptance of cultural diversity is an ambiguous phenomenon. On the one hand, countries with a low incidence of nationalism and a positive disposition towards foreigners may still regard cultural assimilation as a necessity. On the other hand, there are countries that, while accepting minority cultures, think nationalistically and are negatively disposed towards foreigners. This difference is probably due to the fact that the former group of countries is far more exposed to the social problems accompanying mass immigration than the second.

Whether or not individuals or countries accept cultural diversity seems by and large to be a traditional phenomenon. Relationships between acceptance and the characteristics of individuals or countries are unconvincing to say the least. A high degree of tolerance of diversity is either present in a culture or it is not. It is important to note that negative attitudes towards minorities are independent of population density and the proportion of resident foreigners. It is doubtful whether raising educational levels will foster acceptance of diversity.

Notes

1. The major source for this chapter was the *World Values Survey, 1990–1993*. A new world survey was conducted during the period 1995–1997. At the time of writing, the data were not available to the community of researchers. A new edition of *European Values Study* appeared in 1999. The preparation of an international enquiry into religious and moral pluralism (the RAMP-project) started in 1998. So the availability of data is reasonably assured for the future; however, the present issue of the *World Culture Report* called for a temporary solution. The International Social Survey Programme (ISSP) proved useful: information on this programme may be found in *British – and European – Social Attitudes. The 15th report: How Britain Differs* (Jowell et al., 1998). The International Social Survey Programme (ISSP) is an ongoing process covering various topics. The 1995 research examined national identity. The researchers emphasized national and international orientations, feelings of nationalism and attitudes towards minorities.

This subject seemed appropriate to the current report.

2. The formulations for the United Kingdom are used as an example: 'How close do you feel to your neighbourhood (or village), your town or city, your [county], [Britain], [Europe]'? The concepts in square brackets were subject to local adaptation, so that different concepts were inserted in different countries.

3. When the results of the twenty-four countries were pooled, each country's scores were given equal weight statistically in order to prevent inadvertent weighting by the number of respondents in the sample. Each national sample was weighted in such a way that the number of respondents became 1,000.

4. These figures are not quite the same as those reported in the *World Culture Report 1998* (pp. 287–8, Table 22). The question asked (taken from the *World Values Survey*) did not contain the option 'attachment to the neighbourhood', which may account for the fairly high mean score for the 'next higher geographical area' of the home town in the 1998 issue (40% as compared to 30% in Table 1).

5. As the heading of the table indicates, the correlations are based on the pool of respondents from the twenty-four countries. Each national sample has been given equal weight (*n* corresponds to 1,000 for each of the countries). Naturally the pool cannot refer to any meaningful social entity or universe, as for instance the European Community or East Asia. The countries were not selected systematically with the representation of this type of universe in view. Pooling, however, presents the reader with a quick overview of whatever is regular in the data. Inspection of the twenty-four separate correlation matrices shows the pattern of correlations to be virtually the same in all the countries.

6. The formulations for the United Kingdom are used as an example. 'If you could improve your work or living conditions, how willing or unwilling would you be to move to another neighbourhood (or village), etc.?' Possible answers: very willing, fairly willing, neither willing nor unwilling, fairly unwilling, very unwilling, cannot choose.

7. Again the individual responses are pooled. Inspection of the twenty-four separate correlation matrices shows the pattern of correlations are fairly similar.

8. The economic situation may not be the only factor stimulating a willingness to immigrate. This could be the case in the Philippines (6%) and Bulgaria (8%). The percentages of potential immigrants are also rather high, however, in countries that experienced extensive emigration in the past, e.g. Great Britain (8%), Ireland (6%) and the Netherlands (7%). The fairly high percentages for Canada and Sweden (both 9%) are difficult to explain.

9. Which of these statements comes closer to your own view?

1. It is essential that the [United Kingdom] remain one nation.
2. Parts of the [United Kingdom] should be allowed to become fully separate nations if they choose to.

The concepts in square brackets are subject to local adaption. They vary according to the country where the survey takes place.

10. How proud are you of [Britain] for each of the following?

1. The way democracy works.
2. Political influence in the world.
3. Economic achievements.
4. Scientific and technological achievements.
5. Achievements in sports.
6. Achievements in the arts and literature.
7. Armed forces.
8. History.
9. Fair and equal treatment of all groups in society.

11. The share of the truly convinced separatists may also be large enough to influence the results in their totality.

12. The results, however, are not inconsistent with the correlations of the indicators for the pooled data of twenty-four countries.

13. The division is based on a HOMALS analysis depicting the countries in a two-dimensional plane relative to their position on the indexes. The results of the analysis are not reproduced here.

14. The question was worded as follows: 'Some people say the following things are important for being truly [British]. Others say they are not important. How important do you think each of the following is . . .'.

15. The statistical procedure of principal component analysis with varimax rotation with two-factor solution was used on the pooled data (equal weight for each country). 'Being born', 'nationality' and 'having lived' showed high loadings on the first factor. The loading for being a Christian was less important, but could not be neglected. A review of the results per country showed the relationship between religion and the objective factor to be fairly strong in Great Britain, Ireland, Japan, and former Western and Eastern Germany. One might detect faint traces of the 'state church' in these cases. The difference between objective and subjective citizenship tended to be weak in the Czech Republic, the Philippines and Spain. In these cases religion tended to dominate the second factor exclusively.

16. The correlation between ideas about immigration and the opinion on refugees is virtually non-existent at the level of countries. It is 0.14 on the aggregated data, i.e. far too low to draw conclusions. On the level of the individual citizen it could be said that negative thinking in both cases

tends to be comparable. The correlation coefficient is 0.32.

17. The questions were subject to local adaptation. Whenever 'this country' was mentioned, the name of an actual country was inserted.

18. This item was subject to local adaptation.

19. Answers: agree strongly, agree, neither agree nor disagree, disagree, disagree strongly, cannot choose.

20. Exclusive: the answer 'very important' was counted for 'being born in the country', 'being a passport carrier' and 'having lived in the country for the greater part of one's life'.

Inclusive: the answer 'very important' was counted for 'to be able to speak the language', 'respect for the law and political institutions' and 'feeling like a citizen or native'.

21. As usual in this chapter, the data were weighted in such a way that respondents from large and small countries held equal weight.

22. Pooled data, each country having equal weight.

23. Former East Germany was left out, because country-specific background variables were known for former West Germany only.

24. Principal components analysis, three factor solution, varimax rotation, variance explained 54%.

25. The factor scores were used in computing the correlations.

26. Even a correlation of 0.02 or 0.0004 % variance explained is significant at the 5% level.

27. Principal components analysis, three factor solution, varimax rotation, variance explained 73%.

28. In all of the countries individuals tend to link nationalism with economic and national pride. This tendency is, however, not particularly strong (the correlations are about 0.2% or 4% variance explained). When individuals are grouped according to their countries and the general percentages of the samples are taken as country specific characteristics, there is room for a new pattern. Nationalism goes together with cultural pride only. The country influences the relationships found on the individual level. It is to be supposed that in not a few of the countries, traditional thinking and successful propaganda link nationalism to cultural pride rather than pride in economic or political achievement. This tendency is fairly important and is reflected in the analysis.

29. Two influences may be perceived. The analysis is on the basis of aggregated data which makes for high coefficients. The number of observations is small, making it difficult for coefficients to reach a level of any significance. As the countries are not part of a representative sample, significance has to be tested on a *t*-distribution. On twenty-three observations or units of analysis, a correlation has to be 0.4 or more to be significant.

Bibliography

Goldstone, L. 1998. Measuring Culture: Prospects and Limits. In: UNESCO, *World Culture Report*. Paris, UNESCO Publishing.

Jowell R. et al. 1998. *British – and European – Social Attitudes. The 15th report. How Britain Differs*. Aldershot, Ashgate.

McKinley, T. 1998. Measuring the Contribution of Culture to Human Well-being: Cultural Indicators of Development. In: UNESCO, *World Culture Report*. Paris, UNESCO Publishing.

Pérez de Cuéllar. 1995. *Our Creative Diversity. Report of the World Commission on Culture and Development*. Paris, UNESCO.

UNESCO. 1998. *World Culture Report*. Paris, UNESCO Publishing.

Van der Staay, A. 1998. Public Opinion and Global Ethics: A Descriptive Study of Existing Survey Data. In: UNESCO, *World Culture Report*. Paris, UNESCO Publishing.

Escargots and beer,
Sitting on tatami mats,
Leno on T.V.

Paul Kent Oakley

One flower alone
carries the wisdom of time
bouquets promise hope

Amy Lynn Reifsnyder

Hennaed hand in hand
Remember olive trees in
The warmth of gestures

Meghann Ormond

Different people here
Holding hands, erasing fear
Make the world peaceful

Melissa Blackwell

Part Six
Measuring culture: national and international practice

Introduction

In 1998, the Stockholm Action Plan on Cultural Policies for Development made an explicit call for the strengthening of international research on culture and development and, judging from the widespread interest in and positive feedback from the first issue of the *World Culture Report*, the matter of measuring culture and constructing relevant cultural indicators is growing in importance in contemporary research contexts and policy-making agendas.

The first edition of the *World Culture Report* appeared in 1998: the construction of cultural indicators of development was one of its research priorities, conceptualized to complement the work being carried out by the United Nations Development Programme (UNDP) in its *Human Development Report*, and the World Bank in its *Development Indicators*. In pursuing this task, UNESCO has also collaborated closely with other United Nations organizations and institutions, for example with the United Nations Research Institute for Social Development (UNRISD), which launched a series of co-publications on cultural statistics and indicators in 1997.

On the occasion of the 'Culture Counts' Conference in Florence in October 1999, the World Bank and the Government of Italy invited the UNESCO World Culture Report Unit to organize a seminar on cultural indicators in view of the considerable experience of the Organization in this domain and the advances that were made through the publication of the *World Culture Report*.

The seminar entitled 'Measuring Culture and Development: Prospects and Limits of Constructing Cultural Indicators' was organized as a series of interventions by eight international experts[1] and was attended by an audience of some eighty government representatives, heads of national statistical offices and international scholars.

On the basis of UNESCO's specific mandate in the area of culture and its access to research at the international level, the objective of the seminar was to exchange experiences and policies in connection with research on statistics of culture and development. Drawing on existing practices as well as on the complex and multi-faceted nature of world cultural processes, the experts attempted to identify specific implications and concerns in the process of statistical analysis. A more policy-oriented aim of the seminar was to increase awareness among national ministries of culture and finance on the soundness of investing in research on culture and development as a useful tool for decision-making. Edited versions of the Florence Seminar interventions and discussions on national and international practices in cultural statistics from the representatives of Canada, France, Italy, Philippines and UNDP are presented in this section, together with a most interesting proposal for further research.

As efforts are deployed to broaden measurable aspects of culture in the world in the years to come, one of the main challenges is to ensure that the database will provide useful information for the decision-making process in cultural organizations worldwide.

The World Bank's emerging interest in the economic aspects of the impact of culture on sustainable development and the contributions it may make to poverty alleviation is a very positive trend. At the same time, however, there is a risk that action programmes on culture and development may become dispersed into minor, unconnected projects. Indicators must therefore be defined in the framework of the advances made in recent years and the seminar clearly showed the value and necessity of collaborating internationally in this domain.

In order to strengthen the process of broadening measurable and reported aspects of culture in the world, UNESCO, in collaboration with the World Bank, UNDP and the responsible government agencies, plans to pursue a comprehensive research programme that will focus on the creation of new and very relevant data on the linkage between culture and development. The objective should be to develop a fully-fledged international system of statistical information on culture where policy performance at the local level can be understood, measured and assessed against performance in other localities and policy performance at the national level can be compared among countries and across different regions.

UNESCO will therefore reinforce its institutional capacity and scientific excellence with a research agenda focusing on three main areas:

1. Strengthening the work of generating indicators on culture and development within and among countries with the necessary help of the Member States.
2. Reinforcing the notion that cultural indicators are a tool for policy dialogue and guidance and that their creation should therefore be encouraged.
3. Since culture embraces multifaceted realities that cannot be synthesized into a single composite dimension, developing an international framework starting with a few critical dimensions of culture and development in both quantitative and qualitative terms. These dimensions might include cultural diversity; creativity or cultural vitality; cultural income, expenditure and labour force; cultural identity; global ethics; and cultural participation and access.

LEO GOLDSTONE
Director,
World Statistics Ltd. (United States)

1. Lourdes Arizpe, Chair of the Scientific Committee of the World Culture Report, Professor, Researcher at the Centro Regional de Investigaciones Multidisciplinarias (CRIM) UNAM, Mexico; Michel Durand, Chief of the Research and Communication Section of the Culture Statistics Program, Statistics Canada, Ottawa; Arlene K. Fleming, Cultural Resource Specialist and Consultant to the World Bank Culture and Sustainable Development Program, Washington, D.C.; Sakiko Fukuda-Parr, Director of the Human Development Report Office, United Nations Development Programme, UNDP, New York; Paolo Garonna, Director-General of the Italian National Institute for Statistics (ISTAT), Rome, Italy; Leo Goldstone, Director of World Statistics Ltd., New York; Ann-Belinda Preis, Executive Co-ordinator of the World Culture Report in the UNESCO Culture Sector, Paris; Paul Tolila, Director of the Department of Statistical and Prospective Studies of the French Ministry of Culture and Communication, Paris; and Paola Leoncini-Bartoli, Programme Specialist, World Culture Report Unit, UNESCO, Paris.

Chapter 15
Canada's national Culture Statistics Program: a quarter century of development

PAUL McPHIE
Assistant Director, Science Innovation and Electronic Information, Statistics Canada (Canada),
with notes from Michel G. Durand,
Chief, Research and Communication Section, Culture Statistics Program, Statistics Canada (Canada),
John C. Gordon, Chief, Culture Surveys, Culture Statistics Program, Statistics Canada (Canada),
and John Foote, Manager, Economic Research and Analysis, Strategic Planning and Policy Coordination Directorate, Department of Canadian Heritage (Canada)

'Cultural policie and programme are capable wieldin considerabl social an econom influence

Since the 1950s Canada has seen an explosion of popular interest in the creative output of Canadians and a desire to preserve the disappearing heritage of the past. This period has also seen a burgeoning of government involvement in culture and heritage. Public spending on culture and heritage averages more than 1% of government spending per year, peaking at $5.9 billion (all figures in Canadian dollars) in 1992–93, but falling back to $5.6 billion by 1997–98 (Table 26). Canada's wide interest in culture and heritage has been accompanied by a broadening recognition of the role culture plays in sustaining a strong sense of national identity and in stimulating economic growth and prosperity.

The Culture Statistics Program's origins go back to the early 1970s. Statistics Canada was already collecting data on film, libraries and museums at that time, but they were primarily economic in nature and could not be broken down into detail fine enough to address growing information needs. Data and analysis were critical to new policy development, to the evaluation of established programmes and to the growing number of artistic and cultural organizations and their umbrella associations looking for statistics to help them improve their operations and solicit support from private corporations, government and the public in general. Furthermore, the classification system used for existing data and the sampling approach to data collection tended to ignore smaller companies that were often the ones of most interest.

The national Culture Statistics Program is housed in Statistics Canada, the national statistical agency. The operating budget for 1999–2000 is $1.6 million, with a staff of twenty-two excluding the primary data collectors in the agency's regional

TABLE 26
PUBLIC EXPENDITURES ON CULTURE, 1984–98, IN MILLIONS OF C$

(C$ in current millions)	Federal	Provincial	Municipal	All levels of government [1] (current million dollars)	All levels of government [1] (constant 1984 million dollars)
1984–85	2 256	1 246	671	3 933	3 933
1985–86	2 248	1 322	714	4 043	3 903
1986–87	2 451	1 423	818	4 449	4 162
1987–88	2 609	1 447	901	4 717	4 228
1988–89	2 750	1 542	999	5 019	4 338
1989–90	2 891	1 690	1 080	5 376	4 415
1990–91	2 893	1 768	1 237	5 578	4 341
1991–92	2 884	1 909	1 263	5 741	4 292
1992–93	2 883	1 964	1 363	5 875	4 265
1993–94	2 832	1 929	1 413	5 823	4 173
1994–95	2 876	1 868	1 427	5 854	4 130
1995–96	2 923	1 790	1 420	5 825	4 070
1996–97	2 776	1 730	1 443	5 660	3 925
1997–98	2 668	1 716	1 480	5 561	3 812

1. These totals exclude inter-governmental transfers and cannot be derived by adding the three figures.

offices. The Program has two sections: the relatively new Research and Communications Section with a budget of $0.6 million, one quarter of which comes from external partners and clients, and the more traditional Culture Surveys Section with a budget of $1 million, virtually all of which is provided by Statistics Canada.

The Culture Statistics Program has traditionally attempted to respond to the information needs of those who identify themselves with the culture sector rather than those whom we or others may feel should be in the sector. They include the creators, the conservators, all the professional and technical support staff who produce, provide and market artistic, cultural and heritage goods and services, and the associations to which they belong. Thus, much of the focus has been on the suppliers of cultural products and services – an amalgam of publishing, communications, film, sound recording, performing and visual arts industries and heritage institutions. Considerable effort has also been devoted to tracking government spending in this sector, vetting the size and characteristics of the culture sector labour force and measuring consumer demand for cultural products and services.

Research and communications

The creation of the Research and Communications Section came in response to a dilemma common to public service managers. The choice facing the Program was either to remain survey-focused or to move fully into the areas of research, interpretation and communications. By better anticipating the data and information needs of a broad base of potential clients and by developing new products and services to meet them, the Program hoped to demonstrate its real worth to the culture community.

The analytic activities hitherto performed by the Program on an ad hoc basis, and whose scope was limited by the availability of client dollars, have given way to multi-client, multi-year research partnerships in which Statistics Canada is often a financial contributor. Considerable resources are now spent on producing and marketing project proposals to recruit potential clients. Publications containing mostly survey data with limited demand have been dropped in favour of much less expensive data tables. New analytic reports of greater public and professional interest have been created. Programme data are augmented by information from internal and external sources, and the marketing of these products has become extremely important.

Priority has been given to developing standard concepts, definitions and indicators for the culture sector. Clients wished to evaluate the economic impact of the culture sector domestically and to track the size of cultural exports abroad and the competition from foreign cultural imports in the domestic market. These were complex issues requiring a variety of products from a multitude of information sources, and it quickly became apparent that more work had to be done to create measurement consistency among these information sources to avoid creating confusion in the culture community.

The fundamental question was one of knowing how wide to cast the net, regardless of whether the results were to be used for sectoral analysis or to measure the size of the culture sector nationally. Should the definition of the culture sector be governed by what is traditionally viewed as culture (the arts, cultural industries and heritage), or by the UNESCO definition, which also includes photography, design, architecture and sport? Should all aspects of the economic chain from creation to manufacturing and distribution (wholesale and retail) be included? Should those who offer support services, including government culture workers, associations, unions, educators, promoters and studios, be included? What about cultural equipment when no intellectual property is involved? Should new media be included as a separate cultural industry, or festivals and advertising as separate arts categories? Should the heritage sector, in addition to museums and art galleries, also include zoos, botanical gardens, planetariums and archaeological sites? And what about those who view culture as having a much larger social or anthropological dimension? The framework used in Tables 27 and 28 (see below) reflects the conclusions of the federal partnership about how the framework should appear for Canada. However, it also reflects the additional types of decisions that were made to address the needs of the different framework applications.

The framework's scope was almost as broad as that of UNESCO, with some important exceptions. First, the concept of the economic chain from creation to consumption was viewed in Canada, as at UNESCO, as essential to the understanding of the relationships among all cultural actors from the supply of cultural products and services to the domestic and international demand for these products. For the same reason, indigenous output alone would not suffice where the performance of imported products is of research interest. Support structures are included because of their critical importance in the creation of cultural products and also because of their role in the distribution of these products to consumers. These structures include cultural organizations, copyright collectives and government, and they support the cultural community by helping artists achieve the financial and administrative organization necessary for any successful business.

However, the assistance provided by cultural equipment (i.e. musical instruments and home entertainment equipment) was excluded from the framework. Cultural equipment production and sales were seen as outside what could reasonably be considered professional intellectual production by the cultural community, because they are more closely related to the enjoyment of cultural content. It is this relationship to the enjoyment of intellectual property that justifies placing cultural equipment outside the framework. Products such as videotapes, CDs and television programmes require the consumer to invest in cultural equipment. For example, music industry sales are based on the consumer listening to music on the radio or purchasing CDs or sheet music for use with his own entertainment equipment. The sale of radios, instruments and CD players is not a reasonable measure of the viability of the music industry. Nevertheless the Program intends to continue to track the economic activity associated with cultural equipment outside the framework.

The inclusion of New Media as a cultural industry was a somewhat risky addition in the absence of a concrete definition of the products from this industry. Some felt that these products might simply be new output from existing industries, but the general view was that the new category should be added because of what could be missed among culture industry output if it were not.

Under the Arts category, the terms 'festivals' and 'advertising' require some explanation. Festivals with performances or presentations of cultural intellectual property (such as music and film festivals) have been included in the framework, but ethnic-oriented or sociocultural festivals, attractions or other events may not have been. Many festivals of both types are funded through government grant programmes. Concerning advertising, it was felt that the large artistic contribution to advertising products also warranted the inclusion of this area as a separate category.

A broader definition of heritage to include institutions such as zoos and planetariums was adopted, because such institutions are supported by federal, provincial and municipal cultural policies and funding initiatives. These policies are dedicated to the conservation, preservation and promotion of Canadian cultural and natural heritage in its many forms. While the UNESCO framework includes nature and the environment quite broadly defined, the Canadian framework includes only nature parks

TABLE 27
DIRECT ECONOMIC IMPACT OF THE CULTURE SECTOR ON GDP BY FUNCTION, CANADA, 1994–95, IN MILLIONS OF C$

	Direct impact on GDP					
Culture sector: Canada	Creation	Production	Manufacturing	Wholesale	Retail	Total
Arts and cultural industries						
Cultural industries						
Print industry		4 436.3	786.4	201.4	1 061.8	6 485.9
Film		771.5	216.4		400.3	1 388.2
Broadcasting		3 833.2				3 833.2
Music industry[1]	85.3	261.3			231.4	578.0
TOTAL Cultural industries	**85.3**	**9 302.3**	**1 002.8**	**201.4**	**1 693.5**	**12 285.4**
Arts						
Performing arts		580.3				580.3
Visual arts and crafts	53.7	104.2			253.6	411.4
Advertising		1 154.5				1 154.5
Architecture		407.0				407.0
Design		1 235.9				1 235.9
Photography		251.6				251.6
TOTAL Arts	**53.7**	**3 733.5**			**253.6**	**4 040.7**
Festivals		**26.7**				**26.7**
Total Arts and cultural industries	**139.0**	**13 062.4**	**1 002.8**	**201.4**	**1 947.1**	**16 352.7**
Heritage						
Museums and galleries		602.9				602.9
Libraries		1 091.1				1 091.1
Nature areas		259.1				259.1
TOTAL Heritage		**1 953.1**				**1 953.1**
Supporting infrastructure						
Arts and culture education		609.6				609.6
Government		1 246.4				1 246.4
TOTAL		**1 856.0**				**1 856.0**
TOTAL	**139.0**	**16 871.6**	**1 002.8**	**201.4**	**1 947.1**	**20 161.9**

1. Separate data for Music Industry record and CD-pressing-facilities, tape-duplicating facilities, and recording wholesalers are currently unavailable. As a result this table represents an under-coverage of the music industry for manufacturing and wholesaling.

with interpretation programmes and includes them under the heritage category. Sport, however, remains outside our cultural perimeter and is the subject of a separate policy initiative. The Program is now in the third year of a partnership with Sport Canada to develop the underlying infrastructure for the future collection, analysis and presentation of Canadian sport statistics.

Framework applications

Using the Canadian framework, it is estimated that the direct impact of the culture sector on the Canadian economy in 1994–95 was of the order of $20 billion (Table 27). For reasons of credibility and acceptability of these estimates, it was decided to publish only direct impacts based on primary activities and related wages, depreciation, profits and investment income rather than a much larger direct and indirect figure obtained if all other secondary purchases and subsequent spending rounds were added. Constraints included our inability to separate the impact of indigenous from imported cultural activities; to distinguish, within certain cultural industries, between cultural and non-cultural output; or to fill the many data gaps. In estimating the economic impact of culture at the provincial level, only the economic impact of provincial economic activity on Canada, rather than its impact upon the provincial economy, could be calculated. The Program is currently working to address these weaknesses.

Canada has been developing another framework analytical application over the past three years to better monitor the international competitiveness of Canadian artists, cultural industries and institutions. The challenge is to develop concepts for measuring culture trade (i.e. commodities, intellectual property and services) and investment, inventorying available data, closing gaps and delivering analytic products to sponsors and the public. Again, the estimation decisions must be carried out in the context of certain very real limitations: our inability to segregate cultural and non-cultural commodities.

A further research priority is to establish credibility for the culture labour force estimates. The direct impact of the culture sector on the Canadian economy was estimated as 610,000 jobs in 1994–95 (Table 28). This figure is based on the number of culture and non-culture workers in cultural industries, defined by the culture categories and the economic chain in the Canadian framework. If, however, the research requirement is to establish the characteristics of culture workers in both cultural and non-cultural industries and to exclude non-cultural workers or those culture workers in the manufacturing and distribution end of the economic chain, then the final count of culture workers in Canada would appear to be inconsistent with the count in the economic impact application. Unless one were able to explain this difference, the credibility of both figures would appear doubtful. By using the framework as the point of reference, research decisions are better understood and accepted. This project in Canada is limited to the front end of the chain, to cultural workers in both cultural and non-cultural industries, and to primary occupations only because the data sources, the monthly Labour Force Survey and the quinquennial census, are not able to yield more information. There do remain, however, strong policy and industry-related reasons for tracking all employment and self-employment in the culture sector.

Culture surveys

The Culture Surveys Section continues the traditional tasks of managing the collection of data directly from Canada's cultural industries and institutions and releasing the results to the public. The Section directly administers eleven surveys, maintaining its own mailing lists and is the repository and publisher of the results of two others. There are four annual film surveys an annual government expenditures survey, and six biennial surveys covering books, periodicals, the performing arts, public heritage institutions, sound recording and label companies and a newly introduced music publishers survey. Furthermore, using administrative data, the Program creates data banks on radio listening and television viewing with detail at the level of individual programme characteristics in the case of television and station formats in the case of radio.

TABLE 28
DIRECT ECONOMIC IMPACT OF THE CULTURE SECTOR ON EMPLOYMENT BY FUNCTION, CANADA, 1994–95

	Direct impact on employment (number of jobs)					
Culture sector: Canada	Creation	Production	Manufacturing	Wholesale	Retail	Total
Arts and cultural industries						
Cultural industries						
Print industry		73 810	14 153	4 045	44 182	136 190
Film		20 402	3 417		20 087	43 906
Broadcasting		51 004				51 004
Music industry[1]	12 280	2 740			9 627	24 647
TOTAL Cultural industries	**12 280**	**147 956**	**17 570**	**4 045**	**73 896**	**255 747**
Arts						
Performing arts		68 856				68 856
Visual arts and crafts	10 755	2 913			10 552	24 220
Advertising		70 775				70 775
Architecture		25 722				25 722
Design		28 245				28 245
Photography		15 925				15 925
TOTAL Arts	**10 755**	**212 436**			**10 552**	**233 743**
Festivals		**3963**				**3963**
Total Arts and cultural industries	**23 035**	**364 355**	**17 570**	**4 045**	**84 448**	**493 453**
Heritage						
Museums and galleries		21 212				21 212
Libraries		39 566				39 566
Nature areas		8 005				8 005
TOTAL Heritage		**68 783**				**68 783**
Supporting infrastructure						
Arts and culture education		25 364				25 364
Government		22 187				22 187
TOTAL		**47 551**				**47 551**
TOTAL	**23 035**	**480 689**	**17 570**	**4 045**	**84 448**	**609 787**

1. Separate data for Music industry record and CD-pressing facilities, tape-duplicating facilities, and recording wholesalers are currently unavailable. As a result this table represents an under-coverage of the music industry for manufacturing and wholesaling.

Survey elements common to most of the eleven industrial and institutional surveys include information on corporate status, country of controlling interest, international transactions by type, revenues and expenditures by source and type, markets, employment and volunteer action, types and levels of production, the commercial categories and formats of products, origin of products and services (whether Canadian or foreign), sales or attendance figures, the language of products and services, and activities in new technology and multimedia.

Communications with the culture constituency

As part of the initiative to create the Culture Statistics Program within Statistics Canada, there has been extensive liaison with the representatives and associations of the culture and heritage sector. In 1984 a Program advisory body was formed called the National Advisory Committee on Culture Statistics (NACCS) which meets with Program management and staff twice yearly and holds the mandate for advising on the development and strategic direction of statistical activities concerning all facets of arts and culture in Canada. Members are chosen for three-year terms from among professionals in cultural businesses, institutions, government and academia. During the past few years the Program has created statistical profiles on the culture sector in seven out of ten provinces and provided the detailed data for this purpose to an eighth.

Conclusion

Cultural policies and programmes are capable of wielding considerable social and economic influence. While it is always a challenge to evaluate the impact of the culture sector, it is becoming increasingly difficult today to forecast with any degree of certainty the trajectory and pace of change there, because it is, in any event, a traditionally high-risk sector both in commercial cultural industries and in the not-for-profit arts and heritage areas. Changes in the social sphere, in the world economy and in technology are compounding both the complexity of the policy environment and, by extension, the traditional exercise of gathering information to support it.

Information and data urgently need to be collected in Canada on these emerging issues, some of which are already upon us before the funds can be acquired and technical adjustments to survey instruments can be made to evaluate their impact. Today we are witnessing the democratization of culture and its new influence upon world economy and its links to the technology revolution. These and associated trends have raised issues of equitable access, content regulation, competition and productivity. The emergence of new media is a good example of the impact of new technology on new forms of content, new channels of distribution and new audiences. In both the traditional and emerging cultural environments, the continuing evolution of credible, useful cultural indicators and information systems, some quantitative but others qualitative, remains essential to our appreciation of the place of culture in our lives, however broadly or narrowly we define it.

Chapter 16
The Philippine approach to cultural statistics

JAIME C. LAYA
Chairman, National Commission for Culture and the Arts (Philippines)

'A solid factual basis is necessary for the proper evaluation of the effectiveness of cultural policies and programmes.'

Background

The Philippine Development Plan for Culture and the Arts identifies the objective of cultural development as national unity, with plan activities categorized under cultural heritage, artistic expression and cultural dissemination. The plan was approved in 1993 and is now being updated by the National Commission for Culture and the Arts (NCCA). A solid factual basis is necessary for the proper evaluation of the effectiveness of cultural policies and programmes. Globalization and the pervasive influence of international and domestic media, in particular, add to the challenges of maintaining cultural diversity among the country's many cultural communities, of encouraging excellence in artistic creation while also maintaining a distinct Philippine identity, and of promoting public appreciation not only of world culture and arts, but also of the country's heritage and contemporary artistic work.

Various difficulties have been identified in the quantitative monitoring of culture and the arts, since the available data are of varying quality and focus largely on revenue and income, volume of activity and cultural literacy survey results. One difficulty is the definition of variables to be measured. Artists tend to look for something that transcends the material and the quantitative. Relatively few people or organizations engage solely in cultural and arts activities. Major cultural events are often part of people's daily lives, and reciters of epics, singers and dancers at festivals and participants in religious processions are actually farmers, traders and entrepreneurs. Historians, playwrights, poets, musicians and visual artists may well be professors, for example, and thus earn their living from education rather than culture.

Another challenge arises because a significant part of cultural activity is in the non-monetary or informal economy sector. Traditional arts and crafts are created largely for the enjoyment and consumption of the creators and their fellow villagers. Even in the monetary sector many cultural activities are contributed in kind and not all artists issue receipts.

Qualitative differences in artistic output raise the problem of how to cope with variations in the quality and type of cultural work. Critically acclaimed paintings and sculpture, for example, should not be grouped with tourist trade works. Classical dancers

Cultural statistics and poverty

The available cultural statistics under-represent or completely exclude many of the cultural activities of poor nations and of poor people in rich nations. The richer the country, the more cultured it would appear to be. Cultural statistics under-report or exclude poor countries and poor people because, unlike the statistics of other social areas such as education, population and health (but not disease), they are not inclusive. On the contrary, they are patently exclusive, focusing primarily on the production and consumption of cultural goods that can be priced in the market. In fact, cultural statistics may be said at present to be as much a process of discounting as of counting.

A further, and more insidious, aspect of this state of affairs is the extent to which living in poverty deprives people, and in some cases whole countries, of many cultural activities and opportunities as commonly defined. Market-place culture is by far the leading cultural brand with a dominant share of the statistically defined culture market. It is also identified mainly with the rich countries. And the culture that is practised in rich countries is automatically practised by the rich in the not-so-rich countries and, in particular, by the rich in the poor countries. This results in the creation of a self-perpetuating exclusively value-laden definition of culture which is the culture of the comparatively rich as expressed through the market-place.

The absurdity and inequity of this situation are well illustrated by the following. Most of the cultural activities of a poor rural family in a developing country are not reflected at all in culture statistics as at present constituted. Yet should that same poor rural family win the lottery, all its subsequent 'cultural' activities will be fully manifest in those statistics.

LEO GOLDSTONE
Director,
World Statistics Ltd. (United States)

and singers may call attention to the difference between their art and productions inspired by international pop stars. Prize-winning books should not be confused with pulp novels and soap opera scripts.

Industry statistics

One estimation of the value of a culture industry's annual output is the aggregate of the industry's revenue from sales to the public of commodities or services produced and income from private or state subsidy. Alternatively, the value of the industry's production may be determined by estimating the income earned by all the resource providers – actors, painters, composers, scriptwriters, crews and ticket sellers *inter alia* – who make the output possible. This type of data – revenue or income – is routinely estimated by government statisticians who gather and extrapolate data from co-operating government agencies and private companies and other sources such as Income Tax Returns and Securities and Exchange Commission files. Any number of activities and industry classifications can be used to help illuminate aspects of culture and the arts and of the life of cultural communities.

The Philippine Standard Industrial Classification (PSIC) code is the basis for government statistical work on industry status and performance. Modelled on the United Nations industrial classification system, the PSIC is used for census and general statistical purposes, including population and household surveys, family income and expenditure studies, economic activity and employment, and imports and exports. A number of four-digit industries in the PSIC listing belong to or are associated with culture and the arts.

TRADITIONAL CULTURAL COMMUNITIES

The economic basis of the economies of traditional cultural communities can be gauged using certain indicators such as agricultural production (specifically upland paddy), or hunting and fishing activities. Furthermore, since many cultural communities are forest-based, logging operations would give an idea of any difficulty in the maintenance of their culture. It is assumed that transactions captured in the statistics would most likely be understated, since the traditional cultural communities are, for the most part, outside the monetized economy.

CULTURAL DISSEMINATION: LITERARY ARTS

Printing and publishing data are rather general and describe activities in cultural dissemination only to the extent that some of these, such as recorded music, are tracked. Basic education textbooks comprise the most significant part of the book publishing industry. Furthermore, publishers do not specialize but tend to cover the whole range of works, from the sciences and the professions to crafts and religion and even to a mixed bag of books that are broadly considered as cultural, including pulp novels, comics, and glossy art and design books.

MANUFACTURED GOODS

This category includes some products of a cultural nature, although no distinction is made between production for export and production for home consumption, which would be a means of measuring domestic cultural activity. Retail sales would be a significant indicator of public interest in cultural goods. Book sales are a potentially important indicator, showing not only locally published works but also titles published abroad. As indicated above, the bulk of such sales consist of textbooks and school supplies. It may, however, be possible to compile more detailed data to include retail sales of non-textbooks as an indicator of the book-buying and reading habits of the general public.

PERFORMING AND VISUAL ARTS: CULTURAL HERITAGE

Data on architecture – the revenues of architectural firms and individuals – are probably the most reliable of all, since they concern the only recognized profession in all the arts. Among visual artists, professional photographers are those most closely monitored, although statistics include sales not only of art photographs, but also of studio portraits, pictures taken at weddings and other events, photographs for passports and so on.

Cultural activities, including training and symposia, are carried on by professional associations for historians, librarians, archivists, art educators or writers.

A number of cultural industries belong to the category of 'Recreation, culture and sports,' notably the movie and broadcasting industries. The same category includes commercial art galleries, libraries and museums. Adjustments have yet to be made to the industry classification system in order to identify, among other things, companies dealing in ethnic handicrafts.

Quality differences also need to be accounted for. Statistics on art galleries, for example, should include the revenues of both recognized painters and those who produce pictures *en masse* for hotels. Statistics on theatres should also include presentations of original plays of different kinds, Broadway imports and burlesque shows. Similarly, museum statistics should cover exhibitions of all kinds.

Apart from the more active industries (e.g. printing and broadcasting media and cinema), the available statistics show only negligible amounts for most categories. The challenge, as in most statistical work, is to extend coverage for greater accuracy and detail, and so permit more meaningful data analysis. This will call for close co-ordination between the National Statistics Office, the NCCA and private companies, individual artists and cultural workers, non-government organizations, local government units and other data sources so as to comprise a statistically valid cross section of the participants in the culture and arts sector.

Volume indicators

Activity in culture and the arts is also measured by means of physical or volume indicators, such as number of performances, book titles published and motion pictures released. While these elements are subsumed in financial measures, volume data are useful particularly where financial indicators are inadequate. In non-monetarized sectors of the economy, volume indicators may be the best available to measure activity, in particular in the performing and literary arts.

The Government's cultural and communications agencies maintain regular statistical series and conduct surveys on a regular basis or as the need arises. The available series are generally limited to numbers of museums, public libraries and archives, classified by location and source of financing. Data are also available on numbers of visitors or users, and, in the case of libraries, numbers of volumes in collections. In the communications sector, data are compiled on media infrastructure and numbers of radio and television stations, newspapers, magazines and movie houses, classified by location. Market surveys are also conducted from time to time on readership or audience preferences. Government budgetary figures for cultural agencies and cultural activities are available, as are numbers of teachers, textbooks, schoolrooms, equipment and other resource inputs.

NCCA efforts to develop cultural indicators have resulted in preliminary recommendations for indicators in the following categories: production and consumption of material goods and services, development/stock of physical and human capital, the public's allocation of time for culture and arts activities, and indicators of quality of culture and arts output.

Cultural literacy

The final objective of the culture and arts plan, as previously stated, is to achieve national unity while maintaining cultural diversity, including encouraging artistic expression and public appreciation, and patronage of artistic and cultural activities. The degree of success of these objectives might be gauged by means of carefully structured surveys intended to reveal the cultural literacy of key groups. Achievement tests for schoolchildren include questions on the minimum that every educated Filipino should know about Philippine, Asian and Western culture and arts. These have not yet been systematically analysed, and further work should be done to identify the state of cultural literacy among the general public and specific groups such as teachers and students of teacher training institutions.

Surveys should also be developed for use with focus groups. The findings of such surveys will help to identify areas for effective intervention via the family, the school or the media, through improvements to libraries, museums and other cultural institutions, not forgetting the inexhaustible energy of community cultural activity.

Chapter 17
Towards an international system of cultural statistics and indicators: the Italian experience

PAOLO GARONNA
Director, Statistical Division, Economic Commission for Europe;
Former Director, Italian National Institute of Statistics-Istat (Italy)

'The objective should be to develop a fully-fledged international system of statistical information on culture. . . .'

In the field of culture, as in many other fields, there is an increasing demand for a wide range of indicators and statistics, covering activities and products, expenditure and consumption, employment, finance, institutions, costs and prices and so on. The need for measuring, reporting, benchmarking, evaluating and comparing performance has become almost an obsession.

One may well wonder why this is so. Is it that, in the 'quantum' age, a sort of 'data fetishism' has extended its reach over art and culture? Or is it, on the contrary, that the complexity and uncertainty of decision-making, particularly in art and culture, call for more solid infrastructures of information and a more cold-blooded, informed and rational approach, with less 'irrational exuberance' and 'animal spirits' (as Keynes put it)?

There are four outstanding reasons for the widespread popularity of indicators. Firstly, as the Maastricht process showed, peer pressure, reviews and benchmarking can be a very powerful policy tool in the information society to induce the desired response, stimulate reform and guide behaviour. Competition and emulation are indeed quite effective levers. They are the rule in exhibitions, fairs, shows and festivals. What is more important is the fact that peer reviews can succeed today where the more traditional policy tools of the past have failed: regulation has often created distortions and stifled innovation; nationalizing certain cultural activities proved to be too expensive for the taxpayer and led to entrenched inefficiency; public subsidies and tax expenditures often bring about spurious redistributions and disincentive effects. Playing on moral suasion, on the contrary, can have lasting effects, attract public attention, and sanction misbehaviour through exposure to political scrutiny. But it requires clear and policy-relevant indicators, based on sound, comparable and credible statistics.

Secondly, if we wish to contrast under-investment in culture, more transparency is needed in both cultural markets and cultural institutions. The opacity of the markets for art and culture is a well-known phenomenon. The returns on cultural investments are notoriously unpredictable, dispersed and distant in time. The mechanisms for knowledge acquisition or transmission and value generation are still largely unexplored. It is undeniable that innate talents, extraordinary circumstances and chance play a decisive role in cultural outcomes; however, culture is increasingly seen as the result of deliberate effort, commitment, labour and institutional adjustment. Data and information are providing clues for uncovering and unveiling the black box of creativity, beauty and innovation. However, investment in culture still relies too much on acts of faith or on eccentricity, and this is something that does not reach ordinary people easily. More and better information is needed in order to manage risk, allocate resources and time efficiently, focus commitment and invest capital.

Thirdly, under-investment too is largely due to a lack of accountability of public policies for culture. The 'government failures' in the field of arts and culture are well-known, particularly so when the governments in question are national governments. Too often, boosting the national cultural identity has been accompanied by the threat of uniformity, assimilation, fragmentation and intolerance. Making governments more accountable for their actions in the field of culture and the arts is an essential precondition for greater and swifter public support for culture.

Fourthly, international dialogue is yet another crucial factor. Alongside the element of public good in culture, there is an undeniably universal element in all art and culture. Ultimately, culture belongs to humanity as a whole. Thus, exchanging and communicating cultural experiences and assets on a global scale is a fundamental ingredient of cultural progress. But any such exchange needs high-quality statistics and indicators that can be compared and contrasted on the international level.

It is clear, accordingly, that every effort should be made to standardize statistical concepts, definitions and classifications at worldwide level. This is where the fundamental role of UNESCO and other appropriate international organizations operating in the field of culture can be clearly seen and appreciated. The objective should be to develop a fully-fledged international system of statistical information on culture so that policy performance at the local level may be understood, measured and assessed against performance in other localities, or at national level or in different regions of the globe. The international community of statisticians has been working intensively and fairly successfully for several years on this bold enterprise. Indeed considerable progress has been made in evolving a workable international system of culture statistics. Two important European initiatives should be noted.

The first is the Leadership Group on Culture Statistics of the European Union (LEG), set up by Eurostat and led by the Italian National Institute of Statistics (Istat), with the participation of the statistical bureaux and ministries of culture of many European countries. LEG has made considerable efforts, achieving significant results in: revising and updating the classification of cultural activities (NACE), taking stock of the work already done at UNESCO, disaggregating the relevant NACE headings and proposing a table of correspondence between the standard NACE and the specific classification of cultural activities, and establishing a detailed classification of cultural occupations by adapting and disaggregating ISCO'88.

But LEG's main effort has gone into promoting full exploitation of the principal existing surveys in order to get an overview and a better insight into culture, participation and supply: they are the labour force survey, the household budget survey, the multipurpose social survey, and the main enterprise and governmental sector surveys. In this way more in-depth data on cultural activities is not only collected but also linked to standard classifications, concepts, information and indicators in social statistics.

The second major initiative was the creation in 1993 of the Siena Group on Social Statistics grouping social statisticians from national statistics institutes, experts from ministries and other agencies, academics and policy-makers. The Siena Group has done considerable work on measuring ethnicity and cultural or linguistic identity, and in particular on identifying discrimination or areas of vulnerability and cultural disadvantage. A report on the monitoring of multicultural societies was published in 1998 by the Swiss Federal Statistics Office. It deals with the different approaches to the construction of indicators for a multicultural society.

Three main challenges lie ahead in the field of cultural statistics and indicators. The first concerns the establishment of a complete system of cultural statistics and indicators that would be integrated, comprehensive and capable of linking the various sectors of the wide-ranging cultural issues and connecting them to the multiple aspects of social and economic development. This implies linking and networking many sources of data, including those of an administrative nature, and sample surveys, household and enterprise surveys, registers and population and housing censuses, while improving data capturing processing and dissemination methods and techniques.

The second challenge is of an institutional or political nature. Statistics are inherently a matter of trust. Statistical information and transparency are needed in order to generate trust and 'social capital', but, on the other hand, trust and social capital are needed in order to generate good quality statistics. There has to be trust between respondents and interviewers, between the public agency and the media, and between policy-makers and statisticians. The process therefore involves a circular relationship. Trust is particularly important in questions on culture, a field which touches people's minds, hearts, individual freedoms and collective beliefs. Public confidence in culture statistics has to be won, maintained and nurtured through a rigorous allegiance to the principles of public statistics. The role of national statistics institutes in this context is potentially very important, because in most countries – where they are based on a statistical law or some other legal and regulatory framework – they enjoy a relatively autonomous status with a long tradition of involvement in research and confidentiality. If we require more data on cultural aptitudes and beliefs, or seek to interconnect micro-data from separate spheres (e.g. ethnicity with social conditions, employment and participation in cultural activities), or wish to link economic and social development with culture, national heritage and promotion of the arts, then we must invest seriously in public confidence on culture statistics through institutional reform and open communication.

The third challenge – the most complex and intriguing of all – concerns measurement issues. Some of the difficulties with indicators arise, not through lack of data, but rather because of conceptual inadequacy. There is now a growing awareness, not only among specialists but also in the public at large, that cultural expenditure under certain conditions is an investment in social or human capital, and that certain cultural services, produced by volunteer work or at home, should be regarded as products. They have an economic value and should be included in the national product even though they are not exchanged in the market. They are intangible, yet they count none the less like wheat and steel – or even more than these. Finally, some cultural fortunes become a negative investment: for instance, the erasure of cultural diversity or the destruction of culture by war, natural disaster or through pollution or environmental damage. Such phenomena can destroy a country's cultural capital.

Unfortunately, such theoretical concepts have not yet been incorporated into operational ones for standard statistical measurements of output, assets and welfare. Such a lag can lead to mis-measurement and contradictory policies. For instance, governments may pour money into public monopolies (railways, post offices or tanks), and thus invest in public capital, while refusing to support the arts, which are regarded as simply revenue consuming. A similar dichotomy may be observed in families investing in culture and education for their children as opposed to those which push their youngsters to work and earn money for investment in material wealth.

The 1993 System of National Accounts (SNA) has made considerable progress in the treatment of works of art, books, music and historical monuments which are now classified as produced intangible assets and included in gross capital formation. However, research and education are still treated as intermediate consumption and therefore subtracted from the gross domestic product (GDP). But, more importantly, the new SNA permits the creation of satellite accounts to test new concepts and linkages and permit more comprehensive measurement. In other words, accounts of cultural activities are being developed and linked to standard economic and social accounts as a means of measuring the impact of culture on sustainable development. The aim is to produce an adapted set of indicators, or a set of culture-adjusted economic and social accounts, that can measure national productivity, capital, employment, income and welfare in a comprehensive fashion within the context of a broad concept of sustainable development. As in the case of the 'Green GDP', we now have every hope of creating a 'Golden GDP' that will take full account of culture and its impact on development and society.

UNESCO, in collaboration with the European Union, the Conference of European Statisticians and the United Nations Statistical Commission, should take the leadership in this effort requiring an enhanced dialogue between government statisticians and academic experts. What is needed is a shared commitment of the kind that in the post-war period produced the National Accounts, as we now know them, in connection with the Marshall Plan and the reconstruction of Europe. I shall conclude with a quotation on the historical links between culture and statistics, taken from Swiss historian Jacob Burkhardt's work, *The Civilization of the Renaissance in Italy*, written in 1860. In the introductory chapter, under the imaginative title, 'The State as a Work of Art', we read:

> The most elevated political thought and the most valued forms of human development are found united in the history of Florence, which in this sense deserves the name of the first modern State in the world. Here the entire people are busy with what in despotic cities would be the affairs of a single family. The wondrous Florentine spirit, at once keenly critical and artistically creative, was ceaselessly transforming the social and political conditions of the State, and as ceaselessly describing and judging the change. Thus Florence became the home of political doctrines and theories, of experiments and sudden changes, but also, like Venice, the home of statistical science. This statistical view of things was highly cultivated in Florence. The significant point about it is that, as a rule, we can perceive its connection with the higher aspects of history, with art, and with culture in general.

Chapter 18
Culture and its statistics: a glance at French experience

PAUL TOLILA
Director, Department of Statistical and Prospective Studies, Ministry of Culture and Communication (France)

'In a world of rapid globalization, comparability is still the best means of identifying specificities, preserving them and so promoting the diversity of cultures.'

At first glance, culture and statistics do not make a happy couple. Relations in this long-standing alliance are often perceived at worst as stormy and at best as distant. The idea of assessing culture in statistical terms would seem to be either a fanciful challenge or an autocratic demand. Can this contradiction be resolved? Is it possible to break out of the vicious circle where culture, which is synonymous with life itself in being dynamic, varied and filled with vitality, cannot but oppose statistics with their linear, arid tools of analysis and rationality?

The current situation is one of deadlock. The basic, abstract – and, dare one say, metaphysical – terms used to reflect on this problem prompt us quickly, all too quickly, either to return to the essential questions ('What is culture?') or to succumb to the temptation of endless debates over binary oppositions: passion versus reason, freedom versus constraint and pleasure versus auditing. Stated in these terms, there is little to choose within such a circular universe, which then confronts us with the question, 'What on earth do statistics have to do with culture?'

However, let us leave these remote, archetypal territories and return to the world of human experience and day-to-day reality. Here we can ask ourselves a number of straightforward, unpretentious questions: What share of wealth is devoted by such and such a society to what it defines as its culture, and according to which trends, through which channels and with which actors? What are the cultural products of that society and how are they devised and disseminated? How much employment do these sectors provide? What is their contribution to national wealth? Do they have links with non-cultural sectors? What relationships do men and women in that society have with cultural products, commercial or otherwise? What obstacles – financial, geographical, social or educational – continue to stand between entire sections of that society and access to a more developed cultural life? How and on what basis can the various actors involved in culture (citizens, creators, associations, and private and public decision-makers) communicate? How and on what basis – aside from major statements of principle – can states enter into dialogue and co-ordinate their actions in order to stimulate cultural development and co-operation?

These are some of the issues where statistics are not only well-disposed towards culture but are actually contributing increasingly to a potentially fruitful dialogue. But we have yet to master the methodological and tangible means to devise them, monitor them over time and submit them to public scrutiny, while resisting any temptation to turn them into dogma. They are none the less the necessary instruments for global reflection on the part of the players involved (let us call it policy in the broad sense), while they cannot presume to take the place of analysis.

The experience which France has acquired over the past forty years is exemplary and contains many useful lessons. We shall here endeavour to describe this experience briefly in regard to the issues that concern us in order to determine how it can help us reappraise the relations between statistics and culture more accurately.

Culture in France: permanence and significance of public policy

Just over forty years ago, France created a Ministry of Culture. We are often tempted to describe this initiative as the result of a specifically French tradition of state intervention in the cultural domain, a tradition which some believe goes back to Louis XIV (or even earlier). This retrospective viewpoint (and any retrospection has the intrinsic defect of seeking out origins according to an infinitely regressive approach) often misses the very essence of the 1959 innovation, namely, the creation not only of a political structure, but of a public policy, of which the ministry is but the symbol and the medium.

A public policy means a number of things. First of all, the state recognizes the importance of cultural fields, the arts and the aesthetic link with the world in the eyes of the community it serves. It also believes – at the risk of running counter to the most elementary of all democratic requirements – that cultural phenomena cannot depend exclusively on the balance of power at work in society and, more particularly, on market forces. Finally, it recognizes that part of its budget will be allocated to supporting and developing cultural activities and that it will be accountable to the citizens it represents in this regard for the use made of that budget and therefore the results of its policy. For over forty years, ministers have come and gone, and while the particular tone of policies may have shifted, and budgets allocated to culture have fluctuated in opposite directions, yet France has constantly upheld a public policy in the cultural domain.

Forty years of cultural policies as a record is both modest and substantial. Modest because when compared to other fields where the state traditionally intervenes (taxation, defence and foreign relations), cultural policies are still a recent phenomenon. Substantial, in so far as there has been a sustained effort from the days of André Malraux to those of Catherine Tasca, on behalf of culture, which cannot be attributed merely to the cult of the past. We should also consider the passionate commitment of leading ministers, the values shared by all of the democratic parties involved in politics, the commitment of creators and, more widely, of French society itself to the very idea of a cultural policy.

For such a policy to be conducted, established, developed and accounted for, the state and the ministry were conscious from the outset of the need for statistical data so that political action could be taken with a minimum number of stable reference points and due consideration to defining priorities. As long ago as 1963, the Department of Statistical and Prospective Studies (DEP) was set up for this purpose in the wake of a broad-based interministerial consultation. Its task was to collect, process, classify and disseminate all socio-economic data on culture in France. Its responsibility was to serve as a cornerstone for public policies, disseminate all its information and promote any research required. The public it served was composed of decision-makers working for the ministry, the state and the public authorities, the actors involved in the cultural domain and the general public.

As such, the DEP's responsibility amounted to a

challenge and a minor revolution. It was a challenge in so far as nothing or virtually nothing existed as regards classified, correlated cultural data; it was a revolution too because, at the time, there was little awareness of the utility of statistics and a degree of mistrust was still quite common. We should like to pay tribute here to Augustin Girard, founder and first director of the DEP, for his astute, tenacious and patient action as the initiator of a genuine culture of cultural statistics at the ministry, in France and no doubt further afield.

Thus, public cultural policy and statistics emerged hand in hand. In France, the phenomenon led to wide-ranging development of qualitative, quantitative and statistical knowledge. It naturally stimulated vigorous development of the social sciences focused on observable cultural phenomena and extensive debates in every section of society. Is there any need to recall that the statistics originating from studies and investigations conducted over these forty years have never claimed to assess culture with a capital C? Quite the contrary, those statistics have invariably been described as what they are, namely, the quantifiable aspect of very simple phenomena, very carefully defined in regard to the needs of public policies (cultural customs, funding, employment in the cultural sector, the relationship between price and attendance, and so on). Need we underline, furthermore, that these simple statistics have never been presented as indisputable evidence of observed reality, and that they have always been accompanied – for the benefit of decision-makers and the general public alike – by the precautionary principles necessary for their comprehension and a degree of interpretation, leaving the field open to debate and the full responsibility of decision-makers?

Finally, is it necessary to recall that, in contrast with the totalitarian regimes of the past and the ideas of those who are hostile to any state intervention, cultural policies in France have never claimed to represent, make or even, a fortiori, *be* culture itself? They have set themselves modest but ambitious objectives, without which culture itself would have been exposed to mutilation and impoverishment. Their objectives have ever been to encourage creation, preserve heritage, develop cultural industries, broaden access to cultural activities and promote diversity. They have never sought either to dictate what people should like or to impose what should be considered beautiful. They have contributed in their own way to maintaining and expanding the creative capacity of society, to enabling as many people as possible, each according to his or her own choice, to have access to the dimension of aesthetic pleasure and, undoubtedly, to acquire a better understanding of the interests of others. From this point of view, while these statistics enabled long-term policies to be implemented and perhaps opened the way to certain decisions, it will be acknowledged that, aside from the myth that they are a threat to culture, they are, conversely, truly the most reliable agents for its development.

Cultural statistics and the culture of statistics

Statistics are but one aspect of the wide-ranging problem of acquiring knowledge about cultural phenomena. To acquire this knowledge, adequate means must be made available and, more importantly, the task organized efficiently and durably. Over the years, the DEP has developed its activities in four principal areas in order to respond to the whole range of tasks: a survey and research unit where work on the socio-economic aspects of culture is conducted; a statistics unit to encourage tasks such as collecting series over the longer term and managing them in databases (in this regard, it should be said that the DEP is also a ministerial statistical department and, as such, has strong links with the National Statistics Office and hence all the statistics agencies in France and in Europe); a publishing unit in charge of disseminating the research conducted (books, working documents, documentary synopses, briefs and survey abstracts; preparations are under way for making the DEP's research readily available on the Internet); and a documentation unit which, over the past forty years, has been one of the most extensive library sources of the Ministry of Culture and Communication. This centre is the only one of its kind in France and it caters for the staff of the department, the research community, students and actors in the cultural

The Index Translationum on CD-ROM: an analytical tool

The humanities and social sciences, situated as they are at the interface between the various trends of change in society and their interpretation, representation and dissemination, are a privileged area for anyone wishing to assess the dynamics of identity in operation. Without dealing here with the sizeable problem that presupposes acceptance of the terms 'humanities and the social sciences', and the exact scope of the field of investigation entailed, the matter at hand is to provide material for the publication of a book as demonstration of the necessity to communicate within a given social, economic, cultural and political framework.

Consequently, exchange in publications, and especially the process of transfer represented by the publication of a translation in the field of human and social sciences, would seem to be the leitmotif whereby we can apprehend the notion of 'Europe' which has recently been established in temporal terms, or in other words a territory governed by the economic and cultural logic of unrestricted movement and trade. The question that needs to be raised can therefore be worded as follows: to what extent does this network approach to culture genuinely apply to Europe as regards translation in the field under consideration? That being so, it is within this exploratory framework that we turn to the *Index Translationum*, a database that has been available in CD-ROM form since 1994. We therefore propose to focus our attention now on the availability of this computer technology and, consequently, on an extensive data analysis.

The issue is by no means a negligible one. Above and beyond the methodological aspects and empirical conditions of our investigation conducted as an autopsy envisaged in its initial and etymological sense – that of seeing with one's own eyes rather than merely tracing the contours of a geography of cultural affinities – we managed to delineate a cartography of 'complicity' in publishing between five different countries (France, Germany, Italy, Spain and the United Kingdom) over a specific period of time namely, from 1981 to 1992.

The *Index Translationum* CD-ROM lists over 700,000 bibliographical references of works that have been translated and published in every field in some 100 countries and which have been recorded by UNESCO since 1979. More than 60,000 references are added each year to this index and it has replaced the international bibliography of translations which has not appeared in book form since 1989. The data on the CD-ROM are drawn from the mainframe, which is UNESCO's central server. A CDS/ISIS interface allows users to seek, select and cross-check the entries in the *Index Translationum*.

Each bibliographical note contains regular items such as the author's name, the original language, the language of translation and so on. Every work translated and published is reported by a national agency. This ensures not only that the ISO (International Organization for Standardization) standard is observed but also that the various definitions used correspond to the CDU (Classification Décimale Universelle). In spite of recommendations made on these definitions by UNESCO at the General Conference in Sofia in 1985, it is far from certain that they are scrupulously adhered to for every item of data supplied. The precision of the data collected depends on the good will of each particular state, second-hand sources being something of a gamble. Whenever possible, missing data are of course provided by UNESCO's Sector for Culture.

Apart from these methodological and above all epistemological considerations, we divided the humanities and social sciences into four categories, as follows: History/Geography/Biography (7% of all references), Philosophy/Psychology (5%), Law/Social Sciences/Education (11%), and Religion/Theology (6%).

With regard to the *Index Translationum* as a whole, the humanities and social sciences made up 29% (211,888 entries of all references in the 1995 edition of the CD-ROM). In order to provide greater homogeneity in these categories, we deliberately grouped certain disciplines which account for a mere eight references under the heading of Philosophy/Psychology. These include Philosophy/Psychology of Law, and even Applied Psychology, which alone contains four references.

Three search procedures are accessible via the CDS/ISIS: assisted mode, expert mode and dictionary mode. The *Index Translationum* quickly proves to be an excellent consultation tool. On the other hand, a crosscheck analysis, namely, transforming an online list of entries with common fields into a matrix synoptic table with lines and columns, cannot be carried out. This is because the format for dispatching information available in CDS/ISIS is incompatible with the import formats of the Excel and Access software which we use.

Aware of the difficulties that our research faced concerning the export and import of *Index Translationum* data, UNESCO's Centre for Information Exchange suggested personalized retrieval of data from the mainframe capable of interfacing with Access. Containing already itemized criteria, a file of 91,336 entries was communicated to us. These entries are automatically imported via Access on a data table list similar to that on the CD-ROM. However, we are now on a database management system; in other words, we can now conduct search procedures (simple, cross-checked or otherwise) in order to select entries which have at least one common parameter (e.g. country of publication). At this particular point in the search procedure – and, aside from the question of how far back a researcher should be looking, (sufficiently out of reach of any prior judgement to permit a proper understanding of intercultural exchanges), it is quite clear that statistical data have no validity or relevance other than those of the circumstances in which they were collected. Besides, such figures are merely indicative in so far as they refer only to titles rather than print runs or sales figures. One should remember that the mere fact that a book is translated and published is no indication of its importance in the target culture.

To describe the main themes that feature in publishing exchanges in the humanities and social sciences, it may be relevant to link data from the *Index Translationum* with those in the Statistical Yearbooks that UNESCO has also been publishing since 1963. Thus trends in translation rates – the ratio of the number of translations to the number of titles published – show *inter alia*, and with some degree of accuracy, the predominance of such and such a language in terms of translation per discipline.

In short, this analysis of rates of translation shows that, in relative terms, the greatest number of translations are done in Spain, whereas the United Kingdom is at the bottom of the list. However, in absolute terms, Germany publishes the largest number of translations. And if it were possible to assess the time lapse before works are translated, the Italians would lead the list: their curiosity is equalled only by their speed in translating and publishing works that appeal to them. As regards languages, Spanish is the least translated, followed by Italian, while the most translated language is, naturally, English. The dissymetrical rank of the United Kingdom, already pronounced at the outset, was even more so by the end of the period. The picture is quite clear: translation operates from north to south. It is worth noting that the traditional rift between the two main categories of affinity – Latin and Anglo-Saxon – is turning slightly to the advantage of the latter. Religion is now the only field in Italy in which French cultural influence surpasses Anglo-Saxon influence. In that regard, an assessment according to flows reveals its limitations here. While it enables asymmetrical and undulating flows to be identified, it does not propose any principle of comprehension. To quote but one example relating to greater Spanish openness, one need only recall that the collapse of Franco's dictatorship in 1975 brought an end to the censorship which had been imposed on books in Spain until then.

To conclude, it should be stressed that translation rates are falling rapidly throughout the world (in spite of the scarcity of British data, it is certain that this is also the case in the United Kingdom). Out of sixteen trends, four increases may be observed (for Philosophy/Psychology in Germany, Law/Social Sciences/Education section in France and Germany, and lastly Religion/Theology in France) as against twelve significant declines. In the five European countries selected, the number of works translated in the humanities and social sciences fell drastically in the period under consideration.

To conclude, the use of this analytical matrix, made possible by the work conducted on the basis of the *Index Translationum* CD-ROM, opens the way, albeit with all due methodological precautions, to new thinking, whereby systems of interaction in human and social science publishing may be envisaged on a larger scale than that of Europe alone. It goes without saying that such research could contribute to the understanding of intercultural relationships between the main geographical areas of the world.

SYLVIE BOSSER
Doctoral degree student, Department of Information and Communication Sciences, University of Paris VIII (France)

domain. These four units work in constant collaboration with each other.

The DEP has become a focal point both for networks of researchers in the social sciences, which it has managed to nurture over the years and continues to call upon, and for actors and decision-makers who need structured, reliable information. The skills acquired by the department and the way they have been built up are used, first and foremost, for every new project that is launched, and are also disseminated through lectures, consultancy activities and participation in working groups in France and in Europe. The DEP is a research centre, a centre for expertise and a centre of resources for the benefit of the ministry and outside users as well. Each year, according to a rough estimate, the DEP has twenty or more projects of varying size under way, the statistics unit answers over 1,000 requests and the documentation unit receives more than 1,500 inquiries.

To carry out its assignment satisfactorily, the DEP has divided its activities into major programmes focusing on the economics of culture, practices and audiences, the international environment, cultural statistics, education and teaching of the arts, public expenditure and funding, and cultural occupations and professions. Accordingly, the department is able to manage both major recurring surveys and more occasional but thematically integrated research work. The DEP conducts a decennial survey on the cultural practices of the French population revealing figures and trends as observed over nearly forty years. It also carries out a triennial survey on public funding in culture (by central government, the regions, the *départements* and municipal councils) and a survey on cultural spending and consumption patterns of households. It has succeeded in setting up a French observatory of cultural employment which it continues to supplement through specialized research on the various professions. Every year, it publishes a volume of 'key figures' from cultural statistics in every acknowledged field. All these structural arrangements are justified only in the long term since they enable figures to be compared and viewed in a more accurate perspective. Consequently, the figures really speak for themselves, not as such but as part of a lengthy series and on the basis of clearly explicit interpretation criteria.

On the basis of this accumulation of expertise and this corpus of qualitative and quantitative information in which hypotheses and figures are free to interact and enrich each other, the DEP has been able to open up new areas of investigation as yet comparatively unexplored. In this way, the department has been pursuing research on 'street culture' which is closely linked to modern urban life, and on 'cultural geography' in which territorial planning is seen as part of the spatial dynamics of cultural customs. The DEP is also involved in research on festivals and cultural events which bring to light new forms of consumption and sociability, and on the world of new technologies, which appears to raise as many problems as it solves. Lastly, the DEP is investigating the field of international comparisons, where the major issue of irreducible specificities re-emerges.

Certainly, the practical obligation of producing statistics on culture has fortunately enabled the whole range of cultural actors in France to acquire – not without difficulty or controversy – a genuine culture of statistics where figures are no longer seen as a constraint, but rather as objective aspects of the vast and passionate challenge of assessing cultural phenomena.

An example of co-operation: European cultural statistics

At first glance, nothing is more difficult to compare than cultures, if by that we are referring to their unique character which in the eighteenth century would have been called their 'genius'. But we can compare the number and types of jobs which those cultures create, the economic value of the industries they nurture, the funding they attract and the cultural customs of their citizens. On the basis of these questions, the DEP organized a meeting of experts during the French presidency of the European Union in 1995. Two years later a pilot group – the LEG – was created with the support of Eurostat, and a three-year programme was adopted. The overall objective was to define and draw up the conditions for a system of cultural statistics that would be harmonized and comparable at a European level. This involved evaluating existing data and working out a series of key indicators in order to describe the diversity of cultures in Europe and contribute to defining and evaluating cultural policy. Fourteen European countries took part in the project on a voluntary basis and four task forces were set up to deal with methodology, employment, cultural expenditure and funding, and participation in cultural activities. The LEG submitted its report to Eurostat in November 1999. The report concluded that the situation was largely positive due to the definition of a common code (fields, classifications and nomenclature). Naturally, the problems were not all solved, in view of the heterogeneous nature of the existing national sources. Nevertheless, the conclusion of the pilot group's work left a residual spirit of dialogue and comprehension which all the participants were determined to maintain.

Within this context, the DEP was able to play a part commensurate with its expertise, since it was in charge of two of the four task forces (i.e. employment and methodology). The methodology group was a particularly sensitive one because its work served as a basis for all the others. A consensus was therefore reached for the definition of a common cultural field and the activities which structure it. On this basis, it was possible to experiment by collecting data in four different cultural fields (museums, libraries, theatres and the plastic arts).

All the LEG's experimental work was considered so fruitful by the specialized European bodies that it was decided unanimously to create a working group on cultural statistics within Eurostat. New research work (this time in fifteen countries) will begin in the year 2000 and there can be little doubt that this institutional status will give it new impetus and greater legitimacy.

It is quite clear that the path towards international comparability in cultural matters, while it will be a long and difficult one, is now open on condition that care be taken to clearly define the objectives, fields and methods.

By way of conclusion

The experience acquired in France has shown that culture and statistics are far from being the sworn enemies they were long considered to be. There is no fundamental opposition between them: the only substance for such thinking would be a dogmatic use of statistics (let us not forget the terrifying uses to which culture can be put). If, however, we ask the right questions about cultural activities, we should obtain the right figures. And if we then ask the right questions of those figures, they should open the way to new possibilities.

Culture and statistics, viewed in a narrow sense, can become an insurmountable barrier between nations and human beings. They may also be extraordinary opportunities for dialogue if care is taken to prepare the ground and to understand fully what is at stake.

As for comparisons, let us not be afraid to make them. In a world of rapid globalization, comparability is still the best means of identifying specificities, preserving them and so promoting the diversity of cultures. We frequently plead incomparability through fear and ignorance. Yet culture needs knowledge and skills that can be shared. The social sciences and their statistics are there to help us along that road.

Bibliography

DEP. 1993. *Trente ans d'études au service de la culture*. Paris, DEP.

DEP. 2000. *Les dépenses culturelles des Français*. Paris, DEP.

La Documentation Française. 1998. *Les pratiques culturelles des Français*. Paris, La Documentation Française.

——. 1998. *Atlas géographique des activités culturelles*. Paris, La Documentation Française.

——. 2000. *Chiffres-clés, statistiques de la culture*. Paris, La Documentation Française.

Chapter 19
In search of indicators of culture and development: progress and proposals

SAKIKO FUKUDA PARR
Director, Human Development Report Office,
United Nations Development Programme (United States)

'Recognizing tha indicators ar intended t stimulate polic dialogue ha importar implications fo the creation c cultura indicators

Introduction

Since the publication of *Our Creative Diversity* by the World Commission on Culture and Development and the issuing of UNESCO's first *World Culture Report*, increasing attention has been given to culture as a vital part of development. This has led to an exciting debate on indicators of culture. The *World Culture Report* published a number of interesting tables illustrating many aspects of culture in development, although research on cultural indicators is still in its infancy.

Future of cultural indicators

This chapter sets out to present some ideas for future work on developing cultural indicators. It argues that indicators are a tool of policy dialogue and are not the same thing as statistical data. They should contain evaluative, and not merely descriptive, information. The methodology for developing indicators should start by defining a conceptual framework. The definitions of culture and development, and the relationship between the two, were set out clearly in *Our Creative Diversity*.

No single indicator alone can capture the complex reality of culture. Dimensions of culture should be identified in relation to two aspects of development, namely, outcomes and processes. As regards the former, global ethics, cultural vitality and cultural diversity are proposed as key dimensions; and as regards the latter, we propose participation in creative activity, access to culture and respect for cultural identity. The indicators that appeared in the first issue of the *World Culture Report* were related mainly to material achievements of cultural creativity. Future work, however, should seek ways of quantifying other dimensions that were contained in the messages relayed in *Our Creative Diversity*.

Indicators as a tool of policy dialogue

The current interest in developing cultural indicators stems from concern about the fact that development policies are neglecting culture as a factor to be taken into account. It is time for quantitative indicators to contribute to inserting culture in the development policy dialogue. They can help focus the attention of busy policy-makers on the urgency of priority issues and the extent of improvements or setbacks in the field. Indicators are being used increasingly as a tool of policy dialogue through the provision of monitoring information. This is a new trend in the use of data. The conventional use of the latter is to provide material for research and analysis. And whereas data are used by economists and social scientists, indicators are used by politicians, the media and activists.

In launching the *Human Development Report,* Mahbub ul Haq set out deliberately to use indicators as advocacy tools. Going beyond unidimensional indicators, he realized that a composite index was needed to draw attention away from the preoccupation with the gross domestic product (GDP) as an indicator of development. In his special contribution to the report in 1999, Sen noted, 'By skilful use of the attracting power of the human development index (HDI), Mahbub got readers to take an involved interest in the large class of systematic tables and detailed critical analyses presented in [this report]'.[1]

Indeed, the HDI is central to public debate in many parts of the world when it is launched each year. The annual release of the new HDI ranking is a matter of widespread interest. It is indeed of some concern to many heads of state. Newspapers give prominence to the facts. The HDI ranking is the cause of widespread discussion and soul-searching in many countries. These in turn lead to the launching of national human development programmes. National human development reports in many countries publish disaggregated HDIs by region, municipality or ethnic group.

Recognizing that indicators are intended to stimulate policy dialogue has important implications for the creation of cultural indicators. Firstly, indicators should be designed for an evaluative rather than a descriptive purpose (Pattanaik, 1997). Thus they should track progress or recession in terms of specific goals. Secondly, they should be relevant, sending clear messages about issues of current concern and those that can be affected by policy response.

Methodology: conceptual framework, key dimensions and a step-by-step procedure

No indicators can be expected to make sense without a clear conceptual framework. As stimulators of policy debate, they should be developed in such a way as to provide objective data on positive or negative trends. The following questions might be asked: What precisely is the reality to be measured? What is culture and how can it be defined as an aspect of development? How should we evaluate progress in culture and development? What are the key dimensions? Since most social and economic realities are complex and multi-dimensional, no single indicator can be expected to reflect them. Culture is no exception: it is a complex reality that needs to be broken down into key dimensions.

Next, indicators must be selected by asking questions such as these: Are the components quantifiable? Most development goals are complex and may not be so. If not, it is important to acknowledge that only partial indicators can be developed. If so, do measures exist, and if not, are there substitutes? What data are available for the indicators selected? Finally, a composite index should be considered.

The following procedure was used in developing the HDI. First, definitions were established:

- Human development was defined: extending choices to permit the kind of life that people wish to lead.
- The most important features were defined: while an individual may be faced with an infinite range of choices, focus should be on the most important ones, which should include leading a long and healthy life; being knowledgeable; enjoying a decent standard of living; enjoying personal security; participating in the life of a community; enjoying the respect of others.

Second, indicators were selected:

- A long and healthy life: life expectancy measures length of life, but not degree of health.
- Breadth of knowledge: this is difficult to measure against an objective, universal standard. None the less, being literate and attending school are important in acquiring kinds of knowledge that in today's world are

fundamental to giving people choices in life. Thus literacy and school enrolment rates are good indicators of knowledgeability.

- A decent standard of living: a complex concept that varies from one social context to another. However, having minimal access to resources is equivalent to enjoying a decent standard of living. Per capita income is a fair indication; however, this is adjusted (with diminishing marginal returns) to take account of the fact that achieving a decent standard of living does not call for unlimited income.
- Two further dimensions, personal security and participation, are not quantifiable. Moreover, it is difficult to find corresponding indicators for them that have reliable data for a large number of countries.

The key dimensions and indicators of human development were selected in the light of the foregoing and became the components of the HDI. It should be remembered that the concept of human development is far greater than the sum of its parts.

Conceptual framework: unpacking a complex reality

The Report of the World Commission on Culture and Development entitled *Our Creative Diversity* breaks new ground in so far as it provides a solid conceptual foundation for developing cultural indicators.

In the first place, the report presents a conceptual framework which relates to culture and development. It does so by building on the anthropological concept of culture as the distinctive way of life of a people or society and on the concept of development as an extension of the choices that the individual can make to lead the life that he or she values.

Culture has everything to do with what we value most and the way in which we value living together. *Our Creative Diversity* introduces culture into the concept of human development, enriching and enlarging it. Development, seen in this perspective, is 'the opportunity to choose a full, satisfying, valuable and valued way of living together, the flourishing of human existence in all its forms and as a whole'.[2] Thus, culture is the social basis and context and indeed the very purpose of development. This perspective contrasts with the manner in which culture has often been analysed merely as a means to development, with cultural norms and values being regarded as contributors or obstacles to economic growth.

Accordingly, this conception of culture and development is a departure from the more conventional approaches. Culture is defined as a way of living with norms and standards rather than material achievements of intellectual and artistic creativity such as paintings, books and so forth. Development is viewed as an expansion of the individual's choices rather than as growth of material production, and culture is seen as the purpose of development and its social basis, and not as a facilitator of or impediment to economic growth.

In the second place, *Our Creative Diversity* gives a vision of development against which progress may be evaluated. It is a vision in which 'respect for all cultures whose values are tolerant of others and that subscribe to a global ethics is the basic principle'.[3] Its principal tenets include: cultural freedom of both the community and the individual; respect for pluralism that extends beyond tolerance to rejoice in different ways of life and creative diversity; recognition that culture is not static but dynamic, building as it does on creativity which fosters evolution and progress; and the ethos of universalism and universal human rights. This vision therefore reflects unity in diversity – a common ethic in a world made up of 10,000 distinct societies, each with its distinct culture, in and across some 200 countries. The report projects culture as a key factor in current global trends such as growing inequality in economic growth, culture and globalization; ethnic conflict; democracy, environment, the rights of minorities and ethnic peoples; and values and gender.

What indicators can denote the progress made towards achieving this vision? Any such image of culture and development is far too complex to be captured by a single indicator. An attempt has to be made to break this down to major areas or dimensions of culture and development. Can culture and development conceivably be reduced to a single perspective? It is clearly more feasible to consider the key recommendations of *Our Creative Diversity* and to identify

Life expectancy as an integrating concept

Following some scholars' proposals for socio-economic accounting, an attempt could be made to trace life expectancy sequences of certain states for the average person in certain categories. Total life expectancy would be divided into segments: time spent at school, at work, at leisure, on vacation, in pensioned (happy) retirement or unpensioned (miserable) retirement. Another sequence might trace how long a new-born child could expect to spend in unemployment (in view of the unemployment rates of the year), and how long in undesirable states such as incapacitation, in hospital, on a psychiatrist's couch, in prison or in unpensioned retirement, based on current experience. It would be possible to trace how long a person is single, married, widowed, divorced; how long healthy, in hospital; how long free, in prison, on parole. For instance, an increase in the number of university students extends the expected time that a child born today will spend at a university, thus reducing his or her expectation of unemployment.

If desired, these periods could be summed into a single welfare (or 'illfare') index that would not be entirely meaningless, being expressed as a ratio of total life expectancy. This could be desegregated for males and females, rich and poor, rural and urban residents, ethnic or religious minorities. Age-specific rates for these states could also be calculated: hours per day or week or month or year spent sleeping, travelling to work, at leisure. One could include the number of children, the number of marriages, etc. Data could be collected on accidents or arrests or burglaries. These would yield numbers over a lifetime.

Even income over average lifetime rather than per annum could combine economic and social (or human) indicators in a meaningful way. A problem with this factor is that, for example, $4 million might show as the result of 80 years' work with an average annual income of $100,000. This trade-off can be misleading: if we wish to build in an indicator of distribution, we should take the mode or the median of average lifetime income instead of the mean income, which would eliminate the skew at the upper end.

One may wish to trace the time spent on various cultural activities such as attending meetings, participating in amateur theatre, dancing, singing, painting, playing games, athletic activities or other cultural activities such as going to the theatre, opera and concert, reading books, visiting museums; possibly not watching television or films – but that is open to discussion. Of particular relevance to the concern of the *World Culture Report* would be research on the comparison of time spent on various cultural activities among different ethnic, language, religious and economic groups.

PAUL STREETEN
Professor Emeritus of
Boston University, Boston,
Consultant to the United Nations
Development Programme (United States)

areas of priority policy concern, bearing in mind that indicators have to send clear messages about policy-relevant trends of public concern.

The question has already been the subject of serious reflection. To begin with, an important UNESCO/UNRISD workshop held in 1996 identified three areas for study, namely, global ethics, cultural vitality, and cultural diversity:[4]

- Global ethics: a core set has been developed in the form of international standards of human rights. The observance of these human rights – civil, political, economic, social and cultural – is a reliable reflection of a society's practice of global ethics.
- Cultural vitality: this can be measured using conventional cultural development indicators of literacy, media content, popular arts and crafts, preservation of cultural heritage, and access to and participation in cultural performances and activities.
- Cultural diversity: access, participation and equity, with special attention to minorities, including protection of minority rights and minority representation in political forums.

Three further issues were recently identified by Arizpe:[5] namely, participation in creative activity; access to culture; and repositioning cultures: conviviality.

- Participation in creative activity: is there equitable participation of all people in cultural expression? McKinley has explored this complex issue in his proposals for a 'cultural empowerment index';[6] it covers not only material creation by individuals, but group activities, creativity in ideas and science and non-institutionalized and non-marketed activities.
- Access to culture: does everyone have access to the creativity of others, and in particular of groups?
- Repositioning cultures: conviviality. Concern with diversity and respect for cultures is a real issue in today's globalizing world where ethnic conflicts are continually breaking out, very many communities live in fear of cultural imperialism and arguments are heard about the trends of cultural homogenization. Arizpe's notion of conviviality could be thought of as affording space for individuals to express their own cultural identity as a key variable in the development process. Identity as a concept is not directly amenable to quantification and measurement. However, it would be possible to examine whether, in the process of development, efforts are being made to protect language, customs, values and other important aspects of cultural identity. A key question to ask is whether cultural rights are being protected or violated.

These six above-mentioned dimensions appear central to make the vision of the concept of culture and development as set out in *Our Creative Diversity* operational. It is important to note that the first three of these refer to development outcomes while the rest refer to development as processes; the former relate to the vision of culture as the end of development and the latter to culture as the social basis of development.

Indicators of culture: the way forward

Future research on indicators should concentrate on further refining these dimensions. Until now, most indicators have related to cultural vitality and especially to the level of achievement in producing cultural goods or engaging in cultural activities. This has had the unfortunate effect of emphasizing the material achievements of creative activities – the 'reification of culture' – and thereby of overlooking culture as a distinct way of living that is underpinned by values and social institutions.

Priority for further research should therefore focus on the other five dimensions, in other words, global ethics, cultural vitality, cultural diversity, participation in creative activity and access to culture and conviviality. The next steps should focus on asking if each of the six dimensions as identified is amenable to quantification and, if so, whether data are available. A good deal of useful data has already appeared in the first issue of the *World Culture Report*. The statistical tables and cultural indicators in that report relate *inter alia* to newspapers, libraries, books, radio, television, cinema, recorded music, performing arts and museums; cultural practices, including tourism and heritage sites; cultural trade and communications; communications and new technologies and cultural trends that focuses on material achievements as well as communications. These all focus on cultural commodities and communications; sixty-two indicators give information on the production or consumption of cultural commodities or services, and nineteen on communications. Only one set of indicators focuses on values: nineteen indicators concern the ratification of human rights treaties.

However useful such indicators may be, they cover but a small part of the indicator requirements for evaluating culture and development.

- They focus on the material achievements of creative activity and expression, i.e. on cultural vitality and participation, thereby giving virtually no information on other dimensions.
- They are limited to capturing institutionalized and marketed commodities and services, thereby ignoring much of the creative achievements of people that are not in the market or in formal institutions.
- They focus on institutionalized and marketed commodities, thereby leading to a distinct wealth bias, as noted by Goldstone.[7]
- They give virtually no information about values, behaviour patterns and social arrangements that ensure respect for identity, participation, access, global ethics and cultural diversity. Only one set of indicators on the ratification of human rights treaties touch on these issues.

In future work on indicators, attention might well be shifted away from material expressions of creativity to focus instead on social arrangements, behaviour patterns and values. These are more central to the message of *Our Creative Diversity* which seeks progress towards respect for all cultures whose values are tolerant of others and that subscribe to a global ethics. Material culture is far removed from this. It may stand in for creativity and collective identity, but not quite adequately. Somewhat more relevant may be social arrangements – formal or informal institutions and policies – that encourage or discourage cultural vitality, cultural diversity, global ethics, participation in creative activity, access to culture and respect for cultural identity.

The debate on cultural indicators has come a long way. Much has already been accomplished under the guidance of the World Commission on Culture and Development and the *World Culture Report* in terms of defining the conceptual framework. The picture of what should constitute the key elements of desirable trends is clearer now than ever before. The debate still has a great deal of ground to cover. The next steps should focus on finding innovative indicators and building tables of the six dimensions so far identified.

Notes

1. A. K. Sen, in UNDP, *Human Development Report*, New York, OUP, 1999.
2. Pérez de Cuéllar, J. (ed.), *Our Creative Diversity*, Report of the World Commission on Culture and Development, Paris, UNESCO, 1995.
3. World Commission on Culture and Development, op.cit.
4. UNESCO/UNRISD, *Towards a World Report on Culture and Development: Constructing Cultural Statistics and Indicators,* Paris, UNESCO/UNRISD, 1997. (Occasional Paper Series on Culture and Development, 1.)
5. Lourdes Arizpe, in conference at the World Bank/UNESCO/Italy Conference on Culture, Panel on measuring culture and development: prospects and limits of constructing cultural indicators.
6. T. McKinley, *Cultural Indicators of Development,* Paris, UNESCO/UNRISD, 1997. (Occasional Paper Series on Culture and Development, 4.)
7. L. Goldstone, 'Cultural Statistics and Poverty', in ECLAC, *Social Dimensions of Economic Development and Productivity,* LC/R.1873, December 1998.

Bibliography

Goldstone, L. 1998. Cultural Statistics and Poverty. In: *ECLAC, Social Dimensions of Economic Development and Productivity*, LC/R.1873, 29 December.

McKinley, T. 1997. *Cultural Indicators of Development.* Paris, UNESCO/ UNRISD. (Occasional Paper Series on Culture and Development, 4.)

Pattanaik, P. 1997. *Cultural Indicators of Well-being: Some Conceptual Issues.* Paris, UNESCO/UNRISD. (Occasional Paper Series on Culture and Development, 2.)

UNDP. 1990–1999. *Human Development Report.* New York, OUP.

UNESCO/UNRISD. 1997. *Towards a World Report on Culture and Development: Constructing Cultural Statistics and Indicators.* Paris, UNESCO/UNRISD. (Occasional Paper Series on Culture and Development, 1.)

Unify the world.
Show us from a child's eye;
The simplicity.

Brianne Barneman

Walking over grass
sand, dirt, mud, concrete – anywhere
all still just walking

Oscar Cuellar

I am beautiful
see me through my mother's eyes
mirror of her love.

Ilivia L. Osceola

All different people,
We are really just the same.
Let's open our eyes

Brianne Barneman

Part Seven
Statistical tables and culture indicators

Introduction

The Introduction to the Statistical Tables and Culture Indicators part of UNESCO's *World Culture Report 1998* drew attention to the limited coverage and depth of those indicators and undertook to try to broader their country coverage and subject depth in the present report. It stated that 'one of the aims of the report is to start a process of broadening those measurable and reported aspects of world culture in the coming years so that subsequent reports will be able to present a more complete picture'.

In the Introduction to the Statistical Tables and Culture Indicators part of the *World Culture Report 2000* we are able to take the first steps to broaden the scope of the culture indicators by presenting six new tables on previously uncharted multicultural areas, owing in large part to the magnificent response of UNESCO Member States to a special questionnaire prepared and issued by the World Culture Report Unit in Spring 1999.

The new tables deal with a number of central multicultural areas not presented in the indicators of the first report but specifically included in the long list of omitted cultural areas. They include: leading languages; leading religions; national festivals; folk and religious festivals; most-visited cultural sites; and most-visited natural sites. They are found in Tables 6 to 11.

The information presented in these tables is based mainly on the replies of Member States to the special UNESCO questionnaire. One hundred countries replied to the questionnaire and we would like to express our thanks to them for their enthusiastic participation in helping to expand the scope of the culture indicators, thus contributing in a highly significant way to the *World Culture Report*.

This positive response by Member States argues in favour of preparing and issuing a special biennial questionnaire on key cultural areas that are still missing as a regular part of the work programme for future *World Culture Reports*. In this way it will be possible in due course to improve the coverage, depth and representativeness of the culture indicators of the report and to redress some imbalances as pointed out in the introduction to the first report.

The indicators in the report are based on data obtained from some twenty international and professional sources. Official government data received and standardized by the United Nations agencies or other international and professional organizations involved were used wherever possible. As stated above in the case of a number of new tables, the data were received directly from UNESCO Member States in response to a special questionnaire. In cases where there were no reliable published official figures, estimates made by the responsible agency were used when available. In some cases the indicators were obtained directly from the responsible international, professional or trade organizations. In other cases the indicators were specially developed by World Statistics Ltd.

For the benefit of the reader, all new tables and new indicators in existing tables are so indicated.

We welcome comments on and criticism of the indicators and their presentation in order to improve them in future *World Culture Reports*.

LEO GOLDSTONE
Director,
World Statistics Ltd. (United States)

Culture indicator tables

Cultural activities and trends

TABLE 1 NEWSPAPERS AND BOOKS
TABLE 2 LIBRARIES AND CULTURAL PAPER
TABLE 3 RADIO AND TELEVISION
TABLE 4 CINEMA AND FILM
TABLE 5 RECORDED MUSIC

Cultural practices and heritage

TABLE 6 LEADING LANGUAGES
TABLE 7 LEADING RELIGIONS
TABLE 8 NATIONAL FESTIVALS
TABLE 9 FOLK AND RELIGIOUS FESTIVALS
TABLE 10 MOST VISITED CULTURAL SITES
TABLE 11 MOST VISITED NATURAL SITES
TABLE 12 WORLD HERITAGE SITES

Ratifications

TABLE 13 UNESCO AND ILO CULTURAL AND LABOUR CONVENTIONS (1999)
TABLE 14 UNITED NATIONS HUMAN RIGHTS CONVENTIONS (1999)

Cultural trade and communication trends

TABLE 15 TRENDS IN CULTURAL TRADE
TABLE 16 DISTRIBUTION OF CULTURAL TRADE BY TYPE
TABLE 17 TOURISM FLOWS
TABLE 18 INTERNATIONAL TOURISM
TABLE 19 COMMUNICATION
TABLE 20 NEW COMMUNICATION TECHNOLOGY

Translations

TABLE 21 TRANSLATIONS AND BOOKS IN FOREIGN LANGUAGES
TABLE 22 TRANSLATIONS BY ORIGINAL LANGUAGE
TABLE 23 MOST FREQUENTLY TRANSLATED AUTHORS

Cultural context

TABLE 24 EDUCATION
TABLE 25 TERTIARY EDUCATION ABROAD
TABLE 26 HUMAN CAPITAL
TABLE 27 DEMOGRAPHIC AND HEALTH
TABLE 28 ECONOMIC
TABLE 29 SOCIAL SECURITY
TABLE 30 ENVIRONMENT AND BIODIVERSITY

INDEX AND SOURCES OF THE CULTURE INDICATORS
LIST OF COUNTRIES BY REGION

Table symbols

*	New table.
-	None or not ratifying.
..	Not available.
(.)	Less than half the unit shown.
1996-98	A dash between two years indicates that the data refer to any one of the years in the period shown.
1995/98	A slash between two years indicates an average for all the years in the period shown.
Note	The indicator tables consist mainly of the 150 countries and territories with a population of 1 million or more; for reasons of space the names of certain regions and countries have had to be abbreviated. Unless otherwise stated, the regional aggregates found at the end of each table are the appropriately weighted values for each regional or development group (see the List of Countries by Region for the composition of each group). Where the summary measure is a total, the letter 'T' appears at the top of the column.

TABLE 1
CULTURAL ACTIVITIES AND TRENDS: NEWSPAPERS AND BOOKS

Country or territory	Daily newspapers (daily circulation per thousand people)		Annual rate of change (%)	Number of copies of books produced (per 100 people)		Book titles published (per 100,000 people)		Literature and art	
	1980	1998	1980/1998	1980	1994-96	1980	1994-96	Books produced as % of total 1994-96	Book titles as % of total 1994-96
Sub-Saharan Africa									
Angola	20	11	-3.3	..	..	..	..	..	100
Benin	(.)	2	..	..	0.7	..	..	7	7
Botswana	21	27	1.4	..	..	..	..	..	..
Burkina Faso	(.)	1	..	..	0.1	..	..	71	..
Burundi	(.)	3	..	..	..	..	..	..	..
Cameroon	8	1	-11	..	..	..	..	..	..
Central African Rep.	..	2	..	..	..	..	..	..	..
Chad	(.)	(.)	..	..	..	..	..	..	..
Congo	2	8	8.0	..	..	..	..	..	..
Congo (Dem. Rep.)	2	3	1.7	0.4	..	..	..	..	..
Côte d' Ivoire	4	17	8.4	..	..	..	..	..	..
Eritrea	..	..	..	..	..	..	..	..	..
Ethiopia	1	2	3.4	0.4	..	0.4	..	..	..
Gabon	22	30	1.7	..	..	..	..	..	..
Gambia	..	2	..	..	0.8	..	1.2	..	..
Ghana	47	14	-6.5	..	..	0.1	..	..	..
Guinea	..	..	..	..	..	..	..	..	..
Guinea-Bissau	8	5	-2.2	..	..	..	..	..	..
Kenya	13	9	-2.0	1.3	..	1.3	(.)	..	8
Lesotho	33	8	-7.6	..	..	..	..	..	..
Liberia	6	16	5.7	..	..	..	..	..	..
Madagascar	6	3	-4.0	..	2.0	4.6	(.)	32	20
Malawi	3	4	1.2	1.2	..	..	1.1	1	..
Mali	(.)	1	..	..	0.3	..	..	79	79
Mauritania	..	1	..	..	..	..	..	..	..
Mauritius	83	76	-0.5	18	15	8.0	7.3	40	48
Mozambique	5	3	-2.2	..	..	..	..	..	..
Namibia	26	19	-1.7	..	..	..	..	..	..
Niger	(.)	(.)	..	0.1	..	..	..	..	..
Nigeria	17	27	2.6	..	..	2.3	(.)	..	14
Rwanda	(.)	(.)	..	..	..	..	..	..	..
Senegal	6	5	-1.3	..	..	..	..	..	..
Sierra Leone	3	5	2.7	..	..	..	..	..	..
Somalia	1	1	0.0	..	..	..	..	..	..
South Africa	51	26	-3.7	..	80	..	..	25	26
Sudan	6	7	1.2	..	..	..	..	..	..
Tanzania (United Rep. of)	11	4	-5.5	..	..	..	..	..	..
Togo	6	4	-2.3	..	..	..	..	..	..
Uganda	2	2	0.0	..	11	..	..	..	..
Zambia	19	4	-8.3	..	..	..	..	..	..
Zimbabwe	19	9	-4.1	..	..	7.5	..	..	..
Arab States									
Algeria	24	38	2.6	6.9	..	2.7	2.2	..	16
Egypt	39	38	-0.1	..	140	..	..	15	30
Iraq	26	20	-1.4	..	..	..	..	..	..
Jordan	23	2	-13	..	..	..	8.1	..	27
Kuwait	222	377	3.0	..	..	..	..	..	..

Country or territory	Daily newspapers (daily circulation per thousand people)		Annual rate of change (%)	Number of copies of books produced (per 100 people)		Book titles published (per 100,000 people)		Literature and art	
								Books produced as % of total	Book titles as % of total
	1980	1998	1980/1998	1980	1994-96	1980	1994-96	1994-96	1994-96
Lebanon	109	59	-3.4	..	..	..	..	..	..
Libyan Arab Jamahiriya	18	14	-1.4	..	..	..	..	..	42
Morocco	14	27	3.7	..	6.7	..	..	26	26
Oman	..	28	..	..	0.9	..	..	..	14
Saudi Arabia	35	59	2.9	..	..	..	..	..	16
Syrian Arab Rep.	13	20	2.4	..	..	1.4	..	..	..
Tunisia	42	31	-1.7	..	..	2.7	(.)	24	36
United Arab Emirates	149	170	0.7	159	208	8.4	13	..	..
Yemen	..	15	..	..	..	..	..	..	..
South Central Asia									
Afghanistan	6	6	0.0	37	..	..	..	..	..
Armenia	..	24	..	..	..	..	11	11	35
Azerbaijan	..	28	..	..	34	..	..	13	55
Bangladesh	3	9	6.1	..	..	..	..	..	..
Bhutan	..	..	..	..	..	..	..	..	..
Georgia	..	..	..	..	16	..	11	..	35
India	21	28	1.6	..	..	3.0	..	..	40
Iran (Islamic Rep. of)	25	26	0.2	..	13	7.6	..	32	4
Kazakhstan	..	..	..	..	..	..	..	6	24
Kyrgyzstan	..	5	..	..	43	..	..	27	23
Nepal	8	11	1.6	..	..	..	..	..	..
Pakistan	12	21	3.2	1.5	..	2.1	..	..	..
Sri Lanka	30	29	-0.2	119	106	13	22	9	13
Tajikistan	..	21	..	..	17	..	2.2	10	27
Turkmenistan	..	..	..	..	..	..	..	33	31
Uzbekistan	..	4	..	..	..	..	4.3	14	29
East Asia									
China	34	36	0.3	496	478	3.2	..	..	14
Hong Kong SAR	714	786	0.5	..	..	..	..	..	..
Japan	567	577	0.1	561	317	37	45	64	39
Korea (Dem. People's Rep. of)	226	199	-0.7	..	..	..	..	..	..
Korea (Rep. of)	210	394	3.6	296	310	93	..	22	35
Mongolia	106	21	-8.6	29	..	51	..	..	..
South-East Asia and Oceania									
Australia	323	168	-3.6	..	..	..	59	..	23
Cambodia	..	..	..	..	..	..	..	..	..
Indonesia	15	24	2.6	..	3.9	3.8	1.9	22	15
Lao People's Dem. Rep.	4	4	0.0	..	19	..	1.7	5	19
Malaysia	59	115	3.8	58	136	17	27	15	25
Myanmar	10	10	0.0	..	..	..	8.2	..	74
New Zealand	314	223	-1.9	..	..	..	..	..	..
Papua New Guinea	9	15	2.9	..	..	..	..	..	..
Philippines	41	66	2.7	..	..	1.7	2.1	..	18
Singapore	286	273	-0.3	..	..	..	..	..	..
Thailand	57	194	7.0	..	..	12	14	..	13
Viet Nam	10	4	-5.0	..	110	..	7.2	5	27

TABLE 1 (continued)

Country or territory	Daily newspapers (daily circulation per thousand people) 1980	1998	Annual rate of change (%) 1980/1998	Number of copies of books produced (per 100 people) 1980	1994-96	Book titles published (per 100,000 people) 1980	1994-96	Literature and art: Books produced as % of total 1994-96	Book titles as % of total 1994-96
Latin America and the Caribbean									
Argentina	142	62	-4.5	52	110	15	27	27	31
Bolivia	42	55	1.5	..	..	..	..	..	..
Brazil	45	46	0.1	377	63	16	13	8	16
Chile	108	98	-0.5	179	..	12	17	..	38
Colombia	49	27	-3.3	124	..	29	..	..	..
Costa Rica	110	88	-1.2	..	..	..	..	..	..
Cuba	108	118	0.5	424	..	20	..	..	..
Dominican Rep.	39	52	1.6	..	..	..	..	..	..
Ecuador	70	70	0.0	..	0.2	..	0.1	89	92
El Salvador	63	48	-1.5	..	..	..	..	..	..
Guatemala	29	33	0.7	..	..	..	..	..	..
Haiti	7	3	-4.3	..	..	..	..	..	..
Honduras	59	55	-0.4	..	..	..	..	..	..
Jamaica	51	3	-15	..	..	..	..	..	..
Mexico	123	97	-1.3	..	..	..	..	..	..
Nicaragua	47	30	-2.5	..	..	..	..	..	..
Panama	56	62	0.6	..	..	..	..	..	..
Paraguay	51	43	-0.9	..	..	..	2.9	..	20
Peru	81	84	0.2	..	7.4	4.1	2.5	18	18
Trinidad and Tobago	143	123	-0.8	..	..	..	..	..	..
Uruguay	240	293	1.1	29	..	29	28	..	29
Venezuela	195	206	0.3	..	32	..	15	21	28
North America									
Canada	221	167	-1.5	..	..	..	65	..	20
United States	270	201	-1.6	..	..	34	25	..	26
Europe									
Albania	54	37	-2.1	244	..	39	..	..	..
Austria	351	402	0.8	..	..	80	99	..	27
Belarus	243	173	-1.9	496	574	34	37	44	32
Belgium	323	158	-3.9	..	..	278	..	..	..
Bosnia and Herzegovina	..	152	..	..	..	..	..	..	..
Bulgaria	253	134	-3.5	672	245	55	58	36	43
Croatia	..	112	..	..	..	..	38	..	20
Czech Rep.	..	171	..	..	..	..	99	..	38
Denmark	366	300	-1.1	..	..	185	233	..	28
Estonia	..	175	..	..	476	..	188	49	40
Finland	505	455	-0.6	..	..	179	252	..	21
France	192	145	-1.5	..	..	70	59	..	38
Germany	..	303	..	..	..	83	87	..	22
Greece	120	64	-3.4	..	..	..	40	..	44
Hungary	247	167	-2.2	..	527	79	91	..	35
Ireland	229	154	-2.2	..	..	..	..	..	..
Israel	258	288	0.6	299	156	..	..	..	..
Italy	101	104	0.2	255	486	24	61	48	36
Latvia	..	106	..	..	322	..	82	18	23
Lithuania	..	93	..	..	403	..	99	..	29

Country or territory	Daily newspapers (daily circulation per thousand people) 1980	1998	Annual rate of change (%) 1980/1998	Number of copies of books produced (per 100 people) 1980	1994-96	Book titles published (per 100,000 people) 1980	1994-96	Literature and art: Books produced as % of total 1994-96	Book titles as % of total 1994-96
Macedonia (former Yugoslav Rep. of)	..	21	..	..	125	..	45	10	32
Moldova (Rep. of)	..	60	..	..	63	..	21	..	15
Netherlands	326	290	-0.6	..	..	95	217	..	17
Norway	463	588	1.3	..	..	135	157	..	47
Poland	236	108	-4.2	548	208	25	36	36	25
Portugal	49	72	2.2	591	273	88	80	14	61
Romania	181	298	2.8	359	171	30	32	30	32
Russian Federation	..	141	..	..	286	..	25	43	25
Slovakia	..	171	..	..	114	..	70	14	28
Slovenia	..	173	..	..	..	..	172	..	32
Spain	93	106	0.7	727	485	86	117	42	33
Sweden	528	430	-1.1	..	..	97	152	..	26
Switzerland	393	377	-0.2	..	..	137	211	..	2
Turkey	56	61	0.5	..	..	15	10	..	35
Ukraine	..	3	..	306	..	18	12	22	24
United Kingdom	417	317	-1.5	..	135	85	183	..	3
Yugoslavia	..	106	..	..	158	..	51	14	36

Regions	Daily newspapers (daily circulation per thousand people) 1980	1998	Annual rate of change (%) 1980/1998	Number of copies of books produced (per 100 people) 1980	1994-96	Book titles published (per 100,000 people) 1980	1994-96	Literature and art: Books produced as % of total 1994-96	Book titles as % of total 1994-96
World	77	78	0.6	..	..	..	..	..	..
Developing	35	40	0.9	..	..	..	..	..	..
Industrial	281	218	-1.0	..	..	51	56	..	27
Developing excl. India/China	41	48	0.9	..	..	..	..	..	..
Industrial excl. US/Rus. Fed.	285	237	-0.7	..	..	58	73	..	27
Sub-Saharan Africa	13	11	0.2	..	..	..	..	..	..
Arab States	33	36	0.6	..	..	..	..	..	..
South Central Asia	..	24	..	..	..	..	..	..	..
East Asia	92	100	0.4	494	458	9.2	..	..	..
South-East Asia/Oceania	39	57	1.6	..	..	..	7.9	..	26
Latin Am./Carib.	82	70	-0.9	..	..	..	..	..	..
North America	265	198	-1.6	..	..	34	29	..	22
Europe	212	169	-0.8	..	..	62	69	..	27

TABLE 2
CULTURAL ACTIVITIES AND TRENDS: LIBRARIES AND CULTURAL PAPER

Country or territory	Registered public library users (per 100 people)	Population served by public libraries (%)	Number of books in public libraries (per 100 people)		Annual rate of change (%)	Cultural paper[1] consumed (metric tons per person)		Annual rate of change (%)
	1994-97	1994-97	1981-83	1994-97	81-83/94-97	1980	1997	1980/1997
Sub-Saharan Africa								
Angola	..	..	..	..	..	0.6	0.3	-4.0
Benin	(.)	10	..	0.6	..	..	..	..
Botswana	..	..	..	..	..	..	..	..
Burkina Faso	(.)	..	..	..	..	..	0.1	..
Burundi	..	..	..	..	..	..	(.)	..
Cameroon	..	..	..	..	..	0.5	0.8	2.8
Central African Rep.	..	..	..	..	..	..	..	..
Chad	..	..	..	..	..	..	..	..
Congo	..	..	3.2	..	..	..	0.3	..
Congo (Dem. Rep.)	..	..	..	..	..	0.1	0.1	0.0
Côte d'Ivoire	..	..	..	..	..	0.6	0.5	-1.1
Eritrea	..	..	..	..	..	..	(.)	..
Ethiopia	..	..	..	..	..	..	0.2	..
Gabon	..	..	..	..	..	..	..	..
Gambia	..	..	11	7.3	-2.6	..	0.2	..
Ghana	..	..	8.7	..	..	0.5	0.6	1.1
Guinea	..	..	..	..	..	..	0.1	..
Guinea-Bissau	..	..	..	..	..	..	0.1	..
Kenya	0.8	6	..	2.1	..	1.2	1.8	2.4
Lesotho	..	..	..	..	..	..	..	..
Liberia	..	..	..	..	..	..	..	..
Madagascar	..	..	..	..	..	0.5	0.3	-3.0
Malawi	0.4	..	..	..	..	..	0.1	..
Mali	..	..	..	..	..	..	0.2	..
Mauritania	..	..	..	..	..	..	0.2	..
Mauritius	..	..	..	..	..	2.2	3.3	2.4
Mozambique	..	..	..	..	..	0.5	(.)	..
Namibia	..	..	..	..	..	..	..	..
Niger	..	..	..	..	..	..	(.)	..
Nigeria	..	33	0.7	..	..	1.0	0.6	-3.0
Rwanda	..	..	..	..	..	..	0.1	..
Senegal	(.)	58	..	0.1	..	0.5	0.2	-5.2
Sierra Leone	..	..	..	..	..	..	0.9	..
Somalia	..	..	..	..	..	..	(.)	..
South Africa	..	..	..	..	..	14	25	3.5
Sudan	..	..	..	..	..	..	0.1	..
Tanzania (United Rep. of)	..	..	..	..	..	0.6	0.5	-1.1
Togo	0.2	25	..	1.2	..	..	0.2	..
Uganda	0.2	..	0.6	..	..	..	0.3	..
Zambia	..	..	..	..	..	16	0.5	-18
Zimbabwe	..	..	..	..	..	3.4	1.9	-3.4
Arab States								
Algeria	..	..	..	..	..	2.2	3.2	2.2
Egypt	..	..	3.0	2.3	-2.0	4.3	3.2	-1.7
Iraq	..	..	..	..	..	..	2.2	..
Jordan	..	..	2.4	..	..	3.3	5.9	3.5
Kuwait	..	..	21	..	..	30	14	-4.4

Country or territory	Registered public library users (per 100 people)	Population served by public libraries (%)	Number of books in public libraries (per 100 people)		Annual rate of change (%)	Cultural paper [1] consumed (metric tons per person)		Annual rate of change (%)
	1994-97	1994-97	1981-83	1994-97	81-83/94-97	1980	1997	1980/1997
Lebanon	..	..	..	..	..	15	18	1.1
Libyan Arab Jamahiriya	..	..	..	..	..	..	0.3	..
Morocco	..	..	..	..	..	1.7	2.3	1.8
Oman	..	..	..	..	..	..	2.1	..
Saudi Arabia	..	..	..	..	..	6.1	6.2	0.1
Syrian Arab Rep.	..	..	..	..	..	3.9	3.0	-1.5
Tunisia	..	12	14	27	4.7	5.4	6.1	0.7
United Arab Emirates	..	..	..	..	..	..	19	..
Yemen	..	..	..	..	..	0.2	0.7	7.6
South Central Asia								
Afghanistan	..	..	..	..	..	..	(.)	..
Armenia	30	..	..	410	..	..	0.3	..
Azerbaijan	37	88	..	415	..	..	0.4	..
Bangladesh	..	..	..	..	..	0.5	1.1	4.7
Bhutan	0.1		..	0.2	..	..	(.)	..
Georgia	49	44	..	613	..	..	0.5	..
India	..	..	..	..	..	1.2	2.2	3.6
Iran (Islamic Rep. of)	45	80	5.6	24	11.1	2.3	3.9	3.2
Kazakhstan	35	94	..	582	..	..	1.2	..
Kyrgyzstan	20	30	..	304	..	..	0.7	..
Nepal	..	..	..	..	..	..	0.1	..
Pakistan	..	..	0.1	..	..	1.0	1.4	2.0
Sri Lanka	..	..	4.9	..	..	2.4	2.8	0.9
Tajikistan	..	..	..	..	..	..	..	..
Turkmenistan	..	..	..	..	..	..	0.1	..
Uzbekistan	..	..	..	..	..	..	0.1	..
East Asia								
China	0.4	..	..	26	..	2.3	7.8	7.4
Hong Kong SAR	30	100	20	74	9.8	37	150	8.6
Japan	20	..	59	155	7.1	57	118	4.4
Korea (Dem. People's Rep. of)	..	..	..	..	..	0.2	0.1	-4.0
Korea (Rep. of)	87	..	3.7	28	15.6	13	57	9.1
Mongolia	..	..	..	..	..	..	0.3	..
South-East Asia and Oceania								
Australia	..	..	..	..	..	64	89	2.0
Cambodia	..	..	..	..	..	..	0.1	..
Indonesia	..	..	..	..	..	1.4	7.1	10.0
Lao People's Dem. Rep.	..	..	..	..	..	..	0.1	..
Malaysia	9.0	..	18	51	7.7	9.3	28	6.7
Myanmar	..	..	..	..	..	0.6	0.6	0.0
New Zealand	..	..	..	..	..	44	53	1.1
Papua New Guinea	..	..	..	..	..	..	0.8	..
Philippines	..	..	2.1	..	..	3.5	5.0	2.1
Singapore	..	..	..	..	..	45	111	5.5
Thailand	..	..	..	..	..	3.7	14	8.1
Viet Nam	..	..	..	17	..	0.5	1.2	5.3

TABLE 2 (continued)

Country or territory	Registered public library users (per 100 people)	Population served by public libraries (%)	Number of books in public libraries (per 100 people)		Annual rate of change (%)	Cultural paper [1] consumed (metric tons per person)		Annual rate of change (%)
	1994-97	1994-97	1981-83	1994-97	81-83/94-97	1980	1997	1980/1997
Latin America and the Caribbean								
Argentina	..	..	..	37	..	16	16	0.0
Bolivia	1.0	..	..	0.6	..	..	1.2	..
Brazil	..	..	..	..	..	8.9	13	2.3
Chile	..	80	5.2	..	..	10	14	2.0
Colombia	..	..	..	..	..	6.3	7.4	1.0
Costa Rica	..	..	2.4	..	..	8.6	8.4	-0.1
Cuba	..	..	28	..	..	8.1	2.8	-6.1
Dominican Rep.	..	..	..	..	..	6.7	6.3	-0.4
Ecuador	..	..	..	..	..	7.0	3.1	-4.7
El Salvador	..	..	..	..	..	40	7.2	-9.6
Guatemala	..	..	..	..	..	3.4	4.2	1.3
Haiti	..	..	..	..	..	..	0.5	..
Honduras	..	..	..	..	..	3.3	7.4	4.9
Jamaica	..	..	52	..	..	4.9	7.3	2.4
Mexico	..	..	3.6	..	..	12	12	0.0
Nicaragua	..	..	..	..	..	1.7	1.1	-2.5
Panama	..	..	..	..	..	3.8	6.7	3.4
Paraguay	..	..	..	..	..	4.4	3.6	-1.2
Peru	..	..	24	..	..	4.7	4.1	-0.8
Trinidad and Tobago	..	..	..	..	..	8.6	19	4.8
Uruguay	..	..	..	..	..	13	11	-1.0
Venezuela	..	40	6.5	14	5.7	16	8.5	-3.7
North America								
Canada	..	100	185	229	1.5	77	95	1.3
United States	..	..	..	..	..	109	146	1.6
Europe								
Albania	..	..	214	..	..	..	6.2	..
Austria	11	99	70	112	3.4	33	73	4.8
Belarus	42	..	905	..	..	..	..	..
Belgium	23	..	245	302	1.5	69	123	3.5
Bosnia and Herzegovina	..	..	..	..	..	..	2.3	..
Bulgaria	11	96	552	491	-0.8	10	7.8	-1.5
Croatia	11	50	..	101	..	..	12	..
Czech Rep.	14	..	..	521	..	..	36	..
Denmark	..	100	576	593	0.2	67	122	3.6
Estonia	29	100	..	75	..	..	38	..
Finland	48	..	489	708	2.7	88	250	6.3
France	..	60	94	153	3.5	50	72	2.2
Germany	..	..	159	182	1.0	..	94	..
Greece	..	..	..	86	..	14	39	6.2
Hungary	13	100	381	429	0.9	18	27	2.4
Ireland	23	100	218	303	2.4	29	80	6.2
Israel	12	84	..	..	..	22	60	6.1
Italy	..	100	25	72	7.9	35	68	4.0
Latvia	..	20	..	623	..	..	18	..
Lithuania	21	20	..	626	..	..	6.4	..

Country or territory	Registered public library users (per 100 people)	Population served by public libraries (%)	Number of books in public libraries (per 100 people)		Annual rate of change (%)	Cultural paper [1] consumed (metric tons per person)		Annual rate of change (%)
	1994-97	1994-97	1981-83	1994-97	81-83/94-97	1980	1997	1980/1997
Macedonia (former Yugoslav Rep. of)	..	48	..	..	..	..	7.0	..
Moldova (Rep. of)	26	33	..	431	..	..	1.6	..
Netherlands	..	97	217	264	1.4	81	94	0.9
Norway	..	100	344	466	2.2	55	90	2.9
Poland	19	89	266	351	2.0	10	21	4.5
Portugal	..	..	54	49	-0.7	11	43	8.3
Romania	8.9	..	270	224	-1.3	6.3	4.7	-1.7
Russian Federation	37	41	..	667	..	..	5.2	..
Slovakia	14	100	..	358	..	..	41	..
Slovenia	22	21	..	308	..	..	32	..
Spain	..	85	31	83	7.3	24	55	5.0
Sweden	..	100	470	520	0.7	98	78	-1.3
Switzerland	..	98	..	383	..	91	120	1.6
Turkey	1.7	50	11	17	3.3	5.2	7.0	1.8
Ukraine	39	39	742	662	-0.8	..	3.7	..
United Kingdom	57	100	233	225	-0.3	54	113	4.4
Yugoslavia	63	97	..	132	..	..	5.8	..

Region	Registered public library users (per 100 people)	Population served by public libraries (%)	Number of books in public libraries (per 100 people)		Annual rate of change (%)	Cultural paper [1] consumed (metric tons per person)		Annual rate of change (%)
	1994-97	1994-97	1981-83	1994-97	81-83/94-97	1980	1997	1980/1997
World	..	..	..	..	..	14	21	3.9
Developing	..	..	..	..	..	3.1	6.0	4.2
Industrial	28	70	191	294	3.2	62	78	2.8
Developing excl. India/China	..	..	..	..	..	4.7	6.6	2.4
Industrial excl. US/Rus. Fed.	25	78	191	224	3.2	42	68	3.3
Sub-Saharan Africa	..	..	..	..	..	..	2.2	..
Arab States	..	..	..	..	..	3.9	3.6	0.7
South Central Asia	..	..	..	..	..	..	2.0	..
East Asia	5	..	43	38	9.4	7.5	19	7.1
South-East Asia/Oceania	..	..	..	..	..	5.0	11	6.5
Latin Am./Carib.	..	..	..	..	..	10	10	0.2
North America	..	100	185	229	1.5	106	141	1.6
Europe	30	..	221	320	2.4	34	47	3.2

1. Newsprint other printing and writing paper

TABLE 3
CULTURAL ACTIVITIES AND TRENDS: RADIO AND TELEVISION

Country or territory	Radios (per thousand people)		Annual rate of change (%)	Televisions (per thousand people)		Annual rate of change (%)	Radios per televisions		Cultural radio programmes (% of total programmes)	Cultural television programmes (% of total programmes)
	1980	1997	1980/97	1980	1997	1980/97	1980	1997	1989-94	1989-94
Sub-Saharan Africa										
Angola	21	54	10.5	4.3	13	13.5	4.9	4.2	..	..
Benin	66	110	4.4	1.4	11	45.7	47	10	1.1	..
Botswana	99	154	3.7	..	20	..	..	7.7	3.3	..
Burkina Faso	18	34	5.2	2.9	9.1	14.3	6.2	3.7	12.6	8.3
Burundi	39	69	4.5	..	3.9	..	..	18	2.1	8.0
Cameroon	88	163	5.7	..	32	..	..	5.1	..	..
Central African Rep.	52	83	3.5	0.2	5.3	..	260	16	..	..
Chad	168	248	3.2	..	1.4	..	..	177	5.4	10.6
Congo	90	126	2.7	2.2	12	29.7	41	11	6.4	19.2
Congo (Dem. Rep.)	193	376	5.6	0.4	135	..	483	2.8	20.2	2.2
Côte d' Ivoire	122	161	2.1	38	64	4.0	3.2	2.5	5.1	4.9
Eritrea	..	100	..	..	0.4	..	..	250	..	..
Ethiopia	168	202	1.2	0.8	5.5	..	210	37	5.2	0.2
Gabon	152	183	1.4	14	55	17.2	11	3.3	..	..
Gambia	114	165	3.0	..	3.6	..	..	46	..	..
Ghana	157	236	3.4	5.3	93	110	30	2.5	1.1	0.7
Guinea	30	49	4.2	1.3	12	54.9	23	4.1	..	..
Guinea-Bissau	31	43	2.6	..	..	..	..	..	..	..
Kenya	39	108	11.8	3.7	26	35.5	11	4.2	..	..
Lesotho	25	52	7.2	..	27	..	..	1.9	..	..
Liberia	179	329	5.6	11	29	10.9	16	11	..	..
Madagascar	180	209	0.9	5.1	22	19.5	35	9.5	25.8	4.8
Malawi	186	258	2.3	..	..	..	..	..	9.3	..
Mali	15	55	17.8	..	4.3	..	..	13	..	..
Mauritania	129	146	0.8	..	25	..	..	5.8	..	..
Mauritius	269	371	2.5	95	228	9.3	2.8	1.6	..	..
Mozambique	21	40	5.3	0.2	4.9	..	105	8.2	16.1	5.2
Namibia	117	143	1.3	4.9	37	43.7	..	3.9	..	..
Niger	45	70	3.3	0.9	13	..	50	5.4	10.0	16.0
Nigeria	107	226	7.4	8.4	66	45.7	13	3.4	..	..
Rwanda	34	101	13.1	..	0.1	..	..	..	..	..
Senegal	99	141	2.8	1.4	41	189	71	3.4	5.7	6.3
Sierra Leone	176	253	2.9	6.2	12	5.5	28	21	..	..
Somalia	19	53	11.9	..	15	..	..	3.5	..	..
South Africa	290	355	1.5	73	134	5.6	4.0	2.6	..	..
Sudan	225	272	1.2	43	86	6.7	5.2	3.2	10.5	10.0
Tanzania (United Rep. of)	81	280	16.4	0.4	3.3	42.6	203	85	..	9.7
Togo	203	219	0.5	3.8	17	20.4	53	13	..	4.2
Uganda	100	130	1.8	5.5	16	11.2	18	8.1	..	..
Zambia	56	120	6.7	10	32	14.7	5.6	3.8	..	..
Zimbabwe	34	102	13.3	10	33	15.3	3.4	3.1	1.6	..
Arab States										
Algeria	197	242	1.5	52	105	6.8	3.8	2.3	..	..
Egypt	137	317	8.8	32	119	16.0	4.3	2.7	18.9	..
Iraq	161	229	2.8	50	83	4.4	3.2	2.8	2.6	..
Jordan	188	271	2.9	59	82	2.6	3.2	3.3	..	..
Kuwait	284	678	9.2	257	505	6.4	1.1	1.3	8.5	13.7

Country or territory	Radios (per thousand people) 1980	Radios (per thousand people) 1997	Annual rate of change (%) 1980/97	Televisions (per thousand people) 1980	Televisions (per thousand people) 1997	Annual rate of change (%) 1980/97	Radios per televisions 1980	Radios per televisions 1997	Cultural radio programmes (% of total programmes) 1989-94	Cultural television programmes (% of total programmes) 1989-94
Lebanon	749	907	1.4	281	375	2.2	2.7	2.4	..	..
Lybyan Arab Jamahiriya	158	259	4.3	61	140	7.6	2.6	1.9	..	..
Morocco	155	247	4.0	46	115	10.0	3.4	2.1	..	..
Oman	487	607	1.6	31	694	143	16	0.9	18.5	12.6
Saudi Arabia	260	321	1.6	219	262	1.3	1.2	1.2	..	2.5
Syrian Arab Rep.	195	278	2.8	44	70	3.5	4.4	4.0	..	..
Tunisia	155	224	3.0	47	100	7.5	3.3	2.2	..	..
United Arab Emirates	236	355	3.4	84	134	4.0	2.8	2.6	17	9.5
Yemen	..	64	..	..	29	..	..	2.2	5.6	11.7
South Central Asia										
Afghanistan	75	132	4.5	2.8	13	24.3	27	10	5.2	..
Armenia	..	239	..	..	232	..	..	1.0	15.8	11.2
Azerbaijan	..	23	..	..	22	..	..	1.0	..	..
Bangladesh	17	50	11.4	0.9	6.3	..	19	7.9	..	5.3
Bhutan	12	19	3.6	..	5.5	..	..	3.5	..	..
Georgia	..	590	..	..	..	..	..	..	..	7.8
India	38	120	14.4	4.4	65	81.0	8.6	1.8	..	8.1
Iran (Islamic Rep. of)	163	263	3.6	51	71	2.6	3.2	3.7	30.5	16.2
Kazakhstan	..	395	..	..	237	..	..	1.7	..	..
Kyrgyzstan	..	113	..	..	45	..	..	2.5	..	..
Nepal	21	38	4.8	..	5.8	..	..	6.6	8.2	..
Pakistan	64	94	3.1	11	22	6.7	5.8	4.3	1.2	3.6
Sri Lanka	101	211	6.4	2.4	84	200	42	2.5	17.3	0.3
Tajikistan	..	143	..	..	3.4	..	..	42	..	..
Turkmenistan	..	289	..	..	194	..	..	1.5	..	..
Uzbekistan	..	405	..	..	276	..	..	1.5	..	..
East Asia										
China	95	335	16.8	9.0	321	204	11	1.0	..	..
Hong Kong SAR	506	684	2.3	221	283	1.7	2.3	2.4	..	..
Japan	678	956	2.7	539	686	1.6	1.3	1.4	..	..
Korea (Dem. People's Rep. of)	99	146	2.8	7.4	52	40.2	13	2.8	..	..
Korea (Rep. of)	944	1 039	0.7	165	348	6.5	5.7	3.0	35.5	25.1
Mongolia	96	142	3.2	3.4	47	85.5	28	3.0	..	..
South-East Asia and Oceania										
Australia	1 098	1 391	1.8	384	554	2.6	2.9	2.5	1.6	0.1
Cambodia	92	128	2.3	5.4	9.0	4.4	17	14	..	..
Indonesia	119	155	1.8	20	68	16.0	6.0	2.3	..	..
Lao People's Dem. Rep.	109	145	1.9	..	10	..	..	15	..	..
Malaysia	411	434	0.3	87	172	5.7	4.7	2.5	..	..
Syrian Arab Rep.	23	96	18.7	(.)	5.9	..	..	16	..	..
New Zealand	885	997	0.8	332	512	3.6	2.7	1.9	2.3	1.4
Papua New Guinea	58	91	3.8	..	9.3	..	..	10	..	..
Philippines	124	161	1.8	22	52	9.1	5.6	3.1	..	..
Singapore	373	744	5.9	306	388	1.8	1.2	1.9	..	..
Thailand	140	234	3.9	21	254	74.0	6.7	0.9	..	..
Viet Nam	93	107	1.0	34	47	..	..	2.3	..	..

TABLE 3 (continued)

Country or territory	Radios (per thousand people) 1980	Radios (per thousand people) 1997	Annual rate of change (%) 1980/97	Televisions (per thousand people) 1980	Televisions (per thousand people) 1997	Annual rate of change (%) 1980/97	Radios per televisions 1980	Radios per televisions 1997	Cultural radio programmes (% of total programmes) 1989-94	Cultural television programmes (% of total programmes) 1989-94
Latin America and the Caribbean										
Argentina	427	681	4.0	183	223	1.5	2.3	3.1	10.5	5.3
Bolivia	523	673	1.9	56	116	7.1	9.3	5.8	0.2	..
Brazil	312	434	2.6	123	223	5.4	2.5	1.9	..	..
Chile	292	354	1.4	110	215	5.6	2.7	1.6	6.1	..
Colombia	116	524	23.4	79	115	3.0	1.5	4.6	..	7.1
Costa Rica	201	261	2.0	68	140	7.1	3.0	1.9	..	..
Cuba	300	352	1.2	131	239	4.8	2.3	1.5	23.7	9.8
Dominican Rep.	158	178	0.8	70	95	2.4	2.3	1.9	..	..
Ecuador	305	348	0.9	63	130	7.1	4.8	2.7	..	..
El Salvador	338	465	2.5	65	..	..	..	..	8.0	15.0
Guatemala	51	79	3.7	26	61	7.9	2.0	1.3	..	..
Haiti	19	53	10.5	2.9	4.8	4.4	6.6	11	..	..
Honduras	140	410	12.9	18	95	25.2	7.8	4.3	..	..
Jamaica	375	483	1.9	80	183	8.6	4.7	2.6	..	..
Mexico	133	329	9.8	57	272	22.2	2.3	1.2	..	..
Nicaragua	229	265	1.0	55	68	1.6	4.2	3.9	..	..
Panama	154	299	6.3	115	187	4.2	1.3	1.6	..	..
Paraguay	112	182	4.2	22	101	23.9	5.1	1.8	..	..
Peru	159	273	4.8	52	126	9.5	3.1	2.2	..	..
Trinidad and Tobago	277	533	6.2	194	333	4.2	1.4	1.6	..	..
Uruguay	559	603	0.5	126	239	6.0	4.4	2.5	..	..
Venezuela	391	472	1.4	113	180	3.5	3.5	2.6	..	..
North America										
Canada	721	1 067	3.2	432	710	3.8	1.7	1.5	..	0.4
United States	1 973	2 116	0.5	676	806	1.1	2.9	2.6	..	..
Europe										
Albania	150	259	4.8	36	129	15.2	4.2	2.0	22.5	5.8
Austria	507	751	3.2	391	395	0.1	1.3	1.9	19.3	7.9
Belarus	228	292	1.7	218	311	2.8	..	0.9	4.9	5.0
Belgium	731	797	0.6	387	396	0.1	1.9	2.0	3.0	6.4
Bosnia and Herzegovina	..	267	..	..	..	..	..	..	..	..
Bulgaria	395	537	2.4	243	386	3.9	1.6	1.4	3.9	3.5
Croatia	..	337	..	..	272	..	..	1.2	2.6	4.1
Czech Rep.	..	803	..	..	330	..	..	2.4	5.2	14.8
Denmark	927	1 145	1.6	498	453	-0.6	1.9	2.5	16.6	13.2
Estonia	..	..	..	..	418	..	..	..	9.4	7.2
Finland	837	1 498	5.3	414	423	0.1	2.0	3.5	0.3	5.7
France	741	946	1.8	353	382	0.5	2.1	2.5	5.5	20.9
Germany	774	948	1.5	464	454	-0.1	1.7	2.1	..	4.2
Greece	343	475	2.6	171	311	4.8	2.0	1.5	1.5	4.0
Hungary	499	690	2.6	310	366	1.1	1.6	1.9	4.7	7.7
Ireland	375	697	5.7	231	297	1.7	1.6	2.3	1.5	4.2
Israel	245	524	7.6	232	288	1.4	1.1	1.8	..	..
Italy	602	880	3.1	390	334	-0.8	1.5	2.6	34.9	16.2
Latvia	..	715	..	..	..	..	..	..	..	..
Lithuania	..	513	..	..	..	..	..	..	..	..

Country or territory	Radios (per thousand people) 1980	1997	Annual rate of change (%) 1980/97	Televisions (per thousand people) 1980	1997	Annual rate of change (%) 1980/97	Radios per televisions 1980	1997	Cultural radio programmes (% of total programmes) 1989-94	Cultural television programmes (% of total programmes) 1989-94
Macedonia (former Yugoslav Rep. of)	..	206	..	..	257	..	..	0.8	0.3	2.1
Moldova (Rep. of)	..	736	..	..	288	..	..	2.6	10.3	2.5
Netherlands	650	980	3.4	399	427	0.5	1.6	2.3	..	12.7
Norway	661	917	2.6	350	432	1.4	1.9	2.1	6.2	8.7
Poland	298	522	5.0	246	300	1.5	1.2	1.7	12.6	8.9
Portugal	170	306	5.3	158	303	5.4	1.1	1.0	25.1	0.8
Romania	252	319	1.8	180	204	0.9	1.4	1.6	7.2	12.2
Russian Federation	..	417	..	..	311	..	..	1.3	..	..
Slovakia	..	581	..	..	333	..	..	1.7	1.8	..
Slovenia	..	403	..	..	356	..	..	1.1	1.2	3.7
Spain	258	331	1.9	253	306	1.2	1.0	1.1	..	5.5
Sweden	842	932	0.7	461	438	-0.3	1.8	2.1	5.4	27.5
Switzerland	813	979	1.4	364	411	0.8	2.2	2.4	5.0	7.2
Turkey	113	178	3.8	79	330	18.7	1.4	0.5	2.1	10.3
Ukraine	579	882	3.5	255	314	1.6	2.3	2.8	..	..
United Kingdom	950	1 443	3.5	401	408	0.1	2.4	3.5	..	..
Yugoslavia	..	296	..	..	198	..	..	1.5	4.2	2.5

Region	Radios (per thousand people) 1980	1997	Annual rate of change (%) 1980/97	Televisions (per thousand people) 1980	1997	Annual rate of change (%) 1980/97	Radios per televisions 1980	1997
World	274	416	8.5	105	225	73.4	13.4	3.8
Developing	117	244	10.3	25	153	92.0	16.2	4.2
Industrial	854	1 046	2.2	438	496	2.2	2.0	2.0
Developing excl. India/China	162	248	5.1	44	100	19.8	23.1	6.9
Industrial excl. US/Rus. Fed.	591	804	2.8	354	426	2.6	1.7	1.9
Sub-Saharan Africa	120	193	5.8	13	44	35.2	74.3	16.6
Arab States	189	278	4.5	66	127	10.4	3.7	2.4
South Central Asia	49	127	11.6	..	60	..	..	3.1
East Asia	174	409	14.8	61	348	176.5	10.0	1.2
South-East Asia/Oceania	162	216	3.3	40	103	21.8	6.0	3.9
Latin Am./Carib.	250	408	6.0	95	198	8.8	2.8	2.4
North America	1 847	2 011	0.8	651	796	1.4	2.8	2.5
Europe	490	684	2.6	310	346	2.8	1.7	1.9

TABLE 4
CULTURAL ACTIVITIES AND TRENDS: CINEMA AND FILM

Country or territory	Annual cinema attendance (per person)		Percentage change (%)	Cinema screens[1] (per million people)	Number of feature films produced	Of which co-produced	Number of feature films imported	Imported feature films (as % of total films distributed)	Major country of origin of imported films[1]	
	1981-85	1994-98	81-85/94-98	1998	1994-98	1994-98	1994-98	1994-98	First country 1994-98	Second country 1994-98
Sub-Saharan Africa										
Angola	0.9	0.4	-56	..	..	..	..	..	..	..
Benin	0.4	0.1	-44	(.)	..	..	219	..	India	US
Botswana	..	..	..	..	..	..	..	..	..	..
Burkina Faso	0.6	0.7	17	..	..	..	197	..	..	..
Burundi	..	..	..	..	..	..	50	..	..	..
Cameroon	..	..	..	(.)	..	..	..	..	..	..
Central African Rep.	..	..	..	..	..	..	..	..	..	..
Chad	..	..	..	..	..	..	..	..	..	..
Congo	..	..	..	(.)	..	..	43	..	France	US
Congo (Dem. Rep.)	..	..	..	..	..	..	..	..	..	..
Côte d' Ivoire	0.9	0.6	-33	(.)	2	2	152	99	US	India
Eritrea	..	..	..	..	..	..	..	..	..	..
Ethiopia	..	..	..	1	1	..	65	98	..	..
Gabon	2.2	1.6	-27	..	..	..	53	..	US[2]	France
Gambia	..	..	..	..	..	..	..	..	..	..
Ghana	..	..	..	..	..	..	36	..	..	..
Guinea	..	..	..	..	1	1	..	..	US[2]	India
Guinea-Bissau	..	..	..	..	..	..	..	..	..	..
Kenya	0.6	0.6	0	(.)	..	..	..	..	India[2]	US
Lesotho	..	..	..	..	..	..	118	..	..	..
Liberia	..	..	..	..	..	..	..	..	..	..
Madagascar	..	(.)	..	..	..	..	19	..	US[2]	Hong Kong SAR
Malawi	..	..		..	..	..	124	..	..	..
Mali	..	..	..	..	3	2	..	..	..	..
Mauritania	..	..	..	..	..	..	..	..	..	..
Mauritius	..	0.7	..	..	..	..	50	..	France[2]	India
Mozambique	..	..	..	..	..	..	121	..	..	..
Namibia	..	..	..	..	..	..	96	..	..	..
Niger	..	..	..	..	..	..	..	..	..	..
Nigeria	..	..	..	..	..	..	..	..	..	..
Rwanda	0.1	..	..	(.)	..	..	..	..	..	..
Senegal	..	..	..	..	..	..	..	..	..	..
Sierra Leone	..	..	..	..	..	..	..	..	..	..
Somalia	..	..	..	..	..	..	..	..	..	..
South Africa	..	0.8	..	18	10	..	..	..	..	..
Sudan	..	..	..	..	..	..	70	..	..	..
Tanzania (United Rep. of)	0.2	0.1	-50	(.)	..	..	71	..	India[2]	US
Togo	..	..	..	..	..	..	..	..	..	..
Uganda	..	..	..	..	..	..	171	..	..	..
Zaire	..	..	..	..	..	..	..	..	..	..
Zambia	..	..	..	..	..	..	..	..	..	..
Zimbabwe	..	0.2	..	(.)	..	..	215	..	US[2]	UK
Arab States										
Algeria	1.2	0.9	-25	..	3	0	..	..	..	..
Egypt	1.2	0.3	-75	..	16	..	220	93	US[2]	Italy
Iraq	..	..	..	..	..	..	277	..	..	..
Jordan	..	(.)	..	10	..	..	271	..	US[2]	Hong Kong SAR
Kuwait	0.6	0.5	-17	3	..	..	229	..	..	..

Country or territory	Annual cinema attendance (per person) 1981-85	Annual cinema attendance (per person) 1994-98	Percentage change (%) 81-85/94-98	Cinema screens[1] (per million people) 1998	Number of feature films produced 1994-98	Of which co-produced 1994-98	Number of feature films imported 1994-98	Imported feature films (as % of total films distributed) 1994-98	Major country of origin of imported films[1]: First country 1994-98	Major country of origin of imported films[1]: Second country 1994-98
Lebanon	..	..	..	..	5	4	277	98	US[2]	..
Libyan Arab Jamahiriya	..	..	..	..	..	..	..	..	..	..
Morocco	1.5	0.6	-60	7	3	..	394	99	US	India
Oman	..	..	..	..	..	..	..	..	..	..
Saudi Arabia	..	..	..	..	..	..	..	..	..	..
Syrian Arab Rep.	1.1	0.3	-72	..	1	..	122	99	US	..
Tunisia	..	..	..	..	2	..	..	..	..	..
United Arab Emirates	..	..	..	..	..	..	..	..	..	..
Yemen	..	..	..	5	..	..	44	..	..	..
South Central Asia										
Afghanistan	..	..	..	..	..	..	..	..	..	..
Armenia	..	..	..	..	3	1	28	90	US	Russia
Azerbaijan	..	0.4	..	86	4	1	5	56	Russia	India
Bangladesh	..	..	..	..	77	..	..	..	..	..
Bhutan	..	..	..	..	..	..	..	..	..	..
Georgia	..	1.1	..	..	5	0	39	89	US	France
India	6.4	2.9	-55	14	693	..	141	17	US[2]	UK
Iran (Islamic Rep. of)	0.6	0.4	-33	4	60	..	73	55	Japan	Russia
Kazakhstan	..	0.4	..	..	10	0	51	84	US	India
Kyrgyzstan	..	0.1	..	..	..	..	65	..	US[2]	Russia
Nepal	..	..	..	..	..	..	..	..	..	..
Pakistan	..	0.8	..	..	64	..	134	68	US[2]	Hong Kong SAR
Sri Lanka	2.3	1.5	-34	(.)	58	1	61	51	US[2]	India
Tajikistan	..	0.1	..	(.)	1	0	145	99	India	Russia
Turkmenistan	..	..	..	..	..	..	..	..	India	US
Uzbekistan	..	1.3	..	(.)	10	..	53	84	..	..
East Asia										
China	..	0.1	..	53	82	6	..	..	..	..
Hong Kong SAR	..	3.3	..	30	92	20	177	66	US[2]	Japan
Japan	1.3	1.2	-8	16	249	8	352	59	US[2]	France
Korea (Dem. People's Rep. of)	..	..	..	..	..	..	..	..	..	..
Korea (Rep. of)	1.4	1.0	-29	12	43	0	347	89	US[2]	Hong Kong SAR
Mongolia	..	..	..	..	..	..	..	..	..	..
South-East Asia and Oceania										
Australia	..	4.3	..	86	38	1	239	86	US[2]	UK
Cambodia	..	..	..	..	..	..	268	..	..	..
Indonesia	..	1.1	..	11	15	..	150	91	..	..
Lao People's Dem. Rep.	..	0.4	..	(.)	..	..	101	..	Hong Kong SAR	..
Malaysia	..	0.7	..	16	8	..	..	..	..	..
Myanmar	..	..	..	4	..	..	..	..	..	..
New Zealand	..	4.2	..	78	7	0	124	95	US[2]	UK
Papua New Guinea	..	..	..	..	..	..	..	..	..	..
Philippines	..	1.4	..	14	200	..	235	54	..	..
Singapore	..	4.6	..	46	7	..	..	..	..	..
Thailand	..	0.4	..	6	30	..	219	88	..	..
Viet Nam	5.8	..	..	..	..	..	179	..	..	..

TABLE 4 (continued)

Country or territory	Annual cinema attendance (per person)		Percentage change (%)	Cinema screens[1] (per million people)	Number of feature films produced	Of which co-produced	Number of feature films imported	Imported feature films (as % of total films distributed)	Major country of origin of imported films[1]	
									First country	Second country
	1981-85	1994-98	81-85/94-98	1998	1994-98	1994-98	1994-98	1994-98	1994-98	1994-98
Latin America and the Caribbean										
Argentina	2.1	0.9	-57	23	34	6	200	85	..	..
Bolivia	..	0.4	..	..	4	1	149	97	US[2]	Hong Kong China
Brazil	..	0.8	..	11	40	..	..	..	..	..
Chile	1.0	0.6	-40	11	4	2	220	98	US[2]	UK
Colombia	2.4	0.5	-79	8	1	..	418	100	..	..
Costa Rica	0.9	0.5	-44	..	..	..	49	..	US[2]	UK
Cuba	7.6	2.2	-71	..	6	3	55	90	US	..
Dominican Rep.	..	0.6		..	..	..	173	..	..	..
cuador	2.0	0.4	-80	..	1	0	203	100	US[2]	..
El Salvador	..	..	..	..	..	..	200	..	US[2]	France
Guatemala	1.0	0.9	-10	..	..	..	182	..	..	..
Haiti	..	..	..	..	..	..	..	..	..	..
Honduras	..	..	..	..	..	..	..	..	..	..
Jamaica	..	0.8	..	..	..	..	..	..	..	..
Mexico	3.9	1.1	-72	24	7	2	268	97	US[2]	Italy
Nicaragua	..	..	..	..	..	..	..	..	..	..
Panama	..	3.4	..	..	..	..	..	..	..	..
Paraguay	..	1.1	..	5	..	..	..	..	..	..
Peru	..	2.5	..	..	3	..	211	99	..	..
Trinidad and Tobago	..	1.1	..	..	..	..	50	..	US[2]	India
Uruguay	..	0.8	..	20	..	..	..	..	..	..
Venezuela	0.8	0.4	-50	14	10	2	171	94	US[2]	France
North America										
Canada	4.1	3.5	-15	81	60	28	1 115	95	US[2]	France
United States	4.4	5.4	22	128	661	9	477	42	..	..
Europe										
Albania	..	..		..	..	..	..	..	..	..
Austria	2.0	1.9	-5	56	12	5	219	95	US[2]	Germany
Belarus	..	1.2	..	..	2	1	73	97	Russia	..
Belgium	1.8	2.3	28	49	7	6	477	99	US	France
Bosnia and Herzegovina	..	..	..	..	..	..	..	..	..	..
Bulgaria	..	0.3	..	13	3	1	200	99	US[2]	France
Croatia	4.6	0.7	-85	33	4	..	33	89	US[2]	Germany
Czech Rep.	..	0.9	..	70	16	..	109	87	US[2]	France
Denmark	2.2	2.1	-5	63	18	12	150	89	US[2]	UK
Estonia	..	0.7	..	74	1	1	85	99	US[2]	France
Finland	1.4	1.2	-14	65	8	7	131	94	US[2]	UK
France	3.1	2.9	-6	81	183	81	235	56	US[2]	UK
Germany	2.8	1.5	-46	51	119	..	197	62	US[2]	UK
Greece	..	1.1	..	27	20	10	148	88	US[2]	France
Hungary	6.6	2.1	-68	61	11	..	203	95	US	Italy
Ireland	3.3	3.2	-3	71	25	..	137	85	..	..
Israel	..	1.8	..	51	13	..	152	92	US[2]	France
Italy	2.2	2.1	-5	44	92	13	331	78	US[2]	France
Latvia	..	0.5	..	43	2	..	247	99	..	..
Lithuania	..	0.2	..	48	3	1	174	98	US[2]	France

Country or territory	Annual cinema attendance (per person) 1981-85	Annual cinema attendance (per person) 1994-98	Percentage change (%) 81-85/94-98	Cinema screens[1] (per million people) 1998	Number of feature films produced 1994-98	Of which co-produced 1994-98	Number of feature films imported 1994-98	Imported feature films (as % of total films distributed) 1994-98	Major country of origin of imported films[1] First country 1994-98	Major country of origin of imported films[1] Second country 1994-98
Macedonia (former Yugoslav Rep. of)	..	0.1	..	7	1	0	..	..	US[2]	France
Moldova (Rep. of)	..	0.3	..	..	6	2	108	95	US[2]	France
Netherlands	1.1	1.3	18	31	18	5	173	91	US[2]	France
Norway	3.1	2.7	-13	89	14	5	171	92	US[2]	France
Poland	2.9	0.5	-82	22	14	4	126	90	US[2]	France
Portugal	2.0	1.4	-30	36	10	..	195	95	US[2]	UK
Romania	8.4	0.3	-96	17	..	..	101	..	US[2]	France
Russian Federation	..	0.3	..	11	65	..	118	64	US[2]	Italy
Slovakia	..	0.7	..	55	1	1	121	99	US[2]	UK
Slovenia	..	1.4	..	54	3	..	96	97	US[2]	France
Spain	2.6	2.7	4	75	65	18	346	84	US[2]	Germany
Sweden	2.0	1.8	-10	131	20	7	203	91	US[2]	France
Switzerland	2.8	2.2	-21	76	29	11	359	93	US[2]	France
Turkey	0.5	0.3	-40	8	63	..	131	68	..	..
Ukraine	..	0.6	..	..	5	..	164	97	US[2]	Russia
United Kingdom	..	2.3	..	45	87	..	240	73	..	..
Yugoslavia	3.3	0.4	-88	12	6	4	131	96	US[2]	France

1. New indicator
2. More than half the imported films.

Region	Annual cinema attendance (per person) 1981-85	Annual cinema attendance (per person) 1994-98	Percentage change (%) 81-85/94-98	Cinema screens (per million people) 1998	Number of feature films produced 1994-98	Of which co-produced 1994-98	Number of feature films imported 1994-98	Imported feature films (as % of total films distributed 1994-98
World	..	1.4	..	..	3 580	..	17 115	..
Developing	..	1.1	..	..	1 619	..	8 724	..
Industrial	3.1	2.3	-10.8	59	1 961	241	8 391	60
Developing excl. India/China	..	..	..	..	844	..	8 583	..
Industrial excl. US/Rus. Fed.	2.5	1.6	-25.7	44	1 235	232	7 796	76
Sub-Saharan Africa	..	..	..	..	..	..	..	..
Arab States	..	..	..	..	..	..	1 834	..
South Central Asia	..	2.4	..	..	985	..	795	24
East Asia	..	0.2	..	48	466	34	876	63
South-East Asia/Oceania	..	1.2	..	14	305	..	1 515	..
Latin Am./Carib.	..	0.9	..	..	..	..	2 549	..
North America	4.4	5.2	18.3	123	721	37	1 592	51
Europe	2.7	1.3	-30.9	39	946	195	6 084	77

TABLE 5
CULTURAL ACTIVITIES AND TRENDS: RECORDED MUSIC

Country or territory	A leading popular music artist*	Recorded music sales (US$ per capita) [1]	Distribution by type of music			Piracy (%)	Combined tax rates [2] (%)	CD players (per 100 households)
			Domestic popular (%)	International popular (%)	Classical (%)			
		1998	1998	1998	1998	1997-98	1998	1998
Sub-Saharan Africa								
Angola	Waldemar Bastos	..	..	..	..	..	..	..
Benin	Angelique Kidjo	..	..	..	..	..	..	..
Botswana	Steve Kulhman	..	..	..	..	..	..	..
Burkina Faso	..	..	..	..	..	..	..	..
Burundi	..	..	..	..	..	..	..	..
Cameroon	Manu Dibango	..	..	..	..	..	..	..
Cape Verde	Cesaria Evora	..	..	..	..	..	..	..
Central African Rep.	..	..	..	..	..	..	..	..
Chad	..	..	..	..	..	..	..	..
Congo	Bantous de la Capitale	..	..	..	..	..	..	..
Congo (Dem. Rep.)	..	..	..	..	..	..	..	..
Côte d'Ivoire	Serge Kassy	..	..	..	..	50	..	..
Eritrea	..	..	..	..	..	..	..	..
Ethiopia	Aster Aweke	..	..	..	..	..	..	..
Gabon	Pierre Akendengwe	..	..	..	..	..	..	..
Gambia	Foday Mus Soso	..	..	..	..	..	..	..
Ghana	E.T. Mensah	1.3	71	29	(.)	15	18	..
Guinea	Bembeya Jazz	..	..	..	..	..	..	..
Guinea-Bissau	..	..	..	..	..	..	..	..
Kenya	Kabaka	0.1	34	66	(.)	75	15	(.)
Lesotho	..	..	..	..	..	..	..	..
Liberia	..	..	..	..	..	..	..	..
Madagascar	Hanitra Andriamala Harijauna	..	..	..	..	..	..	..
Malawi	..	..	..	..	..	..	..	..
Mali	Salif Keita	..	..	..	..	..	..	..
Mauritania	Dimi Mintabba	..	..	..	..	..	..	..
Mauritius	..	..	..	..	..	..	..	..
Mozambique	..	..	..	..	..	..	..	..
Namibia	..	..	..	..	..	..	..	..
Niger	..	..	..	..	..	..	..	..
Nigeria	Fela Kuti	(.)	66	34	(.)	75	5	..
Rwanda	Mevard Ntamganya	..	..	..	..	..	..	..
Senegal	Lamine Konte	..	..	..	..	..	..	..
Sierra Leone	Geraldo Pino	..	..	..	..	..	..	..
Somalia	..	..	..	..	..	..	..	..
South Africa	Abdullah Ibrahim	4.4	24	70	6	20	14	21
Sudan	..	..	..	..	..	..	..	..
Swaziland	Ladysmith Black Mambazo	..	..	..	..	..	..	..
Tanzania (United Rep. of)	..	..	..	..	..	..	..	..
Togo	..	..	..	..	..	..	..	..
Uganda	Elly Wamala	..	..	..	..	..	..	..
Zambia	..	..	..	..	..	..	..	..
Zimbabwe	Thomas Mapfumo	0.8	65	35	(.)	11	20	..
Arab States								
Algeria	Khaled	..	..	..	..	..	..	..
Egypt	Uma Kolthuum	0.8	81[3]	19	(.)	25	10	(.)
Iraq	..	..	..	..	..	..	..	..
Jordan	..	..	..	..	..	..	..	..
Kuwait	Abdul Kereem Abdullgader	4.5	57	43[3]	(.)	25	17	..

Country or territory	A leading popular music artist*	Recorded music sales (US$ per capita) [1]	Distribution by type of music			Piracy (%)	Combined tax rates [2] (%)	CD players (per 100 households)
			Domestic popular (%)	International popular (%)	Classical (%)			
		1998	1998	1998	1998	1997-98	1998	1998
Lebanon	Matar Muhammad	4	60 [3]	40	(.)	25	..	..
Libyan Arab Jamahiriya	..	..	..	..	..	..	..	..
Morocco	Nas El' Ghiwane	..	..	..	..	..	..	..
Oman	..	0.7	60 [3]	40	(.)	25	..	..
Saudi Arabia	Walid Tawfik	2.7	63 [3]	37	(.)	40	12	10
Syrian Arab Rep.	..	..	..	..	..	..	..	..
Tunisia	Alain Boublil	..	..	..	..	..	..	..
United Arab Emirates	..	15.3	46 [3]	54	(.)	5	4	20
Yemen	..	..	..	..	..	..	..	..
South Central Asia								
Afghanistan	..	..	..	..	..	..	..	..
Armenia	Upper Karabagh	..	..	..	..	..	..	..
Azerbaijan	Aziza Mustafa Zadeh	..	..	..	..	..	..	..
Bangladesh	Ali Akbar Khan	..	..	..	..	..	..	..
Bhutan	Riuchen Namgyel	..	..	..	..	..	..	..
Georgia	..	..	..	..	..	..	..	..
India	Lata Mangeshkar	0.3	96	3	1	30	10	(.)
Iran (Islamic Rep. of)	..	..	..	..	..	..	..	..
Kazakhstan	..	..	..	..	..	..	..	..
Kyrgyzstan	..	..	..	..	..	..	..	..
Nepal	..	..	..	..	..	..	..	..
Pakistan	Nusrat Khan	(.)	90	10	(.)	90	10	2
Sri Lanka	..	..	..	..	..	..	..	..
Tajikistan	..	..	..	..	..	..	..	..
Turkmenistan	..	..	..	..	..	..	..	..
Uzbekistan	..	..	..	..	..	..	..	..
East Asia								
China	Guyi Li	0.1	66	33 [3]	1	60	17	6
Hong Kong SAR	Mei Yan Fang	18.8	42	46 [3]	12	70	0	99
Taiwan	Ah Mei	14.6	67	24	9	25	5	66
Japan	Sandii and The Sunsetz	51.8	78	22	..	3	5	53
Korea (Dem. People's Rep.)	..	..	..	..	..	..	..	..
Korea (Rep. of)	I. Arirang	3.3	39	43	18	18	10	46
Mongolia	..	..	..	..	..	..	..	..
South-East Asia and Oceania								
Australia	INXS	33	20	73	7	4	22	53
Cambodia	..	..	..	..	..	..	..	..
Indonesia	Nasidah Ria	0.3	81	18	1	35	10	25
Lao People's Dem. Rep.	..	..	..	..	..	..	..	..
Malaysia	Raihan	2.4	24	71 [3]	5	70	10	20
Myanmar	..	..	..	..	..	..	..	..
New Zealand	Split Enz	27.0	6	86	8	4	13	64
Papua New Guinea	..	..	..	..	..	..	..	..
Philippines	..	0.6	30	67	3	22	10	2
Singapore	..	15.4	27 [3]	64	9	25	3	99
Thailand	Am Saowalak	1.9	82	18	(.)	25	10	23
Viet Nam	..	..	..	..	..	..	..	..

TABLE 5 (continued)

Country or territory	A leading popular music artist*	Recorded music sales (US$ per capita) [1]	Distribution by type of music			Piracy (%)	Combined tax rates [2] (%)	CD players (per 100 households)
			Domestic popular (%)	International popular (%)	Classical (%)			
		1998	1998	1998	1998	1997-98	1998	1998
Latin America and the Caribbean								
Argentina	Astor Piazzolla	8.5	40	56 [3]	4	15	21	27
Bahamas	Joseph Spence	..	..	..	..	..	..	..
Bolivia	Bolivia Manta	0.8	22	74 [3]	4	85	13	..
Brazil	Caetano Veloso	6.4	73	24 [3]	3	45	17	20
Chile	Inti Illimani	5.7	15	80 [3]	5	14	18	12
Colombia	Orquesto Guayacan	4.2	50	48 [3]	2	15	16	5
Costa Rica	Manuel Chamorro	2.7	70 [3]	25	5	20	12	..
Cuba	Silvio Rodriguez	..	..	..	..	..	..	..
Dominican Rep.	Johnny Pacheco	..	..	..	..	..	..	..
Ecuador	..	1.2	30	65 [3]	5	75	10	..
El Salvador	..	0.6	70 [3]	25	5	85	12	..
Guatemala	..	0.7	70 [3]	25	5	45	12	..
Haiti	..	..	..	..	..	..	..	..
Honduras	..	0.5	70 [3]	25	5	80	12	..
Jamaica	Bob Marley	..	..	..	..	..	..	..
Mexico	Narcisco Martinez	5.7	57	41 [3]	2	45	15	27
Nicaragua	Luis Mejia	0.1	70 [3]	25	5	90	12	..
Panama	Ruben Blades	2.0	70 [3]	25	5	60	12	..
Paraguay	Luis Alberto del Paraná	1.3	35	64 [3]	1	70	10	1
Peru	Yma Sumac	0.7	17	82 [3]	1	80	18	6
St. Kitts	Joan Armatrading	..	..	..	..	..	..	..
Trinidad and Tobago	David Rudder	..	..	..	..	..	..	..
Uruguay	Zitarrosa	5.1	41	49 [3]	10	20	23	1
Venezuela	Oscar D'Leon	4.1	69	28 [3]	3	25	17	9
North America								
Canada	Celine Dion	32.1	11	83	6	3	7	73
United States	Bob Dylan	48.2	91	5	4	3	5	73
Europe								
Albania	..	..	..	..	..	..	..	..
Austria	Franz Kuglmann	42.3	15	73	12	2	20	48
Belarus	..	..	..	..	..	..	..	..
Belgium	Django Renhardt	36.1	20	71	9	4	21	63
Bosnia and Herzegovina	..	..	..	..	..	..	..	..
Bulgaria	Dyana Dafova	0.4	62	38	(.)	80	22	..
Croatia	..	3.9	62	38	(.)	70	22	..
Czech Rep.	Adam Makowicz	7.6	42	48	10	6	22	21
Denmark	Palle Mikkelborg	49.5	35	57	8	1	25	77
Estonia	..	..	..	..	..	..	..	..
Finland	Ultra Bra	26.9	42	48	10	10	22	43
France	Edith Piaf	36.4	44	46	10	3	21	68
Germany	Dagmar Krause	36.6	43	47	10	3	16	75
Greece	Angelique Ionatas	10.9	59	37	4	25	18	22
Hungary	Marta Sebestyen	5.6	32	59	9	25	25	22

Country or territory	A leading popular music artist*	Recorded music sales (US$ per capita) [1]	Distribution by type of music: Domestic popular (%)	Distribution by type of music: International popular (%)	Distribution by type of music: Classical (%)	Piracy (%)	Combined tax rates [2] (%)	CD players (per 100 households)
		1998	1998	1998	1998	1997-98	1998	1998
Iceland	Bjork	56.9	45	55	..	5	25	..
Ireland	U2	31.6	16	79	5	5	21	67
Israel	Ofra Haza	8.3	33	60	7	60	17	27
Italy	Sergio Bruni	10.5	44	51	5	25	20	38
Latvia	..	3.9	47	53	(.)	50	18	4
Lithuania	..	1.7	..	..	..	50	18	..
Macedonia (former Yugoslav Rep. of)	Vlatko Stefanovski	..	..	..	..	..	..	..
Moldova (Rep. of)	..	..	..	..	..	..	..	..
Netherlands	Jan Akkerman	35.7	27	64	9	6	18	99
Norway	Karin Krog	62.8	19	77	4	4	23	44
Poland	..	3.9	22	67	11	40	22	20
Portugal	Amalia Rodriguez	18.7	31	65	4	3	18	30
Romania	Maria Tanase	0.3	41	52	7	80	18	6
Russian Federation	Alla Pugacheva	0.6	68	26	6	70	20	2
Slovakia	..	4.0	19	74	7	15	15	21
Slovenia	..	4.8	23	77	(.)	10	13	..
Spain	Paco de Lucia	17.1	42	51	7	2	16	47
Sweden	Abba	44.2	25	71	4	3	25	60
Switzerland	Hat Art	45.0	8	82	10	4	8	75
Turkey	Nezih Uzel	2.0	79	21	(.)	30	15	..
Ukraine	Sophia Rotoru	0.4	6	92	2	70	20	..
United Kingdom	The Beatles	49.0	48	45	7	1	18	87
Yugoslavia	Franco Milosavijevic	..	..	..	..	..	..	..

*New indicator

1. Retail value of CDs, casettes and records. 2. Including sales taxes and additional special taxes. 3. Including regional popular.

Regions	Recorded music sales (US$ per capita) [1]	Distribution by type of music: Domestic popular (%)	Distribution by type of music: International popular (%)	Distribution by type of music: Classical (%)	Piracy (%)	Combined tax rates [2] (%)	CD players (per 100 households)
	1998	1998	1998	1998	1997-98	1998	1998
World	..	..	..	..	..	..	..
Developing	..	..	..	..	..	..	..
Industrial	28	31	62	7	10	18	52
Developing excl. India/China	..	..	..	..	..	..	..
Industrial excl. US/Rus. Fed	27	27	66	7	11	18	55
Sub-Saharan Africa							
Arab States	..	..	..	..	..	..	..
South Central Asia	..	..	..	..	..	..	..
East Asia	5	..	..	..	21	8	12
South-East Asia/Oceania	3	19	74	7	11	11	23
Latin Am./Carib.	5	50	46	4	32	15	..
North America	47	59	36	5	3	6	73
Europe	17	27	66	7	12	19	42

TABLE 6
CULTURAL PRACTICES AND HERITAGE: LEADING LANGUAGES*

Country or territory	Official languages		Percent of population foreign born 1990-95	Countries where over 50 languages are spoken (X)	Leading languages in daily use[1]				
	Number	Names							
Sub-Saharan Africa									
Angola	1	Portuguese	0.3	-	Umbundu	Mbundu Loanda	Kabyle	Kongo	Portuguese
Benin	1	French	1.0	X	Fon	Yoruba	Adja	Bariba	Gen
Botswana	1	English	1.8	-	Setswana	English	Kalanga	Kgalagadi	Afrikaans
Burkina Faso	1	French	4.7	X	Moore	Fulfulde	Jula	Bissa	Gurma
Burundi	2	Rundi, French	6.1	-	Rundi	Swahil	French	Cham	..
Cameroon	2	French, English	2.4	X	Fulfulde	Pidgin-English	Ewondo	Bassa	Douala
Central African Rep.	2	Sango, French	2.0		Gbaya	Banda	Manza	Sango	Fulfulde
Chad	2	French, Arabic	0.3	X	Arabic	Daza	Maba	Sara	Gulay
Congo	1	French	5.9	X	Munukutuba	Kongo	Lingala	Teke	Mbosi
Congo (Dem. Rep.)	1	French	2.8	X	Lingala	Luba	Kituba	Bangala	Kongo
Côte d'Ivoire	1	French	29.3	X	Dioula	Baule	Bete	Senoufo	We
Eritrea	..	..	..	-	Tigrinya	Afar	Arabic	Saho	Kunama
Ethiopia	1	Amharic	12.1	X	Amharic	Oromigna	Tigrina	Somali	Guaragigna
Gabon	1	French	8.9	-	Fang	Sira	Mbere	Myene	French
Gambia	1	English	11.2	-	Mandinka	Fulfulde	Wolof	Soninke	Jola
Ghana	1	English	0.9	X	Akan	Ewe	Ga	English	Abron
Guinea	1	French	1.7	X	Maninka	Pular	Susu	Kpele	Kissi
Guinea-Bissau	1	Portuguese	1.8	-	Balcanta	Fulfulde	Crioulo	Mandyak	Mandinka
Kenya	2	English, Swahili	0.7	X	Kikuyu	Luo	Luyia	Kalenjin	Kamba
Lesotho	2	Sesotho, English	1.4	-	Sesotho	English		..	..
Liberia	1	English	5.0	-	Pidgin English	Kpelle	Bassa	Mano	Dan
Madagascar	2	Malagasy, French	0.3	-	Malagasy	French			
Malawi	2	English, Chichewa	12.1	-	Chichewa	Lomwe	Yao	Ngoni	Tumbuka
Mali	1	French	1.2	-	Bambara	Soninke	Fulfulde	Malinke	Senoufo
Mauritania	2	Arabic, Wolof	3.3	-	Arabic	Fulfulde	Tamashek	Soninke	Wolof
Mauritius	1	English	0.8	-	Creole	Morisyen	Bhojpuri	Urdu	French
Mozambique	1	Portuguese	0.1	-	Makhuwa	Tsonga	Lomwe	Sena	Shona
Namibia	1	English	0.6	-	Afrikaans	Herero	English	Nama	Owambo
Niger	1	French	1.5	-	Haus	Zarma	Songhai	Fulfulde	Tamajak
Nigeria	1	English	0.3	X	English	Haus	Igbo	Yoruba	Pidgin English
Rwanda	2	French, Kinyarwanda	1.0	-	Kinyarwanda	French	..	..	..
Senegal	1	French	2.5	-	Wuluf	Fulfulde	Serere	Mandinka	Malinke
Sierra Leone	1	English	5.0	-	Mende	Themne	Creole	Limba	Kuranko
Somalia	1	Somali	7.2	-	Somali	Maay	Gabre	Swahili	Jiddu
South Africa	11	(See footnote)	3.1	-	Zulu	Xhosa	Afrikaans	Sepedi	English
Sudan	1	Arabic	3.3	X	Arabic	Dinka	Bedawi	Nuer	Fur
Swaziland	2	English, Siswati	..	-	English	Siswati	..	..	..
Tanzania (United Rep. of)	2	English, Swahili	2.3	X	Swahili	Bemba	English	Gogo	Haya
Togo	1	French	4.1	-	Ewe	Kabiye	Tem	Gen	Moba
Uganda	1	English	1.9	-	Swahili	Ganda	Nyankore	Chiga	Soga
Zambia	1	English	4.1	-	Bemba	Tonga	Niyanja	Lozi	Lalabisa
Zimbabwe	1	English	8.0	-	Shona	Ndebele	English	Kalanga	Tonga
Arab States									
Algeria	1	Arabic	1.5	-	Arabic	Kabyle	Chaouia	Tachelhit	French
Egypt	3	(See footnote)	0.3	-	Arabic	Domari	Nubian	Armenian	Greek
Iraq	1	Arabic	2.8	-	Arabic	Kurdish	Azeri	Farsi	Turkmen
Jordan	1	Arabic	26.4	-	Arabic	Adyghe	Armenian	..	..
Kuwait	1	Arabic	71.7	-	Arabic	..	..	..	..

Country or territory	Official languages Number	Official languages Names	Percent of population foreign born 1990-95	Countries where over 50 languages are spoken (X)	Leading languages in daily use[1]				
Lebanon	2	Arabic, French	11.2	-	Arabic	French	English	Armenian	Kurdish
Libyan Arab Jamahiriya	1	Arabic	12.3	-	Arabic	Nefusi	Zuara	Tamashek	
Morocco	1	Arabic	0.2	-	Arabic	Techelhit	Tamazight	Tarifit	French
Oman	1	Arabic	33.6	-	Arabic	English	Baluchi	Swahili	Farsi
Saudi Arabia	1	Arabic	25.8	-	Arabic	..	..	..	..
Syrian Arab Rep.	1	Arabic	6.6	-	Arabic	Kurdish	Armenian	Azeri	Assyrian
Tunisia	1	Arabic	0.5	-	Arabic	Jerba	French	..	..
United Arab Emirates	1	Arabic	90.2	-	Arabic	Pashto	Baluchi	Somali	Farsi
Yemen	1	Arabic	0.6	-	Arabic	Somali	Soqotri	Mehri	..
South Central Asia									
Afghanistan	2	Pashto, Dari	0.2	-	Pashto	Dari	Hazaragi	Uzbek	Aimaq
Armenia	1	Armenian	..	-	Armenian	Azerbaijani	Russian	Kurdish	Ukrainian
Azerbaijan	1	Azeri	..	-	Azeri	Russian	Turkish	English	French
Bangladesh	1	Bangla	0.7	-	Bangla	English	Urdu	Sylheti	Hindi
Bhutan	1	Dzongkha	..	-	Dzongkha	Nepali	Scharchup	Kebumtamp	Gurtu
Georgia	1	Georgian	..	-	Georgian	Mingrelian	Armenian	Russian	Azeri
India	19	(See footnote)	1.0	X	Hindi	Bengali	Telugu	Marathi	Tamil
Iran (Islamic Rep. of)	1	Farsi	6.2	X	Farsi	Azeri	Kurdish	Arabic	Baluchi
Kazakhstan	1	Kazakh	..	X	Kazakh	Russian	Uzbek	Uigur	German
Kyrgyzstan	1	Kirghiz	..	-	Kirghiz	Russian	Uzbek	Ukrainian	Tatar
Nepal	1	Nepalese	2.1	X	Nepali	Maithali	Bhojpuri	Tharu	Tamang
Pakistan	2	Urdu, English	6.1	X	Urdu	Pashto	Punjabi	Sindhi	Baluchi
Sri Lanka	3	(See footnote)	0.1	-	Sinhala	Tamil	English	Malay	..
Tajikistan	1	Tajik	..	-	Tajik	Uzbek	Russian	Tatar	Kirghiz
Turkmenistan	1	Turkmen	..	-	Turkmen	Russian	Uzbek	Kazakh	..
Uzbekistan	1	Uzbek	..	-	Uzbek	Russian	Kazakh	Tatar	Karakalpak
East Asia									
China	1	Mandarin	(.)	X	Mandarin	Cantonese	Xiang	Min	Hakka
Hong Kong SAR	..	..	40.6	-	Cantonese	Min Nan	English	Vietnamese	..
Japan	1	Japanese	0.7	-	Japanese			..	..
Korea (Dem. People's Rep.)	1	Korean	0.2	-	Korean	..	..	..	..
Korea (Rep. of)	1	Korean	2.1	-	Korean	..	..	..	..
Mongolia	1	Mongolian	0.5	-	Mongolian	Kalmyk	Kazakh	Buriat	Chinese
South-East Asia and Oceania									
Australia	1	English	23.4	X	English	Italian	Greek	Cantonese	Arabic
Cambodia	1	Khmer	0.3	-	Khmer	Vietnamese	Chinese	..	..
Indonesia	1	Bahasa Indonesian	0.1	X	Javanese	Bahasa-Indonesian	Malay	Madura	Minang
Lao People's Dem. Rep.	1	Lao	0.4	X	Lao	Khmu	Tai	Hmong	So
Malaysia	1	Malay	4.2	X	Malay	Chinese	Tamil	Javanese	English
Myanmar	1	Burmese	0.2	X	Burmese	Karen	Shan	Arakanese	Chinese
Nauru	1	English	..	-	Nauruan	English	..	..	..
New Zealand	2	English, Maori	15.5	-	English	Maori	Samoan	Cantonese	Mandarin
Niue	2	English, Niuean	..	-	Niuean	English	..	..	..
Papua New Guinea	1	English	0.7	X	Pidgin-English	Motu	..	..	..
Philippines	2	Tagalog, English	0.1	X	Tagalog	Cebuano	Ilocano	Bicolano	Waray
Samoa	2	Samoan, English	..	-	Samoan	English	French	Tokelauan	..
Singapore	4	(See footnote)	15.5	-	Chinese	Malay	English	Tamil	Thai
Thailand	1	Thai	0.6	X	Thai	Malay	Chinese	Khmer	Karen
Viet Nam	1	Vietnamese	(.)	X	Vietnamese	Tai	Muong	Nung	Chinese

TABLE 6 (continued)

Country or territory	Official languages		Percent of population foreign born 1990-95	Countries where over 50 languages are spoken (X)	Leading languages in daily use[1]				
	Number	Names							
Latin America and the Caribbean									
Antigua	1	English	..	-	English	Spanish	Chinese	Creole-French	..
Argentina	1	Spanish	5.1	-	Spanish	Quechua	Guarani	Mapuche	Toba
Barbados	1	English	..	-	English	..	..	..	..
Belize	1	English	..	-	English	Spanish	Creole-English	Garifuna	Ketchi
Bolivia	3	(See footnote)	1.0	-	Spanish	Quechua	Aymara	German	Chiquitano
Brazil	1	Portuguese	0.7	X	Portuguese	Spanish	English	French	Créole
Chile	1	Spanish	0.8	-	Spanish	Mapudungun	Aymara	Rapa Nui	Huilliche
Colombia	1	Spanish	0.3	X	Spanish	Wayuu	Paez	Embera	Romani
Costa Rica	1	Spanish	5.9	-	Spanish	English	Creole-English	Bribri	Cabecar
Cuba	1	Spanish	0.6	-	Spanish	English	French	..	..
Dominican Rep.	1	Spanish	2.5	-	Spanish	Creole-French	Creole-English	..	..
Ecuador	1	Spanish	0.9	-	Spanish	Quechua	Shuar	Colorado	Chachi
El Salvador	1	Spanish	1.0	-	Spanish	Kekchi	Nahuat	..	..
Guatemala	1	Spanish	0.5	X	Spanish	Quiche	Cakchiquel	Mam	Tzutujil
Haiti	2	French, Creole	0.3	-	Creole	French	..	..	..
Honduras	1	Spanish	0.7	-	Spanish	Garifuna	Arabic	English	Miskito
Jamaica	1	English	0.8	-	Creole-English	English	..	..	..
Mexico	1	Spanish	0.4	X	Spanish	Nahuatl	Maya	Zapoteco	Mixteco
Nicaragua	1	Spanish	2.1	-	Spanish	Miskito	Creole-English	Sumo	Rama
Panama	1	Spanish	2.6	-	Spanish	English	..	..	..
Paraguay	1	Spanish	4.3	-	Guarani	Spanish	German	Chilupi	Pai
Peru	1	Spanish	0.3	X	Spanish	Quechua	Aymara	Campa	Aguaruno
St. Lucia	1	English	..	-	English	Creole-French	..	..	..
St. Vincent	2	English, Creole-English	..	-	English	Creole-English	French	..	..
Trinidad and Tobago	1	English	5.0	-	English	Hindi	Creole-English	Creole-French	Chinese
Uruguay	1	Spănish	3.0	-	Spanish	..	..	..	..
Venezuela	1	Spanish	5.3	-	Spanish	Wayuu	Warao	Pemon	Kariña
North America									
Canada	2	English, French	15.5	X	English	French	Chinese	Italian	German
United States	..	..	7.9	X	English	Spanish	Chinese	Russian	Italian
Europe									
Albania	1	Albanian	0.4	-	Albanian	Macedonian	Macedo Rom.	Romani	Greek
Andorra	1	Catalan	..	-	Catalan	Spanish	French	Portuguese	
Austria	1	German	5.8	-	German	Serbian	Croatian	Slovenian	Turkish
Belarus	1	Byelorussian	..	-	Byelorussian	Russian	Polish	Ukrainian	Tatar
Belgium	3	(See footnote)	9.0	-	Dutch	French	German	Luxembourgeois	..
Bosnia and Herzegovina	1	Bosnian	..	-	Bosnian	Serbian	Croatian	English	..
Bulgaria	1	Bulgarian	0.2	-	Bulgarian	Turkish	Romani	Macedo Rom.	Armenian
Croatia	1	Croatian	..	-	Croatian	Serbian	Italian	Hungarian	Slovenian
Cyprus	2	Greek, Turkish		-	Greek	Turkish	English	..	..
Czech Rep.	1	Czech	..	-	Czech	Slovak	German	Polish	Romani
Denmark	1	Danish	4.1	-	Danish	Turkish	Greenlandic	Faroese	Serb.-Cro.
Estonia	1	Estonian	..	-	Estonian	Russian	Ukrainian	Byelorussian	Finnish
Finland	2	Finnish, Swedish	1.2	-	Finnish	Swedish	English	Russian	Estonian
France	1	French	10.4	-	French	Occitan	Alsatian	Arabic	Breton
Germany	1	German	6.4	-	German	Turkish	Serbo-Croatian	Italian	Kurdish
Greece	1	Greek	3.2	-	Greek	Turkish	Albanian	..	..
Hungary	1	Hungarian	0.3	-	Hungarian	Ukrainian	German	Romani	Romanian
Ireland	2	English, Gaelic	9.3	-	English	Gaelic	..	..	..
Israel	2	Hebrew, Arabic	30.9	-	Hebrew	Arabic	Russian	English	Yiddish
Italy	1	Italian	2.7	-	Italian	Neapolitan	Piemontese	Venetian	Ligurian

Country or territory	Official languages		Percent of population foreign born 1990-95	Countries where over 50 languages are spoken (X)	Leading languages in daily use[1]				
	Number	Names							
Latvia	1	Latvian	..	-	Latvian	Russian	English	German	Polish
Lithuania	1	Lithuanian	..	-	Lituanian	Russian	Polish	Byelorussian	Ukrainian
Macedonia (former Yugoslav Rep. of)	..	..	..	-	Macedonian	Albanian	Turkish	Serbo-Croatian	Romani
Moldova (Rep. of)	1	Moldovan	..	-	Moldovan	Ukrainian	Russian	Bulgarian	Gagauz
Netherlands	2	Dutch. Frisian	7.8	-	Dutch	Frisian	Arabic	Turkish	Papiamcutu
Norway	1	Norwegian	4.4	-	Norwegian	Saami	Swedish	Vietnamese	Danish
Poland	1	Polish	3.6	-	Polish	German	Byelorussian	Kashubian	Russian
Portugal	1	Portuguese	1.4	-	Portuguese	Arabic	Galician	Mirandesa	Calo
Romania	1	Romanian	0.6	-	Romanian	Hungarian	Romani	Turkish	German
Russian Federation	1	Russian	..	X	Russian	Tatar	Ukrainian	Byelorussian	German
San Marino	1	Italian	..	-	Italian	..	..	..	..
Slovakia	1	Slovak	..	-	Slovak	Hungarian	Romani	Ruthenian	Ukranian
Slovenia	1	Slovenian	..	-	Slovenian	German	Hungarian	Italian	..
Spain	1	Spanish	1.8	-	Spanish	Catalan	Valencian	Galician	Basque
Sweden	1	Swedish	8.9	-	Swedish	Finnish	Serbian	Bosnian	Farsi
Switzerland	4	(See footnote)	11.0	-	German	French	Italian	Spanish	Serbian-Croatian
Turkey	1	Turkish	2.0	-	Turkish	Kurdish	Zaza	Kirmanjki	Arabic
Ukraine	1	Ukrainian	..	-	Ukrainian	Russian	Romanian	Bulgarian	Hungarian
United Kingdom	2	English, Welsh	6.5	-	English	Italian	Arabic	Gujarati	Urdu
Yugoslavia	1	Serbian	1.7	-	Serbian	Croatian	Albanian	Romanian	Slovak

*New table.

1. As reported by UNESCO Member States in descending order of use.

Footnote on Official languages (alphabetical order). Belgium: Dutch, French, German. Bolivia: Aymara, Quechua, Spanish. Egypt: Arabic, English, French. India: Assamese, Bengali, English (Associate), Gujarati, Hindi, Kannada, Kashmiri, Konkani, Malayalan, Manipuri, Marathi, Nepali, Oriya, Punjabi, Sanskrit, Sindhi, Tamil, Telugu, Urdu. Singapore: Chinese, English, Malay, Tamil. South Africa: Afrikaans, English, Ndebele, Sepedi, Sesotho, Setswana, Siswati, Tshivenda, Xitsonga, Xhosa, Zulu. Sri Lanka: English, Sinhala, Tamil. Switzerland: French, German, Italian, Romansh.

Region	Official languages		Percent of population foreign born 1990-95	Countries where over 50 languages are spoken (X)
	Number	Names		
	T			
World	225		2.8	37
Developing	172		1.7	33
Industrial	53		5.1	4
Developing excl. India/China	152		2.8	31
Industrial excl. US/Rus. Fed.	52		4.9	2
Sub-Saharan Africa	63		4.1	14
Arab States	17		6.4	0
South Central Asia	38		..	5
East Asia	5		0.4	1
South-East Asia/Oceania	21		1.4	9
Latin Am./Carib.	31		1.3	5
North America	2		8.7	2
Europe	48		4.2	1

TABLE 7
CULTURAL PRACTICES AND HERITAGE: LEADING RELIGIONS*

Country or territory	Leading religions [1]		
Sub-Saharan Africa			
Angola	Animist	Catholic	Protestant
Benin	Animist	Christian	Muslim
Botswana	Protestant	Animist	Catholic
Burkina Faso	Animist	Muslim	Catholic
Burundi	Catholic	Animist	Protestant
Cameroon	Muslim	Christian	Animist
Central African Rep.	Christian	Muslim	Animist
Chad	Muslim	Christian	Animist
Congo	Christian	Animist	Muslim
Congo (Dem. Rep.)	Christian	Animist	Muslim
Cote d'Ivoire	Muslim	Animist	Christian
Eritrea	Muslim	Coptic	Catholic
Ethiopia	Orthodox	Muslim	Protestant
Gabon	Christian	Animist	Muslim
Gambia	Muslim	Christian	Animist
Ghana	Christian	Animist	Muslim
Guinea	Muslim	Christian	Animist
Guinea-Bissau	Animist	Muslim	Christian
Kenya	Protestant	Catholic	Animist
Lesotho	Christian	..	..
Liberia	Christian	Muslim	Animist
Madagascar	Animist	Christian	Muslim
Malawi	Protestant	Catholic	Muslim
Mali	Muslim	Christian	Animist
Mauritania	Muslim	..	..
Mauritius	Hindu	Christian	Muslim
Mozambique	Animist	Christian	Muslim
Namibia	Christian	Animist	Secular
Niger	Muslim	Animist	Christian
Nigeria	Christian	Muslim	Animist
Rwanda	Catholic	Animist	Protestant
Senegal	Muslim	Animist	Christian
Sierra Leone	Muslim	Animist	Christian
Somalia	Muslim	Animist	Christian
South Africa	Christian	Animist	Secular
Sudan	Muslim	Animist	Christian
Swaziland	Christian	Animist	..
Tanzania (United Rep. of)	Christian	Muslim	Animist
Togo	Animist	Christian	Muslim
Uganda	Animist	Christian	Muslim
Zambia	Christian	Hindu	Muslim
Zimbabwe	Christian	Animist	Secular
Arab States			
Algeria	Sunni Muslim	..	..
Egypt	Muslim	Christian	..
Iraq	Shi'a Muslim	Sunni Muslim	Christian
Jordan	Sunni Muslim	Christian	Secular
Kuwait	Sunni Muslim	Shi'a Muslim	Christian

Country or territory	Leading religions [1]			
Lebanon	Shi'a Muslim	Sunni Muslim	Christian	
Libyan Arab Jamahiriya	Muslim	Christian	..	
Morocco	Muslim	Jewish	Christian	
Oman	Ibadhi Muslim	Shi'a Muslim	Sunni Muslim	
Saudi Arabia	Muslim	..	..	
Syrian Arab Rep.	Sunni Muslim	Other Muslim	Christian	
Tunisia	Muslim	Jewish	Christian	
United Arab Emirates	Sunni Muslim	Shi'a Muslim	Christian	
Yemen	Sunni Muslim	Shi´a Muslim	Christian	
South Central Asia				
Afghanistan	Sunni Muslim	Shi´a Muslim	Hindu	
Armenia	Orthodox	Muslim	Secular	
Azerbaijan	Muslim	Christian	Jewish	
Bangladesh	Muslim	Hindu	Christian	
Bhutan	Buddhist	Hindu	..	
Georgia	Orthodox	Muslim	Secular	
India	Hindu	Muslim	Christian	
Iran (Islamic Rep. of)	Shi'a Muslim	Sunni Muslim	Christian	
Kazakhstan	Muslim	Orthodox	Catholic	
Kyrgyzstan	Muslim	Secular	Christian	
Nepal	Hindu	Buddhist	Muslim	
Pakistan	Muslim	Hindu	Christian	
Sri Lanka	Buddhist	Hindu	Muslim	
Tajikistan	Sunni Muslim	Shi´a Muslim	Secular	
Turkmenistan	Secular	Muslim	Orthodox	
Uzbekistan	Muslim	Christian	Secular	
East Asia				
China	China	Secular	Buddhist	Taoist
Hong Kong SAR	Traditional	Christian	Secular	
Japan	Shintoist	Buddhist	Christian	
Korea (Dem. People's Rep. of)	Secular	Buddhist	Christian	
Korea (Rep. of)	Christian	Buddhist	..	
Mongolia	Secular	Buddhist	Muslim	
South-East Asia and Oceania				
Australia	Protestant	Catholic	Secular	
Cambodia	Buddhist	Secular	Traditional	
Indonesia	Muslim	Christian	Hindu	
Lao People's Dem. Rep.	Buddhist	Traditional	Secular	
Malaysia	Muslim	Buddhist	Hindu	
Myanmar	Buddhist	Christian	Muslim	
Nauru	Protestant	Catholic	..	
New Zealand	Protestant	Catholic	Traditional	
Niue	Traditional	Protestant	Catholic	
Papua New Guinea	Protestant	Traditional	Catholic	
Philippines	Catholic	Muslim	..	
Samoa	Congregationalist	Methodist	Catholic	
Singapore	Buddhist	Muslim	Secular	
Thailand	Buddhist	Muslim	Traditional	

TABLE 7 (continued)

Country or territory	Leading religions [1]		
Latin America and the Caribbean			
Antigua	Protestant	Catholic	..
Argentina	Catholic	Protestant	Jewish
Barbados	Protestant	Catholic	..
Bolivia	Catholic	Protestant	Traditional
Brazil	Catholic	Traditional	Protestant
Chile	Catholic	Protestant	Jewish
Colombia	Catholic	Protestant	Secular
Costa Rica	Catholic	Protestant	Secular
Cuba	Secular	Catholic	Protestant
Dominican Rep.	Catholic	Protestant	Traditional
Ecuador	Catholic	Protestant	Secular
El Salvador	Catholic	Protestant	..
Guatemala	Catholic	Protestant	..
Haiti	Traditional	Catholic	Protestant
Honduras	Catholic	Protestant	..
Jamaica	Protestant	Traditional	Catholic
Mexico	Catholic	Protestant	Secular
Nicaragua	Catholic	Protestant	Secular
Panama	Catholic	Protestant	Muslim
Paraguay	Catholic	Protestant	Traditional
Peru	Catholic	Protestant	Traditional
St. Lucia	Catholic	Protestant	..
St. Vincent	Christian	Muslim	Traditional
Trinidad and Tobago	Christian	Hindu	Muslim
Uruguay	Catholic	Protestant	Jewish
Venezuela	Catholic	Jewish	Muslim
North America			
Canada	Catholic	Protestant	Orthodox
United States	Protestant	Catholic	Secular
Europe			
Albania	Muslim	Christian	Secular
Austria	Catholic	Protestant	Secular
Belarus	Orthodox	Secular	Catholic
Belgium	Catholic	Protestant	Secular
Bosnia and Herzegovina	Muslim	Orthodox	Catholic
Bulgaria	Orthodox	Secular	Muslim
Croatia	Catholic	Orthodox	Secular
Czech Rep.	Secular	Catholic	Protestant
Denmark	Lutheran	Muslim	Catholic
Estonia	Lutheran	Orthodox	Secular
Finland	Lutheran	Secular	Orthodox
France	Catholic	Muslim	Jewish
Germany	Protestant	Catholic	Secular
Greece	Orthodox	Muslim	Secular
Hungary	Catholic	Protestant	Secular

Country or territory	Leading religions [1]		
Ireland	Catholic	Protestant	..
Italy	Catholic	Protestant	Jewish
Israel	Jewish	Muslim	Secular
Latvia	Lutheran	Catholic	Orthodox
Lithuania	Catholic	Orthodox	Lutheran
Macedonia (former Yugoslav Rep. of)	Orthodox	Muslim	Catholic
Moldova (Rep. of)	Orthodox	Secular	Catholic
Netherlands	Catholic	Protestant	Muslim
Norway	Lutheran	Secular	Catholic
Poland	Catholic	Secular	Orthodox
Portugal	Catholic	Secular	Protestant
Romania	Orthodox	Catholic	Secular
Russian Federation	Orthodox	Muslim	Secular
Slovakia	Catholic	Protestant	Secular
Slovenia	Catholic	Secular	Protestant
Spain	Catholic	Protestant	Secular
Sweden	Lutheran	Catholic	Muslim
Switzerland	Catholic	Protestant	Secular
Turkey	Muslim	Christian	Jewish
Ukraine	Orthodox	Secular	Muslim
United Kingdom	Christian	Muslim	Sikh
Yugoslavia	Orthodox	Muslim	Secular

*New table.

1. As reported by UNESCO Member States in descending order of importance

TABLE 8
CULTURAL PRACTICES AND HERITAGE: NATIONAL FESTIVALS*

Country or territory	Leading national festivals		
Sub-Saharan Africa			
Angola	..	..	..
Benin	Independence Day (1 Aug)	Gani Festival (Var)	Vandouns Festival (10 Jan)
Botswana	..	..	..
Burkina Faso	..	..	..
Burundi	..	..	..
Cameroon	Unified State Fest (20 May)	Youth Festival (11 Feb)	..
Central African Rep.	Independence Day (1 Dec)	Death of Pres Buganda(29 Mar)	Harvest Festival (Oct)
Chad	..	..	..
Congo	Independence Day (15 Aug)	National Tree Day (6 Nov)	Women´s Day (8 Mar)
Congo (Dem. Rep.)	..	..	..
Côte d'Ivoire	Independence Day (7 Aug)	Death of First President (7 Dec)	Peace Day (15 Nov)
Eritrea	..	..	..
Ethiopia	Ethiopian New Year (12 Sep)	Adwa Victory Day (2 Mar)	Patriots Victory Day (5 May)
Gabon	..	..	..
Gambia	..	..	..
Ghana	..	..	..
Guinea	Independence Day (2 Oct)	Womens`s Day (27 Aug)	Republic Day (3 Apr)
Guinea-Bissau	..	..	..
Kenya	..	..	..
Lesotho	..	..	..
Liberia	Independence Day (26 Jul)	Flag Day (24 Aug)	National Unification Day (25 May)
Madagascar	Donia, Nosy Be Island (Jun)	Independence Movement Day (29 Mar)	..
Malawi	John Chilembwe Day (15 Jan)	Freedom Day (14 Jun)	Republic Day (6 Jul)
Mali	..	..	..
Mauritania	..	..	..
Mauritius	..	..	..
Mozambique	..	..	..
Namibia	..	..	..
Niger	Independence Day (3 Aug)	Republic Day (18 Dec)	World Labour Day (1 May)
Nigeria	Independence Day (1 Oct)	Christmas Day (25 Dec)	Id- El-Fitri (Var)
Rwanda	..	..	..
Senegal	..	..	..
Sierra Leone	..	..	..
Somalia	..	..	..
South Africa	Freedom Day (27 Apr)	Heritage Day (24 Sep)	National Women´s Day (9 Aug)
Sudan	..	..	..
Swaziland	Uhmlanga, Reed Dance (Aug-Sep)	Kingship Ceremony (Dec)	Buganu Fruit Ceremony (Feb-Mar)
Tanzania (United Rep. of)	Saba Saba Trade Festival (7 Jul)	Mei Moisi, Labour Day (1 May)	..
Togo	..	..	..
Uganda	..	..	..
Zambia	..	..	..
Zimbabwe	..	..	..
Arab States			
Algeria	Revolution Day (1 Nov)	Independence Day (5 Jul)	Moudjahid Day (20 Aug)
Egypt	Sinai Liberation Day (25 Apr)	Revolution Day (23 Jul)	Wafaa Al-Neel (Aug)
Iraq	..	..	..
Jordan	..	..	..
Kuwait	National Day (25 Feb)	Liberation Day (26 Feb)	Qurain Culture Festival (Oct-Nov)

Country or territory	Leading national festivals		
Lebanon	Independence Day (22 Nov)	Martyrs´ Day (16 May)	Flag Day (20 Nov)
Libyan Arab Jamahiriya	..	..	..
Morocco	Throne Festival (30 Jul)	Youth Festival (9 Jul)	Independence Festival (18 Nov)
Oman	National Day (18 Nov)	Renaissance Day (23 Jul)	..
Saudi Arabia	National Fest, Heritage+Culture (Jan)	..	..
Syrian Arab Rep.	..	..	..
Tunisia	International Carthage Fest (Jul-Aug)	Hammamet Festival (Jul-Aug)	CarthageTheater+Cinema Days (Oct)
United Arab Emirates	Federation Day (2 Dec)	Shaikh Zayed Bin Accession Day (6 Aug)	Armed Forces Unification Day
Yemen	..	..	..
South Central Asia			
Afghanistan	..	..	..
Armenia	..	..	..
Azerbaijan	Novrooz Bayrami Spring (Mar)	Republic Day (28 May)	Liberty Day (15 Jun)
Bangladesh	Independence Day (26 Mar)	Bangla New Year`s Day (14 Apr)	Mother Tongue Day(21 Feb)
Bhutan	..	..	..
Georgia	..	..	..
India	Independence Day (15 Aug)	Constitution + Republic Day (26 Jan)	Mahatma Gandhi Birthday (2 Oct)
Iran (Islamic Rep. of)	Noveerooz Lunar New Year (13 Favardin)	Yalda Midwinter Night	Fajr Feasts (Feb)
Kazakhstan	Kurban Ayt Sacrifice	Easter (Apr)	Nauryz Eastern New Year
Kyrgyzstan	..	..	..
Nepal	Buddha Jayenti Birthday (30 Apr)	Dashain	..
Pakistan	Pakistan Day (23 Mar)	Independence Day (14 Aug)	Muhammad Ali Jinnah Birthday
Sri Lanka	New Year (13-14 Apr)	Independence Day	National Heroes Day
Tajikistan	..	..	..
Turkmenistan	Independence Day (27-28 Oct)	Neutrality Day (12 Dec)	Revival+Unity Day (18 May)
Uzbekistan	Independence Day (31 Aug-1 Sep)	Navruz, New Year (21 Mar)	Sharq Tarolanari Music Fest (Aug-Sep)
East Asia			
China	National Day (1 Oct)	International Labour Day (1 May)	National Youth Day (4 May)
Hong Kong SAR	..	..	..
Japan	..	..	..
Korea (Dem. People's Rep. of)	..	..	..
Korea (Rep. of)	National Foundation Day (3 Oct)	Liberation Day (15 Aug)	Children`s Day (5 May)
Mongolia	..	..	..
South-East Asia and Oceania			
Australia	Anzac Day (25 Apr)	Australia Day (26 Jan)	Naidoc Week (July)
Cambodia	..	..	..
Indonesia	Independence Day (17 Aug)	Youth Pledge Allegiance Day (28 Oct)	Hero Day (10 Nov)
Lao People's Dem. Rep.	..	..	..
Malaysia	..	..	..
Myanmar	..	..	..
Nauru	Angam Day (26 Oct)	Independence Day (31 Jan)	NPC Handover Day (1Jul)
New Zealand	..	..	..
Niue	Constitution Celebration (Oct)	Thanksgiving Feast (Jan)	Earpiercing + Haircutting Ceremonies
Papua New Guinea	..	..	..
Philippines	Independence Day (12 Jun)	National Heroes Day (30 Aug)	Rizal Day (30 Dec)
Samoa	Independence Day (1-2 Jun)	Teuila Festival (3-9 Sep)	National Youth Day (Apr-May)
Singapore	..	..	..
Thailand	..	..	..
Viet Nam	..	..	..

TABLE 8 (continued)

Country or territory	Leading national festivals		
Latin America and the Caribbean			
Antigua	Carnival (Aug)	Boxing Day 26 (Dec)	New Year`s Day (1 Jan)
Argentina	Navidad (25 Dec)	Pascua de Resurrección(Apr)	Immaculate Conception (8 Dec)
Barbados	Holetown Fest (13-20 Feb)	Crop Over Harvest Fest (Jul-Aug)	..
Belize	Independence Day (21 Sep)	Battle of St George`s Cay (10 Sep)	..
Bolivia	..	..	..
Brazil	..	..	..
Chile	Iquique Naval Combat Day (21 May)	Independence Day (18 Sep)	Día de la Raza (12 Oct)
Colombia	..	..	..
Costa Rica	Independence Day (15 Sep)	Nicoya Day (25 Jul)	Culture Day (12 Oct)
Cuba	Liberation Day (1 Jan)	National Rebellion Day (26 Jun)	War of Independence Day (10 Oct)
Dominican Rep.	Independence Day (27 Feb)	Republic Restoration Day (16 Aug)	Juan Pablo Duarte Day (26 Jan)
Ecuador	Mama Negra Day (24 Sep)	Pasé del Niño (Mar)	..
El Salvador	Agostinas Festivals (Aug)	Christmas+New Year (Dec-Jan)	Independence Day (15 Sep)
Guatemala	..	..	..
Haiti	Independence Day (1 Jan)	Ancestors Day (2 Jan)	Agriculture+Labour Day
Honduras	..	..	..
Jamaica	..	..	..
Mexico	Independence Shout Day (15 Sep)	Cinco de Mayo Day (5 May)	Mexican Revolution Day (20 Nov)
Nicaragua	Independence Day (14-15 Sep)	Revolution Triumph Day (19 Jul)	Ruben Dario Day (18 Jan)
Panama	Independence Day (Spain) (28 Nov)	Independence Day(Columbia) (3 Nov)	First Independence Call (10 Nov)
Paraguay	..	..	..
Peru	Independence Festivals (28-29 Jul)	Oath to the Flag (7 Jun)	Battle of Angamos (8 Oct)
Saint Lucia	Independence Day (22 Feb)	National Day (13 Dec)	St. Lucia Jazz Festival
Saint Vincent	Vincy Mas Carnival (Jun-Jul)	Nine Mornings, Christmas (Dec)	Big Drum Festival (May)
Trinidad and Tobago	Emancipation (1 Aug)	Labour Day (19 Jun)	Carnival (Mar)
Uruguay	General Artigas Birthday (19 Jun)	First Constitution Day (18 Jul)	Independence Day (25 Aug)
Venezuela	Revolution Day (19 Apr)	Simon Bolivar Birthday (24 Jul)	Independence Day (5 Jul)
North America			
Canada	International Jazz Fest Montreal (Jul)	Quebec Summer Fest (Jul)	International Children Fest (May)
United States	..	..	..
Europe			
Albania	..	..	..
Andorra	Meritxell Festival (8 Sep)	Constitution Day (14 Mar)	..
Austria	..	..	..
Belarus	..	..	..
Belgium (Fl)	Ommegang Pageant (Jun-Jul)	Giants Procession (26 Aug)	Flemish Painting Parade (6 Aug)
Belgium (Fr)	Communauté Francophone Day (27 Sep)	Wallonie Festival (Sep)	Communauté Germanophone (15 Nov)
Bosnia and Herzegovina	..	..	..
Bulgaria	..	..	..
Croatia	Dubrovnik Summer Fest (Jul-Aug)	Eurokaz Modern Theatre Fest (Jun)	Varazdin Baroque Evenings (Sep-Oct)
Cyprus	Liberation Day (1 Apr)	Independence Day (1 Oct)	Commemoration Day (9 Jul)
Czech Rep.	Kutna Hora (Jun)	Cesky Krumlov Rose Fest (Jun)	Znojmo Grape Harvest (Sep)
Denmark	Grundslovsdag Constitution Day (5 Jun)	International Workers´Day (1 May)	..
Estonia	Song Festival (Jun-Jul)	Dance Festival	Old Town Days (1-4 Jan)
Finland	Helsinki Festival (Aug-Sep)	Pori Jazz Festival (Jul)	Tampere Int Theatre Fest (Aug)
France	National Festival (14 Jul)	Second World War End (8 May)	First World War Armistice (11 Nov)

Country or territory	Leading national festivals		
Germany	German Unification Day (3 Oct)	Second World War Beginning (1 Sep)	Liberatión From Nazi Regime (8 May)
Greece	Athens Festival (Jun-Aug)	Epidaurus Festival (Jul-Aug)	Olympus Festival (Jun-Aug)
Hungary	..	..	..
Ireland	..	..	..
Israel	..	..	..
Italy	Liberation Day (25 Apr)	Labour Day (1 May)	Ferragosto (15 Aug)
Latvia	Song+Dance Festival (Jun-Jul)	Midsummer Solstice (23-24 Jun)	Republic Day (18 Nov)
Lithuania	Statehood Day (6 Jul)	Trakai Festival (Jul-Aug)	Vilnius Festival (May-Jul)
Macedonia (former Yugoslav Rep. of)	Krnsevo Republic Day (2 Aug)	..	..
Moldova (Rep. of)	..	..	..
Netherlands	Queen´s Birthday (30 Apr)	Liberation Day (5 May)	Commemoration Day (4 May)
Norway	..	..	..
Poland	..	..	..
Portugal	..	..	..
Romania	..	..	..
Russian Federation	Patriotic War Victory Day	New Year+Christmas (Dec-Jan)	St Cyril+Mephodius (24 May)
San Marino	Captain Regent's Fest (9 May)	San Marino Fest (3 Sep)	St Agatha Fest (5 Feb)
Slovakia	..	..	..
Slovenia	..	..	..
Spain	San Fermin Fest Pamplona (Jul)	Sevilla Festival (Apr-May)	Valencia Fallas (Cardboard Figures)
Sweden	..	..	..
Switzerland	National Festival (1 Aug)	Basel Carnival (Mar)	Berne Onion Market Day (27 Nov)
Turkey	Republic Day (29 Oct)	Sovereignty+Children`s Day (23 Apr)	Ataturk Youth + Sport Day (19 May)
Ukraine	Independence Day (24 Aug)	New Year´s Day (1 Jan)	Victory Day (9 May)
United Kingdom	Guy Fawkes Day (5 Nov)	Queen`s Birthday (10 Jun)	St. George´s Day (23 Apr)
Yugoslavia	..	..	..

*New Table
Fest=Festival
Var=Variable

TABLE 9
CULTURAL PRACTICES AND HERITAGE: FOLK AND RELIGIOUS FESTIVALS*

Country or territory	Leading folk and religious festivals		
Sub-Saharan Africa			
Angola	..	..	..
Benin	Lacustre People´s Festival	Art+Culture Day	Regional Festivals (Nov-Dec)
Botswana	..	..	..
Burkina Faso	..	..	..
Burundi	..	..	..
Cameroon	Ngondo Festival (Dec)	Ngouon Festival (Dec)	Nyem Nyem Fest (Jan)
Central African Rep.	Christmas (25 Dec)	Easter (Apr)	Ramadan (Var)
Chad	..	..	..
Congo	Panafrican Music Festival	..	..
Congo (Dem. Rep.)	..	..	..
Côte d'Ivoire	Bonoua Masked Carnival (Apr)	Grand Bassam Carnival (Oct)	Bouake Carnival (Var)
Eritrea	..	..	..
Ethiopia	Meskel Festival (28 Sep)	Timekt Epiphany (20 Jan)	El Alfeter - Ramadan (Var)
Gabon	..	..	..
Gambia	..	..	..
Ghana	..	..	..
Guinea	Drum Festival	Hunter's Festival	..
Guinea-Bissau	..	..	..
Kenya	..	..	..
Lesotho	..	..	..
Liberia	Christmas (25 Dec)	Ramadan (Var)	Fast + Prayers Day (May 14)
Madagascar	Ankaramalaza Pilgrimage (Jul-Aug)	Fanompoambe/Fitampoha Cleansing (Apr)	Famadihana Shrouds (Winter)
Malawi	Gonapamhanya Fest (Var)	Chizangala Fest (Var)	Ngwanda Harvest Fest (Oct)
Mali	..	..	..
Mauritania	..	..	..
Mauritius	..	..	..
Mozambique	..	..	..
Namibia	..	..	..
Niger	Bianou Muhammed`s Birthday	Budin Daji, Animist Fest	Hottungo, New Year
Nigeria	Durbar Kano Festival	Argungu Fishing Fest	Mmanwu Enugu Masked Fest
Rwanda	..	..	..
Senegal	..	..	..
Sierra Leone	..	..	..
Somalia	..	..	..
South Africa	Christmas (25 Dec)	Easter (Apr)	..
Sudan	..	..	..
Swaziland	Somklolo Praise Festival (22 Jul)	Siyavuka Arts Festival	..
Tanzania (United Rep. of)	Nane Nane Peasants Day (8 Aug)	Idd El Fitr (Var)	Christmas (25 Dec)
Togo	Agbogbozan Fest, Ewe	Epe Ekpe Fest, Guen (Sep)	Evala Kabye Fest (Jul)
Uganda	..	..	..
Zambia	..	..	..
Zimbabwe	..	..	..
Arab States			
Algeria	Maoussem Taghit (Oct-Nov)	Yennayer (11 Jan)	Sebiba Festival, Djanet
Egypt	..	..	..
Iraq	..	..	..
Jordan	..	..	..
Kuwait	Ramadan, Eid-Al-Fater (Var)	Eid Al Adha (Var)	Hejira New Year

Country or territory	Leading folk and religious festivals		
Lebanon	Eid Adha Moubarak	Ascension Day (15 Aug)	Karme Festival, Zahle (Sep)
Libyan Arab Jamahiriya	..	..	..
Morocco	Popular Art Fest, Marrakesh	Sacred Music Fest, Fez	Guaoua Festival, Essaouira
Oman	Eid-Al-Fitr (Var)	Eid-Al-Adhha (Var)	Molid Al Rasoul
Saudi Arabia	Eid-Al Feter (Var)	Eid-Al-Adhuah (Var)	..
Syrian Arab Rep.	..	..	..
Tunisia	Aid El-Fitr (Var)	Aid El-Idha (Var)	Lunar New Year, Muharrem
United Arab Emirates	Eid-Al Fitr (Var)	Al- Adha Holy Eid (Var)	The Prophet`s Birthday (25 Jun)
Yemen	..	..	..
South Central Asia			
Afghanistan	..	..	..
Armenia	..	..	..
Azerbaijan	Khary Bul-Bul Fest	Mougam Traditional Music Fest	Gadjibekov Classical Music Fest
Bangladesh	Eid-Ul-Fitr Festival (Var)	Durga Puja	Christmas Day (Dec)
Bhutan	..	..	..
Georgia	..	..	..
India	Diwali Festival of Lights	Dussehra, Good Over Evil	Holi, Fest of Colours (Harvest Time)
Iran (Islamic Rep. of)	Imam Ali`s Birthday (13 Rajab)	Imam Mahdi`s Birthday (15 Sha'aban)	Imam Hussein Mourning, Ashura
Kazakhstan	Traditional Music Festival	Classical Dance Fest (Apr-May)	Int Popular Music Fest (Jul-Aug)
Kyrgyzstan	..	..	..
Nepal	Indra Jatra	Losar, Tibetan New Year (6 Feb)	Godavari Mela Fair
Pakistan	Eid-Ul-Fitr (Var)	Eidul Azha (Var)	Aashora (Var)
Sri Lanka	Vesak (May)	Poson (June)	Deepavali (Nov)
Tajikistan	..	..	..
Turkmenistan	Carpet Festival (Mar)	Good Neighbour Day (Dec)	Turkmen Bakshi Music Fest (Sep)
Uzbekistan	Alpomish Bakshi Poetry Fest (Spring)	Folk Societies Fest (Summer)	Navruz Theatre Fest (Jun)
East Asia			
China	Chinese Lunar New Year (5 Feb)	Qing Ming Festival (4 Apr)	Mid Autumn Festival (12 Sep)
Hong Kong SAR	..	..	..
Japan	..	..	..
Korea (Dem. People's Rep. of)	..	..	..
Korea (Rep. of)	Lunar New, Sollal (5 Feb)	Ch'usok Harvest Day (Autumn)	Tano Day (6Jun)
Mongolia	..	..	..
South-East Asia and Oceania			
Australia	Woodford Maleny Folk Fest (Dec-Jan)	Port Fairy Fest (Mar)	Christmas (Dec)
Cambodia	..	..	..
Indonesia	Idul Fitri Fest (Var)	Christmas (Dec)	Waissak Buddha's Birthday (18 May)
Lao People's Dem. Rep.	..	..	..
Malaysia	..	..	..
Myanmar	..	..	..
Nauru	Women's Arts+Crafts Fest (17 May)	Nauru Pacific Arts Fest (9 Aug)	Women's Easter Choral Competition
New Zealand	..	..	..
Niue	Peniaminas´s Day (Oct)	White Sunday (May)	Prayer Week (Jan)
Papua New Guinea	..	..	..
Philippines	All Saints Day (1 Nov)	Black Nazarene of Quiapo (9 Jan)	Pahiyas of Lucban, Quezon (15 May)
Samoa	White Sunday (8 Oct)	Palolo Rise, Seafood (Oct-Nov)	Christmas/New Year (Dec-Jan)
Singapore	..	..	..
Thailand	..	..	..
Viet Nam	..	..	..

TABLE 9 (continued)

Country or territory	Leading folk and religious festivals		
Latin America and the Caribbean			
Antigua	Christmas (25 Dec)	Whit Sunday (Jun)	Easter Weekend (Apr)
Argentina	Cosquin Folklore Festival (Jan)	Jesus+Mary Fest, Cordoba (Feb)	Popular Music Fest, Baradero (Feb)
Barbados	Barbados Jazz Festival (Jan)	Oistin´s Fish Fest (Easter)	..
Belize	Garifuna Settlement Day (19 Nov)	School Fest of Arts+Crafts (Mar)	..
Bolivia	Oruro Carnaval (Var)	..	..
Brazil	..	..	..
Chile	St Peter + St Paul Day (29 Jun)	La Tirana Carnaval (16 Jul)	Jesus Nazareno Chiloe Procession (31 Aug)
Colombia	..	..	..
Costa Rica	San Ramon Nonato Fest (30 Aug)	National Boyero Day (Mar)	Virgin Of Guadalupe Fest (12 Dec)
Cuba	May Pilgrimage (May)	National Cucalambeana Day (Jun-Jul)	Fiesta del Fuego (Jul)
Dominican Rep.	Señora de la Alta Gracia (21 Jan)	Semana Santa (Apr)	Virgen de las Mercedes (24 Sep)
Ecuador	Semana Santa (Apr)	Pendoneros (Jun)	..
El Salvador	Flowers+Palms Fest, Panchimalco	Patron Saints Festival	Ahuachapan Street Lamp Day (7 Sep)
Guatemala	..	..	..
Haiti	Carnaval (Jan- Feb)	Saut d´eau Pilgrimage	..
Honduras	..	..	..
Jamaica	..	..	..
Mexico	Virgen de Guadalupe (12 Dec)	Day of The Dead (1-2 Nov)	La Guelaguetza (Jul)
Nicaragua	Immaculate Conception (Nov-Dec)	St Domingo de Guzman (Aug)	St Jeronimo Doctor, Masaya (Sep)
Panama	Corpus Christi (Jun)	St. Librada de las Tablas (20 Jul)	St de las Mercedes, Guarare
Paraguay	..	..	..
Peru	Inti Raymi Festival, Cuzco	Lord of the Miracles, Lima (Oct)	La Candelaria, Puno
Saint Lucia	Carnival (Jul)	Jounen Kweyol, Creole Day (28 Oct)	Asou Skwe Festival (1-2 Jan)
Saint Vincent	National Music Fest (Mar)	Easterval (Apr)	..
Trinidad and Tobago	Tobago Heritage (Jul-Aug)	Easter (Jun)	Divali Lights Fest (7 Nov)
Uruguay	Carnaval (Feb)	Semana Santa, Criolla (Apr)	Verdum Virgin Pilgrimage (19 Apr)
Venezuela	San Antonio El Tamunangue Fest (13 Jun)	San Juan Fest (24 Jun)	Corpus Christi Dancing Devils (Jun)
North America			
Canada	Winnipeg Folk Fest (Jul)	Vancouver Folk Music Fest (Jul)	Drummondville World Cultures (Jul)
United States	..	..	..
Europe			
Albania	..	..	..
Andorra	Bal de L`Ours (Lent)	Dance de la Sardane (Easter)	..
Austria	..	..	..
Belarus	..	..	..
Belgium (Fl)	Holy Blood Procession (1 Jun)	Penance Procession, Veurne (25 Jul)	World Folklore Fest (Jul)
Belgium (Fr)	Binche Carnaval (Lent)	Mons Festival (Whitsun)	Liege Festival (Nov-Dec)
Bosnia and Herzegovina	..	..	..
Bulgaria	..	..	..
Croatia	International Folklore Fest (19-23 Jul)	Sinjska Alka (4-6 Aug)	Vinkovci Autumn Fest (22-24 Sep)
Cyprus	Easter (Apr)	Kataklysmos Flood Fest (19 Jun)	Anthestiria Flower Fest (May)
Cz··3ep.	Velehrad Pilgrimage (Jul)	Annunciation of the Virgin (Aug)	Jan Hus Festival (6 Jul)
Denmark	Christmas	Easter (Apr)	Whitsun (Jun)
Estonia	Baltica Int Folklore Fest (Summer)	Sacred Music Fest	Credo Orthodox Sacred Music Fest
Finland	Laestadian Summer Services	The Awakened Convention (Summer)	Pentecostal Conference (Midsummer)
France	Lorient Interceltique Fest (6-15 Aug)	..	..

Country or territory	Leading folk and religious festivals		
Germany	Oktoberfest (Oct)	Christmas (Dec)	The Love Parade, Berlin (Summer)
Greece	Anastenaria Fest (20-21 May)	Boula + The Janissaries	Int. String Music Fest, Kassos
Hungary	..	..	..
Ireland	..	..	..
Israel	Shorashim; Roots, Maayan Baruch (Jul)	Carmiel Folk Dancing Fest (Aug)	Arad Folk Singing Fest (Aug)
Italy	Christmas (25-26 Dec)	All Saints Day (1 Nov)	Easter (Apr)
Latvia	Baltica Int Folklore Fest (Summer)	Children+Youth Festival	Aglona Basilica Pilgrimage (15 Aug)
Lithuania	Skamba Skamba, Kankliai	Sea Festival (Jul)	Uzgavenes Winter's End Fest (Feb)
Macedonia (former Yugoslav Rep. of)	Balkan Song+Dance Fest (Jul)	Student Folk Fest (Sep)	Folk Instruments Festival (May)
Moldova (Rep. of)	..	..	..
Netherlands	Christmas (Dec)	Sinterklaas (5 Dec)	Carnival (Mar)
Norway	..	..	..
Poland	..	..	..
Portugal	..	..	..
Romania	..	..	..
Russian Federation	Regional Folklore Festivals	White Nights, St Petersburg	..
San Marino	Ethnic Music Festival	Medieval Crossbow Fest (Jul)	..
Slovakia	..	..	..
Slovenia	..	..	..
Spain	Semana Santa, Sevilla (Apr)	Rocio Romero Pilgrimage (10-12 Jul)	Corpus Cristi, Toledo
Sweden	..	..	..
Switzerland	Wine Growers Fest, Vevey (Jul-Aug)	Yodeller's Fest, Frauenfeld (2-4 Jul)	Int Folklore Meeting, Fribourg
Turkey	Ramadan (Jan)	Hidrellez Winter´s End Fest (6 May)	Nevrouz New Year (21 Mar)
Ukraine	Pokud Folk Fest (Sep)	Children´s Fest, Kharkiv	Polissya Folklore Fest (Jul)
United Kingdom	Easter (Apr)	Hallowe'en (31 Oct)	Christmas (25 Dec)
Yugoslavia	..	..	..

*New Table
Fest=Festival
Var=Variable

TABLE 10
CULTURAL PRACTICES AND HERITAGE: MOST VISITED CULTURAL SITES*

Country or territory	Most visited cultural sites		
Sub-Saharan Africa			
Angola	..	..	..
Benin	Abomey Royal Palaces	Ouida+The Slave Route	Ethnographic Musseum, Porto-Novo
Botswana	..	..	..
Burkina Faso	..	..	..
Burundi	..	..	..
Cameroon	Sultan of Bamoun Palace	Waza Park	Limbe Botanical Garden
Central African Rep.	Bouar Megaliths	Boganda Village	Berengo Imperial Court
Chad	..	..	..
Congo	Ma-Loango Museum	Poto-Poto Painting School	Ste. Anne Du Congo Basilica
Congo (Dem. Rep.)	..	..	..
Côte d'Ivoire	Yamoussoukro Basilica	Grand-Bassam French Quarter	Waraniene Weavers
Eritrea	..	..	..
Ethiopia	Tana and Gonder	Lalibela	Axum
Gabon	..	..	..
Gambia	..	..	..
Ghana	Ashanti Traditional Buildings	Forts+Castles	..
Guinea	Baffa - Rio Pongo	Le Voile de la Mariée	Le Chien Qui Fume
Guinea-Bissau	..	..	..
Kenya			
Lesotho	..	..	..
Liberia	National Museum, Monrovia	Providence Island	Kendeja Cultural Centre
Madagascar	Ambohimanga Museum	Mahavelona Fort	Mahafaly Tombs
Malawi	Nkhotakota Village	Mikolongwe Hill Rock Paintings	Mwalawamphini
Mali	Djenne	Timbuktu	..
Mauritania	Ouadane + Other Ksours	..	..
Mauritius	..	..	..
Mozambique	Mozambique Island	..	..
Namibia	..	..	..
Niger	Gadafana Dinosaur Cemetery	Agadez Mosque	National Museum
Nigeria	Sukur Cultural Landscape	Arochukwu Sacred Grove	Benin Earthworks
Rwanda	..	..	..
Senegal	Goree Island	..	..
Sierra Leone	..	..	..
Somalia	..	..	..
South Africa	Robben Island	Good Hope Castle, Capetown	Sterkfontein
Sudan			
Swaziland	Lobamba	Sibebe Rock	Ngwenya Ancient Iron-Ore Mine
Tanzania (United Rep. of)	Ngorongoro Crater	Olduvai Gorge	Bagamoyo
Togo	Temberma Castles	Kpalime Crafts Centre	Kabye Forges
Uganda	..	..	..
Zambia	..	..	..
Zimbabwe	Great Zimbabwe	World´s View Monument	Matopos National Monument
Arab States			
Algeria	Algiers Casbah	Djemila	Timgad
Egypt	The Pyramids	Luxor	Abu Simbel
Iraq	Hatra	..	..
Jordan	Petra	Quseir Amra	..
Kuwait	National Museum	Kuwait Souk	Dar Al-Athar Al- Islamiyyah

Country or territory	Most visited cultural sites		
Lebanon	Baalbeck	Byblos	Beiteddine
Libyan Arab Jamahiriya	Leptia Magna	Tadrart Acacus Rock Art Sites	Ghadames Old Town
Morocco	Saadien Tombs	El Bahia Palace	Dar Si Said Museum
Oman	Nizwa City	Bahla Fort	Salalah
Saudi Arabia	King Fahed Cultural Centre	King Abdoul Aziz Cultural Centre	King Fahed National Library
Syrian Arab Rep.	Damascus	Palmyra	Aleppo
Tunisia	Carthage	Bardo National Museum	El Jem
Syrian Arab Rep.	Abu Dhabi Cultural Complex	Sharja Culture Department	Abu Dhabi Culture Department
United Arab Emirates	Shibam	Sana`ã Old City	Zabid
South Central Asia			
Afghanistan	..	..	..
Armenia	Haghpat Monastery	..	..
Azerbaijan	Republic Palace	National Fine Arts Museum	History Museum
Bangladesh	Cox's Bazar	The Sundar Bans	Mahsthangar
Bhutan	..	..	..
Georgia	Mtskheja City	Bagrati Cathedral	Upper Svaneti
India	Taj Mahal, Agra	Meenakshi Temple, Madurai	Qutab Minar, Delhi
Iran (Islamic Rep. of)	Isfahan Naqsh-e-Jahan Square	Persepolis	Kerman
Kazakhstan	Tamgaly	Chodza Achmed Jasavy Mausoleum	Taraz
Kyrgyzstan	..	..	..
Nepal	Kathmandu	Patan	Bhaktapur
Pakistan	Lahore Fort	Shalamar Garden	Moenjodaro
Sri Lanka	Anuradhapura	Polonnaruwa	Sigiriya
Tajikistan	..	..	..
Turkmenistan	Old Nisa	Merv Historical Park	Kunya Urgench
Uzbekistan	Bukhara Arkh	Bibihonim Mausoleum, Samarkand	Hazrati Imom Complex, Tashkent
East Asia			
China	Palace Museum	The Great Wall	Qin Emperor Mausoleum
Hong Kong SAR	..	..	..
Japan	..	..	..
Korea (Dem. People's Rep. of)	..	..	..
Korea (Rep. of)	Kyongju City	Hahoe Folk Village	Seoul Historical Area
Mongolia	..	..	..
South-East Asia and Oceania	..	..	..
Australia	Sovereign Hill	War Memorial	Sydney Opera House
Cambodia	Angkor	..	..
Indonesia	Borobudur	Prambanan	Besakih
Lao People's Dem. Rep.	Luang Prabang	..	..
Malaysia	..	..	..
Myanmar	..	..	..
Nauru	World War II Sites	Mythological Sites	..
New Zealand	..	..	..
Niue	Haunaki Museum	Centennial Hall	Misa´s Bushwalk
Papua New Guinea	..		
Philippines	Baroque Churches	Ifugao Rice Terraces	Vigan
Samoa	Apia Town	Robert Louis Stevenson Museum	Falealupo Legend Sites
Singapore	..	..	..
Thailand	Sukhothai	Ayutthaya	Ban Chiang
Viet Nam	Hue Monuments	Hoian	My Son Sanctuary

TABLE 10 (continued)

Country or territory	Most visited cultural sites		
Latin America and the Caribbean			
Antigua	St. John's Cathedral	Antigua Recreation Grounds	Betty's Hope Estate
Argentina	Buenos Aires	Cordoba+The Jesuit Farms	Humauaca Ravine
Barbados	Barbados Museum	Tyrol Cot Village	The Rum Factory
Belize	Xunantunich	Altun Ha	Lubantun
Bolivia	Potosi	Chiquitos Jesuit Missions	Sucre
Brazil	..	..	..
Chile	..	..	..
Colombia	Cartagena	Santa Cruz de Mompox	Tierra de Tro Archeol. Park
Costa Rica	National Museum	National Theatre	Science+Cultural Centre
Cuba	Old Havana Historical Centre	Trinidad City	Morro San Pedro de la Roca Castle
Dominican Rep.	Colon Palace	Santo Domingo Cathedal	Higuey Basilica
Ecuador	Quito Historical Centre	Ingapirca	Cuenca
El Salvador	San Andres	Tazumal	Joya de Ceren
Guatemala	Antigua	Quirigua	..
Haiti	Sans Souci Palace	Henri Christophe Citadel	Ville Bonheur Falls
Honduras	Copan	..	..
Jamaica	..	..	..
Mexico	Teotihuacan	National Anthropological Museum	Mayan Sites
Nicaragua	Granada	León+León Viejo	Old Managua Ruins
Panama	Ruins of Old Panama	El Casco Antiguo	Panama Canal
Paraguay	Parana Jesuit Missions		..
Peru	Machu Picchu	Nasca	Cusco
Saint Lucia	Pigeon Island	Morne	Marguis Estate
Saint Vincent	Fort Charlotte	Layou Petroglyph	Black Point Tunnel
Trinidad and Tobago	Waterloo Sea Temple	Queen's Park Savanah	The Red House
Uruguay	Colonia Del Sacramento	Legislative Palace	National Visual Arts Museum
Venezuela	Caracas University Centre	Los Cabus Cultural Complex	Rio Caroni, Bajo Orinoco
North America			
Canada	Montreal Old Port	Gastown, Vancouver	Quebec City
United States	..	..	..
Europe			
Albania	Voskopoja Churches	Permet Church	Butrinti
Andorra	Meritxell Sanctuary	Areny-Plandolit Museum	Parliament House
Austria	Schönbrunn	Hohensalzburg Fortress	Vienna Art History Museum
Belarus	..	..	..
Belgium (Fl)	Bruges	Grand Place, Brussels	Notre Dame Cathedral, Antwerp
Belgium (Fr)	Bouillon	Dinant	Waterloo
Bosnia and Herzegovina	..	..	..
Bulgaria	Boyana Church	Madara Rider	Kazaniak Thracian Tomb
Croatia	Diocletian's Palace, Split	Dubrovnik	Bishop Euphrasius Basilica
Cyprus	Chirokitia	Nea Pafos	Aphrodite's Sanctuary
Czech Rep.	Prague Castle	Karlstejn Castle	Prague Town Hall
Denmark	The Little Mermaid	Tivoli	Copenhagen Zoo
Estonia	Tallinn Old Town	Tartu University	Palmse Manor House
Finland	Suomenlinna Sea Fortress	Temppeliaukio Church, Helsinki	Uspenski Cathedral
France	Eiffel Tower	Louvre Museum	Notre Dame, Paris

Country or territory	Most visited cultural sites		
Germany	Cologne Cathedral	Neuschwanstein Castle	Sans Souci Castle
Greece	Athens Acropolis	Knossos	Lindos Acropolis
Hungary	Budapest	Holloko	Pannonhalma Monastery
Ireland	Bend of the Boyne	Skellig Michael	..
Israel	Jeruslem	..	..
Italy	Colosseum, Rome	Pompei	Uffizi Gallery, Florenze
Latvia	Riga Historical Centre	Sigulda	Rundale Palace
Lithuania	Trakai Historical National Park	The Hill of Crosses	Rumsiskes Folk Museum
Macedonia (former Yugoslav Rep. of)	Ohrid	Struga	Skopje
Moldova (Rep. of)	..	..	..
Netherlands	Amsterdam Inner City	Kindordijk Windmills	Muiderslot Castle
Norway	Urnes Stave Church	Bryggen	Roros
Poland	Krakow Historical Centre	Warsaw Historical Centre	Zamosc
Portugal	..		
Romania	Biertan	Horezu Monastery	Moldavian Churches
Russian Federation	Moscow District	Saint Petersburg	Golden Ring Ancient Cities
San Marino	Government Palace	The Fortresses	The Basilica
Slovakia	Vikolinek	Banska Stiavnild	Sprsky Hrad
Slovenia	..	..	..
Spain	Prado Museum, Madrid	Alhambra+Generalife, Granada	Reina Sofia Museum, Madrid
Sweden	..	..	..
Switzerland	Fondation Gianadda Martigny	Fondation Beyeler	Jean Tinguely Museum
Turkey	Topkapi Palace	Saint Sophia	Mueulana Museum
Ukraine	St Sophia, Kyiv	Kyiv Pechersk Lavra	Taras Shevchenko Opera House
United Kingdom	Westminster Abbey	Tower of London	York Minster
Yugoslavia	Stari Ras	Kotor	Studenica Monastery

*New Table

TABLE 11
CULTURAL PRACTICES AND HERITAGE: MOST VISITED NATURAL SITES*

Country or territory	Most visited natural sites		
Sub-Saharan Africa			
Angola	..	..	..
Benin	Ganvie Lakeside Town	Pendjari National Park	Tanougou + Kola Falls
Botswana	..	..	..
Burkina Faso	..	..	..
Burundi	..	..	..
Cameroon	Dja Faunal Reserve	Mount Cameroon	Kribi Beaches
Central African Rep.	Manovo-Gounda Park	Dzanga-Sangha Reserve	Boali Falls
Chad	..	..	..
Congo	Mbamou Island	Inoni Cliffs	Djoue Rapids
Congo (Dem. Rep.)	Urunga National Park	Garamba National Park	Okapi Wildlife Reserve
Côte d Ivoire	Grand-Berebi Bay	Comoe National Park	Tai Forest
Eritrea	..	..	..
Ethiopia	Semen National Park	Awash National Park	Bale Mountains
Gabon	..	..	..
Gambia	..	..	..
Ghana	..	..	..
Guinea	Mount Nimba Nature Reserve	Niokolo Badiar Park	Niger Valley Park
Guinea-Bissau	..	..	..
Kenya	Mount Kenya Nat. Park	Sibiloi National Park	..
Lesotho	..	..	..
Liberia	Lake Piso	Kpatawi Falls	Sapo National Park
Madagascar	Bemaraha Tsingy	Nosy Be Island	Southern Landscape
Malawi	Kasungu National Park	Vwaza Wildlife Reserve	Liwonde National Park
Mali	Bandiagara Cliff	..	..
Mauritania	Banc D'Arguin Nat. Park	..	..
Mauritius	..	..	..
Mozambique	Mozambique Island	..	..
Namibia	..	..	..
Niger	L'Aïr + Tenere Reserve	W National Park	Termit Massif
Nigeria	Zuma Rock	Ogbunike Cave	Olumu Rock
Rwanda	..	..	..
Senegal	Niokolo-Koba Nat. Park	Djoudj Nat. Bird Sanctuary	..
Sierra Leone	..	..	..
Somalia	..	..	..
South Africa	Kruger Game Park	Table Mountain	Drakensberg
Sudan	..	..	..
Swaziland	Mantenga Falls	Malolotja Nature Reserve	Mkhaya Game Reserve
Tanzania (United Rep. of)	Mt. Kilimanjaro National Park	Serengeti National Park	Selous National Park
Togo	Akrowa Falls	Lake Togo	Aledjo Fault
Uganda	Bwindi Impenetrable Nat. Park	Rwenzori Mountain Nat. Park	..
Zambia	Victoria Falls	..	..
Zimbabwe	Victoria Falls	Mana Pools	Chiremba Balancing Rocks
Arab States			
Algeria	Ahaggar National Park	Tassili National Park	M'zab Valley
Egypt	Aswan	Al-Kharga Oasis	Al-Baharia Oasis
Iraq	..	..	..
Jordan	..	..	..
Kuwait	Failaka Island	Ukaz Island	Al-Qasr Al-Ahmar

Country or territory	Most visited natural sites		
Lebanon	Jeita	Arz Forest	Wadi Kadicha
Libyan Arab Jamahiriya	..	..	..
Morocco	Ouzoud Falls	Ourika Valley	Marzoga Sand Dunes
Oman	Ras Al Hadd	Gedat Al Harasis	Khoar Salalah
Saudi Arabia	Ibexes Reserve	Al Harra Reserve	Al Khanfa Reserve
Syrian Arab Rep.	..	..	..
Tunisia	Ichkeul National Park	El Feidja National Park	Bouhedma National Park
United Arab Emirates	Siri Bani Yas Island	Al Haili Monuments	Ain Khit
Yemen	..	..	..
South Central Asia			
Afghanistan	..	..	..
Armenia	..	..	..
Azerbaijan	Goy-gol Lake	Gobustan	Zakataly State Reserve
Bangladesh	Madhupur Shalban	Kunkala	Chandra
Bhutan	Srebarna Nature Reserve	Pirin National Park	..
Georgia	..	..	..
India	Corbett National Park	Kaziranga National Park	Bharatpur Ghana Bird Sanctuary
Iran (Islamic Rep. of)	Southern Caspian Coast	Alborz Forest	Al Sadr Cave
Kazakhstan	Burabay	Altyn Amel Nat. Park	Bajanaul National Park
Kyrgyzstan	..	..	..
Nepal	Pokhara	Godavari	Gosainkunda
Pakistan	Muree	Swat and The North	Kirthar Nat .Park, Sindh
Sri Lanka	Horton Plains	Yala	..
Tajikistan	..	..	..
Turkmenistan	Aghia I-Pill Dinosaur Trail	Bakharden Lake	..
Uzbekistan	Chatkal Mountains	Zaamin Mountains	Shakkimardan
East Asia			
China	Li Jiang River	Mount Taishan	Mount Huangshan
Hong Kong SAR	..	..	..
Japan	Yakushima	Shirakami - Sanch	..
Korea (Dem. People's Rep. of)	..	..	..
Korea (Rep. of)	Mount Sorak Nat Park	Chejudo Island	Hallyosudo Waterway
Mongolia	..	..	..
South-East Asia and Oceania			
Australia	Uluru Ayers Rock	Sydney Harbour	Kakadu National Park
Cambodia	..	..	..
Indonesia	Pelabuhan Ratu	Kuta Beach	Toba Lake
Lao People's Dem. Rep.	..	..	..
Malaysia	..	..	..
Myanmar	..	..	..
Nauru	Anibare Bay	Phosphate Field Ruins	Coral Reef
New Zealand	Te Wahipounamu	Tongariro National Park	Sub-Antarctic Islands
Niue	Huvalu Forest	Matapa Chasm	Talava Arches
Papua New Guinea	..	..	..
Philippines	Tubbataha Reef Marine Park	Saint Paul River Park	Batanes
Samoa	Taga Blowholes	Lalomanu Beaches	Palolo Coral Reef Reserve
Singapore	..	..	..
Thailand	Thungai-Huai Kha Khaeng Sanctuaries	..	..
Viet Nam	Ha Long Bay	..	..

TABLE 11 (continued)

Country or territory	Most visited natural sites		
Latin America and the Caribbean			
Antigua	Devil's Bridge	Barbuda Bird Sanctuary	Fig Tree Drive
Argentina	Iguazu National Park	Lanin National Park	Nahuel Huapi Nat. Park
Barbados	Harrisons's Cave	Farley Hill Nat. Park	Welchman Hall Gully
Belize	Barrier Reef	Mountain Pine Ridge	The Blue Hole
Bolivia	..	..	..
Brazil	Iguacu National Park	..	..
Chile	Rapa Nui Nat. Park	Torres del Paine Nat. Park	Atacama Desert
Colombia	Los Katios Nat. Park		
Costa Rica	Poas Volcano	Irazu Volcano	Cocos Islands
Cuba	Viñales Valley	Sierra del Rosario Bios. Reserve	Zapata Peninsula
Dominican Rep.	Pico Duarte	Samana Whale Sanctuary	Los Haitiseis
Ecuador	Cotopaxi National Park	Galapagos National Park	Machalilla National Park
El Salvador	Montecristo National Park	National Zoo	El Imposible Nat. Park
Guatemala	Tikal National Park	..	..
Haiti	Macaya Park	Lake Azuei	Pine Forest
Honduras	Rio Platana Bios. Reserve	..	..
Jamaica	..	..	..
Mexico	Sian Ka'An	Cozumel Reefs	Contoy Island
Nicaragua	Masaya Volcano Nat. Park	Mombacho Volcano	Granada + Ometepe Islets
Panama	Darien National Park	Chiriqui Volcano	La India Dormida, Cocle
Paraguay	..	..	..
Peru	Iquitos	Manu National Park	Huascaran National Park
Saint Lucia	Sulphur Springs	Diamond Falls	Descartiers Forest Trail
Saint Vincent	La Soufrière	Balleine Falls	Tobago Cays
Trinidad and Tobago	Asa Wright Nature Centre	Buccoo Reef	Bird Sanctuary
Uruguay	Rio Plata and Uruguay Coasts	Arapoy Baths	Sierras De Minas
Venezuela	Canaima National Park	Sierra Nevada Nat. Park	Archipelago Las Roques Nat. Park
North America			
Canada	Niagara Falls	Banff	Stanley Park
United States	..	..	..
Europe			
Albania	..	..	..
Andorra	Madriu Valley	Sorteny Valley	Incles Valley
Austria	Wachau	Grosslockner Alpine St Salzburg	Lake Neusiedl
Belarus	Belovezhskaya Forest	..	..
Belgium (Fl)	The Zwin	Planckendael Zoo	Meise Nat. Botanic Garden
Belgium (Fr)	Han-Sur-Lesse	Haut Fagnes Nature Reserve	Meuse Valley
Bosnia and Herzegovina	..	..	..
Bulgaria	Srebarna Nature Reserve	Pirin National Park	..
Croatia	Plitvicka Jezera Nat. Park	Kornati National Park	Krka National Park
Cyprus	Cape Greco Nat. Forest Park	Akamas Peninsula Forest	Troudos Nat. Forest Park
Czech Rep.	Krkonose National Park	Sumava National Park	Karst Morave Grottoes
Denmark	Grenen	Jutland West Coast	Rabjerg Mile
Estonia	Lahemaa National Park	Lake Puhajarve	Taevaskoja
Finland	..	..	..
France	Fontainebleau Forest	Mont Saint-Michel	Pyrenees National Park

Country or territory	Most visited natural sites		
Germany	The Alps	The Rhine Valley	Northern+Baltic Sea Islands
Greece	Samaria National Park	Olympus National Park	Vikos National Park
Hungary	Hortobagy National Park	Aggtelek Karst Caves	..
Ireland	..	..	..
Israel	..	..	..
Italy	Venice	Amalfi Coast	Cinque Terre
Latvia	Gauja National Park	Vidzeme Stony Beach	Kolka Horn
Lithuania	Neringa National Park	Aukstaitija National Park	Zemaitija National Park
Macedonia (former Yugoslav Rep. of)	Ohrid	Mavrovo	Struga
Moldova (Rep. of)	..	..	..
Netherlands	Waddenzee Wetlands	The Tulip Fields	De Hoge Weluwe Nat. Park
Norway	..	..	..
Poland	Bialowieza Forest	..	..
Portugal	..	..	..
Romania	Danube Delta	..	..
Russian Federation	Karelian Isthmus	Seliger Lake + Valdai	Lake Baikal National Park
San Marino	Montecerreto Pines	Montecchio Park	Aus De Dogana Park
Slovakia	Aggtelek Karst Caves	..	..
Slovenia	Skocjan Caves	..	..
Spain	Ordesa Nat. Park	Los Picos De Europa Nat. Park	Teide National Park
Sweden	..	..	..
Switzerland	Rhine Falls, Neuhausen	Jungfraujoch	Cervin
Turkey	Hierapolis	Cappadocia	Troia
Ukraine	Ascania Nova	Crimea	Carpathia
United Kingdom	Hampton Court Gardens	Kew Gardens	Royal Botanic Garden, Edinburgh
Yugoslavia	Durmitor National Park	..	..

*New Table

TABLE 12
WORLD HERITAGE SITES

Country or territory	Properties included in the World Heritage List				Year of inscription		Tentative list of world heritage properties	Endangered heritage sites	
	Cultural [1]	Natural	Combined	Total [1]				World Heritage Committee	World Monument Fund
	1999	1999	1999	1999	1980's	1990's	1999	1999	1998-2000
Sub-Saharan Africa									
Angola	-	-	-	-	-	-	11	-	-
Benin	1	-	-	1	1	-	5	1	1
Botswana	-	-	-	-	-	-	5	-	-
Burkina Faso	-	-	-	-	-	-	4	-	-
Burundi	-	-	-	-	-	-	-	-	-
Cameroon	-	1	-	1	1	-	-	-	-
Central African Rep.	-	1	-	1	1	-	-	1	-
Chad	-	-	-	-	-	-	-	-	-
Congo	-	-	-	-	-	-	-	-	-
Congo (Dem. Rep.)	-	5	-	5	4	1	3	4	-
Côte d' Ivoire	-	3	-	3	3	-	-	1	-
Eritrea	-	-	-	-	-	-	-	-	-
Ethiopia	6	1	-	7	7	-	1	1	1
Gabon	-	-	-	-	-	-	-	-	-
Gambia	-	-	-	-	-	-	3	-	1
Ghana	2	-	-	2	2	-	-	-	-
Guinea	-	1	-	1	1	-	-	1	-
Guinea-Bissau	-	-	-	-	-	-	-	-	-
Kenya	-	2	-	2	-	2	7	-	1
Lesotho	-	-	-	-	-	-	-	-	-
Liberia	-	-	-	-	-	-	-	-	-
Madagascar	-	1	-	1	-	1	6	-	-
Malawi	-	1	-	1	1	-	1	-	-
Mali	2	-	1	3	3	-	4	1	1
Mauritania	1	1	-	2	1	1	-	-	-
Mauritius	-	-	-	-	-	-	-	-	-
Mozambique	1	-	-	1	-	1	3	-	1
Namibia	-	-	-	-	-	-	-	-	-
Niger	-	2	-	2	-	2	6	1	1
Nigeria	1	-	-	1	-	1	8	-	-
Rwanda	-	-	-	-	-	-	-	-	-
Senegal	1	2	-	3	3	-	2	-	-
Seychelles	-	2	-	2	2	-	-	-	-
Sierra Leone	-	-	-	-	-	-	-	-	-
Somalia	-	-	-	-	-	-	-	-	-
South Africa	2	1	-	3	-	3	6	-	-
Sudan	-	-	-	-	-	-	8	-	1
Tanzania (United Rep. of)	1	4	-	5	5	-	3	-	1
Togo	-	-	-	-	-	-	-	-	-
Uganda	-	2	-	2	-	2	5	-	1
Zambia	-	1	-	1	1	-	3	-	-
Zimbabwe	2	2	-	4	4	-	2	-	1
Arab States									
Algeria	6	-	1	7	6	1	-	-	1
Egypt	5	-	-	5	5	-	14	-	4
Iraq	1	-	-	1	1	-	-	-	1
Jordan	3	-	-	3	3	-	-	1	1
Kuwait	-	-	-	-	-	-	-	-	-

Country or territory	Properties included in the World Heritage List: Cultural [1] 1999	Natural 1999	Combined 1999	Total [1] 1999	Year of inscription: 1980's	1990's	Tentative list of world heritage properties 1999	Endangered heritage sites: World Heritage Committee 1999	World Monument Fund 1998-2000
Lebanon	5	-	-	5	4	1	10	-	2
Libyan Arab Jamahiriya	5	-	-	5	5	-	10	-	-
Morocco	6	-	-	6	3	3	16	-	2
Oman	2	1	-	3	2	1	5	1	-
Saudi Arabia	-	-	-	-	-	-	-	-	-
Syrian Arab Rep.	4	-	-	4	4	-	15	-	-
Tunisia	7	1	-	8	7	1	-	1	-
United Arab Emirates	-	-	-	-	-	-	-	-	-
Yemen	3	-	-	3	2	1	-	-	2
South Central Asia									
Afghanistan	-	-	-	-	-	-	-	-	1
Armenia	1	-	-	1	-	1	6	-	-
Azerbaijan	-	-	-	-	-	-	8	-	-
Bangladesh	2	1	-	3	2	1	5	-	-
Bhutan	-	-	-	-	-	-	-	-	-
Georgia	3	-	-	3	-	3	9	-	3
India	17	5	-	22	19	3	7	1	7
Iran (Islamic Rep. of)	3	-	-	3	3	-	17	-	-
Kazakhstan	-	-	-	-	-	-	10	-	-
Kyrgyzstan	-	-	-	-	-	-	-	-	-
Nepal	2	2	-	4	3	1	6	-	3
Pakistan	6	-	-	6	5	1	8	-	2
Sri Lanka	6	1	-	7	6	1	-	-	1
Tajikistan	7	-	-	7	-	7	-	-	-
Turkmenistan	1	-	-	1	-	1	4	-	1
Uzbekistan	2	-	-	2	-	2	19	-	1
East Asia									
China	16	4	3	23	6	17	42	-	7
Hong Kong SAR	-	-	-	-	-	-	-	-	-
Japan	8	2	-	10	-	10	11	-	-
Korea (Dem. People's Rep. of)	-	-	-	-	-	-	-	-	-
Korea (Rep. of)	5	-	-	5	-	5	8	-	-
Mongolia	-	-	-	-	-	-	9	-	1
South-East Asia and Oceania									
Australia	9	-	4	13	8	5	2	-	-
Cambodia	1	-	-	1	-	1	11	1	2
Fiji	-	-	-	-	-	-	-	-	1
Indonesia	3	3	-	6	-	6	16	-	3
Lao People's Dem. Rep.	1	-	-	1	-	1	3	-	1
Malaysia	-	-	-	-	-	-	-	-	2
Myanmar	-	-	-	-	-	-	8	-	-
New Zealand	-	2	1	3	-	3	1	-	-
Papua New Guinea	-	-	-	-	-	-	3	-	-
Philippines	3	2	-	5	-	5	11	-	4
Singapore	-	-	-	-	-	-	-	-	-
Solomon Is	-	2	-	2	2	-	-	-	-
Thailand	3	1	-	4	-	4	-	-	1
Viet Nam	3	1	-	4	-	4	6	-	2

TABLE 12 (continued)

Country or territory	Properties included in the World Heritage List: Cultural[1] 1999	Natural 1999	Combined 1999	Total[1] 1999	Year of inscription: 1980's	1990's	Tentative list of world heritage properties 1999	Endangered heritage sites: World Heritage Committee 1999	World Monument Fund 1998-2000
Latin America and the Caribbean									
Argentina	2	3	-	5	3	2	5	-	2
Barbados	-	-	-	-	-	-	-	-	1
Belize	-	1	-	1	-	1	-	-	1
Bolivia	4	-	-	4	2	2	1	-	2
Brazil	9	3	-	12	7	5	23	-	3
Chile	1	-	-	1	-	1	20	-	5
Colombia	4	1	-	5	1	4	7	-	-
Costa Rica	-	3	-	3	1	2	1	-	-
Cuba	4	1	-	5	2	3	2	-	5
Dominica	-	1	-	1	-	1	-	-	-
Dominican Rep.	1	-	-	1	-	1	-	-	1
Ecuador	2	2	-	4	3	1	6	1	1
El Salvador	1	-	-	1	-	1	6	-	1
Guatemala	2	-	1	3	3	-	-	-	-
Guyana	-	-	-	-	-	-	4	-	-
Haiti	1	-	-	1	1	-	-	-	-
Honduras	1	1	-	2	2	-	-	1	-
Jamaica	-	-	-	-	-	-	-	-	2
Mexico	19	2	-	21	8	13	17	-	13
Nicaragua	-	-	-	-	-	-	6	-	-
Panama	2	2	-	4	3	1	1	-	1
Paraguay	1	-	-	1	-	1	3	-	-
Peru	5	2	2	9	7	2	3	1	7
St. Kitts	1	-	-	1	-	1	3	-	-
Suriname	-	-	-	-	-	-	2	-	1
Trinidad and Tobago	-	-	-	-	-	-	-	-	-
Uruguay	1	-	-	1	-	1	1	-	-
Venezuela	1	1	-	2	-	2	2	-	1
North America									
Canada	5	8	-	13	10	3	9	-	1
United States	8	12	-	20	17	3	72	2	15
Europe									
Andorra	-	-	-	-	-	-	2	-	-
Albania	1	-	-	1	-	1	4	1	1
Austria	5	-	-	5	-	5	14	-	2
Belarus	-	1	-	1	1	-	1	-	-
Belgium	4	-	-	4	-	4	9	-	3
Bosnia and Herzegovina	-	-	-	-	-	-	2	-	2
Bulgaria	7	2	-	9	9	-	11	1	2
Croatia	4	1	-	5	3	2	8	2	7
Cyprus	3	-	-	3	1	2	1	-	-
Czech Rep.	9	-	-	9	-	9	5	-	7
Denmark	2	-	-	2	-	2	8	-	-
Estonia	1	-	-	1	-	1	5	-	-
Finland	5	-	-	5	-	5	7	-	-
France	25	1	1	27	17	10	15	-	4
Germany	21	1	-	22	8	14	25	-	3

Country or territory	Properties included in the World Heritage List: Cultural[1] 1999	Natural 1999	Combined 1999	Total[1] 1999	Year of inscription: 1980's	1990's	Tentative list of world heritage properties 1999	Endangered heritage sites: World Heritage Committee 1999	World Monument Fund 1998-2000
Greece	14	-	2	16	10	6	6	-	2
Hungary	4	1	-	5	2	3	6	-	2
Ireland	2	-	-	2	-	2	8	-	2
Israel	1	-	-	1	1	-	-	1	3
Italy	31	-	-	31	6	25	67	-	20
Latvia	1	-	-	1	-	1	5	-	1
Lithuania	1	-	-	1	-	1	3	-	1
Luxembourg	1	-	-	1	-	1	2	-	-
Macedonia (former Yugoslav Rep. of)	-	-	1	1	1	-	-	-	-
Malta	3	-	-	3	3	-	7	-	1
Moldova (Rep. of)	-	-	-	-	-	-	-	-	-
Netherlands	6	-	-	6	-	6	14	-	-
Norway	4	-	-	4	4	-	-	-	2
Poland	8	1	-	9	5	4	2	1	4
Portugal	9	1	-	10	6	4	5	-	1
Romania	6	1	-	7	-	7	17	-	3
Russian Federation	8	5	-	13	-	13	18	-	10
Slovakia	3	1	-	4	-	4	9	-	2
Slovenia	-	1	-	1	1	-	3	-	-
Spain	27	2	2	31	16	15	85	-	2
Sweden	8	-	1	9	-	9	11	-	-
Switzerland	3	-	-	3	3	-	1	-	-
Turkey	6	-	2	8	6	2	2	-	6
Ukraine	2	-	-	2	-	2	8	-	3
United Kingdom	14	4	-	18	14	4	26	-	5
Yugoslavia	3	1	-	4	4	-	11	1	1

Regions	Properties included in the World Heritage List: Cultural[1] 1999	Natural 1999	Combined 1999	Total[1] 1999	Year of inscription: 1980's	1990's	Tentative list of world heritage properties 1999	Endangered heritage sites: World Heritage Committee 1999	World Monument Fund 1998-2000
World	496	128	22	646	327	319	1 023	28	232
Developing	214	80	8	302	171	131	495	19	114
Industrial	282	48	14	344	156	188	528	9	118
Developing excl. India/China	181	71	5	257	146	111	446	18	100
Industrial excl. US/Rus. Fed.	266	31	14	311	139	172	438	7	93
Sub-Saharan Africa	20	33	1	54	40	14	96	11	11
Arab States	47	2	1	50	42	8	70	3	13
South Central Asia	50	9	0	59	38	21	99	1	19
East Asia	29	6	3	38	6	32	70	0	8
South-East Asia/Oceania	23	11	5	39	10	29	61	1	16
Latin Am./Carib	62	23	3	88	43	45	113	3	47
North America	13	20	0	33	27	6	81	2	16
Europe	252	24	9	285	121	164	433	7	102

1. Plus two cultural sites in the World Heritage list in the Holy See.

TABLE 13
RATIFICATIONS: UNESCO AND ILO CULTURAL AND LABOUR CONVENTIONS (1999)

Country or territory (Date of convention)	Protection of the world heritage (UNESCO 1972)	Protection of cultural property in armed conflict (UNESCO 1954)	Illicit trade/ transfer of cult. prop. (UNESCO 1970)	Discrimi-nation in education* (UNESCO 1960)	Discrimi-nation in employment/ occupation* (ILO 1957)	Equal remune-ration for men and women for equal work* (ILO 1957)	Indigenous and tribal people* (ILO 1980)	Abolition of forced labour* (ILO 1957)	Freedom of association and right to organize* (ILO 1948)	Total score
Sub-Saharan Africa										
Angola	X	-	X	-	X	X	-	X	-	10
Benin	X	-	-	X	X	X	-	X	X	12
Botswana	X	-	-	-	-	-	-	X	X	4
Burkina Faso	X	X	XX	-	X	X	-	X	X	16
Burundi	X	-	-	-	X	X	-	X	X	10
Cameroon	X	X	X	-	X	X	-	X	X	14
Cape Verde	X	-	-	-	X	X	-	X	-	8
Central African Rep.	X	-	X	X	X	X	-	X	X	14
Chad	-	-	-	-	X	X	-	X	X	8
Congo	X	-	-	X	-	-	-	X	X	8
Congo (Dem. Rep.)	X	X	X	-	-	X	-	-	-	8
Côte d' Ivoire	X	X	XX	-	X	X	-	X	X	15
Eritrea	-	-	-	-	-	-	-	-	X	2
Ethiopia	X	-	-	-	X	-	-	-	X	6
Gabon	X	X	-	-	X	X	-	X	X	12
Gambia	X	-	-	-	-	-	-	-	-	2
Ghana	X	X	-	-	X	X	-	X	X	12
Guinea	X	X	XX	X	-	X	-	X	X	16
Guinea-Bissau	-	-	-	-	-	X	-	X	-	4
Kenya	X	-	-	-	-	-	-	X	-	4
Lesotho	-	-	-	-	-	-	-	-	X	2
Liberia	-	-	-	X	X	-	-	X	X	8
Madagascar	X	X	X	X	X	X	-	-	X	14
Malawi	X	-	-	-	X	X	-	X	X	10
Mali	X	X	X	-	X	X	-	X	X	14
Mauritania	X	-	X	-	X	-	-	X	X	10
Mauritius	X	-	X	X	-	-	-	X	-	8
Mozambique	X	-	-	-	X	X	-	X	X	10
Namibia	-	-	-	-	-	-	-	-	X	2
Niger	X	X	X	X	X	X	-	X	X	16
Nigeria	X	X	X	X	-	X	-	X	X	14
Rwanda	-	-	-	-	X	X	-	X	X	8
Senegal	X	X	XX	X	X	X	-	X	X	18
Seychelles	X	-	-	-	-	-	-	X	X	6
Sierra Leone	-	-	-	X	-	X	-	X	X	8
Somalia	-	-	-	-	X	-	-	X	-	4
South Africa	X	-	-	-	-	X	-	X	X	8
Sudan	X	X	-	-	X	X	-	X	-	9
Tanzania (United Rep. of)	X	X	X	X	-	-	-	X	-	9
Togo	X	-	-	-	X	X	-	X	X	10
Uganda	X	-	-	X	-	-	-	X	-	6
Zambia	X	-	XX	-	X	X	-	X	X	14
Zimbabwe	X	X	-	-	-	X	-	X	-	7
Arab States										
Algeria	X	-	X	X	X	X	-	X	X	14
Bahrain	X	-	-	-	-	-	-	X	-	4
Egypt	X	X	X	X	X	X	-	X	X	16
Iraq	X	X	X	X	X	X	-	X	-	14
Jordan	X	X	X	X	X	X	-	X	-	14
Kuwait	-	X	X	X	X	-	-	X	X	12
Lebanon	X	X	X	X	X	X	-	X	-	14
Libyan Arab Jamahiriya	X	X	X	X	X	X	-	X	-	14
Morocco	X	X	-	X	X	X	-	X	-	12
Oman	X	X	X	-	-	-	-	-	-	5

Country or territory (Date of convention)	Protection of the world heritage (UNESCO 1972)	Protection of cultural property in armed conflict (UNESCO 1954)	Illicit trade/ transfer of cult. prop. (UNESCO 1970)	Discrimi- nation in education* (UNESCO 1960)	Discrimi- nation in employment/ occupation* (ILO 1957)	Equal remune- ration for men and women for equal work* (ILO 1957)	Indigenous and tribal people* (ILO 1980)	Abolition of forced labour* (ILO 1957)	Freedom of association and right to organize* (ILO 1948)	Total score
Qatar	X	X	X	-	X	-	-	-	-	7
Saudi Arabia	X	X	X	X	X	X	-	X	-	13
Syrian Arab Rep.	X	X	X	-	X	X	-	X	X	14
Tunisia	X	X	X	X	X	X	-	X	X	16
United Arab Emirates	-	-	-	-	-	-	-	-	-	0
Yemen	X	X	-	-	X	X	-	X	X	12
South Central Asia										
Afghanistan	X	-	-	-	X	X	-	X	-	8
Armenia	X	X	X	X	X	X	-	-	-	12
Azerbaijan	X	X	-	-	X	X	-	-	X	10
Bangladesh	X	-	X	-	X	-	-	X	X	10
Bhutan	-	-	-	-	-	-	-	-	-	0
Georgia	X	X	XX	X	-	-	-	X	X	14
India	X	X	X	-	X	X	-	-	-	10
Iran (Islamic Rep. of)	X	X	X	X	X	X	-	X	-	14
Kazakhstan	X	X	-	-	-	-	-	-	-	4
Kyrgyzstan	X	X	X	X	X	X	-	X	X	15
Maldives	X	-	-	-	-	-	-	-	-	2
Nepal	X	-	X	-	X	X	-	-	-	8
Pakistan	X	X	XX	-	X	-	-	X	X	14
Sri Lanka	X	-	X	X	-	X	-	-	X	10
Tajikistan	X	X	X	X	X	X	-	X	X	16
Turkmenistan	X	-	-	-	-	-	-	X	X	6
Uzbekistan	X	X	X	-	-	-	-	X	-	7
East Asia										
China	X	-	XX	X	-	X	-	-	-	10
Hong Kong SAR	-	-	-	-	-	-	-	-	X	2
Japan	X	-	-	-	-	X	-	-	X	6
Korea (Dem People's Rep. of)	X	-	X	-	-	-	-	-	-	4
Korea (Rep. of)	X	-	X	-	-	-	-	-	-	4
Mongolia	X	X	X	X	X	X	-	-	X	13
South-East Asia and Oceania										
Australia	X	X	X	X	X	X	-	X	X	15
Cambodia	X	X	XX	-	-	-	-	-	X	10
Fiji	X	-	-	-	-	-	-	X	-	4
Indonesia	X	X	-	X	-	X	-	X	X	12
Lao People's Dem. Rep.	X	-	-	-	-	-	-	-	-	2
Malaysia	X	X	-	-	-	-	-	-	-	4
Myanmar	X	X	-	-	-	-	-	-	X	6
New Zealand	X	-	-	X	X	X	-	X	-	10
Papua New Guinea	X	-	-	-	-	-	-	X	X	6
Philippines	X	-	-	X	X	X	-	X	X	12
Singapore	-	-	-	-	-	-	-	-	-	0
Thailand	X	X	-	-	-	-	-	X	-	6
Viet Nam	X	-	-	X	X	-	-	-	-	6
Latin America and the Caribbean										
Antigua	X	-	-	-	X	-	-	X	X	8
Argentina	X	X	X	X	X	X	-	X	X	15
Bahamas	-	-	X	-	-	-	-	X	-	4
Belize	X	-	X	-	-	-	-	X	X	8
Bolivia	X	-	XX	-	X	X	X	X	X	16

Table 13 (continued)

Country or territory (Date of convention)	Protection of the world heritage (UNESCO 1972)	Protection of cultural property in armed conflict (UNESCO 1954)	Illicit trade/ transfer of cult. prop. (UNESCO 1970)	Discrimi- nation in education* (UNESCO 1960)	Discrimi- nation in employment/ occupation* (ILO 1957)	Equal remune- ration for men and women for equal work* (ILO 1957)	Indigenous and tribal people* (ILO 1980)	Abolition of forced labour* (ILO 1957)	Freedom of association and right to organize* (ILO 1948)	Total score
Brazil	X	X	XX	X	X	X	-	X	-	16
Chile	X	-	-	X	X	X	-	X	X	12
Colombia	X	X	X	-	X	X	X	X	X	16
Costa Rica	X	X	X	X	X	X	X	X	X	18
Cuba	X	X	X	X	X	X	-	X	X	16
Dominica	X	-	-	X	X	X	-	X	X	12
Dominican Rep.	X	X	X	X	X	X	-	X	X	15
Ecuador	X	X	XX	X	X	X	-	X	X	18
El Salvador	X	-	X	-	-	-	-	X	-	6
Grenada	X	-	X	-	-	X	-	X	X	10
Guatemala	X	X	X	X	X	X	-	X	X	16
Guyana	X	-	-	-	X	X	-	X	X	10
Haiti	X	-	-	-	X	X	-	X	X	10
Honduras	X	-	X	-	X	X	X	X	X	14
Jamaica	X	-	-	-	X	X	-	X	X	10
Mexico	X	X	X	-	X	X	X	X	X	16
Nicaragua	X	X	X	X	X	X	-	X	X	16
Panama	X	X	X	X	X	X	-	X	X	15
Paraguay	X	-	O	-	X	X	X	X	X	13
Peru	X	X	XX	X	X	X	X	X	X	20
St. Kitts	X	-	-	-	-	-	-	-	-	2
St. Lucia	X	-	-	-	X	X	-	X	X	10
Suriname	X	-	-	-	-	-	-	X	X	6
Trinidad and Tobago	-	-	-	-	X	-	-	X	X	6
Uruguay	X	-	X	-	X	X	-	X	X	12
Venezuela	X	-	-	X	X	X	-	X	X	12
North America										
Canada	X	X	X	-	X	X	-	X	X	13
United States	X	-	X	-	-	-	-	X	-	6
Europe										
Albania	X	X	-	X	-	X	-	X	X	12
Andorra	X	-	-	-	-	-	-	-	-	2
Austria	X	X	-	-	X	X	-	X	X	12
Belarus	X	X	X	X	X	X	-	X	X	16
Belgium	X	X	-	-	X	X	-	X	X	12
Bosnia and Herzegovina	X	X	X	X	X	X	-	-	X	14
Bulgaria	X	X	X	X	X	X	-	X	X	16
Croatia	X	X	XX	X	X	X	-	X	X	18
Cyprus	X	X	X	X	X	X	-	X	X	16
Czech Rep.	X	X	X	X	X	X	-	X	X	16
Denmark	X	-	-	X	X	X	X	X	X	14
Estonia	X	X	X	-	-	-	-	X	X	9
Finland	X	X	O	X	X	X	-	X	X	15
France	X	X	XX	X	X	X	-	X	X	18
Germany	X	X	-	X	X	X	-	X	X	14
Greece	X	X	X	-	X	X	-	X	X	14
Hungary	X	X	X	X	X	X	-	X	X	16
Iceland	X	-	-	-	X	X	-	X	X	10
Ireland	X	-	-	-	-	X	-	X	X	8
Israel	-	X	-	X	X	X	-	X	X	12

Country or territory (Date of convention)	Protection of the world heritage (UNESCO 1972)	Protection of cultural property in armed conflict (UNESCO 1954)	Illicit trade/ transfer of cult. prop. (UNESCO 1970)	Discrimi- nation in education* (UNESCO 1960)	Discrimi- nation in employment/ occupation* (ILO 1957)	Equal remune- ration for men and women for equal work* (ILO 1957)	Indigenous and tribal people* (ILO 1980)	Abolition of forced labour* (ILO 1957)	Freedom of association and right to organize* (ILO 1948)	Total score
Italy	X	X	XX	X	X	X	-	X	X	18
Latvia	X	-	-	-	X	X	-	X	X	10
Lithuania	X	X	XX	-	X	X	-	X	X	16
Luxembourg	X	X	XX	X	-	X	-	X	X	16
Macedonia (former Yugoslav Rep. of)	X	X	X	-	-	-	-	-	X	8
Malta	X	-	-	X	X	X	-	X	X	12
Moldova (Rep. of)	-	-	-	X	-	-	-	X	X	6
Monaco	X	X	-	-	-	-	-	-	-	4
Netherlands	X	X	O	X	X	X	-	X	X	15
Norway	X	X	-	X	X	X	X	X	X	16
Poland	X	X	X	X	X	X	-	X	X	16
Portugal	X	-	XX	X	X	X	-	X	X	16
Romania	X	X	XX	X	X	X	-	X	X	18
Russian Federation	X	X	XX	X	X	X	-	X	X	18
San Marino	X	X	-	-	X	X	-	X	X	12
Slovakia	X	X	X	X	X	X	-	X	X	12
Slovenia	X	X	X	X	X	X	-	X	X	12
Spain	X	X	X	X	X	X	-	X	X	16
Sweden	X	X	-	X	X	X	-	X	X	14
Switzerland	X	X	O	-	X	X	-	X	X	13
Turkey	X	X	X	-	X	X	-	X	X	14
Ukraine	X	X	X	X	X	X	-	-	X	14
United Kingdom	X	-	-	X	-	X	-	X	X	10
Yugoslavia	X	X	X	X	X	X	-	-	X	14

* New indicator.

X: Convention only.

XX: Also signed the 1995 Unidroit Convention on stolen or illegally exported cultural objects

O: Signed only the 1995 Unidroit Convention

Regions (Date of convention)	Protection of the world heritage (UNESCO 1972)		Protection of cultural property in armed conflict (UNESCO 1954)		Illicit trade/ transfer of cult. prop. (UNESCO 1970)		Discrimi- nation in education* (UNESCO 1960)		Discrimi- nation in employment/ occupation* (ILO 1957)		Equal remune- ration for men and women for equal work* (ILO 1957)		Indigenous and tribal people* (ILO 1980)		Abolition of forced labour* (ILO 1957)		Freedom of association and right to organize* (ILO 1948)		Total score
	T	%	T	%	T	%	T	%	T	%	T	%	T	%	T	%	T	%	
World	154	90	93	54	94	55	79	46	114	66	119	69	9	5	125	73	125	73	11
Developing	107	87	56	48	64	52	47	38	76	62	76	62	7	6	93	63	79	57	11
Industrial	47	96	37	76	30	61	32	65	38	78	43	88	2	4	42	69	46	90	13
Developing excl. India/China	105	87	55	46	62	51	46	38	75	62	74	61	7	6	93	64	71	58	11
Industrial excl. US/Rus. Fed	45	96	36	77	28	60	31	66	37	79	42	89	2	4	40	70	46	92	13
Sub-Saharan Africa	34	79	15	35	16	37	13	30	25	58	28	65	0	0	36	84	32	74	9
Arab States	14	88	13	81	12	75	10	63	13	81	11	69	0	0	13	81	6	38	11
South Central Asia	16	94	10	59	11	65	6	35	10	59	9	53	0	0	9	53	8	47	9
East Asia	5	83	1	17	4	67	2	33	1	17	3	50	0	0	0	0	3	50	7
South-East Asia/Oceania	12	92	6	46	2	15	5	39	4	31	4	31	0	0	7	54	6	46	7
Latin Am./Carib	29	94	12	39	20	65	13	42	25	81	24	77	7	23	30	97	27	87	12
North America	2	100	1	50	2	100	0	0	1	50	1	50	0	0	2	100	1	50	10
Europe	42	96	35	80	27	61	30	68	35	80	39	89	2	5	28	86	42	95	13

TABLE 14
RATIFICATIONS: UNITED NATIONS HUMAN RIGHTS CONVENTIONS

Country or territory (Date of convention)	Economic, social and cultural rights (1966)	Civil and political rights (1966)	Elimination of all forms of racial discrimination (1965)	Elimination of all forms of discrimination against women (1979)	Prevention and punishment of the crime of genocide (1948)	Rights of the child (1989)	Torture and other cruel, inhuman or degrading treatment or punishment (1984)	Status of refugees (1951)	Total score
Sub-Saharan Africa									
Angola	X	X	-	X	-	X	-	X	10
Benin	X	X	X	X	-	X	X	X	13
Botswana	-	-	X	X	-	X	-	X	8
Burkina Faso	X	X	X	X	X	X	X	X	16
Burundi	X	X	X	X	X	X	X	X	16
Cameroon	X	X	X	X	-	X	X	X	14
Central African Rep.	X	X	X	X	-	X	-	X	12
Chad	X	X	X	X	-	X	X	X	14
Congo	X	X	X	X	-	X	-	X	12
Congo (Dem. Rep.)	X	X	X	X	X	X	X	X	16
Côte d'Ivoire	X	X	X	X	X	X	X	X	16
Eritrea	-	-	-	X	-	X	-	-	4
Ethiopia	X	X	X	X	X	X	X	X	16
Gabon	X	X	X	X	X	X	X	X	15
Gambia	X	X	X	X	X	X	X	X	15
Ghana	-	-	X	X	X	X	-	X	10
Guinea	X	X	X	X	-	X	X	X	14
Guinea-Bissau	X	-	-	X	-	X	-	X	8
Kenya	X	X	-	X	-	X	X	X	12
Lesotho	X	X	X	X	X	X	-	X	14
Liberia	X	X	X	X	X	X	-	X	12
Madagascar	X	X	X	X	-	X	-	X	12
Malawi	X	X	X	X	-	X	X	X	14
Mali	X	X	X	X	X	X	X	X	16
Mauritania	-	-	X	-	-	X	-	X	6
Mauritius	X	X	X	X	-	X	X	-	12
Mozambique	-	X	X	X	X	X	-	X	12
Namibia	X	X	X	X	X	X	X	X	16
Niger	X	X	X	X	-	X	X	X	14
Nigeria	X	X	X	X	-	X	X	X	13
Rwanda	X	X	X	X	X	X	-	X	14
Senegal	X	X	X	X	X	X	X	X	16
Sierra Leone	X	X	X	X	-	X	X	X	13
Somalia	X	X	X	-	-	-	X	X	10
South Africa	X	X	X	X	X	X	X	X	15
Sudan	X	X	X	-	-	X	X	X	11
Tanzania (United Rep. of)	X	X	X	X	X	X	-	X	14
Togo	X	X	X	X	X	X	X	X	16
Uganda	X	X	X	X	X	X	X	X	16
Zambia	X	X	X	X	-	X	X	X	14
Zimbabwe	X	X	X	X	X	X	-	X	14
Arab States									
Algeria	X	X	X	X	X	X	X	X	16
Egypt	X	X	X	X	X	X	X	X	16
Iraq	X	X	X	X	X	X	-	X	14
Jordan	X	X	X	X	X	X	X	-	14
Kuwait	X	X	X	X	X	X	X	-	14

Country or territory (Date of convention)	Economic, social and cultural rights (1966)	Civil and political rights (1966)	Elimination of all forms of racial discrimination (1965)	Elimination of all forms of discrimination against women (1979)	Prevention and punishment of the crime of genocide (1948)	Rights of the child (1989)	Torture and other cruel, inhuman or degrading treatment or punishment (1984)	Status of refugees (1951)	Total score
Lebanon	X	X	X	X	X	X	-	-	12
Libyan Arab Jamahiriya	X	X	X	X	X	X	X	-	14
Morocco	X	X	X	X	X	X	X	X	16
Oman	-	-	-	-	-	X	-	-	2
Saudi Arabia	-	-	X	-	X	X	X	-	8
Syrian Arab Rep.	X	X	X	-	X	X	-	-	10
Tunisia	X	X	X	X	X	X	X	X	16
United Arab Emirates	-	-	X	-	-	X	-	-	4
Yemen	X	X	X	X	X	X	X	X	16
South Central Asia									
Afghanistan	X	X	X	X	X	X	X	-	13
Armenia	X	X	X	X	X	X	X	X	16
Azerbaijan	X	X	X	X	X	X	X	X	16
Bangladesh	X	-	X	X	X	X	X	-	12
Bhutan	-	-	X	X	-	X	-	-	5
Georgia	X	X	X	X	X	X	X	-	14
India	X	X	X	X	X	X	X	-	13
Iran (Islamic Rep. of)	X	X	X	-	X	X	-	X	12
Kazakhstan	-	-	X	X	X	X	X	X	12
Kyrgyzstan	X	X	X	X	X	X	X	X	16
Nepal	X	X	X	X	X	X	X	-	14
Pakistan	-	-	X	X	X	X	-	-	8
Sri Lanka	X	X	X	X	X	X	X	-	14
Tajikistan	X	X	X	X	X	X	X	X	16
Turkmenistan	X	X	X	X	-	X	X	-	12
Uzbekistan	X	X	X	X	-	X	X	-	12
East Asia									
China	X	X	X	X	X	X	X	X	14
Hong Kong SAR	-	-	-	-	-	-	-	-	-
Japan	X	X	X	X	-	X	X	X	14
Korea (Dem. People's Rep. of)	X	X	-	-	X	X	-	-	8
Korea (Rep. of)	X	X	X	X	X	X	X	X	16
Mongolia	X	X	X	X	X	X	-	-	12
South-East Asia and Oceania									
Australia	X	X	X	X	X	X	X	X	16
Cambodia	X	X	X	X	X	X	X	X	16
Indonesia	-	-	X	X	-	X	X	-	8
Lao People's Dem. Rep.	-	-	X	X	X	X	-	-	8
Malaysia	-	-	-	X	X	X	-	-	6
Myanmar	-	-	-	X	X	X	-	-	6
New Zealand	X	X	X	X	X	X	X	X	16
Papua New Guinea	-	-	X	X	X	X	-	X	10
Philippines	X	X	X	X	X	X	X	X	16
Singapore	-	-	-	X	X	X	-	X	8
Thailand	X	X	-	X	-	X	-	-	8
Viet Nam	X	X	X	X	X	X	-	-	12

TABLE 14 (continued)

Country or territory (Date of convention)	Economic, social and cultural rights (1966)	Civil and political rights (1966)	Elimination of all forms of racial discrimination (1965)	Elimination of all forms of discrimination against women (1979)	Prevention and punishment of the crime of genocide (1948)	Rights of the child (1989)	Torture and other cruel, inhuman or degrading treatment or punishment (1984)	Status of refugees (1951)	Total score
Latin America and the Caribbean									
Argentina	X	X	X	X	X	X	X	X	16
Bolivia	X	X	X	X	X	X	X	X	14
Brazil	X	X	X	X	X	X	X	X	16
Chile	X	X	X	X	X	X	X	X	16
Colombia	X	X	X	X	X	X	X	X	16
Costa Rica	X	X	X	X	X	X	X	X	16
Cuba	-	-	X	X	X	X	X	-	10
Dominican Rep.	X	X	X	X	X	X	X	X	14
Ecuador	X	X	X	X	X	X	X	X	16
El Salvador	X	X	X	X	X	X	X	X	16
Guatemala	X	X	X	X	X	X	X	X	16
Haiti	-	X	X	X	X	X	-	X	12
Honduras	X	X	-	X	X	X	X	X	14
Jamaica	X	X	X	X	X	X	-	X	14
Mexico	X	X	X	X	X	X	X	-	14
Nicaragua	X	X	X	X	X	X	-	X	15
Panama	X	X	X	X	X	X	X	X	16
Paraguay	X	X	-	X	X	X	X	X	13
Peru	X	X	X	X	X	X	X	X	16
Trinidad and Tobago	X	X	X	X	-	X	-	-	10
Uruguay	X	X	X	X	X	X	X	X	16
Venezuela	X	X	X	X	X	X	X	-	14
North America									
Canada	X	X	X	X	X	X	X	X	16
United States	X	X	X	X	X	X	X	-	11
Europe									
Albania	X	X	X	X	X	X	X	X	16
Austria	X	X	X	X	X	X	X	X	16
Belarus	X	X	X	X	X	X	X	-	14
Belgium	X	X	X	X	X	X	X	X	16
Bosnia and Herzegovina	X	X	X	X	X	X	X	X	16
Bulgaria	X	X	X	X	X	X	X	X	16
Croatia	X	X	X	X	X	X	X	X	16
Czech Rep.	X	X	X	X	X	X	X	X	16
Denmark	X	X	X	X	X	X	X	X	16
Estonia	X	X	X	X	X	X	X	X	16
Finland	X	X	X	X	X	X	X	X	16
France	X	X	X	X	X	X	X	X	16
Germany	X	X	X	X	X	X	X	X	16
Greece	X	X	X	X	X	X	X	X	16
Hungary	X	X	X	X	X	X	X	X	16
Ireland	X	X	-	X	X	X	-	X	14
Israel	X	X	X	X	X	X	X	X	16
Italy	X	X	X	X	X	X	X	X	16
Latvia	X	X	X	X	X	X	X	X	16
Lithuania	X	X	X	X	X	X	X	X	16

Country or territory (Date of convention)	Economic, social and cultural rights (1966)	Civil and political rights (1966)	Elimination of all forms of racial discrimination (1965)	Elimination of all forms of discrimination against women (1979)	Prevention and punishment of the crime of genocide (1948)	Rights of the child (1989)	Torture and other cruel, inhuman or degrading treatment or punishment (1984)	Status of refugees (1951)	Total score
Macedonia (former Yugoslav Rep. of)	X	X	X	X	X	X	X	-	14
Moldova (Rep. of)	X	X	X	X	X	X	X	-	14
Netherlands	X	X	X	X	X	X	X	X	16
Norway	X	X	X	X	X	X	X	X	16
Poland	X	X	X	X	X	X	X	X	16
Portugal	X	X	X	X	X	X	X	X	16
Romania	X	X	X	X	X	X	X	X	16
Russian Federation	X	X	X	X	X	X	X	X	16
Slovakia	X	X	X	X	X	X	X	X	16
Slovenia	X	X	X	X	X	X	X	X	16
Spain	X	X	X	X	X	X	X	X	16
Sweden	X	X	X	X	X	X	X	X	16
Switzerland	X	X	X	X	-	X	X	X	14
Turkey	-	-	X	X	X	X	X	X	11
Ukraine	X	X	X	X	X	X	X	-	14
United Kingdom	X	X	X	X	X	X	X	X	16
Yugoslavia	X	X	X	X	X	X	X	X	16

X denotes signature not followed by ratification.

Regions (Date of convention)	Economic, social and cultural rights (1966)		Civil and political rights (1966)		Elimination of all forms of racial discrimination (1969)		Elimination of all forms of discrimination against women (1979)		Prevention and punishment of the crime of genocide (1948)		Rights of the child (1989)		Torture and other cruel, inhuman or degrading treatment or punishment (1984)		Status of refugees (1951)		Total score
	T	%	T	%	T	%	T	%	T	%	T	%	T	%	T	%	
World	129	86	129	86	137	91	140	93	118	79	148	99	115	77	112	75	13
Developing	88	82	88	82	94	97	98	90	78	72	106	98	74	60	75	69	13
Industrial	41	98	41	98	43	98	42	100	40	95	42	100	41	98	37	88	15
Developing excl. India/China	86	81	86	82	92	87	96	90	76	72	104	98	72	59	74	70	13
Industrial excl. US/Rus. Fed.	39	98	39	98	41	98	40	100	38	95	40	100	39	98	36	90	15
Sub-Saharan Africa	36	88	36	88	37	90	38	93	20	49	40	98	27	56	39	95	13
Arab States	11	79	11	79	13	93	10	71	12	86	14	100	9	64	6	43	12
South Central Asia	13	81	12	75	16	100	15	94	13	81	16	100	13	81	6	38	13
East Asia	6	83	5	83	4	67	4	67	4	67	5	83	3	33	3	50	10
South-East Asia/Oceania	5	42	6	50	8	67	12	100	10	83	12	100	5	42	6	50	11
Latin Am./Carib.	20	91	21	96	20	91	22	100	21	96	22	100	19	86	18	82	15
North America	2	100	2	100	2	100	2	100	2	100	2	100	2	100	1	50	14
Europe	36	97	6	97	37	100	37	100	36	97	37	100	37	100	33	89	16

TABLE 15
CULTURAL TRADE AND COMMUNICATION TRENDS: TRENDS IN CULTURAL TRADE

Country or territory	Cultural trade [1]						Cultural exports as % of total cultural trade	
	US$ Mill. 1980	US$ Mill. 1997	US$ per capita 1980	US$ per capita 1987	As % of GNP 1980	As % of GNP 1997	1980	1997
Sub-Saharan Africa								
Angola	..	..	..	..	..	..	..	..
Benin	..	..	..	..	..	..	..	..
Botswana	..	..	..	..	..	..	..	..
Burkina Faso	..	..	..	..	..	..	..	..
Burundi	..	..	..	..	..	..	..	..
Cameroon	18	..	2	..	0.3	..	4.4	..
Central African Rep.	..	..	..	..	..	..	..	..
Chad	..	..	..	..	..	..	..	..
Congo	..	..	..	..	..	..	..	..
Congo (Dem. Rep.)	..	..	..	..	..	..	..	..
Côte d'Ivoire	..	..	..	..	..	..	..	..
Eritrea	..	..	..	..	..	..	..	..
Ethiopia	6	..	(.)	..	0.1	..	1.6	..
Gabon	..	..	..	..	..	..	..	..
Gambia	..	..	..	..	..	..	..	..
Ghana	..	..	..	..	..	..	..	..
Guinea	..	..	..	..	..	..	..	..
Guinea-Bissau	..	..	..	..	..	..	..	..
Kenya	42	143	3	5	0.6	1.5	5.3	7.8
Lesotho	..	..	..	..	..	..	..	..
Liberia	..	..	..	..	..	..	..	..
Madagascar	12	28	1	2	0.4	0.7	0.9	2.5
Malawi	..	..	..	..	..	..	..	..
Mali	..	..	..	..	..	..	..	..
Mauritania	..	..	..	..	..	..	..	..
Mauritius	11	92	11	84	1.0	2.1	1.9	6.6
Mozambique	..	..	..	..	..	..	..	..
Namibia	..	..	..	..	..	..	..	..
Niger	..	..	..	..	..	..	..	..
Nigeria	..	..	..	..	..	..	..	..
Rwanda	..	..	..	..	..	..	..	..
Senegal	20	..	4	..	0.7	..	25	..
Sierra Leone	..	..	..	..	..	..	..	..
Somalia	..	..	..	..	..	..	..	..
South Africa	..	..	..	..	..	..	..	..
Sudan	..	..	..	..	..	..	..	..
Tanzania (United Rep. of)	..	5	..	(.)	..	0.1	..	13
Togo	3	..	1	..	0.3	..	3.0	..
Uganda	..	..	..	..	..	..	..	..
Zambia	..	..	..	..	..	..	..	..
Zimbabwe	..	183	..	16	..	2.6	..	11
Arab States								
Algeria	80	308	4	10	0.2	0.7	0.3	0.6
Egypt	39	674	1	10	0.2	0.9	3.1	4.5
Iraq	35	..	..	..	..	..	..	..
Jordan	..	..	..	..	..	..	..	..
Kuwait	..	364	..	212	..	..	..	4.6

Country or territory	Cultural trade [1] US$ Mill. 1980	US$ Mill. 1997	US$ per capita 1980	US$ per capita 1987	As % of GNP 1980	As % of GNP 1997	Cultural exports as % of total cultural trade 1980	1997
Lebanon	..	..	..	..	..	..	..	..
Libyan Arab Jamahiriya	..	..	..	..	..	..	..	..
Morocco	47	328	2	12	0.3	0.9	0.6	3
Oman	25	340	22	142	0.8	..	8.3	25
Saudi Arabia	..	..	..	..	..	..	..	..
Syrian Arab Rep.	..	..	..	..	..	..	..	..
Tunisia	44	303	7	33	0.5	1.6	14	17
United Arab Emirates	..	..	..	..	..	..	..	..
Yemen	..	..	..	..	..	..	..	..
South Central Asia								
Afghanistan	..	..	..	..	..	..	..	..
Armenia	..	..	..	..	..	..	..	..
Azerbaijan	..	..	..	..	..	..	..	..
Bangladesh	14	..	(.)	..	0.1	..	0.7	..
Bhutan	..	..	..	..	..	..	..	..
Georgia	..	..	..	..	..	..	..	..
India	18	2 558	(.)	3	(.)	0.6	42	30
Iran (Islamic Rep. of)	..	..	..	..	..	..	..	..
Kazakhstan	..	..	..	..	..	..	..	..
Kyrgyzstan	..	..	..	..	..	..	..	..
Nepal	..	..	..	..	..	..	..	..
Pakistan	18	618	(.)	4	(.)	1.0	3.4	59
Sri Lanka	20	..	1	..	0.5	..	1.5	..
Tajikistan	..	..	..	..	..	..	..	..
Turkmenistan	..	..	..	..	..	..	..	..
Uzbekistan	..	..	..	..	..	..	..	..
East Asia								
China	..	30 461	..	24	..	3.3		64
Hong Kong SAR	2 167	33 535	430	5 005	8.3	21.2	57	8.8
Japan	13 404	70 261	115	556	1.2	1.7	92	53
Korea (Dem People's Rep. of)	..	..	..	..	..	..	..	..
Korea (Rep. of)	1 263	23 342	33	506	1.4	6.3	76	63
Mongolia	..	..	..	..	..	..	..	..
South-East Asia and Oceania								
Australia	1 042	10 442	72	564	0.9	2.7	12	14
Cambodia	..	..	..	..	..	..	..	..
Indonesia	139	4 668	1	23	0.2	3.4	5.9	71
Lao People's Dem. Rep.	..	..	..	..	..	..	..	..
Malaysia	..	29 007	21	1 355	1.3	36.4	24	72
Myanmar	..	254	..	57	..	..	..	..
New Zealand	180	2 036	58	536	0.9	3.6	9.6	13
Papua New Guinea	..	..	..	..	..	..	..	..
Philippines	79	5 741	2	79	0.2	7.3	18	45
Singapore	1 968	72 322	815	20 633	17.9	76.0	62	63
Thailand	80	15 925	2	264	0.3	11.8	14	66
Viet Nam	..	..	..	..	..	..	..	..

TABLE 15 (continued)

Country or territory	Cultural trade[1] US$ Mill. 1980	US$ Mill. 1997	US$ per capita 1980	US$ per capita 1987	As % of GNP 1980	As % of GNP 1997	Cultural exports as % of total cultural trade 1980	1997
Latin America and the Caribbean								
Argentina	649	2 910	23	81	1.2	0.9	12	9.4
Bolivia	20	148	4	19	0.7	1.9	0.5	1.7
Brazil	422	6 185	4	37	0.2	0.8	45	24
Chile	218	1 796	20	121	0.9	2.5	3.3	14
Colombia	126	1 380	5	34	0.4	1.3	32	15
Costa Rica	28	264	12	70	0.6	2.7	20	6.8
Cuba	..	..	..	..	..	..	..	..
Dominican Rep.	..	..	..	..	..	..	..	..
Ecuador	36	289	5	24	0.4	1.6	2.5	0.8
El Salvador	13	183	3	31	0.4	1.6	19	3.7
Guatemala	29	266	4	25	0.4	1.5	13	3.5
Haiti	..	..	..	..	..	..	..	..
Honduras	15	128	4	21	0.7	2.8	0.6	3.6
Jamaica	10	131	5	52	0.4	3.0	23	0.7
Mexico	567	22 774	8	238	0.3	6.0	16	66
Nicaragua	6	80	2	17	0.3	..	1.6	21
Panama	34	239	17	85	1	2.8	0.6	1.8
Paraguay	6	296	2	57	0.1	3.2	0.2	1.1
Peru	62	839	4	34	0.4	1.4	6.3	1.8
Trinidad and Tobago	29	115	27	88	0.6	2.0	2.4	7.9
Uruguay	28	285	10	86	0.3	1.4	14	11
Venezuela	483	922	32	40	0.8	1.1	1.3	3.6
North America								
Canada	2 452	32 498	100	1 062	1	5.3	26	51
United States	11 290	177 474	49	648	0.4	2.2	42	41
Europe								
Albania	..	19	..	4	..	0.7	..	1.1
Austria	1 203	9 579	159	1 182	1.6	4.4	38	55
Belarus	..	..	..	..	..	..	..	..
Belgium	3 246	19 447	330	1 925	2.6	7.5	60	50
Bosnia and Herzegovina	..	..	..	..	..	..	..	..
Bulgaria	..	217	..	37	..	2.1	..	25
Croatia	..	691	..	154	..	3.3	..	19
Czech Rep.	..	2 976	..	289	..	5.7	..	30
Denmark	648	..	126	..	1	..	35	..
Estonia	..	691	..	494	..	14.1	..	40
Finland	554	10 472	116	2 014	1.1	8.4	42	74
France	5 117	45 786	95	780	0.8	3.1	37	44
Germany	..	68 352	..	833	..	3.2	..	44
Greece	128	1 642	13	155	0.3	1.3	11	11
Hungary	..	5 517	..	546	..	12.1	..	55
Ireland	335	25 680	99	6 940	2	38.0	28	65
Israel	180	4 839	46	807	0.9	5.1	49	54
Italy	2 939	24 321	52	424	0.7	2.1	43	43
Latvia	..	196	..	82	..	3.3	..	16
Lithuania	..	410	..	111	..	4.6	..	29

Country or territory	Cultural trade [1]						Cultural exports as % of total cultural trade	
	US$ Mill. 1980	US$ Mill. 1997	US$ per capita 1980	US$ per capita 1987	As % of GNP 1980	As % of GNP 1997	1980	1997
Macedonia (former Yugoslav Rep. of)	..	..	..	..	..	..	..	..
Moldova (Rep. of)	..	..	..	..	..	..	..	..
Netherlands	3 438	51 296	243	3 267	2	13.2	43	49
Norway	471	12 534	115	2 849	0.9	8.2	11	74
Poland	..	3 630	..	94	..	2.4	..	..
Portugal	249	3 372	25	341	1.1	3.2	54	35
Romania	..	570	..	25	..	1.8	..	6.9
Russian Federation	..	3 214	..	22	..	1.0	..	42
Slovakia	..	1 021	..	189	..	5.1	..	30
Slovenia	..	824	..	412	..	4.2	..	46
Spain	1 323	14 912	35	377	0.7	2.7	38	35
Sweden	1 213	16 324	146	1 834	1.0	7.2	28	57
Switzerland	2 045	12 000	324	1 644	1.9	4.2	35	33
Turkey	19	2 614	(.)	41	(.)	1.3	13	22
Ukraine	..	..	..	..	..	..	..	..
United Kingdom	6 392	77 906	113	1 329	1.4	6.2	45	48
Yugoslavia	..	268	..	25	..	..	..	7.9

Regions	Cultural trade [1]						Cultural exports as % of total cultural trade	
	US$ Mill. 1980	US$ Mill. 1997	US$ per capita 1980	US$ per capita 1987	As % of GNP 1980	As % of GNP 1997	1980	1997
	T	T						
World	..	..	..	..	..	..	..	..
Developing Industrial	57 850	714 030	77	608	0.8	3.1	53	46
Developing excl. India/China Industrial excl. US/Rus. Fed.	46 560	533 343	91	709	1.1	3.7	56	48
Sub-Saharan Africa	..		..	..	..	..	..	..
Arab States	..		..	..	..	..	..	..
South Central Asia	..		..	..	..	..	..	..
East Asia	16 834	157 599	105	110	1.5	2.8	86	47
South-East Asia/Oceania	3 488	140 395	14	331	2.4	14.6	40	60
Latin Am./Carib.	2 781	39 230	8.5	84	0.5	2.1	16	44
North America	13 742	209 972	54	690	0.4	2.4	39	43
Europe	..	421 320	..	585	..	4.4	..	48

1. Exports plus imports of books and pamphlets; newspapers, newsprint and periodicals; typewrietrs and word and data processors; music-related goods; cinema and photography; radio, television and VCRs; visual arts and antiques; and sporting goods.

TABLE 16
CULTURAL TRADE AND COMMUNICATION TRENDS: DISTRIBUTION OF CULTURAL TRADE[1] BY TYPE

Country or territory	Books and pamphlets (%) 1997	Newspapers, newsprint and periodicals (%) 1997	Typewriters, word and data processors (%) 1997	Music-related goods (%) 1997	Cinema and photography (%) 1997	Radio, television and VCRs (%) 1997	Visual arts and antiques (%) 1997	Sporting goods (%) 1997
Sub-Saharan Africa								
Angola	..	..	..	..	..	..	..	..
Benin	..	..	..	..	..	..	..	..
Botswana	..	..	..	..	..	..	..	..
Burkina Faso	..	..	..	..	..	..	..	..
Burundi	..	..	..	..	..	..	..	..
Cameroon	..	..	..	..	..	..	..	..
Central African Rep.	..	..	..	..	..	..	..	..
Chad	..	..	..	..	..	..	..	..
Congo	..	..	..	..	..	..	..	..
Congo (Dem. Rep.)	..	..	..	..	..	..	..	..
Côte d'Ivoire	..	..	..	..	..	..	..	..
Eritrea	..	..	..	..	..	..	..	..
Ethiopia	..	..	..	..	..	..	..	..
Gabon	..	..	..	..	..	..	..	..
Gambia	..	..	..	..	..	..	..	..
Ghana	..	..	..	..	..	..	..	..
Guinea	..	..	..	..	..	..	..	..
Guinea-Bissau	..	..	..	..	..	..	..	..
Kenya	10.4	12.3	36.6	2.3	22.5	12.7	0.1	3.1
Lesotho	..	..	..	..	..	..	..	..
Liberia	..	..	..	..	..	..	..	..
Madagascar	14.1	6.9	23.2	8.4	6.7	35.9	0.2	4.6
Malawi	..	..	..	..	..	..	..	..
Mali	..	..	..	..	..	..	..	..
Mauritania	..	..	..	..	..	..	..	..
Mauritius	11.7	7.9	34.4	7.0	8.8	24.7	0.1	5.4
Mozambique	..	..	..	..	..	..	..	..
Namibia	..	..	..	..	..	..	..	..
Niger	..	..	..	..	..	..	..	..
Nigeria	..	..	..	..	..	..	..	..
Rwanda	..	..	..	..	..	..	..	..
Senegal	..	..	..	..	..	..	..	..
Sierra Leone	..	..	..	..	..	..	..	..
Somalia	..	..	..	..	..	..	..	..
South Africa	..	..	..	..	..	..	..	..
Sudan	..	..	..	..	..	..	..	..
Tanzania (United Rep. of)	12.4	12.7	27.3	4.4	7.1	30.8	0.4	4.9
Togo	..	..	..	..	..	..	..	..
Uganda	..	..	..	..	..	..	..	..
Zambia	..	..	..	..	..	..	..	..
Zimbabwe	9.9	4.1	46.3	7.8	8.0	21.6	0.2	2.1
Arab States								
Algeria	3.9	3.2	36.3	3.9	9.8	40.1	0.1	2.7
Egypt	3.0	2.9	30.8	2.4	10.9	46.4	(.)	3.6
Iraq	..	..	..	..	..	..	..	..
Jordan	..	..	..	..	..	..	..	..
Kuwait	2.9	5.8	17.2	7.9	9.0	50.7	0.1	6.4

Country or territory	Books and pamphlets (%) 1997	Newspapers, newsprint and periodicals (%) 1997	Typewriters, word and data processors (%) 1997	Music-related goods (%) 1997	Cinema and photography (%) 1997	Radio, television and VCRs (%) 1997	Visual arts and antiques (%) 1997	Sporting goods (%) 1997
Lebanon	..	..	..	..	..	..	..	..
Libyan Arab Jamahiriya	..	..	..	..	..	..	..	..
Morocco	8.1	8.9	40.9	9.5	10.0	19.8	0.1	2.7
Oman	..	..	..	..	..	..	..	..
Saudi Arabia	3.5	1.7	46.5	7.4	4.9	30.4	0.2	5.4
Syrian Arab Rep.	..	..	..	..	..	..	..	..
Tunisia	7.4	6.4	37.2	6.0	9.3	30.2	0.1	3.4
United Arab Emirates	..	..	..	..	..	..	..	..
Yemen	..	..	..	..	..	..	..	..
South Central Asia								
Afghanistan	..	..	..	..	..	..	..	..
Armenia	..	..	..	..	..	..	..	..
Azerbaijan	..	..	..	..	..	..	..	..
Bangladesh	..	..	..	..	..	..	..	..
Bhutan	..	..	..	..	..	..	..	..
Georgia	..	..	..	..	..	..	..	..
India	4.3	17.1	38.1	13.2	11.9	14.5	(.)	0.9
Iran (Islamic Rep. of)	..	..	..	..	..	..	..	..
Kazakhstan	..	..	..	..	..	..	..	..
Kyrgyzstan	..	..	..	..	..	..	..	..
Nepal	..	..	..	..	..	..	..	..
Pakistan	4.3	19.1	26.1	4.0	13.2	31.4	0.7	1.2
Sri Lanka	..	..	..	..	..	..	..	..
Tajikistan	..	..	..	..	..	..	..	..
Turkmenistan	..	..	..	..	..	..	..	..
Uzbekistan	..	..	..	..	..	..	..	..
East Asia								
China	0.5	2.5	39.6	2.7	7.5	44.6	0.2	2.4
Hong Kong SAR	0.9	0.8	38.4	3.1	8.7	40.5	0.5	7.1
Japan	1.0	1.9	56.6	5.9	5.4	19.6	1.8	7.8
Korea (Dem. People's Rep. of)	..	..	..	..	..	..	..	..
Korea (Rep. of)	1.0	0.5	41.6	9.2	16.9	24.8	0.7	5.3
Mongolia	..	..	..	..	..	..	..	..
South-East Asia and Oceania								
Australia	4.9	3.6	52.6	8.0	7.3	17.4	1.2	5.0
Cambodia	..	..	..	..	..	..	..	..
Indonesia	2.2	3.7	23.2	3.5	13.5	52.5	0.2	1.2
Lao People's Dem. Rep.	..	..	..	..	..	..	..	..
Malaysia	1.0	2.1	59.2	3.9	3.7	28.4	0.1	1.6
Myanmar	1.6	1.2	27.7	3.1	10.5	54.6	0.1	1.2
New Zealand	6.7	4.3	42.4	10.6	8.1	20.7	0.7	6.5
Papua New Guinea	..	..	..	..	..	..	..	..
Philippines	1.5	0.8	46.3	2.1	4.3	43.8	0.1	1.1
Singapore	0.8	0.4	63.2	8.3	4.0	21.9	0.2	1.2
Thailand	0.9	1.6	59.0	10.4	4.9	21.9	(.)	1.3
Viet Nam	..	..	..	..	..	..	..	..

TABLE 16 (continued)

Country or territory	Books and pamphlets (%) 1997	Newspapers, newsprint and periodicals (%) 1997	Typewriters, word and data processors (%) 1997	Music-related goods (%) 1997	Cinema and photography (%) 1997	Radio, television and VCRs (%) 1997	Visual arts and antiques (%) 1997	Sporting goods (%) 1997
Latin America and the Caribbean								
Argentina	4.1	4.5	41.2	10.0	8.2	28.8	0.1	3.1
Bolivia	8.8	8.3	18.6	5.3	4.2	54.1	0.1	0.6
Brazil	5.5	8.4	33.8	4.2	8.2	37.1	0.2	2.6
Chile	3.7	1.7	40.2	7.9	7.3	34.7	0.2	4.3
Colombia	6.3	6.7	44.2	10.4	10.1	19.9	0.2	2.2
Costa Rica	8.3	10.6	37.9	10.8	8.1	20.7	0.4	3.1
Cuba	..	..	..	..	..	..	..	..
Dominican Rep.	..	..	..	..	..	..	..	..
Ecuador	12.8	9.2	33.2	7.5	8.6	24.1	0.1	4.5
El Salvador	9.0	7.5	43.7	5.3	6.9	24.4	0.1	3.1
Guatemala	6.9	10.3	36.3	7.2	8.5	27.8	0.1	2.9
Haiti	..	..	..	..	..	..	..	..
Honduras	5.3	8.8	38.6	5.3	8.3	28.3	0.2	5.2
Jamaica	17.1	5.9	40.5	3.8	7.2	22.6	0.1	2.8
Mexico	3.5	1.7	34.6	7.7	7.7	40.7	0.2	3.9
Nicaragua	16.7	5.9	40.7	5.8	8.3	20.3	0.1	2.2
Panama	6.3	7.5	37.5	8.0	7.4	28.1	0.3	4.9
Paraguay	4.7	3.5	28.2	8.0	8.2	40.2	0.1	7.1
Peru	4.7	5.2	36.7	7.1	7.9	34.4	(.)	4.0
Trinidad and Tobago	13.9	8.5	43.7	5.9	6.7	18.5	(.)	2.8
Uruguay	0.2	2.6	36.9	5.3	7.4	42.4	0.1	5.1
Venezuela	5.6	9.2	40.9	8.8	7.2	25.9	0.2	2.2
North America								
Canada	7.2	4.7	64.1	10.0	6.2	0.2	0.6	7.0
United States	1.6	4.0	70.6	4.3	6.0	2.4	3.6	7.5
Europe								
Albania	2.3	11.4	24.1	2.6	3.6	53.2	0.1	2.7
Austria	9.7	8.1	32.9	11.8	8.3	19.1	1.0	9.1
Belarus	..	..	..	..	..	..	..	..
Belgium	4.8	4.3	42.6	8.6	9.7	24.2	0.8	5.0
Bosnia and Herzegovina	..	..	..	..	..	..	..	..
Bulgaria	2.0	5.9	48.8	3.7	4.8	29.1	(.)	5.7
Czech Rep.	3.4	2.7	41.5	7.7	5.2	26.5	8.4	4.6
Denmark	..	..	..	..	..	..	..	..
Estonia	1.8	10.4	40.9	2.9	3.2	38.1	(.)	2.7
Finland	1.9	1.7	55.9	7.2	5.5	24.0	0.1	3.7
France	2.6	3.0	53.5	7.9	7.7	19.9	0.6	4.8
Germany	1.6	3.1	56.7	7.1	7.0	18.0	1.3	5.2
Greece	4.5	6.3	31.4	9.6	10.3	27.8	1.8	8.3
Hungary	1.3	2.5	50.9	6.1	2.4	34.8	0.5	1.5
Ireland	1.4	1.6	80.7	7.2	1.2	6.6	0.1	1.2
Israel	1.9	4.6	52.4	9.2	5.9	22.9	1.0	2.1
Italy	1.5	3.2	50.6	8.8	8.0	22.5	0.4	5.0
Latvia	3.2	6.1	52.8	5.5	6.8	20.9	(.)	4.7
Lithuania	3.7	4.1	34.2	5.8	9.5	39.1	0.1	3.5

Country or territory	Books and pamphlets (%) 1997	Newspapers, newsprint and periodicals (%) 1997	Typewriters, word and data processors (%) 1997	Music-related goods (%) 1997	Cinema and photography (%) 1997	Radio, television and VCRs (%) 1997	Visual arts and antiques (%) 1997	Sporting goods (%) 1997
Macedonia (former Yugoslav Rep. of)	..	..	..	..	..	..	..	..
Moldova (Rep. of)	..	..	..	..	..	..	..	..
Netherlands	0.9	1.4	72.4	4.9	4.1	12.1	0.2	4.0
Norway	3.9	2.6	52.3	9.7	5.2	20.1	1.1	5.1
Poland	5.3	3.5	48.2	5.1	5.9	28.6	0.2	3.2
Portugal	4.0	6.0	38.1	8.2	7.8	31.5	0.2	4.2
Romania	4.0	4.2	36.2	3.1	5.8	45.1	(.)	1.6
Russian Federation	8.9	12.6	23.4	6.8	11.8	33.5	0.2	2.8
Slovakia	4.5	4.6	47.3	7.7	4.4	28.2	0.1	3.2
Slovenia	2.7	5.7	47.1	8.8	7.2	22.5	0.1	5.9
Spain	2.1	4.3	41.7	7.6	7.6	29.8	1.0	5.7
Sweden	2.5	1.3	45.1	6.3	5.7	34.6	0.2	3.7
Switzerland	5.6	4.8	45.1	10.6	5.8	12.9	10.8	4.4
Turkey	1.9	9.1	42.7	7.2	10.3	26.4	0.3	2.1
Ukraine	..	..	..	..	..	..	..	..
United Kingdom	2.8	3.2	57.2	6.5	6.2	15.8	4.4	3.9
Yugoslavia	..	..	..	..	..	..	..	..

Regions	Books and pamphlets (%) 1997	Newspapers, newsprint and periodicals (%) 1997	Typewriters, word and data processors (%) 1997	Music related goods (%) 1997	Cinema and photography (%) 1997	Radio, television and VCRs (%) 1997	Visual arts and antiques (%) 1997	Sporting goods (%) 1997
World	..	..	..	..	..	..	..	..
Developing	..	..	..	..	..	..	..	..
Industrial	2.4	3.3	60.3	6.5	6.1	13.8	1.8	5.8
Developing excl. India/China	..	..	..	..	..	..	..	..
Industrial excl. US/Rus. Fed.	2.6	3.0	56.3	7.4	6.1	18.2	1.2	5.2
Sub-Saharan Africa	..	..	..	..	..	..	..	..
Arab States	..	..	..	..	..	..	..	..
South Central Asia	..	..	..	..	..	..	..	..
East Asia	0.9	1.6	47.1	5.2	8.2	29.7	1.1	6.2
South-East Asia/Oceania	1.3	1.3	58.7	7.2	4.7	24.9	0.2	1.7
Latin Am./Carib.	4.3	3.7	35.8	7.4	7.9	37.1	0.2	3.6
North America	2.5	4.1	69.6	5.2	6.0	2.1	3.1	7.4
Europe	2.5	3.1	55.5	7.4	6.3	19.7	1.1	4.4

1. Exports plus imports

TABLE 17
CULTURAL TRADE AND COMMUNICATIONS TRENDS: TOURISM FLOWS

Country or territory	Foreign tourists: leading countries of origin			Nationals touring abroad: leading countries of destination		
	First country 1998	Second country 1998	Third country 1998	First country 1998	Second country 1998	Third country 1998
Sub-Saharan Africa						
Angola	Portugal	South Africa	France	Namibia	South Africa	Brazil
Benin	..	..	..	Côte d'Ivoire	Togo	Burkina Faso
Botswana	South Africa	Zimbabwe	UK	South Africa	Namibia	Zambia
Burkina Faso	France	Cote D'Ivore	Senegal	Togo	Côte d'Ivoire	Ghana
Burundi	..	..	..	Belgium	Egypt	India
Cameroon	France	US	Germany	Nigeria	Côte d'Ivoire	US
Central African Rep.	..	..	..	Nigeria	Côte d'Ivoire	Spain
Chad	France	US	Germany	Nigeria	Libya	Egypt
Congo	France	Congo Dem	US	Congo Dem	Côte d'Ivoire	Nigeria
Congo (Dem. Rep.)	Congo	Belgium	France	Zambia	Belgium	South Africa
Côte d'Ivoire	France	US	Burkina Faso	Nigeria	Ghana	Burkina Faso
Eritrea	Ethiopia	Italy	US	Egypt	US	Lebanon
Ethiopia	US	Italy	UK	Eritrea	Lebanon	India
Gabon	..	..	..	Côte d'Ivoire	Morocco	US
Gambia	UK	Germany	Netherlands	Nigeria	US	Belgium
Ghana	Nigeria	UK	US	Nigeria	US	Côte d'Ivoire
Guinea	..	..	..	Côte d'Ivoire	Nigeria	Morocco
Guinea-Bissau	..	..	..	Spain	Belgium	Hong Kong SAR
Kenya	Germany	UK	Tanzania	Tanzania	India	South Africa
Lesotho	South Africa	Zimbabwe	Botswana	South Africa	Botswana	US
Liberia	..	..	..	Nigeria	Russia	Ghana
Madagascar	France	Germany	Italy	Mauritius	Reunion	Comoros
Malawi	Mozambique	Zambia	..	South Africa	Zambia	US
Mali	France	Italy	Germany	Nigeria	Côte d'Ivoire	Algeria
Mauritania	..	.	..	Côte d'Ivoire	Tunisia	Morocco
Mauritius	France	UK	South Africa	Reunion	Singapore	South Africa
Mozambique	..	..	..	South Africa	Zimbabwe	Tanzania
Namibia	South Africa	Angola	Germany	South Africa	Angola	Mauritius
Niger	France	US	Germany	Nigeria	Côte d'Ivoire	Burkina Faso
Nigeria	Niger	Benin	Ghana	Gana	UK	US
Rwanda	..	..	..	Uganda	Belgium	Egypt
Senegal	France	Italy	Germany	Côte d'Ivoire	Nigeria	Spain
Sierra Leone	UK	France	..	Nigeria	Russia	China
Somalia	..	..	..	U.A.E.	Libya	Egypt
South Africa	Lesotho	Swaziland	Zimbabwe	Zimbabwe	UK	Swaziland
Sudan	China	Egypt	Canada	Egypt	Nigeria	Syria
Tanzania (United Rep. of)	Kenya	UK	US	Kenya	Zambia	India
Togo	France	Burkina Faso	Benin	Nigeria	Ghana	Côte d'Ivoire
Uganda	Kenya	Tanzania	Congo Dem	Kenya	US	India
Zambia	Zimbabwe	South Africa	UK	Zimbabwe	South Africa	Botswana
Zimbabwe	South Africa	Zambia	Mozambique	South Africa	Botswana	Zambia
Arab States						
Algeria	France	Tunisia	Mali	Tunisia	Spain	France
Egypt	Italy	Israel	Germany	Libya	UK	Lebanon
Iraq	Jordan	Syria	..	Egypt	Turkey	Syria
Jordan	Saudi Arabia	Israel	US	Syria	Egypt	Israel
Kuwait	Saudi Arabia	India	Egypt	Jordan	Egypt	Lebanon

Country or territory	Foreign tourists: leading countries of origin			Nationals touring abroad: leading countries of destination		
	First country 1998	Second country 1998	Third country 1998	First country 1998	Second country 1998	Third country 1998
Lebanon	Saudi Arabia	France	Jordan	Syria	Israel	Egypt
Libyan Arab Jamahiriya	Tunisia	Egypt	Algeria	Tunisia	Egypt	Malta
Morocco	France	Germany	Spain	Spain	Tunisia	Libya
Oman	..	..	..	India	Jordan	Egypt
Saudi Arabia	..	..	..	Bahrain	Jordan	Egypt
Syrian Arab Rep.	Lebanon	Jordan	France	Turkey	Egypt	Russia
Tunisia	Germany	Libya	France	Libya	Morocco	Turkey
United Arab Emirates	UK	India	..	US	Egypt	Thailand
Yemen	Germany	France	Italy	Egypt	India	Syria
South Central Asia						
Afghanistan	..	..	..	Iran	Pakistan	Turkmenistan
Armenia	Russia	US	UK	Russia	Ukraine	Iran
Azerbaijan	..	..	..	Russia	Iran	Ukraine
Bangladesh	India	UK	Pakistan	India	Singapore	Thailand
Bhutan	Japan	US	UK	Thailand	India	Nepal
Georgia	Russia	Turkey	US	Russia	Ukraine	Poland
India	UK	Bangladesh	Sri Lanka	Singapore	UK	US
Iran (Islamic Rep. of)	Azerbaijan	Pakistan	Turkey	Turkey	Turkmenistan	U. A. E.
Kazakhstan	..	..	..	Russia	China	Poland
Kyrgyzstan	Russia	China	Turkey	Russia	China	Turkmenistan
Nepal	India	Germany	Japan	India	Hong Kong SAR	Thailand
Pakistan	UK	India	US	Iran	U.A.E.	UK
Sri Lanka	Germany	UK	India	India	Singapore	Thailand
Tajikistan	..	..	..	Russia	Turkmenistan	Iran
Turkmenistan	Turkey	Russia	Uzbekistan	Russia	Ukraine	China
Uzbekistan	..	..	..	Russia	Turkmenistan	Ukraine
East Asia						
China	Japan	Russia	US	Hong Kong SAR	Macao, China	Russia
Hong Kong SAR	China	Taiwan, China	US	Macao, China	Japan	Taiwan, China
Japan	Taiwan, China	Korea Rep.	US	US	Italy	Korea Rep.
Korea (Dem. People's Rep. of)	..	..	..	China	Russia	India
Korea (Rep. of)	Japan	US	Hong Kong SAR	Japan	China	US
Mongolia	China	Russia	Japan	China	Russia	Korea Rep.
South-East Asia and Oceania						
Australia	Japan	New Zealand	UK	UK	US	France
Cambodia	Taiwan, China	Japan	US	Viet Nam	Thailand	China
Indonesia	Singapore	Japan	Malaysia	Singapore	Malaysia	Hong Kong SAR
Lao People's Dem. Rep.	Thailand	Viet Nam	US	Thailand	VietNam	China
Malaysia	Singapore	Thailand	Japan	Thailand	China	Singapore
Myanmar	Japan	Thailand	France	Singapore	Indonesia	China
New Zealand	Australia	US	UK	Australia	US	UK
Papua New Guinea	Australia	US	New Zeland	Australia	Singapore	N. Zealand
Philippines	US	Japan	Taiwan, China	Hong Kong SAR	China	Korea Rep.
Singapore	Indonesia	Japan	Malaysia	Malaysia	Indonesia	Thailand
Thailand	Malaysia	Japan	Singapore	Malaysia	Singapore	China
Viet Nam	China	US	Taiwan, China	Laos	Thailand	China

TABLE 17 (continued)

Country or territory	Foreign tourists: leading countries of origin			Nationals touring abroad: leading countries of destination		
	First country 1998	Second country 1998	Third country 1998	First country 1998	Second country 1998	Third country 1998
Latin America and the Caribbean						
Argentina	Uruguay	Brazil	Chile	Uruguay	Brazil	Chile
Bolivia	Peru	Argentina	US	Argentina	Brazil	Chile
Brazil	Argentina	US	Paraguay	US	Argentina	Italy
Chile	Argentina	Peru	Bolivia	Argentina	US	Peru
Colombia	US	Panama	Venezuela	US	Ecuador	Panama
Costa Rica	US	Nicaragua	Panama	US	Nicaragua	Panama
Cuba	Italy	Germany	Spain	Colombia	US	Costa Rica
Dominican Rep.	US	Germany	UK	US	Colombia	Panama
Ecuador	Colombia	US	Peru	US	Colombia	Panama
El Salvador	Guatemala	US	Honduras	US	Guatemala	Nicaragua
Guatemala	US	El Salvador	Mexico	El Salvador	US	Belize
Haiti	US	Canada	Dom Rep	US	Panama	Cuba
Honduras	US	Nicaragua	El Salvador	Nicaragua	El Salvador	US
Jamaica	US	UK	Canada	US	Cayman	Canada
Mexico	US	Canada	..	US	Spain	Canada
Nicaragua	Honduras	US	Costa Rica	Costa Rica	El Salvador	US
Panama	US	Colombia	Costa Rica	US	Colombia	Costa Rica
Paraguay	Argentina	Brazil	Chile	Brazil	Argentina	Uruguay
Peru	US	Chile	Argentina	Chile	US	Bolivia
Trinidad	US	Canada	UK	US	Venezuela	Barbados
Uruguay	Argentina	Brazil	Paraguay	Argentina	Brazil	US
Venezuela	US	Germany	Canada	US	Aruba	Spain
North America						
Canada	US	UK	Japan	US	UK	France
United States	Canada	Mexico	Japan	Mexico	Canada	UK
Europe						
Albania	Italy	Greece	US	Turkey	Bulgaria	Macedonia
Austria	Germany	Netherlands	Italy	Czech Rep.	Hungary	Italy
Belarus	Russia	Germany	UK	Poland	Russia	Lithuania
Belgium	Netherlands	Germany	UK	France	Spain	UK
Bosnia and Herzegovina	..	..	..	Croatia	Yugoslavia	Slovenia
Bulgaria	Turkey	Romania	Yugoslavia	Hungary	Romania	Greece
Croatia	Italy	Germany	Slovenia	Hungary	Slovenia	Austria
Czech Rep.	..	..	..	Croatia	Poland	Slovakia
Denmark	Sweden	Germany	Norway	Germany	France	UK
Estonia	Finland	Latvia	Russia	Poland	Russia	Finland
Finland	Sweden	Russia	Germany	Russia	Estonia	Germany
France	Germany	UK	Netherlands	Spain	UK	Italy
Germany	Netherlands	US	US	France	Spain	Austria
Greece	Germany	UK	Yugoslavia	France	Italy	Bulgaria
Hungary	Germany	Romania	Austria	Czech Rep.	Romania	Poland
Ireland	UK	US	Germany	UK	Spain	US
Israel	US	Germany	Germany	Egypt	US	UK
Italy	Germany	US	France	France	Spain	UK
Latvia	Russia	Finland	Germany	Poland	Russia	Ukraine
Lithuania	Russia	Germany	Poland	Poland	Russia	Ukraine

Country or territory	Foreign tourists: leading countries of origin			Nationals touring abroad: leading countries of destination		
	First country 1998	Second country 1998	Third country 1998	First country 1998	Second country 1998	Third country 1998
Macedonia (former Yugoslav Rep. of)	Bulgaria	Yugoslavia	Albania	Bulgaria	Yugoslavia	Slovenia
Moldova (Rep. of)	..	..	..	Ukraine	Romania	Russia
Netherlands	Germany	UK	US	France	Spain	Germany
Norway	Germany	Sweden	Denmark	Sweden	UK	Denmark
Poland	Germany	Czech Rep.	Ukraine	Czech Rep.	Russia	Ukraine
Portugal	Spain	UK	Germany	Spain	France	UK
Romania	Moldova	Hungary	Germany	Hungary	Bulgaria	Turkey
Russian Federation	Ukraine	Finland	Georgia	Poland	Hungary	Germany
Slovakia	Czech Rep.	Germany	Poland	Ukraine	Poland	Bulgarria
Slovenia	Italy	Germany	Austria	Croatia	Hungary	Austria
Spain	Germany	UK	France	Portugal	France	UK
Sweden	Germany	Norway	Denmark	Spain	Germany	UK
Switzerland	Germany	US	UK	France	Spain	Italy
Turkey	Germany	Russia	UK	Bulgaria	Russia	Germany
Ukraine	Russia	Moldova	Belarus	Poland	Hungary	Romania
United Kingdom	France	US	Germany	France	Spain	US
Yugoslavia	Russia	Moldova	Greece	Hungary	Greece	Turkey

TABLE 18
CULTURAL TRADE AND COMMUNICATION TRENDS: INTERNATIONAL TOURISM

Country or territory	Arrivals of foreign visitors (per 100 people)		Annual rate of change (%)	Departures of nationals abroad (per 100 people)	International tourism accounts			
					Receipts (mill US$)	Expenditures (mill US$)	Receipts (US$ per tourist)	Expenditures (US$ per tourist abroad)
	1980	1998	1980/98	1998	1998	1997	1998	1997
Sub-Saharan Africa								
Angola	..	0.4	..	1.7	9	73	200	351
Benin	..	10	..	3.2	33	7	57	38
Botswana	..	68	..	31	185	140	171	281
Burkina Faso	..	1.2	..	0.3	39	32	283	1 032
Burundi	..	0.2	..	(.)	1	..	91	..
Cameroon	..	0.2	..	0.4	40	107	1 212	2 019
Central African Rep.	..	0.2	..	0.2	..	..	..	..
Chad	..	1.0	..	0.5	10	24	143	667
Congo	..	1.3	..	0.4	3	..	81	..
Congo (Dem. Rep.)	..	0.1	..	1.0	2	7	56	179
Côte d'Ivoire	..	0.5	..	0.5	97	..	322	..
Eritrea	..	5.2	..	0.1	75	..	399	..
Ethiopia	..	0.2	..	0.5	40	40	342	135
Gabon	..	14	..	1.0	8	178	48	1 483
Gambia	..	7.6	..	0.9	33	16	363	1 455
Ghana	..	1.7	..	0.6	274	22	843	196
Guinea	..	1.3	..	0.4	..	23	..	821
Guinea-Bissau	..	..	..	0.2	..	..	..	..
Kenya	..	3.5	..	0.5	400	194	400	1 426
Lesotho	..	16	..	59	20	8	59	6
Liberia	..	..	..	2.4	..	..	892	..
Madagascar	..	0.6	..	0.2	74	48	..	2 087
Malawi	..	1.0	..	0.7	..	17	424	227
Mali	..	0.6	..	0.6	28	42	..	712
Mauritania	..	..	..	1.2	11	24	..	774
Mauritius	..	51	..	7.1	. 502	177	900	2 269
Mozambique	..	..	..	2.3	..	..	..	..
Namibia	..	30	..	13.0	339	99	675	465
Niger	..	0.2	..	2.8	18	24	947	86
Nigeria	..	1.2	..	0.2	124	..	101	..
Rwanda	..	(.)	..	0.2	17	..	..	..
Senegal	..	4.0	..	0.5	165	77	527	1 750
Sierra Leone	..	0.6	..	0.5	..	2	..	83
Somalia	..	0.2	..	0.1	..	..	..	..
South Africa	2.4	14	27	5.1	2 366	1 947	435	978
Sudan	..	0.2	..	0.4	6	34	95	330
Tanzania (United Rep. of)	..	1.1	..	0.5	431	..	1 197	..
Togo	..	2.1	..	0.4	15	19	163	487
Uganda	..	0.8	..	0.4	142	137	888	1 651
Zambia	..	4.1	..	5.8	90	59	249	116
Zimbabwe	..	13	..	11	246	118	164	96
Arab States								
Algeria	5.1	2.3	-3.1	2.9	20	64	29	73
Egypt	2.9	5.2	4.4	0.6	3 838	..	1 111	..
Iraq	..	2.0	..	0.4	..	..	..	..
Jordan	..	20	..	5.6	790	398	629	1 131
Kuwait	..	150	..	18	188	2 558	70	8 121

Country or territory	Arrivals of foreign visitors (per 100 people) 1980	Arrivals of foreign visitors (per 100 people) 1998	Annual rate of change (%) 1980/98	Departures of nationals abroad (per 100 people) 1998	International tourism accounts: Receipts (mill US$) 1998	Expenditures (mill US$) 1997	Receipts (US$ per tourist) 1998	Expenditures (US$ per tourist abroad) 1997
Lebanon	..	20	..	9.5	1 384	..	2 193	..
Libyan Arab Jamahiriya	..	16	..	21	6	215	7	195
Morocco	7.3	12	3.6	0.6	1 600	315	493	1 780
Oman	..	15	..	3.1	112	47	321	627
Saudi Arabia	10	17	3.9	11	1 462	..	436	..
Syrian Arab Rep.	..	5.8	..	2.9	1 050	545	1 180	1 233
Tunisia	25	51	5.8	3.1	1 550	160	329	544
United Arab Emirates	30	2.0	-5.2	13	..	..	..	..
Yemen	..	0.5	..	0.5	69	81	821	910
South Central Asia								
Afghanistan	..	(.)	..	0.5	1	1	..	9
Armenia	..	0.9	..	15	14	41	452	81
Azerbaijan	..	..	..	13	160	72	..	73
Bangladesh	..	0.1	..	0.4	65	170	378	312
Bhutan	..	0.3	..	0.4	6	..	120	..
Georgia	..	6.2	..	22	440	228	1 388	201
India	0.2	0.2	(.)	0.2	3 168	1 342	1 343	782
Iran (Islamic Rep. of)	..	1.1	..	1.2	400	253	541	298
Kazakhstan	..	..	..	2.8	289	445	..	959
Kyrgyzstan	..	1.3	..	3.2	7	4	119	27
Nepal	..	2.0	..	0.5	124	103	276	873
Pakistan	..	0.3	..	0.4	111	364	296	551
Sri Lanka	..	21	..	1.5	233	180	612	659
Tajikistan	..	..	..	5.1	..	..	..	..
Turkmenistan	..	7.8	..	6.9	119	125	358	421
Uzbekistan	..	..	..	2.7	21	..	..	..
East Asia								
China	0.4	0.6	2.8	0.5	12 500	10 166	1 759	1 766
Hong Kong SAR	35	143	17	60	7 114	..	743	..
Japan	0.7	3.3	21	20	4 154	33 041	1 012	1 338
Korea (Dem. People's Rep. of)	..	0.5	..	0.4	..	..	..	..
Korea (Rep. of)	2.6	9.2	14	13	5 700	6 262	1 341	1 079
Mongolia	..	5.2	..	20	23	21	170	41
South-East Asia and Oceania								
Australia	6.2	23	15	30	8 575	6 129	2 058	1 097
Cambodia	..	20	..	1.5	143	12	653	77
Indonesia	0.3	2.4	39	1.1	5 138	2 436	1 020	1 047
Lao People's Dem. Rep.	..	10	..	0.7	68	21	136	553
Malaysia	7.5	26	14	16	3 369	2 478	607	704
Myanmar	..	0.4	..	0.3	35	25	179	164
New Zealand	15	39	8.9	43	1 883	1 451	1 267	903
Papua New Guinea	..	1.5	..	1.3	75	81	1 119	1 397
Philippines	2.0	2.9	2.5	2.5	2 421	1 936	1 127	..
Singapore	107	178	3.7	210	6 501	3 224	1 042	438
Thailand	4.0	12	11	3.4	6 392	1 888	876	928
Viet Nam	..	2.0	..	0.2	86	..	57	..

TABLE 18 (continued)

Country or territory	Arrivals of foreign visitors (per 100 people) 1980	Arrivals of foreign visitors (per 100 people) 1998	Annual rate of change (%) 1980/98	Departures of nationals abroad (per 100 people) 1998	International tourism accounts: Receipts (mill US$) 1998	Expenditures (mill US$) 1997	Receipts (US$ per tourist) 1998	Expenditures (US$ per tourist abroad) 1997
Latin America and the Caribbean								
Argentina	4.0	13	13	14	5 363	2 680	1 103	541
Bolivia	..	5.0	..	6.7	185	172	465	323
Brazil	1.0	2.9	11	2.0	2 776	6 583	577	1 970
Chile	3.8	12	12	8.5	991	946	561	752
Colombia	2.1	3.3	3.2	1.9	955	958	714	1 207
Costa Rica	..	25	..	9.5	730	358	774	989
Cuba	..	1.1	..	0.5	..	..	..	..
Dominican Rep.	6.7	28	18	3.2	2 151	242	922	927
Ecuador	..	4.3	..	2.4	285	227	539	772
El Salvador	..	6.5	..	6.5	125	75	323	192
Guatemala	..	5.9	..	4.0	280	119	440	275
Haiti	..	1.9	..	0.9	96	37	644	514
Honduras	..	5.3	..	6.0	173	62	539	169
Jamaica	19	49	8.8	13	1 196	..	976	..
Mexico	18	20	0.6	10	7 850	3 892	406	389
Nicaragua	..	8.6	..	7.1	90	65	219	190
Panama	..	15	..	12	376	164	891	485
Paraguay	..	6.7	..	18	710	195	2 029	207
Peru	..	2.6	..	2.3	878	485	1 353	857
Trinidad and Tobago	..	25	..	17	108	7	333	32
Uruguay	37	70	5.0	55	695	264	299	145
Venezuela	..	3.6	..	4.1	1 229	3 281	1 468	3 450
North America								
Canada	52	62	1.1	66	9 133	11 304	485	560
United States	10	17	4.1	24	74 240	51 220	1 600	788
Europe								
Albania	..	1.8	..	2.2	27	5	482	74
Austria	183	214	0.9	162	12 164	10 992	701	383
Belarus	..	3.4	..	37	26	114	73	30
Belgium	18	60	13	118	5 375	8 275	890	697
Bosnia and Herzegovina	..	..	..	6.3	15	..	..	..
Bulgaria	62	91	2.6	13	361	222	48	203
Croatia	..	91	..	20	2 740	521	66	585
Czech Rep.	..	167	..	20	3 609	2 380	2 161	1 144
Denmark	19	39	5.8	80	3 627	4 128	1 750	973
Estonia	..	207	..	54	483	118	167	156
Finland	..	36	..	56	1 972	2 270	1 061	784
France	56	115	5.9	38	29 700	16 576	441	736
Germany	14	20	2.4	96	16 840	46 200	1 020	585
Greece	50	95	5.0	17	3 925	1 325	390	721
Hungary	88	171	5.2	39	2 568	1 153	149	296
Ireland	66	143	6.5	85	3 159	3 223	598	1 024
Israel	29	34	1.0	40	2 700	278	1 343	116
Italy	39	52	1.9	31	30 427	16 631	1 025	922
Latvia	..	9.2	..	40	211	326	959	338
Lithuania	..	8.5	..	50	418	290	1 323	156

Country or territory	Arrivals of foreign visitors (per 100 people) 1980	Arrivals of foreign visitors (per 100 people) 1998	Annual rate of change (%) 1980/98	Departures of nationals abroad (per 100 people) 1998	International tourism accounts: Receipts (mill US$) 1998	Expenditures (mill US$) 1997	Receipts (US$ per tourist) 1998	Expenditures (US$ per tourist abroad) 1997
Macedonia (former Yugoslav Rep. of)	..	7.9	..	9.0	15	27	96	151
Moldova (Rep. of)	..	..	..	68	..	..	..	..
Netherlands	20	58	11	150	5 749	10 232	633	434
Norway	31	98	12	61	2 212	4 496	513	1 674
Poland	16	50	12	20	..	6 900	..	903
Portugal	28	103	15	24	4 772	2 164	469	892
Romania	15	13	-0.7	19	547	793	184	187
Russian Federation	..	11	..	3.9	7 107	10 113	450	1 779
Slovakia	..	15	..	13	480	439	578	617
Slovenia	..	49	..	51	931	544	953	532
Spain	62	121	5.3	32	29 585	4 467	620	349
Sweden	..	87	..	76	3 755	6 579	488	968
Switzerland	..	98	..	164	8 208	6 904	1 142	574
Turkey	2.1	14	31	3.1	8 300	1 716	926	853
United Kingdom	22	44	5.6	83	21 295	27 710	835	567
Ukraine	..	12	..	19	280	305	45	31
Yugoslavia	..	2.7	..	26	39	..	138	..

Regions	Arrivals of foreign visitors (per 100 people) 1980	Arrivals of foreign visitors (per 100 people) 1998	Annual rate of change (%) 1980/98	Departures of nationals abroad (per 100 people) 1998	International tourism accounts: Receipts (mill US$) 1998	Expenditures (mill US$) 1997	Receipts (US$ per tourist) 1998	Expenditures (US$ per tourist abroad) 1997
World	..	11	..	9.0	411 500	362 300	1 060	1 053
Developing	..	3.4	..	1.9	99 900	60 800	1 097	1 110
Industrial	22	36	8.7	35	311 600	301 500	924	867
Developing excl. India/China	..	6.2	..	3.4	84 200	46 300	597	833
Industrial excl. US/Rus. Fed.	26	47	10.6	44	230 300	240 200	777	728
Sub-Saharan Africa	..	4.5	..	1.5	5 843	3 695	395	722
Arab States	..	10	..	3.1	12 069	4 383	702	998
South Central Asia	..	0.8	..	0.6	5 158	3 328	1 067	674
East Asia	0.7	1.8	4.8	2.9	29 491	49 490	1 672	1 703
South-East Asia/Oceania	3.0	6.9	24.6	4.7	34 686	19 681	813	870
Latin Am./Carib.	..	8.9	..	5.7	27 242	20 812	688	1 207
North America	14	22	3.8	28	83 373	62 524	1 488	765
Europe	32	48	8.4	40	213 622	198 416	651	825

TABLE 19
CULTURAL TRADE AND COMMUNICATIONS TRENDS: COMMUNICATION

Country or territory	Post offices (per 100,000 people)	Letter post items posted		Main telephones lines			Outgoing international telephone calls		Cost of a three minute telephone call*	
		(per person)	(per person sent or received from abroad)	(per thousnd people)	(per thousnd people)	Annual rate of change (%)	(minutes per person)	Major interna-tional partner	Local [1] (US$)	Inter-national to the US (US$)
	1997	1997	1997	1980	1998	1980/98	1997	1997	1997	1997
Sub-Saharan Africa										
Angola	1	(.)	(.)	..	6	..	2	..	0.09	2.92
Benin	3	1.0	0.6	..	7	..	1	France	0.13	7.24
Botswana	13	24	7.3	9	56	10.7	24	South Africa	0.03	5.52
Burkina Faso	1	0.8	..	..	4	..	1	..	0.10	11.52
Burundi	(.)	1.0	1.3	..	3	..	(.)	Belgium	0.04	11.75
Cameroon	3	..	..	..	5	..	2	US	0.07	12.02
Central African Rep.	1	..	..	..	3	..	1	France	0.20	20.56
Chad	1	1.3	1.2	..	1	..	(.)	France	0.17	12.34
Congo	4	0.5	0.6	..	8	..	2	..	0.12	..
Congo (Dem. Rep.)	1	..	..	..	(.)	..	..	..		.. ..
Côte d' Ivoire	3	1.3	0.8	..	12	..	3	..	0.11	7.15
Eritrea	1	0.4	0.3	..	7	..	1	..	0.03	8.24
Ethiopia	1	0.4	0.2	..	3	..	(.)	..	0.03	7.82
Gabon	5	1.1	2.6	..	33	..	16	..	0.15	..
Gambia	..	..	..	..	21	..	5	..	0.34	5.88
Ghana	6	3.3	6.3	..	6	..	1	..	0.08	..
Guinea	1	0.3	0.8	..	5	..	1	France	0.11	7.82
Guinea-Bissau	2	..	..	..	7	..	3	..	0.09	..
Kenya	4	12	3.1	..	9	..	1	UK	0.06	11.17
Lesotho	8	25	29	..	10	..	15	..	0.04	..
Liberia	..	..	..	..	2	..	2	..	..	..
Madagascar	5	1.3	0.4	..	3	..	1	..	0.10	23.22
Malawi	3	5.7	6.3	..	4	..	1	Botswana	0.03	11.02
Mali	1	0.2	2.1	..	3	..	1	France	0.17	15.42
Mauritania	3	0.3	1.5	..	5	..	2	..	0.13	..
Mauritius	9	44	18	24	212	12.9	22	France	0.05	5.11
Mozambique	3	0.1	2.6	..	4	..	1	..	0.04	..
Namibia	7	..	..	..	61	..	31	South Africa	0.04	..
Niger	1	0.3	0.2	..	2	..	1	..	0.15	..
Nigeria	3	3.1	3.3	..	4	..	(.)	..	0.26	..
Rwanda	(.)	0.2	0.1	..	3	..	(.)	..	..	..
Senegal	2	0.7	1.1	3	15	9.4	3	..	0.09	8.20
Sierra Leone	1	0.1	0.2	..	4	..	1	..	0.07	..
Somalia	..	..	..	..	2	..	..	..	..	..
South Africa	6	52	5.3	55	107	3.8	9	Namibia	0.07	..
Sudan	2	0.1	0.1	..	6	..	1	Saudi Arabia	0.03	8.02
Tanzania (United Rep. of)	2	0.8	0.6	..	4	..	(.)	..	0.10	4.46
Togo	1	0.7	1.2	..	7	..	2	France	0.10	11.56
Uganda	2	0.5	0.6	..	3	..	(.)	UK	0.19	8.31
Zambia	5	1.3	1.3	6	9	2.3	2	US	0.09	3.91
Zimbabwe	4	29	10.0	14	17	1.1	4	UK	0.03	6.49
Arab States										
Algeria	11	21	7.5	17	53	6.5	5	France	0.02	4.78
Egypt	6	3.5	3.0	..	60	..	2	Saudi Arabia	0.01	6.82
Iraq	..	3.8	2.8	19	32	2.9	..	..	..	..
Jordan	14	17	9.3	..	70	..	16	Saudi Arabia	0.03	..
Kuwait	4	24	64	114	231	4.0	90	Egypt	0.00	5.44

Country or territory	Post offices (per 100,000 people)	Letter post items posted (per person)	Letter post items posted (per person sent or received from abroad)	Main telephones lines (per thousnd people)	Main telephones lines (per thousnd people)	Main telephones lines Annual rate of change (%)	Outgoing international telephone calls (minutes per person)	Outgoing international telephone calls Major interna-tional partner	Cost of a three minute telephone call* Local[1] (US$)	Cost of a three minute telephone call* Inter-national to the US (US$)
	1997	1997	1997	1980	1998	1980/98	1997	1997	1997	1997
Lebanon	9	1.2	..	..	194	..	19	..	0.05	7.29
Libyan Arab Jamahiriya	7	2.9	4.3	..	68	..	6	..	0.03	..
Morocco	5	7.8	1.3	9	54	10.5	5	France	0.08	6.30
Oman	4	..	..	13	92	11.5	32	..	0.08	..
Saudi Arabia	7	30	31	34	142	8.3	41	Egypt	0.02	6.41
Syrian Arab Rep.	5	1.0	0.4	28	88	6.6	6	Saudi Arabia	0.05	33.41
Tunisia	11	12	1.7	18	71	7.9	10	Italy	0.06	5.70
United Arab Emirates	9	39	41	116	389	7.0	310	India	0.00	3.78
Yemen	2	0.2	0.3	2	13	11.0	2	Saudi Arabia	0.02	..
South Central Asia										
Afghanistan	2	..	..	..	1	..	..	..		.. ..
Armenia	..	..	..	97	150	2.5	14	Russia		.. ..
Azerbaijan	23	1.3	0.5	55	89	2.7	8	..	0.19	3.85
Bangladesh	8	4.3	1.0	..	3	..	(.)	..	0.04	..
Bhutan	6	0.7	0.3	..	10	..	2	..	..	..
Georgia	22	0.1	0.2	63	114	3.3	..	..	0.00	..
India	17	16	0.6	3	19	10.8	(.)	Saudi Arabia	0.02	6.10
Iran (Islamic Rep. of)	6	2.8	0.4	23	101	8.6	3	UAE	0.01	6.02
Kazakhstan	21	..	..	44	108	5.1	7	..	0.00	6.69
Kyrgyzstan	20	15	1.9	40	77	3.7	6	..	..	8.73
Nepal	10	4.0	1.8	..	9	..	1	..	0.02	..
Pakistan	11	3.3	..	4	19	9.0	1	Saudi Arabia	0.05	..
Sri Lanka	23	26	3.6	4	28	11.4	2	..	0.04	6.76
Tajikistan	12	0.4	1.4	30	37	1.2	2	Russia	0.00	10.50
Turkmenistan	40	..	..	38	82	4.4	2	..	..	..
Uzbekistan	13	0.4	0.2	36	65	3.3	3	..	..	..
East Asia										
China	11	5.5	0.1	2	56	20.3	1	Hong Kong, China	0.01	6.66
Hong Kong SAR	2	182	35	254	561	4.5	264	China	0.00	2.63
Japan	20	202	4.1	342	479	1.9	14	US	0.08	3.72
Korea (Dem. People's Rep. of)	..	..	..	..	48	..	..	..	..	..
Korea (Rep. of)	8	85	1.7	71	444	10.7	19	US	0.05	3.15
Mongolia	32	0.2	0.1	..	37	..	1	Russia	0.02	10.25
South-East Asia and Oceania										
Australia	22	218	18	323	514	2.6	53	US	0.19	2.94
Cambodia	1	0.2	0.4	..	2	..	1	..	0.09	..
Indonesia	8	3.4	0.5	3	27	13.0	2	Singapore	0.04	4.69
Lao People's Dem Rep.	4	0.5	0.3	..	6	..	1	..	..	7.16
Malaysia	5	47	4.7	29	198	11.3	34	Singapore	0.03	5.33
Myanmar	3	1.9	0.2	..	5	..	(.)	..	0.17	26.86
New Zealand	..	..	..	361	486	1.7	107	Australia	0.00	3.95
Papua New Guinea	..	..	..	8	11	1.8	7	..	0.13	..
Philippines	6	12	4.5	9	29	6.7	3	US	0.00	6.22
Singapore	34	184	39	235	543	4.8	374	Malaysia	0.03	2.42
Thailand	7	22	2.4	8	80	13.6	5	Japan	0.10	5.87
Viet Nam	..	..	..	..	21	..	1	..	0.11	..

TABLE 19 (continued)

Country or territory	Post offices (per 100,000 people)	Letter post items posted (per person)	Letter post items posted (per person sent or received from abroad)	Main telephones lines (per thousnd people)	Main telephones lines (per thousnd people)	Main telephones lines Annual rate of change (%)	Outgoing international telephone calls (minutes per person)	Outgoing international telephone calls Major interna-tional partner	Cost of a three minute telephone call* Local[1] (US$)	Cost of a three minute telephone call* Inter-national to the US (US$)
	1997	1997	1997	1980	1998	1980/98	1997	1997	1997	1997
Latin America and the Caribbean										
Argentina	20	11	2.6	67	203	6.4	6	Uruguay	0.10	7.08
Bolivia	2	0.7	0.9	24	69	6.0	3	Argentina	..	..
Brazil	7	27	..	40	121	6.3	3	US	0.09	4.36
Chile	4	23	1.8	33	180	9.9	21	US	..	3.22
Colombia	5	3.5	1.6	41	176	8.4	4	US	0.01	3.82
Costa Rica	15	69	3.6	69	162	4.9	19	US	0.04	4.93
Cuba	4	1.2	1.9	..	34	..	3	Mexico	0.00	7.35
Dominican Rep.	3	..	..	19	88	8.9	14	US	..	..
Ecuador	4	0.5	0.9	28	82	6.2	6	US	0.02	5.32
El Salvador	5	1.8	2.2	15	80	9.7	11	US	0.05	..
Guatemala	5	6.7	4.0	12	41	7.1	5	El Salvador	0.03	..
Haiti	2	..	..	..	8	..	2	US	0.00	7.07
Honduras	8	3.0	4.6	8	37	8.9	7	US	0.06	6.40
Jamaica	32	17	10	25	140	10.0	26	Trinidad	0.06	5.45
Mexico	10	10	2.4	38	104	5.8	13	US	0.14	3.79
Nicaragua	5	..	..	11	31	5.9	9	Costa Rica	0.11	..
Panama	10	3.8	3.7	65	134	4.1	15	Colombia	0.00	5.20
Paraguay	7	0.6	0.7	16	43	5.6	4	Argentina	0.06	..
Peru	4	0.4	0.6	18	68	7.7	4	US	0.09	4.81
Trinidad and Tobago	19	16	11	40	207	9.6	49	US	0.04	3.31
Uruguay	8	6.4	2.1	75	250	6.9	21	Argentina	0.19	4.98
Venezuela	2	6.0	1.1	54	117	4.4	7	US	0.07	4.48
North America										
Canada	64	..	..	415	621	2.3	143	US	0.00	1.16
United States	17	705	9.0	414	644	2.5	85	Canada	0.09	..
Europe										
Albania	21	(.)	(.)	10	37	7.5	11	Italy	0.04	7.19
Austria	32	371	33	290	491	3.0	123	Germany	0.20	3.11
Belarus	36	68	3.4	75	241	6.7	15	Ukraine	0.01	3.53
Belgium	16	329	39	248	468	3.6	121	France	0.17	2.54
Bosnia and Herzegovina	6	1.6	0.9	..	90	..	18	..	0.04	3.08
Bulgaria	38	..	..	102	323	6.6	9	..	0.01	..
Croatia	24	64	9.6	79	348	8.6	51	Germany	0.03	5.04
Czech Rep.	33	75	9.7	..	364	..	30	Germany	0.07	3.97
Denmark	24	335	40	434	633	2.1	115	Germany	0.17	2.19
Estonia	39	34	24	135	343	5.3	46	Finland	0.05	4.33
Finland	30	379	15	364	551	2.3	72	Sweden	0.14	2.95
France	29	384	15	295	570	3.7	58	Germany	0.13	1.52
Germany	25	249	12	332	566	3.0	59	Austria	0.14	2.49
Greece	12	..	..	235	522	4.5	57	Germany	0.04	3.18
Hungary	31	107	7.5	58	304	9.6	28	Germany	0.12	3.21
Ireland	53	161	51	142	411	6.1	191	UK	0.17	2.20
Israel	12	97	11	222	450	4.0	58	US	0.07	3.07
Italy	25	111	5.6	231	451	3.8	41	Germany	0.20	2.28
Latvia	40	11	3.8	161	383	4.9	18	Russia	0.08	6.09
Lithuania	26	11	4.7	115	300	5.5	15	Russia	0.02	7.88

Country or territory	Post offices (per 100,000 people)	Letter post items posted		Main telephones lines			Outgoing international telephone calls		Cost of a three minute telephone call*	
		(per person)	(per person sent or received from abroad)	(per thousnd people)	(per thousnd people)	Annual rate of change (%)	(minutes per person)	Major interna-tional partner	Local[1] (US$)	Inter-national to the US (US$)
	1997	1997	1997	1980	1998	1980/98	1997	1997	1997	1997
Macedonia (former Yugoslav Rep. of)	1	10	3.5	..	199	..	25	..	0.01	4.50
Moldova (Rep. of)	29	9.8	2.4	..	150	..	13	Russia	0.10	6.36
Netherlands	14	..	..	346	566	2.8	98	Germany	0.09	2.32
Norway	36	555	28	293	621	4.3	109	Sweden	0.11	1.64
Poland	19	40	2.4	55	228	8.2	14	Germany	0.06	4.12
Portugal	70	110	9.9	107	413	7.8	40	France	0.08	3.35
Romania	23	12	1.1	73	167	4.7	5	Germany	0.01	4.98
Russian Federation	30	38	..	70	183	5.5	7	Ukraine	..	7.55
Slovakia	33	80	7.2	94	286	6.4	30	..	0.05	4.46
Slovenia	27	197	14	..	364	..	57	Croatia	0.03	4.71
Spain	12	106	8.5	193	414	4.3	40	France	0.09	2.66
Sweden	20	503	25	580	679	0.9	120	Finland	0.13	1.81
Switzerland	51	..	..	444	661	2.2	276	Germany	0.14	2.07
Turkey	31	20	5.3	26	254	13.5	9	Germany	0.07	2.34
Ukraine	31	6.5	1.6	76	185	5.1	10	Russia	0.10	..
United Kingdom	32	332	23	332	542	2.8	93	US	0.20	1.16
Yugoslavia	17	..	..	..	218	..	20	Germany	0.01	6.19

Regions	Post offices (per 100,000 people)	Letter post items posted		Main telephones lines			Outgoing international telephone calls		Cost of a three minute telephone call*	
		(per person)	(per person sent or received from abroad)	(per thousnd people)	(per thousnd people)	Annual rate of change (%)	(minutes per person)	Major interna-tional partner	Local a/ (US$)	Inter-national to the US (US$)
	1997	1997	1997	1980	1997-8	1980/98	1997	1997	1997	1997
World	14	79	3.0	73	136	3.5	14		0.08	6.3
Developing	10	25	1.4	12	51	8.5	3		0.07	7.8
Industrial	25	282	9.6	259	448	3.1	51		0.09	3.6
Developing excl. India/China	7	11	2.7	26	61	4.8	6		0.07	7.8
Industrial excl. US/Rus. Fed.	27	174	9.8	240	430	3.3	47		0.09	3.5
Sub-Saharan Africa	3	7	2.4	..	13	..	2		0.10	9.5
Arab States	7	10	6.6	20	69	7.0	13		0.03	8.9
South Central Asia	15	13	0.7	7	24	7.6	1		0.04	
East Asia	12	69	0.7	35	107	6.4	4		0.03	5.3
South-East Asia/Oceania	8	20	2.6	27	60	4.6	9		0.08	7.3
Latin Am./Carib	8	15	2.1	39	118	6.4	7		0.06	5.1
North America	22	705	9.0	414	642	2.5	91		0.04	1.2
Europe	27	141	10.8	181	367	4.0	41		0.09	3.7

* New indicator.

1. Within the same exchange area using the subcriber's equipment, i.e. not from a public phone.

TABLE 20
CULTURE TRADE AND COMMUNICATION TRENDS: NEW COMMUNICATION TECHNOLOGY*

Country or territory	Mobile cellular telephone subcribers (per 10,000 people)		Mobile cellular telephone subcribers Percentage change (%)	Facsimile machines (per 10,000 people)		Facsimile machines Percentage change (%)	Personal computers (per 10,000 people)		Personal computers Percentage change (%)	Internet hosts (per 10,000 people)
	1995	1997-98	95/97-98	1992-95	1997-98	92-95/97-98	1995	1997-98	95/97-98	1997-98
Sub-Saharan Africa										
Angola	2	8	200	..	..	..	..	7	..	(.)
Benin	2	11	450	2	2	0	..	9	..	(.)
Botswana	..	..	..	22	22	0	..	134	..	3.6
Burkina Faso	..	2	..	..	..	..	..	7	..	(.)
Burundi	1	1	0	(.)	6	..	..	..	..	..
Cameroon	2	3	50	..	..	..	..	15		(.)
Central African Rep.	..	2	..	1	1	0	..	..	..	(.)
Chad	..	..	..	(.)	(.)	..	..	..	..	..
Congo	..	..	..	(.)	1	..	..	..	..	..
Congo (Dem. Rep.)	2	2	0	1	1	0	..	..	..	..
Côte d' Ivoire	..	64	..	..	..	..	..	33	..	0.2
Eritrea	..	..	..	2	4	100	..	..	..	..
Ethiopia	..	..	..	(.)	(.)	..	..	..	..	(.)
Gabon	25	83	23	..	4	..	45	75	67	(.)
Gambia	13	40	208	6	9	50	..	26	..	0.1
Ghana	4	12	200	3	3	0	12	16	33	0.1
Guinea	..	28	..	(.)	3	..	2	3	50	(.)
Guinea-Bissau	..	1	..	5	4	-25	..	..	..	0.1
Kenya	1	2	100	1	1	0	7	23	299	0.2
Lesotho	..	..	..	3	3	0	..	..	..	..
Liberia	..	..	..	..	..	..	..	..	..	..
Madagascar	..	3	..	..	..	..	..	13	..	(.)
Malawi	..	10	..	1	1	0	..	..	..	..
Mali	..	4	..	..	..	..	..	6	..	(.)
Mauritania	..	..	..	..	16	..	..	53	..	(.)
Mauritius	104	527	407	182	254	40	319	789	147	1.8
Mozambique	..	4	..	5	4	20	..	16	..	(.)
Namibia	23	119	417	..	..	..	..	186	..	4
Niger	..	1	..	(.)	(.)	..	..	2	..	(.)
Nigeria	1	1	0	..	..	..	41	51	24	(.)
Rwanda	..	..	..	..	1	..	..	..	..	..
Senegal	..	25	..	..	..	..	72	114	58	0.1
Sierra Leone	..	..	..	2	4	100	..	..	..	..
Somalia	..	..	..	..	..	..	..	..	..	..
South Africa	129	369	186	..	13	..	265	416	57	28
Sudan	..	3	..	2	4	100	..	..	..	..
Tanzania (United Rep. of)	..	..	..	..	1	..	..	16	..	(.)
Togo	..	17	..	..	39	..	..	58	..	0.1
Uganda	..	15	..	1	1	0	5	14	180	(.)
Zambia	2	4	100	1	1	0	..	..	..	0.2
Zimbabwe	..	9	..	..	4	..	30	97	223	0.5
Arab States										
Algeria	2	6	200	3	2	-50	30	42	40	(.)
Egypt	..	14	..	4	5	25	34	73	115	0.3
Iraq	..	..	..	..	6	..	..	..	..	..
Jordan	26	118	354	..	56	..	80	87	9	0.4
Kuwait	707	1 179	69	219	233	6	571	829	45	23

Country or territory	Mobile cellular telephone subcribers (per 10,000 people)		Mobile cellular: Percentage change (%)	Facsimile machines (per 10,000 people)		Facsimile: Percentage change (%)	Personal computers (per 10,000 people)		Personal computers: Percentage change (%)	Internet hosts (per 10,000 people)
	1995	1997-98	95/97-98	1992-95	1997-98	92-95/97-98	1995	1997-98	95/97-98	1997-98
Lebanon	300	1 567	422	..	8	..	125	318	154	3.6
Libyan Arab Jamahiriya	..	17	..	..	..	..	..	..	..	..
Morocco	11	42	282	3	7	133	17	25	47	0.5
Oman	..	433	..	8	27	238	..	151	..	2.9
Saudi Arabia	..	311	..	42	74	77	251	436	74	(.)
Syrian Arab Rep.	..	..	..	4	14	250	..	17	..	(.)
Tunisia	4	8	100	28	33	18	67	86	28	0.1
United Arab Emirates	542	2 096	287	104	208	100	484	840	74	8.2
Yemen	..	5	..	..	17	..	..	12	..	(.)
South Central Asia										
Afghanistan	..	..	..	..	..	..	..	..	..	..
Armenia	..	16	..	1	(.)	..	..	..	..	1.2
Azerbaijan	..	72	..	3	3	..	..	..	..	0.5
Bangladesh	..	2	..	(.)	(.)	..	..	..	..	..
Bhutan	..	..	..	..	5	..	..	..	..	(.)
Georgia	..	55	..	1	1	0	..	..	.	0.8
India	..	..	..	1	2	100	13	21	62	0.1
Iran (Islamic Rep. of)	..	37	..	5	5	0	..	327	..	(.)
Kazakhstan	3	7	133	..	1	..	..	..	..	0.7
Kyrgyzstan	..	3	..	..	..	..	..	..	..	0.3
Nepal	..	..	..	(.)	(.)		..	..	..	0.1
Pakistan	3	8	167	..	11	..	12	45	275	0.1
Sri Lanka	28	94	236	..	6	..	11	41	272	0.4
Tajikistan	..	1	..	2	4	100	..	..	..	(.)
Turkmenistan	2	6	200	..	..	..	..	..	..	(.)
Uzbekistan	..	7	..	..	1	..	..	..	..	(.)
East Asia										
China	..	106	..	(.)	16	..	22	60	173	0.1
Hong Kong SAR	1 290	3 429	166	467	519	11	1 163	2 308	99	104
Japan	815	3 746	360	480	1 267	164	1 525	2 024	33	93
Korea (Dem. People's Rep. of)	..	..	..	1	1	0	..	..	..	..
Korea (Rep. of)	366	1 502	310	84	87	4	1 208	1 507	25	27
Mongolia	..	8	..	9	25	178	..	54	..	0.1
South-East Asia and Oceania										
Australia	1 277	2 889	126	267	486	82	2 758	3 622	31	539
Cambodia	15	57	280	..	3	..	..	9	..	0.1
Indonesia	11	52	373	4	9	125	37	80	116	0.5
Lao People's Dem. Rep.	..	12	..	1	1	0	..	11	..	11
Malaysia	434	752	73	29	70	141	397	416	5	15
Myanmar	..	2	..	(.)	(.)	(.)	..	..	..	..
New Zealand	1 080	1 491	38	186	171	-8	2 227	2 639	19	447
Papua New Guinea	..	..	..	2	2	0	..	..	..	0.1
Philippines	73	180	147	5	7	40	114	136	19	0.6
Singapore	977	2 734	180	191	286	50	1 724	3 995	132	186
Thailand	185	333	80	10	25	150	153	198	29	204
Viet Nam	2	17	750	2	3	50	..	46	..	..

TABLE 20 (continued)

Country or territory	Mobile cellular telephone subcribers			Facsimile machines			Personal computers			Internet hosts (per 10,000 people)
	(per 10,000 people)		Percentage change (%)	(per 10,000 people)		Percentage change (%)	(per 10,000 people)		Percentage change (%)	
	1995	1997-98	95/97-98	1992-95	1997-98	92-95/97-98	1995	1997-98	95/97-98	1997-98
Latin America and the Caribbean										
Argentina	99	781	689	22	19	-14	246	392	59	5.6
Bolivia	..	149	..	..	..	..	..	..	..	0.7
Brazil	80	486	508	13	30	131	130	263	120	7.3
Chile	138	280	103	11	27	145	378	541	43	12
Colombia	71	491	592	28	42	50	162	334	106	2.8
Costa Rica	55	178	223	7	22	214	..	..	..	8.2
Cuba	2	3	50	(.)	(.)	(.)	..	..	..	0.1
Dominican Rep.	42	161	283	3	3	0	..	..	..	6.0
Ecuador	46	253	450	..	27	..	39	130	233	0.9
El Salvador	25	176	604	..	..		..	..	..	0.3
Guatemala	28	61	118	10	9	-10	28	30	7	0.7
Haiti	..	..	..	..	..	..	..	..	..	..
Honduras	..	23	..	..	..	..	..	..	..	0.1
Jamaica	179	..	..	..	6	..	..	46	..	1.1
Mexico	70	345	393	20	30	25	261	373	43	4.4
Nicaragua	11	45	309	..	..	..	..	..	..	1.2
Panama	..	62	..	..	..	..	..	..	..	3.7
Paraguay	32	166	419	..	4	..	..	123	..	0.6
Peru	31	179	477	6	6	0	59	60	2	1.4
Trinidad and Tobago	43	187	335	15	18	20	192	190	-1	7.2
Uruguay	126	596	373	34	33	-3	220	232	6	32
Venezuela	180	867	382	8	30	275	167	366	119	1.7
North America										
Canada	865	1 756	103	180	327	82	1 928	2 706	40	280
United States	1 284	2 560	99	539	766	82	3 280	4 067	24	770
Europe										
Albania	..	9	..	..	2	..	..	..	..	0.3
Austria	476	1 437	202	313	352	14	1 242	2 107	70	134
Belarus	6	12	100	9	15	67	..	..	..	0.7
Belgium	232	957	313	163	189	16	1 383	2 353	70	105
Bosnia and Herzegovina	..	69	..	..	..	..	..	..	..	1.0
Bulgaria	25	84	236	18	22	22	215	297	38	8.2
Croatia	71	407	473	80	111	38	209	220	5	18
Czech Rep.	..	939	..	71	100	41	532	825	55	55
Denmark	1 573	2 737	74	481	472	-2	2 705	3 602	33	321
Estonia	205	1 699	729	87	93	7	67	151	125	109
Finland	1 992	5 728	188	328	381	16	1 821	3 107	71	946
France	238	1 878	689	259	477	84	1 343	1 744	30	60
Germany	428	1 695	296	178	682	282	1 649	2 555	55	138
Greece	261	891	241	15	46	207	334	448	34	27
Hungary	259	695	168	44	119	171	392	490	25	67
Ireland	441	1 462	232	222	270	22	1 450	2 413	66	109
Israel	535	2 832	429	259	233	-10	998	1 861	87	147
Italy	674	3 553	427	35	314	797	837	1 130	35	44
Latvia	60	625	942	3	4	33	..	79	..	29
Lithuania	..	723	..	10	17	70	..	65	..	11

Country or territory	Mobile cellular telephone subcribers (per 10,000 people) 1995	Mobile cellular telephone subcribers (per 10,000 people) 1997-98	Mobile cellular telephone subcribers Percentage change (%) 95/97-98	Facsimile machines (per 10,000 people) 1992-95	Facsimile machines (per 10,000 people) 1997-98	Facsimile machines Percentage change (%) 92-95/97-98	Personal computers (per 10,000 people) 1995	Personal computers (per 10,000 people) 1997-98	Personal computers Percentage change (%) 95/97-98	Internet hosts (per 10,000 people) 1997-98
Macedonia (former Yugoslav Rep. of)	..	60	..	9	15	67	..	..	..	2.4
Moldova (Rep. of)	11	21	91	1	2	100	21	38	81	0.6
Netherlands	332	1 098	231	325	382	18	2 005	2 803	40	250
Norway	2 244	4 739	111	302	500	66	2 730	3 608	32	664
Poland	..	498	..	14	14	0	285	362	27	23
Portugal	344	3 088	798	36	71	97	605	744	23	43
Romania	..	89	..	9	9	0	53	89	68	6.0
Russian Federation	6	33	45	3	7	133	177	320	81	10
Slovakia	..	865	..	84	103	24	410	558	36	27
Slovenia	136	470	246	78	90	15	477	1 889	296	98
Spain	241	1 791	643	55	177	222	816	1 221	50	50
Sweden	2 294	4 641	102	369	506	37	1 925	3 503	82	394
Switzerland	635	2 352	270	281	284	1	3 480	3 949	14	267
Turkey	70	525	650	16	17	91	125	207	66	5.6
Ukraine	3	11	267	(.)	(.)	..	..	56	..	2.8
United Kingdom	980	2 523	157	308	340	10	1 862	2 424	30	168
Yugoslavia	..	226	..	..	14	..	118	..	..	4.6

Regions	Mobile cellular telephone subcribers (per 10,000 people) 1995	Mobile cellular telephone subcribers (per 10,000 people) 1997-98	Mobile cellular telephone subcribers Percentage change (%) 95/97-98	Facsimile machines (per 10,000 people) 1992-95	Facsimile machines (per 10,000 people) 1997-98	Facsimile machines Percentage change (%) 92-95/97-98	Personal computers (per 10,000 people) 1995	Personal computers (per 10,000 people) 1997-98	Personal computers Percentage change (%) 95/97-98	Internet hosts (per 10,000 people) 1997-98
World	..	613	..	62	110	98	..	550	..	59
Developing	..	163	..	5	13	79	..	113	..	4.7
Industrial	651	1 822	263	243	444	139	1 559	1 989	44	240
Developing excl. India/China	..	197	..	12	17	65	..	201	..	9.9
Industrial excl. US/Rus. Fed.	544	1 896	368	186	414	161	1 203	1 585	43	106
Sub-Saharan Africa	..	42	..	2	4	..	..	73	..	2.4
Arab States	51	119	237	13	20	58	74	111	76	0.6
South Central Asia	..	16	..	1	3	..	..	..	..	0.1
East Asia	..	486	..	46	128	105	198	289	156	9.6
South-East Asia/Oceania	125	249	333	17	31	89	256	296	73	62
Latin Am./Carib.	77	417	454	15	27	78	174	295	86	5.0
North America	1 242	2 479	99	503	722	82	3 144	3 930	26	721
Europe	344	1 243	321	102	206	161	861	1 171	54	72

*New table

TABLE 21
TRANSLATIONS: TRANSLATIONS AND BOOKS IN FOREIGN LANGUAGES

Country or territory	Translations published 1980	Translations published 1994-96	Major language translated: First language 1980	Second language 1980	Third language 1980	Major language translated: First language 1994-96	Second language 1994-96	Third language 1994-96	Percentage of titles published in foreign languages 1991-95	Percentage of titles published in two or more languages 1991-95
Sub-Saharan Africa										
Angola	11	..	French	English	..	..	..	..	..	..
Benin	..	..	..	..	..	..	..	..	..	..
Botswana	..	..	..	..	..	..	..	..	..	..
Burkina Faso	..	..	..	..	..	..	..	..	..	..
Burundi	..	..	..	..	..	..	..	..	..	..
Cameroon	..	..	..	..	..	..	..	..	..	..
Central African Rep.	..	..	..	..	..	..	..	..	..	..
Chad	..	..	..	..	..	..	..	..	..	..
Congo	2	..	..	..	..	..	..	..	..	..
Congo (Dem. Rep.)	..	..	..	..	..	..	..	..	..	..
Côte d' Ivoire	..	..	..	..	..	..	..	..	..	..
Eritrea	..	..	..	..	..	..	..	..	79	..
Ethiopia	..	..	..	..	..	..	..	..	14	..
Gabon	..	..	..	..	..	..	..	..	..	..
Gambia	..	..	..	..	..	..	..	..	10	..
Ghana	..	..	..	..	..	..	..	..	..	..
Guinea	..	..	..	..	..	..	..	..	..	..
Guinea-Bissau	..	..	..	..	..	..	..	..	..	..
Kenya	..	..	..	..	..	..	..	..	..	..
Lesotho	..	..	..	..	..	..	..	..	..	..
Liberia	..	..	..	..	..	..	..	..	..	..
Madagascar	13	8	French	English	..	French	English	Italian	4	3
Malawi	3	1	English	..	..	English	..	..	26	..
Mali	..	..	..	..	..	..	..	..	..	..
Mauritania	..	..	..	..	..	..	..	..	..	9
Mauritius	4	2	French	..	..	French	Hindi	..	..	..
Mozambique	..	..	..	..	..	..	..	..	..	..
Namibia	..	11	..	..	..	Afrikaans	German	..	..	..
Niger	39	..	English	..	..	..	..	..	..	..
Nigeria	9	..	English	..	..	..	..	..	1	..
Rwanda	..	..	..	..	..	..	..	..	..	..
Senegal	..	..	..	..	..	..	..	..	..	..
Sierra Leone	..	..	..	..	..	..	..	..	..	..
Somalia	..	..	..	..	..	..	..	..	..	..
South Africa	..	..	..	..	..	..	..	..	7	6
Sudan	..	..	..	..	..	..	..	..	..	..
Tanzania (United Rep. of)	..	..	..	..	..	..	..	..	..	..
Togo	..	..	..	..	..	..	..	..	..	..
Uganda	..	..	..	..	..	..	..	..	..	..
Zambia	..	..	..	..	..	..	..	..	..	..
Zimbabwe	..	..	..	..	..	..	..	..	..	..
Arab States										
Algeria	..	2	..	..	..	Arabic	English	..	49	..
Egypt	123	..	English	French	German	..	..	..	11	..
Iraq	53	..	English	Arabic	..	..	..	..	..	..
Jordan	10	81	English	..	..	English	French	..	1	..
Kuwait	19	5	French	English	..	English	Russian	..	..	..

Country or territory	Translations published		Major language translated			Major language translated			Percentage of titles published in foreign languages	Percentage of titles published in two or more languages
	1980	1994-96	First language 1980	Second language 1980	Third language 1980	First language 1994-96	Second language 1994-96	Third language 1994-96	1991-95	1991-95
Lebanon	10	11	French	..	Spanish	French	English	..	..	..
Libyan Arab Jamahiriya	4	..	French	..	..	..	..	..	..	..
Morocco	..	..	..	..	..	..	..	..	..	..
Oman	..	..	..	..	..	..	..	..	..	..
Saudi Arabia	2	24	English	..	..	English	German	..	..	..
Syrian Arab Rep.	44	114	French	English	Russian	French	English	..	..	..
Tunisia	7	7	..	..	..	Arabic	French	..	35	..
United Arab Emirates	..	23	..	..	..	English	Arabic	..	14	..
Yemen	..	..	..	..	..	..	..	..	..	..
South Central Asia										
Afghanistan	..	..	..	..	..	..	..	..	..	..
Armenia	..	..	..	..	..	..	..	..	..	..
Azerbaijan	..	..	..	..	..	..	..	..	4	4
Bangladesh	..	..	..	..	Classical	English	..	..	..	..
Buthan	..	..	..	..	..	..	..	..	..	..
Georgia	..	..	..	..	..	..	..	..	..	..
India	685	164	English	Sanskrit	German	English	Bengali	Sanskrit	..	..
Iran (Islamic Rep. of)	7	..	English	..	..	..	..	..	..	..
Kazakhstan	..	..	..	..	..	..	..	..	..	..
Kyrgyzstan	..	3	..	..	..	Kirghiz	Tadzik	..	..	..
Nepal	..	..	..	..	..	..	..	..	..	..
Pakistan	79	32	English	Arabic	Russian	English	Kazahskij	Panjabi	5	..
Sri Lanka	30	32	English	Russian	..	English	French	Sinhala	46	25
Tajikistan	..	..	..	..	..	..	..	..	..	..
Turkmenistan	..	..	..	..	..	..	..	..	..	..
Uzbekistan	..	..	..	..	..	..	..	..	17	(.)
East Asia										
China	..	..	..	..	..	..	..	..	..	..
Hong Kong SAR	..	..	..	..	..	..	..	..	..	..
Japan	1 966	5 375	English	French	German	English	French	German	..	..
Korea (Dem People's Rep)	..	..	..	..	..	..	..	..	..	..
Korea (Rep. of)	363	1 326	English	French	German	English	French	German	..	..
Mongolia	..	..	..	..	..	..	..	..	..	..
South-East Asia and Oceania										
Australia	113	..	English	Classical	French	..	..	..	..	..
Cambodia	..	..	..	..	..	..	..	..	..	..
Indonesia	377	354	English	French	Arabic	English	French	..	..	..
Lao People's Dem. Rep.	..	..	..	..	..	..	..	..	17	..
Malaysia	331	343	English	Arabic	..	English	Arabic	..	40	4
Myanmar	47	..	English	Chinese	..	..	..	..	..	..
New Zealand	21	101	English	..	..	English	Tongan	Samoan	..	..
Papua New Guinea	..	..	..	..	..	..	..	..	2	..
Philippines	29	4	English	Classical	..	Iloko	..	..	36	(.)
Singapore	70	..	English	Arabic	..	..	..	..	..	..
Thailand	95	108	English	Russian	French	English	Chinese	..	7	..
Viet Nam	..	..	..	..	..	..	..	..	..	..

TABLE 21 (continued)

Country or territory	Translations Published 1980	Translations Published 1994-96	Major language translated: First language 1980	Second language 1980	Third language 1980	Major language translated: First language 1994-96	Second language 1994-96	Third language 1994-96	Percentage of titles published in foreign languages 1991-95	Percentage of titles published in two or more languages 1991-95
Latin America and the Caribbean										
Argentina	248	1 009	English	French	German	English	French	..	(.)	..
Bolivia	..	..	..	..	..	..	..	..	..	..
Brazil	716	2 075	English	French	German	English	French	Spanish	64	..
Chile	24	166	English	French	French	English	French	German	..	..
Colombia	48	191	English	French	German	English	German	French	..	..
Costa Rica	1	21	..	..	..	Spanish	..	..	..	..
Cuba	..	18	..	..	..	Spanish	French	..	..	..
Dominican Rep.	1	..	..	..	..	..	..	..	..	..
Ecuador	1	..	..	..	..	..	..	..	..	..
El Salvador	..	..	..	..	..	..	..	..	..	..
Guatemala	..	..	..	..	..	..	..	..	..	..
Haiti	..	..	..	..	..	..	..	..	..	..
Honduras	..	..	..	..	..	..	..	..	..	..
Jamaica	..	..	..	..	..	..	..	..	..	..
Mexico	2 702	..	English	French	..	..	..	..	..	..
Nicaragua	..	..	..	..	..	..	..	..	..	..
Panama	9	8	English	..	..	English	French	..	..	..
Paraguay	..	..	..	..	..	..	..	..	1	..
Peru	19	9	English	..	..	Korean	..	..	10	..
Trinidad and Tobago	..	2	..	..	..	Spanish	French	..	..	..
Uruguay	11	14	English	French	..	English	..	..	..	..
Venezuela	15	5	French	English	..	German	English	Spanish	..	..
North America										
Canada	360	680	English	French	Classical	English	French	German	2	14
United States	1 390	1 721	German	French	Russian	German	French	Spanish	..	..
Europe										
Albania	173	112	Russian	French	English	English	French	Italian	43	(.)
Austria	327	430	English	French	German	English	French	German	7	2
Belarus	..	256	..	..	..	English	Russian	French	1	..
Belgium	1 149	23	English	German	French	English	Swedish	French	10	3
Bosnia and Herzegovina	..	..	..	..		..	..	..	..	..
Bulgaria	656	1 221	Russian	English	French	English	German	French	5	2
Croatia	..	656	..	..	..	English	Croatian	German	8	(.)
Czech Rep.	..	2 776	..	..	..	English	German	French	11	3
Denmark	1 913	2 280	English	Swedish	French	English	Swedish	German	17	3
Estonia	..	787	..	..	..	English	Estonian	German	23	5
Finland	1 476	1 164	English	Swedish	German	English	Swedish	..	16	(.)
France	5 691	6 542	English	German	Italian	English	German	Italian	11	2
Germany	7 681	9 931	English	French	Russian	English	French	German	..	..
Greece	358	683	English	French	Russian	English	French	..	..	..
Hungary	1 121	1 489	French	English	German	English	German	French	6	1
Ireland	..	215	..	..	..	English	German	..	..	..
Israel	330	198	English	German	French	English	French	..	..	..
Italy	2 055	1 958	English	French	German	English	French	..	9	3
Latvia	..	248	..	..	..	English	German	French	21	..
Lithuania	..	746	..	..	..	English	French	German	13	1

Country or territory	Translations published 1980	Translations published 1994-96	Major language translated: First language 1980	Second language 1980	Third language 1980	Major language translated: First language 1994-96	Second language 1994-96	Third language 1994-96	Percentage of titles published in foreign languages 1991-95	Percentage of titles published in two or more languages 1991-95
Macedonia (former Yugoslav Rep. of	..	199	..	..	..	Macedonian	English	German	..	..
Moldova (Rep. of)	..	96	..	..	..	Moldavian	Russian	English	23	6
Netherlands	1 846	4 561	English	German	..	English	German	French	19	..
Norway	1 175	1 245	English	Swedish	German	English	Swedish	Danish	14	..
Poland	883	1 528	English	Russian	German	English	German	French	5	(.)
Portugal	839	1 444	French	English	German	English	French	..	39	2
Romania	609	882	Hungarian	French	Russian	English	French	German	..	..
Russian Federation	..	3 235	..	..	French	English	French	German	8	1
Slovakia	..	409	..	..	..	English	German	Czech	21	5
Slovenia	..	643	..	..	..	English	German	..	13	..
Spain	6 366	3 233	English	French	German	English	French	German	5	1
Sweden	2 189	2 188	English	Scandinavian	German	English	German	Norwegian	18	3
Switzerland	811	945	English	German	French	English	German	French	18	..
Turkey	684	322	English	French	Arabic	English	French	..	4	1
Ukraine	..	363	..	..	..	English	French	..	10	7
United Kingdom	1 348	1 560	French	German	Russian	French	German	..	..	..
Yugoslavia	..	809	..	..	French	English	Serbian	Russian	20	10

Regions of publication	Translations Published 1980	Translations Published 1994-96	Percentage of titles published in foreign languages 1991-95	Percentage of titles published in two or more languages 1991-95
	T	T		
World	..	..	..	..
Developing	..	..		..
Industrial	43 530	63 254	13	3
Developing excl. India/China	..	..	..	..
Industrial excl. US/Rus. Fed.	42 140	58 298	13	3
Sub-Saharan Africa	..	..	..	..
North Af. / West Asia	272	267	..	..
South Central Asia	..	..	..	..
East Asia	..	..	..	..
South-East Asia/Oceania	1 083	..	..	..
Latin Am. / Carib.	3 795	3 518	..	..
North America	1 750	2 401	2	14
Europe	39 680	55 377	13	2

TABLE 22
TRANSLATIONS: TRANSLATIONS BY ORIGINAL LANGUAGE

Original language	Number of translations published *		Major languages into which translated 1980		Major languages into which translated 1996		
	1980	1996	First language 1980	Second language 1980	First language 1996	Second language 1996	Third language 1996
Abhazskij	15	2	..	..	Russian	..	..
Afrikaans	..	10	..	..	Dutch	German	English
Albanian	118	22	English	French	French	English	Italian
American Indian	..	5	..	..	German	English	..
Arabic	230	195	French	English	French	German	English
Aramaic	..	6	..	..	English	French	..
Armenian	54	7	Russian	English	English	Bulgarian	..
Azerbaijani	47	2	Russian	German	Turkish	..	..
Baskirskij	18	16	..	..	Tatarskij	Russian	..
Byelorussian	98	11	Russian	English	Russian	German	Bulgarian
Bengali	77	33	English	..	Hindi	English	Assamese
Bosnian	..	22	..	..	German	English	Macedonian
Breton	..	16	..	..	French	Occitan	English
Bulgarian	239	23	Russian	German	English	French	Russian
Catalan	27	149	Spanish	English	Spanish	French	German
Chinese	187	247	French	English	Japanese	English	German
Chuvash	14	4	..	..	Barkirskij	French	..
Croatian	..	103	..	..	English	German	Italian
Czech	651	186	Slovak	German	German	Slovak	French
Danish	649	373	Swedish	German	English	Norwegian	German
Dutch	409	516	German	English	German	English	French
Old Egyptian	..	7	..	..	German	French	..
English	22 415	36 528	German	French	German	French	Japanese
Middle English	..	8	..	..	English	German	..
Estonian	124	103	Russian	English	Russian	English	German
Euskera	..	14	..	..	Spanish	English	French
Finnish	165	105	Swedish	English	Estonian	German	Danish
French	5 972	4 623	Spanish	German	German	English	Spanish
Middle/Old French	17	25	French	German	French	English	..
Gallego	..	23	..	..	Calalan	Spanish	Eushera
Georgian	71	8	Russian	German	English	Russian	..
German	4 823	5 561	English	French	Czech	French	English
Middle High German	20	23	German	..	German	French	..
Classical Greek	458	426	German	Spanish	French	German	Spanish
Modern Greek	86	3	English	German	French	German	English
Gujarati	..	5	..	..	English	Oriya	..
Hebrew	181	271	English	Spanish	German	English	French
Hindi	63	18	English	Tamoul	Tamoul	English	French
Hungarian	633	187	English	German	German	English	French
Icelandic	39	30	English	German	Danish	German	French
Indonesian	..	9	..	..	German	Dutch	Japanese
Irish	..	9	..	..	German	English	..
Italian	1 476	1 621	Spanish	French	French	German	Spanish
Japanese	199	321	English	German	French	English	German
Kannada	..	5	..	..	English	Hindi	..

Original language	Number of translations published *		Major languages into which translated 1980		Major languages into which translated 1996		
	1980	1996	First language 1980	Second language 1980	First language 1996	Second language 1996	Third language 1996
Kazakh	66	2	Russian	..	Tatarskij	Lithuanian	..
Kirghiz	68	4	Russian	German	French	..	..
Korean	21	41	French	English	Japanese	German	French
Kurdish	..	5	..	..	German	Byelorussian	..
Latin	537	441	German	French	German	French	English
Latvian	77	7	Russian	..	Lithuanian	Estonian	..
Lithuanian	99	55	Russian	..	English	Russian	Polish
Macedonian	36	90	..	..	Albanian	English	Turkish
Malayalam	..	9	..	..	Tamil	English	..
Marathi	26	11	..	..	English	French	Japanese
Moldavian	45	53	Russian	..	Russian	English	French
Old Norse	..	11	..	..	Nynorsil	German	Dutch
Norwegian	358	342	Danish	Swedish	German	Danish	English
Occitan	23	19	French	..	French	English	..
Oriya	..	5	..	..	Assamese	Bengali	..
Pali	..	10	..	..	French	English	..
Panjabi	..	6	..	..	English	Hindi	..
Persian	96	48	English	French	French	German	English
Polish	608	298	German	English	German	Ressian	English
Portuguese	198	217	Spanish	French	French	English	German
Romanian	392	57	English	Hungarian	French	German	English
Russian	6 450	964	English	German	English	German	French
Samoan	..	15	..	..	Niuean	Tongan	..
Sanskrit	204	53	English	German	English	Russian	French
Serbian	382	164	English	German	English	French	German
Slovak	148	54	Hungarian	Russian	Czech	Hungarian	German
Slovene	41	155	..	..	English	German	Croatian
Spanish	851	1 240	French	German	English	French	German
Swahili	..	5	..	..	German	French	..
Swedish	1 225	183	Danish	Norwegian	Danish	Norwegian	German
Tadzijskij	22	1	Russian	..	Jakut	..	..
Tamoul	24	5	..	..	French	German	..
Tatarskij	32	15	Russian	..	Russian	Baskirskij	..
Telugu	..	9	..	..	German	Tamoul	..
Thai	..	6	..	..	Danish	English	..
Tibetan	14	42	German	English	English	French	German
Tongan	..	7	..	..	Niuean	Rarotongan	..
Turkish	52	40	German	French	German	French	English
Turkmenskij	30	1	..	..	Russian	..	..
Ukranian	158	24	Russian	English	Russian	German	English
Urdu	37	5	English	..	English	Albanian	..
Uzbek	64	1	Russian	..	Urdu	..	..
Valencian	..	6	..	..	Catalan	Spanish	..
Vietnamese	11	17	..	..	French	English	Dutch
Welsh	..	5	..	..	Breton	German	..
Yiddish	69	50	English	Russian	German	English	Polish

*Not including 590 translations of another 120 languages with less than five entries in either year.

TABLE 23
TRANSLATIONS: MOST FREQUENTLY TRANSLATED AUTHORS[1]

Rank 1980	Authors 1980	Associated country 1980	Number of translations 1980	Number of countries translating 1980	Rank 1996	Authors 1996	Associated country 1996	Number of translations 1996	Number of countries translating 1996
1	Lenin V. I.	USSR	468	15	1	Christie A.	UK	192	25
2	The Bible	Palestine	232	48	2	Steel D.	US	141	22
3	Christie A.	UK	189	20	3	King S.	US	137	21
4	Verne J.	France	172	21	4	Shakespeare W.	UK	125	25
5	Blyton E.	UK	147	12	5	Cartland B.	UK	115	11
6	Marx K.	Germany	136	20	6	Stine R.L	US	107	8
7	Cartland B.	UK	135	13	7	Blyton E.	UK	94	9
8	Engels F.	Germany	132	17	8	Koontz D. R.	US	82	14
9	Shakespeare W.	UK	112	22	9	Vandenberg P.	Germany	78	2
10	Breznev L. I.	USSR	109	14	10	Austen. J	UK	74	19
11	Grimm J.	Germany	103	14	11	Brown S.	US	73	15
12	Goscinny R.	France	101	10	11	Holt V.	UK	73	11
13	London J.	US	93	20	11	Sheldon S.	US	73	19
14	Andersen H. C.	Denmark	91	17	14	Verne J.	France	72	20
15	Twain M.	US	88	21	15	Courths Mahler H.	Germany	65	3
16	Dostoevskij F. M.	Russia	85	16	16	The Bible	Palestine	64	20
17	Asimov I.	US	82	17	17	Andersen H. C.	Denmark	60	20
17	Simenon G.	Belgium	82	21	18	Twain M.	US	60	19
19	Tolstoj L. N.	Russia	79	22	19	Andrews V. C.	US	58	13
20	Konsalik H. G.	Germany	72	10	19	Clark M. H.	UK	57	16
21	Buck P. S.	US	70	13	21	Gardner E. S.	US	54	8
21	Joannes Paulus II	Holy See	70	16	21	Steiner R.	Germany	54	16
23	Hemingway E.	US	64	21	23	Grimm W.	Germany	53	18
24	Greene G.	UK	63	17	23	Lindsey J.	US	53	10
24	Stevenson R. L.	UK	63	19	23	Pilcher R.	UK	53	11
26	Hesse H.	Germany	62	13	26	Doyle A. C.	UK	51	15
27	Robbins H.	US	60	17	26	Grimm J.	Germany	51	18
28	Dickens C.	UK	59	14	26	Montgomery L. M.	Canada	51	12
28	Grover M.	US	59	3	29	Chase J. H.	UK	50	8
28	Kolmogorov A. N.	USSR	59	1	29	Rendell R.	UK	50	13
31	Maclean A.	UK	57	14	31	Wilde O.	UK	48	17
32	Masterson L.	Norway	55	5	32	Roberts N	US	47	11
33	Gardner E. S.	US	54	11	33	Clancy T.	US	46	15
34	Tito J. B.	Yugoslavia	52	1	33	Grisham J.	US	46	15
35	Cehov A. P.	Russia	51	24	33	Peters E.	UK	46	10
36	Defoe D.	UK	50	17	36	Deveraux J.	US	45	12
36	Dumas (Père) A.	France	50	17	37	Cook R.	US	44	13
38	Lindgren A. E.	Sweden	49	16	37	Follett K.	UK	44	14
39	Balzac H. de	France	48	14	39	Kipling R.	UK	43	19
39	Doyle A. C.	UK	48	14	39	Lindgren A.	Sweden	43	15
39	Singer I. B.	US	48	12	41	Balzac H. de	France	42	13
42	Uderzo A.	France	46	8	41	Jordan P.	US	42	11
43	Peyo	Belgium	45	6	43	Eco U.	Italy	41	13
43	Sartre J.-P.	France	45	12	43	London J.	US	41	14
43	Shaw I.	US	45	18	45	Bradford B. T.	US	40	20

Rank 1980	Authors 1980	Associated country 1980	Number of translations 1980	Number of countries translating 1980	Rank 1996	Authors 1996	Associated country 1996	Number of translations 1996	Number of countries translating 1996
46	Makarycev J. N.	Russia	44	1	46	Dumas (Père) A.	France	39	14
46	Pushkin A. S.	Russia	44	11	46	Garcia Marquez G.	Colombia	39	16
46	Stratemeyer E. L.	US	44	1	46	McBain E.	US	39	13
49	De Villiers G.	France	43	6	46	Parker J.	..	39	5
49	Miller H.	US	43	9	51	May K.	Germany	38	8
49	Poe E. A.	US	43	11	51	Pratchett T.	UK	38	9
52	Homerus	Greece	42	13	51	Weis M.	..	38	8
53	Caldwell T.	US	41	6	54	Dahl R.	UK	37	10
53	Hoxha E.	Albania	41	4	54	Rajneesh B. S.	India	37	13
53	Plato	Greece	41	15	54	Scarry R.	US	37	9
56	Cronin A. J.	UK	40	13	57	Bradley M. Z.	US	36	10
56	Gorkij M.	USSR	40	13	57	Camus A.	France	36	19
56	Lobsang T. R	UK	40	7	57	Crichton M.	US	36	14
59	Carroll L.	UK	39	10	60	Anderson K.J.	US	35	7
59	Fromm E.	US	39	13	60	Chopra D.	India/US	35	17
59	Mather A.	..	39	7	60	Francis R. S.	UK	35	11
59	Tolkien J. R.	UK	39	12	63	Dickens C.	UK	34	13
63	Cooper J. F.	US	38	12	63	Kafka F.	Austria	34	17
63	Heyer G.	UK	38	6	63	Ludlum R.	US	34	11
63	Scott W.	UK	38	15	66	Hesse H.	Germany	33	16
66	Stalin I. V.	USSR	38	5	66	Lamb C.	UK	33	10
66	Steiner R.	Germany	38	11	68	Cookson C.	UK	32	11
68	Nietzsche F. W.	Germany	37	9	68	Fogle B.	..	32	17
69	Solohov M. A.	USSR	36	7	68	Homer	Greece	32	12
70	Carter N.	US	35	4	68	Mark W.	..	32	2
70	Freud S.	Austria	35	9	68	Rice A.	US	32	13
70	Garcia Marquez G.	Colombia	35	19	73	Dostoevskij F. M.	Russia	31	15
70	Goethe J. W. von	Germany	35	12	73	Higgins J.	UK	31	15
70	McBain E.	US	35	6	73	Kundera M.	Czech R.	31	15
70	Schultz C. M.	US	35	8	73	Le Carre J.	UK	31	13
70	Slaughter F. G.	US	35	9	73	Stout R.	US	31	9
77	Arabian Nights[2]	Persia	34	5	73	Tolstoy L. N.	Russia	31	13
77	Klepinina Z. A.	Russia	34	1	73	Unger G.F	Germany	31	1
77	Le Carre J.	UK	34	9	80	Asimov I.	US	30	12
77	Mann T.	Germany	34	13	80	Castaneda C.	Mexico	30	13
77	Molière	France	34	16	80	Defoe D.	UK	30	15
77	Morris M.	Belgium	34	4	80	Macomber D.	US	30	11
77	Winspear V.	..	34	6	80	Rilke R.M.	Germany	30	14
77	West M. L.	Austria	34	9	80	White E.G.	US	30	13
85	Flaubert G.	France	33	16	86	Dark J.	..	29	1
85	Perrault C.	France	33	10	86	Flaubert G.	France	29	4
87	Gogol N. V.	Russia	32	13	86	Gaarder J.	Norway	29	17
87	Huxley A.	UK	32	11	86	Llamas A.	Spain	29	3
87	Wahloo P.	Sweden	32	8	86	Nietzsche F. W.	Germany	29	17
90	Amado J.	Brazil	31	12	86	Redfield J.	US	29	13

TABLE 23 (continued)

Rank 1980	Authors 1980	Associated country 1980	Number of translations 1980	Number of countries translating 1980	Rank 1996	Authors 1996	Associated country 1996	Number of translations 1996	Number of countries translating 1996
90	Arthur R.	UK	31	4	86	Wallace E.	US	29	7
90	Hodakov J. V.	Russia	31	1	93	Chmielewska J.	Poland	28	2
90	Kent L.	US	31	3	93	Eddings D.	US	28	9
90	Kipling R.	UK	31	9	93	Hay L. L.	US	28	11
90	Shuttleworth C.	UK	31	1	93	James H.	US	28	10
90	Werner L.	Denmark	31	3	93	Lee M.	US	28	6
97	Camus A.	France	30	14	93	Rushdie S.	India/UK	28	9
97	Lem S.	Poland	30	11	93	Stevenson R. L.	UK	28	16
97	Maupassant G. de	France	30	13	93	Tolkien J. R. R.	UK	28	13
97	Sjowall M.	Sweden	30	8	101	Burroughs E.R.	US	27	8
97	Vilenkin N. S.	Russia	30	1	101	Cehov A. P.	Russia	27	13
97	Wolde G.	Sweden	30	5	101	Conrad J.	UK	27	9
97	Woolf V.	UK	30	11	101	Cornwell P.D.	US	27	9
104	Buhovcev B. B.	Russia	29	2	101	Davis J.	US	27	5
104	Harper C.	..	29	1	101	Goethe J. W. von	Germany	27	13
104	Holt V.	UK	29	29	101	Goscinny R.	France	27	9
104	Johns W. E.	UK	29	5	101	Gray J.	US	27	18
104	Melville H.	US	29	15	101	Irving J.	US	27	12
104	Mjakisev G. J.	Russia	29	3	101	Konsalik H.G.	Germany	27	7
104	Steinbeck J.	US	29	13	101	Parker D.	..	27	4
111	Aristotle	Greece	28	28	101	Randell B.	New Zealand	27	1
111	Brecht B.	Germany	28	13	101	Waller R.J.	US	27	14
111	Conrad J.	UK	28	14	114	Arabian Nights[2]	Persia	26	13
111	Hampson A.	US	28	6	114	Carroll L.	UK	26	12
111	Heinlein R. A.	US	28	6	114	Clarke A. C.	UK	26	12
111	Kafka F.	Austria	28	12	114	Inkpen M.	..	26	6
111	Lawrence D. H.	UK	28	10	114	Jung C. G.	Austria	26	11
111	Nin A.	France	28	12	114	Krishnamurti J.	India	26	11
111	Popov S. G.	Russia	28	2	114	Saint-Exupery A. de	France	26	13
111	Swift J.	UK	28	14	114	Uderzo A.	France	26	7
121	Farmer P.J.	US	27	6	122	Auster P.	US	25	9
121	Gilman G. G.	UK	27	3	122	Beckett S.	Ireland	25	9
121	Goodman L.	US	27	6	122	Bukowski C.	US	25	10
121	Hugo V.	France	27	13	122	Calvino I.	Italy	25	13
121	Keene C.	US	27	6	122	Carnefif D.	US	25	11
121	L'Amour L.	US	27	7	122	Coulter C.	US	25	6
121	Moravia A.	Italy	27	12	122	Duras M.	France	25	10
121	Pendleton D.	US	27	4	122	Eliade M.	Romania	25	13
121	Sagan F.	France	27	8	122	Ende M.	Germany	25	10
121	Scarry R.	US	27	7	122	Grafton S.	US	25	9
121	Srebnickij A. K.	Russia	27	1	122	Lessing D.	U.K	25	9
121	Wilde O.	UK	27	8	122	Perrault C.	France	25	14
133	Chandler R.	US	26	8	122	Steinbeck J.	US	25	10
133	Collodi C.	Italy	26	10					
133	de Beauvoir S.	France	26	8					

Rank 1980	Authors 1980	Associated country 1980	Number of translations 1980	Number of countries translating 1980	Rank 1996	Authors 1996	Associated country 1996	Number of translations 1996	Number of countries translating 1996
133	Du Maurier D.	UK	26	9					
133	Fischer M. L.	Germany	26	4					
133	Hargreaves R.	..	26	4					
133	Wallace E.	US	26	6					
133	Wells H. G.	UK	26	12					
141	Ajtmatov C.	USSR	25	5					
141	Deighton L.	UK	25	9					
141	Fleming I.	UK	25	6					
141	Franquin A.	Belgium	25	4					
141	Hailey A.	UK	25	14					
141	Kardelj E.	Yugoslavia	25	3					
141	Leguin U. K.	US	25	16					
141	Lewis C. S.	UK	25	11					
141	Maugham W. S.	UK	25	11					
141	Simmel J. M.	Germany	25	11					

1. Twenty five or more translations.

2. Alf Laila Wa-Laila

TABLE 24
CULTURAL CONTEXT: EDUCATION

Country or territory	Enrolment Ratios (%) Primary (net) Male	Primary (net) Female	Secondary (net) * Male	Secondary (net) * Female	Tertiary (gross) * Male	Tertiary (gross) * Female	Tertiary students in fine arts and humanities [1] as % of all tertiary students* Total	Female	Public expenditure on education as % of GNP	as % of total public expen-diture*
	1997	1997	1997	1997	1994-97	1994-97	1994-97	1994-97	1995-97	1995-97
Sub-Saharan Africa										
Angola	35	34	34	28	.. 1	..	..	..	..	..
Benin	85	50	38	18	5	1	..	..	3.2	15.2
Botswana	78	83	..	..	6	5	..	..	8.6	20.6
Burkina Faso	39	25	16	9	1	(.)	..	..	3.6	11.1
Burundi	38	33	20	14	1	(.)	..	..	4.0	18.3
Ca·meroon	64	59	45	35	.. 3	..	..	..	..	..
Central African Rep.	55	38	26	13	3	1	..	..	2.3	..
Chad	61	35	26	10	1	(.)	..	..	1.7	..
Congo	81	76	..	..	10	2	..	..	6.1	14.7
Congo (Dem. Rep.)	69	48	46	29	..	..	..	..	..	..
Côte d' Ivoire	66	50	45	24	9	3	20	25	5.0	24.9
Eritrea	31	28	41	34	2	(.)	5	6	1.6	..
Ethiopia	44	27	32	18	1	(.)	..	..	4.0	13.7
Gabon	..	..	..	..	..	..	..	..	2.9	..
Gambia	74	58	42	25	2	1	..	..	4.9	21.2
Ghana	45	42	..	..	2	1	..	..	4.2	19.9
Guinea	58	33	22	7	2	(.)	..	..	1.9	26.8
Guinea-Bissau	66	39	32	16	..	..	..	..	..	..
Kenya	63	67	63	57	2	1	20	18	6.5	16.7
Lesotho	63	74	..	..	2	3	7	8	8.4	..
Liberia	..	..	..	..	..	..	..	..	..	..
Madagascar	58	59	..	..	2	2	..	..	1.9	16.1
Malawi	97	99	91	54	1	(.)	..	..	5.4	18.3
Mali	45	31	23	13	2	1	..	..	2.2	..
Mauritania	66	60	..	..	6	1	..	..	5.1	16.2
Mauritius	96	97	66	70	8	6	..	..	4.6	17.4
Mozambique	45	34	28	17	1	(.)	..	..	..	..
Namibia	89	94	77	84	6	10	12	12	9.1	25.6
Niger	30	19	12	7	.. 1	..	..	..	2.3	12.8
Nigeria	..	..	..	..	.. 4	..	..	..	0.7[2]	11.5[2]
Rwanda	78	79	..	..	..	..	..	..	..	..
Senegal	65	54	24	16	5	2	..	..	3.7	33.1
Sierra Leone	49	39	..	..	.. 1	..			..	..
Somalia	9	5	..	..	..	..			..	..
South Africa	99	99	93	97	18	16	12	16	8.0	23.9
Sudan	40	35	23	20	3	3	18	17	..	9.0
Tanzania (United Rep. of)	47	48	..	..	1	(.)	..	..	..	..
Togo	94	70	77	40	6	1	..	..	4.5	24.7
Uganda	64	58	15	9	3	1	7	6	3.6	21.4
Zambia	73	72	49	35	4	1	..	..	2.2	7.1
Zimbabwe	94	92	62	56	9	4	..	..	7.1	..
Arab States										
Algeria	99	93	73	64	14	10	13	20	5.1	16.4
Egypt	99	90	80	70	24	16	19	25	4.8	14.9
Iraq	80	70	52	34	..	..	..	..	..	..
Jordan	..	..	..	..	..	..	18	25	7.9	19.8
Kuwait	66	64	63	63	15	24	..	..	5.0	14.0

Country or territory	Enrolment Ratios (%)						Tertiary students in fine arts and humanities [1] as % of all tertiary students*		Public expenditure on education	
	Primary (net)		Secondary (net) *		Tertiary (gross) *					
	Male	Female	Male	Female	Male	Female	Total	Female	as % of GNP	as % of total public expenditure*
	1997	1997	1997	1997	1994-97	1994-97	1994-97	1994-97	1995-97	1995-97
Lebanon	77	75	..	..	27	27	27	30	2.5	8.2
Libyan Arab Jamahiriya	99	99	99	99	18	15	..	..	..	..
Morocco	86	67	43	32	13	9	36	45	5.3	24.9
Oman	69	67	68	65	9	7	3	3	4.5	16.4
Saudi Arabia	62	58	62	53	17	15	19	15	7.5	22.8
Syrian Arab Rep.	99	91	45	39	18	13	27	39	3.1	13.6
Tunisia	99	99	76	72	15	12	24	28	7.7	19.9
United Arab Emirates	83	81	76	80	5	21	..	..	1.8	16.7
Yemen	..	..	..	..	.. 4	..	..	..	7.0	21.8
South Central Asia										
Afghanistan	66	33	30	14	2	1	..	..	..	..
Armenia	..	..	..	..	11	14	12	17	2.0	10.3
Azerbaijan	..	..	..	..	17	18	5	..	3.0	18.8
Bangladesh	80	70	27	16	7	1	..	..	2.2	8.7
Bhutan	14	12	..	..	..	..	..	..	4.1	7.0
Georgia	89	89	76	75	40	44	14	21	5.2	6.9
India	83	71	71	48	8	5	..	..	3.2	11.6
Iran (Islamic Rep. of)	91	89	86	76	22	13	13	18	4.0	17.8
Kazakhstan	..	..	..	..	29	37	12	17	4.4	17.5
Kyrgyzstan	99	99	77	79	11	13	4	4	5.3	23.5
Nepal	93	63	68	40	.. 5	..	..	..	3.2	13.5
Pakistan	..	..	..	..	4	2	..	..	2.7	7.1
Sri Lanka	99	99	73	79	6	4	19	24	3.4	8.9
Tajikistan	..	..	..	..	27	13	..	..	2.2	11.5
Turkmenistan	..	..	..	..	.. 22	..	..	..	..	..
Uzbekistan	..	..	..	..	.. 32	..	..	..	7.7	21.1
East Asia										
China	99	99	74	65	7	4	6	..	2.3	12.2
Hong Kong SAR	90	93	67	72	24	20	..	..	2.9	17.0
Japan	99	99	99	99	44	36	18	29	3.6	9.9
Korea (Dem. People's Rep. of)	..	..	..	..	..	..	..	..	..	..
Korea (Rep. of)	99	99	99	99	82	52	17	26	3.7	17.5
Mongolia	83	88	48	64	10	24	16	17	5.7	15.1
South-East Asia and Oceania										
Australia	99	99	81	82	77	83	..	..	5.5	13.5
Cambodia	99	99	47	31	2	1	..	..	..	2.9..
Indonesia	99	99	59	53	15	8	6	8	1.4[2]	7.9
Lao People's Dem. Rep.	77	69	74	53	4	2	..	..	2.1	8.7
Malaysia	99	99	60	69	11	12	9	11	4.9	15.4
Myanmar	99	99	55	53	4	7	..	..	1.2	14.4
New Zealand	99	99	92	94	53	73	22	24	7.3	17.1
Papua New Guinea	85	73	..	..	4	2	..	..	..	..
Philippines	99	99	77	79	25	33	..	..	3.4	15.7
Singapore	92	91	76	75	37	31	..	..	3.0	23.4
Thailand	87	89	48	47	17	20	4	..	4.8	20.1
Viet Nam	99	99	56	54	.. 7	..	..	..	3.0	7.4

TABLE 24 (continued)

Country or territory	Enrolment Ratios (%)							Tertiary students in fine arts and humanities [1] as % of all tertiary students*		Public expenditure on education	
	Primary (net)		Secondary (net) *		Tertiary (gross) *						
	Male	Female	Male	Female	Male		Female	Total	Female	as % of GNP	as % of total public expen-diture*
	1997	1997	1997	1997	1994-97		1994-97	1994-97	1994-97	1995-97	1995-97
Latin America and the Caribbean											
Argentina	99	99	74	80	..	36	..	11	..	3.5	12.6
Bolivia	99	95	43	37	..	21	..	22	..	4.9	11.1
Brazil	99	94	75	77	..	15	..	9	12	5.1	..
Chile	92	89	83	87	34		29	4	..	3.6	15.5
Colombia	89	89	75	78	16		17	3	4	4.4	19.0
Costa Rica	91	93	55	57	33		28	6	..	5.4	22.8
Cuba	99	99	67	73	10		15	23	24	6.7	12.6
Dominican Rep.	89	94	75	82	19		27	4	..	2.3	13.8
Ecuador	99	99	51	51	..	20	..	1	..	3.5	13.0
El Salvador	89	89	36	37	18		18	..	..	2.5	16.0
Guatemala	77	70	38	32	..	8	..	..	..	1.7	15.8
Haiti	19	20	..	..	2		1	..	..	..	..
Honduras	86	89	34	38	11		9	1	2	3.6	16.5
Jamaica	96	96	68	72	9		7	..	..	7.5	12.9
Mexico	99	99	68	64	17		15	3	3	4.9	23.0
Nicaragua	77	80	49	53	11		12	2	2	3.9	8.8
Panama	90	90	71	72	..	32	..	11	12	5.1	16.3
Paraguay	96	97	62	60	10		11	..	..	4.0	19.8
Peru	94	93	87	81	..	26	..	16	..	2.9	19.2
Trinidad and Tobago	99	99	71	79	9		7	..	..	4.4	10.3
Uruguay	94	95	79	89	..	30	..	..	..	3.3	15.5
Venezuela	81	84	44	54	..	28	..	..	..	5.2	22.4
North America											
Canada	99	99	96	94	81		95	9	10	6.9	12.9
United States	97	96	97	96	71		92	13	..	5.4	14.6
Europe											
Albania	95	97	..	..	9		11	21	26	3.1	..
Austria	99	99	98	97	48		49	16	21	5.4	10.4
Belarus	..	..	..	..	39		49	22	..	5.9	17.8
Belgium	99	99	99	99	55		57	10	12	3.1	6.0
Bosnia and Herzegovina	..	..	..	..	..					..	..
Bulgaria	97	99	80	75	31		52	8	10	3.2	7.0
Croatia	99	99	72	73	27		29	8	11	5.3	..
Czech Rep.	99	99	99	99	24		23	8	11	5.1	13.6
Denmark	99	99	94	95	43		53	19	23	8.1	13.1
Estonia	99	99	85	87	38		46	12	11	7.2	25.5
Finland	99	99	95	96	68		80	14	18	7.5	12.2
France	99	99	99	99	45		57	25	30	6.0	10.9
Germany	99	99	96	95	50		44	15	21	4.8	9.6
Greece	99	99	90	93	47		46	4	5	3.1	8.2
Hungary	98	97	96	98	22		26	12	15	4.6	6.9
Ireland	99	99	99	99	39		43	..	..	6.0	13.5
Israel	99	99	..	..	36		41	..	..	7.6	12.3
Italy	99	99	94	96	42		52	15	23	4.9	9.1
Latvia	99	99	81	81	27		40	9	11	6.3	14.1
Lithuania	99	99	..	..	25		38	9	11	5.5	22.8

Country or territory	Enrolment Ratios (%)						Tertiary students in fine arts and humanities [1] as % of all tertiary students*		Public expenditure on education	
	Primary (net)		Secondary (net) *		Tertiary (gross) *					
	Male	Female	Male	Female	Male	Female	Total	Female	as % of GNP	as % of total public expen-diture*
	1997	1997	1997	1997	1994-97	1994-97	1994-97	1994-97	1995-97	1995-97
Macedonia (former Yugoslav Rep. of)	86	84	..	..	17	22	11	14	5.1	20.0
Moldova (Rep. of)	..	..	..	..	24	29	4	..	10.6	28.1
Netherlands	99	99	99	99	48	46	8	11	5.1	9.8
Norway	99	99	97	98	53	71	12	14	7.4	15.8
Poland	99	99	85	89	21	28	12	15	7.5	24.8
Portugal	99	99	88	91	33	44	8	11	5.8	11.7
Romania	99	99	75	76	21	24	9	11	3.6	10.5
Russian Federation	99	99	85	91	37	49	7	10	3.5	9.6
Slovakia	..	..	..	..	22	23	8	9	5.0	..
Slovenia	99	99	..	..	31	41	8	10	5.7	12.6
Spain	99	99	91	93	47	56	10	12	5.0	11.0
Sweden	99	99	99	99	43	57	16	18	8.3	12.2
Switzerland	99	99	87	80	40	25	14	21	5.4	15.4
Turkey	99	98	68	49	27	15	5	6	2.2	14.7
Ukraine	..	..	..	..	35	47	14	..	7.3	15.7
United Kingdom	99	99	..	..	49	56	15	18	5.3	11.6
Yugoslavia	..	..	..	..	20	24	13	18	..	..

Countries and Regions	Enrolment Ratios (%)						Tertiary students in fine arts and humanities [1] as % of all tertiary students*		Public expenditure on education *	
	Primary (net)		Secondary (net) *		Tertiary (gross) *					
	Male	Female	Male	Female	Male	Female	Total	Female	as % of GNP	as % of total public expen-diture*
	1997	1997	1997	1997	1994-97	1994-97	1994-97	1994-97	1995-97	1995-97
World	90	85	72	63	19	19	..	..	4.8	..
Developing	87	82	67	56	10	7	..	..	3.8	..
Industrial	98	98	92	92	48	56	13	18	5.1	13.7
Developing excl. India/China	83	77	59	54	14	11	..	..	4.2	..
Industrial excl. US/Rus. Fed.	99	99	91	90	42	45	14	19	4.9	13.8
Sub-Saharan Africa	53	45	43	33	4	3	..	..	5.6	..
Arab States	90	82	66	57	18	14	21	27	4.5	16.8
South Central Asia	85	71	67	46	9	5	..	..	3.4	
East Asia	99	99	77	69	13	8	14	28	3.4	15.5
South-East Asia/Oceania	97	97	61	58	18	17	..	..	4.4	16.2
Latin Am./Carib	94	93	69	70	17	16	7	..	4.5	15.4
North America	97	96	97	96	72	92	13	10	5.5	13.7
Europe	99	99	88	88	38	44	12	16	5.3	13.7

*New indicator.

1. Art studies, drawing and painting, sculpturing, handicrafts, music, drama, photography, cinematography, interior design, history and philosophy of art, languages and literature, linguistics, comparative literature, interpreters and translators programmes, history, archaeology, philosophy, religion and theology.

2. Central government only.

TABLE 25
CULTURAL CONTEXT: TERTIARY EDUCATION ABROAD

Country or territory	Number of students abroad (thousnds)	Leading countries of study			Number of foreign students (thousnds)	Leading countries of origin			Foreign students as % of students abroad
		First country	Second country	Third country		First country	Second country	Third country	
	1994-97	1994-97	1994-97	1994-97	1994-97	1994-97	1994-97	1994-97	1994-97
Sub-Saharan Africa									
Angola	3.3	Portugal	Russia	Ukraine	..	..	..	..	..
Benin	1.9	France	Russia	Germany	0.7	Niger	Cameroon	Togo	37
Botswana	1.7	UK	US	South Africa	0.3	..	..	..	18
Burkina Faso	1.2	France	Morocco	Ukraine	0.8	..	..	..	67
Burundi	0.7	Belgium	Canada	France	0.5	..	..	..	71
Cameroon	8.8	France	Germany	Belgium	0.2	..	..	..	2
Central African Rep.	0.5	France	US	Canada	0.2	..	..	..	40
Chad	0.6	France	Algeria	Russia	0.1	..	..	..	17
Congo	3.8	France	Ukraine	Cuba	0.2	..	..	..	5
Congo (Dem. Rep.)	6.2	Belgium	France	US	..	..	..	..	..
Côte d'Ivoire	3.9	France	US	Canada	..	..	..	..	..
Eritrea	0.4	Egypt	Syria	Jordan	0.1	Ethiopia	..	..	25
Ethiopia	4.4	US	Germany	UK	0.1	..	..	..	2
Gabon	1.8	France	Canada	US	0.2	..	..	..	11
Gambia	0.6	US	UK	Norway	..	..	..	..	..
Ghana	4.1	US	UK	Germany	0.1	..	..	..	2
Guinea	1.3	France	Canada	US	(.)	Cameroon	Liberia	..	..
Guinea-Bissau	0.7	Portugal	Cuba	Russia	..	..	..	..	..
Kenya	5.9	US	UK	Canada	..	..	..	..	..
Lesotho	0.6	South Africa	UK	US	0.1	Zimbabwe	Swaziland	Burundi	17
Liberia	0.5	US	UK	Germany	..	..	..	..	..
Madagascar	3.5	France	Russia	Ukraine	0.7	..	..	..	20
Malawi	0.8	UK	US	South Africa	(.)	..	..	..	..
Mali	1.7	France	Russia	Ukraine	..	..	..	..	..
Mauritania	1.9	France	Syria	Morocco	0.5	..	..	..	26
Mauritius	2.3	UK	France	US	(.)	..	..	..	..
Mozambique	1.5	Portugal	Cuba	UK	0.1	..	..	..	7
Namibia	2.5	South Africa	Tunisia	UK	0.4	..	..	..	16
Niger	0.9	France	Morocco	US	..	..	..	..	..
Nigeria	6.3	US	UK	Germany	..	..	..	..	..
Rwanda	1.1	Belgium	France	Germany	0.3	..	..	..	27
Senegal	4.8	France	US	Canada	1.9	..	..	..	40
Sierra Leone	0.9	US	UK	Russia	..	..	..	..	..
Somalia	1.1	Italy	Norway	UK	..	..	..	..	..
South Africa	3.6	US	UK	Germany	12.6	Zimbabwe	Namibia	..	350
Sudan	4.4	Egypt	Germany	US	0.8	..	..	..	18
Tanzania (United Rep. of)	2.5	US	UK	Canada	..	..	..	..	..
Togo	1.8	France	Germany	US	0.5	Nigeria	Benin	Cameroon	28
Uganda	1.6	US	UK	Germany	..	..	..	..	..
Zambia	1.5	UK	US	South Africa	..	..	..	..	..
Zimbabwe	5.3	South Africa	UK	US	..	..	..	..	..
Arab States									
Algeria	22.3	France	Belgium	Germany	2.6	Palestine	Morocco	Tunisia	12
Egypt	9.8	Lebanon	US	Germany	6.7	Palestine	Sudan	Kuwait	68
Iraq	2.7	Jordan	Germany	UK	..	..	..	..	..
Jordan	14.3	Lebanon	Syria	US	11.0	Palestine	Malaysia	Yemen	77
Kuwait	4.8	US	UK	Egypt	2.7	Saudi Arabia	Bahrain	Oman	56

Country or territory	Number of students abroad (thousnds) 1994-97	Leading countries of study			Number of foreign students (thousnds) 1994-97	Leading countries of origin			Foreign students as % of students abroad 1994-97
		First country 1994-97	Second country 1994-97	Third country 1994-97		First country 1994-97	Second country 1994-97	Third country 1994-97	
Lebanon	10.3	France	US	Syria	18.3	Syria	Egypt	Jordan	178
Libyan Arab Jamahiriya	1.9	UK	Egypt	Germany	..	..	..	..	..
Morocco	38.2	France	Germany	Belgium	3.6	Tunisia	Mauritania	Algeria	9
Oman	2.6	Jordan	UK	US	..	..	..	..	..
Saudi Arabia	7.6	US	UK	Kuwait	5.4	Yemen	Palestine	Jordan	71
Syrian Arab Rep.	15.0	Lebanon	France	Russia	11.8	Palestine	Jordan	Yemen	79
Tunisia	10.4	France	Morocco	Germany	2.9	Morocco	Namibia	Algeria	28
United Arab Emirates	3.5	US	UK	Egypt	1.6	Oman	Jordan	Palestine	46
Yemen	6.1	Jordan	Syria	Saudi Arabia	1.0	..	..	..	16
South Central Asia									
Afghanistan	3.0	Russia	Germany	Ukraine	0.2	..	..	..	7
Armenia	2.7	Russia	Ukraine	US	0.9	India	Syria	Iran	33
Azerbaijan	4.6	Russia	Turkey	Ukraine	4.0	Georgia	Turkey	Russia	87
Bangladesh	5.8	US	Japan	Ukraine	0.2	..	..	..	3
Bhutan	0.1	India	UK	US	..	..	..	..	..
Georgia	7.7	Russia	Azerbaijan	Ukraine	0.1	..	..	..	1
India	40.4	US	UK	Ukraine	12.8	Nepal	Kenya		32
Iran (Islamic Rep. of)	26.4	Germany	US	France	0.6	Afghanistan	Iraq	Pakistan	2
Kazakhstan	15.5	Russia	US	Ukraine	2.9	Uzbekistan	Russia	China	19
Kyrgyzstan	3.2	Russia	Kazakhstan	Tajikistan	0.1	..	..	..	3
Nepal	2.2	India	US	Ukraine	..	..	..	..	..
Pakistan	10.9	US	UK	Germany	0.9	Afghanistan	Palestine	..	8
Sri Lanka	5.1	US	India	UK	0.1	..	..	..	2
Tajikistan	1.4	Russia	Ukraine	Kazakhstan	6.7	Uzbekistan	Russia	Kyrgyz Rep.	479
Turkmenistan	1.5	Russia	Ukraine	Turkey	..	..	..	..	..
Uzbekistan	10.4	Russia	Tajikistan	Kazakhstan	..	..	..	..	..
East Asia									
China	121.4	US	Japan	UK	22.8	Japan	Korea Rep.	US	19
Hong Kong SAR	36.5	US	UK	Australia	1.0	China	UK	..	3
Japan	64.3	US	China	UK	53.5	China	Korea Rep.	Malaysia	83
Korea (Dem. People's Rep. of)	0.6	US	China	Germany	..	..	..	..	..
Korea (Rep. of)	71.8	US	Japan	China	2.1	China	Japan	US	3
Mongolia	1.7	Russia	Kazakhstan	Germany	0.3	Russia	China	Turkey	18
South-East Asia and Oceania									
Australia	5.4	US	UK	China	102.3	Malaysia	Hong Kong, China	Singapore	1 894
Cambodia	1.6	France	Russia	Germany	..	..	..	..	..
Indonesia	22.1	US	Australia	Germany	1.1	Malaysia	Japan	Korea Rep.	5
Lao People's Dem. Rep.	1.1	France	Russia	US	0.1	Viet Nam	China	Japan	9
Malaysia	49.4	UK	US	Australia	..	..	..	..	..
Myanmar	0.7	US	Japan	UK	..	..	..	..	..
New Zealand	6.0	Australia	US	UK	6.4	Malaysia	Thailand	Hong Kong SAR	107
Papua New Guinea	0.6	Australia	UK	New Zealand	0.3	..	..	..	50
Philippines	5.1	US	Japan	Australia	4.9	China	Korea. Rep.	Indonesia	96
Singapore	18.1	UK	Australia	US	..	..	..	..	..
Thailand	17.1	US	UK	Australia	..	..	..	..	..
Viet Nam	6.3	Germany	France	US	..	..	..	..	..

TABLE 25 (continued)

Country or territory	Number of students abroad (thousnds) 1994-97	Leading countries of study			Number of foreign students (thousnds) 1994-97	Leading countries of origin			Foreign students as % of students abroad 1994-97
		First country 1994-97	Second country 1994-97	Third country 1994-97		First country 1994-97	Second country 1994-97	Third country 1994-97	
Latin America and the Caribbean									
Argentina	4.7	US	Spain	France	12.7	Peru	Chile	Bolivia	270
Bolivia	3.1	Argentina	US	Germany	..	..	..	..	..
Brazil	12.9	US	France	Germany	..	..	..	..	..
Chile	5.0	Argentina	US	Germany	0.6	..	..	..	12
Colombia	6.4	US	France	Germany	..	..	..	..	..
Costa Rica	1.2	US	Germany	France	..	..	..	..	..
Cuba	0.6	Spain	US	Germany	4.2	Angola	Zimbabwe	Ghana	700
Dominican Rep.	1.0	US	France	Spain	..	..	..	..	..
Ecuador	2.3	US	Germany	France	..	..	..	..	..
El Salvador	1.0	US	Germany	France	0.5	US	Honduras	Nicaragua	50
Guatemala	1.0	US	Germany	France	..	..	..	..	..
Haiti	1.4	US	France	Canada	..	..	..	..	..
Honduras	1.0	US	Spain	France	0.5	..	..	..	50
Jamaica	3.6	US	UK	Canada	0.1	..	..	..	3
Mexico	12.3	US	UK	France	..	..	..	..	..
Nicaragua	1.2	US	Cuba	Germany	0.3	US	Honduras	El Salvador	25
Panama	1.6	US	Spain	Russia	0.7	..	..	..	44
Paraguay	2.0	Argentina	US	Italy	..	..	..	..	..
Peru	8.5	Argentina	US	Germany	..	..	..	..	..
Trinidad and Tobago	3.0	US	UK	Canada	0.1	Malaysia	US	Canada	3
Uruguay	2.2	Argentina	US	Spain	..	..	..	..	..
Venezuela	7.0	US	Spain	Portugal	..	..	..	..	..
North America									
Canada	29.6	US	UK	France	35.5	Hong Kong SAR	China	France	120
United States	30.4	UK	Germany	France	454.8	China	Japan	Korea Rep.	1 496
Europe									
Albania	1.9	Italy	Rumania	US	0.5	..	..	..	26
Austria	10.7	Germany	UK	US	27.1	Italy	Germany	Turkey	253
Belarus	7.2	Russia	Poland	Ukraine	3.7	Russia	China	Lebanon	51
Belgium	8.3	UK	France	Germany	35.0	France	Italy	Morocco	422
Bosnia and Herzegovina	2.8	Germany	Austria	Turkey	..	..	..	..	..
Bulgaria	6.2	US	France	Austria	8.5	Greece	Moldova	Turkey	137
Croatia	5.0	Germany	Austria	US	0.7	Italy	Slovenia	..	14
Czech Rep.	2.9	Germany	US	Poland	3.9	Slovakia	Greece	Poland	134
Denmark	5.7	UK	US	Sweden	9.0	Norway	Iran	Germany	158
Estonia	2.4	Russia	Finland	US	..	Finland	Lithuania	Latvia	..
Finland	6.8	Sweden	UK	Germany	3.8	China	Estonia	Sweden	56
France	39.2	UK	Germany	US	138.2	Morocco	Algeria	Germany	353
Germany	49.4	UK	US	France	166.0	Turkey	Iran	Greece	336
Greece	54.1	UK	Germany	Italy	1.5	..	..	..	3
Hungary	5.3	Germany	US	Ausria	6.4	Romania	Greece	Macedonia	121
Ireland	20.2	UK	US	Germany	6.0	UK	US	Germany	30
Israel	9.8	US	UK	Germany	..	..	..	..	..
Italy	40.7	Holy See	Germany	Austria	24.9	Greece	Germany	Switzerland	61
Latvia	1.5	Russia	US	Germany	0.9	Russia	Lebanon	Sri Lanka	60
Lithuania	2.1	Russia	Poland	US	0.4	Lebanon	China	Poland	19

Country or territory	Number of students abroad (thousnds) 1994-97	Leading countries of study			Number of foreign students (thousnds) 1994-97	Leading countries of origin			Foreign students as % of students abroad 1994-97
		First country 1994-97	Second country 1994-97	Third country 1994-97		First country 1994-97	Second country 1994-97	Third country 1994-97	
Macedonia (former Yugoslav Rep. of)	1.3	Hungary	Bulgaria	Germany	0.3	Yugoslavia	Albania	Bulgaria	23
Moldova (Rep. of)	8.2	Romania	Russia	Ukraine	1.2	Syria	Ukraine	Romania	15
Netherlands	13.0	Belgium	UK	Germany	11.4	Germany	Suriname	Belgium	88
Norway	7.2	US	Germany	Sweden	11.2	Iran	Sweden	Denmark	156
Poland	13.5	Germany	US	UK	5.2	Ukraine	Belarus	Lithuania	39
Portugal	7.6	France	Germany	US	6.1	Angola	Brazil	Cape Verde	80
Romania	7.0	France	UK	Germany	14.2	Greece	Moldova	Israel	203
Russian Federation	21.1	US	Ukraine	Germany	73.1	Ukraine	Kazakhstan	Belarus	346
Slovakia	2.1	Czech Rep.	Austria	Germany	1.7	Czech Rep.	Greece	Poland	81
Slovenia	1.1	Germany	Austria	US	0.4	Bosnia	Yugoslavia	Croatia	36
Spain	25.6	UK	US	France	21.4	France	Germany	UK	84
Sweden	10.6	US	UK	Germany	12.2	Finland	Iran	Norway	115
Switzerland	7.8	Germany	US	Italy	24.1	Germany	Italy	France	309
Turkey	41.9	Germany	US	UK	14.7	Cyprus	Azerbaijan	Greece	35
Ukraine	22.0	Russia	US	Poland	18.3	Russia	Moldova	India	83
United Kingdom	25.1	US	France	Germany	198.8	Malaysia	Ireland	Greece	792
Yugoslavia	7.2	Germany	Austria	France	1.2	Greece	Iran	Romania	17

Region	Number of students abroad (thousnds) 1994-97	Number of foreign students (thousnds) 1994-97	Foreign students as % of students abroad 1994-97
	T	T	
World	1 470	1 676	114
Developing	830	171	21
Industrial	640	1 505	235
Developing excl. India/China	669	135	20
Industrial excl. US/Rus. Fed.	589	977	166
Sub-Saharan Africa	103	22	21
Arab States	150	68	45
South Central Asia	141	30	21
East Asia	296	80	27
South-East Asia/Oceania	134	115	86
Latin Am./Carib.	83	..	..
North America	60	490	817
Europe	505	852	169

TABLE 26
CULTURAL CONTEXT: HUMAN CAPITAL

Country or territory	Estimated adult literacy rate (age 15+)			Estimated young adult literacy rate (age 15-24)			Female education disparity * (female as % of male)		
	Total (%) 2000	Male (%) 2000	Female (%) 2000	Total (%) 2000	Male (%) 2000	Female (%) 2000	Mean years of schooling (age 25+) 1992	Adult literacy rate (age 15+) 2000	Young adult literacy rate (age 15-24) 2000
Sub-Saharan Africa									
Angola	..	..	..	..	..	..	50	..	..
Benin	38	52	34	53	71	36	27	65	51
Botswana	77	74	80	88	84	92	96	108	110
Burkina Faso	23	33	13	33	45	21	67	39	47
Burundi	48	56	41	..	..	..	43	73	..
Cameroon	75	82	69	93	94	93	31	84	99
Central African Rep.	47	60	35	66	76	58	31	58	76
Chad	54	67	41	..	..	..	40	61	..
Congo	81	88	74	97	98	97	35	84	99
Congo (Dem. Rep.)	..	..	..	..	..	..	33	..	..
Côte d' Ivoire	47	55	39	65	70	59	31	71	84
Eritrea	..	..	..	..	..	..	..	..	..
Ethiopia	36	44	33	55	55	54	47	75	98
Gabon	71	80	62	..	..	..	33	78	..
Gambia	37	44	30	57	65	49	22	68	75
Ghana	70	80	61	89	93	86	45	76	92
Guinea	41	55	27	..	..	..	20	49	..
Guinea-Bissau	37	53	21	55	71	39	14	40	55
Kenya	83	89	76	95	96	94	42	85	98
Lesotho	84	74	94	91	84	99	146	127	118
Liberia	53	70	37	69	85	53	24	53	62
Madagascar	..	..	..	..	..	..	65	..	..
Malawi	60	75	47	71	81	61	46	63	75
Mali	40	48	33	64	71	58	14	69	82
Mauritania	40	51	30	48	57	39	14	59	68
Mauritius	84	88	81	93	93	94	67	92	101
Mozambique	44	60	38	60	75	45	55	63	60
Namibia	82	83	81	92	90	94	..	98	104
Niger	16	34	8	22	31	13	50	24	42
Nigeria	65	72	56	87	90	84	29	78	93
Rwanda	67	74	61	84	85	82	33	82	96
Senegal	37	47	28	50	59	42	33	60	71
Sierra Leone	36	51	23	..	..	..	29	45	..
Somalia	..	..	..	..	..	..	40	..	..
South Africa	85	86	84	81	81	81	90	98	100
Sudan	57	68	46	77	83	72	50	68	87
Tanzania (United Rep. of)	75	84	67	91	93	88	46	80	95
Togo	57	72	43	75	87	64	33	60	74
Uganda	67	78	57	79	86	73	38	73	85
Zambia	78	85	71	88	91	85	46	84	93
Zimbabwe	93	96	90	99	100	99	40	94	99
Arab States									
Algeria	63	75	51	79	87	71	19	68	82
Egypt	55	67	44	70	76	72	40	66	95
Iraq	..	..	..	..	..	..	68	..	..
Jordan	90	95	84	100	99	100	67	88	101
Kuwait	82	84	80	93	92	94	79	95	102

Country or territory	Estimated adult literacy rate (age 15+)			Estimated young adult literacy rate (age 15-24)			Female education disparity * (female as % of male)		
	Total (%)	Male (%)	Female (%)	Total (%)	Male (%)	Female (%)	Mean years of schooling (age 25+)	Adult literacy rate (age 15+)	Young adult literacy rate (age 15-24)
	2000	2000	2000	2000	2000	2000	1992	2000	2000
Lebanon	86	92	80	95	98	93	66	87	95
Libyan Arab Jamahiriya	80	91	68	96	100	92	25	75	92
Morocco	49	62	36	67	76	58	36	58	76
Oman	72	80	62	98	100	96	21	78	96
Saudi Arabia	76	83	67	93	95	91	25	81	96
Syrian Arab Rep.	74	88	60	87	95	79	60	68	83
Tunisia	71	81	60	93	97	88	39	74	91
United Arab Emirates	77	75	80	91	88	95	102	106	108
Yemen	46	67	25	64	83	45	13	37	54
South Central Asia									
Afghanistan	36	51	21	54	68	39	13	41	57
Armenia	..	..	..	..	..	..	..	..	..
Azerbaijan	..	..	..	..	..	..	..	..	..
Bangladesh	41	52	30	50	60	39	29	58	65
Bhutan	47	61	34	..	..	..	40	56	..
Georgia	..	..	..	..	..	..	..	..	..
India	56	69	42	70	79	60	34	61	76
Iran (Islamic Rep. of)	77	84	70	94	96	92	67	83	96
Kazakhstan	..	..	..	..	..	..	..	..	..
Kyrgyzstan	..	..	..	..	..	..	..	..	..
Nepal	41	59	24	59	75	42	31	41	56
Pakistan	43	58	28	57	71	42	24	48	59
Sri Lanka	96	95	89	97	97	96	79	94	99
Tajikistan	99	99	99	..	..	..	..	100	..
Turkmenistan	..	..	..	..	..	..	..	..	..
Uzbekistan	..	..	..	..	..	..	..	..	..
East Asia									
China	85	92	77	98	91	97	60	84	107
Hong Kong SAR	93	97	90	99	99	100	63	93	101
Japan	..	..	..	..	..	..	98	..	..
Korea (Dem. People's Rep. of)	..	..	..	..	..	..	62	..	..
Korea (Rep. of)	98	99	96	..	..	..	61	97	..
Mongolia	99	99	99	100	99	100	95	100	101
South-East Asia and Oceania									
Australia	..	..	..	..	..	..	98	..	..
Cambodia	..	..	..	..	..	..	74	..	..
Indonesia	87	92	82	98	98	97	58	89	99
Lao People's Dem. Rep.	62	74	51	..	..	..	58	69	..
Malaysia	88	92	84	98	97	98	88	91	101
Myanmar	85	89	81	91	91	91	70	91	100
New Zealand	..	..	..	..	..	..	104	..	..
Papua New Guinea	78	84	68	..	..	..	54	81	..
Philippines	95	96	95	99	99	99	90	99	100
Singapore	92	96	88	100	100	100	67	92	100
Thailand	96	97	94	99	100	99	77	97	99
Viet Nam	93	96	91	97	97	97	58	95	100

TABLE 26 (continued)

Country or territory	Estimated adult literacy rate (age 15+)			Estimated young adult literacy rate (age 15-24)			Female education disparity * (female as % of male)		
	Total (%) 2000	Male (%) 2000	Female (%) 2000	Total (%) 2000	Male (%) 2000	Female (%) 2000	Mean years of schooling (age 25+) 1992	Adult literacy rate (age 15+) 2000	Young adult literacy rate (age 15-24) 2000
Latin America and the Caribbean									
Argentina	97	97	97	99	99	99	106	100	100
Bolivia	86	92	79	96	98	94	60	86	96
Brazil	85	85	85	93	91	94	95	100	103
Chile	96	96	95	99	99	99	91	99	100
Colombia	92	92	92	97	96	98	105	100	102
Costa Rica	96	96	96	98	98	99	97	100	101
Cuba	96	97	96	100	100	100	103	99	100
Dominican Rep.	84	84	84	92	91	92	87	100	101
Ecuador	92	94	90	98	98	97	91	96	99
El Salvador	79	82	76	88	89	87	91	93	98
Guatemala	69	76	61	79	85	72	86	80	85
Haiti	49	51	46	62	62	62	115	90	100
Honduras	72	73	72	80	79	81	93	99	103
Jamaica	87	83	91	93	90	97	98	110	108
Mexico	91	93	89	97	97	96	96	96	99
Nicaragua	64	64	65	68	68	69	109	102	101
Panama	92	93	91	97	97	96	106	98	99
Paraguay	93	94	92	97	97	97	88	98	100
Peru	90	95	85	97	98	95	79	89	977
Trinidad and Tobago	98	99	98	100	100	100	101	99	100
Uruguay	98	97	98	99	99	100	112	101	101
Venezuela	93	93	93	98	97	99	97	100	102
North America									
Canada	..	..	..	..	..	..	97	..	..
United States	..	..	..	..	..	..	102	..	..
Europe									
Albania	..	..	..	..	..	..	72	..	..
Austria	..	..	..	..	..	..	90	..	..
Belarus	99	100	99	..	..	..	..	100	..
Belgium	..	..	..	..	..	..	100	..	..
Bosnia and Herzegovina	..	..	..	..	..	..	..	..	..
Bulgaria	99	99	98	100	100	100	84	99	100
Croatia	98	99	97	100	100	100	..	98	100
Czech Rep.	..	..	..	..	..	..	..	..	..
Denmark	..	..	..	..	..	..	98	..	..
Estonia	..	..	..	..	..	..	..	..	..
Finland	..	..	..	..	..	..	98	..	..
France	..	..	..	..	..	..	102	..	..
Germany	..	..	..	..	..	..	91	..	..
Greece	97	99	96	100	100	100	89	97	100
Hungary	99	100	99	..	..	..	102	99	..
Ireland	..	..	..	..	..	..	102	..	..
Israel	96	97	94	100	100	100	83	97	100
Italy	99	99	98	..	..	..	99	99	..
Latvia	100	100	100	..	..	..	..	100	..
Lithuania	99	100	99	..	..	..	..	100	..

Country or territory	Estimated adult literacy rate (age 15+) Total (%) 2000	Male (%) 2000	Female (%) 2000	Estimated young adult literacy rate (age 15-24) Total (%) 2000	Male (%) 2000	Female (%) 2000	Female education disparity * (female as % of male) Mean years of schooling (age 25+) 1992	Adult literacy rate (age 15+) 2000	Young adult literacy rate (age 15-24) 2000
Macedonia (former Yugoslav Rep. of)	..	..	..	..	..	..	..	..	..
Moldova (Rep. of)	99	100	98	..	..	..	..	98	..
Netherlands	..	..	..	..	..	..	105	..	..
Norway	..	..	..	..	..	..	98	..	..
Poland	100	100	100	..	..	..	92	100	..
Portugal	92	95	90	100	100	100	77	95	100
Romania	98	99	97	100	100	100	89	98	100
Russian Federation	99	100	99	..	..	..	..	100	..
Slovakia	..	..	..	..	..	..	..	..	..
Slovenia	100	100	100	..	..	..	..	100	..
Spain	98	99	97	100	100	100	93	98	100
Sweden	..	..	..	..	..	..	100	..	..
Switzerland	..	..	..	..	..	..	93	..	..
Turkey	85	94	77	97	99	94	49	82	95
Ukraine	..	..	..	..	..	..	..	..	..
United Kingdom	..	..	..	..	..	..	102	..	..
Yugoslavia	..	..	..	..	..	..	..	..	..

Regions	Estimated adult literacy rate (age 15+) Total (%) 2000	Male (%) 2000	Female (%) 2000	Estimated young adult literacy rate (age 15-24) Total (%) 2000	Male (%) 2000	Female (%) 2000	Female education disparity * (female as % of male) Mean years of schooling (age 25+) 1992	Adult literacy rate (age 15+) 2000	Young adult literacy rate (age 15-24) 2000
World	..	..	..	..	..	..	66	..	..
Developing	71	77	65	83	86	79	59	80	90
Industrial	..	..	..	..	..	..	94	..	..
Developing excl. India/China	71	77	65	83	86	79	59	80	90
Industrial excl. US/Rus. Fed.	..	..	..	..	..	..	94	..	..
Sub-Saharan Africa	58	67	50	73	79	68	44	72	84
Arab States	71	80	61	87	91	83	47	75	90
South Central Asia	60	70	49	..	..	..	47	65	..
East Asia	94	97	91	99	96	99	73	94	103
South-East Asia/Oceania	86	91	82	97	97	97	75	89	100
Latin Am./Carib	86	88	85	92	92	92	96	97	100
North America	..	..	..	..	..	..	99	..	..
Europe	..	..	..	..	..	..	93	..	..

* New indicator.

TABLE 27
CULTURAL CONTEXT: DEMOGRAPHIC AND HEALTH

Country or territory	Population (millions)	Urban population (as % of total population)	Percentage of population: Under age 15	Percentage of population: 60 and over	Life expectancy at birth (years)	Average female age at first marriage	Average family size	Total fertility rate (per woman)	Number of births to 1,000 women age 15-19	Contraceptive prevalence rate (% of females 15-49)	Maternal mortality rate (per 100,000 live births)
	1998	1997	1998	1998	1995-2000	1980-90	1980-90	1995-2000	1991-96	1990-98	1990-97
Sub-Saharan Africa											
Angola	12.1	32	48	5	46	17.9	..	6.8	1 180	..	1 500
Benin	5.8	40	47	4	53	18.3	5.4	5.8	720	16	500
Botswana	1.6	35	43	4	47	26.4	4.8	4.3	500	33	250
Burkina Faso	11.3	25	47	4	44	17.4	6.2	6.6	785	8	930
Burundi	6.5	8	47	4	42	21.9	5.2	6.3	300	9	1 300
Cameroon	14.3	46	44	6	55	18.8	5.2	5.3	705	16	550
Central African Rep.	3.5	40	43	6	45	17.3	5.1	4.9	735	15	700
Chad	7.3	23	46	5	47	16.5	..	6.1	960	4	840
Congo	2.8	60	46	5	49	19.6	5.3	6.1	730	..	890
Congo (Dem. Rep.)	49.1	31	48	4	51	20.1	5.5	6.4	1 155	8	870
Côte d'Ivoire	14.3	45	44	5	47	18.9	..	5.1	755	11	810
Eritrea	3.6	18	44	5	51	..	..	5.7	700	5	1 000
Ethiopia	59.6	16	46	5	43	17.5	..	6.3	845	4	1 400
Gabon	1.2	52	40	9	52	17.7	..	5.4	795	..	500
Gambia	1.2	30	41	5	47	..	3.4	5.2	855	12	1 050
Ghana	19.2	37	44	5	60	19.4	4.8	5.1	615	20	740
Guinea	7.3	31	45	4	47	16.0	6.7	5.5	1 205	2	880
Guinea-Bissau	1.2	23	43	6	45	18.3	..	5.8	945	..	910
Kenya	29.0	30	44	4	52	20.3	5.2	4.4	550	33	650
Lesotho	2.1	26	40	6	56	20.5	..	4.8	455	23	610
Liberia	2.7	48	46	5	47	19.4	5.0	6.3	1 150	6	560
Madagascar	15.1	28	44	4	58	20.3	4.5	5.4	775	17	500
Malawi	10.3	14	47	4	39	17.8	4.3	6.8	865	22	620
Mali	10.7	28	47	5	53	16.4	5.0	6.6	945	7	580
Mauritania	2.5	54	44	5	53	19.4	5.5	5.5	665	3	800
Mauritius	1.1	41	26	9	71	21.7	4.8	1.9	230	75	110
Mozambique	18.9	36	45	5	45	17.6	4.3	6.3	655	6	1 100
Namibia	1.7	38	42	6	52	..	..	4.9	555	29	2 0
Niger	10.1	19	48	4	49	15.8	..	6.8	1 095	4	590
Nigeria	106.4	41	44	5	50	18.7	..	5.1	750	6	1 000
Rwanda	6.5	6	46	4	40	21.2	4.6	6.2	300	21	1 300
Senegal	9.0	45	45	4	52	18.3	..	5.6	775	13	510
Sierra Leone	4.6	35	44	5	37		..	6.1	1 060	..	1 800
Somalia	9.2	28	48	4	47	20.1	..	7.3	1 040	..	1 600
South Africa	39.4	50	35	6	55	22.8	..	3.3	360	50	230
Sudan	28.3	33	40	5	55	18.7	6.3	4.6	295	10	370
Tanzania (United Rep. of)	32.1	26	46	4	48	18.6	..	5.5	670	18	530
Togo	4.4	32	46	5	49	18.6	5.1	6.1	630	12	640
Uganda	20.6	13	50	3	40	17.7	4.5	7.1	900	15	550
Zambia	8.8	44	48	4	40	19.4	5.0	5.5	725	25	650
Zimbabwe	11.4	33	42	4	44	20.4	5.2	3.8	645	48	280
Arab States											
Algeria	30.1	57	38	6	69	21.0	7.0	3.8	130	52	140
Egypt	66.0	45	37	6	66	21.4	5.5	3.4	310	47	170
Iraq	21.8	75	42	5	62	20.8	6.3	5.3	245	14	310
Jordan	6.3	73	42	4	70	22.6	6.6	4.9	245	35	150
Kuwait	1.8	97	36	3	76	22.9	6.5	2.9	205	35	20

Country or territory	Population (millions)	Urban population (as % of total population)	Percentage of population		Life expectancy at birth (years)	Average female age at first marriage	Average family size	Total fertility rate (per woman)	Number of births to 1,000 women age 15-19	Contraceptive prevalence rate (% of females 15-49)	Maternal mortality rate (per 100,000 live births)
			Under age 15	60 and over							
	1998	1997	1998	1998	1995-2000	1980-90	1980-90	1995-2000	1991-96	1990-98	1990-97
Lebanon	3.2	88	33	8	70	..	..	2.7	160	53	300
Libyan Arab Jamahiriya	5.3	86	39	5	70	18.7	..	3.8	550	40	220
Morocco	27.4	53	33	7	67	22.3	6.0	3.1	185	50	370
Oman	2.4	13	45	4	71	..	..	5.8	610	22	300
Saudi Arabia	20.2	84	41	4	71	..	..	5.8	620	..	18
Syrian Arab Rep.	15.3	53	42	5	69	20.7	6.3	4.0	285	36	180
Tunisia	9.3	63	32	8	70	24.3	5.6	2.5	85	60	170
United Arab Emirates	2.4	85	29	4	75	18.0	5.2	3.4	395	27	26
Yemen	16.9	35	48	4	58	17.8	6.8	7.6	510	13	1 400
South Central Asia											
Afghanistan	21.4	22	43	5	45	17.8	6.2	6.9	765	2	1 700
Armenia	3.5	69	26	13	70	..	..	1.7	260	22	21
Azerbaijan	7.7	56	30	10	70	..	..	2.0	110	17	44
Bangladesh	124.8	19	37	5	58	16.7	5.7	3.1	690	49	890
Bhutan	2.0	6	43	6	61	..	..	5.5	430	19	1 600
Georgia	5.1	59	23	18	73	..	..	1.9	255	17	19
India	982.2	27	34	7	63	18.7	5.5	3.1	580	41	440
Iran (Islamic Rep. of)	65.8	60	39	6	69	19.7	5.0	2.8	480	65	120
Kazakhstan	16.3	60	29	11	68	..	..	2.3	175	59	53
Kyrgyzstan	4.6	39	36	9	68	..	..	3.2	225	60	32
Nepal	22.8	13	42	6	57	17.9	5.8	4.4	460	29	1 500
Pakistan	148.2	35	42	5	64	19.8	6.7	5.0	465	18	340
Sri Lanka	18.5	23	27	9	73	24.4	5.0	2.1	170	66	30
Tajikistan	6.0	32	41	7	67	..	..	4.1	180	21	58
Turkmenistan	4.3	45	39	6	65	..	..	3.6	110	20	44
Uzbekistan	23.6	42	39	7	68	..	..	3.4	195	56	31
East Asia											
China	1 255.7	32	26	10	70	22.4	4.0	1.8	25	83	95
Hong Kong SAR	6.7	95	18	14	78	25.3	3.7	1.3	35	86	7
Japan	126.3	78	15	22	80	25.1	3.0	1.4	20	59	18
Korea (Dem. People's Rep. of)	23.3	62	28	8	72	..	..	2.0	25	62	70
Korea (Rep. of)	46.1	83	22	10	72	24.1	4.1	1.6	20	79	30
Mongolia	2.6	62	36	6	66	..	..	2.6	155	61	65
South-East Asia and Oceania											
Australia	18.5	85	21	16	78	23.5	3.0	1.8	110	76	9
Cambodia	10.7	22	42	5	53	21.3	..	4.6	60	..	900
Indonesia	206.3	37	32	7	65	21.1	4.8	2.6	310	55	390
Lao People's Dem. Rep.	5.2	22	44	5	53	..	..	5.8	255	19	660
Malaysia	21.4	55	35	6	72	23.5	5.1	3.2	145	48	34
Myanmar	44.5	27	29	7	60	22.4	5.2	2.4	175	17	580
New Zealand	3.8	86	23	15	76	22.7	2.9	2.0	170	75	25
Papua New Guinea	4.6	17	39	5	56	..	4.5	4.6	115	26	370
Philippines	72.9	56	37	6	68	22.4	5.6	3.6	240	48	210
Singapore	3.5	100	22	10	77	26.2	4.7	1.7	40	74	10
Thailand	60.3	21	26	8	69	22.7	4.6	1.7	255	74	200
Viet Nam	77.6	21	35	7	67	..	4.8	2.6	225	65	105

TABLE 27 (continued)

Country or territory	Population (millions)	Urban population (as % of total population)	Percentage of population: Under age 15	Percentage of population: 60 and over	Life expectancy at birth (years)	Average female age at first marriage	Average family size	Total fertility rate (per woman)	Number of births to 1,000 women age 15-19	Contraceptive prevalence rate (% of females 15-49)	Maternal mortality rate (per 100,000 live births)
	1998	1997	1998	1998	1995-2000	1980-90	1980-90	1995-2000	1991-96	1990-98	1990-97
Latin America and the Caribbean											
Argentina	36.1	89	28	13	73	22.9	3.9	2.6	350	74	100
Bolivia	8.0	62	40	6	61	22.1	4.4	4.4	410	45	370
Brazil	165.9	80	30	7	67	22.6	4.4	2.3	365	77	160
Chile	14.8	84	29	10	75	23.6	4.5	2.4	280	43	65
Colombia	40.8	74	33	7	70	22.6	5.1	2.8	400	72	100
Costa Rica	3.8	50	33	7	76	21.7	4.7	2.8	265	75	55
Cuba	11.1	77	22	13	76	19.9	4.1	1.5	335	70	36
Dominican Rep.	8.2	64	34	6	71	19.7	4.8	2.8	455	64	110
Ecuador	12.2	60	35	7	70	21.1	4.8	3.1	395	57	150
El Salvador	6.0	46	36	7	69	19.4	5.0	3.2	525	53	300
Guatemala	10.8	41	44	5	64	20.5	5.2	4.9	615	31	190
Haiti	8.0	33	42	5	54	23.8	..	4.4	270	18	600
Honduras	6.1	45	43	5	69	20.0	5.7	4.3	635	50	220
Jamaica	2.5	55	32	9	75	25.2	4.2	2.5	475	62	120
Mexico	95.8	75	34	7	72	20.6	5.5	2.8	385	67	110
Nicaragua	4.8	63	44	5	68	20.2	..	4.4	745	49	160
Panama	2.8	56	32	8	74	21.2	4.6	2.6	455	58	55
Paraguay	5.2	54	40	5	70	21.8	5.2	4.2	435	56	190
Peru	24.8	72	34	7	68	22.7	5.1	3.0	315	64	280
Trinidad and Tobago	1.3	73	27	9	74	22.3	4.2	1.6	300	53	90
Uruguay	3.3	91	25	17	74	22.4	3.3	2.4	310	..	85
Venezuela	23.2	93	35	6	72	21.2	5.3	3.0	505	49	120
North America											
Canada	30.6	77	19	17	79	26.1	2.8	2.5	130	75	6
United States	274.0	77	22	16	77	23.3	2.6	2.0	315	76	12
Europe											
Albania	3.1	38	30	9	73	..	..	2.5	70	..	28
Austria	8.1	56	17	20	77	25.7	2.7	1.4	110	71	10
Belarus	10.3	72	20	19	68	..	3.8	1.4	140	50	22
Belgium	10.1	97	17	22	77	24.9	2.7	1.5	45	79	10
Bosnia and Herzegovina	3.7	49	20	14	73	23.3	..	1.3	155	..	..
Bulgaria	8.3	70	17	21	71	21.9	2.9	1.2	300	76	20
Croatia	4.5	64	18	20	73	23.2	..	1.6	160	..	12
Czech Rep.	10.3	66	17	18	74	21.5	..	1.2	210	69	7
Denmark	5.3	85	18	20	76	28.2	2.4	1.7	45	78	9
Estonia	1.4	74	19	19	69	23.0	..	1.3	165	70	52
Finland	5.2	64	18	19	77	26.9	2.6	1.7	55	80	11
France	58.7	75	19	20	78	26.1	2.7	1.7	45	75	15
Germany	82.1	87	16	22	77	26.0	2.4	1.3	65	75	22
Greece	10.6	65	16	23	78	24.4	3.1	1.3	90	..	10
Hungary	10.1	61	17	20	71	21.6	2.8	1.4	175	73	14
Ireland	3.7	58	22	15	76	25.9	3.7	1.9	75	60	10
Israel	6.0	91	28	13	78	23.5	3.5	2.7	95	..	7
Italy	57.4	67	14	24	78	25.6	3.0	1.2	40	78	12
Latvia	2.4	73	19	20	68	22.4	2.4	1.3	175	48	15
Lithuania	3.7	73	20	18	70	..	..	1.4	130	59	13

Country or territory	Population (millions)	Urban population (as % of total population)	Percentage of population: Under age 15	Percentage of population: 60 and over	Life expectancy at birth (years)	Average female age at first marriage	Average family size	Total fertility rate (per woman)	Number of births to 1,000 women age 15-19	Contraceptive prevalence rate (% of females 15-49)	Maternal mortality rate (per 100,000 live births)
	1998	1997	1998	1998	1995-2000	1980-90	1980-90	1995-2000	1991-96	1990-98	1990-97
Macedonia (former Yugoslav Rep. of)	2.0	61	24	14	73	22.8	..	2.1	220	..	22
Moldova (Rep. of)	4.4	53	25	14	68	..	..	1.8	195	74	23
Netherlands	15.7	89	18	18	78	26.6	2.5	1.5	35	79	12
Norway	4.4	74	20	20	78	26.2	2.7	1.8	80	74	6
Poland	38.7	64	21	16	73	21.6	3.1	1.5	140	75	10
Portugal	9.9	37	17	21	75	24.5	3.3	1.4	110	66	15
Romania	22.5	57	19	18	70	22.1	3.1	1.2	235	57	41
Russian Federation	147.4	77	19	18	67	..	2.9	1.3	405	67	53
Slovakia	5.4	60	21	15	73	21.2	..	1.4	215	74	8
Slovenia	2.0	63	17	18	74	24.1	..	1.3	140	..	13
Spain	39.6	77	15	21	78	25.3	3.5	1.1	50	59	7
Sweden	8.9	83	19	22	79	27.8	2.2	1.6	60	78	7
Switzerland	7.3	62	18	19	79	27.3	2.5	1.5	25	71	6
Turkey	64.5	72	29	8	69	20.6	5.2	2.5	295	63	180
Ukraine	50.9	71	19	20	69	17.4	3.7	1.4	215	..	30
United Kingdom	58.6	89	19	21	77	25.7	2.7	1.7	..	82	9
Yugoslavia	10.6	58	21	18	73	23.8	..	1.8	205	55	12

Regions	Population (millions)	Urban population (as % of total population)	Percentage of population: Under age 15	Percentage of population: 60 and over	Life expectancy at birth (years)	Average female age at first marriage	Average family size	Total fertility rate (per woman)	Number of births to 1,000 women age 15-19	Contraceptive prevalence rate (% of females 15-49)	Maternal mortality rate (per 100,000 live births)
	1998	1997	1998	1998	1995-2000	1980-90	1980-90	1995-2000	1991-96	1990-98	1990-97
World	5 880	46	30	10	67	21.3	4.5	2.8	328	57	277
Developing	4 630	38	33	7	64	20.7	4.9	3.1	362	54	345
Industrial	1 250	75	19	18	75	23.7	3.0	1.6	194	71	28
Developing excl. India/China	2 390	46	37	6	62	20.6	5.3	3.8	450	43	436
Industrial excl. US/Rus. Fed.	830	75	18	19	76	24.1	3.1	1.6	116	70	28
Sub-Saharan Africa	607	32	45	5	49	19.0	5.2	5.5	750	15	820
Arab States	228	57	39	6	67	21.3	6.1	4.2	301	41	283
South Central Asia	1 457	29	35	7	63	..	..	3.3	549	40	466
East Asia	1 461	38	25	11	71	22.8	3.9	1.8	25	80	85
South-East Asia/Oceania	529	37	32	7	66	22.1	4.9	2.7	247	55	298
Latin Am./Carib.	496	75	32	8	69	21.9	4.8	2.8	388	67	150
North America	305	77	22	16	77	23.6	2.6	2.1	296	76	11
Europe	798	74	19	19	73	23.6	3.1	1.5	190	71	36

TABLE 28
CULTURAL CONTEXT: ECONOMIC

Country or territory	GNP per capita (US Dollars)	PPP estimates of GNP per capita (Current int'l $)	Ratio of household income share: Richest 10% to poorest 10%	Ratio of household income share: Richest 20% to poorest 20%	Population below an international poverty line [1] * %	Labour force participation rate (% age 15-64): Male	Labour force participation rate (% age 15-64): Female	Employment to population ratio *: Male	Employment to population ratio *: Female
	1998	1998	1988-98	1988-98	1988-98	1997	1997	1995-97	1995-97
Sub-Saharan Africa									
Angola	340	840	..	..	..	91	76	..	..
Benin	380	1 250	..	..	..	84	77	..	..
Botswana	3 600	8 310	..	..	61	63	49	..	..
Burkina Faso	240	1 020	18.0	10.0	..	91	79	..	..
Burundi	140	620	..	..	..	94	86	..	..
Cameroon	610	1 810	..	..	..	87	50	..	..
Central African Rep.	300	1 290	..		..	88	69	..	..
Chad	230	900	..	..	..	90	70	..	..
Congo	690	1 430	..	..	..	84	58	..	..
Congo (Dem. Rep.)	110	750	..	..	..	86	64	..	..
Côte d' Ivoire	700	1 730	10.2	6.5	55	89	45	..	..
Eritrea	200	950	..	..	..	87	77	..	..
Ethiopia	210	500	11.2	6.7	89	86	59	..	..
Gabon	3 950	6 660	..	..	..	86	66	..	..
Gambia	340	1 430	25.1	12.0	..	91	70	..	..
Ghana	390	1 610	7.3	5.0	..	83	82	..	..
Guinea	540	1 760	12.3	7.4	50	88	81	..	..
Guinea-Bissau	160	750	84.8	28.0	97	92	59	..	..
Kenya	330	1 130	19.4	10.0	78	90	76	..	..
Lesotho	570	2 320	48.2	21.5	74	86	49	..	..
Liberia	..	..	..	..	..	84	56	..	..
Madagascar	260	640	19.3	10.2	93	90	71	..	..
Malawi	200	750	..	..	..	87	79	..	..
Mali	250	550	22.4	12.2	..	91	75	..	..
Mauritania	410	1 540	13.0	7.4	68	88	66	..	..
Mauritius	3 700	9 400	..	..	..	85	42	..	..
Mozambique	210	900	..	..	..	91	84	..	..
Namibia	1 940	4 950	..	..	..		84	56	..
Niger	190	830	44.3	20.5	92		94	72	..
Nigeria	300	820	24.2	12.4	60		88	49	..
Rwanda	230	690	5.8	4.0	89	89	87	..	..
Senegal	530	1 710	42.3	18.7	80	87	63	..	..
Sierra Leone	140	390	87.2	57.6	..	85	45	..	..
Somalia	..	..	..	..	..	88	65	..	..
South Africa	2 880	6 990	41.7	22.3	50	83	49	..	..
Sudan	290	..	..	..	..	86	33	..	..
Tanzania (United Rep. of)	210	490	10.8	6.7	..	89	84	..	..
Togo	330	1 390	..	..	..	88	55	..	..
Uganda	320	1 170	12.0	7.0	92	92	82	..	..
Zambia	330	860	24.5	13.0	98	88	67	..	..
Zimbabwe	610	2 150	26.1	15.6	68	87	67	..	..
Arab States									
Algeria	1 550	4 380	9.6	6.1	18	79	26	29	
Egypt	1 290	3 130	6.8	4.7	52	76	23	67	17
Iraq	..	..	..	..	..	76	17	..	..
Jordan	1 520	3 230	14.5	8.5	24	78	23	..	..
Kuwait	18 000	..	..	..	..	80	40	..	..

Country or territory	GNP per capita (US Dollars) 1998	PPP estimates of GNP per capita (Current int'l $) 1998	Ratio of household income share: Richest 10% to poorest 10% 1988-98	Ratio of household income share: Richest 20% to poorest 20% 1988-98	Population below an international poverty line [1] * % 1988-98	Labour force participation rate (% age 15-64): Male 1997	Labour force participation rate (% age 15-64): Female 1997	Employment to population ratio *: Male 1995-97	Employment to population ratio *: Female 1995-97
Lebanon	3 560	6 150	..	..	..	80	30	..	..
Libyan Arab Jamahiriya	..	..	..	..	..	80	24	..	..
Morocco	1 250	3 120	10.9	7.0	20	83	42	..	..
Oman	5 000	8 140	..	..	..	81	17	..	..
Saudi Arabia	7 000	..	..	..	..	84	19	..	..
Syrian Arab Rep.	1 020	3 000	..	..	..	81	27	..	..
Tunisia	2 050	5 160	13.3	7.8	23	83	37	..	..
United Arab Emirates	18 220	..	..	..	..	91	32	..	..
Yemen	300	740	13.4	7.6	..	84	3	..	..
South Central Asia									
Afghanistan	..	..	..	..	..	88	49	..	..
Armenia	480	..	..	..	..	79	70	..	..
Azerbaijan	490	1 820	..	..	..	78	58	56	
Bangladesh	350	1 100	5.8	4.0	..	90	57	76	50
Bhutan	400	1 260	..	..	..	91	60	..	..
Georgia	930	..	..	..	..	80	65	..	..
India	430	1 700	6.1	4.3	89	88	44	..	..
Iran (Islamic Rep. of)	1 770	..	..	..	..	81	26	..	..
Kazakhstan	1 310	3 400	8.0	5.4	12	81	68	..	..
Kyrgyzstan	350	2 200	9.7	6.3	55	78	67	42	
Nepal	210	1 090	9.3	5.9	87	88	58	..	..
Pakistan	480	1 560	6.8	4.4	57	85	13	66	10
Sri Lanka	810	..	6.6	4.4	41	82	45	..	..
Tajikistan	350	..	..	..	..	78	60	63	47
Turkmenistan	700	..	4.0	6.4	..	81	66	..	..
Uzbekistan	870	2 900	..	..		78	66	69	51
East Asia									
China	750	3 220	14.0	8.6	58	90	80		76
Hong Kong SAR	23 670	22 000	8.4	..	..	84	55	74	47
Japan	32 380	23 180	..	..	4b	85	59	75	49
Korea (Dem. People's Rep.)	..	..	..	..	..	84	67	..	..
Korea (Rep. of)	7 970	12 270	..	..	..	76	53	74	48
Mongolia	400	1 520	8.4	5.6	..	87	76	..	..
South-East Asia and Oceania									
Australia	20 300	20 130	9.9	5.8	8b	82	63	66	48
Cambodia	280	1 240	..	..	..	84	80	..	..
Indonesia	680	2 790	8.4	5.6	59	84	55	79	47
Lao People's Dem. Rep.	330	1 300	6.3	4.2	..	91	77	..	..
Malaysia	3 000	6 990	19.9	11.7	27		83	49	.. ..
Myanmar	..	..	..	..	..	90	68	..	..
New Zealand	14 700	15 840	..	..	..	84	67	70	53
Papua New Guinea	890	2 700	23.8	12.6	..	89	69	..	..
Philippines	1 050	3 540	14.0	8.4	65	84	51	76	45
Singapore	30 060	28 620	..	..	..	83	56	76	50
Thailand	2 200	5 840	14.8	9.4	24	86	72	78	64
Viet Nam	330	1 690	8.3	5.6	..	86	79	..	..

TABLE 28 (continued)

Country or territory	GNP per capita (US Dollars)	PPP estimates of GNP per capita (Current int'l $)	Ratio of household income share: Richest 10% to poorest 10%	Ratio of household income share: Richest 20% to poorest 20%	Population below an international poverty line [1] * %	Labour force participation rate (% age 15-64): Male	Labour force participation rate (% age 15-64): Female	Employment to population ratio *: Male	Employment to population ratio *: Female
	1998	1998	1988-98	1988-98	1988-98	1997	1997	1995-97	1995-97
Latin America and the Caribbean									
Argentina	8 970	10 200	..	..	..	76	41	48	27
Bolivia	1 000	820	13.8	8.6	..	78	58	..	..
Brazil	3 640	6 160	59.9	25.7	44	86	55	..	..
Chile	4 570	12 890	32.9	17.4	39	80	39	71	33
Colombia	2 600	7 500	46.9	19.8	22	82	56	..	..
Costa Rica	2 780	6 620	26.7	13.0	44	85	39	78	34
Cuba	..	..	..	..	..	85	53	..	..
Dominican Rep.	1 770	4 700	24.8	13.3	48	87	39	47	26
Ecuador	1 530	4 630	16.3	9.7	66	83	51	..	..
El Salvador	1 850	2 850	31.9	14.7	..	82	43	62	34
Guatemala	1 640	4 070	77.7	30.0	77	90	33	..	..
Haiti	410	1 250	..	..	..	83	59	..	..
Honduras	730	2 140	35.1	17.1	76	90	43	70	34
Jamaica	1 680	3 210	13.3	8.2	25	84	74	66	49
Mexico	3 970	8 190	30.6	16.2	40	87	41	82	38
Nicaragua	400	1 790	24.9	13.1	75	87	46	..	..
Panama	3 080	6 940	62.6	26.3	46	85	47	74	34
Paraguay	1 760	3 650	66.6	27.1	..	89	37	..	..
Peru	2 460	..	22.1	11.6	..	81	57	..	..
Trinidad and Tobago	4 430	6 720	..	..	..	80	51	64	37
Uruguay	6 180	9 480	..	..	..	85	58	..	..
Venezuela	3 500	8 190	23.7	12.0	32	83	43	74	36
North America									
Canada	20 020	24 050	8.5	5.2	6b	82	68	66	52
United States	29 340	29 340	19.0	9.4	14b	84	71	71	57
Europe									
Albania	810	..	..	..	..	86	65	..	..
Austria	26 850	22 740	4.4	3.2	..	77	58	64	44
Belarus	2 200	..	6.6	4.4	6	82	73	..	..
Belgium	25 380	23 480	5.5	3.6	12b	72	53	56	36
Bosnia and Herzegovina	..	..	..	..	..	79	49	..	..
Bulgaria	1 230	..	7.5	4.7	24	77	72	47	39
Croatia	4 520	..	..	..	..	76	58	..	..
Czech Rep.	5 040	..	5.1	3.6	55	81	64	68	49
Denmark	33 260	23 830	5.7	3.6	8b	85	74	69	55
Estonia	3 390	..	11.9	6.7	33	77	66	..	..
Finland	24 110	20 270	5.1	3.6	4b	78	71	61	53
France	24 940	22 320	10.0	5.6	12b	74	60	56	41
Germany	25 850	20 810	6.1	4.1	12b	79	61	62	42
Greece	11 650	13 010	..	..	..	77	46	59	31
Hungary	4 510	..	5.9	3.9	11	67	49	55	40
Ireland	18 340	18 340	11.0	6.4	..	76	50	61	38
Israel	15 940	17 310	9.6	6.2	..	68	53	57	42
Italy	20 250	20 200	8.2	5.1	..	71	44	55	29
Latvia	2 430	..	6.8	4.5	..	77	65	58	46
Lithuania	2 440	4 310	8.2	5.2	19	78	65	..	..

Country or territory	GNP per capita (US Dollars) 1998	PPP estimates of GNP per capita (Current int'l $) 1998	Ratio of household income share: Richest 10% to poorest 10% 1988-98	Ratio of household income share: Richest 20% to poorest 20% 1988-98	Population below an international poverty line [1] * % 1988-98	Labour force participation rate (% age 15-64) Male 1997	Labour force participation rate (% age 15-64) Female 1997	Employment to population ratio * Male 1995-97	Employment to population ratio * Female 1995-97
Macedonia (former Yugoslav Rep. of)	1 290	3 660	..	..		73	48	..	..
Moldova (Rep. of)	410	..	9.6	6.0	31	81	70	51	
Netherlands	24 760	21 620	8.5	5.0	14b	82	62	69	48
Norway	34 330	24 290	5.2	3.5	3b	85	76	75	65
Poland	3 900	6 740	5.5	3.9	15	73	60	60	44
Portugal	10 690	14 380	..	..	..	77	61	63	46
Romania	1 390	3 970	6.1	4.2	71	78	64	68	54
Russian Federation	2 300	3 950	26.7	12.6	11	81	72	66	49
Slovakia	3 700	..	3.6	2.6	85	75	61	59	45
Slovenia	9 760	..	6.1	4.2	..	72	63	61	49
Spain	14 080	16 060	9.0	5.4	21b	77	48	54	27
Sweden	25 620	19 480	5.4	3.6	5b	79	75	66	60
Switzerland	40 080	26 620	9.9	5.9	..	90	73	75	55
Turkey	3 160	..	..	..	26	79	29	70	26
Ukraine	850	..	26.3	12.1	..	76	70	54	
United Kingdom	21 600	20 640	10.3	5.6	13b	84	68	66	51
Yugoslavia	..	..	..	..	..	76	57	..	..

Regions	GNP per capita (US Dollars) per capita 1998	PPP estimates of GNP 10% to (Current int'l $) 1998	Ratio of household income share: Richest 20% to poorest 10% 1988-98	Ratio of household income share: Richest poverty poorest 20% 1988-98	Population below an international (% age 15-64) line [1] * % 1988-98	Labour force participation rate (% age 15-64) Male 1997	Labour force participation rate (% age 15-64) Female 1997	Employment to population ratio * Male 1995-97	Employment to population ratio * Female 1995-97
World	5 030	6 880	14.7	8.2	..	85	59	..	
Developing	1 320	3 210	14.9	8.4	..	87	58	..	..
Industrial	18 610	20 380	14.5	7.6	15	80	62	66	47
Developing excl. India/China	1 980	3 830	20.3	10.6	..	85	51	..	..
Industrial excl. US/Rus. Fed.	17 960	20 340	9.4	5.4	16	79	58	64	43
Sub-Saharan Africa	570	1 720	21.8	11.6	..	88	63	..	..
Arab States	2 020	3 820	..	..	..	80	24	..	..
South Central Asia	510	1 640	6.2	4.3	..	87	43	..	..
East Asia	4 320	5 630	14.0	..	..	89	77	76	73
South-East Asia/Oceania	2 110	4 430	10.8	6.9	..	85	62	77	50
Latin Am./Carib.	3 620	6 720	43.4	19.8	42	84	49	71	36
North America	28 400	28 810	18.0	9.0	13	84	71	71	57
Europe	12 670	16 720	13.1	7.0	18	78	60	62	43

*New indicator.

1. An international poverty line of US$2 per day (1985 PPP dollars) is used for almost all developing countries; one of US$14.40 per day is used for 16 industrial countries and is market b.

TABLE 29
CULTURAL CONTEXT: SOCIAL SECURITY

Country or territory	Old age, disability, death	Family allowances	Sickness and maternity	Work injury	Unemployment
Sub-Saharan Africa					
Angola	-	-	-	-	-
Benin	X	X	-	X	-
Botswana	-	-	-	X	-
Burkina Faso	X	X	-	X	-
Burundi	X	-	-	X	X
Cameroon	X	X	-	X	-
Central African Rep.	X	X	-	X	-
Chad	X	X	-	X	-
Congo	X	X	-	X	-
Congo (Dem. Rep.)	X	X	-	X	-
Côte d' Ivoire	X	X		X	
Eritrea	-	-	-	-	-
Ethiopia	X	-	-	X	-
Gabon	X	X	-	X	-
Gambia	X	-	-	X	-
Ghana	X	-	-	X	-
Guinea	X	X	-	X	-
Guinea-Bissau	-	-	-	-	-
Kenya	X	-	-	X	-
Lesotho	-	-	-	-	-
Liberia	X		-	X	-
Madagascar	X	X	-	X	-
Malawi	-	-	-	X	-
Mali	X	X	-	X	-
Mauritania	X	X	-	X	-
Mauritius	-	-	-	-	-
Mozambique	X	X	-	X	-
Namibia	-	-	-	--	
Niger	X	X	-	X-	
Nigeria	X	-	-	X	-
Rwanda	X	-	-	X	-
Senegal	X	X	-	X	-
Sierra Leone		-	-	X	-
Somalia	X	-	-	X	-
South Africa	X	-	-	X	X
Sudan	X	-	X	X	-
Tanzania (United Rep. of)	X	-	-	X	-
Togo	X	X	-	X	
Uganda	X	-	-	X	-
Zambia	X	-	-	X	-
Zimbabwe	X	-	-	X	-
Arab States					
Algeria	X	X	X	X	X
Egypt	X	-	X	X	X
Iraq	X	-	X	X	-
Jordan	X	-	-	X	-
Kuwait	X	-	-	-	-

Country or territory	Old age, disability, death	Family allowances	Sickness and maternity	Work injury	Unemployment
Lebanon	X	X	X	X	-
Libyan Arab Jamahiriya	X	-	X	X	-
Morocco	X	X	X[1]	X	-
Oman	X	-	-	X	-
Saudi Arabia	X	-	-	X	-
Syrian Arab Rep.	X			X	
Tunisia	X	X	X	X	X
United Arab Emirates	-	-	-	-	-
Yemen	X	-	-	X	-
South Central Asia					
Afghanistan	X	-	X[1]	X	-
Armenia	X	X	X	X	X
Azerbaijan	X	X	X	X	X
Bangladesh	-	-	X	X	X
Bhutan					
Georgia	X	X	X	X	X
India	X	-	X	X	-
Iran (Islamic Rep. of)	X	X	X	X	X
Kazakhstan	X	X	X	X	X
Kyrgyzstan	X	X	X	X	X
Nepal	X	-	-	X	-
Pakistan	X	-	X	X	-
Sri Lanka	X	X	-	X	-
Tajikistan	-	-	-	-	-
Turkmenistan	X	X	X	X	X
Uzbekistan	X	X	X	X	X
East Asia					
China	X	-	X	X	X
Hong Kong SAR	X	X	X[1]	X	X
Japan	X	X	X	X	X
Korea (Dem. People`s Rep. of)	-	-	-	-	-
Korea (Rep. of)	X	-	-	X	-
Mongolia	-	-	-	-	-
South-East Asia and Oceania					
Australia	X	X	X	X	X
Cambodia	-	-	-	-	-
Indonesia	X	-	-	X	-
Lao People´s Dem. Rep.	X	X	X	X	X
Malaysia	X	-	-	X	-
Myanmar	-	-	X	X	-
New Zealand	X	X	X	X	X
Papua New Guinea	X	-	-	X	-
Philippines	X	-	X	X	-
Singapore	X	-	-	X	-
Thailand	X	-	X	X	-
Viet Nam	X	-	X	X	-

TABLE 29 (continued)

Country or territory	Old age, disability, death	Family allowances	Sickness and maternity	Work injury	Unemployment
Latin America and the Caribbean					
Argentina	X	X	X	X	X
Bolivia	X	X	X	X	-
Brazil	X	X	X	X	X
Chile	X	X	X	X	X
Colombia	X	X	X	X	-
Costa Rica	X	X	X	X	-
Cuba	X	-	X	X	-
Dominican Rep.	X	-	X	X	-
Ecuador	X	-	X	X	X
El Salvador	X	-	X	X	-
Guatemala	X	-	X	X	-
Haiti	X	-	-	X	-
Honduras	X	-	X	X	-
Jamaica	X	-	-	X	-
Mexico	X	-	X	X	-
Nicaragua	X	X	X	X	-
Panama	X	-	X	X	-
Paraguay	X	-	X	X	-
Peru	X	-	X	X	-
Trinidad and Tobago	X	-	X[1]	X	-
Uruguay	X	X	X	X	X
Venezuela	X		X	X	X
North America					
Canada	X	X	X	X	X
United States	X	-	-	X	X
Europe					
Albania	X	X	X	X	X
Austria	X	X	X	X	X
Belarus	X	X	X	X	X
Belgium	X	X	X	X	X
Bosnia and Herzegovina	-	-	-	-	-
Bulgaria	X	X	X	X	X
Croatia	X	X	X	X	X
Czech Rep.	X	X	X	X	X
Denmark	X	X	X	X	X
Estonia	X	X	X	X	X
Finland	X	X	X	X	X
France	X	X	X	X	X
Germany	X	X	X	X	X
Greece	X	X	X	X	X
Hungary	X	X	X	X	X
Ireland	X	X	X	X	X
Israel	X	X	X	X	X
Italy	X	X	X	X	X
Latvia	-	-	-	-	-
Lithuania	X	X	X	X	X

Country or territory	Old age, disability, death	Family allowances	Sickness and maternity	Work injury	Unemployment
Macedonia (former Yugoslav Rep. of)	-	-	-	-	-
Moldova (Rep. of)	X	X	-	X	X
Netherlands	X	X	X	X	X
Norway	X	X	X	X	X
Poland	X	X	X	X	X
Portugal	X	X	X	X	X
Romania	X	X	X	X	X
Russian Federation	X	X	X	X	X
Slovakia	X	X	X	X	X
Slovenia	X	X	X	X	X
Spain	X	X	X	X	X
Sweden	X	X	X	X	X
Switzerland	X	X	X	X	X
Turkey	X	-	X	X	-
Ukraine	X	X	X	X	X
United Kingdom	X	X	X	X	X
Yugoslavia	-	-	-	-	-

Regions	Old age, disability, death		Family allowances		Sickness and maternity		Work injury		Unemployment	
	T	%	T	%	T	%	T	%	T	%
World	129	86	75	50	83	55	133	89	60	40
Developing	91	84	40	37	47	44	95	88	23	21
Industrial	38	91	35	83	36	86	38	91	37	88
Developing excl. India/China	89	84	40	38	45	43	93	88	22	21
Industrial excl. US/Rus. Fed.	36	90	34	85	35	88	36	90	35	88
Sub-Saharan Africa	32	76	17	41	1	2	35	83	2	5
Arab States	13	93	4	29	7	50	12	86	3	21
South Central Asia	13	81	9	56	12	75	14	88	9	56
East Asia	4	67	2	33	3	50	4	67	3	50
South-East Asia/Oceania	10	83	3	25	7	58	11	92	3	25
Latin Am./Carib.	22	100	8	36	20	91	22	100	6	27
North America	2	100	1	50	1	50	2	100	2	100
Europe	33	89	31	84	32	87	33	89	32	87

*New table.

1. Cash only

TABLE 30
CULTURAL CONTEXT: ENVIRONMENT AND BIODIVERSITY

Country or territory	Total land area (thousnd sq km) 1999	Population density (population per sq km) 1998	Nationally protected areas (% of total area) 1999	Biodiversity* Vertebrate [1/] species (hundreds) 1996	% of vertebrate species threatened 1996	Plant species (hundreds) 1996	% of plant species threatened 1996	Total forest area (% of total land area) 1995	Average annual deforestation (hundred sq km) 1990-95	(% of total forest area) 1990-95
Sub-Saharan Africa										
Angola	1 247	10	6.6	11	3.3	52	0.6	18	24	5.0
Benin	111	51	7.1	5.0	2.4	22	0.2	42	6.0	6.0
Botswana	567	3	19	7.5	1.4	22	0.3	25	7.1	2.5
Burkina Faso	274	41	11	4.8	1.7	11	(.)	16	3.2	3.5
Burundi	26	232	5.5	5.6	2.0	25	(.)	12	0.1	2.0
Cameroon	465	30	4.5	9.9	5.1	83	1.1	42	13	3.0
Central African Rep.	623	6	8.2	7.5	1.9	36	(.)	48	13	2.0
Chad	1 259	6	9.1	5.0	3.6	16	0.8	9	9.4	4.0
Congo	342	8	4.5	6.5	2.3	60	0.1	57	4.2	1.0
Congo (Dem. Rep.)	2 267	21	4.5	13	5.0	110	0.7	48	74	3.5
Côte d'Ivoire	318	44	6.3	7.7	4.3	37	2.6	17	3.1	3.0
Eritrea	101	30	5.0	4.3	2.8	..	..	3	(.)	(.)
Ethiopia	1 000	54	5.5	8.8	6.4	66	2.5	14	6.2	2.5
Gabon	258	4	2.8	6.6	2.9	67	1.4	69	9.1	2.5
Gambia	10	109	2.0	3.9	1.6	10	0.1	9	0.1	4.5
Ghana	228	80	4.8	7.5	3.6	37	2.8	40	12	6.5
Guinea	246	30	0.7	6.0	4.5	30	1.3	26	7.5	5.5
Guinea-Bissau	28	32	(.)	3.5	2.3	10	(.)	82	1.0	2.0
Kenya	581	50	6.1	15	4.9	65	3.7	2	0.3	1.5
Lesotho	30	68	0.3	0.9	7.7	16	1.3	(.)	(.)	(.)
Liberia	96	24	..	..	..	..	..	47	1.5	3.0
Madagascar	582	26	1.9	7.0	13	95	3.2	26	13	4.0
Malawi	94	87	11	9.1	1.8	38	1.6	36	5.5	8.0
Mali	1 220	9	3.7	5.5	3.6	17	0.9	10	11	5.0
Mauritania	1 025	2	1.7	3.3	5.1	11	0.3	1	(.)	(.)
Mauritius	2	559	4.9	0.4	48	7.5	39	6	(.)	(.)
Mozambique	784	24	6.1	7.4	4.2	57	1.6	22	12	3.5
Namibia	823	2	13	6.6	3.5	32	2.4	15	4.2	1.5
Niger	1 267	8	7.6	5.3	2.6	12	(.)	2	(.)	(.)
Nigeria	911	115	3.3	11	3.6	47	0.8	15	12	4.5
Rwanda	25	251	15	6.6	2.3	23	(.)	10	(.)	1.0
Senegal	193	46	11	5.4	4.8	21	1.5	8	5.0	3.5
Sierra Leone	72	64	1.1	6.1	3.9	21	1.4	18	4.3	15
Somalia	627	14	..	..	..	..	..	1	(.)	(.)
South Africa	1 221	32	5.4	12	6.2	234	9.7	7	1.5	1.0
Sudan	2 376	11	..	9.5	3.5	31	0.3	18	35	4.0
Tanzania (United Rep. of)	884	34	16	15	4.3	100	4.4	37	32	5.0
Togo	54	77	7.9	5.9	2.0	22	0.2	23	1.9	7.0
Uganda	200	87	9.6	14	2.1	54	0.3	31	5.9	4.5
Zambia	743	12	8.6	9.2	2.3	47	0.3	42	26	4.0
Zimbabwe	387	29	7.9	11	1.7	44	2.3	23	5.0	3.0
Arab States										
Algeria	2 382	13	2.5	2.8	8.5	32	4.5	1	2.3	6.0
Egypt	995	66	0.8	3.4	9.4	21	4.0	(.)	(.)	(.)
Iraq	437	50	(.)	3.4	6.2	..	..	(.)	(.)	(.)
Jordan	89	64	3.4	2.2	5.4	21	0.4	1	0.1	13
Kuwait	18	102	1.7	0.7	8.3	2.3	(.)	(.)	(.)	(.)

Country or territory	Total land area (thousnd sq km)	Population density (population per sq km)	Nationally protected areas (% of total area)	Biodiversity*				Total forest area (% of total land area)	Average annual deforestation	
				Vertebrate [1/] species (hundreds)	% of vertebrate species threatened	Plant species (hundreds)	% of plant species threatened		(hundred sq km)	(% of total forest area)
	1999	1998	1999	1996	1996	1996	1996	1995	1990-95	1990-95
Lebanon	10	307	(.)	1.5	7.8	30	0.2	5	0.5	39
Libyan Arab Jamahiriya	1 760	3	0.1	1.7	9.6	18	3.1	(.)	(.)	(.)
Morocco	446	61	0.7	3.2	9.8	37	5.1	9	1.2	1.5
Oman	212	11	16	2.3	8.4	12	2.5	(.)	(.)	(.)
Saudi Arabia	2 150	9	2.3	4.2	6.3	20	0.4	(.)	0.2	4.0
Syrian Arab Rep.	184	83	(.)	2.7	5.2	30	0.3	1	0.5	11
Tunisia	155	57	0.3	3.5	5.4	22	1.1	4	0.3	2.5
United Arab Emirates	84	28	(.)	1.3	7.0	..	..	(.)	(.)	(.)
Yemen	528	32	(.)	2.9	7.0	..	..	8	(.)	(.)
South Central Asia										
Afghanistan	652	33	..	..	..	..	..	2	12	34
Armenia	28	119	7.4	..	..	..	..	12	-0.2	14
Azerbaijan	87	89	5.5	..	..	..	..	11	(.)	(.)
Bangladesh	130	866	0.8	5.4	11	50	0.5	8	-6.9	4.0
Bhutan	47	43	..	..	..	..	..	59	(.)	(.)
Georgia	70	73	2.7	..	..	..	..	43	(.)	(.)
India	2 973	299	4.8	18	9.2	160	7.7	22	-0.7	(.)
Iran (Islamic Rep. of)	1 636	40	5.1	8.4	5.3	80	(.)	1	2.8	8.5
Kazakhstan	2 671	6	2.7	..	..	..	..	4	-19	-9.5
Kyrgyzstan	192	23	3.6	..	..	..	..	4	(.)	(.)
Nepal	137	162	7.8	8.9	6.7	70	0.3	35	5.5	5.5
Pakistan	771	186	4.8	7.2	6.2	50	0.3	2	5.5	15
Sri Lanka	65	281	13	5.2	6.4	33	14	28	2.0	5.5
Tajikistan	141	42	4.2	..	..	..	..	3	(.)	(.)
Turkmenistan	488	9	4.2	..	..	..	..	8	(.)	(.)
Uzbekistan	414	53	2.0	..	..	..	..	22	-23	-14
East Asia										
China	9 326	131	6.4	21	8.6	322	1.0	14	8.7	0.5
Hong Kong SAR	1	6 373	40	2.0	7.7	20	0.5	(.)	(.)	(.)
Japan	377	334	6.8	5.0	16	56	13	67	1.3	0.5
Korea (Dem. People's Rep. of)	120	194	2.6	..	..	29	0.1	51	..	..
Korea (Rep. of)	99	466	6.9	2.0	13	29	2.3	77	1.3	1.0
Mongolia	1 567	2	10	5.5	4.7	23	(.)	6	..	..
South-East Asia and Oceania										
Australia	7 644	2	7.3	19	8.9	156	14	5	-1.7	(.)
Cambodia	181	59	16	5.4	9.3	..	..	56	16	8.0
Indonesia	1 812	108	11	27	9.2	294	0.9	61	108	5.0
Lao People's Dem. Rep.	231	22	(.)	7.6	8.4	..	..	54	13	6.0
Malaysia	329	65	4.5	12	7.4	155	3.2	47	40	12
Myanmar	658	66	0.3	14	6.8	70	0.5	41	39	7.0
New Zealand	270	14	24	2.0	29	24	8.9	29	-4.3	-3.0
Papua New Guinea	463	10	(.)	13	7.3	115	0.8	82	13	2.0
Philippines	298	243	4.9	8.0	18	89	4.0	23	26	18
Singapore	1	5 624	(.)	1.6	9.8	22	1.3	7	(.)	(.)
Thailand	511	118	14	12	8.0	116	3.3	23	33	13
Viet Nam	325	234	3.0	10	9.7	105	3.3	28	14	7.0

TABLE 30 (continued)

Country or territory	Total land area (thousnd sq km) 1999	Population density (population per sq km) 1998	Nationally protected areas (% of total area) 1999	Biodiversity* Vertebrate [1/] species (hundreds) 1996	% of vertebrate species threatened 1996	Plant species (hundreds) 1996	% of plant species threatened 1996	Total forest area (% of total land area) 1995	Average annual deforestation (hundred sq km) 1990-95	(% of total forest area) 1990-95
Latin America and the Caribbean										
Argentina	2 737	13	1.7	16	4.9	94	2.6	12	8.9	1.5
Bolivia	1 084	7	14	119	2.8	174	1.3	45	58	6.0
Brazil	8 457	19	4.2	29	6.8	562	2.4	65	255	2.5
Chile	757	20	19	5.0	7.6	53	6.2	11	2.9	2.0
Colombia	1 039	36	9.0	32	3.5	512	1.4	51	26	2.5
Costa Rica	51	75	14	12	3.0	121	4.4	24	4.1	15
Cuba	110	100	17	3.1	9.3	65	14	17	2.4	6.0
Dominican Rep.	48	169	25	3.0	8.8	57	2.4	33	2.6	8.0
Ecuador	277	43	43	25	3.8	194	4.3	40	19	8.0
El Salvador	21	287	0.5	4.8	1.7	29	1.4	5	0.4	17
Guatemala	108	99	17	10	2.0	87	4.1	35	8.2	10
Haiti	28	287	0.4	2.3	9.7	52	1.9	1	0.1	17
Honduras	112	55	9.9	8.0	2.2	57	1.7	37	10	12
Jamaica	11	231	(.)	1.9	12	33	23	16	1.6	36
Mexico	1 909	49	3.7	22	5.5	261	6.1	29	51	4.5
Nicaragua	121	37	7.4	9.0	1.6	76	1.3	46	15	7.5
Panama	74	37	19	13	2.5	99	13	38	6.4	11
Paraguay	397	13	3.5	11	3.7	79	1.6	29	33	13
Peru	1 280	19	2.7	25	4.8	182	5.0	53	22	1.5
Trinidad and Tobago	5	250	3.9	4.6	2.0	23	0.9	31	0.3	7.5
Uruguay	175	19	0.3	3.2	5.0	23	0.7	5	(.)	(.)
Venezuela	882	25	36	19	3.1	211	2.0	50	50	5.5
North America										
Canada	9 221	3	10	7.0	2.3	33	8.5	27	-18	-0.5
United States	9 159	29	13	16	8.6	195	24	23	-59	-1.5
Europe										
Albania	27	108	2.9	3.4	2.9	30	2.6	38	(.)	(.)
Austria	83	97	28	3.3	3.9	31	0.7	47	(.)	(.)
Belarus	207	50	4.1	..	..	..	..	36	-6.9	-5.0
Belgium	31	332	2.5	2.6	3.4	16	0.1	22	(.)	(.)
Bosnia and Herzegovina	51	72	0.4	..	..	..	..	53	(.)	(.)
Bulgaria	111	75	4.4	3.7	7.0	36	3.0	29	-0.1	(.)
Croatia	56	79	6.6	..	..	..	..	33	(.)	(.)
Czech Rep.	77	130	16	..	..	..	..	34	(.)	(.)
Denmark	42	122	32	2.6	1.9	15	0.1	10	(.)	(.)
Estonia	42	32	12	2.9	2.0	..	..	48	-2.0	-5.0
Finland	305	15	6.0	3.2	2.5	11	0.5	66	1.7	0.5
France	550	106	11	4.3	5.9	46	4.2	27	-16	-5.5
Germany	349	230	27	3.5	3.8	27	0.5	31	..	..
Greece	129	80	2.4	4.1	7.3	50	11	51	-14	-12
Hungary	93	109	6.8	3.1	6.2	22	1.4	19	-0.9	-2.5
Ireland	69	52	0.9	1.7	1.8	10	0.1	8	-1.4	-14
Israel	21	284	15	2.7	9.2	23	1.4	5	(.)	(.)
Italy	294	190	7.3	4.0	6.3	56	5.6	22	-0.6	-0.5
Latvia	62	38	13	3.2	3.1	12	(.)	46	-2.5	-4.5
Lithuania	65	57	10	2.9	3.1	..	..	31	-1.1	-3.0

Country or territory	Total land area (thousnd sq km) 1999	Population density (population per sq km) 1998	Nationally protected areas (% of total area) 1999	Biodiversity*: Vertebrate [1] species (hundreds) 1996	Biodiversity*: % of vertebrate species threatened 1996	Biodiversity*: Plant species (hundreds) 1996	Biodiversity*: % of plant species threatened 1996	Total forest area (% of total land area) 1995	Average annual deforestation (hundred sq km) 1990-95	Average annual deforestation (% of total forest area) 1990-95
Macedonia (former Yugoslav Rep. of)	25	78	7.1	..	..	..	..	39	0.0	(.)
Moldova (Rep. of)	33	130	1.2	2.7	3.8	..	..	11	(.)	(.)
Netherlands	34	384	7.1	2.7	3.4	12	0.1	10	(.)	(.)
Norway	307	14	31	3.1	2.3	17	0.7	26	-1.8	-1.5
Poland	304	120	9.6	3.4	4.7	25	1.1	29	-1.2	-0.5
Portugal	92	107	6.4	3.2	6.9	51	5.3	31	-2.4	-4.5
Romania	230	95	4.6	3.8	7.7	34	2.9	27	0.1	(.)
Russian Federation	16 889	9	3.1	9.8	7.6	..	..	45	..	..
Slovakia	46	110	22	..	..	..	..	41	-0.2	-0.5
Slovenia	20	98	5.5	3.0	4.7	..	..	54	(.)	(.)
Spain	500	79	8.4	4.4	8.7	51	20	17	..	..
Sweden	412	20	8.8	3.3	2.7	18	0.7	59	0.2	(.)
Switzerland	40	177	18	3.0	3.3	30	1.0	29	(.)	(.)
Turkey	770	83	1.4	5.4	8.0	87	22	12	..	..
Ukraine	579	84	1.6	..	..	..	..	16	-0.5	-0.5
United Kingdom	242	240	21	3.0	2.0	16	1.1	10	-1.3	-2.5
Yugoslavia	102	104	(.)	..	..	..	..	17	..	..

Regions	Total land area (thousnd sq km) 1999	Population density (population per sq km) 1998	Nationally protected areas (% of total area) 1999	Biodiversity*: Vertebrate [1] species (hundreds) 1996	Biodiversity*: % of vertebrate species threatened 1996	Biodiversity*: Plant species (hundreds) 1996	Biodiversity*: % of plant species threatened 1996	Total forest area (% of total land area) 1995	Average annual deforestation (hundred sq km) 1990-95	Average annual deforestation (% of total forest area) 1990-95
	T			T		T			T	
World	126 840	45	7.1	1 050	5.2	8 000	4.2	28	..	..
Developing	76 970	57	5.8	900	5.0	6 800	3.0	25	1 243	5.3
Industrial	49 870	25	8.0	150	6.5	1 200	10.9	29	..	..
Developing excl. India/China	64 673	35	5.8	860	4.8	6 324	3.0	26	1 235	5.0
Industrial excl. US/Rus. Fed.	23 821	36	9.4	125	6.2	991	8.3	21	..	..
Sub-Saharan Africa	23 055	24	6.4	290	3.8	1 688	2.8	22	369	3.9
Arab States	9 450	24	1.8	36	7.3	245	2.3	4.6	5	9.3
South Central Asia	10 084	133	3.9	..	..	..	..	11	..	3.7
East Asia	11 490	124	6.9	36	9.2	478	2.4	16	11	0.7
South-East Asia/Oceania	12 209	41	8.0	132	9.3	1 147	3.8	20	297	6.6
Latin Am./Carib.	18 975	25	6.9	378	3.8	3 042	3.7	47	577	7.4
North America	18 380	16	12	23	6.7	227	21.8	25	-77	-1.0
Europe	23 198	36	5.1	102	5.1	723	6.7	40	..	..

New indicator.

1. Vertebrates: Include mammals, reptiles, amphibians and birds, but not whales, porpoises and fish.

Index and sources of culture indicators

Indicators	Indicator tables	Basic data sources [1]	New *World Culture Report* indicators [2]
Archives, metres	WCR 1998	UNESCO	X
personnel	WCR 1998	UNESCO	X
user visits	WCR 1998	UNESCO	X
Biodiversity, vertebrate species	30	WCMC	X
plant species	30	WCMC	X
Book titles, published	1	UNESCO	X
Books produced	1	UNESCO	X
literature and art	1	UNESCO	X
Cinema attendance	4	UNESCO, SDG	
Cinema screens	4	SDG	
Compact-disc players	5	IFPI	
Computers, personal	20	ITU	
Contraceptive prevalence	27	UNFPA	
Cultural conventions, ratifications	13	UNESCO	
total score	13	UNESCO	X
Cultural paper, consumption	2	UNESCO	X
Deforestation, total	30	FAO	
as % of forest area	30	FAO	X
Education expenditure,			
public as % of GNP	24	UNESCO	
as % of public expenditure	24	UNESCO	
Enrolment ratio, primary female net	24	UNESCO	
primary male net	24	UNESCO	
secondary female net	24	UNESCO	
secondary male net	24	UNESCO	
tertiary female gross	24	UNESCO	
tertiary male gross	24	UNESCO	
tertiary enrolment in fine arts, female	24	UNESCO	X
tertiary enrolment in fine arts, male	24	UNESCO	X
Employment-to-population ratio, male	28	ILO	
female	28	ILO	
Exports, cultural	15	UNSTAT	X
Facsimile machines	20	ITU	X
Family size	27	UNPOP	
Feature films, produced	4	UNESCO, SDG	
co-produced	4	UNESCO, SDG	
imported	4	UNESCO	
imported as % of total	4	UNESCO	X
imported, leading countries of origin	4	UNESCO	X
Fertility, total	27	UNPOP	
young women	27	UNPOP	X
Festivals, national	8	MSU	X
folk or religious	9	MSU	X
Foreign language publications	21	UNESCO	X
Foreign remittances	WCR 1998	IMF	X

Indicators	Indicator tables	Basic data sources [1]	New *World Culture Report* indicators [2]
Foreign students, total	25	UNESCO	
leading countries of origin	25	UNESCO	X
as % of students abroad	25	UNESCO	X
Forest area	30	FAO	
GNP per capita, US dollars	28	WBANK	
international dollars (PPP)	28	WBANK	
Heritage sites, total	12	UNESCO	
cultural	12	UNESCO	
natural	12	UNESCO	
combined	12	UNESCO	
tentative	12	UNESCO	
endangered	12	UNESCO, WMF	
most visited cultural	10	MSU	X
most visited natural	11	MSU	X
Human rights conventions, ratifications	14	UNCHR	
total score	14	UNCHR	X
Income share of households			
highest 20% to lowest 20%	28	WBANK	X
highest 10% to lowest 10%	28	WBANK	X
Internet hosts	28	ITU	
Labour conventions, ratifications	13	ILO	
total score	13	ILO	X
Labour-force participation, female	28	ILO	
male	28	ILO	
Land area	30	FAO	
Languages, official names	6	MSU	X
numbers	6	MSU	X
leading	6	MSU	X
over fifty spoken	6	MSU	X
Letters posted	19	UPU	X
to or from abroad	19	UPU	X
Library (public), books	2	UNESCO	X
users	2	UNESCO	X
population served	2	UNESCO	
Life expectancy	27	UNPOP	
Literacy, adult	26	UNESCO	
young adult	26	UNESCO	
female disparity, years of schooling	26	UNESCO/UNDP	X
adult literacy	26	UNESCO	X
young adult literacy	26	UNESCO	X
Marriage (first), female age	27	UNPOP	
Maternal mortality	27	WHO	
Migrants (international), total	WCR1998	UNPOP	
female	WCR1998	UNPOP	

Indicators	Indicator tables	Basic data sources [1]	New *World Culture Report* indicators [2]
Museums, attendance	WCR1998	UNESCO	X
personnel	WCR1998	UNESCO	X
Music, popular artist	5	WSL	X
Music (recorded), sales	5	IFPI	X
domestic popular	5	IFPI	
international popular	5	IFPI	
classical	5	IFPI	
piracy	5	IFPI	
ıates	5	IFPI	X
Newspapers, daily circulation	1	UNESCO, WAN	
Performing arts, establishments	WCR1998	UNESCO	X
performances	WCR1998	UNESCO	X
attendance	WCR1998	UNESCO	X
foreign tours	WCR1998	UNESCO	X
Population, total	27	UNPOP	
urban	27	UNPOP	
under 15	27	UNPOP	
60 and over	27	UNPOP	
Population density	30	UNPOP	
Post offices	19	UPU	
Poverty line, population below	28	WBANK, ILO	X
Protected areas	30	WCMC	
Public holidays	WCR 1998	JPM	X
Radios	3	UNESCO	
Radios per televisions	3	UNESCO	X
Radio programmes, cultural	3	UNESCO	X
Refugees, country of origin	WCR 1998	UNHCR	X
country of asylum	WCR 1998	UNHCR	X
Religions, leading	7	MSU	X
Schooling, mean years total	WCR 1998	UNESCO, UNDP	X
female	WCR 1998	UNESCO, UNDP	X
male	WCR 1998	UNESCO, UNDP	X
Social security, old age, disability, death	29	ILO	
family allowances	29	ILO	
sickness and maternity	29	ILO	
work injury	29	ILO	
unemployment	29	ILO	
Students abroad, total	25	UNESCO	
leading countries of study	25	UNESCO	X

Telephones, total	19	ITU	
mobile	20	ITU	X
Telephone calls (international), minutes	19	ITU	
major partner	19	ITU	X
cost of an international call	19	ITU	
cost of a local call	19	ITU	
Televisions	3	UNESCO	
Television programmes, cultural	3	UNESCO	
Tourism (foreign), arrivals of visitors	18	WTO	X
departures of nationals	18	WTO	X
leading countries of origin	17	WTO	X
leading countries of destination	17	WTO	X
receipts	18	WTO	X
expenditures	18	WTO	X
Translations, total published	21	UNESCO	
leading languages translated	21	UNESCO	X
multilingual publications	21	UNESCO	
by original language	22	UNESCO	
leading languages into which translated	22	UNESCO	X
authors most translated	23	UNESCO	X
Trade (cultural), total	15	UNSTAT	
per capita	15	UNSTAT	X
as % of GNP	15	UNSTAT	X
books and pamphlets	16	UNSTAT	X
newspapers, newsprint and periodicals	16	UNSTAT	X
typewriters, word and data processors	16	UNSTAT	X
music-related goods	16	UNSTAT	X
radio, television, VCRs	16	UNSTAT	X
cinema and photography	16	UNSTAT	X
visual art and antiques	16	UNSTAT	X
sporting goods	16	UNSTAT	X

1. See list of acronyms on page 13. The first source listed is the main source for the indicator. When data originally came from more than one source, or when a second organization has published the data in a more convenient form, the leading secondary source follows the main source.
2. New indicator developed by World Statistics Ltd (New York) for the *World Culture Report*.

List of countries by region*

SUB-SAHARAN AFRICA

Angola
Benin
Botswana
Burkina Faso
Burundi
Cameroon
Central African Republic
Chad
Congo
Côte d'Ivoire
Democratic Republic of the Congo
Eritrea
Ethiopia
Gabon
Gambia
Ghana
Guinea
Guinea-Bissau
Kenya
Lesotho
Liberia
Madagascar
Malawi
Mali
Mauritania
Mauritius
Mozambique
Namibia
Niger
Nigeria
Rwanda
Senegal
Sierra Leone
Somalia
South Africa
Sudan
Togo
Uganda
United Republic of Tanzania
Zambia
Zimbabwe

ARAB STATES

Algeria
Egypt
Iraq
Jordan
Kuwait
Lebanon
Libyan Arab Jamahiriya
Morocco
Oman
Saudi Arabia
Syrian Arab Republic
Tunisia
United Arab Emirates
Yemen

SOUTH CENTRAL ASIA

Afghanistan
Armenia
Azerbaijan
Bangladesh
Bhutan
Georgia
India
Iran (Islamic Republic of)
Kazakhstan
Kyrgyzstan
Nepal
Pakistan
Sri Lanka
Tajikistan
Turkmenistan
Uzbekistan

EAST ASIA

China
Hong Kong SAR
Democratic People's Republic of Korea
Japan
Mongolia
Republic of Korea

* For reasons of space, country names have been abbreviated and/or modified in the preceding tables; the correct and full names of states appear in this list.

SOUTH-EAST ASIA AND OCEANIA

Australia
Cambodia
Indonesia
Lao People's Democratic Republic
Malaysia
Myanmar
New Zealand
Papua New Guinea
Philippines
Singapore
Thailand
Viet Nam

LATIN AMERICA AND THE CARIBBEAN

Argentina
Bolivia
Brazil
Chile
Colombia
Costa Rica
Cuba
Dominican Republic
Ecuador
El Salvador
Guatemala
Haiti
Honduras
Jamaica
Mexico
Nicaragua
Panama
Paraguay
Peru
Trinidad and Tobago
Uruguay
Venezuela

NORTH AMERICA

Canada
United States of America

EUROPE

Albania
Austria
Belarus
Belgium
Bosnia and Herzegovina
Bulgaria
Croatia
Czech Republic
Denmark
Estonia
Finland
France
Germany
Greece
Hungary
Ireland
Israel
Italy
Latvia
Lithuania
Netherlands
Norway
Poland
Portugal
Republic of Moldova
Romania
Russian Federation
Slovakia
Slovenia
Spain
Sweden
Switzerland
the former Yugoslav Republic of Macedonia
Turkey
Ukraine
United Kingdom of Great Britain and Northern Ireland
Yugoslavia

Millennium guide to cultural resources on the web

This CD-ROM is planned to operate as an interface between a personal computer and the World Wide Web to facilitate access to web cultural information. Two types of thematic resource have been explored for all UNESCO Member States: museum websites and heritage management websites.

More than 3,000 sites have been referenced to give a picture of cultural resources on the web in the year 2000. The CD-ROM also indicates best practices and the potential ICTs to promote cultural subjects and participation in the information society.

We wish to thank Lab Production (Paris, France) and the Centro Regional de Investigaciones Multidisciplinarias (CRIM) for its invaluable contribution to the production of the CD-ROM.

Achevé d'imprimer par Corlet, Imprimeur, S.A. - 14110 Condé-sur-Noireau (France)
N° d'Imprimeur : 50011 - Dépôt légal : octobre 2000 - *Imprimé en U.E.*